THE GATES OF HELL

THE GATES OF HELL

Sir John Franklin's Tragic Quest
for the North West Passage

ANDREW LAMBERT

Yale University Press
New Haven & London

First published in the United States in 2009 by Yale University Press.
First published in the United Kingdom in 2009 by Faber and Faber Limited.

Typeset by Faber and Faber Limited.
Printed in the United States of America.

Library of Congress Control Number: 2009921883
ISBN 978-0-300-15485-6 (hardcover : alk. paper)

A catalogue record for this book is available from the British Library.
This paper meets the requirements of ANSI/NISO Z39.48-1992 (Permanence of Paper).

10 9 8 7 6 5 4 3 2 1

This book is dedicated to my Arctic companions: John Murray, who started it all, Saul Aksalook, who made sure we got back, Jon Woods, who captured it on film, and Peter Bate, who directed proceedings.

It was an honour to travel with you.

Contents

List of Illustrations ix
Acknowledgements xi
Prologue: Erebus – the Gates of Hell 1

BOOK ONE: THE PURSUIT OF SCIENCE

1 The North West Passage – Designs and Delusions 7
2 John Franklin – Navigator 22
3 Another Career 44
4 Scientific Empires 61

BOOK TWO: PUBLIC VISIONS

5 From Van Diemen's Land to Tasmania, 1836–43 93
6 Science, Culture and Civilisation 110
7 'The nucleus of an iceberg' 141
8 Magnetic Empires 167

BOOK THREE: THE POLITICS OF TRAGEDY

9 'Till our provisions get short' 179
10 Defeated, Deceived and Defrauded 204
11 Belcher 227
12 Martyrs of Science 247
13 Arctic *Fox* 276

BOOK FOUR: THE COST OF THE PAST

14 Big Art, Brazen Lies and the 'Great Explorer' 307
15 Terror: What Really Happened? 336

Notes 353
Bibliography 395
Index 407

Illustrations

1 'The Sea of Ice', Caspar David Friedrich, 1824. Hamburger Kunsthalle, Hamburg, Germany/The Bridgeman Art Library

2 Sir John Franklin. National Maritime Museum, Greenwich, London

3 Hudson's Bay Company trading posts. Jari Patenan, 2001

4 Dip circle. National Maritime Museum, Greenwich, London

5 The expeditions of the Royal Navy. Jari Patenan, 2001

6 Lithograph from *Franklin Sketches*, a series of fourteen sketches made during the voyage up Wellington Channel in search of Sir John Franklin, published with a short account of each drawing by Commander Walter May, RN, in 1855

7 Lithograph from *Franklin Sketches*, a series of fourteen sketches made during the voyage up Wellington Channel in search of Sir John Franklin, published with a short account of each drawing by Commander Walter May, RN, in 1855

8 'The Arctic Council Planning a Search for Sir John Franklin', Stephen Pearce, 1899. National Portrait Gallery, London

9 'Lady Jane Franklin', Amélie Romilly, 1816. National Portrait Gallery, London

10 Photo of letter by Fitzjames and Crozier © Andrew Lambert

11 'The Icebergs', Frederic Edwin Church, 1861. Dallas Museum of Art

12 'Man Proposes, God Disposes', Sir Edwin Landseer, 1864. Royal Holloway College, University of London/The Bridgeman Art Library

13 Skulls of members of the Franklin expedition discovered and buried by William Skinner and Paddy Gibson. Library and Archives, Canada

14 Smith Sound © Andrew Lambert

15 Graves on Beechey Island © Andrew Lambert

Acknowledgements

IN THE COURSE of researching and writing this book I have incurred many debts, their number and geographical dispersion providing evidence of the lengths that an obsession can achieve. Without John Murray and Peter Bate I would never have gone to the Arctic, or spent so long discussing Franklin at Chiswick, Gjoahaven, Point Victory, in various departure lounges and on board an ice-breaker.

For the opportunity to research in Australia in the summer of 2005 I am indebted to Captain Richard McMillan RAN and Dr David Stevens of the RAN Sea Power Centre and to Dr John Reeve and the staff of the Australian Defence Academy, while Professor Michael Bennett of the University of Tasmania not only arranged for a lecture visit but provided hospitality and local guidance that went far beyond the call of duty. Along with his family and his colleagues he transformed a flying visit into a remarkably productive stay. A timely invitation to provide the annual Vaughan Evans Lecture from the director of the Australian Maritime Museum facilitated work at the Mitchell Library, where the Director and Professor John Gascoigne of the University of New South Wales were most generous with their time and expertise. In Britain, staff at the National Archives, the National Maritime Museum, the Archives of the Royal Society, the Geological Society, the archivists of Scott Polar Research Institute, the Royal Geographical Society, the Geological Society, the National Maritime Museum, the Hartley Library (University of Southampton) and the British Library offered much appreciated support and assistance, including permission to quote from archival material in their collections. Opportunities to lecture on Franklin in Canberra, Hobart, Greenwich, Falmouth, Chatham and London have provided valuable feedback.

Among those who have followed the project with interest are

Professor John Beeler, Professor Gary Weir and Professor Glyndwr Williams, Michael Tapper, Sarah Ingham, and my mother, Nola Lambert, who generously agreed to read the draft and provided valuable criticism. It was a noble gesture, and much valued. Hard as others have tried, the flaws and failings of the author endure, and for them I am uniquely responsible.

At Faber and Faber my editor, Julian Loose, boldly accepted this book in lieu of something else, a decision that I trust he will not regret. His confidence is a valued commodity, and along the way the support of everyone at Great Russell Street has made for a rewarding working relationship. My colleagues and students have tolerated the somewhat eccentric pursuit of Arctic visions and scientific notions, my family have embraced my Franklin quest from the first mention of a trip north to the final submission of the manuscript. For my parents, and for Zohra and Tama, this must have been as laborious to live through as it has been pleasurable to write. They have endured the North West Passage, and they deserve my love and thanks.

PROLOGUE

Erebus – the Gates of Hell

WE DON'T KNOW when it started, or who took the decision, but some time in May 1848 British sailors from HMS *Erebus* and HMS *Terror* began butchering and eating their comrades.[1] We do not know if they killed the living, picking out the weak, the young and the expendable, or whether they confined their attentions to the dead. But make no mistake they ate their shipmates, not one or two, but forty or fifty. British sailors carefully and deliberately used their knives, vital symbols of their profession, to strip the flesh from men who had been their friends. Their sharp blades left tell-tale marks on the victims' bones, marks that have endured to this day. To remove the maximum amount of flesh they cut the bodies into joints, removing the muscle tissue. These men were hungry, and they did not waste anything. They cracked open the larger bones to extract the marrow. In most cases of survival cannibalism the heads and hands are removed and discarded, too human to be eaten. These men were not so squeamish. They took the heads, ripped off the jaw bones and stove in the bases of the skulls to get at the nutritious and easily digested brain. After the heads were done they scavenged for scraps, defleshing the fingers, stripping off every last remnant with the grim efficiency of a meat-recovery machine.

How many men were eaten, and how many ate, we will never know. No one was keeping score, and no one lived to tell. This was fortunate; when Inuit hunters reported the story those at home comforted themselves with the illusion that British men could never do such a thing. Even now there are still those who insist it did not happen, but forensic science is a precise art, and the evidence is overwhelming. The Arctic expedition of Captain Sir John Franklin ended in large-scale cannibalism.

I

Hell is a curious place; it exists in the minds of men and can be reached by a variety of routes. Some of these routes are peculiar and even personal; some, like cannibalism, are almost universal. Eating human flesh is the final taboo among Western societies, one that retains the power to shock even the jaded sensibilities of a postmodern twenty-first-century world, reminding us just how thin is the veneer of civilisation that separates us from primeval savagery.

In the Arctic, death can be slow, the human body will endure prolonged periods of cold, shortage of food and vitamins, and even dehydration. Eventually scurvy, muscle wastage, enervation and lassitude create a desperate longing for sleep, rest and release. Mind and body simply shut down – it was, as Captain Scott observed, 'a painless end'.[2] On 5 August 2004 I finally understood what he meant. That summer I travelled across King William Island in the Canadian Arctic, tracing the death march of a doomed expedition from Victory Point to Starvation Cove. The day ended by the beach in Erebus Bay, after a fruitless search for locations and insight. We were just yards from the shoreline, behind a low ridge of shattered limestone slabs. The wind was blowing hard from the NNW, straight down the McClintock Channel, across multi-year polar ice. The ambient temperature was already below zero, the wind chill must have been minus twenty. There was no cover. After pitching the tent I left the others to get the stove alight and went to collect driftwood. A fire would help. There was enough wood, and with the encouragement of a little petrol the logs were soon blazing, but the wind pushed the flames sideways across the beach. There was no warmth to be had here, not even at the fireside. At least it was a cheerful sight amid the cold desolation of a bay named for the very gates of hell, and there was hot food, a pleasant change from the endless routine of chewing frozen energy bars on the move. (In case you need to know, the yoghurt coated bars were the best: they remained slightly moist.)

Everyone tried to be positive, but it had been a terrible day, too cold to work, an energy-sapping struggle to find the way ahead. This was an awful place, gloomy, cold and desolate, a cold hell. Nothing could lift the mood that evening. Cold, tired and dirty, I would have given anything to get out, go home, take a shower and get into a clean bed. Instead solace came in the smelly form of half-cured cari-bou and musk-ox hide, a serious sleeping bag and two sets of long underclothes. Fortunately sleep comes quickly, and with it dreams of home, hot water and four strong walls. I'm not sure how long I could take this sort of travelling, and have no desire to find out. The next morning it was time to get up and strike camp. Jon cooked up something hot, I checked the bikes – oil, petrol and tyres – then we lashed our world to our machines, started our engines and rode off.

The Arctic appeared in many guises, at once sublime and loaded with horrific memories. History is about questions, and I came back from King William Island with a journal full of them. Why did apparently sane men keep coming into this wilderness for forty years, and why had the story of Sir John Franklin been so heavily reconstructed? What was the fabled North West Passage they sought, and was it ever open for shipping? How could such a large expedition be lost completely? A second expedition, travelling north on the Russian ice-breaker *Kapitan Khlebnikov*, and further study of the literature on Arctic exploration only added to the uncertainty. One thing was certain: something terrible had happened.

BOOK ONE

THE PURSUIT OF SCIENCE

I

The North West Passage – Designs and Delusions

THE FRANKLIN DISASTER had its origins in the Peruvian Andes. In 1802 Prussian nobleman Alexander von Humboldt measured the magnetic intensity of the earth at Cajamarca, effectively on the equator; his figures served as a reference point for the next half-century of geomagnetic science.[1] Both Humboldt's expedition to South America and his science had been inspired by Captain James Cook's voyages to the South Pacific in the 1760s and 1770s. Meeting Georg Forster, scientist on the second Cook voyage, in 1790 connected Humboldt with a world of science, travel and literature that shaped the rest of his life. Soon after they met, Forster took Humboldt to England, where he introduced him to Sir Joseph Banks.[2] Banks had sailed on Cook's first voyage and now ruled British science as president of the Royal Society. It was a fateful meeting, for between them Banks and Humboldt would create and sustain the scientific impulse behind naval exploration from the 1780s to the 1850s. They laid the foundations for Franklin's final voyage: they determined that men should go the Arctic in pursuit of science, and decided which science had priority.

Not that Humboldt was a man for the frozen wastes. Inspired by Forster's descriptions and South Sea images he encountered in London, Humboldt set his course for the steamy tropics.[3] An inveterate observer, Humboldt began to amass geomagnetic data in Europe and shared it with Banks. This work continued on the American expedition that made him a celebrity, a journey recorded with British navigational instruments.[4] Yet for all his careful observation, mapping and science Humboldt achieved celebrity status only after climbing the volcanic Mount Chimborazo, Ecuador's highest summit, in 1802, a feat that would be recalled for decades to come.[5] In his attempt to comprehend the deeper meaning of the

7

chain of volcanoes Humboldt laid the foundations of plate tectonics. Shortly after climbing Chimborazo, Humboldt crossed the equator and took his critical magnetic readings, readings that demonstrated magnetic intensity increased with latitude and that were to form the basis of Carl Gauss's theory of magnetic fields.[6]

Wittingly or otherwise Humboldt used exploration to secure an audience for cutting-edge science – transmitting his experiences, observations, data and images to a breathless public in a monumental series of books.[7] The first instalments of his American journey ensured that magnetic observations were an essential element of the first British Arctic mission of the nineteenth century. These observations measured the extent to which the compass needle was deflected from true north by local magnetism – declination. Although the English astronomer Edmund Halley published an Atlantic chart of declination readings early in the eighteenth century it would be another century before the Frenchman Jean-Charles de Borda produced an inclinometer capable of making accurate measurements, to study his theory that declination was not consistent across the globe. Humboldt took Borda's ideas and one of his instruments to South America. The data he collected required a systematic explanation, which in turn inspired Humboldt to seek magnetic data from many points on the globe. Both data and concept were critical to the rapid development of magnetic science.[8] Humboldt kept on observing, and refining his technique. Gradually he persuaded others that his endless vigils in a Berlin back garden, with musical accompaniment provided by Moses Mendelssohn's brilliant children, produced significant useable results, and that similar work would be profitable. In 1822 Humboldt organised the first international scientific congress in Berlin for the leading figures in European magnetic science.

Humboldt's American expedition took three decades and many volumes to publish. Costly books filled with specially commissioned art, maps, data and theories ruined the author financially. Overwhelmed by the immensity of his experience, Humboldt simply took the established eighteenth-century travel narrative and expanded it to unprecedented scale, with detailed scientific appendices that required separate volumes. The example was not lost on English critic John Barrow, the *Quarterly Review* contributor chosen to assess Humboldt's offerings. Not that Barrow was very gracious, rightly observing that Humboldt was a prolix and ill-disciplined author, unable to sustain an argument or a narrative without digressing.[9] That said, Humboldt taught the world to see nature subjectively as well as objectively, to report how it appeared, as well as what could be measured. He combined art and science by providing a theoretical programme for landscape painting.[10] Humboldt's work evoked a sensual response. It was his vision that brought the Arctic to the attention of the Western world, not for the size or temperature of its icebergs, but for their grandeur and beauty.

Humboldt and his *Cosmos* provided an all-embracing scientific explanation of a world in which natural forces were in constant conflict, and each had to be examined in detail. Significantly, Humboldt managed to harmonise his liberal, progressive political views with a fixed physical universe, a package that proved irresistible to the Anglican churchmen and university graduates who led British science down to 1859. It was a global vision that attracted the narrow focused work of specialists: having defined the world Humboldt left his followers to develop his ideas in ever greater sophistication, through endless travel, data gathering, reflection and publication. 'In the first part of the nineteenth century "Humboldtian Science" was perhaps the most inspirational and comprehensive program for the investigation of nature.'[11] Critically it was a programme defined by exploration and data gathering.

The North West Passage

Nowhere was the need for a Humboldtian voyage of scientific discovery more obvious than the Arctic. In the sixteenth century English mariners, merchants and explorers sought a sea route north of the American continents. Access to the alluring markets and opportunities of the Indian and Pacific Oceans was barred by Spanish and Portuguese fleets. English merchants tried the Arctic, both to the north-east and the north-west. Their hopes were blasted by ice, storms, mutiny and the lure of gold. In the seventeenth century the decline of Iberian power opened the Indian Ocean to British traders, and interest in the Arctic decreased. For the next two hundred years various haphazard efforts to find a North West Passage proved tragic or farcical.[12] Yet after a twenty-two-year hiatus while Britain fought Revolutionary and Napoleonic France, the Arctic mission revived.

After Trafalgar the Royal Navy lacked opposition worthy of its skill and power; the heirs of Nelson needed new challenges. They found a new raison d'être attacking piracy, the slave trade and the natural world. The most successful fighting force on earth made war on the Arctic in the interests of ownership, commerce and science. It would be many years before the contest was decided, but the navy had finally found a foe that it could not overcome. After forty years the expeditions stopped – the ice had triumphed.

However, defeat was the last thing anyone expected when the Royal Navy set out for the north. The Arctic quickly became a theatre of the sublime, the awe-inspiring power of the natural world exerting an irresistible appeal on the art and literature of the Romantic age. Although Elizabethan navigators provided first-hand accounts of the Arctic the inner meaning of the desolate, lifeless polar wastes emerged as a cultural force only with Coleridge's 'Rime of the Ancient Mariner'. Although set in the Antarctic, Coleridge employed Arctic imagery from whaling voyages, and his contemporaries saw no difference between the two frozen extremities. This potent place made men question God. Mary Shelley's *Frankenstein* of 1818 employed the Arctic as a theatre for the display of human pride and vanity, the perfect setting for a final scene. These imaginative writings predated the first nineteenth-century expeditions. The voyages of Parry and Franklin gave sensation-starved audiences access to new wonders, described in suitably understated fashion by naval officers who were men of science, not art.[13] If Emily Brontë worshipped Edward Parry, she was not alone. Parry's narrative inspired Caspar David Friedrich's startling picture 'The Sea of Ice'. In a scene created entirely from his own imagination the artist represented the very personal grief for the loss of a brother.[14] This is how the Arctic was understood: huge, dangerous and empty, a place without life, hope or God. Whatever his intentions, Friedrich encapsulated the Arctic impulse in a single, stark image long before the reality had been recognised, or the darkest truths told.

Narrative accounts of early nineteenth-century Arctic exploration were best-sellers, making heroes of their authors. These voyages flirted with disaster, overwintering in the ice and avoiding catastrophe by the narrowest margins. Yet the providential survival of such expeditions only encouraged more risk taking, by men made over-confident by good fortune.

In 1817 there were practical reasons for these missions: territory and trade, the commercial and strategic concerns of the British state. Although the Napoleonic Wars had ended with Britain dominant on the world's oceans her policy makers saw no occasion for complacency. The challenge of imperial Russia, which emerged after 1815 as Britain's principal rival in European and Asian affairs, was soon manifest in the polar region. With Arctic lands in Siberia and Alaska, Russia controlled the Bering Strait, threatening to move eastwards and challenge the commercial interest of the Hudson's Bay Company – the chartered company that harvested the animal pelts of the Canadian Arctic and sub-Arctic. Mapping and charting the Arctic would legitimate British claims.

Such immediate concerns were an ideal complement for the possible discovery of a new commercial route and the lure of science. They provided a frisson of danger to prompt the British government, desperate to save money and pay off the massive national debt arising from more than twenty years of war, to fund a major new project. The same issues were at stake around the globe, and John Barrow (1783–1847), permanent secretary to the Board of Admiralty, was heavily involved in their resolution.[15]

As the long-serving human face of a large, amorphous organisation, Barrow is usually credited with a dominant role in British attempts to find a North West Passage in the first half of the nineteenth century. Alongside his official post Barrow was also a councillor of the Royal Society and a founder of the Royal Geographical Society. His passionate belief that a passage existed, his administrative abilities and his official position convinced many that he should lead the project and set the agenda.[16] The inevitable consequence was that he is blamed for the Franklin catastrophe. This version of the story has been told many times, without anyone wondering how a permanent civil servant without private means could achieve so much, or why the British state, and British statesmen, were so stupid as to let him to play out his dreams at their expense, and at the cost of many lives. In reality Barrow managed, facilitated and promoted the mission, linking the many disparate agendas of the key players. His prominence in polar literature is a convenient shorthand for more complex processes, and obscures vital elements of the story – a development that began immediately after his death.

Setting an agenda

Nowhere is the over-estimation of Barrow's role more significant than in the field of science. Humboldt's impact on the ideas and methods of exploration and science, and the impulse he gave to geological and especially magnetic science, is incalculable. Barrow knew his works. As literary director of the Arctic project, Barrow used Humboldt's publications as the model for quasi-official narratives published by John Murray, the Admiralty printer, but he did not share Humboldt's scientific interests.

Narrative histories have focused on the drama of the search for a North West Passage, the suffering, endurance and resolve of the navigators, but the Arctic mission was a broad church. While the Passage was an obvious and enduring headline, these costly missions had to be funded, despite Treasury opposition, by a cash-strapped post-war Royal Navy. Here the support of non-governmental scientific pressure groups proved critical. If they wanted to take their Humboldtian science into the Arctic to study geology, biology, oceanography, ice, anthropology and above all terrestrial magnetism, they needed to join a naval expedition. Cook's first Pacific voyage in the 1760s had been primarily one of science and navigation, and so were the Arctic voyages of the early nineteenth century. They employed scientific seamen and travelling scientists to satisfy the curiosity of the world, extend the frontiers of knowledge and secure economic rewards. The attraction of the Arctic for scientists was obvious from the outset. The voyagers spent more time recording data than sailing, their long dark winters occupied with endless observations of terrestrial magnetism, astronomy and meteorological phenomena, taking geological samples while subjecting the flora and fauna to the deadly categorisation of the preserved specimen.

When the Arctic mission resumed in 1817, the Royal Society was the only scientific body with the standing to influence ministerial decisions, reflecting the status of its president, botanist, voyager and imperial economic expert Sir Joseph Banks. Under Banks the Royal Society actively supported exploration, the combination of observational science and discovery providing a route to the top of the scientific community for able men. The ideal of an improved understanding of the world propelled many missions and opened the way to new generations with different agendas. The close relationship between the Admiralty and the Royal Society went back to the latter's founding in the 1660s and increased in the late eighteenth century as science and technology exerted ever greater influence on naval activity. Solving the key navigational problem of longitude had opened the way for further exploration and data collection in ever more inclusive schemes of study. Cook was one of many prominent naval scientists to be awarded the prestigious appellation FRS: Fellow of the Royal Society.

However, the Royal Society was far too genteel to function as a public pressure group: Banks preferred to lobby key individuals. In the nineteenth century other scientific societies would emerge to challenge the Royal Society's primacy. After 1830 the Royal Geographical Society, the Geological Society and the British Association for the Advancement of Science played important roles in the Arctic mission, working with or without the Royal Society. More significantly, new scientific administrators would emerge to assume the mantle of Sir Joseph Banks and achieve something of his eminence. Because the Admiralty was not the only organisation promoting Arctic exploration skilled players of the bureaucratic game could use science to outmanoeuvre opponents in government and the navy.

In reality the hard work of Arctic exploration was largely conducted in London. When promoting new voyages, men such as Barrow, with more than one power base, were particularly effective. The assistance of the press and print media was equally important, in the form not just of the odd polemical pamphlet, by this time an outmoded eighteenth-century approach, but the review article, the key opinion-former of the age. It is because he reviewed all the Arctic books in John Murray's prestigious Tory *Quarterly Review*, and wrote the standard narratives of the Arctic mission, that John Barrow has been given more credit for their genesis than is his due. Barrow, as permanent secretary, directed Admiralty press relations, providing opportunities to use the media for his own ends. He was also a reliable if pedestrian author and had no qualms about adjusting his argument to suit his audience. Contemporaries recognised his utility, and his limitations. They used him to promote Arctic voyages at the Admiralty and in public. That did not make him the chief architect of Arctic exploration, just the chief spin-doctor.

The Admiralty and the Royal Society had co-operated on Arctic missions in the eighteenth century. The 1773 Spitsbergen expedition of Captain Constantine Phipps produced important observations on natural phenomena, from magnetism to meteorology, although the exploration proved less successful. Thereafter war and crisis effectively precluded further naval expeditions, but interest in exploiting natural resources, primarily whales, ensured the subject was not forgotten. Banks visited Iceland, and retained a research interest in the Arctic for the rest of his life. In 1807 he began corresponding with William Scoresby Jr, a Whitby whaling captain and talented amateur scientist. Recognising a unique Arctic resource Banks furthered Scoresby's education and loaned him essential scientific instruments. Like all professional seamen Scoresby was particularly concerned with magnetic phenomena that affected navigation, deflecting the compass needle from true to magnetic north, an issue 'so important to our maritime concerns'.[17] During the Napoleonic Wars Banks relied on Scoresby's ability to combine science with a successful career as a whale catcher.[18] Knowing more about whales, winds and way-finding paid healthy dividends. His sustained interest in magnetism was equally pragmatic: at high latitudes the compass was unreliable.[19]

In October 1817 Scoresby reported that Baffin Bay was open to navigation, apparently for the first time since the seventeenth century, and that he might resolve the mystery of a North West Passage that season.[20] Banks brought Scoresby's report to the Council of the Royal Society in November, launching nineteenth-century Arctic exploration. The Council urged the Admiralty to send an official voyage to determine if Baffin Bay existed, and to search for a North West Passage. Although the mission was based on Scoresby's work, when the time came to send an expedition he was sidelined.

In his declining years Banks came to rely on the quietly efficient Barrow to manipulate the Council of the Royal Society, and ensure it was filled with suitable councillors. Having risen from a humble background on undoubted talent and a willingness to serve the great, Barrow had no desire to be supplanted in Banks's favour by a whaler. He used Scoresby's news to produce an article in the October issue of the *Quarterly Review* indicating the Admiralty wished to resume the Arctic mission. In all probability Banks had used Barrow to prime the naval pump before sending the official Royal Society letter to Lord Melville, First Lord of the Admiralty, on 20 November. Referring to recent meteorological and glacial changes that Scoresby had observed, and the scientific possibilities they opened, Banks suggested the time had come to

correct and amend the very defective geography of the Arctic Regions more especially on the side of America . . . and to endeavour to ascertain the practicability of a passage from the Atlantic to the Pacific Ocean, along the Northern Coast of America. These objects may be considered as peculiarly interesting to Great Britain, not only from their proximity and the national advantages which they involve but also for the marked attention they called forth and the Discoveries made in consequence thereof in the very early periods of our foreign navigation.[21]

Evidently Sir Joseph had been reading the voyage narratives compiled by Elizabethan geographer Richard Hakluyt. Perhaps Barrow had pointed out the relevant passages. However, Banks had other interests in the Arctic, scientific concerns that secured Royal Society support for the mission.[22] In part the mission was a fraud; Scoresby already knew that Baffin Bay existed, and did not believe in an economically viable North West Passage.

John Barrow did not want Scoresby's negative views to spoil 'his' Arctic mission. An adept player of the power game, he exploited his dual role as Admiralty secretary and Royal Society councillor to sideline them. Scoresby was a commercial seaman, not a naval officer. Rather than giving him command of a vessel, or the post of sailing master, Barrow invited Scoresby to offer his services to the Navy Board, the administrative body that handled naval bureaucracy. This calculated insult excluded the best qualified man from the expedition. Whether Barrow saw Scoresby as a rival for the ear of the elderly Banks, or genuinely believed that the navy should conduct the mission, his conduct was devious.[23] Barrow was a man whose hatreds endured to the grave, and his cursory treatment on this and other occasions effectively ended Scoresby's role in Arctic exploration. He went back to the more profitable business of whaling, but not before publishing the first major book on the Arctic.[24] Pioneer Arctic navigators John Ross and Edward Parry acknowledged their debt to Scoresby – and he continued his scientific work, first while at sea, and then as a clergyman.

Having unceremoniously dismissed Scoresby, Barrow soon found his agenda threatened by a voice from the past. In December 1817 Rear Admiral James Burney, companion of Cook and historian of Pacific exploration, read a paper at the Royal Society arguing that Asia and America were connected to the north of the Bering Strait. He had sailed in this area on Cook's third, fatal expedition.[25] Appearing just as the government was preparing to send expeditions north to find a navigable sea route across the top of America, the paper caused a minor sensation when a transcript appeared in the popular *Gentleman's Magazine*. Burney had real authority, combining local knowledge with expertise on regional history and geography. If he was correct there was no point searching for a North West Passage. Barrow responded with 'On the Polar Ice and Northern Passages to the Pacific', an unsigned article in the October issue of the *Quarterly Review*. (Despite the date, Barrow wrote his article after Burney's paper had been read in December; the October 1817 issue actually appeared in February 1818.) The effect was startling; Barrow's paper added 2,000 copies to the usual sale of 10,000, launching Murray's long and profitable association with Arctic literature. In the spring of 1818, after Burney's paper had been published, Barrow produced 'Burney on Behring's Strait and the Polar Basin'. Once again sales of the *Quarterly* rose.[26] In a manner that would become familiar to his victims Barrow opened a comprehensive dismissal of Burney with a fulsome if unctuous tribute to his eminence and his 'orthodoxy', before citing Cook and implying Burney was senile. In fact Cook's account supported Burney, something Barrow chose to ignore. His mission was too important to be derailed by a living connection with the heroic age of exploration. Burney spent 1818 compiling his *Chronological History of North-Eastern Voyages of Discovery and of the Early Eastern Navigations of the Russians*. The book appeared in 1819, too late to influence the first round of Arctic voyages, but Russian ambition would be a key element in sustaining the impulse, adding an alarmist theme to Barrow's work.

After the commercial success of his two lengthy Arctic reviews Murray invited Barrow to write a book.[27] In his foreword, dated London, 1 August 1818, Barrow noted that 'the two expeditions recently fitted out for exploring a northern communication between the Atlantic and Pacific Oceans were of a nature to excite public attention'. His aim was to set the record straight by providing a brief history. To disarm critics and disguise his agenda he archly confessed that the work was a quick compilation, with 'no pretensions to authorship', providing 'a general knowledge of what has been and what remains to be accomplished'. This was the Arctic manifesto, a carefully crafted narrative that inexorably led the casual reader to accept the logic of the mission, and the likelihood of success. The chapter on the eighteenth century ended with the Russian voyages.[28] Although Barrow claimed this was no more than a discussion of Coxe's *Account of Russian Discoveries*, the real object was to pre-empt Burney and establish the Russians as credible rivals for the Passage.

Barrow focused on Russian attempts to navigate between the White Sea and the Pacific, and attributed their failure to the very Russian fault of having hugged the coast. Convinced that an open Polar Sea existed, he argued the ice would be less difficult further from the shore. Russia had suspended voyages of discovery during the French wars, and the first post-war mission was a privately financed attempt to transit the American north from west to east. Lieutenant Kotzebue, another disciple of Humboldt,[29] reached 68°N, 160°W around Norton Sound, where he met Inuit who corresponded with Cook's description. However, Kotzebue's fantastical descriptions of icebergs and other phenomena did not agree with Cook's. Favoured with an interview by Kotzebue, Barrow repeated his claims, and praised him for bringing back all but one of his men.[30] When discussing the latest British voyages, Barrow took care not to mention Scoresby.[31] He was less concerned by the posthumous republication of Daines Barrington's 1775 pamphlet calling for an approach to the pole via Spitsbergen, which had been anticipated by an Admiralty mission.[32] Barrow dismissed Burney with the same coldly efficient hatchet job he had employed to defeat Scoresby. This ensured the Admiralty's response to the Royal Society was quick and positive. On 8 January 1818 Banks reported to his Council that the Admiralty would send two missions, each with two ships: one would attempt to find the Passage, the other to reach the North Pole by way of Spitsbergen.

However, there were other reasons the Admiralty was anxious to send expeditions north, for the entire mission was intimately linked to the navigational needs of the British Empire. An Act of Parliament of 10 June 1818 offered a reward for any ship passing 100°w at a longitude about halfway between Baffin Bay and the Bering Strait.[33] This replaced legislation dating back over a century, designed to reward the determination of longitude at sea, and set up a new body to adjudicate claims, effectively deputing the task to the Royal Society.[34] In case anyone doubted the importance of navigational science in the dispatch of the first nineteenth-century polar missions the same commissioners who deliberated on navigational improvements would judge the success of Arctic voyages, and oversee the publication of the *Nautical Almanac*, the vital reference for oceanic navigators. The Astronomer Royal, professors from Oxford and Cambridge and the president of the Royal Society were commissioners *ex officio*, while the salaries of three paid commissioners and a secretary were covered by the Navy Estimates.

While the Royal Society was happy to support the development of navigational science, it had another major project in hand that would benefit from a polar voyage. Following the success of geodesic work by Captain Henry Kater in 1817 the Royal Society was anxious to continue this work in high latitudes.[35] In addition it provided advice on other scientific subjects, and sent Captain Edward Sabine, Royal Artillery, on the mission seeking the passage.[36] Many of the key Arctic figures of the next thirty years served on the ships that went north in 1818: John and James Clark Ross, Edward Parry, John Franklin, George Back and Sabine. Banks played a key role in selecting these officers. Edward Parry was the son of a scientific friend, John Franklin the legacy of another scientific officer. Banks opened his remarkable London library to the Arctic officers, and they saluted him as 'the father of the Enterprise'. Parry named his westernmost discovery for Banks, but the old man did not live to learn of that honour.[37]

While the science was a success, the Spitsbergen voyage of David Buchan and John Franklin, like Phipps's fifty years before, was hampered by thick ice and made no geographical discoveries. Scoresby had seen it all before, and in rather easier ice conditions. The other expedition, led by Danish linguist and ice navigator Captain John Ross, confirmed the existence of Baffin Bay and charted much of the south-western shore, but they went little further. A mountainous mirage persuaded Ross that Lancaster Sound was a dead end, and he turned back. Both expeditions were back in England before the end of 1818. At least Ross had claimed Baffin and Bylot Islands for the Crown.[38] Every subsequent expedition would repeat the time-honoured process of landing on terra firma, erecting a flagstaff, delivering a pompous speech in English (just in case the locals wanted to argue), hoisting the Union Jack and firing a salute.

The failure to find a North West Passage threatened Barrow's status and his role as co-ordinator of a global geographical mission. His response was quick and decisive. John Ross was sacrificed to save the mission, replaced by his pliable second, Parry. The deed was easily done because Ross had not consulted Parry over the 'Croker Mountains' mirage. Ross compounded his error by publicly criticising Sabine's performance as a naturalist. This left him open to a devastating riposte.[39] He had claimed credit for Sabine's scientific observations, and if that impropriety were not enough, added insult to the injury by producing them 'incomplete, imperfect, and printed incorrectly'. Little wonder Sabine became a lifelong ally of Barrow. For a seasoned naval officer and linguist Ross was surprisingly cavalier with facts, credit and money. Many doubted Ross's honesty, and some his sanity. The mirage added to a long list of failings in a venomous *Quarterly Review* of Ross's narrative which never strayed above a tone of harsh mockery, unless it was to express wholly unjustified criticism. Although the article was unsigned, no one doubted Barrow was responsible, or that he was obliged to attack because Ross's failure was the only argument he could advance that would warrant a second expedition.[40] The rival *Edinburgh Review* was better disposed to Ross, observing that Barrow's review was dominated by personal feelings on the question of the existence of a passage.

That so much heat had been generated by scientific data may explain why Parry's first mission was more concerned with magnetic science than Ross's, adopting the magnetic North Pole as a realistic target. Parry, a fine observational scientist, proved more accurate and thorough than the slipshod Ross. The key lesson of 1818 was to avoid giving hostages to fortune, balancing one measure of success – finding the Passage – with magnetic and other scientific objectives 'likely to prove of almost equal importance'.[41] In 1819 Parry quickly sailed through Ross's 'Croker Mountains' and kept heading west. When the sea ice formed in late September, he secured the ships in winter quarters. Sabine then built a magnetic observatory far enough away from the ships to avoid the influence of their iron fittings, and settled down to a long, cold winter of readings, briefly enlivened by a fire that threatened his instruments. The following August the ships were cut out of harbour and pushed west to 113°48', the westernmost discovery, receiving the name of Banks Island. At this point the ice was too thick for any further progress. This was a dead end for 200-ton wooden sailing vessels, and Parry suggested a route further south might be more successful.[42]

Scoresby's version

Scoresby's two-volume study of the Arctic and the whale fishery appeared in 1820. He recognised that the existence of a navigable sea passage between Europe and China was the most contentious geographical problem, and had no doubt that Barrow, whom he took care not to mention by name, was only the latest in a long line of men to deceive themselves into believing in this mirage. 'It is not a little surprising that, after nearly a hundred different voyages have been undertaken, . . . all of which have failed, Britain should again revive and attempt the solution to this interesting problem.'[43] Having examined the evidence and the region Scoresby concluded that even if a passage 'really exists, it could never be practicable in one year'; consequently it 'could never be of any advantage to our commerce with China or India'.[44] The main results of such voyages to the west and the east had been the extension of whale and seal fisheries, and the trade of the Hudson's Bay Company. Rather than pursuing the popular but wholly chimerical North West Passage he advocated voyages to address realistic geographical, commercial and scientific issues, including magnetic variation.[45] This advice may be the burden of conversations with Ross and Parry in Banks's library. After that discussion Scoresby knew that for all their nautical skill and bravery naval officers were inexperienced in ice navigation, and suggested employing Hudson's Bay Company officers on shore to follow up the work of Alexander Mackenzie and Samuel Hearne, who had traced the course of Canadian rivers to the Arctic coast a generation earlier.[46] The key to exploration by sea would be the state of the ice, which fluctuated considerably from year to year. Between 1813 and 1817 the coast of Spitsbergen had been largely open, and in 1817 and 1818 remarkably so. A table of thermometer readings backed up his analysis. In a late addition Scoresby noted that Lieutenant John Franklin had been appointed to command an overland expedition: 'From this officer's known zeal and activity, and from the promising character of this mode of making discoveries, the most satisfactory results are to be anticipated.'[47]

2

John Franklin – Navigator

THERE IS SOMETHING about a tragedy wrapped up in a mystery
that keeps a good story fresh. A terrible death in the Arctic wastes,
given a flesh-chilling frisson of horror by rumours of cannibalism,
keeps us coming back. The final, fatal mission of John Franklin has
come to define the history of the Arctic, a tale of doomed endeavour
endlessly retold for moral improvement, morbid curiosity or the
spread of geographical knowledge. The North West Passage opened
the Arctic, but it killed Franklin and his men. And at the heart of
every Arctic story stands John Franklin. Franklin has been analysed
many times: for some he is the 'pathetic blunderer' and 'bungler'
who led his men, like some latter-day Grand Old Duke of York, to
their icy doom.[1] Others focus on his age and his physical condition –
he was fifty-nine, and in modern terms morbidly obese – to argue
that he was the wrong man for the job. Even his apologists are content to leave him as the archetypal 'heroic explorer', a brave but
simple soul, a type beloved by the Victorians.

The truth, as ever, is very different. While Franklin has had many
biographers, he remains an elusive subject.[2] Born on 15 April 1786 in
the Lincolnshire village of Spilsby, John was the fifth son and ninth
child of Willingham Franklin, local merchant and banker. By the time
he reached school age his elder brothers were on their way to impressive careers: Willingham became chief justice at Madras, while James
entered the East India Company as a military engineer and played a
prominent part in the survey of India. Once he had seen the sea
Franklin was determined to join the navy, and eventually overcame
parental opposition. Whether he chose the sea from a desire to travel,
to escape from the bottom of the family heap, or just from the exu-
berance of youth is unknown. He had a local role model in Matthew
Flinders, a relative by marriage and a close friend of brothers Thomas

and Willingham.³ In the autumn of 1800 Franklin joined the Royal Navy, on board the sixty-four-gun battleship HMS *Polyphemus*.

He joined a navy at war, desperately stretched by the demands of a global conflict with France and Spain. While Franklin was coming to terms with his new life, living in the evil-smelling airless bowels of the ship, working on the deck and climbing the rigging, his country faced a crisis. The neutral powers of northern Europe were infuriated by Britain's aggressive use of naval power against France, especially the use of force to stop their highly profitable abuse of neutral rights to trade through the blockade. In late 1800 Paul I, the mad tsar of Russia, dragooned Sweden, Denmark and Prussia into a coalition to demand concessions. If Britain backed down she would lose the war with France, if she rejected the demands she would face four new enemies. The response was simple: by March 1801 a powerful fleet had assembled, with Lord Nelson as second in command. Nelson chose twelve ships to attack the Danish fleet guarding Copenhagen, including the *Polyphemus*. On 1 April, a fortnight short of his fifteenth birthday, John Franklin found himself at the terrifying heart of a vicious naval battle. The two fleets fought to the finish. The Danes could not move: they had no sails; the British were equally immobile, held in place by the iron will of their admiral. Many men died that day, smashed to pulp by heavy iron shot or cut to ribbons by jagged oak splinters. After hours of stunning, cacophonous cannonade the Danes accepted an armistice, and Nelson persuaded them to leave the coalition. Copenhagen was a savage baptism of fire, bringing Franklin face to face with the grim reality of his profession at a tender age. Although his ship had been in the thick of the action, he was not among *Polyphemus*'s thirty casualties.

Polyphemus returned to Britain just in time for Franklin to take up a midshipman's berth on Flinders's ship, HMS *Investigator*. They sailed that July to chart the coast of a continent Flinders would christen Australia. Family connections secured Franklin the post, and Flinders, in loco parentis, would report back to Lincolnshire on the progress of his young protégé.

There was good reason to report. Franklin had joined the remarkable dynasty of oceanic navigators that began with James Cook. Cook trained Bligh on his final, fatal voyage, while Bligh trained

Matthew Flinders on his successful second journey to Tahiti. In turn Flinders would teach Franklin the business of navigation on the first circumnavigation of Australia.

Before they left England, Flinders told Franklin's brother:

He is a very fine youth and there is every probability of his doing credit to the *Investigator* and to himself . . . after a few months he will be sufficiently of an astronomer to be my right hand man in that way. His attention to his duty has gained him the esteem of the first lieutenant who scarcely knows how to talk enough in his praise.[4]

This voyage was the key to Franklin's character, ambitions and abilities. He left Britain a stunned schoolboy, and returned a proven seaman, raised in the school of Cook. Matthew Flinders was a living link with heroic voyages that had fired the imagination of the Western world. Sir Joseph Banks, Cook's scientific companion, selected Flinders to combine the coastal survey of the entire continent with a large scientific programme. As commanding officer Flinders was responsible for the education of his midshipmen. He provided rich opportunities for practical and theoretical study, a forcing house of seamanship and science. Franklin was an enthusiastic student.[5] He profited from the fact that his captain needed competent deck officers, surveyors and scientific observers when he reached Australia. When Humboldt took his readings in Peru, Franklin was on the south coast of Australia, recording compass deviation, taking astronomical observations and maintaining the critical chronometers. Flinders communicated an enthusiasm for navigation, and Franklin learned 'everything that we can show him'.[6] Four years on a frigate might have made him a skilled handler of ships under sail, and an able tactician, but an unimpressive, leaky merchant ship offered him so much more, not least her suggestive original name: *Xenophon*. Franklin mastered the key elements of navigation and charting. Patience and thoroughness made him a trustworthy observer, and he had opportunities to demonstrate judgement and leadership.

The voyage was a typical mixture of long sea passages of almost interminable boredom, interspersed with periods of frenetic activity ashore and in the surveying boats. Whatever Flinders did, Franklin was close by, and along with his naval lessons received a master class in leadership. By 1804 Franklin was an adept student of navigation, astronomy and the other observational sciences that featured on the voyage. He also picked up Flinders's obsession with the navigational problems caused by the deviation of the magnetic compass. Flinders demonstrated that the ironwork of the ship was a major culprit, and his findings were published by Banks in the Royal Society journal *Philosophical Transactions* in 1805.

On the Australian coast Franklin also buckled down to the study of French, a decision prompted by the unusual experience of meeting the crew of a French warship during the brief Peace of Amiens and finding that their only common language was Latin. Franklin also worked his way through Flinders's library, a fine collection of contemporary naval, exploration, cultural and scientific material. Above all he profited from the example of his captain. Shipwrecked on the Barrier Reef, Flinders demonstrated how to lead men in adversity, calmly building camp and salvaging supplies before sailing an open boat back to Sydney for help.

After rescuing his men Flinders, anxious to bring his work before the Admiralty, took the first ship home. There was little space on board, so he had to leave most of his officers and men behind. Franklin was fortunate to be among them as Britain and France were once more at war. When he landed on Mauritius, Flinders was arrested by General Decaen, the angry, punctilious French governor, and detained for the better part of a decade without good cause. Not that Franklin was safe. He sailed from Sydney to Canton to take a passage home on an East India ship. French warships were at large in the Indian Ocean looking for prizes, and there were none richer than an East India convoy. Convoy Commodore George Dance was no fool; he knew that his ships could not run or hide, so he prepared for trouble. His fleet of eighteen lumbering merchant Argosies was intercepted in the Banda Strait by five powerful French warships, but Dance was ready. He had prepared his fleet to masquerade as battleships. The deception was almost credible, at a distance – the East Indiamen were big two-decked vessels – but any officer worth his salt would quickly see through the disguise. They were too narrow in the beam, too lightly manned, and armed with pop guns. Undeterred by such obvious flaws in his scheme Dance drilled the convoy to behave like a battle squadron, his naval passengers providing signals expertise. Dance took the initiative, sailing towards Admiral Linois's squadron and conducting a series of smartly executed naval manoeuvres that bluffed the Frenchman into retreating. While Linois became the laughing stock of the French navy, Franklin, Dance's signal officer during the encounter, earned a commendation for his 'zeal and alacrity'. Evidently he had read the naval tactical and signalling material in Flinders's library with some attention.

The day after returning to Britain, Franklin was appointed to HMS *Bellerophon*, a famous old seventy-four-gun battleship, already distinguished in two great battles: the 'Glorious First of June' 1794 and the Nile. After a spell of blockade duty off Brest the *Bellerophon* was detached to Cadiz, and on 21 October 1805 earned the ultimate battle honour in Lord Collingwood's division. Once again Franklin was the signals officer, but this time the quarterdeck lived up to its nickname 'the slaughter pen'. Forty-seven men stood there that day, of whom only seven, including Franklin, avoided death or injury. Many, like Nelson on the *Victory*, were hit by musket fire from the French ships. Not until the last French marksman was shot down by the *Bellerophon*'s marines was Franklin safe. Captain John Cooke was not so fortunate: his death placed First Lieutenant William Pryce Cumby in command, securing instant promotion to captain.[7] Cumby and Franklin were lifelong friends, but Trafalgar left Franklin stunned and deafened. His hearing never fully recovered, and although impaired hearing was not unusual for a career naval officer, it proved to be a serious handicap when he moved into another profession.

With the shattered *Bellerophon* under repair Franklin moved to another 'seventy-four', HMS *Bedford*. This time his luck ran out. For the next decade he could only inch his way up the promotion ladder, lacking well-placed patrons or the chance to secure promotion by some signal act of personal bravery. Eventually, he was commissioned lieutenant on 11 February 1808, aged twenty-two. Nelson had been a captain at twenty, and so had many of Franklin's contemporaries. Cruising service off Rio de Janeiro and the River

Scheldt provided little opportunity for distinction. With Flinders far away and unable to help him, Franklin was doomed to a slow career. To make matters worse brother Thomas managed to lose the family's business and most of its savings. Franklin scraped together what he could of his meagre pay to help out.

In April 1814 Franklin's career prospects took a turn for the worse: Napoleon abdicated, peace was restored and the navy would be paid off. There were far more lieutenants than the navy could hope to employ in peacetime, and he had little hope of promotion. It seemed that his career was as good as over when the *Bedford* joined the Duke of Clarence's fleet to escort the victorious allied sovereigns to England. Finally, Flinders died on the eve of fame.[8] Anxious to catch any opportunity for advancement Franklin wrote to *Investigator* shipmate botanist Dr Robert Brown, now installed as Banks's librarian, amanuensis and confidant. From the comfort of Banks's Soho Square office Brown enquired if Franklin would be interested in a naval expedition, since voyages of discovery were to resume now that peace had returned. If so, Brown would be happy to recommend him.[9] Banks added Flinders's relative to his list of scientific seamen. Franklin was too wise in the ways of officialdom to give an unqualified acceptance. He was interested, but left Brown in no doubt that he would expect promotion in return for years of service and possible loss of health – Flinders had died of renal failure. Having made his terms he stressed his anxiousness to serve on the type of scientific mission that Banks had in mind.

For the moment Franklin was fortunate that Britain had other enemies. His luck changed when *Bedford* was ordered to the West Indies in late 1814, joining the fleet off New Orleans to take part in one of the final battles of the War of 1812. The British planned an amphibious operation to capture the city from the Americans, despite the difficulties posed by impassable terrain, vile weather and even the enemy. Franklin's character shone amid the ruins of a desperate, ill-starred enterprise. The British planned to cut into the Mississippi river from the east, across Lake Borgne, but the lake was occupied by five American gunboats. The gunboats had to be taken before the troops were landed. Franklin commanded one of the *Bedford*'s boats in a daring attack on the powerful American craft.

Fifty British boats sailed across the lake to a point just beyond range of the American guns, a distance of about two miles. There they anchored, took lunch and rested for an hour. Suitably refreshed, the men rowed into the attack. All five American vessels were taken by boarding, at a cost of seventeen dead and seventy-eight wounded. Franklin displayed exemplary leadership, being the first to board his chosen target, and was slightly wounded in the process. He spent the next nine weeks on detached service with the army, helping to land and sustain the troops as they prepared to attack the city. This was dismal work, perpetually cold and wet. On the day of battle he led a party of seamen assisting General Thornton's troops to cross the river and attack a key American battery. Thornton's men, the sailors well to the front, stormed the American position under heavy fire. The operation had been entirely successful, but just as they prepared to turn the captured American guns to enfilade American General Andrew Jackson's trenches on the left bank they were recalled. The British commander-in-chief General Pakenham had not waited to learn the result of Thornton's operation, launching a hopeless frontal assault on well-prepared entrenchments on the right bank. Pakenham and many of his men were killed in a one-sided exchange, and once again the navy had to evacuate a demoralised army. Finally, Franklin had made a name for himself; General Lambert, the senior surviving British general, mentioned him in dispatches, and recommended him for promotion. However, the battle had been lost, and with it Franklin's chance of promotion to commander.[10]

Returning to Britain, the *Bedford* paid off on 5 July and two days later Franklin was appointed first lieutenant of HMS *Forth*, captained by Nelson's nephew Sir William Bolton, serving during Napoleon's 'Hundred Days' and the second Bourbon restoration. Sir William was only a few years older than Franklin, but had been promoted quickly. If Franklin was going to make a career he had many years to catch up on such sons of fortune. His wartime career had not been without honour or merit, but promotion had been painfully slow. Flinders's imprisonment had cost Franklin dear; his death could have been a disaster. After reading Flinders's narrative Franklin regretted the book was too dry for the general reader. It would establish Flinders's 'character as a good navigator' but he was disappointed not to be mentioned more favourably.[11] His own narratives would be more highly coloured, in the Humboldtian manner, and better received by the popular audience.

Although stingy with praise, Flinders bequeathed to Franklin his telescope (that he might see his way ahead), an interest in magnetism and the patronage of fellow Lincolnshire man Sir Joseph Banks. That Banks, Flinders and Franklin were born not five miles apart emphasised Banks's personal approach to patronage. It was through Banks that Franklin first entered the ice. Flinders taught Franklin another vital lesson when his irascible temper cost him six years' detention on Mauritius. Franklin would be the very model of calm dignity. Flinders's name was made by a great voyage and a great narrative; Franklin followed the model and reaped the rewards.

While the prospect of promotion may have seemed distant when Franklin paid off in September 1815, he had been thinking about his career options. The First Lord of the Admiralty confirmed in writing that the only hope of promotion lay in service abroad. Once ashore he took the opportunity to pay his respects to Flinders's widow, visit his family in Lincolnshire and call on Sir Joseph at nearby Revesby Abbey. Banks recommended studies 'that would better prepare me for the service of any other expedition which might offer'. Never one to miss a hint, Franklin applied himself to mastering marine surveying, 'as a source of amusement and improvement during the time of my being unemployed, and even when employed I shall hope to have opportunities of practising, what I now learn by theory'.[12] The results of his studies would soon be seen on the Arctic chart.

Service abroad soon returned to the top of Franklin's agenda. He was lucky not to be selected for the first post-Napoleonic mission: the 1816 Congo expedition under James Tuckey made some progress upriver, but tropical diseases killed most of the crew. Instead the Arctic became Franklin's theatre. He was appointed to command the Lincolnshire-built merchant ship *Trent*.[13] By February 1818 Banks was briefing him and expedition leader Captain Buchan on Scoresby's observations.[14] Expectations ran high: their instructions included the delivery of copies of their journals to the governor of Kamchatka, in Russia's far north-east, before returning home the

way they came, securing British territorial claims with an unequivocal demonstration of priority. Many of the leading scientists of the
day crowded onto the two ships at Deptford, leaving behind a number of experiments for Buchan and Franklin to conduct. In taking
small projects into a new environment, there are obvious parallels
with modern space missions. The Arctic gripped the scientific community, from Banks's expansive vision to the humblest amateur. After
twenty years of war the backlog of ideas and projects was immense.
Although slightly overawed by the eminence of his new friends,
Franklin found himself surprisingly comfortable in this heady environment.[15] He might not have a university pedigree, or the status of a
Fellow of the Royal Society, but he had been round the world, made
observations, and fought the king's enemies. He was somebody, and
if this venture paid off he could expect to be promoted.

After a formal inspection by the Board of Admiralty the two expeditions sailed from the Thames and met at Lerwick in May 1818.
Franklin took the opportunity to discuss the magnetic project with
fellow voyagers Parry and Sabine, and practise making observations. Despite his experience under Flinders he was anxious to learn.
He wrote to Captain Henry Kater Royal Engineers, leader of the
Royal Society geodetic project, 'I wish you could have been of the
party, you were such a warm advocate of our cause, and have been
so anxious to contribute to our comfort and our success.' Kater, an
expert in the latest geodetic and magnetic research, was well worth
cultivating.[16] Franklin also wrote a letter to Banks to ensure he was
not forgotten whenever a scientific expedition was projected.[17] If
Franklin's letters stopped just short of sycophancy, their purpose
was to establish him in the expeditionary branch of the Royal Navy
through his scientific attainment and attention to detail. He was
already looking for patterns in the results, to develop hypotheses
and advance scientific understanding.[18]

While the expedition failed to reach Kamchatka, only sighting the
coast of Spitsbergen, it inspired Franklin with a passion for Arctic
travel. Surrounded by icebergs and driven by storms both ships came
close to destruction, but Franklin proved either the more competent
or the luckier of the two commanders and HMS *Trent* escorted
Buchan's *Dorothea* home. Six months after leaving they were back in

London, but unlike Ross's expedition there was no suggestion they should have done more. While no one would be promoted for a six-month cruise among the icebergs, Franklin knew that science was the key to sustaining his naval career. A prominent place was occupied by compass deviation, a study pioneered by Flinders and one with practical implications for navigators. In addition he had taken great care with the observations that interested Banks, sending details at every opportunity. Above all his magnetic research had linked atmospheric and terrestrial phenomena.[19] Little wonder his services were retained – he was exactly what the scientists were looking for: calm, capable, and intellectually sophisticated. In addition he had achieved a degree of popular fame. An Arctic panorama opened in Leicester Square which included a portrait of Franklin. Always a reluctant celebrity, bashful John stayed away for fear of being recognised.

Arctic hero

When Barrow renewed his Arctic mandate, Franklin was given command of an overland expedition. In 1819 he travelled to Canada via Hudson's Bay with midshipmen George Back and Robert Hood and surgeon John Richardson to follow the Coppermine river to the Arctic coast. John Ross's magnetic results had convinced Barrow and Franklin that Samuel Hearne's position for the Coppermine delta must be seriously inaccurate, and Barrow had included the land expedition alongside a second Arctic voyage to establish accurate navigational fixes for the river and the coastline as part of the Arctic mission. Franklin was not sent to 'explore': indeed, Barrow pointedly recommended him for the command as 'an officer well skilled in astronomical and geographical science, and in the use of instruments, to ascertain the points above mentioned'.[20] His instructions included a significant magnetic element, notably observations for dip, declination and intensity, along with the effect of the aurora borealis on the magnetic needle and other phenomena 'likely to lead to the future development of its cause, and the laws by which it is governed'.[21] The Admiralty hoped he would link up with Parry's expedition.[22]

As a career naval officer Franklin had neither training for nor experience of overland travel.[23] The Colonial Office relied on the

Hudson's Bay and North West Companies to provide essential technical and logistical support. This proved unwise, since the companies were effectively at war over trade and territory. Left to make the best of a bad situation, Franklin knew that he had to carry out his orders to have any hope of future employment. To make matters worse the heavy load of scientific hardware necessary to fix positions and record magnetic data significantly delayed the 'exploring' mission.

Franklin spent the first winter comfortably in purpose-built accommodation with ample food, taking numerous scientific observations and preparing his base camp for a second winter. In the summer of 1821 the party took canoes down the Coppermine river, propelled by a dozen Canadian voyageurs. They surveyed and recorded the Arctic coast, looking for commercial harbours and Parry's expedition, surviving storms and heavy seas in fragile river craft.[24] Having mapped a considerable section of coast and collected further scientific readings, Franklin fatally delayed his return. The journey back to base was a disaster. Franklin's journal and his astronomical readings were lost. Starving and exhausted the voyageurs carrying the equipment began to falter as winter set in. With the whole party reduced to eating rock lichen and their untreated leather boots Franklin, like Flinders, divided his party and pressed on to get help. He left the weaker men to follow as best they could while he went ahead with Back and the fittest voyageurs.[25] Tragically the local Native American tribe, having agreed to stock the larder, didn't believe the crazy white men would return, and didn't waste good food filling the store. When Franklin reached camp, the cupboard was bare. Back set off to find the hunters, but Franklin and the others were too weak to carry on, or to go back for Richardson, Hood, Seaman Hepburn and the remaining voyageurs. Eventually Richardson and Hepburn struggled into camp with a tale of absolute horror. One of the men, half-Iroquois Michel, had killed and eaten at least one of his comrades and then murdered Hood, who had been too sick to continue. Richardson and Hepburn agreed that Michel planned to kill them next, so the doctor shot him.[26] Both Englishmen had eaten human flesh, and this, with the death of Hood, was the key to their survival. It is not clear how much cannibalism Richardson and his party indulged in, or if they were even aware of the fact, but their survival depended on adequate food. Back's return after a heroic journey brought relief to the base camp just as the expedition faced death. Altogether ten voyageurs had died of starvation and hypothermia, some hastened into the next world by hungry comrades.

Nursed back to health by the local chief, Franklin returned home in 1822. On this expedition he had much to learn, and he learned quickly. He never made the same mistake twice. But his performance had not been about competence, it had been about leadership, motivating men who believed themselves as good as dead. He inspired them to cross rivers and carry on when common sense told them to lie down and die quietly. He defeated the fatal drift of hypothermia, providing a sensation-starved world with a stunning example of human fortitude.

Despite the disasters Franklin added hundreds of miles of coastline to the Arctic chart and produced useful magnetic readings while Richardson collected a wealth of botanical and zoological specimens.[27] Furthermore the expedition narrative, helped by sensational press coverage, was a runaway best-seller, combining exotic frozen wastes, high drama, contact with hitherto unknown Inuit peoples, suffering, murder, a hint of cannibalism and a last-gasp rescue. It was simply too improbable for fiction and provided the navy with an Arctic celebrity. Little wonder the Admiralty secretaries Barrow and Croker were anxious to see it in print.[28] The book was cast in the model of Humboldt: high drama and obscenity while searching for knowledge at the edge of the world.[29] This 'powerfully interesting production' made Franklin famous, widely known as 'the man who ate his boots'.[30] The narrative was an innocent production; Franklin did not reflect on his own culpability for the disasters, and felt no need to obscure the unpalatable.[31] He provided potent insights into his experience at the edge of existence, connecting readers with a world of horror hitherto found only in the pages of fiction. Man, mission and manuscript were the toast of the season. Almost unnoticed at the time, and excised from later editions, were seven weighty scientific appendices running to 260 pages. Ninety of those pages were devoted to magnetic phenomena, and links between atmospheric and terrestrial magnetism.[32] By reprinting such narratives without their Humboldtian scientific apparatus publishers seriously distorted popular understanding of the objects and achievements of Arctic expeditions.

Whatever else had been achieved, Franklin had demonstrated a rare talent for leadership. Soon after returning to England he was contemplating another expedition. Excused any enquiry into the 'execution' of Michel, Richardson was happy to go back, but only under Franklin's leadership.[33] Franklin returned a hero, but more significantly he was now a commander, having been promoted in his absence. Once the Admiralty understood the magnitude of his achievement he received a second promotion to post captain. The next promotion, to admiral, depended on seniority. Franklin had caught up with his contemporaries.

The celebrity effect did not falter: he was elected a Fellow of the Royal Society on 20 February 1823, backed by a stellar cast comprising Sabine, Francis Beaufort, Charles Babbage, James Horsborough,[34] Edward Troughton[35] and Robert Brown. His claims were those of 'a gentleman well versed in various branches of natural philosophy . . . geographical and hydrographical discoveries, for which this country has long been celebrated and who has evinced his zeal for science by two expeditions to the North Polar regions'.[36] Above all he had made a major addition to geomagnetic knowledge, and the possibility of accurate compass correction.[37] Franklin spent much of his time moving in the scientific and intellectual circles of the day. His connection with the Royal Society and Royal Institution, which was 'managed' by Edward Sabine, allowed him to develop his interest in magnetic science. He would return to the Arctic with a more extensive collection of instruments and experiments, at least one of which was a personal favour for Michael Faraday.[38] In 1824 Franklin was a founder member of the Athenaeum Club, 'for cultivators of science, letter and art'. He kept company with leading statesmen, scientists, explorers and authors, artists and sculptors. Other founders included his future father-in-law John Griffin, Algernon Percy – later the Duke of Northumberland – an old naval friend and Edward Sabine of magnetic fame. At the Athenaeum explorers rubbed shoulders with statesmen and scientists: Lord

Aberdeen, Michael Faraday, Hudson Gurney (whose son would be the first man to walk across the North West Passage), John Herschel, Sir Robert Inglis, Captain Henry Kater RA, Captain Philip Parker King RN, Charles Lyell, Captain George Lyon RN, Lord Palmerston, Sir Robert Peel and the engineering brothers John and George Rennie among others.[39] Many of these men had their names added to the map of the American Arctic coast, testament to the friendship of John Franklin.

Yet Franklin was not content with his fame, and found unemployment hard to bear. His main comfort came from the same direct and unwavering faith that had sustained him in battle, shipwreck and the Arctic wastes:

the reliance which every one ought to feel on the Almighty and more especially those who undertake services of great hazard and peril. It should surely be their endeavour to seek his heavenly support, guidance and protection by constant fervent prayer, and by the steady use of his appointed means.

Faith and work gave him constant strength.

Amid the hectic social round of 1823 Franklin found time to marry Eleanor Porden, a bright, determined young poet and daughter of a leading architect. The marriage revealed the intellectual aspects of Franklin, while his hitherto single-minded evangelical Christianity was tempered by his wife's determination to continue writing. On 3 June 1824 their daughter, also Eleanor, was born. It seemed he had it all: fame, career, wife and family; but the Arctic had bitten deep into John Franklin's soul and he would not give up his mission half finished. That was not the naval way. Flinders had charted the whole coast of Australia and Franklin was not going to leave any blanks on the map. It was fortunate that his anxiety for further service coincided with a renewed phase of Anglo-Russian tension. He was soon planning a three-pronged assault on the Arctic and preparing to return to the Canadian north.

Russia

The primary impulse for further Arctic exploration in the mid-1820s was the fear of Russian encroachment from their base in Alaska.

Trade and Empire in Arctic America, both of which had been subcontracted to the Hudson's Bay Company since the seventeenth century, were at risk. Well aware that Russia had been identified as Britain's main security concern after Waterloo, Barrow had exploited the threat from the outset while Parry and Franklin were quick to play on his fears to promote their second expeditions.[40] After Kotzebue's voyage the fur trade inside the Bering Strait had been pioneered by American merchants.[41] Suitably alarmed, a Russian imperial decree of 28 September 1821 claimed exclusive use of the Arctic seas on the Siberian and Alaskan coasts far beyond their current occupation, or their charts. Foreign Secretary Lord Castlereagh rejected claims of exclusive sovereignty or navigation, with support from the leading British international lawyer.[42] It was important to tell the Russians that the British government would never concede their claims, but diplomatic procedure could be slow. It would be quicker and more certain to send an expedition to take physical possession, reduce the coast to a chart and own the ground. By producing a map and, if necessary, burying some Englishmen in the corner of a forgotten field Russian claims would be disproved. The primary importance of the publication of Arctic narratives, and those of other exploring missions, lay in demonstrating to the world that the results were British. This 'Imperial Exploration' carried the strongest possible claim to title, short of an international treaty. Accurate maps marked the ground, and enabled others to check the results. This imperative explains why the British translated otherwise obscure Russian voyage narratives: they wanted to check Russian claims. That the otherwise secretive Russians were publishing their narratives was proof positive that publication served a purpose beyond the transmission of scientific or even geographical knowledge. Reviews of these narratives, usually published in German, enabled the British to check the Muscovite version and prepare a British response.

Both Russians and British used the Humboldtian model. The base travel narrative and maps demonstrated that the journey had been made. Scientific appendices, often in separate volumes, conveyed a different kind of ownership. They proved that the travellers had reduced the local world to taxonomic order, naming not just mountains and rivers but animals, birds, minerals and atmospheric phenomena. If this were not enough, all significant exploration texts were given far wider publication through the *Reviews*, in pared-down twenty- to forty-page versions. John Murray, the Admiralty printer, retained a stranglehold over Arctic and other 'official' voyage narratives, notably that of Charles Darwin, for the rest of Barrow's life. Barrow provided editorial support, and ensured the final product supported official policy. It helped that the Arctic was a popular subject, adding thousands to Murray's sales.[43]

In 1823 the Russian card proved a winner. Barrow used Franklin's argument that a new mission would secure 'the naval character and commercial interests of Britain' to obtain Colonial Office support for a second overland expedition.[44] At the same time Parry, who had suggested seeking a passage further south after his first voyage, would link up with the chart of Franklin's first land expedition at the most easterly point he reached on the Arctic coast, the aptly named Point Turnagain. Franklin would return to the Canadian Arctic coast, extend his charting west and link up with Frederick Beechey in HMS *Blossom* coming eastward through the Bering Strait. If the three expeditions met, the North West Passage would be completed in a season, neatly establishing British primacy in the frozen north and precluding further Russian expansion. Barrow developed Franklin and Parry's original concept, securing support from the Colonial Office and the Hudson's Bay Company. This required a commitment to serve the Company's commercial interests. Franklin sold the mission to George Simpson, governor of the Company's Northwest Territories, by promising to secure rich fur lands from potential Russian interlopers. Little wonder the Company proved helpful.[45]

The second expedition

Although Franklin planned a second land expedition he was anxious to command the exploring ships if Parry decided not to go.[46] His objects were to chart the coast and reach Icy Cape, a known eastern terminus for the Bering Strait route, to block the encroachment of Russian fur traders, and gather scientific data in the process.[47] He had proved an adept player of the politics of exploration, twisting the Russian threat, the scientific impulse and pure geographical curiosity with as much skill as he used to flatter the aspirations of the Hudson's Bay Company. While preparing for the second expedition, Franklin attended a lecture course at the Geological Society which addressed the revolutionary ideas of Charles Lyell, the geological concepts that inspired Darwin's theory of evolution. He ordered the full establishment of scientific equipment for his expedition, not least magnetic needles and circles.

Tragically his last months in England were clouded by the knowledge that his wife was dying of tuberculosis. She would not hear of him abandoning his quest; after all she had married a polar explorer for better or worse, and she knew just what it meant to him. Somehow Eleanor kept herself alive to see him off, and even put on a show of recovery. She died five days after he sailed and was carried to the grave by his friends Beaufort, Buchan, Lyon and Beechey.[48] On 22 February 1825 John Franklin became a widower after only twenty-two months of marriage. It was perhaps fortunate that the news reached him as he prepared to set off into the wilderness: it was too late to turn back; he could bury his grief in his work. The second mission profited from the bitter experience of the first. It was essentially incident-free, with ample time for science. In 1826 Franklin travelled down the Mackenzie river to the Arctic Ocean, and then along the coast to the west. The plan was to reach Icy Cape and rendezvous with Beechey.

On this second land expedition Franklin matured as a scientist. Shut up in base camp through the long, dark winter of 1825–6 he had the opportunity to reflect on his magnetic and atmospheric readings. By the spring he could see significant correlations between these phenomena: 'It would appear that there are many Laws and effects of Magnetism to be developed. Our observations lead us to suppose that the motions of the needle often depend on Atmospheric changes – on three occasions for instance, an Easterly Gale has produced an increase of variation.'[49] The instructions he produced for the magnetic, astronomical and meteorological experiments of the expedition reveal a man thoroughly versed in the latest magnetic research, and well aware of the interconnection between phenomena in areas hitherto considered quite distinct.[50] He also provided an extensive collection of rock samples, complete with a Humboldtian analysis of their formation.[51]

This time Franklin knew what to do, what to take, and whom to trust. Much was achieved, although the three voyages did not meet. Once again Franklin provided a master class in navigational skill, science and leadership. Along the way he named coastal features for his friends, his heroes and those who might be flattered. Among the first was Point Sabine. Once again human nature caused a crisis. The expedition encountered a large tribal group of Inuit, and when their boat grounded, the Inuit began to plunder it with the avidity of a people who had never seen a European, but had traded for Russian goods. In part the violence reflected the threat that new traders posed to established networks.[52] Most officers would have opened fire, trusting to their weapons, but Franklin ordered his men to use nothing more than their own strength to secure the stores and equipment that were vital to their survival. Back was able to refloat his boat and ordered his men to level their muskets. This disconcerted the Inuit and gave Franklin the chance to pull off the beach. When the Inuit rushed to their kayaks to pursue him, Franklin had his interpreter warn them off. Franklin's calm, judicious and thoughtful conduct saved the expedition: if anyone had fired a gun they would all have died. It was typical of Franklin to think before acting, to avoid loss of life and defer the use of violence until all other options had been exhausted. At the cost of a few non-essential items and some bruises the expedition was able to continue unmolested.

Turning for home

Franklin would face a far graver challenge than Inuit pilfering before the summer was out. By 18 August 1826 he had pushed 374 miles west from the delta of the Mackenzie river, where he took the hardest decision of his career. Well aware that he stood no chance of making the Icy Cape rendezvous with Beechey in *Blossom* at the assigned time, in part due to delays caused by fog, and unwilling to risk another winter journey, he turned back. In the event *Blossom*'s sailing master had taken a boat far beyond the Icy Cape rendezvous.[53] Even so, the two expeditions were still 146 miles apart, outside the time frame set for the meeting and had no means of communicating. Franklin could not rely on Beechey reaching the rendezvous, and would not expect him to wait if he did. A man who went to the Arctic seeking glory would have pushed on, but Franklin knew the price of failure. He never forgot the appalling events of 1821. He abandoned his dreams in order to save his men, and never regretted the choice. His decision reflected the highest moral courage, demonstrating that Franklin was a careful commander, not one to take unwarranted risks. This time he brought all his men back, and was devastated when two of them died on the 'easy' journey home from base camp. He had done his best, 'but the Almighty has shown that human hopes are vain, and we should praise him that his will has spared so many lives, through such an accumulation of perils'.[54]

Ultimately it was his leadership that inspired John Richardson, who had been with him when they faced certain death, to compose a eulogy:

However high his brother officers may rate his courage and talents, either in the ordinary line of his professional duty or in the field of discovery, the hold he acquires upon the affections of those under his command by a continued series of the most conciliatory attentions to their feelings and a uniform and unremitting regard to their best interests is not less conspicuous.[55]

If other men equalled Franklin as a navigator none could match his leadership, or his power to inspire. Franklin trained, encouraged and rewarded his followers. During the second land expedition he took Edward Kendall under his wing, developed his observational skills and pushed his career at the Admiralty.[56] Once Kendall had been commissioned, Franklin persuaded his friend Henry Foster to take him on another scientific mission,[57] and when Kendall fell out with Foster, did all he could to sustain his career, an anxiety increased by the fact that Kendall married Franklin's niece Mary Kay in 1832.

By the time he returned to base camp in 1826 Franklin was convinced the North West Passage existed. He reached London with Richardson on 29 September 1827. Finding no one at the Colonial Office they went to the Admiralty, met the Lord High Admiral's

Council, headed by Admiral Sir George Cockburn, and spent two hours explaining their mission to the Lord High Admiral, William, Duke of Clarence.[58] In the process Franklin secured a new patron. The Colonial Office ordered him to publish his narrative, much to Barrow's delight.[59] The second narrative was a less innocent production than the first. Franklin consciously improved the style, focusing on drama and spectacle at the expense of science and navigation. Having presented an official report he was free to address another audience, the public who had bought four editions of his first book. This expedition had been too successful, lacking the danger and drama of the first. It sold only a single edition.[60]

Although the three expeditions had not met they achieved their wider territorial and scientific missions. By late 1827 the possibility of further Arctic exploration, with or without scientific agendas, was waning. Improved relations with Russia and the settlement of Russian claims to Alaska deprived Barrow and the explorers of an obvious enemy. New foreign secretary George Canning had secured access to the Bering Strait for British whalers, kept the Russians west of the Rocky Mountains and established the Mackenzie river delta as exclusively British.[61]

Inevitably further honours were bestowed: Franklin was knighted alongside Parry in 1829 and received an honorary degree from the University of Oxford. Franklin was quick to re-enter the social circle of his scientific colleagues, notably his 'dear friend', geologist Roderick Murchison.[62] However, there were more pressing issues than science. Franklin had an infant daughter to bring up. He needed a partner and chose Jane Griffin, a friend of his late wife. A petite woman without any pretension to glamour, Jane was intelligent, widely travelled and ferociously independent.[63] Her father, a successful lawyer, had his name installed on the Arctic chart during Franklin's second mission. Already a mature woman, Jane had rejected other suitors. So what did she see in Franklin? In essence he had become a romantic hero, a cultural icon, and it was perhaps this image that she married. The real Franklin was a curious compound of elevated religious zeal and personal integrity dedicated to the pursuit of naval service, exploration and scientific work as divinely ordained duties. His manner was described as calm, dignified yet resolute. Franklin's physique always surprised those who knew him only by reputation: he was below middling height, certainly no more than 5' 6", and very stout. In 1830 he weighed fifteen stone, which would be considered morbidly obese today. In a contemporary version of the jibe 'Who ate all the pies?' one Tasmanian correspondent was convinced he put away a whole sheep at a sitting![64]

In June 1828 the Lord High Admiral invited Franklin to plan a mission to complete the Passage. He advised crossing the land to the west of Repulse Bay and then dividing the party into two, one to head west to Point Turnagain as in 1821, the other heading north to find Parry's Fury and Hecla Strait. Franklin also advised sending a party by canoe and boat down the Great Fish river to link up with the Repulse Bay party. When the region was finally surveyed, years later, the second route proved impassable. This time it was not tested, for the plan was rejected the next day. Anything on such an extended scale was impossible under existing economic and political conditions. Whatever his private opinions Clarence was rapidly losing his grip on the Admiralty, because the Duke of Wellington's government wanted to control the expenditure and patronage of this powerful department. Franklin's proposal made it clear that the North West Passage would be achieved only when the sea route had actually been navigated.[65]

As Dr John Richardson concluded:

The search after the passage has employed three centuries but now that it may be considered as completed the discovery will I suppose be committed like Juliet to the tomb of the Capulets, unless something more powerful than steam can render it available for the purposes of mercantile gain.[66]

This opinion was almost universal after Franklin and Parry's second expeditions. Scoresby had been right: a North West Passage might exist, but it was economically useless. Without the threat of Russian activity there was no pressing need for another naval mission while the Admiralty budget was coming under increasing pressure from economic reformers. In 1830 one of those reformers, Sir James Graham, became First Lord of the Admiralty, paring the estimates to the bone to fund the political programme of the new Whig ministry. Scientific expeditions, in any quarter, were at a discount while political crises across Europe meant there were never enough warships to meet the demands of the Foreign Office. In 1831 Franklin and Beechey planned a mission to rescue John Ross from the North West Passage, and complete the Arctic chart. Once again rigid economy blocked their way more surely than pack ice.[67] The First Lord of the Admiralty preferred to obtain scientific kudos by offering astronomer John Herschel a free passage to the Cape, a cheap gesture that would annex Herschel's science to imperial interests.[68] Little wonder Franklin rejoined the mainstream naval service.[69]

3

Another Career

WITH NO PROSPECT of an early return to the Arctic, Franklin travelled to Russia, where he was received as an honoured personal guest by Tsar Nicholas I and met the leading Russian geographers and navigators, including Kotzebue and Admiral Krusenstern. Back in England he celebrated Trafalgar Day with Cumby under the *Bellerophon*'s famous flag, listening to the Reverend Alexander Scott's Nelson anecdotes. Nelson's courage, self-sacrifice, reliance on God and anxiety to earn his rewards provided a potent example for naval men, especially Trafalgar veterans. In 1829 the Australian Company offered Franklin £2,000 a year to manage their estates in New South Wales. Anxious not to lose touch with his profession, or the possibility of another Arctic mission, he declined. Parry was quick to accept the offer that Franklin had declined, but as Jane Franklin was equally quick to point out, he was not quite a gentleman. Franklin wanted to serve the state, not a company of land speculators.

Franklin and Jane were married on 5 November 1828. Jane became his professional and personal conscience, recognising his anxiety for service and his preference for Arctic exploration. Having married the romantic hero who ate his boots she had a vested interest in sustaining his fame. Jane was quick to judge the merits of other Arctic explorers, and did not scruple to apply a spur to her husband, describing their married life before he received orders for sea as a 'career of vanity, trifling and idleness'.[1] Life would not provide much peace for Franklin; pricked by his religious conscience and spurred into action by Jane he was condemned to perpetual motion if not to increase his fame, then certainly to sustain it. Fortunately he took some pleasure in the fact that he had finally arrived.[2] Now he could escape the shadow of his older brothers, criticising James Franklin for an untimely visit to England that cost him a lucrative post and threatened his retirement. In addition James's marriage was a disaster, hardly improved by the belated birth of a daughter. His own marriage was altogether more soundly based:

My dear Jane and I have the best foundation for the assurance that we shall live together in the full enjoyment of every earthly blessing. Similar in taste, feelings and affection, no separate desire exists. Blessed with numerous friends, and with a competency for the supply of every moderate desire, blessed too with our dear child . . . we may with the blessing of God justly look forward to substantial comfort & happiness.

The 'competency' was largely Jane's, the rest had been Eleanor's and destined for their daughter. The Franklins took their honeymoon in Paris, where the Geographical Society presented him with a gold medal 'worth about 40 guineas', and elected him a corresponding member. Among 'the leading men of science and literature' Humboldt's friend François Arago invited him to breakfast at the Paris Observatory.[3] Unlike brother James he did not return home a Francophile (few naval officers made such a terrible mistake).[4] Recognising the dangers of celebrity Franklin struggled to retain his integrity. He revealed something of the tension to his sister Henrietta: 'I hope and earnestly pray that where so many Honours are pouring in upon me I may be humble, and that they may only seem, as they ought to be, an additional stimulant to me in my professional career.'[5]

Franklin's scientific interests frequently took him to the Royal Society, the Royal Institution, and the Royal Geological Society, of which he became a fellow in 1829 and a councillor in 1830.[6] He was also instrumental in founding the Geographical Society, soon to receive William IV's royal patronage, serving as vice-president. Socially, the Franklins were very much part of the scientific community: Murchison, Sabine, Faraday, Beaufort and Buckland were frequent visitors.[7] In May 1829 he dined at Babbage's as part of a Royal Society Committee deputed to report on the famous calculating engine. This was no mechanical curiosity, having been conceived to ensure the accurate calculation and printing of the *Nautical Almanac*.[8] Although Franklin hoped the government would renew the Arctic mission, John Ross, funded by gin distiller Felix Booth, made the next polar voyage. Ross set off on 23 May 1829 and Franklin was among the last to shake his hand.[9]

At sea again

By 1830 Captain Sir John Franklin had turned his lacklustre naval career into a success story. Further promotion would have to wait on the numbingly slow procession of elderly officers shuffling off their mortal coil. With no system of retirement for age Franklin finally became an admiral in 1852. There remained another way forward: distinguished service could secure choice rewards, plum naval postings, civil service or perhaps a spell as aide de camp to the new king, former naval officer William IV. But did Franklin possess any talent in the regular line of his profession? Was he any use as a naval officer? His war record was mixed, opportunities to demonstrate skill and courage interspersed with the inevitable longueurs of blockade duty. However, polar fame earned him an interview with First Naval Lord Admiral Sir George Cockburn, who promised to put his name before the First Lord of the Admiralty, Lord Melville.

On 23 August 1830 Franklin was ordered to the twenty-eight-gun ship-rigged sloop HMS *Rainbow* for service in the Mediterranean, the station of 'ambition with the men of rank and influence', and an interesting region packed with history and culture.[10] The 500-ton *Rainbow* was one a large class of new ships that would feature in campaigns and exploration for half a century. Her sisters included the *Rattlesnake* and the *Herald*, which saw distinguished service in the Pacific, while the appropriately named *North Star* became an Arctic depot ship.[11] Too small for the battle fleet, these ships were ideal for detached service. Many deployed to the Mediterranean between 1827 and 1834 as the chaos and instability surrounding the foundation of a Greek state forced the British government to spread naval power across a wide arc of the Aegean and Ionian seas.

The *Rainbow* sailed from Portsmouth in November 1830; four days later the Duke of Wellington's government was defeated in a general election, ending three decades of Tory rule. This was only the latest in a series of shocks and surprises to disturb the European political landscape that year, headed by revolutions in France and Belgium. However, such matters were of limited interest to a new captain anxious to get his ship into prime condition before he arrived on station, to ensure he made a good impression on his commander-in-chief. Despite packing a crew of 175 men into such a small vessel Franklin quickly proved that he could inspire regular Jack Tars with the same brand of care and consideration that had persuaded Richardson, Kendall and Hepburn to follow him to the gates of Hell. Franklin delighted in his new authority, while officers and men responded to his leadership, his faith and the fact that he was far too sensible to dragoon them into excessive worship. Franklin's nephew Henry Kay observed that on the infrequent occasions he had to order corporal punishment – flogging with the dread 'cat o'nine tails' – Sir John was physically distressed.[12] Soon after she joined the fleet, officers and men alike began to refer to the 'Celestial *Rainbow*' or 'Franklin's Paradise'. Officers with scientific or exploring ambitions queued up to join. Young Owen Stanley secured an interview with Jane through Edward Parry, his uncle by marriage. Winner of the Royal Naval College Gold Medal in 1826 and a qualified surveyor trained by Franklin's friend Captain Philip Parker King, Parry's recommendation and the scientific connections of his father, the Bishop of Norwich, gave Stanley tremendous 'interest'. Stanley used his talents and connections to secure a transfer to the *Rainbow* in July 1831.[13] A friendship formed on *Rainbow*'s quarterdeck would endure. Shared magnetic, navigational and polar interests ensured the two men moved in the same circles. They would meet again in Hobart, off Stromness and perhaps in a corner of heaven set aside for great navigators.

Greece

The *Rainbow* joined the Mediterranean station in troubled times. Greece had been granted independence from Ottoman Turkish rule after four centuries of subjugation, but the country was far from stable. Independence had been secured by Britain, France and Russia at the climactic battle of Navarino on 20 October 1827, when the allies annihilated the Turco-Egyptian fleet. Having made Greece free, the European powers were desperately seeking a young prince to install as ruler, but few were interested in the job. An interim Russian-backed provisional government held office, but was profoundly unpopular; warlords and bandits held power in key areas and most Greek armed vessels turned to piracy. The British and French had no faith in the provisional government, in part because it was Russian-backed and in part because it was unable to maintain law and order. The Russian agenda was to co-operate with the allies in public, but covertly support the pro-Russian government, hoping to secure a Mediterranean naval base.[14]

Franklin immediately made a good impression on commander-in-chief Vice-Admiral Sir Pulteney Malcolm:

> a very likely person to be at the Board of Admiralty, for he is a most intimate friend of Sir James Graham's and I know he is also of Captain Elliot and Sir Thomas Hardy and that he warmly enters into all their views and I believe he will promote mine if he can for I was a favourite of his on this station.[15]

Over time such hopes faded: Malcolm did not join the Board, and had other, better-connected officers to support.[16]

His successor as commander-in-chief, Vice-Admiral Sir Henry Hotham, was, if anything, a superior potential patron. Hotham had a stellar war record, had been a senior member of the Board of Admiralty until 1830 and possessed considerable diplomatic skills – a vital asset when working with difficult allies to uphold joint policy. Armed diplomacy would be the key to the success of British policy in the region between 1830 and 1834, when a new king was finally delivered to Athens by a Royal Navy warship.

The problem facing the new British government of Earl Grey was simple, but almost insoluble. A succession of European revolutions and crises was drawing naval force and diplomatic effort into a variety of theatres. These were addressed in order of importance: Greece was a long way down the list, behind the revolution that created modern Belgium, the civil war in Portugal, the instability of Spain and the future of Ottoman Turkey. The fleet had to hold the line while the foreign secretary Lord Palmerston worked his way round to Greece. Eventually Palmerston decided that Turkey could be reformed and developed as a bulwark against Russian expansion in the region, holding the critical Bosphorus Straits that separated the Russian-controlled Black Sea from the Mediterranean. Consequently he limited the size of Greece.[17] Britain's ownership of the Ionian islands was an additional complication: it provided a useful base at Corfu, but Ionian merchants had a significant share in the trade between mainland Greece and Britain. In combination with British commercial houses operating in the region, these merchants would look to the consular service for protection in unstable times, protection Palmerston was committed to provide.[18]

Franklin played a small but significant part in the naval mission to maintain order ashore and support the interests of British merchants while European diplomacy sought a ruler for Greece. His first season in the Mediterranean was largely untroubled, much of his time being spent around Corfu, where he checked mastodon fossils for Murchison and examined the Ionian lighthouses and charts for Francis Beaufort, the new Hydrographer of the Navy.[19] In return Beaufort kept him informed of polar developments.[20]

After carrying dispatches to ships operating off Smyrna, Franklin became senior British officer at Napoli di Romania (present-day Nafplion), attending the British minister to the interim Greek government based in the town. Like many naval officers of his generation Franklin was an educated man. Anchored at the edge of the Plain of Argos he visited the ancient cities of the area. At Mycenae he was struck by the 'Tomb of Agamemnon', Cyclopean masonry and the Lion Gate. Argos offered a theatre, shrines, an acropolis and aqueducts. He noticed that stones from classical temples had been reused in the early Christian churches. 'You can imagine the delight I feel at being employed on this station where there is at every step so much to excite enquiry and research.'[21] High culture and Charles Lyell's revolutionary geology book kept his mind active. Later that year he visited Athens, which he found depressing both on account of the destruction wrought by war and the raw façade of the Parthenon, which still bore evidence of Lord Elgin's quarrying activities. Like most liberal Englishmen Franklin had been sympathetic to the Greek cause – at a safe distance it was easy to contrast the heirs of Aristotle and Pericles with the 'barbarian' Turks – but a brief stay at the interim Greek capital changed

Franklin's opinion. Closer inspection suggested there was little to choose between Greek and Turk, since neither showed the slightest connection with classical civilisation. Although retaining sympathy for a people who were fellow Christians only recently released from heathen oppression, he was disgusted by the endless quarrelling and idleness of the Greek government and the apparent absence of honesty and integrity among their leaders.

Most nineteenth-century naval wives stayed dutiful and demure at home, but the intrepid Jane was not going to miss an opportunity to travel. She was soon in the Mediterranean and after a bizarre meeting on a rock in the middle of Malta's Valletta harbour, the only location permitted by local quarantine regulations, she and Franklin spent the winter of 1831–2 at Corfu. Once Franklin went off to his duty, Jane, rather than wait for his return, made a grand tour of the eastern Mediterranean, taking in Greece, Palestine and Egypt. Among the British travellers she encountered none struck her as quite so ridiculous as the affected young romantic Benjamin Disraeli, with his oiled ringlets and blue velvet suit.[22] Twenty years later she would be begging favours from him.

Franklin's charming stay at Corfu had been interrupted by the assassination of Count Capo d'Istria, leader of the interim government, in October 1831. This act of political violence heralded the breakdown of central authority. With rival factions at war Franklin was ordered to Patras in the spring of 1832 to join French and Russian warships to maintain order, support the British consul and protect British citizens and their property. Patras was a significant trading centre on the southern coast of the Gulf of Corinth. Franklin faced factional interests ashore, and awkward colleagues afloat. While the three captains had identical instructions, only the Frenchman supported Franklin; the Russian, Captain Zanetsky, backed one of the local political factions, following the interests of his government. Franklin protected the Ionian merchants from the local warlord with the same tact, firmness and forbearance that he had displayed when facing a plundering tribe of Inuit, always preferring to negotiate but on the clear understanding that armed force would be used if the limits of his forbearance were breached.

When the seasonal dried-fruit harvest was ready to be sent to Britain, Franklin had to resolve another revenue dispute. The local power broker tried to levy export duties to pay his armed followers, but Franklin and the consul secured the cargo's dispatch in return for Franklin's promise that duty would be paid to the lawfully appointed collector of customs. His word was enough. There would be fruit in the nation's Christmas pudding.[23]

The work at Patras was tedious and slow, but Franklin stuck to his task with the same grim determination he had displayed in the Arctic. The biggest problem was Captain Zanetsky, who accused him of conspiring with a faction ashore and refused to accept Franklin's word that he had not. Incensed by the imputation of dishonesty, Franklin publicly humiliated the unfortunate Captain Zanetsky by contrasting his conduct with the honour the tsar had paid him in St Petersburg. In private Zanetsky admitted that he was acting on the orders of his superior, Admiral Rikord. Franklin reported his problems to Sir Henry Hotham, who found Rikord equally difficult to work with, and Zanetsky was eventually removed. By December, Jane was living ashore in the consul's house and Franklin could anticipate an end to the chaos.

Early the following year Greece gained a king, or at least a rather sad apology for one. The conflicting interests of the Great Powers led them to compromise on Otho, the seventeen-year-old son of King Ludwig of Bavaria. Otho proved feeble, capricious and idle. Greece would not make much progress until he was removed thirty years later. However, that was very much in the future when the king arrived on board HMS *Madagascar*, an occasion Admiral Hotham used to demonstrate British naval power to the assembled Greek ministers, foreign diplomats and naval leaders. Within days Patras passed bloodlessly into government hands and the *Rainbow* was withdrawn. For twelve months Franklin had been the master of the situation, dealing with dishonest Russians and capricious Greeks to uphold law and order, British commercial interests and international harmony. The exercise of individual responsibility was nothing new to him, unlike the application of international law and the maintenance of allied co-operation. But in all three fields Hotham valued his work:

In concluding the operations of the service you have so long and so ably conducted in the Gulfs of Patras and Lepanto I have great satisfaction in repeating
the approbation which I have already at different times expressed of your measures in the interests of Greece and in the maintenance of the honour and
character of the English nation and of His Majesty's Navy on that station,
wherein you have entirely fulfilled my instructions and anticipated my wishes. I
also take this opportunity of commending the judgement and forbearance
which you have exhibited under circumstances of repeated opposition and
provocation. To your calm and steady conduct may be attributed the preserva-
tion of the town and inhabitants of Patras, the protection of commerce, and the
advancement of the benevolent intentions of the Allied Sovereigns in favour of
the Greek nation.[24]

This was no routine testament, for Hotham was no routine admiral. His untimely death at Malta on 19 April 1833 robbed the navy
of an outstanding officer.[25] The local consul was equally effusive,
and lamented the loss of Franklin's company. After a run down to
Istanbul, where Franklin visited the Turkish admiral on his immense
flagship and took in the sights, the *Rainbow* joined the fleet in
Besika Bay close to the fields of Troy, an irresistible draw for John
Franklin the cultural tourist.[26]

If he gained no glory keeping the peace off Patras, moderating the
rapacity and corruption of interregnum Greece, Franklin led the allied
squadron with confidence and, despite the severe provocation offered
by Greek warlords and a Russian colleague, never lost his self-
control. More significantly for British policy he possessed a very sure
touch, anticipating the wishes of his distant admiral with insight and
good sense. This was no ordinary test: many of his contemporaries
signally failed to meet the challenge. During the *Rainbow* commission
Franklin established a solid reputation in the regular line of his profession. Even so, he had little hope of further sea commands, for the
same economic pressures that precluded further Arctic exploration
kept the navy on a tight rein and preference for the handful of
appointments available went to unemployed sprigs of Whig nobility.

The 'Celestial *Rainbow*' arrived back at Portsmouth on Christmas
Day 1833. Franklin's friend King William IV awarded him his personal order, making him a Knight Commander of the Guelphic
Order of Hanover, a treasured token of royal favour that remained
with him to the end. King Otho added the Order of the Redeemer.

Unwelcome leisure[27]

Much as he disliked the bustle of 'society' and longed for the quiet happiness of a retired domestic life in the country Franklin recognised that 'the calls of duty and other considerations professional and private are not likely to favour my wishes'.[28] To make matters worse he quickly realised that his hard work in Greece would count for little back in England. He called at Brighton and King William, who liked nothing better than the company of naval officers, immediately summoned him for an interview. The king was not much interested in Greece; he wanted to know about the current imbroglio between the pasha of Egypt and his nominal suzerain the Ottoman sultan, and the policy of Russia. Usually a delightfully even-handed xenophobe, William reserved a special contempt for the Russians. He despised most foreign nations with the condescension of the great, but the Russians were powerful, and in 1833–4 many anticipated an Anglo-Russian war for the future of European liberty and global empire. William wanted to know how the Russian interest stood in Greece, but he was especially concerned to learn about the fortifications of the Dardanelles, the vital strait connecting Istanbul with the Mediterranean, and the state of Turkish opinion. The king was also concerned by the rising power of Mehmet Ali's Egypt, which had seized Syria from the Turks, prompting the highly undesirable appearance of a Russian amphibious task force at Istanbul. After the glittering vulgarity of George IV's court, dining with the king had become a rather bourgeois affair, not that Franklin objected. A few days later Sir James Graham, First Lord of the Admiralty, repeated many of the royal questions. Both king and minister wanted to know if the fleet could pass the Dardanelles and drive the Russians out of Istanbul. The Greeks were very small cogs in the political machine, which Franklin regretted on their and his own behalf. No one in London cared about Greece. His expertise was at a discount.

Anxious to exploit a fleeting opportunity Franklin pressed Graham for employment, stressing that in thirty-four years' service he had hardly ever been unemployed. The Admiralty, as Franklin knew very well, operated a rota system, attempting to give as many officers as possible an opportunity to serve. This was fair, but left many fine captains to sit out a forty-year term in that rank with three or at best six years at sea. Franklin's only hope was a war, which seemed quite likely, or a renewed phase of exploration, which did not. At least Graham, aware of his services and the favourable opinions of his admirals, promised a ship 'if there was any stir'. The brief war fever passed as the Baltic ice cleared in the spring of 1834 and the Russians evacuated Istanbul, leaving the field to British money and diplomacy. Franklin used his remaining credit at the Admiralty to promote two warrant officers and provide good berths for his midshipmen.

A new Arctic mission

While there remained the possibility of a war, and with it a ship, Franklin waited in London, close to the Admiralty, rather than join Jane, who had remained in the Mediterranean, and was now in Egypt. Those prospects were fading by late February 1834 and, as they did, Arctic ambitions, prompted by his wife, took centre stage. The Arctic mission had not stood still in Franklin's absence. While Parry's unsuccessful attempt on the geographical North Pole via Spitsbergen in 1826 ended the first phase of naval expeditions, the hiatus proved short-lived. John Ross persuaded London distiller Felix Booth to fund a steam-powered attempt on the Passage in 1829, with some support from the Admiralty and the scientific community. All he found was an opportunity to demonstrate outstanding leadership in a truly hopeless position. After a four-year endurance test the crew escaped to Baffin Bay, where they were rescued by the whaler *Isabella*, the very ship Ross had commanded in 1818. Having been widely presumed dead, Ross achieved considerable celebrity and his voyage narrative sold well. Predictably Barrow savaged it in the *Quarterly*, fearing that Ross's declaration that 'there are now fewer temptations than ever to make any fresh attempt for solving this problem' would close the North West Passage. Ross was equally dismissive of the economic possibilities Barrow envisaged.[29] Coming from a man who had survived four winters in the Arctic, in circumstances little short of miraculous, such remarks carried real weight.

The disappearance of the Ross expedition renewed interest in the Arctic, and prompted a rescue mission. Franklin had no doubt Ross was dead, and feared any government search would be cheaply done – sending a junior officer, not a full-fledged captain. Furthermore, the stout captain had to acknowledge that his overland exploring days were over: 'I much question whether I could bear the fatigue and anxiety of service by land without doing great injury to my constitution. I would try, however, if anything were to offer . . .' Despite Beaufort's assurance that George Back was not qualified for the command, Franklin's fears proved well founded. He realised that senior officers who knew and appreciated his work had other, better connected men to push forward.[30] His mood was not improved by Jane, who wrote from the Mediterranean to echo his desire for further polar service and, as if he needed reminding, where his duty lay. She greatly preferred being the wife of a polar hero than the wife of a mere captain in the regular line of the Royal Navy – employed or otherwise. Franklin, the 'chieftain' of the polar men, should resume his rightful place.[31] When the Ross party returned safely, rumours began to circulate of an Antarctic mission, and another attempt on the North West Passage. Surely Franklin could secure one of these commands? She even suggested that he should never have left the discovery service – and urged him to consult Beaufort.[32] Franklin replied that the Admiralty was unaware of a mission to either pole, and he trusted Beaufort to keep him abreast of developments. The polar rumours originated among the scientists, and had not been addressed to the Admiralty. He stressed that he had no interest in travelling for its own sake, or 'for the empty shadow of increasing my fame'. However, he hated the thought that his colleagues might think him content to repose on his laurels.[33]

More significantly, Ross's expedition had revived the Arctic impulse by providing it with a new focus. Lieutenant James Clark Ross had located magnetic north, providing a pole to Humboldt's equator. It was a matter of considerable national pride that Ross had annexed a major scientific landmark for the British Empire, formally taking possession under the Union Jack.[34] John Ross's gin expedition also put Franklin's name on the map. On an epic sledge journey James Ross reached King William Land, naming the most westerly land he could see Point Franklin, being the closest point he reached to Franklin's Point Turnagain of 1821. Reinforcing the honour by calling the nearest promontory Cape John Franklin was 'less than the merits of that officer deserve', so he named another for Jane.[35]

That summer Franklin had other reasons to reflect on mortality, ambition and duty. His last surviving brother, Major General James Franklin, died, leaving a niece whom he effectively adopted. In his last weeks James had ventured ever deeper into the dark, resigned faith of their shared childhood. Grief and depression needed some relief. This time he could not hide his misery amid an Arctic endeavour. Fortunately Jane returned from the Mediterranean in the autumn. In 1835 the Franklins visited Ireland, not, as his first biographer would have it, as an indulgence[36] but in pursuit of knowledge. Franklin attended a meeting of the British Association for the Advancement of Science in Dublin. His companions included Edward Sabine and Humphrey Lloyd, leaders of the magnetic movement, and it was not polite chatter that they exchanged.[37] Having crossed the Irish Sea he made a more extensive tour of the island, observing local conditions. Later that year he was called before the Royal Commission on the Irish fishing industry. He recommended enlightened self-help, the encouragement of fishing on the west coast, the education of local fishermen to secure pilots for the many anchorages, and the training of deep-water square-rig seamen for the Royal Navy. This would be the most effective use of government aid.

While James Ross located a pole, his father George demanded a publicly financed overland search for the lost expedition. It was sent, with limited, grudging support from the Admiralty, rather more useful support from the self-interested Hudson's Bay Company and the entire annual income of the Royal Society. Perhaps the society had been impressed by George Ross's claim that the search had scientific potential. Lieutenant George Back and Dr Richard King had already overwintered at base camp when news arrived that Ross was safe, and their mission was hastily converted to focus on science and exploration.[38] The following spring they travelled down the Great Fish (now Back) river to the Arctic coast. Back's magnetic observations and report on the aurora borealis were of a high standard, as might be expected after three voyages under Franklin's tuition.[39]

Those voyages left him older and wiser: he turned for home at the river estuary, to the disgust of novice traveller King.

By a curious coincidence Back was still in Canada looking for the Rosses when the Admiralty sent newly returned James Clark Ross in a hastily reinforced whaler to rescue eleven whaleships beset in the Davis Strait and fitted out the bomb vessels *Terror* and *Erebus* for Arctic service.[40] Although neither ship was needed, the *Terror* was ready for the Arctic, and the temptation to send another expedition to navigate the Passage proved irresistible. When Back returned, the Royal Geographical Society, representing Barrow's view of the Arctic mission, pressed for another expedition to settle the remaining cartographic questions of the North West Passage, on the plan Franklin had outlined in 1827. This one-ship mission was given to recently promoted Captain Back. While Franklin was understandably disappointed, since he had never rated Back as a navigator or a human being, he visited the *Terror* as she set off in June 1836. Although the primary purpose was to complete the Passage, every opportunity was given for scientific work, especially if the ship was forced to overwinter. The mission was an utter failure, redeemed only by the survival of the ship and most of her crew. Trying to pass the Fury and Hecla Strait, *Terror* became hopelessly trapped in shifting sea ice, a far cry from the safe winter harbours that Parry and Ross had found, and was all but destroyed. Fortunate to reach the coast of Ireland, Back ran his shattered ship onto a beach before she sank.[41] *Terror* was rebuilt, but George Back's fifth Arctic voyage would be his last.[42] Nor was Franklin impressed by Richard King's bold but sketchy plan to complete the coastal survey, advising the Royal Geographical Society not to support it.[43] By a curious irony King's object was to delineate the coast of Boothia, which, had it been successful, would have offered Franklin a priceless advantage a decade later.

Back's voyage, driven primarily by Barrow's geographical concerns, was the last of its type. A new Arctic imperative had emerged from the scientific results of the Parry, Franklin and Ross missions. Geomagnetism dominated the second round of polar exploration, a development largely obscured by the promotional activity of John Barrow. While Barrow remained the chief spin-doctor of the Arctic, he did not set the agenda. The scientists left public advocacy to Barrow and his geography but they had different objects in mind, and they needed leaders with a far higher profile to direct a new polar campaign.

Franklin at fifty

Having missed out on the latest Arctic commands Franklin sent the Admiralty a testimonial of his services. Within weeks he was offered employment by the Colonial Office. His idleness was at an end. Even so, he only accepted the new career after Beaufort, Barrow and First Sea Lord Sir Charles Adam assured him that colonial government would not harm his naval career.[44] The government of Van Diemen's Land was just one of the many tokens that marked Franklin out from the common run of naval officers, and of polar explorers. Far from the dull plodder of most modern accounts, or even the worthy, humane leader of Victorian biography, John Franklin was an ornament to his profession. His scientific interests, diplomatic talent, powers of observation and anxiety to serve King and Country as the best way to employ his God-given talents drove him to find useful labour. In truth he found rest morally reprehensible; the imperious call to duty that had animated his idols Nelson and Flinders ran deep in Franklin's soul. With Jane at his elbow he was doomed to pursue that duty to the ends of the earth, and the end of his life.

In 1836 Franklin was fifty, famous and fat: a favourite with his king, universally admired by the British people and an international celebrity. His public character was beyond question, combining honour, dignity and moral weight. He had no need for more fame, yet his wife, and perhaps Franklin also, believed that he had to remain in employment to sustain his reputation. This obsession with public duty would be his downfall: it sent him to rule in Australia, and it sent him north for one last attempt to locate the philosopher's stone.

Was it anything more than little Johnny Franklin trying to fill his elder brother's boots? After years of being the underachieving lightweight, Franklin had made his mark, and outlived his brothers to become the head of the family. It was a situation he relished. Like any successful self-made man Franklin had responsibilities, not the obvious catalogue of his immediate family, Eleanor and Jane, or even his nephews and nieces, but a wider Franklin tribe. He would make naval careers for nephews by marriage such as Kendall, find worthwhile opportunities for many more relatives and even find suitable husbands for his nieces.

Franklin had a wide range of connections and responsibilities, and he took them very seriously. He cultivated the great and good to secure further opportunities for his circle, and in the process became quite the gentleman. Colonial government was just the type of dignified office that a gentleman would take, believing it to be his duty. It was also an ideal vehicle for advancing his family at the public expense without any hint of impropriety. He would not make any money in Van Diemen's Land, but he would show himself to be a true leader by enriching his tribe. Many of his naval contemporaries took posts at an advanced age for the same reason, to promote sons, nephews, sons-in-law and the children of old friends.

If Franklin regretted the lack of further Arctic employment after 1827, he did not rest on his laurels. In the Mediterranean he demonstrated leadership, judgement and diplomatic talent. The public testimony of Sir Henry Hotham is clear: Franklin was a very good naval officer. Had any of the multiple crises that occupied the attention of European statesmen in the early 1830s turned into a shooting war he would have been employed. When the prospect of war faded, he tried to rejoin his own branch of service, only to find that the economic pressures of the decade cut him out. When his scientific friends and colleagues began to develop an Antarctic expedition, Franklin accepted that it was pencilled in for James Clark Ross because he understood the scientific imperative, and because of the claim that Ross had made by reaching magnetic north.

The prospects before him were of a long wait for another sea command, and even longer before he achieved flag rank. Parry had married into the Whig political family of Lord Stanley of Alderley, making his post-polar career in a succession of shore postings. Franklin did not have such connections, so he shifted his focus to another area. He was already well known at the Colonial Office, which had been heavily involved in his two overland missions, and with the support of his king found a suitable role.

John Franklin was no ordinary naval officer. Educated by Matthew Flinders and given his chance by Sir Joseph Banks he used three Arctic expeditions to secure promotion, a knighthood, the Fellowship of the Royal Society and the patronage of his monarch. He earned further plaudits in the regular line of naval service, but his faith and his conscience would not let him rest. Instead Franklin went to Van Diemen's Land, leaving his scientific and naval friends to lobby for magnetic expeditions to both poles. The character of polar exploration had changed fundamentally in the decade since his return from the Mackenzie river; science was now the dominant concern and as a scientific man he was content to follow that trend. Franklin had many vital qualities, above all leadership, loyalty, honour, humanity and courage; he was a seaman, a navigator and a scientist. This was a man whom politicians and colleagues trusted. They placed their ships and expeditions, colonial governments and scientific projects in his hands. Those who seek to blame him for the catastrophic end of the 1845 expedition, in whole or in part, have signally failed to assess the bigger questions thrown up by such assumptions. If he was incompetent or unsuitable, why was he given the command? Surely either the prime minister, the First Lord of the Admiralty, the president of the Royal Society or the naval and scientific communities would have noticed? After all, they were responsible public figures. Franklin was given the command because he was best man for the job.

4

Scientific Empires

The reason why

AMONG THE TRAGIC collection of Franklin expedition hardware found scattered on the beach at Point Victory was a six-inch dip circle, complete with leather case, built by the London instrument maker Robinson.[1] In use until the ships were abandoned, this instrument was one of the last routines that linked the expedition to the world beyond their terrifying prison. The magnetic data it recorded would exert a powerful, sickening fascination long after the men who had used it had been given up for dead. The expedition had been sent to gather data at the outer limits of human knowledge. 'Arctic and then Antarctic naval commanders were left in no doubt that magnetic studies were scientifically the most important part of their mandate.'[2] Franklin had been at the heart of the magnetic crusade from the outset. He took command in 1845 because he had impeccable credentials, extensive Arctic experience, proven leadership and above all because he was a first-rate magnetic scientist.

John Franklin was not an explorer, a traveller or a discoverer. John Franklin was a navigator. He voyaged to make a path for others, recording and charting the seas. To record and chart, Franklin needed to know where he was, to locate himself and the features he was recording on the surface of the globe. Only through scientific precision could he 'prove' his findings and produce results useful to other navigators. The key to scientific precision in Arctic navigation was geomagnetism, and by 1845 this had been Franklin's study for over forty years.

Scientific organisation

For many years the Royal Society had represented scientific interests to government, but Banks's death in 1820 and a decisive shift from applied to pure science broke that link. The society lost interest in exploration, limiting its support to the scientific element of expeditions. Although the society provided financial support for Parry's Arctic voyages, it had not helped Franklin's overland expeditions, despite making Franklin an FRS in 1823.[3] After Banks's death his universal scientific empire fragmented, creating several new vehicles to promote Arctic exploration. While single-interest societies, notably the Geological, Astronomical and Geographical, were useful, it was only when the broadly based British Association for the Advancement of Science emerged in the late 1830s that the voice of British science gained any influence with government. In effect Banks's universal scientific society was replaced by a constellation of interests, harnessed to a particular view of science by a core leadership of gentlemen scientists who acknowledged Banks's vision and envied his eminence.

Banks's grand concept, harmonising science to the practical interests of an expanding commercial empire through the focused development of newly professional disciplines, was too good a system to be in abeyance for long. Ultimately Banks's mantle settled on the industrious shoulders of Sir Roderick Impey Murchison (1792–1871), soldier, scientist, empire builder and administrator.[4] Murchison had attended the Royal Institution science lectures in 1812, but resigned his commission after Waterloo and drifted into a world of country sports, Tory politics and travel. He married a bright, wealthy woman who encouraged a growing interest in geology. Facing bankruptcy in 1823, he gave up hunting, moved to London and returned to the Royal Institution to work with Sir Humphry Davy. Murchison attacked his new interest with military discipline and immense energy, the basic tools of his public career. In 1825 Davy secured his election as a Fellow of the Geological Society. When the Royal Society followed suit in 1826, Murchison had arrived. The scientific value of exploration was always at the forefront of his mind. He met Franklin at a geology lecture shortly before the second Arctic land expedition, shared scientific and social contacts creating a friendship that would endure to the grave. Both men had reason to promote Arctic expeditions and both were important players in a global attempt to measure, catalogue and control the natural world that it might be reduced to order, placed under the British flag and exploited for commercial gain. Franklin made his career within the framework of imperial science, knowledge, power and piety in the service of the state.

Murchison's geology was done in the field, where his relentless energy and a soldier's ability to read the land enabled him to master vast swathes of country at an unrivalled pace. He quickly developed a basic geological chronology and used it to locate coal-bearing seams. Like Banks he concentrated on economically significant research, because this was the key to selling science to politicians, many of them gentlemen amateurs with a scientific bent. In 1828 Murchison became foreign secretary of the Geological Society, establishing a European network of correspondents. Suitably impressed, the society elected him president in 1831 and kept him in harness down to 1869. He was also a councillor of the Royal Society and in 1849 a vice-president. His will to dominate led him into controversies with other geologists, battles he won with a rich mixture of energy and self-confidence. Never one to admit a mistake, Murchison's scientific views were as unyielding as the granite he studied. Like many of his generation he would not countenance Darwin's theory of evolution. He was a disciple of Humboldt and his descriptive science was to assemble data rather than developing theories.

Humboldt's example and that of similar societies in Paris and Berlin were critical to the foundation of the Royal Geographical Society in 1830, although John Barrow set the formal agenda that transformed the Raleigh dining club into a formal body. No longer in a position of power at the Royal Society after 1820, Barrow used the newly founded Royal Geographical to push an Arctic mission with an emphasis on charts and discovery. Geography was of paramount importance to a maritime nation with 'extensive foreign possessions'. 'Every accession', he declared, 'to hydrographical knowledge . . . must be of great importance to navigation, and a fit object for promulgation by the Society.'[5] The membership included politicians, soldiers, sailors, diplomats and antiquarians, widening the support network and research opportunities. The new society provided a public forum with imperial service at the heart of its agenda. As Captain William A. B. Hamilton RN explained,

'Geography is the mainspring of all operations of war, and of all the negotiations of a state of peace.'[6] Gathering and disseminating intelligence was the key to British power, and the precision of such data was the main concern of the society. Here naval officers were privileged as trained and experienced data gatherers in the science of navigation. Murchison's contribution was the organisational model of the Geological Society. To ensure the Geographical ran smoothly and reflected his interests he served as a councillor from the outset, and took the presidential chair in the critical year 1843–4.

With the sound, practical agenda of discovering and recording the unknown the Royal Geographical Society (RGS) provided Barrow and Murchison with a base from which to advance Arctic and other exploring agendas. While they took distinctly different positions on the science to be served, both men were adept players of the political game – advancing the mission, the society and themselves with remarkable facility across several decades. The link with John Murray ensured that a succession of key geography narratives appeared under his imprint. Murchison's astute stewardship made the RGS into a clearing house for exploration and science, and the stage on which Arctic men displayed themselves to admiring audiences, burning with ambition and bedecked with frosty laurels. The Waterloo Place meeting rooms would also be the headquarters of the Franklin search.[7] Robert Brown and Edward Sabine were founder members, along with scientific naval officers including Francis Beaufort, W. H. Smyth, Basil Hall and John Franklin.[8] Little wonder the North West Passage was a Royal Geographical mission, and its solution worthy of a gold medal or two.[9]

Despite serving the strategic and economic aims of the state the Geographical lacked the influence to advance major causes single handed. It needed the support of other scientific and public bodies.[10] Once again Murchison was at hand, helping to found the British Association for the Advancement of Science (BAAS), an overtly political lobby group, in 1832. The energy and bureaucratic skills of the soldier-geologist made him a vital cog in the new machine. He served as general secretary from 1836 to 1845, accepting the post because it was the office of power, and within half a decade the association had become a highly effective pressure group. This plurality of offices open to a man with the wealth to fund his science reflected ability and overweening ambition. Murchison wanted to be known and rewarded: he liked decorations, titles and honours and enjoyed having his name emblazoned on newly discovered topographical features, be they mountains, waterfalls, lakes or capes. His work was rewarded with a knighthood, a baronetcy and the presidency of every society he ever joined, save the Royal.

Murchison was a master of influence, organisational politics and contacts. His steady rise in the Geological, Geographical and Royal Societies was secured by organisational skill and hard labour, with not a little bullying and back stabbing along the way. He held the key to public funding for science. However, his ambition was not without foundation, the publication of his geological masterpiece *The Silurian System* in 1839 made his name, and advertised the utility of his subject by locating coal. 'Siluria' remained his bailiwick for the rest of his life, constantly expanding his rocky empire and beating off his rivals. While Victorian science was shaped and administered from Murchison's desk, those who crossed him rarely prospered. When the British Isles proved too small for his ego, Murchison secured an invitation to Russia, expanding his empire with a Humboldtian programme of data recording and sample collecting while fawning on the tsar. His visit secured lasting fame, a minor order and, unlike his hero, a lifelong admiration for Romanov autocracy.[11] On his return Murchison moved into Belgrave Square, courtesy of his wife's inheritance, and his house replaced Banks's Soho residence as the social centre of British science. Nor was he a stranger to the political arena. Sir Robert Peel's Tory administration gave him permission to wear his Russian order and a knighthood, but Murchison switched his allegiance to Palmerston's Liberals. Both geologist and geographer, he took the chair as president of the BAAS at the association's 1846 meeting, an honour that 'canonised' his work and confirmed his status.

Murchison's interest in the Arctic was obvious. Navigators and explorers recognised his contribution to their mission, and were only too willing to collect rock samples for him. Every expedition extended his Silurian empire and enhanced his stratigraphy. Curiously, when their journals were reprinted those earnest rocky appendices were expunged, along with all the other sciences. While this was a purely commercial decision, it exacerbated the tendency to misrepresent the expeditions as mere exploration. That said, the appendices were mind-numbingly dull, none more so than those containing geomagnetic data.

Edward Sabine

In Britain this novel science quickly became the special province of one man, Captain, later General, Sir Edward Sabine of the Royal Artillery (1788–1883).[12] After active service in Canada during the War of 1812 Sabine entered the London scientific community. In Banks's Royal Society a gentleman amateur could always secure an opening, and Sabine was assigned to Ross's 1818 Arctic mission to conduct a broad range of scientific and astronomical observations. After he fell out with Ross, Barrow orchestrated Sabine's election to the Fellowship of the Royal Society in 1818, and remembered Sabine's role in damning John Ross for the rest of his life. Barrow had no interest in science but he hated Ross with a passion. Sabine went back to the Arctic with Parry, continuing his magnetic observations. These earned him the prestigious Copley Gold Medal. After further voyages he took part in efforts to standardise units of magnetic measurement across Europe, working with some of the greatest names in earth science. His military training reinforced strong administrative traits which he used to take a major role in the Royal Society, holding secretarial offices of great influence. He was a late but powerful adherent to the BAAS, acting as general secretary for over twenty years from 1839, and by the late 1830s Sabine and Murchison had a powerful grip on British science. In addition Sabine and his talented wife translated key texts from German, notably Humboldt's *Cosmos* and Admiral Wrangel's *Narrative of an Expedition to the Polar Sea*. They were powerful weapons for a campaign to advance magnetic research in the Arctic.[13]

In the early 1830s Sabine launched his 'magnetic crusade', an international co-operative science project on the largest scale. Following Humboldt's lead he wanted to obtain magnetic readings from across the globe. For this he needed government support and naval expeditions. He argued that improved understanding of the causes and consequences of terrestrial magnetism would solve practical problems the phenomenon posed for navigation and develop a general theory. Efficient administration transformed learned societies into effective lobby groups, the foot soldiers of his campaign. From the outset the Arctic was critical, and Sabine used James Clark Ross's location of magnetic north in 1831 to secure magnetic surveys of Ireland, Scotland and England, with Ross as a colleague. Nor was this the end of Sabine's ambition, or his use of naval assets.[14]

For the next thirty years Sabine drove British magnetic research with the single-minded dedication of a Victorian empire builder, persuading most British scientists to endorse his work. The exceptions, computer pioneer Charles Babbage and Astronomer Royal George Airy, despised Sabine, his science and his feeble mathematics.[15] Sabine preferred to work with scientific naval officers: James Ross, Francis Beaufort and John Franklin recognised the vital importance of his work for navigation. Sabine linked magnetic theory and navigational practice. His organisational talent ensured that the scientific community supported terrestrial magnetic research, driving the process as a secretary at the Royal Society, switching to the British Association when he realised that the new body was more dynamic. After 1838 the British Association was effective because the general secretaries were Sabine and Murchison. In the 1840s Sabine reinvigorated the Royal Society when he needed every asset to secure government support.

While Sabine was ruthless, relentless and remorseless, the theoretical foundations of his work were uncertain. Before 1815 Humboldt and Jean-Baptiste Biot had propounded theories that informed Sabine's work on the Ross and Parry missions. In the 1830s Sabine favoured the work of Christopher Hansteen, based on the existence of two magnetic axes, but by 1839 Carl Gauss provided a very different theoretical model, one that Airy adopted. Sabine was never convinced, largely because the mathematics were beyond his competence. He responded to Gauss's work by stressing the need for observational data to test his theories, and subsume them into a data-based model. To this end Sabine assembled and digested the results of an ever widening global empire of numbers. His success in keeping this project going through political changes, economic shifts and conflict is the ultimate proof of his genius. Rather more worrying was his military insistence on subordinating his colleagues of whatever rank to the role of mere collectors of data.

The powerful strategic and commercial concerns of early Victorian Britain were taken into science by Sabine and Murchison, the military minds of British science, empire builders of knowledge. The prominence of the Arctic in their work reflected the importance of magnetic readings taken at the pole; such readings provided a contrast with Humboldt's equatorial baseline, and established Britain's place in this new, high-profile discipline. Going to the magnetic poles was the British response to Gauss's theoretical work – typically practical. Franklin has been consistently omitted from Sabine's magnetic circle, a curious development when the two men were close friends. After all, Franklin had been interested in magnetism from his coming of age on board the *Investigator*, collected magnetic data on his Arctic expeditions and helped to improve the instruments.

Francis Beaufort

To ensure his science was conducted across the globe Sabine needed an ally at the Admiralty. While Barrow was friendly, he remained ignorant and uninterested. Captain Sir Francis Beaufort, Hydrographer of the Navy, was a willing convert. Although Arctic expeditions were not part of his surveying empire, either by origin or by budget, Beaufort was a Fellow of the Royal and Royal Geographical Societies, and by far the most scientific officer in the Admiralty building. Sabine consulted him before approaching the Admiralty for support. Beaufort made his name with a brilliant survey of the Anatolian coast in 1812. Elected to the Royal Society in 1814 he soon mastered Flinders's work on the growing importance of terrestrial magnetism for accurate charting. By the early 1820s Beaufort, discussing magnetic and meteorological phenomena with Parry and Franklin, recognised that an improved understanding of magnetic deviation in high latitudes was essential for accurate navigation and charts. As the naval confidant of the scientific elite, Beaufort served on the councils of the Royal Astronomical Society and the Royal Society. In 1829 he was the obvious man to replace Parry as Hydrographer, combining surveying skill with expertise in meteorology, terrestrial magnetism and astronomy. He had much to gain from the Arctic mission, not least the improvement of the charts, always his watchword for success. Beaufort's London house soon became the social centre of naval science: Franklin, James Ross and Parry met there with Charles Babbage, Humphry Davy, John Herschel and George Everest.

The new post combined Beaufort's interests with his work. Every survey ship he sent out would compile more observational data. Furthermore his 'office' occupied a suite of seven rooms on an upper floor of the Admiralty building in Whitehall, placing him quite literally on top of the naval world. Here he was close at hand for consultation, or the exercise of discreet but effective influence. Beaufort joined Barrow at the heart of the naval administration, and for two decades they provided their Lordships, a rather transient body, with carefully selected information to shape exploration and the survey programme. They soon became the institutional memory, a process reinforced when John Barrow Jr took control of the Admiralty library and records. From inside the building these men could insinuate their ideas into the debate without putting anything on paper. Unlike their political and naval masters who left town when Parliament rose, these official men remained at their posts. That they shared an agenda in exploration was obvious. Leaving Barrow to promote exploration, Beaufort focused on the scientific and surveying results that could be translated into reliable intelligence and charts, both of which were of enormous value to an imperial government. Both men were active in the Geographical Society, and Beaufort had influence in the Royal.

In 1831 the Hydrographer's Office became a separate department within the Admiralty, giving Beaufort control of his own budget. He used this power to focus attention on the growing gap in knowledge between what had only been explored and what had been accurately surveyed and could therefore be safely used by mariners. This difference of emphasis distinguished him from the discovery-minded Barrow. Beaufort's operations were shaped by a massive expansion of commercial navigation, both in scale and in scope. Shipping tonnages doubled, new ocean routes were opened and steamships posed new problems for navigation and charting, demanding new routes and deeper passages. Although his resources were often redirected to wars in distant regions, Beaufort always kept an eye on the core task. His surveyors received close, careful instructions, including the collection of extensive observational data. Beaufort anticipated the development of theoretical structures to explain these phenomena as part of an improved navigational art. Little wonder he was chosen to be on the Royal Society's Board of Visitors for the Royal Observatory – the original temple to navigational science. Beaufort was the bridge between the navy and the scientific community: he alone of those in office recognised the value of advanced scientific research for navigation, and possessed a truly imperial vision of his discipline.[16]

However, Arctic and Antarctic expeditions were organised and funded by the Admiralty rather than the Hydrographer's Department. Therefore Beaufort had to rely on influence to advance his interest in those remote regions. Fortunately he could mobilise the disparate talents of John Barrow, Arctic officers and learned societies to support his cause. When the Royal Society divided on the question of admitting amateurs to the Fellowship in 1828, Beaufort stood shoulder to shoulder with Babbage and the hardline scientists.[17] He also played a key role in setting up the Royal Geographical Society, persuading a reluctant Barrow to set the agenda and obtain royal patronage. Beaufort served the RGS for the rest of his life, his surveyors providing a significant body of copy for the *Geographical Journal*. He was also closely involved in the Royal Astronomical Society, and from his seat on the councils of these societies often found occasion to write to the Admiralty, knowing full well that the scientific appeal he had drafted in the evening would end up on his own desk the next morning for an expert opinion. Nowhere was this conflict of interests more obvious than advocating a new search for the North West Passage in his role as an RGS councillor before judging his pet project as Hydrographer.[18] Not that Beaufort's double-dealing was limited to areas of unanimity among his colleagues. In 1839 he had worked with John Herschel and

Edward Sabine to secure the Antarctic expedition of James Ross as part of a global magnetic survey. Then he had to get Barrow, who had no interest in the area or the science, to ensure the necessary orders were issued before the ministry fell. A new Admiralty Board would require a tedious and long-drawn-out round of persuasion and minute writing. The episode reveals Beaufort's steely determination to promote the scientific mission against opposition from ignorant, penny-pinching blockheads.[19] It is equally clear that his conduct was wholly improper. Little wonder he slept no more than 5½ hours a night. His conscience may have been troubling him – although he had other reasons for insomnia, not least an incestuous relationship with his sister.[20]

Beaufort's little world of interlocking interests, responsibilities and resources came unstuck in his last decade. The Franklin expedition reflected all his obsessions and interests, his ability to manipulate the world of science, his friendships and above all a curiously illogical streak in the mind of a man noted for scientific precision.

Beaufort was involved in the Arctic mission from the start. By the early 1830s he was confident of success: 'I feel more confident than I have ever previously ventured to feel that the probability of accomplishing a Passage is now so great as to fully justify the attempt.'[21] Anticipating a new trade route to Asia and the Pacific, in 1836 he took a prominent part in lobbying the Royal Society to set up a committee, hoping to influence the Admiralty. At the same time he wrote to the Royal Geographical Society:

That there is an open and, at times, a navigable sea passage between the Straits of Davis and Behring there can be no doubt in the mind of any person who has duly weighed the evidence, and it is equally certain that it would be an intolerable disgrace to this country were the flag of any other nation to be borne through it before our own.[22]

Beaufort's only evidence for such optimism was the limited distance that lay between the known eastern and western ends of the passage. This failure of common sense was amply revealed by the abject failure of Back's 1836 expedition. Hope revived after the Dease–Simpson overland expedition of 1839 reduced the doubtful navigation to little more than seventy miles, between Cape Herschel on the south coast of King William Land and Ross's Point Victory on the north-east shore. In 1846 Franklin's expedition would sail into this terrible space, only to discover that seventy miles can be a very long way.

Despite Beaufort's efforts the polar mission had stalled by 1836 – the Russian threat had been countered and the North West Passage had been largely mapped and recognised as highly likely to exist but absolutely useless for all practical purposes. Only the Hudson's Bay Company had any reason to continue the search, to secure a trade monopoly and more animal pelts, objects that could be obtained by an overland mission to map the littoral. Geographical curiosity was not going to reopen the Arctic. The charts were incomplete, but they were perfectly adequate to sustain British ownership of the region between Baffin Bay and the Icy Cape. It would require a high-profile international scientific 'crusade' to reopen the Arctic mission, part of a campaign that spanned the globe. Murchison, Sabine and Beaufort used their administrative talent, determination and self-interest to secure an official expedition. That expedition would be dominated by magnetic research, part of a global magnetic mission. The scientists had turned from imperial task forces to international co-operation to provide the answers.

Geomagnetism

Magnetic science and navigation are intimately connected. The earth's magnetic field affects the functioning of the compass; understanding how this influence varied across the globe would be a great prize for a maritime nation. The scientific difficulties were largely practical, getting to such obvious reference points as the magnetic poles to take readings being an obvious example. A comprehensive, predictive chart of magnetic variation might solve the problems of longitude and position finding in fog. Little wonder the Royal Navy supported magnetic science: it generated a valuable, practical product for compass correction and charting, and held out the promise of a nineteenth-century version of the satellite-based Global Positioning System. To secure this prize a maritime empire would willingly risk a great deal of blood and treasure.

The earth possesses a magnetic field that varies with location and time. Geomagnetism, or 'terrestrial magnetism' as it was known in Franklin's day, is the scientific study of this phenomenon. The earth is composed of a liquid metallic core, a rocky outer crust, an atmosphere and the enveloping plasma. Geomagnetism is caused by electric currents in the spinning molten iron core. Because the core is rotating at different speeds from the rocky outer crust the earth's magnetic fields are constantly moving, along with the magnetic poles. These processes are frequently disrupted by electromagnetic storms, energy flaring out from the sun. The earth's magnetic field can trap plasma bubbles travelling from the sun, manifested as the 'northern lights' or aurora borealis, which interfere with all electrical and magnetic equipment, from simple compasses to satellite-based navigation systems.[23]

From the earliest discovery of magnetic attraction it has been harnessed for navigation. Exactly when this first occurred is uncertain, but European mariners were using compasses to determine north by the twelfth century AD.[24] The wider implications of magnetic phenomena, for navigation and later for other sciences, emerged more slowly.

The four basic elements of geomagnetism are:

Declination – the angle between true north and the horizontal component of the field, counted from north through east (the amount by which the compass 'declines' to point towards true north). This phenomenon was termed 'variation' by mariners, for whom it posed a serious problem. It is measured by recording the horizontal angle between a freely suspended magnet and geographic north.

Inclination (or 'dip' in the nineteenth century) – the angle between the direction of the field and the horizontal, reckoned downwards from the horizontal. The vertical angle between the needle and the local horizontal plane records inclination.

Horizontal intensity – the amount of the horizontal component of the field.

Total intensity – the magnitude of the vector field, both vertical and horizontal components.[25] This varies in space and time.

These concepts developed slowly, as did the instruments to measure the data and the theoretical tools to analyse the results. Declination was the first area to be studied, because it had a direct effect on the compass. Early compasses were crude and unreliable, and when used at sea aboard moving ships with significant amounts of iron in their hulls produced inconsistent or contradictory results. Humboldt credited Columbus with pioneering work in this field on his Atlantic voyages, but his evidence was unreliable.[26] However, Portuguese navigators named the southernmost point of Africa Cabo das Agulhas – Cape of Needles – in the 1490s because magnetic and true north were aligned. In 1538 Portuguese navigators took a series of declination readings on a voyage to India, but kept such valuable information secret. Half a century later the phenomenon was well understood, frequently measured on land and represented on declination charts. The assumption that lines of declination were meridians led Sebastian Cabot to argue that they could be used to determine longitude – the master problem of maritime navigation for the next two centuries.

Inclination was first observed in the mid-sixteenth century: English hydrographer Robert Norman built a basic dip circle and published his findings as a guide for navigators. Reprinted down to 1720, this popular work was the first wholly devoted to the practical use of magnetic knowledge at sea. William Gilbert followed Norman, constructing the first practical dip circle and publishing *De Magnete* in 1600. He recognised the magnetic nature of the earth, but erroneously asserted that declination at any position was constant, a claim that encouraged the idea that it could be used to determine longitude. In 1634 Henry Gellibrand, the professor of astronomy at Gresham College, recognised that the declination in London had altered significantly since Gilbert published, establishing the phenomenon of secular variation.[27] His work coincided with the advance of observational astronomy.

As a seafaring nation, the English were drawn to relevant scientific enquiries. Charles II established the Royal Society in 1662 to advance practical science, especially navigation. In the same year a committee of the Royal Society was established to consider employing 'secular change in the variation of the magnetic needle' to determine positions at sea, an alternative method of navigation without reference to the heavens.[28] In 1675 King Charles II founded the Royal Observatory at Greenwich 'for the practical purpose of accurate navigation out of sight of land'. The other great observatory of the age, at Paris, was concerned with geodesy, determining the size and shape of the earth. By the late seventeenth century the importance of the heavens for accurate navigation was established. The charter of the Royal Observatory declared that the positions and motions of the stars must be recalculated to improve accuracy 'so as to find out the so-much-desired longitude of places for the perfecting the art of navigation'.[29] It was this practical approach to science that prompted Charles to found the Observatory, and from 1710 the Royal Society acted as the Crown's advisory body, or 'visitors', to ensure the Observatory met the obligation imposed in its charter to publish useful results.

If the movements of the heavenly bodies could be accurately recorded and predicted they would provide a reliable system for positional fixes. If navigators could be supplied with accurate forecasts of the predicted positions of the stars, and could keep an accurate record of the time at a known point, they could fix their location. These forecasts were published as the *Nautical Almanac* from 1766. The importance of the *Almanac* was obvious: 10,000 copies of the 1781 edition were sold on publication.[30]

However, such results required decades of work, work that revealed the complex factors that affected the accuracy of heavenly and earthly readings. 'Almost as soon as the Astronomer began to peer into the heavens his concern with navigation ensured he was also interested in geomagnetism.'[31] The second Astronomer Royal, Edmond Halley (1720–42), conducted oceanic research in geomagnetism. His voyages, the first undertaken for purely scientific research, produced pioneering isogonic charts 'of the greatest value for practical navigation and the theory of geomagnetism'.[32] Halley realised the magnetic field was drifting westward, and hypothesised that the earth's inner core was rotating at a different speed from the outer shell, but his primary interest was the practical use of the phenomenon for navigation.[33] Unfortunately most isogonic lines run east to west, and were therefore of little use for determining longitude in the North Atlantic, the longest oceanic crossing then regularly made.[34] Halley's contemporary William Whiston argued that his charts, when combined with a chart of magnetic dip, would enable seamen to navigate. Such hopes persisted to the end of the century, but while 'theoretically sound, its practical application is hindered by the inaccuracy of the measurements on ships, due to their motion (and their iron)'.[35] This was the state of geomagnetic knowledge when John Franklin first encountered the subject on board HMS *Investigator* in 1801.

The importance of determining longitude at sea led Parliament to pass an Act in 1714 offering a £20,000 prize for a practical method. After his magnetic experiments Halley decided that the answer lay in the lunar distance method, which used the transit of the moon across the meridian as the time signal. The complications caused by variations in the moon's orbit and the complex mathematics required to reduce observations to useful results made this method the preserve of advanced navigators such as James Cook.[36] Cook used lunar distance to calculate longitude on his first Pacific voyage, and although he used John Harrison's pioneer marine chronometer on the second, regularly checked the timepiece against lunar distance calculations.

In the mid-eighteenth century international co-operation produced simultaneous readings with improved instruments, revealing the magnetic dimension of solar storms and diurnal variation.[37] Despite setting off from Paris armed with French magnetic instruments and instructions, Humboldt consciously built on the practical legacy of Halley and Gilbert. Inspired by Cook's voyages Humboldt produced a sketch of isodynamic zones to show how magnetic intensity reduced from the poles to the equator. He recorded his evidence by counting the swings of a suspended needle for ten minutes. This was 'le résultat le plus important de mon voyage américain'.[38] Nor was it of purely theoretical interest: 'I showed, from my own observations in the Pacific that, under certain circumstances . . . the latitude might be determined from magnetic inclination with sufficient accuracy for the purposes of navigation.'[39]

When Humboldt provided an equatorial baseline and suggested looking to the Arctic, the Royal Society equipped the polar voyages of 1818 to gather magnetic data. Edward Sabine joined Ross's search for the North West Passage, rather than Buchan's attempt on the geographic pole, because Ross would sail closer to magnetic north than any previous scientific mission and might, with the latest instruments, provide a new absolute to join Humboldt's reading. Knowledge of local magnetic variations was critical to the safe use of the compass in unknown waters, especially in the far north where the pursuit of whales had drawn a significant number of British vessels. It is no coincidence that the first scientist to study magnetic phenomena in the Arctic was Whitby whaler William Scoresby, or that he was influenced by Humboldt.[40]

Following Astronomer Royal John Pond's call to improve links between Greenwich and the Admiralty, the Observatory was placed under Admiralty control in 1818, rather than the Board of Ordnance. The same year, Pond began taking regular declination readings, passing the results to the Hydrographer.[41] A landslip in 1824 rendered the magnetic building unsafe and ended the project. Similar navigational concerns saw the Observatory take charge of the navy's chronometers in 1821, maintaining, rating (checking the rate at which they gained or lost time) and issuing. The installation of the time ball in 1833 also served the needs of navigators. When the Royal Society proposed setting up an Observatory at the Cape of Good Hope in 1820, the Admiralty was quick to agree. The Cape station reflected the expanding horizons of British observational science – being dedicated to an accurate catalogue of the heavenly bodies of the southern hemisphere, a vital navigational tool.[42] That said, the Admiralty took a dim view of Pond's failure to produce a reliable *Nautical Almanac* in 1818. After consulting the Royal Society the Admiralty eventually established a separate naval department dedicated to the task in 1834, run by a naval officer. Incessant Admiralty demands for the quick and accurate publication of Greenwich and Cape results persuaded Pond to resign in 1835.

Gauss

In 1822 Humboldt organised the world's first international scientific congress in Berlin specifically to advance magnetic science, a meeting that inspired the formation of the British Association for the Advancement of Science in 1831.[43] Following Humboldt several European states had established magnetic observatories. Critically, the theoretical implications of Humboldt's work had been taken up by the mathematician Carl Friedrich Gauss (1777–1855), astronomer at Göttingen University. In 1803 Gauss had been struck by a newspaper article on geomagnetism and navigation, and recognised a promising field for mathematics. In 1828 Humboldt persuaded him to return to the subject. Gauss soon realised that in order to understand secular variation, which was then the major problem, he would require absolute readings for the intensity and direction of the magnetic field. Humboldt's relative intensities were useless for this purpose. Gauss's system, published in 1833, measured length, mass and time on fixed scales to determine absolute results, opening a new era of terrestrial magnetic research.[44] He devised an oscillation–deflection method of measuring total intensity. His bifilar magnetometer allowed continuous readings of total intensity against a graduated scale.[45] However, such readings took at least forty-five minutes, long enough for the intensity to alter.[46] They must have been very difficult to make on a pitching deck or in a frozen tent, but with suitable portable apparatus it was possible. Gauss developed his initial theoretical position from limited data as a guide to the collection of further data, a waypoint on the road to more concrete conclusions. These could only be obtained if the results were uniform, and uniformly accurate to a high standard. His work included determining the influence of temperature on readings, so that this factor could be controlled for. At every stage his work depended on highly developed mathematics.[47]

New instruments and methods enabled Gauss to 'transcend previous accuracy in the measurement, at any moment, of the intensity, the declination, and the inclination, and of their variations'.[48] The inexact measures produced by Humboldt and the early Arctic navigators were useless. Having devised standardised measures, equipment and methods, and designed a non-magnetic observatory, Gauss recruited an international network of observers. They provided him with observations, taken simultaneously on predetermined days at five-minute intervals for twenty-four hours. Initially the observations were limited to declination, which Gauss considered 'the geo-magnetic element of most practical interest for seamen and geodesists', but he was developing better instruments to record the other elements of geomagnetism.[49] The impact of these new ideas in Britain was immediate. In 1833 the BAAS published Samuel Hunter Christie's glowing report, with suggestions for improved data-gathering methods.[50] The society's 1834 meeting emphasised the importance of magnetic science. Humboldt's friend Arago was present, calling for magnetic observatories to be established across the British Empire. Suitably impressed, the association recommended that the government and the East India Company take up the challenge. At this meeting Humphrey Lloyd of Trinity College Dublin opened a career devoted to Gaussian research. He was already working with Sabine on the magnetic survey of Ireland.

In 1836 Sabine staged his most audacious coup to date. Fresh from completing the magnetic survey of the British Isles he solicited a letter from Humboldt to the Royal Society. The grand old man of science provided the crusade with impeccable scientific credentials and proposed establishing colonial observatories on the Gaussian system. The data they produced could be charted to show lines of equal declination and inclination, information of great value to advanced navigators. Navigational utility was the critical issue in selling Gauss's ideas to 'the first maritime and commercial nation of the globe'.[51] Sabine used the letter to lever open the Treasury, and in the process outmanoeuvred his old enemy Airy.

Between 1836 and 1841 Gauss produced six annual reports of the Magnetische Verein (Magnetic Union), charting the development of data-gathering equipment and scientific theory. His *Allgemeine Theorie des Geomagnetismus* of 1838 provided a major boost to the subject, demonstrating that the origin of the phenomenon lay within the earth. In February 1838 Humboldt recommended Gauss's apparatus and methods to the Royal Geographical Society, 'which by degrees will be employed in all our great observatories', and explicitly linked Gaussian science to British concerns:

As I think that the subject is not without importance to seamen, I beg to invite the influential members of your society to be good enough to propagate Gauss's manner of observing in all new stations where intelligent people can be found.

Points near the magnetic equator and those which are in high latitudes in the southern hemisphere . . . would be most desirable if they would observe at the same epochs indicated by M. Gauss.[52]

Gauss's theory was quickly translated into English by Sabine's wife, to ensure it could be used by British observers.[53] The Göttingen Magnetic Union persuaded most European observers to standardise instruments and observation techniques, and pool their results. Gauss hoped that German, Swedish, Italian and British observatories would produce enough evidence to sustain a scientific theory to explain the phenomenon. This would enable navigators to use terrestrial magnetism for practical purposes – a classic Humboldtian approach. Simultaneous observations were conducted at fifty locations at prearranged times. Dublin and Greenwich were the British bases, along with eight colonial stations; four of them, at Toronto, St Helena, the Cape and Hobart, were under Sabine's direction, while an Antarctic expedition would be part of the process. The Royal Society instructions to the new magnetic stations, fixed and floating, adopted Gauss's methods and his fixed dates for observations.[54] Between 1830 and 1845 geomagnetism made remarkable progress, and recruited an international following.

Rivals

While the development of magnetic science is usually recorded as a steady evolution with occasional breakthrough events such as Halley's voyages, Humboldt's journey and Gauss's theory, there were other, darker currents running through the geomagnetic world. Personal rivalries and intellectual disagreements coloured the way in which the British state responded to the new opportunities. Humboldt's ideas and his concern to gather data appealed, but Sabine was never convinced by Gauss's theoretical work, in part because he lacked the mathematical and theoretical training to operate at this level. Relations between Humboldt and Gauss were strained, mirroring those between their English followers Sabine and Airy.[55]

Astronomer Royal George Biddell Airy (1801–92) combined Sabine's passion for administration with a commanding personality and a terrifying work ethic. Hampered by poor eyesight, Airy conducted relatively little observational astronomy. Instead he focused on the major scientific problems that faced the Admiralty in an era of rapid technological change. His primary task was to improve practical navigation.[56] Airy was not an easy man to work for or with. His rigid standards left little room for human failings, close professional relationships or personal friendship. In upholding the dignity and authority of his office Airy had serious disagreements with the men who would shape the Franklin mission, Edward Sabine and Francis Beaufort.

Airy arrived at the Observatory in 1835 to find the institution dominated by the assessment and regulation of naval chronometers, 'rather than as a place of science'. Although the Astronomer needed to work closely with the Hydrographer, the two men disagreed fundamentally about chronometers. Airy wanted to reduce the time and effort his staff devoted to clock maintenance; Beaufort required a steady supply of these vital instruments for his surveyors and the fleet. Airy appealed to the Admiralty and the system was changed. Beaufort was furious, and used his position on the Observatory Board of Visitors to block the printing of Airy's first three annual reports.[57] Their relationship never recovered.

While the dispute with Beaufort was not directly related to magnetic science, it had a knock-on effect.[58] Beaufort was already working closely with Sabine, who was building his own magnetic empire. Airy, as Astronomer Royal, had a national role in magnetic science. After Gauss's Magnetic Union of 1833 had catapulted geomagnetism to the top of the international scientific agenda Airy secured Admiralty funds for 'an extensive series of magnetic observations'.[59] His observatory began work in 1838: he added meteorological readings in 1840 because, like Franklin far away in the northern wastes of Canada, Airy was searching for connections. Consequently the Royal Society asked Airy and Samuel Christie to report on Humboldt's 1836 letter. Their emphatic endorsement helped to persuade both government and Admiralty to act. It is probable Airy did not know that the letter had been solicited by Sabine.

In June 1838 Airy and John Herschel argued the case for a global network of Gaussian magnetic observatories at the Admiralty.[60] Airy greatly improved the instrumentation at Greenwich and began to

record data using Gauss's local time in Göttingen (he had corresponded with Gauss before beginning work). The contemporaneous
publicity provided by Ross's location of the magnetic North Pole
and his Antarctic mission led to an increase in staff and observing
work, but by the mid-1840s Airy, like Gauss, was convinced the
time had come to cut back on observations, process the data and
begin analysis. He accepted Gauss's argument that priority should
be shifted to processing the data in hand and developing theory.
Sabine disagreed. Had their disagreement been restricted to scientific
ideas and methods the two men might have been able to co-operate.
Sadly other issues intervened. A shared lust for bureaucratic power
made them rivals, their uncompromising natures made them enemies. An Observatory Board of Visitors that included Beaufort, and
was heavily influenced by Edward Sabine's BAAS, overruled Airy's
proposed cutback.[61] The Treasury funded further observation: Airy
responded by developing self-recording instruments for magnetic
and meteorological work.[62]

The British magnetic mission

In the Arctic, Sabine realised that magnetic data could be gathered by
trained naval officers and some, notably James Clark Ross and John
Franklin, became scientists. All nineteenth-century polar voyages collected magnetic data. This process reached a climax in 1831 when
James Clark Ross reached magnetic north. This secured his place as
the Royal Navy's pre-eminent magnetic officer. That Ross was promoted, rewarded and paid for his role in a private expedition funded
by a London gin distiller reflected the anxiety of the state to annex
this discovery for the Empire. He had legitimised British claims to the
Canadian Arctic and established the standing of British science. His
portrait shows a naval hero, sword in hand, and an Arctic scientist,
his magnetic dip circle perched on an ice table. Some Arctic books
crop the image to remove the dip circle. It seems they have no place
for such prosaic tools, or the prosaic truth they tell.

Ross's discovery was a timely boost to British magnetic science,
which had been lagging behind that of the Europeans. Sabine used
the ability of naval expeditions to reach parts of the globe closed to

European rivals to establish priority in this international crusade. By the time the BAAS was ready to act several theories that attempted to explain geomagnetic activity were in circulation, but the limited geographical range from which existing data had been obtained provided a powerful incentive for further expeditions. Initially Sabine tried to advance his research through the Royal Society, which had a long-standing connection with magnetic science. In 1831 the society approached the Admiralty, requesting their Lordships to set up observatories in South Africa and New South Wales.[63] The failure of this initiative only emphasised the need for a better lobby group, and the political value of Ross's achievement.

It was fortunate that the 1831 approach did not succeed, as it antedated Gauss's theoretical and practical breakthrough. Not that British instrument makers lagged behind: Robert Were Fox built an improved dip instrument that greatly enhanced the accuracy of readings taken on a rolling ship, largely by reducing friction. Franklin, the first to inspect the new instrument, immediately recognised its importance, recommending it to Colonel Chesney's Euphrates expedition and to his friend Beaufort for naval use.[64] Beaufort, Ross and Sabine tested the dip circle in Beaufort's garden one night in April 1836 and hastily loaded it onto HMS *Terror*. Lieutenant Owen Stanley reported the instrument performed perfectly, but many of the adjusting screws were too small for frozen fingers.[65] The two Fox instruments that went with Ross to the Antarctic 'contributed more to a knowledge of the geographical distribution of terrestrial magnetism than any other recent invention'.[66] Even so, shipboard observations were not ideal: the presence of iron rendered readings taken afloat relative. Absolute readings could be secured ashore in a suitable non-magnetic observatory with Professor Humphrey Lloyd's improved unifilar magnetometer. Ultimately Lloyd's work made it possible to observe accurately at sea.[67]

In 1834 the BAAS appealed to the government for additional magnetic research funding. Woolwich Academy physicist Samuel Christie stressed that accurate observation would produce charts of equal variation and magnetic meridians which would help to understand the phenomenon, 'and might indicate relations which have hitherto been overlooked'.[68] The implication was clear: practical results might flow from further research, and better instruments were under development.

Scientists found the lure of a magnetic pole to combine with Humboldt's equatorial readings irresistible. This placed the search for a North West Passage in an entirely different light. In the hands of a proven observer like Ross a fresh attempt at the Passage would produce a wealth of data to advance their agendas. Interested in geomagnetism, not geography, the scientists did not care whether a Passage existed, only that the attempt to find it passed close by the magnetic pole. Predictably Edward Sabine organised the attack, hoping Ross's reputation and his anxiety to complete the Passage would persuade the Admiralty to make an attempt.[69] Ross was ready to go, and believed the government was disposed to send another expedition: 'The national character for perseverance and enterprise is deeply involved with the solution of a problem which has occupied its energies for so many years and having produced such extensive discoveries in geographical and natural science.' The science that Ross and Sabine pursued was the key to Franklin's final mission.[70] Empire, science and discovery formed a magnetic nexus in Edward Sabine's hands.

These hopes proved unfounded. Sabine and Ross made their play in July 1834, only to be confounded by frequent changes of leadership at the Admiralty and a change of government in December.[71] In 1835 Back's overland expedition added to the impetus, and Franklin became closely involved.[72] The plan was to attempt the North West Passage with *Erebus* and *Terror*, conveniently prepared for ice navigation as part of Ross's whaleship rescue mission. After that the ships could be sent to find magnetic south.[73] It was widely assumed that Ross would take command, if the government could be persuaded.

The British Association initiative failed, and Humboldt refused an invitation to bless the project at the 1835 Dublin meeting.[74] It required Roderick Murchison's political skills to translate Franklin and Ross's Dublin Antarctic Committee into action. The key argument was that data gathered on this mission would enable scientists to produce predictive tables of magnetic variation 'for at least a century'.[75] This would be priceless navigational information. Murchison proposed using the committee resolutions to brief John Barrow, because 'he will eventually be the person to lead the government into the project'.[76] Although a life member of the British Association, First Lord of the Admiralty Lord Minto had already informed its leader William Whewell that 'he did not think the government would be likely to accede to such a recommendation'. At this stage the BAAS held back, to avoid the danger of a public rejection. Suitably chastened, the scientists recognised that a polar mission would have to be sold to ministers and the public as a question of national prestige, a more effective if less honest argument.[77] As magnetic science was never going to hit the headlines, the Passage became the cover story. Whewell elected to wait for Sabine's report on terrestrial magnetism in Ireland, which would appear at the 1836 meeting to revive the issue.[78] Co-authored by Humphrey Lloyd and James Ross, Sabine's report provided the scientific focus that ultimately led to Antarctic and Arctic missions.

By the spring of 1836 the magnetic impulse was reaching a crescendo. The Royal Society argued that the Admiralty should fund magnetic observations at the Royal Observatory because they were 'highly important to the interests of science and practical navigation'.[79] Insiders Barrow and Beaufort placed the subject on the Admiralty agenda. Beaufort was the scientist's mole, Barrow the public voice of exploration. The scientists had turned the British Association into a potent political vehicle. It included men with real talents for arm-twisting, ear-bending and lobbying – Whewell mobilised Murchison for another scientific assault on the Admiralty, and pointed out that a mutual friend was already hard at work:

Sir J[ohn] F[ranklin] writes me word that there appears to be a good opportunity of urging upon the Admiralty the southern expedition. The *Terror* which had been strengthened and fitted up for the service in which Capt. Ross is employed will not be wanted for that object, and so there is a ship ready for a polar sea. The suggestion of making this an opportunity of applying to the Admiralty comes from Beaufort. Do you think it worth acting upon? And will you see some of the members of the Committee appointed about this matter, and ascertain whether there is a feeling that we ought to make a push?[80]

After his attempt to rescue the whalers in Baffin Bay, Ross was optimistic:

I am quite delighted to perceive that the North West Passage question has been so much agitated during my absence & am in great hopes of being able to get an expedition equipped next spring. If Back were to return this season, I should have no doubt on this subject. Both Barrow and Beaufort are very sanguine about it & the Admiralty appears, so far as I can judge well disposed. By the time that shall be completed you will be ready with your South Polar scheme, or if that should not be ready, the southern one must be attempted.

He did not forget Sabine's concern to get magnetic data from the South Pole: 'I would sometimes almost give a preference to that Expedition, were it not that the N W Passage has been so long my hobby.' In any event there was a splendid scientific harvest to be reaped in the south, unless the Yankees got there first: 'that would really be most provoking'.[81]

The other element of the campaign was the letter Humboldt wrote to the Royal Society in April, urging the establishment of a world-wide chain of magnetic observatories (he mentioned Canada, Australia, St Helena, Jamaica, Ceylon and the Cape) and the dispatch of an Antarctic expedition.[82] An appeal from the internationally renowned father of the discipline would be hard to resist. It would have been entirely in character for Sabine to prompt Humboldt, and it is revealing that he took no part in the Royal Society response.[83]

By late 1836 Sabine had harnessed the Royal Society and the BAAS to his chariot, and with the help of key allies would drive this powerful combination through the next decade towards a global empire of magnetic data.[84] His single-minded pursuit of the magnetic project, assumption of power in the Royal Society and the British Association, and his ability to co-opt other labourers made him a far more effective scientific promoter than university-based clerical savants. It was highly significant that his friend Murchison became the senior general secretary of the BAAS in September 1837. Murchison's political contacts and public profile made him an ideal coadjutor for backstairs manipulator Sabine.[85] Having assembled his team Sabine launched his appeal for an Antarctic expedition at the 1838 British Association meeting, circulating his report on terrestrial magnetism in the British Isles among those who would sit in judgement on his magnetic plans. He added Beaufort's assurance 'that if the discussion terminates in the adoption of a suitable recommendation to government, it will certainly be done'. Beaufort and Ross were already planning the naval mission.

Ultimately the results of Sabine's crusade were significant only as part of a global imperial science project. Ross's mission would be a national 'victory' in a new and glorious form of competition.[86] This was a game that required ample resources and skilled players. It was not necessarily about facts. Sabine knew that one man held the key to his magnetic campaign. Anxious to avoid any hint of dissent that might call the whole project into question, Sabine secured the support of John Herschel.[87]

By the late 1830s Herschel was universally acknowledged to be the exemplar of British professional science. He had established this primacy on a truly Humboldtian private expedition to the Cape, where he surveyed the southern heavens while collecting, measuring, recording and even travelling in a suitably heroic style. On his return to Britain in 1838 Herschel was swept up in the magnetic project. He became the key advocate for a global system and was largely responsible for the selection of the Cape Astronomical Observatory as a magnetic station.[88] His was the name that ministers looked for on any submission, his endorsement the one that mattered. Herschel doubted key elements of Sabine's agenda, but kept quiet in the interests of the scientific community.

The timing of Herschel's return was perfect for, as Lloyd stressed, the science had been greatly improved in the three years since the subject was first mooted. Gauss's system of simultaneous observation and improved instruments together with Sabine's latest finding on the global distribution of magnetic force had fundamentally altered the task. Now everything was ready for Britain to recover 'the great distance she has suffered herself to fall behind the nations of the Continent in magnetic discovery'.[89]

Just in case that was not enough to push the ministers into a new polar mission the association secured a high-powered guest speaker. For all the interest sparked by Humboldt, Ross and Gauss it required a Frenchman to complete the process. At the 1838 meeting Arago declared that France was building suitable observatories not just in Europe, but also in her colonies.[90] Shortly after the meeting the British Association, in league with the Royal Society, presented a resolution to the government calling for a major project to locate the magnetic South Pole and establish imperial observatories throughout the Empire.

Unfortunately Murchison tried to rig the results by pushing aside the nominated president of the meeting, the troublesome Babbage, to ensure Herschel took the chair. He did this without telling either man. Not only was Babbage openly contemptuous of Sabine and his work, but the scientists needed Herschel's name on the recommendation. Babbage exploded, and Herschel refused the presidency.[91] Fortunately the Marquis of Northampton stepped in and spoke for the association with the not inconsiderable weight of a president of the Royal Society. In case anyone thought this was pure science he noted that 'if the improvements of our knowledge of magnetism, etc. should at any time save only one ship of the line, the whole expense of an expedition will have been well laid out, without any reference to the scientific objects of the expedition'.[92] Fortunately Babbage held his tongue.

Caught red-handed, Murchison was obliged to resign, but suggested that Sabine replace him as general secretary.[93] Sabine accepted because the office would enable him to control co-operation with the Royal Society, the key to securing the Antarctic mission, while drawing the entire scientific community into his nexus.[94] Soon afterwards he and Lloyd travelled to Berlin. The 'delightful reception' they received from Humboldt effectively 'blessed' the British magnetic mission and certified that Edward Sabine was his English disciple.[95] Sabine also took care to keep on good terms with Gauss, sending frequent harvests of British observational data.[96]

Ultimately Sabine's global empire comprised seven magnetic stations: the East India Company administered Simla, Madras and Singapore, the army ran Toronto, St Helena and the Cape of Good Hope, but the Royal Navy controlled the key station. Herschel noted:

The station at Van Diemen's Land is of such vital importance to the General result of the whole undertaking that even should all the others be abandoned, this must be retained, and manned as best can be done by supernumerary naval officers attached to the expedition by orders from the Admiralty.[97]

Initially the stations would conduct pre-planned readings for three years, with significant bursts of activity on Gauss's 'term days', when the international network would be following the same system.

Antarctic expedition

Sabine secured the dispatch of James Clark Ross's Antarctic mission by harnessing the combined efforts of the Royal Society and the British Association, aided by the political instincts of Murchison and the influence of the Marquis of Northampton. Northampton's 1838 presidential address to the Royal Society had stressed the imminence of long-sought magnetic results: 'We are rapidly approaching great and comprehensive generalisations, which can only be completely established or disproved by very widely distributed and, in many cases, by absolutely simultaneous observations.'[98] Along the way Sabine inflicted another unwarranted humiliation on that eminent, reverend and worthy man William Scoresby, whose ideas and methods he had been pirating for many years, blocking his application for a grant to study magnetic needles.[99] Tainted by his origins in 'trade', Scoresby was too clever by half for the manipulative, controlling Sabine's liking.

As a leading figure in the terrestrial magnetic survey work, intimately involved with Sabine, and an experienced polar navigator, Ross was chosen to combine naval command with magnetic observation. This time Lord Minto offered official support. Beaufort's Physics and Meteorology Committee of the Royal Society provided a hundred-page manual of scientific procedure for magnetic and meteorological work, largely Mrs Sabine's translation of Gauss. Significantly the Geological, Zoological and Botanical Committees provided altogether less bulky guidance.[100] Magnetic science was 'the great scientific object of the Expedition',[101] a point Herschel rammed home in the *Quarterly Review*. He emphasised the practical nature of the science and the need to focus on North America: 'the deficiency of trustworthy magnetic observations in all that vast region being lamentable'.[102]

Beaufort's long-standing concern to improve the accuracy of ship's compasses was tied to the question of magnetic variation. After Ross sailed he and Sabine redesigned the magnetic compass in anticipation of a sophisticated compass-based navigational system.[103] In the event Ross did not reach magnetic south. Unable to find a safe winter anchorage and facing a significant mountain barrier he used the Fox instruments to record at sea, and calculated the position. This was hardly a failure: it was not until 1909 that Shackleton's *Nimrod* expedition reached the magnetic South Pole. National pride was salved when Ross recalculated the position of the pole, correcting Gauss's predicted location.[104] Once again German mathematical genius had been matched by British endeavour.

By demonstrating that Gauss's theoretical placement of the magnetic South Pole was incorrect Ross provided a powerful spur to renew Arctic endeavour. Magnetic scientists acknowledged that 'the difficulty of getting adequate observations in high latitudes, where closely spaced observations are most needed', hampered their work.[105] In 1847 Humboldt argued that the needs of navigation and science should ensure the sustained development of the subject, and the extension of large, state-funded research projects.[106] Magnetic data gathering using the new Gauss-type instruments would be the primary purpose of the 1845 expedition.

When Franklin accepted the governorship of Van Diemen's Land, magnetic science was fast becoming the dominant vehicle for the promotion of polar exploration – the one agenda that had enough support across the naval, scientific, and political worlds to open the Treasury's emaciated coffers. When James Clark Ross reached magnetic north, his success was immediately annexed to the imperial glory of Britain. His discovery used the new international language of science to validate British dominion in the Arctic: an irresistible combination of power and wisdom. Little wonder the next round of polar voyages sought magnetic data; charts would be a by-product.

BOOK TWO

PUBLIC VISIONS

5

From Van Diemen's Land to Tasmania,
1836–43

A new career

THE BIG PROBLEM for pioneering Arctic heroes Franklin, Parry and Ross was what to do next. When publicly funded polar exploration ended in the late 1820s, they needed paid employment, but only John Ross found a private backer for a further Arctic voyage. Both Parry and Franklin married well, twice over, but neither was prepared to live on his wife's income. While Parry proved a poor Hydrographer of the Navy, and only a moderate administrator of agricultural societies, Poor Law boards, steam engineering and hospitals, he never went back to sea. It was Franklin who secured the greatest prizes, a full commission in command of a regular warship, a colonial governorship and one more expedition. This was hardly surprising. Franklin was the defining hero of the Arctic mission, a great leader and scientist.

Jane Franklin managed Sir John's career in a thoroughly modern manner, considering his options and protecting his reputation. After the *Rainbow* commission Franklin was unlikely to get another ship for many years: the list of eligible captains was long, the number of ships in commission painfully small. Franklin considered entering mercenary service, like Lord Cochrane, but such work did not appeal to honest John. He feared for his commission, since it was illegal to serve in a foreign fleet, and in any case he was no warrior. Nor was he attracted to Ross's approach, commanding a private expedition.[1] However, colonial administration was a useful alternative employment as the Empire, unlike the fleet, was constantly expanding. With the active support of his patron 'Sailor King' William IV, Franklin had an entrée into any government office.[2] He turned down the governorship of Antigua because it was a subordinate post that reported to a regional governor of the same military rank, rather than directly to Whitehall. Both the colonial secretary Lord Glenelg and the Admiralty were suitably impressed.[3] This was

93

telling: he was in earnest to govern, and had no desire for a dignified retreat as some have argued.[4]

However, colonial government was no sinecure for senior sailors. Long accustomed to the strict subordination of the quarterdeck, many found the give and take of local politics, the assertive, brash colonials and their licentious press a trial. Few made the transition with credit; John Franklin, Robert Fitzroy and Charles Hotham ended their terms under a cloud, respectively recalled, ruined and dead. Franklin's friend Captain James Stirling at the Swan River Settlement, later Fremantle, returned home with his reputation intact, but he was not a celebrity when he set off for colonial government.[5]

A combination of royal patronage and his own resolute character secured Franklin a high-profile appointment, a six-year term as lieutenant-governor of Van Diemen's Land, now Tasmania. He accepted the post only when the Admiralty assured him it would not prevent future naval employment.[6] His ultimate ambitions remained naval and polar. To reinforce the point Lord Minto, First Lord of the Admiralty, sent his son Henry as ADC to 'one of the finest characters that ever lived'.[7] The Admiralty also sent a surveying officer to help Franklin with a key part of his mission, improving local navigation. His friend Beaufort selected Lieutenant Thomas Burnett for the task. Other Admiralty connections proved less useful. John Barrow sent ne'er-do-well son Peter, who came close to causing a rift between Franklin and his father. Beaufort advanced Captain Alexander Maconachie RN, one-time secretary of the Geographical Society,[8] who undermined Franklin's administration.[9]

The appointment was publicly announced in April 1836, giving Franklin four months to prepare. He was under no illusions, confessing to the Colonial Office official responsible for Australasian policy: 'I am about to execute duties very different to my professional habits, and feel that I shall require every friendly aid.'[10] He also consulted Parry, who had considerable Australian experience,[11] and called on his preferred source of strength: 'I pray God that his Grace may be given us to direct our hearts to him and that he will help me in the important and interesting duties I shall be called on to perform.'[12] This last resource proved critical to his sense of purpose, and his conduct of government.

Franklin's mission statement for the government of Van Diemen's Land was written by close friend Thomas Arnold. Headmaster of Rugby School, social reformer and historian, Arnold shared many of Franklin's religious and social views.

I sometimes think that if the Government would make me a Bishop, or principal of a College or school, – or both together, – in such a place as Van Diemen's Land, and during your government, I could be tempted to emigrate with all my family for good and all. There can be, I think, no more useful or more sacred task, than assisting in forming the moral and intellectual character of a new society; it is the surest and best kind of missionary labour. But our colonial society has been in general so Jacobinical in the truest sense of the word; every man has lived so much to and for himself, and the bonds of law and religion have been so little acknowledged as the great sanctions and securities of society – that one shrinks from bringing up one's children where they must in all human probability become lowered, not in rank or fortune, but in what is infinitely more important, in the intellectual and moral and religious standards by which their lives would be guided.

Feeling this, and holding our West Indian colonies to be one of the worst stains in the moral history of mankind, a convict colony seems to me to be even more shocking and more monstrous in its very conception. I do not know to what extent Van Diemen's Land is so; but I am sure that no such evil can be done to mankind as by thus sowing with rotten seed, and raising up a nation morally tainted in its very origin. Compared with this, the bloodiest exterminations ever effected by conquest were useful and good actions. If they will colonize with convicts, I am satisfied that the stain should last, not only for one whole life, but for more than one generation; that no convict or convict's child should ever be a free citizen; and that, even in the third generation, the offspring should be excluded from all the offices of honour or authority in the colony. This would be complained of as unjust or invidious, but I am sure that distinctions of moral breed are as natural and as just as those of skin or of arbitrary caste are wrong and mischievous; it is the law of God's Providence which we cannot alter, that the sins of the father are really visited upon the child in the corruption of his breed, and in the rendering impossible, many of the feelings which are the greatest security to a child against evil.

Forgive me for all this; but it really is a happiness to me to think of you in Van Diemen's Land, where you will be I know, not in name nor in form, but in deed and in spirit, the best and chief missionary.[13]

Arnold's potent mix of evangelical faith and moral purpose would be the key to Franklin's government.

Formally presented to his king on 20 August, Franklin, his

extended family and staff embarked on the merchant ship *Fairlie* a week later. Suitably equipped with reports, books and charts he used the long sea voyage to study the island.[14] He would learn more about human nature in Hobart than he had in all his years traversing the barren wilderness of the Arctic Circle.

Yet there were other, darker stories that linked Franklin with his new home. In 1822 a party of convicts, escaping into the virgin rain forest inland of Macquarie harbour, had resorted to cannibalism. The story was so horrific that the authorities refused to believe it. Two years later one of the convicts, Alexander Pearce, escaped again, and ate another convict. This time the cannibal was given his due – publicly hanged rather than shot in private. His story became a staple of the dark mythos of Van Diemen's Land.[15]

While he had no expectations of private gain,[16] Franklin headed south confident he could make a real contribution to the moral, social and economic development of the colony, establish Hobart as the cultural capital of the Australian colonies and advance his navigational and scientific agenda. Despite the pressures of an overcrowded ship, shared with another 173 passengers including a large number of place-hunting social climbers, Franklin worked on his mission statement. He arrived ready to act along the lines Arnold had provided. He was not going to dwell on the convict past. He came to improve and enlighten, deploying his own unique combination of evangelical piety and Humboldtian science to reduce the island to order and open up its riches for human endeavour while improving the moral and physical well-being of his subjects. However, the colonial context was deeply flawed, and he met serious opposition from people and systems left in place by his predecessor.

Van Diemen's Land

Like the rest of the Empire, Van Diemen's Land had a role in the national interest of the British state, to which all other considerations were subordinate. That role was the provision of a large penal establishment to discipline malefactors and terrorise the lower orders in Britain at the expense of the local community. While the colony's existence relied on the economic activity of free settlers, free settlement was a nuisance. The settlers expected metropolitan support and political rights, which ran counter to the main function of the colony. In attempting to reconcile penal servitude and free settlement Franklin faced no easy task.

Only settled in 1804 to forestall the French, Van Diemen's Land was linked with New South Wales, with which it shared the schizophrenic social mix of convicts and free settlers. In the early years this final frontier of the British imperial diaspora attracted wild lawless men, men who turned chaos to their advantage, the governors being little better than the governed. Hobart, the first and only port of call between the Cape and Sydney, grew quickly. It soon acquired a veneer of culture, and a growing collection of stone buildings erected by convict masons. In 1825 the colony was placed in direct contact with the Colonial Office in London, and welcomed its first 'professional' governor. George Arthur was experienced, tough-minded, puritanical and committed. A relentless administrator with a passion for order and an anxiety to please his superiors back in London, he acted with vigour to end the menace of bush-rangers – escaped convicts who terrorised the outlying settlements – shifted the convict station for repeat offenders to the new model prison at Port Arthur and declared martial law to drive the remnants of the aboriginal peoples out of the settled areas, while raising standards of probity and morality in public office and private life. For every step he took that the settlers approved they complained of two more. Convicts who behaved themselves after landing were assigned to settlers as free labour, for no more than the cost of food and clothing. Access to cheap labour of both sexes helped to push the colony forward, integrate the convicts, who were gradually released on tickets of leave, and keep the cost of the convict establishment, which was borne by the colony, at a low level. Arthur tightened up the rules on land and convict labour, which upset many leading settlers; he also abused his position, taking land grants and lending money.[17] This was common knowledge, but Arthur had the political skill to see off his critics. Nor was it a surprise that his political opponents were also his commercial rivals, for Arthur did not discriminate between public good and private profit. He rejected demands for a free press, trial by jury and a representative assembly as incompatible with a penal colony.

Having settled on a career in colonial government Arthur did his best to make Van Diemen's Land conform to the wishes of London, which were that it remain a cheap, quiet repository for the outcasts of British and increasingly imperial society. By meeting his masters' wishes Arthur would die a wealthy man. After running the colony for more than a decade George Arthur had amassed a significant private fortune in land and investment. He departed leaving the colonial administration in the hands of two men who had married his nieces, both of whom owed him a significant amount of money.[18]

The free population despised Arthur and his minions for their self-aggrandisement and hoped that Franklin, a man of international renown, would remove the old order and begin again. This was entirely characteristic of free settlers, as a rule antagonistic to any form of metropolitan control, obsessed with status, money and public ostentation, and quarrelsome and vindictive. They invariably thought better of their rulers after their departure. The self-importance of the settlers reflected a burgeoning economy, propelled by wool, wheat and whale oil, that translated into a desire for self-government.

Unaware of the extent to which men and measures had become inextricably intertwined, Franklin planned to keep Arthur's old administrative team in office while steadily changing the character of the regime. He knew this would be a tall order, but the man who had eaten his boots and commanded the 'Celestial *Rainbow*' possessed both determination and rare leadership qualities. Unfortunately, while a great leader of the willing and an inspiration to those facing disaster, Franklin was not cut out by art or nature to deal with the petty self-interested politics of the tiny, fractious court at Hobart. To make matters worse he had been partly deaf since the battle of Trafalgar, a serious social drawback that made him appear hesitant or ignorant in noisy gatherings.[19] It also encouraged his wife to intercede, to ensure he had heard the conversation, which could be interpreted by the malign as unwarranted interference.

Arrival

The *Fairlie* arrived at Hobart on 6 January 1837. As the harbour opened before him, Franklin was 'much pleased with the appearance of the scenery': a ribbon of settlement at the water's edge on the western shore of the River Derwent, dwarfed by a majestic mountain backdrop.[20] Coming closer he could see a neat town with many stone buildings.

A carriageway ran for a mile along the shore to Battery Point and, from the waterfront, buildings rose one behind the other like tiers in an amphitheatre. The wide and well lit streets, lined with handsome houses and shops, would not have disgraced a country town in England.[21]

Addressing his subjects for the first time Franklin did not mention convicts, instead pointing out that he had been on the island before any of them, serving with the immortal Flinders. He hoped to complete that legacy and set out his vision: a free colony, representative government and a dynamic economy driven by scientific knowledge of the island's natural resources. These hopes would be frustrated by policy changes in London, which adversely affected everyone on the island, paralysing progress for a decade.

Two issues dominate the early history of Tasmania: the convict system and the destruction of the aboriginal people.[22] In both cases Franklin's involvement was limited. The colony had a European population of 42,944, of whom 29,096 were free. He inherited a smooth-running if brutal penal policy from Arthur that was both cheap and popular with the free settlers, many of whom exploited the assignment of convicts as a source of cheap labour. Any hopes Franklin had of reforming the system for the better were wrecked by a disloyal private secretary and shifting political views in London. The government altered the rules with abandon, leaving Franklin to deal with increased transportation and the end of assignment. Furthermore he had to fund these changes from a threadbare colonial Treasury just as the local economy went into recession.[23]

Similarly, the destruction of the indigenous Tasmanians was essentially complete before Franklin arrived. Arthur had confined them to an island in the Bass Strait, where they slowly died out. Franklin was 'moved to pity' by the plight of the last survivors, but he took the advice of self-proclaimed 'expert' George Robinson, who ran the island. It was already far too late to save this tragic people from the onslaught of European diseases, European agriculture and European violence.[24]

Although of critical import to the settlers, who looked to Franklin for security and prosperity, such issues only exercised his masters in the Colonial Office when there were problems. In their view Franklin's task was to keep the colony quiet and avoid the settler complaints that had marked the latter part of Arthur's regime. Legislators in Britain preferred a convict station to free settlement because a penal colony served metropolitan interests. Throughout his seven years in office Franklin, not for the first time, found the tide set against him. He had expected to end convict transportation and introduce local government. Instead the Colonial Office sent more convicts, laying the cost on local funds, and rejected the call for representative government. No one could have sold these measures to the colonists. In his efforts to conciliate and explain, Franklin struck those used to the harsh dictates of George Arthur as indecisive and feeble, but here, as elsewhere, good manners and a thoughtful approach masked his inner resolve. Franklin's leadership, built on piety, humanity and a powerful example, provided him with precious few resources to combat the malign, the dishonest and the corrupt. Unable to comprehend such conduct, and reluctant to believe ill of anyone, he was slow to condemn, but once resolved his judgement was final. Even then he was anxious to conciliate, and this proved his undoing.

From his home and office in the rambling, uncomfortable Government House on Elizabeth Street, at the heart of the island's growing capital, Franklin could see the key public buildings and observe the movement of ships and cargoes on the River Derwent. To the rear the ground rose steadily up the slopes of Mount Wellington, giving Hobart the appearance of a gigantic stadium. The old Government House building was demolished in the mid-nineteenth century and replaced by a palatial structure on the edge of town. In its place stands a statue of Sir John, the only governor of the colony to be given a public memorial by his one-time subjects. The tribute was well merited. Franklin provided Van Diemen's Land with effective leadership for seven years, weathering a number of crises, mostly of London's making, along with local problems like the economic downturn and the development of a rival colony in Victoria. At the same time he began the process that saw the island offically renamed Tasmania in 1855, and transformed its cultural life. Yet instead of the customary commendation, or even a note of thanks, he would be summarily dismissed in circumstances which implied he had failed. For a man with a profound sense of justice this was unbearable: this was not the way his career was meant to end – he had a reputation to consider.

Culture versus control, convict versus free

At heart the problem of Van Diemen's Land was simple. The colonial authorities in London wanted a locally funded convict station to remove the criminal classes from home without further cost to the British taxpayer. Lieutenant-governors had been largely free to make policy so long as they avoided cost or complaint. Unfortunately, for the colony to support the convict establishment it had to be successful, which meant land-owning, logging, whaling and other labour-intensive occupations. Free settlement carried an expectation of self-government which thoroughly alarmed the Convict Department in London. They sent George Arthur to stem the trend and ensure that the cost of the convicts would still fall on the island. This was mission impossible: Arthur could only meet his masters' expectations by assigning convicts to the settlers and establishing a single prison fortress to contain recidivists. He explained his philosophy to London: he was running a penal colony, civil liberty was restricted and free settlers 'should be looked on as Visitors'.[25] Little wonder they opposed his government.

The very fabric of society in Van Diemen's Land was distorted by the presence of convicts as a significant proportion of the population. Convict labour gave free working men a status far beyond that available in Britain, and unprecedented social mobility. This social mobility was soon apparent at Hobart, where an illusion of gentility was created by the emergence of a polite society with all the attributes of contemporary culture. It was a classic second-generation development, created by those unheralded arbiters of social change, the wives of the newly wealthy. These women replaced the rough-

and-ready frontier lifestyle of the original settlement with church services and weddings, keeping the convicts down and the morally suspect out. Franklin would step into this curious cross-grained world with a vision diametrically opposed to that of Arthur. He came not to run the gaol, but to build a better society, a society in which science and the culture of knowledge would enlighten his subjects while the Church ministered to spiritual needs that had hitherto been assuaged by the contents of a bottle. Science would engage the higher faculties while building vital social and personal links between colonial officers and leading settlers that were vital to effective administration. Because he anticipated the end of transportation and the arrival of representative government Franklin considered the convict question peripheral.[26] He would bring education, culture and civilisation to transform the colony, building a new society out of the dangerous, divisive legacy of George Arthur. While Hobart remained the first port of call for ships travelling to Australia, and the connection with Britain remained strong, Franklin's vision of his colony as a civilised satellite of the metropolis endured.[27] Curiously, it would be his navigational work that broke the communication link with London, heralding the long drawn-out decline of Hobart from cultural centre to colonial backwater.

After an initial outburst of enthusiasm for their famous new lieutenant-governor, the leading colonists were alarmed to hear Franklin praise his unpopular predecessor. While his remarks reflected Colonial Office opinion rather than his own judgement, or his long-term intentions, it persuaded many that the new man would be a tool of the remaining elements of the Arthur regime, especially the colonial secretary John Montagu. Montagu was thoroughly alarmed by Franklin's ideas, and even more so by those of prison-reforming private secretary Captain Alexander Maconochie RN. In response he tried to detach the governor from his supporters. For an old friend, and a nominee of steady, reliable Francis Beaufort, Maconochie proved to be a liability.[28] He went behind Franklin's back, sending his highly partisan views on Arthur's convict system to the Colonial Office in one of Franklin's dispatches.

Maconochie did not disguise his opinion that the settlers were slave masters, hardly the ideal way to build support for Franklin's regime.

His attack on the convict system reached Lord John Russell and Lord Howick, both reforming Whig ministers. Their response undermined Franklin's regime, sustained transportation and postponed the settlers' hopes for representative government. Maconachie's arrogance and stupidity did more to continue the Arthurite vision of Van Diemen's Land than the most ardent proponent of penal servitude. Just when Franklin needed a tough-minded man of business to run his office Maconachie turned out to be an innocent abroad, his head filled with noble ideas. Once the petitions started to come in from outraged settlers Franklin had no option but to dismiss him. Franklin's explanation reveals why he had decided to act slowly:

I really pity Maconachie, but he surely had been his own enemy. He ought not to have thought of sending such a paper home while serving as my private secretary. His warmest friends could not say he was acting justly towards me. It was injudicious as regards himself for I repeatedly told him on the passage out and after our arrival that Lord Glenelg and Sir Geo. Grey and Mr Stephen [the Senior Civil Servant at the Colonial Office] spoke highly of Sir George Arthur as a governor and a man.[29]

To make matters worse Franklin had to explain his actions to old friends like Beaufort.[30] Maconachie's crass act weakened Franklin, forcing him into an undesirable alliance with Montagu and the Arthur clique just when he was beginning to advance his own policy. More than two years of his government were wasted dealing with the consequences of Maconachie's madness.[31] Consequently, popular and wise gestures such as opening the proceedings of the Legislative Council to the public were forgotten. Instead, some, including John West, contemporary historian of the island, came to see him as amiable but weak and idle. Although West recognised the laudable absence of corruption, these virtues did not excuse 'delay and indecision' in government.[32] For his part Franklin considered his subjects 'inconveniently excitable' on public affairs, a characteristically kind interpretation of their behaviour.

From the start Franklin's enemies, those who feared that change and improvement would loosen their grip on the island, interpreted his trusting, generous nature as weakness. Clearly unversed in the darker side of human nature, Franklin tried to retain the friendship of those he had to dismiss, even when they had behaved in the most outrageous manner. Nor was he helped by the Colonial Office, which sent even more convicts and wrecked any hopes he had of ameliorating their lot or introducing representative government. The officials back in London did not provide him with the support that a governor had a right to expect, preferring to criticise, often in shrill tones verging on the contemptuous.

Franklin knew the convict issue was divisive. Maconachie's implication that the colonists were effectively slave owners cut deep into the infant self-esteem of the free settlers. Two public meetings were held to condemn Maconachie, and to get up a petition to Queen Victoria to end transportation. Privately Franklin shared their hopes.[33] He made the same case in his public dispatches, but supported his argument with logic. In reality the assignment system, for all its faults, was the only way in which Van Diemen's Land could deal with mass transportation, unless the imperial government were prepared to fund the convict establishment. However, the imperial government decided, against Franklin's expectations, that it would continue convict transportation, even though it had been abolished in New South Wales, and increase the rate. The island would be the last dumping ground for the criminal classes of a global empire. Assignment would be replaced by chain gangs. Franklin would have to increase the sale of public land to defray the cost. While he had opposed the assignment system as unjust and open to abuse, there was no economic alternative. The decision to adopt a chain-gang system struck him as illogical and misguided, prompting a powerful minute to the Legislative Council:

In an island where provisions are dear, where eligible overseers in sufficient numbers cannot be found, where even could they be got, their wages would be very high, while their abstraction from the ordinary industry of the country would be a colonial injury of by no means a trivial amount: much better would it be, if such a system be preferable to the one in which assignment holds the prominent place, to conduct it in some distant retirement in Great Britain.

Having let his subjects know exactly how he felt Franklin then sent the minute to the colonial secretary.[34]

The government decision was peculiarly ill-timed. The local economic boom was ending, land sales dried up, and free settlers began to leave with their flocks for Port Phillip Bay and the new city of

Melbourne that was growing around it. The Colonial Office seemed oblivious to the problem, merely advising Franklin to inform the settlers that free immigrants would supply their need for labour. Instead the property holders of the island revolted against the cost of the convict settlement in 1839, demanding that the imperial government pay two-thirds of the cost of police and gaols, of administering, housing and feeding the chain gangs and of surveying new areas of the island for the 'public works' that were meant to fill their days. Then the Colonial Office vastly increased the number of convicts: 5,633 arrived in 1842 alone. For every high-profile Tolpuddle Martyr, Canadian rebel and Irish insurgent condemned for political crimes there were many more hardened criminals, often with mental health problems. Already beyond reform or reintegration they would exist in the terrifying twilight world of Port Arthur long after transportation had ended; an enduring legacy of human degradation. The massive influx of convicts postponed the attempt to build a new society. Franklin's vision of harmonising all elements into a single polite society would not be realised in his term of office. Instead the convict establishment would expand, both to run the chain gangs and to handle the increased influx of squalid humanity. Furthermore, the settlers would have to pay the price.[35] The one gesture that would have given satisfaction to the settlers, a legislative assembly, was explicitly denied; the Colonial Office, like George Arthur, considered representative government incompatible with a penal station. New South Wales was once again ahead of Van Diemen's Land, achieving local government in 1842.[36] This distressed Franklin, who was acutely conscious of the need to keep pace with developments on the mainland.[37]

Franklin's confidence that the convicts could be 'improved' must have been shaken on a visit to the factory staffed by female convicts. The prisoners, bored by the chaplain's patronising dull sermon, turned their backs on the official party, lifted their skirts and, as one, smacked their bare backsides.[38] At least Franklin did not laugh, though the rest of his party showed less self-control.

Jane: a partner in government?

The most potent (and unwarranted) criticism of Franklin's admin-istration was that he depended upon or was directed by his wife. Indeed, as we shall see later, John Montagu insinuated undue female influence in orchestrating Franklin's removal: Lord Stanley accepted it as a fact and promptly dismissed him.[39] In reality the Franklins were closely attuned in many areas of public and private life, sharing a vision of duty propelled by religion, culture and serv-ice. Unlike the perennially pregnant Lady Arthur, Jane was well educated, opinionated and energetic.[40] Never a retiring wallflower, she soon found a role in moral and religious work, her concern for the welfare of the female convicts being rather different from that of earlier governors, who took the prettiest to bed. She was also the driving force behind plans for improved schools and higher educa-tion. Nor was she willing to stay at home, travelling far more than her husband while they were in Tasmania. Her knowledge of early voyages touching on the island, local botany and other issues reflected a genuine, intellectually sophisticated engagement with the island.[41] Yet for all her good works and civic spirit there was some-thing slightly odd about Jane. Her fear of snakes fed a colonial killing spree at a shilling a head, though it failed to eradicate either the problem or her complex.[42]

Franklin recognised the unusual qualities of his consort, and often sought her advice on aspects of policy. Her travels as a research assistant and unofficial emissary took her to places Franklin never reached. In early 1839 she toured the south and west coasts of the island, accompanied by scientists Ronald Gunn and John Gould. This expedition, like her visit to Port Phillip and the surrounding area, was largely a fact-finding mission. Franklin expected her to bring back 'whatever information or suggestions may present themselves, and strike her as likely to be useful in this colony'.[43] In 1842 Jane went to the wild frontier in New Zealand. Only a man of Franklin's conviction would have allowed her to make such a voyage, trusting that his naval friends would ensure she returned safely.

Running the colony: land sales and settlement policy

The role of the colonies in the early nineteenth-century world view of British statesmen was clear. They should satisfy the demands of the metropole, especially the pursuit of wealth and power. Consequently the main drivers of policy were domestic economic and social conditions. London remained insulated from the realities of colonial conditions by vast distances and considerable time. To sustain the penal settlement in Australia, Crown land was sold, which brought in revenue, encouraged settlement and improved economic returns. Until the late 1820s convict accommodation dominated the view from London. The burgeoning wool export of New South Wales saw the policy modified: land would be sold at prices that would encourage the establishment of a pastoral society closely modelled on that of Britain. In 1831 the reforming and desperately hard-up Whig government added a new aim. They would relieve wage pressure on the labouring poor by providing a safety valve through assisted emigration. Land sales would fund the passage of free labourers to the Antipodes. This approach, which in part reflected the influence of the popular theorist Edward Gibbon Wakefield on colonial policy, made sense in fast-expanding New South Wales. However, Van Diemen's Land was far smaller, and obtained most of its labour from assigned or emancipated convicts. In reality the economy of the island was dominated by convict labour and the large expenditure of the convict establishment on locally produced foodstuffs. Furthermore, most of the good land had already been sold or given away, so there was neither the need nor the opportunity to fund significant free immigration. Little wonder the colonists wanted a representative legislature: they wanted to take control of the Crown lands, and adopt policies that would suit their needs, not the theories or the needs of a doctrinaire British administration.[44] George Arthur was equally certain that the new policy was wrong, and actively subverted it as far as he dared with large grants of free land. He realised assisted emigrants would compete with the system of assigned convict labour that kept the colony solvent.[45] Arthur left little money in the colonial Treasury to fund immigration, while the attraction of the island began to falter as large new areas on the mainland were opened up.

The agricultural model which London favoured, because it could sustain a new Britain down under, failed in the face of poor-quality badly irrigated land and the rapid rise of the wool economy in New South Wales. While wool easily carried the cost of shipment to Britain, there was no export market for agricultural produce, and labour costs were high.[46] Wool came to dominate London's view of Australia, and New South Wales became the model for colonial policy. It was granted an end to convict transportation and allowed representative government, because these measures would encourage mass immigration. The knock-on effect quadrupled transportation to Van Diemen's Land, effectively ending voluntary immigration until the same reforms reached Hobart. Subsequent changes in convict discipline merely reinforced the impact of a disastrous series of decisions for Van Diemen's Land. Franklin's government was doomed by the reluctance of London to recognise the very different demands of the two Australian colonies.

The opening of the Port Phillip region of Victoria, a reluctant concession by London to settler movement, ended the economic boom in Van Diemen's Land. The island could not compete with the open spaces available just across the Bass Strait. This process was hastened by the decision to raise the price of Crown land from five shillings an acre to twelve in mid-1838. This exposed the real weakness of the island economy: a paucity of capital. Franklin protested that the increase would end land sales, cutting revenue vital to the colonial Treasury.[47] The local effects of the global economic downturn of the early 1840s left Van Diemen's Land with an adverse balance of trade and too much capital locked up by the speculative, overpriced land purchases of the mid-1830s. In late 1841 the Immigration Committee in London misread the signs and persuaded Franklin to commit £60,000 of scarce funds to assist immigration, only to find that there was no shortage of labour. Many of the 2,448 free immigrants who arrived in 1842 found themselves unemployed on arrival. Consequently immigration remained insignificant until the end of the decade.[48]

To add to Franklin's woes the Colonial Office unilaterally raised the price of land from twelve shillings an acre to one pound. As average income per acre never exceeded nine shillings, he protested, and cut the amount of land on offer, hoping to hold up prices without draining away too much capital in speculation. Warning the colonial secretary that this measure 'will I fear soon render apparent a decided inadequacy of the Revenue to the Exchequer and a complete exhaustion of the Treasury', was hardly going to make him any friends in Whitehall.[49] Consequently, Conservative colonial secretary Lord Stanley decided to replace Franklin with a more biddable client. The figures support Franklin's analysis. With no more than 1,500 acres sold in any year between 1844 and 1850, land revenue collapsed.[50] Franklin had realised something that his masters back in London only grudgingly accepted after his death: 'Colonial conditions were bound to triumph over imperial policy, however enlightened.'[51]

Those who criticise Franklin's role in his final polar mission find themselves obliged to extend this negative treatment to his administration of Tasmania, as if the two scenarios were identical. In reality convicts and local government were not the only issues that emerged during Franklin's government.

6

Science, Culture and Civilisation

ALTHOUGH HOBART was a very long way from the centre of the magnetic crusade Franklin remained a major player. Rather than treating his time in Tasmania as a failure, a negative experience that sent him back to exploration, it should be seen as a positive achievement, a further step in his development as a magnetic scientist and the major reason why he was given the command of such an important expedition.

Franklin set off for Hobart deeply committed to the development of local science and the cultivation of useful knowledge. Franklin's government coincided with a new phase of imperial science, directed from the metropolis by his friends John Herschel, Francis Beaufort, Edward Sabine and Roderick Murchison. In his absence they pushed magnetic science to the top of the agenda, reviving the dormant polar mission to serve magnetic ends. Their British Association for the Advancement of Science persuaded Lord Melbourne's government to back an Antarctic magnetic mission commanded by James Clark Ross. Not that Franklin was ignored. The decision to establish the only naval manned station in the global network of magnetic observatories in Hobart reflected his presence, as did the instructions given to hydrographic vessels, explorers and scientists heading south. Franklin's happiest hours in Tasmania were spent exploring the island or discussing scientific subjects with high-profile guests.

Education and culture

Franklin's vision of government went beyond George Arthur's self-serving obsession with minutiae, the day-to-day penny pinching that kept the books balanced and the Colonial Office happy. He saw an opportunity for long-term improvement, for a cultural and religious renaissance that would transform the colony. The Colonial Office generally left him to his own devices, and while it did not criticise him for laying the odd foundation stone for a new church it was anxious that colonial funds should not be diverted into such trivia. In late 1838 Franklin began to canvass for an improved educational establishment, designed by his friend Thomas Arnold. A non-denominational colonial version of Rugby would form the pinnacle of the Tasmanian system, and develop into a university. Despite James Stephen's petty carping the Treasury agreed to build the school. When Franklin needed a headmaster for his new Christ's College, Arnold offered the post to one of his brightest pupils, John Philip Gell:

It is a noble field, and in Franklin himself you would have a fellow-labourer and a Governor with and under whom it would do one's heart good to work. He wants a Christian, a gentleman, and a scholar . . . to become the father of the education of a whole quarter of the globe, and to assist, under God's blessing . . . in laying the foundations of all good and noble principles, not only in individual children, but in an infant nation, which must hereafter influence the world largely for good or for evil.[1]

Having persuaded Gell to take the post (Gell would later marry Franklin's daughter Eleanor), Arnold secured the support of the Colonial Office.[2]

Jane took Christ's College as her pet project, but the Arthur faction did everything they could to oppose it. Stephen's argument that the colony would not support a college to educate the sons of gentlemen proved prophetic. The institution did not outlive the Franklin regime, too costly and too academic for local tastes, while those who could afford education sent their sons home to Britain. Franklin's evangelical faith was further tested by bickering religious communities demanding denominational schools. Even the Church of England rejected his vision. Despite such setbacks Franklin oversaw the critical shift from a colony where the children were less well educated than their parents to one where the need for his college would emerge in the rising generation. His vision was noble, and if his design ran ahead of local and imperial opinion it was ultimately borne out.

Cape Town

Not that anyone could fault Franklin for lack of ambition when it came to the promotion of his favourite public utility. His baggage was stuffed with scientific instruments, including two of Sabine's magnetic needles.[3] The voyage south was broken by a lengthy stop at Cape Town, where his friend John Herschel provided a model of imperial science at the periphery. Having established an observatory to map the southern stars, Herschel did far more than chart the skies. During his four-year residence he travelled, conducted large-scale botanical experiments, dissected specimens, collected meteorological and tidal data and attempted to harness the disparate efforts of local enthusiasts into an effective scientific society with regular publication.[4] He proved that a single savant with a broad curiosity about the natural world could stimulate the wider community into action. Although the ideas and ambitions that drove Herschel were the common currency of early nineteenth-century British scientists, Franklin was mightily impressed by his scientific empire.

Alongside his own research Herschel contributed to the development of practical astronomy, the sort that sailors used to navigate. As he sailed south to the Cape in 1834 he calculated longitude by the lunar distance method, used the results to rate his chronometers and sent his observations to the director of the *Nautical Almanac*, the key practical output of the Royal Observatory at Greenwich. He knew the serious navigators, and their leader, Francis Beaufort. At the Cape he found more scientific naval officers: Robert Wauchope, inventor of the time ball, and James Bance, port captain and tidologist. Herschel processed Bance's data and sent it to William Whewell of the BAAS. In December 1835 Lord Auckland stopped at the Cape, en route to take up the government of India. He took away copies of Herschel's 'Meteorological Instructions' to give 'a fillip to that and such matters in India. He appears to take an interest in promoting scientific objects – seems fond especially of botany & enquired much about Cape Plants.'[5] Lack of time and instruments prevented Herschel following Gauss's new magnetic system, but that did not stop him endorsing the Magnetic Union and recommending that a new observatory at Bombay be fitted to conduct observations on the Gauss system: 'Pray let this be mentioned to Gauss that he may see that I am not unmindful of him.'[6] Herschel's vision included other outposts of the southern Empire such as Mauritius which required practical men to conduct observations in all the key sciences, but especially terrestrial magnetism.[7] In September 1836 Herschel was trying to get the local Literary and Philosophical Society to publish regularly.[8] Franklin arrived two months later and such concerns may have inspired him to try a similar scheme in Hobart: monthly meetings to hear papers on scientific subjects with the intention of publishing for local and London audiences.[9]

The Franklins' visit lasted a fortnight, from 14 to 29 November 1836. Jane insisted on seeing everything, climbing Table Mountain despite Franklin's reservations, travelling into the interior and collecting information on the resources and potential of the Cape. She met all the travellers, savants and visiting naval officers. Herschel's house, and more especially his telescope, were on her list of things to see. On 20 November the Franklins dined at Herschel's home and took turns looking through his enormous telescope at the Magellanic Clouds of the solar system. Even so, Lady Herschel noted, 'they can only spare us one day out of the fortnight which they intended to spend here'.[10] Jane had more important things to do than pass the time in idle gossip: she visited the museum of the South African Literary and Philosophical Institution, of which Herschel was the president, along with the local botanical garden, and bought as many Cape books as she could find.[11] Her efforts would bear fruit in Tasmania. As the Roaring Forties drove his ship eastward, Franklin pondered what he had seen at the Cape, and dipped into Jane's books. His conclusions were clear.

A learned society for the Antipodes

Franklin finally had an opportunity to write to Herschel nine months after they met. (Few ships ever sailed westward from Hobart.) His letter was full of scientific news, enquiries about friends at the Cape and local meteorological and tidal data.[12] A year later he had more to report:

We are endeavouring here to get up a small scientific society composed at first of only 6 or 8 members, as many individuals I believe as we can muster, who take any interest in anything but what relates to party politics, wool or oil; they are to meet at Govt. House quietly every fortnight, and in the course of a short time we may be able to bring forward something in the shape of a journal of original matter. Were you less eminent than you are, or I a less utterly insignificant votary of science, I might with more modesty prefer to you a request that if in any leisure moments (I am aware they must be rare indeed) you would cast a spare thought upon us poor folks at the Antipodes. We should be raised in our own estimation & that of the world by your so doing. A line or two occasionally received from Herschel would in particular stamp a character on our meetings which would go far to render them respectable in the eyes of the Community and give an impulse to our feeble researches into the resources of our interesting & little known quarter of the Globe.

I do not expect any great things from our little Philosophical Society, it lacks a head, & is composed of people who have sufficient work on their hands of other kinds, to be incapacitated from giving anything like an individual attention to scientific enquiries. Nevertheless, if it should tend to excite an interest & disseminate anything like a taste for pursuits which have no tendency to excite the inflammatory propensities of our oddly constituted community it will have a moral advantage which is not only not to be despised but of which we are greatly in want.

Stripped of Franklin's innate modesty this is a ringing endorsement of Herschel's scientific vision.[13] Herschel replied the very day the letter arrived, passing on the latest news of Ross's expedition and the local magnetic observatory.[14] Far from accepting Franklin at his own assessment Herschel considered him a critical member of the Humboldtian scientific project. Excited by the new magnetic enterprise in the southern hemisphere Herschel had no doubt that Franklin was a key player.

In 1838 Franklin was ready. 'The main objects of the Tasmanian Society were to encourage investigation into the plant and animal life of Tasmania; and into the mineralogical character and fossil content of its rocks, and to obtain as far as possible, faithful and trustworthy records of the interesting forms and laws under which mineral, plant and vegetable existence exhibit themselves in Tasmania.'[15] This local fact-collecting approach was the only option for a tiny body of amateur savants at the outermost reaches of the known world. The choice of name was critical, Tasmania honoured the navigator who located the island, it represented Franklin's vision of the future: Van Diemen's Land, named for a distant administrator, would always be George Arthur's convict hell.

There had been two earlier short-lived 'scientific' societies' in Hobart, and Arthur had founded a botanical garden in 1827 using convict labour. The garden was primarily a way station to acclimatise English varieties to local conditions under the supervision of an award-winning English gardener. Arthur spent £300 a year on the garden; Franklin raised that to £800. Ever the practical scientist, Franklin used the colonial garden, originally intended for his personal use, to supply visiting expeditions with fresh vegetables. At the same time he remained a protégé of Banks, calling on Herschel, Murchison and other scientific friends to secure a colonial botanist.[16] Failing that, Ronald Gunn's Hobart Town Horticultural Society spread economically useful plants and improved cultivars, with at least one prize funded by Lady Franklin. Elsewhere Franklin provided the Mechanics' Institute with a small grant and space in the Customs House for their museum and meetings. Popular science lectures attracted audiences of over two hundred members.

Because Franklin was a member of many imperial scientific bodies he acted as a clearing house for queries on all manner of local issues, a point of contact for travelling savants and a one-man ambassador for local science. He expected the Tasmanian Society to gather information on 'the Natural History, Agriculture, Statistics etc., of this country from local gentlemen'.[17] It met fortnightly at Government House, although Franklin was not infrequently sound asleep, but the papers were published, encouraging further efforts. One lecturer, young Joseph Hooker, son of his friend, the director of Kew Gardens Sir William, noted the audience comprised Franklin, Lady Jane, Gunn, his private secretary, Captain Ross and the Chaplain of the *Erebus*.[18] While largely devoted to data gathering and husbandry, the society had access to cutting-edge magnetic science. The establishment of the Rossbank magnetic observatory put Tasmania on the scientific map. Sanctioned by the imperial government and funded by the Admiralty this was one project which the Colonial Office could neither interfere in nor criticise.

To explain what was done at Rossbank, Franklin directed his

nephew Lieutenant Kay to write on magnetic science for the *Tasmanian Journal of Science*.[19] He recruited John Richardson to report on a collection of fish taken at Port Arthur, while an interview with Dumont d'Urville, captain of the French exploring expedition in the Southern Ocean, also appeared. The Frenchman claimed to have located the magnetic South Pole, a claim Ross would dispute. D'Urville thanked Franklin and the colonial authorities for their support, which 'materially added to the success of the mission . . . in short a real and sincere sympathy in the work which he has earnestly endeavoured to accomplish in the promotion of science and navigation'.[20] By 1841 the society boasted thirty-one residing members, and thirty-eight corresponding members, including James Clark Ross, Francis Crozier and Joseph Hooker, radical cleric Bishop Colenso and Captain Berard of the French navy. Well aware that colonial science had limits, Franklin deliberately restricted the local effort to data collection. He left the great work of theoretical analysis to the metropole, but the society and the sciences were performing an important service on moral and religious grounds 'by opening the minds of the colonists to interests above the mundane'.[21]

Although it was easy to scoff and sneer at this tiny outpost of Humboldtian enterprise in the Southern Ocean, surrounded by ignorance and the unknown, there were always enough enlightened minds to keep the flame alight. Franklin took great pride in the *Journal*, persuading John Murray to market it in London.[22] The first volume appeared in 1841 and Franklin included it in a dispatch to the colonial secretary, explaining that it had been printed by the Official Printer (James Barnard, a founder member of the society and an authority on statistics) because he was the only printer who possessed the necessary type.[23] When a commercial Hobart printer complained, the Colonial Office criticised Franklin for failing to act on free-trade principles, ignoring his irresistible rationale. The contents of the *Journal* passed without comment – little wonder George Arthur stuck to penny pinching.

By early 1842 a third volume was at the press. Franklin noted that 'the papers which most engage the attention of the colonists are those of Captain Cotton on Irrigation which all the land holders and Flock masters begin to feel is almost the one thing needful to ensure steady crops and good feeding in this country'.[24] Ronald Campbell Gunn, initially in the Convict Department and then Franklin's private secretary, developed a major reputation as a botanist. He edited the *Journal*, collected plants for Kew Gardens and cultivated seeds brought in by Ross's expedition. Although Tasmanian concern with science was essentially parochial, the *Journal* was a serious contribution to the field. It astonished the intellectual community in Sydney, emphasising the fact that Hobart had secured cultural primacy among the imperial outposts of the Southern Ocean.

Franklin was anxious to establish a museum, another key instrument of nineteenth-century enlightened civilisation, a building to inform and educate. With no hope of Colonial Office support Lady Franklin purchased the 400-acre Ancanthe (Vale of Flowers) estate in the Kangaroo valley. Franklin laid the foundations on 12 March 1842. The museum was 'built on the classical model' and dedicated to science, 'the productions of nature in this country, and a retreat for her ministers and interpreters' with a library of Tasmanian-published works, and others relating to Tasmania.[25] Among the exhibits were Franklin's pistols, symbolising his rejection of warlike pursuits for a career in science and government.[26] Ancanthe was a temple to Franklin's vision of science, a museum of the modern world for the improvement of colonial ideas. For one historian of Hobart the implication of the building was simple: it reflected the society of ancient Athens, 'where men educated in the English classics tradition formed a tight, elite community served by slaves and visited by traders; with leisure and isolation and time to contemplate the things of quality'.[27] The Franklins certainly hoped that the building and its contents would remain in place until a university (for the elite) could be established. Instead it was soon empty and abandoned, 'a monument to enthusiasm and a victim of colonial philistinism'.[28]

Scientific host

Instead Franklin himself proved to be the key contribution to the development of Tasmanian science. His reputation attracted scientists to the island, his hospitality encouraged them to stay, often far longer than they had planned, to the inestimable benefit of the colony and science. Among the first was John Gould, the man who opened Darwin's eyes to the evolutionary implications of his Galapagos finch collection.[29] A pioneer publisher of large-scale illustrated works on ornithology, Gould arrived in late 1838 bearing letters of introduction from friends and colleagues including Lord Glenelg, the Duke of Sussex (president of the Royal Society) and Captain John Washington RN, secretary of the RGS. Barrow had directed captains of ships on the Australian coast to further Gould's aims by giving him free passage.[30] Recognising Gould's value to the colony, Franklin invited the family to live at Government House, children, stuffed birds and all. Gould collected in the Government House garden, the Hobart botanical gardens, on Jane's estate and further afield, where a letter from the governor opened many doors. In return Gould provided a paper for Franklin's journal and named his son for his benefactor. This was only fitting since the boy had entered the world under Franklin's roof. Gould quickly reduced the local avian population to order, killing and skinning his specimens before reproducing them as art. The first instalment of the massive *Birds of Australia* (8 vols, 1840–8) became, if Joseph Hooker is to be believed, a local status symbol. Three hundred no-doubt largely unopened copies were sold in Hobart, where pianos that few could play were also popular.[31]

Soon after the family returned to Britain, Mrs Gould died. Franklin sent heartfelt condolences and advocated the comforts of his religion, which required 'a well grounded faith in the never failing goodness of God'.[32] It was a hard lesson for a man who had lost his wife, the mother of his children and the artist of his publications. But Gould recognised Franklin's humanity and piety and took the advice. Gould was not alone: the Franklins played a critical role in promoting Tasmanian art as part of their scientific vision. There were many talented amateurs in the colony, and art was a key tool for recording and transmitting scientific achievements – be it as botanical illustrations or heroic portraits of learned men, warriors for knowledge.[33]

While the locals were quick to see the merit of Gould's work, and some could be inspired by the ideals and ambitions of Enlighten-

ment science, it required a different type of savant to make fundamental discoveries in Tasmania. None would do more for the island
than Count Paul Strzelecki, travelling Polish geologist and fellow
Humboldtian (predictably Strzelecki named a mountain for the
great man).[34] He arrived intent on a scientific survey of Tasmania and
armed with a recommendation from Governor George Gipps of
New South Wales. Invariably short of money the count lived a rather
tortuous hand-to-mouth existence as he toured Australia. Having
begged a barometer, he secured Franklin's open-ended support and
Jane's undying admiration.[35] Accompanying Franklin on visits to
Port Arthur and inland towns Strzelecki recognised the value of irrigation to the colony. With Franklin's support he began a survey in
the Bass Strait region, travelling on colonial vessels. No one who visited Franklin's kingdom so amply represented the Humboldtian
nexus of knowledge, science and progress. The result of Franklin's
enlightened, open-handed patronage was a classic of geographical
and geological literature, Strzelecki's *Physical Description of New
South Wales and Van Diemen's Land*, which remained in print for
the next forty years. Having signed the dedication of Ancanthe,
Strzelecki also produced the first geological map of the island, and
linked the maps with the coastal charts. Critically he located key
mineral resources, especially coal, which was plentiful in Recherche
Bay.[36] The Count published four articles in the *Tasmanian Journal*.
Sharing Franklin's admiration for the elegant learned Pole, Jane
ordered a fine portrait for the Ancanthe Museum.[37] Strzelecki
returned to London armed with letters of introduction from
Franklin to John Murray and geological chieftain Roderick
Murchison. Murchison followed Franklin's advice, persuading the
British government to support the publication of Strzelecki's results
and ensuring he received the Royal Geographical Society Copley
Gold Medal in 1846.[38]

When Franklin left Hobart, the Tasmanian Society regretted the
departure of their founder, a 'benefactor of unsparing liberality . . .
whose scientific experience has given effect to our feeble exertions,
and invested them with an importance which they could not otherwise have obtained'. This was no mere flattery. In response Franklin
praised the work of the society which had elevated the colony 'in the

estimation of the European Community' and promised to secure further support for their work.[39] His successors took a far narrower view of colonial science, but they were not scientists, their mission being to administer the colony, not act on its behalf.

Franklin raised the intellectual and cultural horizons of his subjects without distracting them from the critical role of data gathering to serve the imperial project. He did so for moral as well as scientific purposes, while his *Journal* raised the international profile of the island. Little wonder the intelligent element of the community loved him. In the years that followed, his society was reformed on a more parochial level, 'to store up and record useful information', once more under the convict-stained name of Van Diemen's Land. A later lieutenant-governor, Sir William Denison, personally examined the susceptibility of local timbers to the dread ship-boring worm *Teredo navalis* before driving the piles to form Franklin Wharf in Hobart harbour.[40] Sir John would have appreciated the compliment.

Adrift on the Southern Ocean

Van Diemen's Land depended on sea communications for immigrants, the steady inflow of economically attractive convicts and the funds that sustained them, the export of wheat and wool, the whaling trade, and the connection with the rest of the world. In 1837 over three hundred ships used the harbours of Van Diemen's Land, carrying a wealth of imports and exports and delivering immigrants, more often in chains than free. This level of shipping required a range of services from improved wharfage and repair facilities to navigational marks, charts and lights. These were issues that Franklin was well equipped to address.

For most lieutenant-governors, landsmen, soldiers and administrators facing the endless demands of government and convict administration, land settlement and the maintenance of order, the sea was little more than a scenic backdrop. Franklin took a very different view, trying to shift the island's focus to the ocean. He turned orphan apprentices into seamen to sustain the growing maritime trade of the island.[41] Some convict boys even joined the crew of HMS *Favourite*, the ship on which Jane would sail to New Zealand in 1842.[42]

While the primary purpose of convict settlements at Macquarie harbour and later Port Arthur had been to segregate and discipline recidivists, both locations were chosen to exploit virgin forests of prime timber. Convict labour was used not only to cut and transport the trees, many of which were exported to the mainland, but also in a large-scale shipbuilding industry that produced a substantial output of ships of up to three hundred tons. An industrial slipway and a shipwright's cottage still feature on the Port Arthur tourist trail. In a testament to the quality of local materials and convict labour one Port Arthur ship, the whaler *Lady Franklin*, completed twenty-five voyages between 1858 and 1883. Yet even as Franklin sailed from Hobart for the final time the writing was on the wall for wooden shipbuilding when the British-built iron steam vessel *Thames* arrived to work on the Derwent.[43] Unable to keep pace with the latest technology, colonial shipbuilding collapsed, and with it the market for high-grade timber.

To develop the colony's maritime character Franklin inaugurated a regatta at Hobart on 1 December 1838, the anniversary of Tasman's arrival. Jane stood sponsor and large crowds turned out to see a series of boats race under sail and oar on the Derwent estuary.[44] Franklin considered that the crowds enjoyed themselves a little too much for his sober taste and withdrew government support, but the regatta survived.

Defence

The first task for any colonial administration was to ensure external security. By the time Franklin reached the Antipodes any lingering French hopes of establishing a naval base and penal colony in Australia had passed: British Western Australia and two abortive northern settlements had closed off the options.[45] However, the French were steadily taking control of Tahiti and considering New Zealand.[46] There were always French warships in the region, and a succession of crises made war seem likely.

The prospect of war began to trouble the Colonial Office in the mid-1830s, and it sent two Royal Engineers officers to design forts in Australia, one to New South Wales, the other to Van Diemen's

Land. At the same time the senior naval officer in the region, Captain Charles Bethune of HMS *Conway*,[47] reported that the defences of Hobart were inadequate, criticism the Admiralty passed to the Board of Ordnance. The poverty of local defence was glaringly exposed by the unseen, unexpected arrival of two American warships in Sydney harbour. One December evening in 1839 Captain Charles Wilkes anchored his two ships close off the town and was not spotted until the following morning.[48] While he came in peace, leading an exploring expedition, he had accurate charts of the harbour and could easily have destroyed the shipping and the town.[49] The threat of war with France in 1840, and then with the United States in 1841–2 – given a suitably hysterical twist by the length of time it took for news to reach the Antipodes, the presence of warships of both nations in the region and the absence of any British force – prompted Franklin and Governor Gipps in New South Wales to assign colonial funds to defence projects, despite Colonial Office policy. Recognising the need to fortify Hobart harbour Franklin rebuilt Mulgrave Battery, now Battery Point.[50] Later he began building six gunboats, but when the Colonial Office rebuked him for unauthorised spending, the only complete vessel was sold to the Bishop of Hobart, who needed to visit his flock.[51] In 1842 the new Prince of Wales Battery, designed by the resident Royal Engineer, saluted Franklin's belated return from an overland journey with heavy 32-pounder cannon.[52] He advocated acquiring an armed steamer to keep up contact with Port Arthur and support local defences, but this proved to be a vision too far. James Ross shared his concern at the relatively defenceless state of the southern colonies and advocated the establishment of a permanent Australian station.[53] The new station would be established in 1859, once Sydney had a dry dock to service the Royal Navy's cruisers.[54]

Despite the threat of war it was the ever-present danger of convict insurrection that sustained the local garrison, calculated against the number of convicts on the island. In 1840 Franklin had 767 officers and men: 330 were in Hobart, 76 in Launceston and 121 guarded Port Arthur; the rest, spread across the island in platoons, guarded local centres. When transportation to Van Diemen's Land was increased, he requested more troops, and when the request was ignored, simply stripped out the guard detachments from passing convict ships. The Horse Guards and the Colonial Office criticised him, but doubled the number of regiments in the garrison and increased their effective strength from 800 men to 1,000. This action took years to implement, but by 1846 there were 2,009 soldiers on the island.[55] However, its safety ultimately depended on ships, not troops and batteries.

Naval visits

While the possibility of war made the visit of British warships welcome, Franklin, who delighted in the presence of like-minded officers and the sight of a well-manned ship of war, extended the same courtesies to French warships. His support for fellow seamen ranged from high culture and advanced science to more prosaic but invaluable gifts: As Hooker observed, 'The Governor's House was open to us, and he gave all the ship's company vegetables from his garden every day, with fruit for the officers.'[56] He had done the same for the scurvy-ridden men of d'Urville's expedition. For Franklin scurvy was an old enemy, one that he could fight but could not conquer. So broad were Franklin's interests and human sympathies that everyone who passed was pressed for information, and sent away with suitable recompense for their trouble. A humble lieutenant working for the South Australian Company went home with a letter to John Barrow Jr, requesting that he be introduced to his father, 'who I dare say may wish to ask him some questions respecting that newly settled country'.[57]

Navigation, charts and safety at sea

Having first seen Tasmania thirty-five years earlier, from the deck of Flinders's *Investigator*, Franklin considered the improvement of local navigation a personal legacy. He would turn the colony towards the ocean, making it easier and safer to approach. Perhaps it was this connection that made him look on his new post as 'a privilege' and 'a source of the highest and purest enjoyment'. To prepare for his labours he brought a significant library of Australian voyages, texts and charts that would be a major resource for fellow survey-ors.[58] Although Franklin was an accomplished hydrographer, he would have little time for such pleasant work. At his request the Admiralty sent out Lieutenant Thomas Burnett as the colonial sur-veying officer:

to resurvey the channels leading to the principal ports of the Island. The numer-ous wrecks that have recently occurred in & near these channels seem to render a fresh survey necessary, though I am inclined to attribute much of these evils to negligence and indifference on the part of the masters. The sailing directions and the charts do not appear to be sufficiently precise & ample for the increas-ing trade of the Island – which has become very considerable.[59]

New charts and lighthouses would transform maritime safety. Sadly such work was not without risk. Burnett drowned on 21 May 1837 after his boat capsized while surveying Actaeon reef in the D'Entrecasteaux Channel. He had been in the colony little more than four months. Colonial coast and harbour charting would have to wait, forcing Franklin to concentrate on extending the map inland.[60] He knew that ships were coming to survey the demanding Bass Strait passage and lost little time in completing Burnett's work. The D'Entrecasteaux Channel chart was sent home in April 1838.[61] Franklin exploited the arrival of HMS *Pelorus* to push forward his survey, loaning *Pelorus*'s officers the colonial vessel *Tamar* to settle the contested location of the south-west tip of the Island. Dissatisfied with the work and the attitude of Captain King, the port officer and superintendent of transports at Hobart, Franklin replaced him with Captain William Moriarty RN, a ranking com-mander of considerable experience who was then working as an assistant police magistrate. Moriarty proved an excellent choice, and under Franklin's direction he established the lighthouse network and developed the charts alongside his duties concerning the convict ships.[62] Lieutenant Matthew Friend FRS, port officer at Launceston, was another talented naval scientist.[63]

The *Beagle* and the Bass Strait

The close relationship between Franklin and the Hydrographer Francis Beaufort, friends, navigators and fellow naval scientists made it inevitable that when Beaufort dispatched HMS *Beagle*, this time *sans* Darwin, back to Australian waters, Captain John Wickham was advised to 'wait on Sir John Franklin; it is probable that he will detach Lieutenant Burnett to co-operate with you in the survey of the Bass Strait, and it is certain that the Governor will do everything in his power to assist your labours'.[64] Franklin did all he could, but Burnett had drowned two weeks before Beaufort wrote his instructions.

Recent shipping losses in the strait which separated the island from the mainland had prompted this diversion of surveying effort, otherwise largely deployed on the north and west coasts of Australia. Not only were the locations of known hazards uncertain, but there was also every possibility that unknown dangers lurked amid the constellation of islands off Tasmania's north coast. Wickham should leave harbour surveys to the colonial surveyor, if Franklin could complete them in reasonable time.[65] Wickham had no doubt Franklin would live up to Beaufort's promise. Arriving in a storm, Wickham was thankful for the new lighthouse Franklin had erected on Bruny Island, part of the chain of beacons planned to illuminate both the treacherous storm-blasted Bass Strait and the approaches to Hobart.[66] Lights were placed at the southern end of the D'Entrecasteaux Channel and the mouth of the River Tamar. Franklin asked the governor of New South Wales to establish more lights in the main strait, where half a dozen ships had been lost in recent years. The Legislative Council agreed to fund the Tasmanian lighthouses, leaving Franklin to settle their location.[67]

In late February 1842 another Captain, John Lort Stokes, took HMS *Beagle* into Hobart, ready to continue the Bass Strait survey. Delighted to escape the humdrum hostile world of colonial government, Franklin enjoyed Stokes's report of a passage on the track of the *Investigator* and shared Strzelecki's maps with him. Among Stokes's officers was Lieutenant Graham Gore, a talented artist with experience of war and ice.[68] Franklin lent Stokes the 70-ton cutter *Vansittart*, complete with a ticket-of-leave convict crew, only to be rebuked by the Colonial Office, who considered her bound to the convict service for which she had been built. Fortunately the results amply repaid Franklin's 'invaluable assistance', effectively doubling the area of Stokes's survey.[69] The survey identified the best location for new lighthouses, enabling Franklin to tame the fearsome Bass Strait.[70] This overriding concern for maritime safety ensured that his last public act on Tasmanian soil was to lay the foundation stone of a lighthouse on Swan Island, with the island's bishop on hand to give it his blessing: Franklin concluded the event with a beautiful extempore prayer.[71] However, Franklin's success would be the death of Hobart. The town had been the first port of call for all shipping heading to Australia, but it would be by-passed when the Bass Strait could be safely used to sail direct to Sydney. Other traffic was diverted to Melbourne. When ships from Britain stopped calling at Hobart, the long slow decline of Tasmania began. Later the Torres Strait route, opened by Blackwood and Owen Stanley, the Suez Canal and the compound engine shifted the focus of Australian shipping from south to north.

Even at the far end of the world Franklin remained committed to his profession. News of naval events, visits from warships, British and foreign, along with opportunities to reflect on aspects of his Arctic and magnetic careers provided vital relief from the routines of public administration, long hours of desk work and constant exposure to the vulgarity and selfishness of his charges. News of the capture of the fortress at Acre and the defeat of Egypt in the brief Syrian campaign of 1840, 'one of the most brilliant deeds of modern times', reminded Franklin that the Royal Navy was still the finest fighting force on earth, and the reason Britain ruled Van Diemen's Land.[72]

Any Royal Navy warship calling at Hobart was certain of a warm welcome, and the hospitality of Government House, where many officers quickly became good friends. In return their officers were happy to assist the Governor. In 1842 HMS *Favourite* took Jane to the wild frontier of New Zealand, Franklin merely asking Owen Stanley, the senior officer in the area, to ensure she returned safe and well.[73] Franklin was only disappointed that he could not join her, the opportunity to see 'the management of a ship of war under sail' being always 'a great treat'.[74] It is highly significant that he did not go – the call of duty overrode both his curiosity and any wish for self-gratification.

Scientific officers, from any navy, were Franklin's favourite guests. Hydrographers, astronomers, magnetic savants, in fact anyone with a curiosity about the world and how it worked, provided a relief from the banal business of balancing off convict management and settler ambition. This was starkly revealed at the turn of 1841, when two warships arrived. While the fifty-gun frigate HMS *Vindictive* was the most powerful warship to call at Hobart in Franklin's time, her stay was not a happy occasion. As Jane observed, Captain John Toup Nicolas was not their type. A bluff, ignorant man spoiling for a fight and hoping to find some desperate glory in these far-off seas, he insisted on holding a succession of gunnery exercises, firing broadsides of shot and shell across the Derwent despite the presence of a French warship. While Nicolas had a high opinion of himself, it was not one that found much support elsewhere in the navy. Both Franklin and Jane found their other naval guest, Captain Berard of the twenty-gun French corvette *Le Rhin*, more to their taste. A scientific and cultured man, a member of the Institut Français and a friend of the great scientist Arago, Berard dined with the Franklins, became a corresponding member of the Tasmanian Society and presented Jane with a large, rare shell from Madagascar. Such hospitality earned the Franklins a high reputation throughout the French navy.[75] Hearing an Anglo-French crisis was brewing in Tahiti, Nicolas rushed north seeking orders, leaving the Derwent strangely silent.[76] This was the closest Franklin came to war – a lot of sound and fury, but nothing very serious.

Antarctic voyagers

The highlight of Franklin's administration would be the arrival at Hobart of a succession of Antarctic voyagers, men of science and learning. The first, the Frenchman Cyrille Laplace in the *Artémise*, arrived at Hobart in January 1839. Despite the fine appearance of the town his sailors quickly located the seedier side of life, and got involved in a brawl. Laplace reported home on the prisons, which struck him as too indulgent, and secured fresh supplies for his scurvy-ridden crew. He also began the tradition of providing a farewell on board his ship.[77] In view of the strained relations then existing between Britain and France, and the flashpoint at Tahiti, Jane ensured her guest was in no doubt that Sir John's civility and scientific concerns did not override political and military questions.[78]

A second French expedition, that of Dumont d'Urville, was compelled by scurvy to refit at Hobart in 1839–40. D'Urville had pre-empted the Ross mission, and shared the Humboldtian impulse to locate the magnetic South Pole. He too would adorn one of his discoveries with the name of the great scientist. As one would expect, Franklin proved a gracious host to his guest, a Fellow of the Institut Français and a capable linguist. He invited the officers to Government House, visited the ships, helped them take magnetic readings on Mount Wellington, much as the location must have grated, listened intently to accounts of their Antarctic voyage and inspected their observatory and their instruments with an expert eye. D'Urville had been anxious to meet Franklin, he was charmed by Lady Jane, became a member of the Tasmanian Society and provided exhibits for the museum. At the most practical level Franklin supplied the scorbutic Frenchmen with garden produce.[79] Franklin earned the admiration of his French guests. D'Urville was especially struck by the powerful synthesis between the colony and the home base, which 'produces undeniable advantages for her trade and seapower'.[80] He also confided in Franklin as a fellow scientist and explorer.[81]

D'Urville arrived at Hobart anxious for news of the American exploring expedition of Captain Charles Wilkes USN. However, Franklin knew nothing: the Americans had not stopped at Hobart. Wilkes had orders not to pass any information, and to make certain no one else did. While at Sydney he sent James Clark Ross details of his route, and a chart of his discoveries. Years later he condemned Ross for failing to reply, and for disparaging the American achievement, but by then he had other reasons to vent his spleen on the Royal Navy.[82] In fact Ross had acknowledged Wilkes's letter in his account of the voyage.[83] Franklin never did get to see the Wilkes expedition, something the Americans may have regretted. In stark contrast to Wilkes's pathological secrecy d'Urville called at Hobart after his second southern voyage, proudly telling Franklin that he had fixed the position of the magnetic South Pole. This information would be passed to Ross, Franklin's most intimate professional friend.

Although a world away from the Arctic, and the centre of naval and scientific power in London, Franklin kept in touch with polar progress. This was still 'his' mission, but he never betrayed a hint of jealousy towards his fellow navigators. Beaufort sent him the latest Arctic chart, marked with the discoveries of Dease and Simpson, confident that Simpson would finish the job by determining whether Boothia was insular or peninsular.[84] Franklin congratulated Henry Pelly of the Hudson's Bay Company, his letter suffused with the collegial spirit of a man confident of his own achievements and anxious to see the job completed.[85] When Beaufort sent Sabine's translation of Baron Wrangel's voyage, Franklin recognised its political purpose and that of Barrow's tightly argued review, which once again undervalued science.[86]

However, the future of the Arctic mission was intimately linked with the Antarctic. Ross's expedition was essentially scientific; exploration was secondary, although essential for the success of the science.[87] While the driving force came from Sabine, Beaufort and Ross, they were careful to work through the British Association, with the endorsement of Sir John Herschel, the support of the Royal Society and ringing endorsements from Humboldt and Gauss. This carefully prepared position made it nearly impossible for a cultured government to resist. Franklin was delighted that Ross had the command, and that Hobart would be the site for a magnetic observatory.[88] Ross's official instructions established that this was a magnetic mission, with Franklin and Van Diemen's Land occupying a prominent place in the scheme. Indeed, Franklin's active participation was taken for granted by his scientific friends.[89] Beaufort kept Franklin informed as the project developed, and used him as a southern post office for passing scientific sailors, British and French.[90]

Where Gauss had estimated the location of the magnetic South Pole, Ross, with his ice-strengthened ships, would attempt to get there, or at least to get close enough to secure a reliable fix. On his way south Ross set up three magnetic observatories, at St Helena, the Cape and Hobart, and the two ships conducted constant readings and set up a temporary observatory ashore whenever possible. The new observatories would join Ross in observing on the

European term days, when Gaussian science came together across the world to take magnetic readings every five minutes. One such day in Hobart found Ross, Crozier, Kay and Franklin observing every 150 seconds, their entire lives seemingly summed up in the fluctuation of a magnetised needle observed through a telescope. After discussing the work with Franklin, Ross relayed his findings to Edward Sabine, presiding genius of the project, in weekly letters.[91]

Ross arrived in Hobart on 17 August 1840, and spent the winter refitting. Having received orders to prepare for the construction of an observatory, and authority to draw on military funds, Franklin was ready with materials and convict labour. On the 18th Ross and Franklin selected a site close by the projected Government House where the local sandstone had been quarried to a sufficient depth to ascertain the geological character of the area, a critical issue for a magnetic station.[92] Soon the 48 x 16-foot wood and stone building, held together without a single piece of iron, was taking shape. Ross warped his ships up the nearby cove, leaving his officers to conduct the refit while he supervised the observatory. Franklin's preparations and ample convict labour ensured the observatory was ready for term-day observations on 27 August 1840, only nine days after Ross arrived, even allowing a day of rest for the Sabbath which neither Ross nor Franklin would violate. This was far earlier than Ross had dared hope, and ensured that the permanent instruments, the portable observatory and the ship's own instruments produced three sets of data. Ross and Crozier took charge of distinct areas of observation, with Franklin as a relief observer on the second term day on 23 September.[93] Delighted to have his friend in town, Franklin was 'bustling and frisky and merry'. The two navigator/scientists had much to discuss.[94] If shared experience of polar hardships and endless scientific observation gave them common cause, professionalism and evangelical faith bound them like brothers. It was a bond that only death could break, one that Franklin recognised when he named the observatory Rossbank, repaying Ross's decision to name the westernmost headland of King William Land Point John Franklin. Jane commissioned a painting to show Ross, Franklin, Crozier and Lieutenant Joseph Henry Kay on the site. Sent to England as a gift for Edward Sabine, it had pride of place in his front room.[95]

When Ross sailed for the Antarctic, he left Kay and mates Peter Scott and Joseph Dayman with two marines to run the establishment. Kay was to consult Franklin when necessary, the governor committing himself to assist the observers on term days. The observatory was his garden shed, a happy release from the cares of office. Here Franklin could lose himself in the demanding but specific routine of data collection, and dream of future polar travels. He savoured the precision, the detail and simultaneity of the instruments, the remarkable concordance of the results – the unalloyed delight of 'almost daily' visits to the southernmost station of imperial science.[96] Fresh magnetic labours prompted him to reconsider the theoretical possibilities of his polar observations in the light of the latest thinking:

I see in them much that tends to confirm opinions I had formed from the Registers kept on my Polar Voyages respecting the influence which atmospheric changes produced on the needle and also regarding the Lunar Motion, but which in the then imperfect state of my knowledge of the intricate questions bearing on magnetic Science, I did not venture to put forth in my published narrative so fully as my own notes would have furnished.[97]

Clearly Franklin's interest in magnetic theory and his concern with Arctic data had not faded during his years in colonial government. His reflections may have been inspired by conversations with Ross, who was already corresponding with Sabine about a magnetically engineered attempt on the North West Passage. At this stage Franklin had no reason to think about leading the mission himself: he was still in harness. Rossbank exemplified the scientific impulse behind Franklin's regime in Van Diemen's Land: it was a task that he was supremely well equipped to direct, but above all it was a critical link in the chain of global imperial science. To ensure his subjects understood what was going on in their back yard a chosen few were given guided tours by Ross, while Kay was directed to write 'Terrestrial Magnetism' and 'The Instruments Employed in the Magnetical Observatory, Tasmania' for the first issue of the *Tasmanian Journal*.[98] Kay set out the navigational utility of magnetic knowledge, the state of theory after Gauss and the tools and methods of observation.

Ross's young naturalist/surgeon Joseph Hooker had an immediate entrée into Government House. While Jane was delighted by Hooker's praise of her mountain garden, he got into trouble with Her Ladyship for botanising at Port Arthur on a Sunday, even though he waited until after the sermon.[99] Despite her concerns, which were shared by Ross, Hooker collected assiduously. *Flora of Tasmania* would be a critical stage in the career of a scientific giant, and a key supporter of Darwin. Hooker never forgot those pioneering days: a medallion of Franklin hung in his office to the end of his life.[100] Ross assisted with the collection of tidal data, another Humboldtian project, using results taken at Port Arthur by meteorologist Thomas Lempriere and tables provided by Herschel.[101] Franklin had been supplying Whewell, Beaufort and Herschel with Lempriere's tidal and astronomical output for some time.[102] Although backed by the BAAS, tidology failed to hit the same dizzy heights of national support as the magnetic crusade.

When the ships departed on 12 November, Franklin accompanied his friends out to sea, as if desperate to go with them. Ross had been annoyed to find his voyage instructions had become public knowledge, and that both the French under d'Urville and the Americans under Wilkes had chosen to follow his intended route.[103] As neither French nor American ships were strengthened for ice navigation, he chose a new line of latitude, and sailed far closer to the southern land mass. Reflecting on his time in Hobart, Ross eulogised his friend, whose 'wise and judicious government' placed the colony in 'a flourishing condition', but blasted 'the sad mismanagement of our colonial legislators in England'.[104]

During the Antarctic voyage Ross honoured Franklin by fixing his name to the most southerly land he encountered, making a pair with the westernmost tip of King William Island, the highest tribute that he could pay. He also applied the names of his ships to Antarctic mountains, a long way from their final resting places, along with those of Sabine, Beaufort, Murchison and other luminaries of the BAAS. On his return to Hobart, Ross was delighted to report sailing over eighty miles south of a mountain range laid down by Wilkes's expedition: 'and thus was stamped the proper value on their pretended discoveries in this quarter'. The French positions were more accurate.[105] Evidently Ross, like many others, had taken a great dis-

like to Captain Wilkes.[106] Franklin was overjoyed that Ross had
fixed the position of the magnetic South Pole, using the latest instruments and techniques.[107] This was a key contribution to the global
terrestrial magnetic chart. It would be necessary to repeat the
process at the magnetic North Pole to complete the survey. News
that Sabine had been promoted and would remain at Woolwich for
some years was equally welcome.[108] Without Sabine's science it was
hard to see how any more polar missions would be generated.

Such considerations seemed a long way off when Ross's expedition wintered (7 April to 7 July 1841) at Hobart. Once again there
was work to be done at Rossbank, and Franklin was delighted to
report that 'on those days when an increased number of observers is
required to keep the watches – I have the pleasure of being enlisted
into the service'.[109] In truth, as his niece Sophia Cracroft observed:
'all his spare hours, however few are devoted to visiting the observatory – he is so much interested in the subject of terrestrial
magnetism'.[110] Franklin did all he could to facilitate magnetic science, directing a series of magnetic observations at Launceston. At
the same time the two celebrity ships, the *Erebus* and the *Terror*, and
their eligible young officers were treated to an unprecedented display of local hospitality. In response the officers used their own
money to provide a grand ball. The two ships were moored close
alongside at the end of the Government House garden, housed over
Arctic style and connected with the shore by a bridge of boats.
Nothing in the history of Van Diemen's Land had prepared the
colonists for an event that would live long in the memories of all
who attended.[111] Everyone who had shown the expedition their hospitality was invited, three hundred people danced on the *Erebus*,
music provided by a band stationed around the mainmast. They sat
down to dinner on the *Terror*. In replying to a toast from Ross,
Franklin reminded the audience that the day set aside by Captain
Ross was one of which 'Englishmen might well be proud; it was the
anniversary of one of the most splendid naval victories that adorned
the pages of our history [Lord Howe's triumph at 'The Glorious
First of June' in 1794] – it was a day rendered historical by the battle of the *Shannon* and the *Chesapeake* – and it was a day also
rendered sacred to *science* by the discovery by the gallant officer

who had proposed his health, of the magnetic North Pole'. To a second toast Franklin responded: 'The British Navy', and then called his own toast to Ross, Crozier, their officers, and with the captains' permission, the seamen. 'It was without exception the most pleasant gala ever given in this town' the *Hobart Town Advertiser* concluded.[112] Ross often referred to the 'deep-felt gratitude' that he and all his crew felt for Franklin's unqualified support. He also purchased 400 acres in the Huon valley, with Jane's help.[113]

The connection between the Ross mission and Franklin's final Arctic voyage is generally restricted to a passing mention that Franklin took the same ships, and some of their officers. In reality these two voyages form the twin poles of British scientific enterprise. They were designed to gather data at the last frontiers of magnetic science, something that would have become obvious had Franklin or his journals ever returned. Franklin was one of the architects of the original magnetic mission within the BAAS, working closely with Beaufort, Sabine and Murchison to secure Admiralty support.[114] Events in the Arctic during his governorship of Tasmania, notably the Dease and Simpson expedition, had reduced the unknown elements of the North West Passage to the apparently trifling matter of making the final connection between the segments of the route.[115] With the unknown shrinking fast another naval expedition was hardly necessary. It would be magnetic science, not geographical curiosity, that inspired the final Arctic expedition. As a central figure in the magnetic crusade, Franklin's correspondence and his discussions with Ross left him in no doubt that an Arctic follow-up to the current magnetic expedition had been projected, or that science rather than a passage would be the key to a new voyage.[116] The observations taken at Rossbank were a potent symbol of the mission-defining imperative of magnetic science.

Although Ross sailed away, naval magnetic science continued. Captain Owen Stanley was delighted with the observatory, and struck by Franklin's 'interest and zeal'.[117] Franklin thought very highly of Stanley, a fine practical astronomer who had sailed with King in the *Beagle*.[118] Captain Francis Blackwood spent the autumn of 1842 at Hobart setting up his instruments before beginning an arduous survey in the Torres Strait.[119] His ships HMS *Fly* and HMS

Bramble took up the Yacht Cove anchorage used by *Erebus* and *Terror*, raising the spirits of the rather isolated magnetic survey party at the top of the hill.[120]

Expedition

Franklin's scientific world was not, of course, restricted to magnetic work. He combined the Humboldtian impulse to understand, record and categorise with a governor's concern for economic utility. Herschel's example bore much fruit. In the autumn of 1842 Franklin led an expedition through the wild rain forest that separated the Derwent valley from the abandoned west-coast convict station at Macquarie harbour. Although part of the route had been pioneered by government surveyor James Calder in the two previous summers, this was far from a picnic or a folly. It was an entirely characteristic element in the Enlightenment approach to colonial government. Franklin was anxious to locate new land to sell, and new resources to harvest. This was obvious from his decision to head for Macquarie harbour, a key timber region – the journey would pass through stands of valuable Huon pine.[121] Anxious to boost colonial revenue, Franklin hoped that science and geography could stimulate economic activity. A delay at Macquarie harbour offered ample opportunity to inspect the derelict convict and shipbuilding facilities, and the local timber resources.[122]

Reading between the lines it seems that Franklin relished the opportunity to exchange the savagery of colonial politics for the hardships of the wilderness. With twenty-eight people under his 'command' Franklin set off on a sixty-six-mile transit of the unknown through some of the wettest, most overgrown and difficult terrain on the island. Even now the route is considered close to suicidal. Jane was carried in a palanquin while the going was good, but she ended up marching more than half the distance. Facing incessant rain, wet ground and limited supplies Franklin ran the expedition like an Arctic voyage. He made sure the porters had more of the scarce rations than the explorers.[123] Like many another who travelled under his leadership James Calder worshipped Franklin. Two years later Franklin was delighted to find that bearings he had taken at Macquarie harbour were used on the new map of the island along with the track of his route.[124] He sent Murchison another collection of rocks, complete with a location map, settling the internal geography of the island, especially the alignment of the mountain range.[125]

Franklin and the ideals of a lost age

Franklin's time in Australia exemplified the ruling ideas of the age. The Enlightenment concept of improvement as applied to the land was seen as a civilising mission. The political leaders of the new colonies were persuaded that the same system and science that had generated the English agricultural revolution of the eighteenth century would work in the new world, re-creating contemporary British society in the Antipodes. Science would reduce this *terra nullis* to order, and provide a higher intellectual purpose elevating colonial minds above the everyday business of existence. However, the cost of 'official' science was not one that the early colonists wished to bear, so the emphasis was on amateur efforts. Here Franklin proved adept, using colonial resources, mostly labour, raw materials and hospitality, to support government missions like those of Ross and Stokes, as well as unattached savants such as Strzelecki. The patient assembly of samples and data would exploit local interest and connect the periphery with the metropole. A scientific catalogue, like a travel narrative, was a key demonstration of imperial possession. Who could deny the British ownership of a land they had catalogued, mapped and named?

Exploration served the colony by opening new lands for 'improvement', while the attendant scientific results helped to justify occupation. Consequently the priceless experience of local peoples was ignored for over a century, leaving the mainland colonists to battle with a natural world that did not conform to their model. In Tasmania the climate and conditions were altogether closer to the British pattern, and the rapid introduction of British and European species provided an early impulse to economic development. As an evangelical Christian and an observational scientist Franklin understood the mission, and his governorship was dominated by a version of science that could be seen as God's purpose revealed on earth. In

136

pursuit of this noble aim Franklin and Jane 'breathed scientific and intellectual life into Hobart Society'.[126] Nor did his tenure pass without note. When the time came for him to depart, the citizens of the colony presented him with a printed memorial, well aware that they would never see his like again:

We have the fullest confidence that, in discharging the obligations of your high office, your own separate interests have never been contemplated; and that it has been the great and leading aim of your official conduct to promote what you believed to be the intellectual, moral and religious interests of the Community.[127]

Recall

Franklin always considered colonial government an interlude in his naval career, hoping to complete his Arctic mission when the opportunity arose. He found the minutiae of government exhausting, and the politics of the colony physically distressing.[128] For a man of faith, used to the honest, open and frank world of naval service where the national good outweighed personal ambition, the experience was traumatic. He had seen human nature up close, and it was far more terrifying than any Arctic wasteland. His nemesis would be John Montagu, the most powerful of George Arthur's clique. Despising Franklin and hating Jane, Montagu spread vicious rumours of petticoat government through his newspaper contacts and used Arthur's controlling interest in the Derwent Bank to buy support. Although ostensibly acting as Arthur's agent, he used Arthur's money and influence to advance his own agenda. For all his administrative skill Montagu was fundamentally dishonest and Arthur would live to regret lending him money.[129] Ross saw that behind the façade of professional disinterest lay 'a man who deals in strong words without one elevated sentiment.'[130] The tragedy was that Franklin had been forced to stick with Montagu because of Maconachie's astonishing behaviour.

Montagu's hostility reflected heavy losses suffered in local investments, losses made unbearable because the money had been borrowed from George Arthur. Not only was Arthur furious at Montagu's inability to pay his debts, but he found Montagu's tactics offensive and disgraceful. Ending his correspondence with Montagu, Arthur salvaged what he could from the wreckage of his Tasmanian empire.[131]

After a long period of leave in England Montagu returned to Hobart, where Franklin could no longer tolerate his scarcely veiled hostility and corruption. Having managed the government both more effectively and, of far greater importance, more harmoniously in Montagu's absence Franklin was not prepared to accept dictation from the self-interested colonial secretary. Montagu forced his hand by sarcastically impugning his memory at a public meeting. Franklin dismissed him and sent him back to London. Foolishly he provided Montagu with a reference which, together with Montagu's insinuation of female influence and the inability of the Franklin regime to balance the budget to London's satisfaction, persuaded James Stephen, never an admirer of Sir John, and his political master Lord Stanley to sack him. The charge of petticoat government was widely believed in London, but quite unfounded. Jane was an unusual woman, intelligent, inquisitive and well-informed, with a passion for adventure and a vision of a better world. She was a vital part of Franklin's life, but she did not control him.[132] Later Stanley would claim that he had delayed sending the recall until after Franklin's six-year term of office was up to avoid any suggestion that his dissatisfaction was linked to the Montagu case. This was not true, as Stanley well knew. He had ignored the facts and been swayed by the self-interested slanders of a man Franklin had dismissed from his post. As if to prove that neither Stanley nor the office over which he presided cared a jot for Franklin, they gave Montagu a copy of the official recall and sent the dispatch in a slow vessel.

The new lieutenant-governor set out on a fast vessel not long after. Consequently Sir John Eardley-Wilmot MP arrived at Hobart three days before the official letter of recall, leaving Franklin to wait for a ship at the Governor's Cottage in New Norfolk. His possessions were not packed and his farewells were unspoken. Deeply distressed by the ingratitude and the injustice of the Montagu affair Franklin opened his soul to Ross, begging him to pass the news to his friends Parry, Beaufort and Richardson.[133]

The new governor was a supporter of Stanley's faction within the disintegrating Tory Party. He also had his salary raised from the paltry £2,500 that Franklin had invariably overspent to £4,000. However, Stanley gave Eardley-Wilmot an impossible task, balancing the budget and imposing London's vision of how the colony should be run. Franklin realised he was a feeble man, 'a hunter after popularity – who is best pleased the more the crowd approve of his actions'.[134] His downfall was occasioned by an attempt to reduce Franklin's Tasmanian Society to a local agricultural research unit, using government funds to run the colonial garden. Where Franklin had given the men of Hobart a global vision, showing them the world of science and learning, Wilmot wanted to put them back in the potting shed.[135] This touched a raw nerve. Bishop Nixon reported Wilmot's unbecoming conduct with convict girls, a far cry from the straight-laced behaviour of his predecessor. His letter reached a new colonial secretary, that paragon of upright moral rectitude William Gladstone. Recalled in disgrace, Eardley-Wilmot was dead within two years.[136]

In some ways Franklin's recall was a relief to a man tired of government and anxious to rejoin his profession,[137] but both Franklin and Jane were deeply attached to the colony whose convict-stained name they had replaced with Tasmania.[138] This was typical: he cared about these people, even those who had done their best to make his work difficult. The worst that can be said of Franklin in colonial government is that he cared too much, that he trusted too many, and that his devout, humane leadership was wasted on Montagu and his like. Soon his recall would be seen as a matter of universal regret; his were 'the golden days of Tasmania'.[139]

If Franklin left the island despondent and bitter at the manner of his dismissal it was entirely in character that he stopped to inaugurate a Bass Strait lighthouse and regretted his inability to call on Captain Philip Parker King at Sydney, because

I feel that you are the only person in NSW of colonial interests and feelings as regards the improvement of the Navigation and the welfare of the shipping – and I should have liked among many other subjects to have conversed with you on these points and especially to have ascertained your opinion as to whether there might be any advantage in striving to secure the erection of the lighthouses on your side of Bass's Strait.[140]

Already hearing the siren call of sea duty, Sir John expected to reverse Lord Stanley's judgement by reason and evidence.[141] He had the backing of many friends in the navy and the scientific world. Indeed, it was his fellow scientists who did most to fight his corner. Unfortunately Stanley was not the man to admit a mistake, and he made far bigger errors than dismissing Franklin.

Franklin's culture, science and humanity transformed the colony, put 'Tasmania' on the world map, ensured there were maps and charts to enable the world to come to his island, and the geological and botanical knowledge to make it useful. In an expansive age his scientific, Christian vision of empire might have been seen as heroic – instead it was damned as costly and irresolute by small-minded, self-interested partisans and penny-pinching bureaucrats. Those who cared for the island and hoped to see it prosper praised Franklin's enlightened, benevolent and charismatic government. If Franklin's term as lieutenant-governor ended in controversy this was through no fault of his. He had been traduced by a corrupt official and summarily dismissed by a hasty minister unwilling to admit his error. That the minister replaced him with a political acolyte, recalled in genuine disgrace only two years later, merely reinforced the injustice.[142]

When Montagu's replacement James Bicheno arrived, he was struck by Franklin's businesslike work habits, insight and powers of expression.[143] Later Montagu wrote to him, admitting that Franklin was an amiable private character, while boasting: 'we shall never hear anything more of the old imbecile'.[144] In fact the world would hear a great deal more of John Franklin before the decade was out – and nothing more of John Montagu.[145]

7

'The nucleus of an iceberg'

AS THE *RAJAH* sailed past Port Philip Head, Franklin faced an uncomfortable passage: it was not the ocean but the sudden end of his governorship that troubled him. Only months before, he had every reason to expect another triumphant return, having conducted his public service with success. Suddenly good government and the transformation of the local cultural landscape with his unique compound of evangelical and Humboldtian concerns seemed irrelevant. Believing he had done his duty, Franklin felt the abrupt, unceremonious recall could only be read as a disgrace. Rather than adding public thanks to his Arctic laurels it seemed he had squandered his reputation in the Antipodes. Never one to give up in the face of adversity, Franklin reminded the Admiralty of his naval and magnetic achievements in Tasmania and requested employment.[1] In his mind further employment and reversing Lord Stanley's judgement were quite separate issues.

The magnetic mission

Franklin remained a central player in the polar mission throughout his Antipodean service. Correspondence with Beaufort, Lloyd and Sabine, hosting Ross's expedition and overseeing the Hobart observatory ensured that he never forgot that the Arctic was a magnetic question. The successful BAAS lobby for an Antarctic mission had been a major step forward: the international collaborative magnetic question, rendered irresistible by the endorsement of the great Humboldt, finally opened Treasury coffers. Although Ross's Antarctic data brought a theory of terrestrial magnetism that much closer, Humboldt was not satisfied. His global project would remain incomplete until observers returned to the magnetic North Pole.[2]

Gauss, Airy and Herschel disagreed, but they were overpowered by Sabine's crusade. Everything hinged on the scientific argument because after the last round of exploration no territorial or economic reasoning would stand up to serious investigation. Such ideas, very much the province of Sir John Barrow, could be tacked on to a science-led proposal; alone they were useless. For all the prominence accorded to 'discovery' the size, equipment and timing of the Franklin expedition were driven by magnetic science. The element of discovery merely satisfied public curiosity, providing a simple mission concept that all could understand – unlike the tedious, unromantic slog of magnetic observations.

Ross, Sabine, Beaufort and Franklin knew that the vital magnetic sites were beyond the reach of overland expeditions. The magnetic pole could be visited only by an overwintering naval expedition, which would complete the last unknown section of the Passage in the process. For this purpose the returning Antarctic ships were ideal: strengthened for ice navigation and thoroughly tested they were otherwise perfectly useless. The availability of these two ships had been a key argument for polar missions since Franklin and Beaufort first raised the idea at the British Association in 1836.[3]

With his customary combination of single-minded determination and bureaucratic skill Sabine had been preparing the ground. While he often described the northern mission as an attempt to complete the North West Passage, it is evident from the impulse of his life's work, and his language, that this was no more than a convenient shorthand. Those who had worked with him for two decades did not need to be reminded that Sabine's project would not be complete until a naval expedition, led by a magnetic officer, had passed through the eastern half of the Passage, reaching the point where Ross had stood a decade earlier. Only with the full set of modern Gaussian instruments, the latest term-day readings and a significant number of observers could Sabine secure the data he craved. He wanted to deploy an observatory at the magnetic pole. Ross was the obvious leader; he had located both magnetic poles and had no peer as a naval magnetic scientist.

Sabine seized every opportunity to advance his agenda. He edited Thomas Simpson's Arctic journals at the request of the Hudson's

Bay Company, to recover the magnetic data and keep the Passage question open.[4] In 1840 his wife's translation of Baron Wrangel's 1821–3 expedition to the Siberian coast appeared

> very opportunely to correct the universally prevailing opinion that the North West Passage was now finally settled by Messrs Dease & Simpson. So far as I have heard it has done that very well; people are satisfied that the survey of the coast, & the NW Passage are two very distinct things – and the interest with which the work is read by the public, an interest much exceeding our most sanguine expectations, will it trust keep alive in the public mind the desire to finish gloriously the labour of so many years. Barrow I hear is writing a review of it; but whether for the next *Quarterly*, or for the Sept. number I do not know. Parry has said something or other to Beaufort about his desire to go again, but one can scarcely believe him serious – or that he can seriously meditate such a step – if he does however I shall most cordially rejoice, and hope that his attempt will be made whilst you are at the South Pole: that would be glorious, one of you in the Arctic, the other in the Antarctic Circle!! But I need scarcely say that that is the only case in which I would unreservedly rejoice in a N W expedition of which you are not the leader.
>
> PS Beaufort sends Franklin a copy of Wrangel.[5]

Sabine's carefully targeted introduction to this text would be critical to the geographical element of the mission – it secured the support of John Barrow, highlighted Russian activity, and argued for renewed activity.[6] At this stage Franklin was not considered for the command: he was busy in Hobart. Instead Sabine expected Ross to command the northern mission after locating the magnetic South Pole, the primary aim of the Antarctic mission. He left Barrow to raise public awareness in the pages of the *Quarterly Review* and keep the polar flame alight in the Admiralty boardroom, with scientific and navigational support from Beaufort on the floor above. Franklin shared Sabine's magnetic agenda, and understood that Barrow's utility was limited by his failure to grasp the primacy of science:

> I entirely agree with him this writer in the desire to urge on the Govt. the necessity of sending out another Sea Expedition to try the NW Passage – and I trust he will be able to add another Laurel to his brow by causing vessels to be equipped for that service. I do not, however, agree with his remarks respecting the secondary value of researches which are carrying forward in this Hemisphere.[7]

From his headquarters at Woolwich, Sabine co-ordinated a British magnetic crusade, linking Humboldtian science with the practical business of getting men, equipment and ships into position for the term days.[8] He liaised with Beaufort to ensure that survey vessels sent to distant waters carried magnetic instruments, and officers trained to use them.[9] In his anxiety to obtain a system of predictive compass-correction data, serving the same function as the astronomical tables of the *Nautical Almanac*, Beaufort tied himself to Sabine's magnetic chariot. He could hardly refuse Sabine's request that his favourite surveyor, Captain Edward Belcher, should make magnetic observations for minimum magnetic force on his Pacific voyage: 'a very important and valuable service . . . towards the theory of Terrestrial Magnetism'. Belcher had the necessary instruments 'and has shewn himself to be an indefatigable and accurate observer'.[10] Well aware of the value to be gained by a little judicious flattery Sabine told Beaufort that Belcher's last cruise in HMS *Sulphur* was

undoubtedly the most extensive and valuable contribution that has been made by any Individual or expedition (with the exception of the expedition under Captain James Ross of which such observations form the specific object), towards the theory of Terrestrial magnetism.[11]

Even if the Franklin mission had *not* been primarily magnetic Sabine and Beaufort would have ensured it generated the necessary data. However, the precise specification of that data was still in flux. Sabine relied on Professor Humphrey Lloyd at Trinity College Dublin to develop the most effective data sets, and the instruments to record them. The remarkable progress of magnetic science in the preceding twenty years provided a key argument for the new mission: the old data sets were of limited value, better instruments and techniques had appeared, while the international term days and global collaboration made data collection on specific, prearranged days essential. In April 1843 Lloyd reported a critical breakthrough that reinforced the need to go north:

I find that the total force can be determined absolutely, in latitudes from 80° to 90° inclination, with much more accuracy than by the old method – viz. through the intervention of the horizontal component. All that is wanting is a small dip circle, with a few additions which are very simple of construction.[12]

Sabine expected Ross to take command: 'You need not fear being left in the lurch if you should take an additional year for completing your work. No one will go to the North Pole until you return; but all is waiting for you and Crozier.'[13] While he did not specify which northern pole he meant, only one was of any interest, or physically possible. In the interval he continued networking:

I had a long conversation with Sir John Barrow on Saturday about refitting the ships for the North West. He does not anticipate any difficulty with the Admiralty and the public are decidedly more favourable to such undertakings than when you sailed. Your success has done that. However we both agreed that though we could make any preliminary arrangements privately, no public or official step should be taken until your return – and until we should hear from yourself what rest you would like to have at home.

However, international magnetic co-operation would end in December 1845, setting the terminal date for any Arctic expedition. To square the circle Sabine suggested that Ross write his Antarctic narrative on the passage home from Rio, complete the scientific appendices over the winter of 1843–4 and depart for the north the following summer. Later, confident he could keep the colonial observatories running for another year, he offered an extension.[14] However, these assumptions quickly unravelled. Ross arrived home in September 1843, physically and mentally drained by a demanding five-year mission. Rather than rush back to the icy seas he got married, promising his wife that his polar days were done. He also took far longer to begin the Antarctic narrative than Sabine expected.[15] The final mission, capstone of a global project, had stalled.

Sabine failed to anticipate Ross's mental and physical state because he had grown used to success. His magnetic world empire was about to reach its apogee. In 1841 he had secured the old Royal Observatory at Kew for the British Association, and ensured it was commissioned as a temple to his own Humboldtian project. While he left long-term ally Murchison to propose a vote of thanks to the Queen at the 1842 BAAS meeting, the gratitude was Sabine's. He also secured research grants from the association: £200 for the observatory, £50 for Herschel's magnetic and meteorological project and another £20 to publish the latest batch of magnetic results. As Sabine had nominated the advisory committee, the outcome of his applications was predictable.[16] In late September 1844 the BAAS met at York. Once again the Kew observatory secured a significant grant and Sabine reported the latest magnetic findings from the Toronto station. The meeting concluded with the Council, dominated by Sabine and Murchison, issuing a call to magnetic arms. They proposed

to invite to the meeting in Cambridge in 1845 the men of science in foreign countries, who have distinguished themselves by attention to magnetical science, – with a view to a conference regarding the propriety of continuing the magnetic observations for three years, or a longer period, and the best mode of continuing them.[17]

Neatly prompted by Humboldt, Sabine's imperial science would renew its mandate and ensure the government kept the colonial observatories open. The foreigners were largely window dressing, too learned to be understood by ministers and yet so eminent that their pronouncements could not be ignored, once Sabine had translated them into everyday English. It was equally important for Sabine that the association's chair should be held in 1845 by the most eminent British scientist, Sir John Herschel – the one name that carried real weight with government. Now Sabine reaped the rewards of astute patronage: Herschel felt obliged to keep his doubts about the mission to himself. Only one man was missing when the British magnetic brotherhood met at York – John Franklin.

Franklin returns

Long before the *Rajah* reached England in June 1844 Franklin's scientific friends had sprung to his defence. Their actions spoke volumes about their regard for him both as a man and as a scientist. As Count Strzelecki reported to Philip Parker King:

Poor Sir John is expected: How shamefully he was treated. I knew of the appointment of his successor Sir Wilmot in China, the *Beagle* met with him at the Cape, and I am very glad to tell you that Stokes took every opportunity of disabusing the new Governor of the preconceived opinions which he derived from Montagu, who as you know is at the Cape. Stokes told Wilmot of all the intrigues which thwarted Sir John's government, and warned him rightly from the rubs and stumbling blocks which he may encounter in his administration too.[18]

Strzelecki's next report was equally positive: Franklin 'is every-where highly esteemed – though perhaps at the Colonial Office the intrigue got the better of him'.[19] Beaufort and John Richardson co-ordinated the unofficial Franklin defence campaign while scientists William Buckland and *Investigator* shipmate Robert Brown approached Prime Minister Sir Robert Peel. Through Peel, a life member of the British Association and a great admirer of Buckland's Christian geology, they secured an interview with Lord Stanley.[20]

When he reached London, Franklin discovered the 'disgrace' of Van Diemen's Land had not affected his standing at the Admiralty or the Treasury.[21] Now he expected Lord Stanley to give him justice, to acknowledge that he had been wrong to act on Montagu's slanders. However, he had underestimated his erstwhile political master, a haughty, unbending aristocrat.[22] Having discovered that Stanley was his equal in resolve, and far less scrupulous, Franklin decamped to Hampshire to consult Richardson.[23] These Tasmanian concerns kept him from the York meeting where Sabine and Lloyd secured their international symposium.[24]

Wounded and angry, Franklin decided to publish his case, the usual recourse of the disappointed. He did not display much tactical skill or political insight, committing himself to publication before exhausting other options. Stanley was unimpressed, leaving Franklin little choice but to lay his version of the affair before the public. Well aware that such pamphlets rarely had much effect beyond lowering the reputa-tions of all concerned, cooler heads like Parry and Buckland sought a compromise. They hoped to secure an honour for Franklin without forcing Stanley into a public climbdown, and then let the matter blow over. Parry dreaded 'the very painful measure of publication, . . . on Lady Franklin's account . . . If the Press once begin to be employed, I see no end to the vexation and annoyance it will produce.[25]

They had reckoned without Franklin's ironclad integrity. He politely but firmly rejected the idea of a compromise honour:

I have asked of Lord Stanley justice, and can I say to him 'but instead of this I will take from you rank or honour if you will give it me?' Why I might be sus-pected even of aggravating my grievances and persisting in grumbling for the very purpose of driving a bargain. I should not be the first person who has adopted such a course.

These observations must not lead you to suppose that I undervalue the endeavours of my friends to produce in Lord Stanley's mind a conviction of the injustice he has done me . . . nothing but anxiety for my poor wife who cannot be left out in the story leads me to regard publication of the intrigues of which I and I may even say the Colony have been the victims, in any other light than as my sole and only course.[26]

Soon he was hard at work, with niece Sophia Cracroft as his amanuensis. His friends helped: Brown analysed the correspondence and Richardson drafted sections.[27] Most hoped to avoid a public statement, but Franklin proved unshakeable and, for the while, Antipodean anxieties took precedence over polar projects.

Defining the mission

While Sabine provided the agenda for a new Arctic mission, Barrow would present the case at the Admiralty. It was curiously appropriate that he did so on the eve of retirement. Having reached his eightieth year Barrow would leave office on 28 January 1845, but his central role in Arctic missions led the Board to direct that he continue to receive copies of the latest polar dispatches.[28] The scientists enlisted Barrow because his interest was easily roused and his ability to compile a good minute unimpaired. His role was advocacy, initially within the Admiralty and in retirement with a public statement to sustain the cause after the expedition had sailed, repeating the formula employed in 1817. In December 1844 Barrow delivered his memorandum to Lord Haddington, First Lord of the Admiralty. The paper harmonised his ideas with those of Beaufort and Parry, but Sabine provided the clinching magnetic argument and controlled the way science spoke to government. This much was clear in the very first sentence of Barrow's 'Proposal for an Attempt to Complete the Discovery of a North West Passage':

There is a feeling generally entertained in the several scientific societies, and individuals attached to scientific pursuits, and also among officers of the Navy, that the [expense of the] discovery . . . may be met by observing that one season only would suffice for its decision, and the cost not more than one-third of that of the late Antarctic expedition under Sir James Ross, while one of the objects would be precisely the same as that of the other, namely, observations on terrestrial magnetism – considered of such importance, that magnetic observatories have been established, through the influence of England, in almost every part of the globe.

Barrow followed his economical boast by quoting Sabine:[29]

Lieutenant Colonel Sabine, who has been named by the President and Council of the Royal Society for the reduction of all these observations, has stated that magnetic observations made in this part of the Arctic regions would be most desirable, and he further observes that he has no hesitation in saying 'that a final attempt to make a North-West Passage would render the most important service that now remains to be performed towards the completion of the Magnetic Survey of the globe'.[30]

There can be no doubt that magnetic science was the key to the expedition; as Richard Cyriax established seventy years ago, Sabine's 'Report' was written before Barrow's proposal.[31] For Sabine the Passage was the route to the magnetic pole. Barrow merely reversed the original emphasis for effect. This was deliberate – such papers ended up in Parliamentary Blue Books, the official record of government action, and their compilers were well advised to use familiar arguments and well-worn mission statements. That the key 'exploration' task was linked to the magnetic pole is evident from Franklin's decision to enter Peel Sound, which he believed to be a dead end.

Prompted by Prime Minister Peel, Haddington referred the proposal to the Royal Society for a report on the anticipated scientific advantages. Barrow admitted that magnetic science was the key, and stressed that he had already consulted the naval experts. He sent his memorandum to the Royal Society, 'according to former precedents, in order to obtain from that Society, those points of scientific investigation which such a voyage might afford, together with suitable instructions'.[32] These 'points' would be defined by Sabine, and he would write the necessary instructions for investigating them.[33] While Admiralty officials Beaufort and Parry necessarily obscured their role in the genesis of the mission, they provided authority for the line that the voyage might be completed inside a year. Barrow also reused the old line that the country was at peace and the revenue flourishing, before raising the scare tactics, revving the Russian bogey before declaring: 'it would be most mortifying and not very creditable to let another naval power complete what we had begun'. That the British had escaped thus far with the loss of only one gentleman, midshipman Robert Hood, a few sailors and ten Canadian voyageurs would be a key argument for the resumption of the mission in 1844 (Barrow conveniently forgot the Canadians). He ended by recommending Parry, Franklin, Back, James Ross, Beaufort, Beechey and Commander Fisher[34] as the best officers to judge the merits of the scheme. He already knew they agreed with him.

Of those whose opinions were taken, Parry had no doubt a passage existed, quoting Wrangel's experience to support Barrow's notion that the Beaufort Sea was open water. As the Admiralty's controller of steam machinery he urged the use of steam-powered vessels, but concluded his report with a discussion of magnetic possibilities. He linked the voyage to the global research effort, observing that research in such high latitudes would 'constitute in itself an object not unworthy of such an expedition'.[35] As president of the Royal Society, the official voice of British science, the Marquis of Northampton backed Barrow with a Resolution of Council. Apart from geographical knowledge the results of the mission would

consist chiefly in the extension of our information with regard to the magnetical phenomena in regions hitherto unexplored with that object, and . . . if the expedition were deferred beyond the present season, the important advantages now discoverable from the co-operation of the observers with those who are at present carrying out a uniform system of magnetic observation in various parts of the world, would be lost.[36]

Time would be of the essence if the mission were primarily scientific. Consequently, while Franklin agreed with Parry he gave greater emphasis to magnetic science. Even if the expedition failed to find the North West Passage it would increase geographical knowledge and make 'important additions to the series of magnetical observations which are now carrying on in every part of the world'.[37] By this time he was confident that the command would be his.[38] James Ross concurred, again emphasising the importance and time-critical nature of the magnetic mission. He added a financial lure, arguing that increased yields from the northern whale fishery had more than repaid the cost of previous polar exploration.[39] Sabine's paper was emphatic. Existing polar magnetic observations were inadequate; they were twenty-five years old, made with inferior instruments and based on outmoded ideas. He therefore had 'no hesitation in saying that a final attempt to make the North West passage would also render the most important service that now remains to be performed towards the completion of the magnetic survey'.[40] He did not care if the Passage was found; only that he obtained magnetic readings from the magnetic pole.

Magnetic science dominated the genesis and direction of the Franklin expedition.[41] Without a magnetic impulse there would have been no Arctic mission. Furthermore the magnetic data had to be collected in 1845 if it were to contribute to the global project. This was Sabine's agenda, one he shared with Ross, Beaufort and Franklin. As Sabine and Franklin had met several times since Franklin returned from Tasmania, it was hardly a surprise that they agreed on the key point, namely that the expedition would be justified by magnetic research. It did no harm to remind Sir Roderick Murchison, 'one of my earliest playfellows in geology', that other sciences would also benefit on a Franklin expedition, and sending a carefully collated collection of Tasmanian rock samples that extended the Silurian empire into new quarters of the globe.[42]

However, Sabine's long-cherished expectations that Ross would take command were dashed. Ross wrote privately to Beaufort, begging him not to offer a command he would have to refuse. Instead he advanced Franklin's claims 'to complete a work which he so well began, on which he was so long engaged and being so pre-eminently qualified for the command of such an Expedition', so that he might feel 'the less reluctance in declining an honour which a few years ago was the highest object of my ambition'. In addition, fitting the ships with steam engines 'would be sufficient reason for not wishing to undertake the service as it is proposed at present'.[43] Bound like brothers by faith and profession, Ross told Franklin everything that passed between himself, Sabine and Beaufort. It is not clear if his refusal came before or after a letter from Jane urging Franklin's need for 'honourable and immediate employment'.[44]

Having ruled himself out of the expedition before Barrow's memorandum reached Lord Haddington, Ross advised Franklin to call at the Admiralty and discuss the subject with Barrow, Beaufort and Parry.[45] Those discussions left Franklin confident he had secured the command.[46] Parry advised him to wait, and reread the Arctic voyages. Franklin took the none-too-subtle hint, and on New Year's Day he attended Hudson's Bay House in the City to consult the journals of Thomas Simpson and Peter Dease.[47]

At least a week before the 'experts' reported to Lord Haddington the mission had been agreed – only the details were left, and Franklin was happy to tell a Tasmanian friend: 'there is little doubt I shall be called upon.'[48]

Sabine pressed Ross to reconsider, but his decision was final. He supported Franklin.[49] The only barrier to Franklin taking the command was Sabine. He persuaded the Admiralty to consult Parry and Richardson, hoping they would disqualify Franklin on account of age or health. Instead both men reported him in robust health, and desperate to go north. On 5 February, when he discussed with Lord Haddington the possibility of travelling to the pole, there can be no doubt both men understood the pole in question to be magnetic.[50] Franklin was confirmed in command of the 'north polar' expedition on 7 February.[51] He repaid Ross by offering the post of second-in-command to his friend Crozier.[52] With the basic arrangements settled Franklin dined at the Admiralty with Third Naval Lord Rear Admiral William Bowles.[53]

Franklin prepares

In his conversation with Lord Haddington, Franklin observed, 'I've nothing to gain by it.'[54] Indeed, command of the expedition hardly interrupted the flow of words and ideas generated by his Tasmanian grievances. While he appreciated that he had not been obliged to apply for the position, 'deeming my position entitles me to be sought for', he would not give up his quixotic quest for justice simply because he had secured a naval command. In his mind the two issues were quite unconnected. Once he took command of the Arctic expedition Franklin had little time for the Tasmanian pamphlet, which left Jane to bear the burden.[55] The matter remained unresolved when he left England, and he arranged for his friends 'to look after the

Montagu affair' in his absence.[56] None provided more help than Edward Sabine.[57] Franklin also had an opportunity to thank Barrow, joining the other Arctic naval heroes in selecting a piece of plate to commemorate his polar work on the occasion of his official retirement.[58] Evidently Franklin was not aware just how strongly the old baronet had argued for Commander James Fitzjames to have the command. Barrow's preference revealed his marginal role in the new polar project. The expedition commander needed extensive polar and magnetic experience and Fitzjames had neither. On 3 March 1845 *Erebus* and *Terror* were ordered to fit for sea, with Franklin and Crozier in command. They were already under refit at Woolwich.

Meanwhile Sabine and Lloyd were planning the magnetic research effort. The key issues were the frequency at which readings were to be taken and the connection with earlier results from locations on the expedition's route. The profile of magnetic science had never been higher; it stood at the frontier of knowledge, and the only regret was 'that the Expedition should start before the Cambridge Magnetic Congress, as otherwise they could give valuable co-operation in any new plan which may be adopted'.[59] Arctic navigation compelled Franklin to depart in May; the association would meet in June.

Following Lloyd's work Falmouth instrument maker Robert Fox applied the necessary modifications to a small dip circle, enabling a careful Arctic navigator to measure dip and absolute intensity at high magnetic latitudes.[60] It was critical to the success of the expedition that these instruments be deployed as close to the magnetic pole as possible. Sabine and Lloyd also adopted Fox's new magnetic needle, which would reduce the number of observations required, even as Franklin left the Thames.[61] By no coincidence at all the assistant superintendent of magnetic observatories at Woolwich C. J. B. Riddell produced a new operator's handbook for portable magnetic observatories.[62]

Erebus and *Terror* were refitted and equipped with steam engines at Woolwich dockyard, less than a mile from Sabine's headquarters at the Woolwich Academy, giving Sabine and Franklin ample opportunity to discuss magnetic issues and ensure the ships were fully equipped.[63] Sabine's staff trained expedition officers without previous magnetic experience. The most senior new boy was Commander James Fitzjames. Fitzjames made his name on Chesney's Euphrates expedition in the late 1830s, which had included magnetic observations, adding further laurels in the China War. Contemporaries were struck by his sense of humour, strength and adventurous nature.[64] As Franklin's second in command on *Erebus*, he was left to select most of the junior officers. He did so without reference to Arctic or surveying experience, and consequently there were only three experienced scientific observers on the expedition: Franklin, Crozier and Graham Gore, who had sailed with Back in the *Terror* and met Franklin in Tasmania. As the officers were appointed only two months before the ships sailed, most of them on 4 March, there was precious little time to complete their training. Sabine would need every day. On a typical surveying expedition, such as Francis Blackwood's aboard HMS *Fly*, it took two to three weeks to provide instruments and train officers to use them.[65] Franklin's was far from an ordinary surveying mission – there were two ships carrying enough magnetic instruments to equip an entire colonial observatory – yet the officers were largely ignorant of the work. Franklin and Crozier knew the demand for trained observers on term days would be heavy; they would need every officer to take a turn, along with the surgeons, leaving the ships to be handled by the masters. It would be unthinkable to return home without Sabine's magnetic data, so every spare minute was used to train the observers. Despite Sabine's efforts these novices would be dependent on Franklin's leadership. Franklin's scientific credentials secured him the command.

Anxious to improve their magnetic novices, Sabine and Franklin left the instruments at Woolwich Observatory after the ships dropped down to their final anchorage at Greenhithe, 'in order that the officers of the Expedition might have an opportunity of practising with them until the latest convenient moment'. When the date of departure was put back, Franklin responded by leaving the instruments at Woolwich for a fifth day: 'for the practice of the officers, without risk of detention of the ships, as they are not to be paid till Friday the 16th'.[66]

Although the need to record critical data in the high Arctic in what might be the final magnetic season dominated the mission, it did not neglect other scientific enquiries. Dr Harry Goodsir, assistant surgeon on the *Erebus*, shared Charles Darwin's interest in barnacles. Darwin secured an introduction to the expedition through his friend Joseph Hooker, who knew both Crozier and Goodsir.[67]

Franklin's commission, dated 3 March, was issued only ten weeks before he was due to sail. Although preparations were already well in hand, Franklin asked Ross to help him obtain ice masters, clerks, warrant officers and information on recent ice conditions from the whaling community. Unfortunately Ross had been called north by the sudden death of his father-in-law, and Parry was seriously ill. Franklin agreed his officers with the First and Second Naval Lords, Admirals Sir George Cockburn and Sir William Gage, on 24 February, properly leaving Crozier to select his own First Lieutenant for the *Terror*.[68]

Meanwhile the ships made good progress. By 21 March the lower masts had been installed and were about to be rigged and the shipwrights were busy installing the steam plant and propellers. Anxious to secure an experienced crew but tied up at Somerset House and the Admiralty dealing with provisions and scientific instruments, Franklin sent the two ice masters to recruit seamen in the whaling ports. In addition to this demanding schedule there were the inevitable dinners to attend and celebrities to entertain. The Royal Artillery hosted the expedition at the Woolwich Officers' Mess on 20 March, dining over 100 officers and scientists. Returning the thanks of the expedition, Franklin emphasised the scientific work of the Royal Artillery and their role in 'the Magnetic Observations which were now engaging the attention of the World'.[69] On 30 April Franklin attended a meeting at Crosby Hall in Bishopsgate to raise funds for a new seamen's church in London with Admiral Lord Radstock, Parry and leaders of the shipping community; Lord Haddington took the chair.[70] That evening he dined at the Geological Society with Buckland and Murchison.[71] A seemingly endless stream of high-profile visitors appeared at Woolwich, although none had quite the impact of the photographer from the *Illustrated London News* who captured Franklin and the *Erebus*'s officers for all eternity. He also provided them with a camera. The

Illustrated printed over 60,000 copies a week, providing a massive public-relations boost for the mission.[72] Unfortunately Franklin was sick; he looked dreadful alongside his jaunty juniors. Plagued by influenza since his return from the Antipodes, he did not recover until he went to sea.[73]

The decision to equip the exploration vessels with steam engines prompted some speculation about their effect on the voyage. Surveyor of the Navy Captain Sir William Symonds considered the screw propeller threatened the structural integrity of wooden ships – and was not above claiming, years later, that the propellers might have caused the disaster.[74] Parry, the controller of the steam department, was instrumental in the installation of the system, 'for pushing through the narrow and ever varying channels between the masses of ice – when there are no other means of doing so'.[75] He recommended installing a second-hand railway locomotive in the hold, driving a screw propeller. The novel combination of engines and ice navigation ended Ross's already limited interest in the command but Parry, who had seen more of the Passage than any man, was unlikely to have made a mistake. Although small, the engines propelled the ships at four knots, more than enough for the intricate business of following leads through the ice in a flat calm.

The engines had two unwelcome side effects. They took up a lot of space in the already overcrowded hold and, more seriously, their installation dominated the hectic two-month period when the expedition was fitting out, although much of the burden fell on Parry.[76] Franklin had little time to focus on engines, although he met Parry and Joshua Field of the marine engineering firm Maudslay, Son & Field on board in late April, after the engines and propellers had been fitted. Even then the decks could not be fixed until the machinery had been tested and adjusted. Franklin invited Count Rosen, the European agent for propeller patentee John Ericsson, to dine with Sabine and John Gould.[77] Quite what Sabine thought about filling the hold of his magnetic-research vessels with several tons of iron is unknown, but he ensured the Admiralty instructions included an order to ascertain the ship's magnetism. Whatever else they achieved the engines emphasised the importance of setting up an observatory on land.

On 24 April, the refit and engine installation complete, *Erebus* and *Terror* were inspected by Naval Lords Cockburn and Gage, Sir John Barrow and artillery expert Sir Howard Douglas. A few days later the ships tried their machinery, reaching four knots just as Parry had predicted. On 8 May Franklin, Crozier and Fitzjames attended an official Admiralty dinner with Barrow, Parry, Ross, Back and Sabine. The following day the Marquis of Northampton PRS inspected the ships. Having moved into his cabin on the *Erebus* on 24 April, Franklin gained no relief from the constant, disrupting stream of visitors until the ships moved downriver to Greenhithe on 12 May.

Among the select few to visit Franklin at Greenhithe, Count Strzelecki presented a copy of his newly published geological *magnum opus*, the *Physical Description of New South Wales and Van Diemen's Land*. Franklin had subscribed £100 to help publish the book, and accepted the dedication. The fulsome citation ended with a heartfelt wish:

> may the enviable lot of solving this still pending geographical problem fall to your share! And may that good fortune be united with a prosperous voyage, and a safe return to your country and your friends![78]

The Polish count had helped Sir John with his pamphlet, and spent a few days at Greenhithe before the ships sailed. Seeing Franklin in his natural element only increased his admiration. He described the transformation to mutual friend Philip Parker King:

> Sir John disclosed during the outfit and on the moment of departure, most astonishing vigour of body and mind. I was with him at Greenwich [he meant Greenhithe] for a couple of days before the final departure, and was struck with the influence and reaction of his old pursuit and profession upon his frame. He was born for the sea. Great regard has been paid to him throughout the time that he was fitting out, and when the moment of his leaving the anchorage arrived he left it amid the best wishes of every one ... take him for all in all, we never shall look upon his like again.[79]

Delighted with the dedication, which counter-balanced Tasmanian disappointments, Franklin finished the book before he entered the ice. This spectacular testament to his scientific status gave him great pleasure in those very different latitudes.[80]

Franklin's sailing orders, his mission statement, were issued on 5 May. They reflected the Admiralty secretary's distillation of the collected wisdom of Parry, Franklin, Ross, Beaufort and Sabine. While they state that the main object was the completion of the North West Passage, the weight of words makes it clear that magnetic science dominated the mission.[81] The orders comprised twenty-three distinct sections, of which eight were purely scientific. They were dominated by the global magnetic project, an imperial science that had been heavily supported by Britain: 'and the more desirable is this co-operation in the present year, when these splendid establishments which do so much honour to the nations who have cheerfully erected them at a great expense are to close'. This imperative, clearly ascribed to Sabine, determined every other detail of the voyage. The ships were equipped with the same instruments as the colonial observatories. They were to be used on board ship, and in the portable shore observatories, far from the magnetic signature of Parry's railway engines. The Franklin expedition was the final link in the imperial network, and this alone justified the enormous cost.

Fitzjames was given responsibility for the daily observations and ordered to attend Sabine's academy for the necessary training. As only two weeks remained before the ships sailed, this last instruction was clearly ex post facto.[82] Like many naval officers of the era Fitzjames was soon converted, hoping to bring Franklin's dispatches home via Kamchatka so that he could make magnetic observations there.[83] He would not be the last to fall for Sabine's Siberian solution.[84] Sabine provided fresh, detailed instructions for the magnetic observations.[85] While Crozier was annoyed that Fitzjames had been given this task, the decision was perfectly sensible.[86] When observations were conducted on board ship, the captain could be distracted by the demands of ice navigation. Once the portable observatory was established ashore – the core of the mission – Franklin and Crozier would take control. For all his anxiety to appoint Ross, Sabine now realised Franklin was his superior as a leader, and probably the better man for the job. Unlike Ross, Franklin was happy to delegate and to give credit to his subordinates; he inspired the devotion of officers and men in a way that the ambitious, self-promoting Ross never managed. Ever the optimist, Franklin was happy with his officers, agreeing with Parry that they were a better set than on any previous expedition.[87]

Amid the hectic last few weeks of preparation for a voyage into the unknown, charged with a complex and challenging scientific agenda, the only discordant note was the frequency with which Franklin referred to his other concern – justice. Three weeks before his departure he admitted: 'We are now very busy writing the fair copy of the pamphlet for printing, and we hope to have it done in a few days.'[88] On the day the expedition sailed he was busy with Tasmanian correspondence, assessing new evidence and commenting on the unpopularity of Lord Stanley, who had already seen some advance sheets from the pamphlet.[89]

From Woolwich to the Whale Fish Islands

Anxious to add her own personal touch to the voyage, Jane begged John Gould to find her a monkey for the *Erebus*:

> I can easily conceive that the dressing him up would be a source of great fun to them – they complain of having no pet onboard. I should like also to give something of the sort to the *Terror*, but not knowing whether Captain Crozier would approve of a monkey I think I had better get a cockatoo, or some other talking bird.[90]

It is not clear if Gould was able to oblige; the monkey would have needed a lot of dressing up.

On Monday 12 May the ships were towed from Woolwich to Greenhithe, where they embarked gunpowder, the last of their food and the magnetic instruments. Then the crew was paid and the ships' compasses adjusted. Jane and the rest of Franklin's extended family took rooms at the local inn until the ships sailed.[91] Eleanor and Sophia Cracroft made themselves useful arranging the books in his cabin.[92] Departure had been set for the 15th, but the late delivery of provisions delayed them until the 19th. Franklin took the opportunity to lead divine service on Sunday 18th, with his family in attendance, an event that Fitzjames among others found profoundly moving.

Monkey or no, Franklin sailed with high hopes:

My friend Crozier is my Second and the Admiralty have appointed a Commander unsolicited on my part to my ship – all the officers have been of my own selection in both ships and they are a fine set of young men, active zealous and devoted to the Service. Equally good are the crew – and many say that no ships could go to sea better appointed than we are. I trust also my dear friend that we shall all proceed on our voyage, not trusting in our own strength or judgement but in the merciful guidance of the Almighty, with whom alone must rest the issue of it – It was gratifying to me that yesterday (Sunday) the Officers and Crew assembled on board their respective ships to offer their thanksgiving to God for His infinite mercies already vouchsafed to them and their prayers for the merciful continuance of His Gracious protection and blessing to them. I had the happiness of seeing my dearest wife my child and niece assembled with the crew of this ship on that occasion whose prayers no doubt were as fervent on our behalf as ours were on theirs.

This circumstance tended with many others to soothe their sorrow at the prospect of my long separation from them, – and they were also much supported in becoming personally known to the officers and seeing that there was every prospect of our living and acting most happily together, – no one ever embarked on an expedition with more causes of rejoicing than ourselves – it is not therefore to be wondered at that we commenced our hazard in the highest spirits and full of hope that it may please God to prosper our effort to successful termination.[93]

On Monday 19 May 1845 the heavily laden, sluggish exploration vessels were towed to sea by the screw steamer HMS *Rattler*, the small tug HMS *Monkey* hauling the transport *Barretto Junior* in their wake. They went to sea buoyed up by boundless euphoria and good wishes. From the chair of the Royal Geographical Society, Sir Roderick Murchison predicted a successful return, and handing over the post to his 'judicious and enterprising friend', who would do all he could 'for the promotion of science'.[94] This was a Victorian expedition, it could not fail, the men were already heroes. There were a few doubters, disappointed, bitter men whose opinions were inevitably discounted. Sir John Ross believed the ships and their crews were too large for such work.[95] He preferred a small, lightly manned steampowered exploring party. But this was incompatible with the extensive scientific programme. Another to underestimate the role of science was George Back, who had done his utmost to deny Franklin the command. At least he did not want the job. The same could not be said of his companion on the Great Fish river Dr Richard King.

King had the Cassandra-like ability to be both absolutely right, and so arrogant that no one would listen. A proponent of lightweight overland efforts, he found some amusement in the naval expedition: 'I told Sir John Barrow publicly at the time Franklin sailed that he was sending him to form *the nucleus of an iceberg*.'[96]

Franklin sailed north along the east coast of Britain, anchoring briefly at Aldeburgh to wait out a storm. Among the last to see them was Owen Stanley, commanding the survey steamer HMS *Blazer*; he joined the squadron off Aberdeen and captured the exploration vessels on paper.[97] Stanley had been appointed expedition magnetic officer in January, but withdrew his name.[98] *Blazer* remained in company, while *Rattler* went into Cromarty to clear a fouled propeller, and Franklin kept her to replace the departed *Monkey*.[99] At Orkney one man was discharged from the *Terror* and the ships took on fresh beef. Then Franklin continued north, well past Stromness. On 8 June he sent his letters across to *Rattler* and set course for Greenland.[100] As they parted company, *Rattler* and *Blazer* cheered the expedition. Now it was time to begin work, Franklin gave the magnetic instructions to Fitzjames and urged every officer to take part in the scientific endeavour.

The expedition made a good passage across the Atlantic, sighting Greenland on 25 June. On the 30th they crossed the Arctic Circle, reaching the Whale Fish Islands on the west coast of Greenland on 4 July for their final stop. Here they transferred stores from the *Barretto Junior*, adding a year's supply of provisions. Their last letters included Fitzjames's lively pen portraits of his fellow officers and his belief that the mission would be completed that year. As befits a more experienced man, Franklin was less optimistic, but still saw every reason to expect good progress. He begged Ross, Richardson, Parry and Sabine to help his family deal with the troubling days when they might doubt his safe return. By contrast Crozier's last letter was despondent. Franklin did his best but the Irishman, depressed by Sophia Cracroft's rejection of his marriage proposal, found it hard to see his way ahead without the dominating presence of James Ross. Franklin carefully avoided mentioning his niece and Crozier was warming to his task as they set off for the unknown.[101] They did so loaded to the limits: Crozier sent back his large cutter, iron stanchions and anything else he could spare, cramming food into every possible space. Franklin's cabin was packed with tinned potatoes.[102] Although they would set off grossly overloaded, Franklin looked to maintain a good sailing trim, arriving at the Bering Strait on the correct load line.[103]

Franklin went ashore to test his magnetic and astronomical instruments and collect botanical specimens at the tiny sealing settlement of Disco. His results confirmed the position Parry had set for the town twenty-five years earlier. Fitzjames and Crozier produced readings for magnetic dip and variation with the instruments belonging to their respective ships, although Fitzjames confessed he needed Crozier's assistance. 'Sir John is very well and full of life and energy – and we are all as happy as possible, looking forward to the commencement of our <u>real</u> work.'[104] Franklin praised his lively commander: 'I see well however that Fitzjames will need no spur, for he goes at his observations with alacrity & cheerfulness. So I must add do each of the officers to the observations which they have had more independently placed under their charge.'[105] He hoped to reach Lancaster Sound without much obstruction.[106]

Although the expedition was making excellent time, Franklin was still tormented by Tasmania. He had discussed it with his officers, many of whom had read the pamphlet, and Crozier, who knew the island, spoke 'in the strongest terms of indignation at the conduct of Lord Stanley'. As for Montagu's unmanly attack on Lady Franklin, 'may God forgive him – and me also for having my mind dwelling so frequently on his baseness'. Franklin hoped the transport would carry away 'his last thoughts about this painful affair. I at least shall endeavour to shake them from my mind.'[107] Yet the vehemence with which he expressed the hope proved that he would carry the worries of Van Diemen's Land with him into the ice. Once Robert Brown had completed the introduction Jane published the pamphlet, despite the entreaties of her friends. They realised it would do no good.[108]

Plans

Franklin's sailing orders anticipated finding a route to the Bering Strait, his ultimate navigational objective, by sailing west along

Lancaster Sound, Parry's original route, and then heading south-west after passing Cape Walker at 98°w, rejoining the North American coast somewhere near the Coppermine river. At a late stage in the drafting process the possibility that this route would be blocked led to the addition of an alternative route due north up the Wellington Channel – perhaps a concession to Barrow's mirage of an open Polar Sea which would prove a rich source of confusion in the years that followed. Franklin did not believe in it, although he was prepared to try it if the south-westerly route were blocked.

Although distracted by Tasmania and occupied with the day-to-day business of command, Franklin used the voyage west to reread his reference library and his Arctic correspondence, focusing on the way ahead.[109] It helped to write out his thoughts and send the results home to his polar companions. Franklin's last letters reported that his health was excellent, his officers and men in fine form and the weather good. His Arctic friends received privileged insight into his plans and ideas as he sailed into the unknown. They learned that the magnetic work was going ahead, and that he had settled on a course:

I shall, of course, despatch parties on boats, and by land to examine into and find out passages in places where it may be difficult and only productive of delay in taking the ships. I have had great pleasure in reading over a letter I received from Krusenstern[110] soon after my return from Russia, and Sir John Ross had sailed – to find that he feels certain of an expedition succeeding in the NW Passage if the ships can be got to any point we were at, on the coast of America. I admit with you that Regent's Inlet seems to be the most certain way of attaining that point, but the more I reflect upon the voyages hitherto made into that Inlet the more convinced I am that James Ross and Parry are right in supposing that ships of our size, if they ever once got down among the islets and strong tides at the bottom of that Inlet, they would never be got out again. The coast in that part must be surveyed in boats. But once to the west of Point Turnagain our ships might with safety go. Should we be entirely obstructed in forcing our passage between the parallels of Banks and Wollaston Lands we must try the Wellington Channel or some other of the channels to the north, but I cannot find any good reason for (supposing that) we are to find it open, though Barrow will have it.[111]

However, he warned, 'we may be so circumstanced at the end of the first winter, and even of the second as to wish to try some other part, in case we have not previously succeeded – and having abundance of provisions and fuel, we may do that with safety'.[112] The same day, he told Ross he believed there was a passage between Banks Land and Wollaston Land because the presence of musk oxen on Melville Island suggested that a chain of islands linked the two larger masses. He did not believe in an open Polar Sea, considering Wrangel's experience irrelevant, and closed, as he did all his letters from Disco, by asking Ross to pray for him.[113] He thanked Parry for the loan of a signal book devised decades before to direct two ships navigating in ice, and ended, 'I never was in better health'.[114] The day before the transport departed Franklin wrote final letters to his wife and his sister Isabella, begging them to pray, but not to worry.[115]

Franklin's plans were dominated by his chart collection. Among them was John Ross's 1834 chart showing his nephew's sledge travel and the magnetic pole. James Clark Ross's journey ended at Victory Point, which the map connected by a straight line bearing W 10° S to Franklin's Point Turnagain 222 miles away. Peter Dease and Thomas Simpson had closed the gap between Point Turnagain and Back's Great Fish river, and marked Cape Herschel on the southern shore of King William Land in 1838–9. Franklin knew the distance from Cape Felix to the Dease and Simpson Strait was about seventy miles.[116] While Dease and Simpson's expedition had secured the renewal of the Hudson's Bay Company charter, it left King William Land cartographically connected to the mainland. The implication was clear. If Franklin could reach Point Victory the line of advance was obvious. That he might was highly likely, given the proximity of Point Victory to the magnetic pole. However, Ross's map was inaccurate in a critical area, one that would have a major influence on Franklin's route. Ross had marked a hatched line east from King William Land to Boothia, which he called Poctes Bay.[117] This line made King William Land a peninsula of Boothia, but it was based on no more than hazy vision and fleeting acquaintance. Dease and Simpson did not reach the area, leaving King William Land a peninsula. For Franklin the fact that the lines in question had been based on James Clark Ross's work invested them with a degree of certainty that they would not have possessed had they been inscribed by any other hand. In a last letter to Ross, Franklin confirmed that he accepted Cape Felix was part of Boothia, that Poctes Bay was a fact.

Ross's dotted lines told him to proceed to the west of King William Land.[118]

Not that death and the divine were ever far from Franklin's thoughts. Writing to his niece Mary Kendall on 12 July he expressed his sympathy with her and her children on the early death of her husband: 'it is one of my most cherished anticipations, if God spares my life, to do what I can in your and their behalf'. Never was the sincerity of his faith more transparent: 'I am sure my dear Mary Anne we shall have the benefit of your prayers also – and I assure you that neither yourself nor your children will be forgotten by me in my humble petitions before the throne of God.'

At least he was in good health:

You will be glad to know the coming to sea has had its usual good effect on me – my cough at once disappeared – and every remnant of my attack of influenza. I never in fact was in better health. I have every reason also to be happy – blessed as I am by having zealous & good young officers – and an active, well disposed crew. Each of whom appears to be ardent in the service we are upon. I trust also that each of us have been taught and see the necessity of placing our trust in God. 'We are not sufficient of ourselves to do anything as of ourselves – but our sufficiency is of God.' His aid, protection and guidance we most earnestly seek in the full assurance of faith and hope that he will order all things as seem the best to his infinite wisdom – and enable each of us to do our duty to the praise and glory of his Holy Name.

He hoped to leave the anchorage that night, 'so that we may be able to get well clear out to sea in time to have prayers, which we have each Sunday morning and evening'.[119]

July 12 was 'another lovely and clear day'. The ships were swung to correct the compasses just before leaving harbour, Franklin sent a final report to the Admiralty, and wrapped up a sixteen-page cumulative letter to Jane by stressing he might be away for three years, that he put his faith in God and trusted his friends would be a comfort to her and to Eleanor. He even found time to consider the future: perhaps they would buy the country estate he had always wanted.[120]

Secure in his faith, his fate resigned to his God, Franklin sailed into the unknown shortly after *Barretto Junior* set course for England bearing his last words to the outside world, spare stores and four very lucky invalids. Never again would Franklin's hopes and fears, his achievements and his failings, reach his wife and daughter, friends and colleagues. Sir John Franklin's public life had almost two years left to run, but his correspondence would pile up in his cabin, along with the magnetic readings and log books that explained his actions. But whatever he committed to paper is as irretrievably lost as the rest of his expedition. There is no evidence of Franklin's intentions or his state of mind after 12 July 1845. Thereafter everything is guesswork and speculation.

There was one last fleeting glimpse of the outside world. Two weeks later, approaching Lancaster Sound, *Erebus* and *Terror* encountered Peterhead whalers *Enterprise* and *Prince of Wales*. Franklin told Captain Martin of the *Enterprise* that he had provisions for five years, but that he could make them suffice for seven.[121] At that moment his men were busy salting down freshly killed sea birds. Later some of the expedition's officers visited Martin, but he would not pass up a favourable wind to dine with them.[122] With that Franklin was gone.

Although officially described as an attempt to complete the transit of the North West Passage, the real object of the Franklin expedition was to observe at or near the magnetic North Pole as the final element in a global 'imperial science' project. The ships carried enough magnetic hardware to equip a colonial observatory, along with a large body of officers trained in the latest techniques at Woolwich. They were commanded by a Fellow of the Royal Society with extensive experience of collecting magnetic data in high latitudes; his second, Captain Crozier, was another experienced polar observer. Magnetic science determined they must depart in May 1845. Without the magnetic impulse this mission would never have sailed.

However, Franklin set sail for the Arctic tormented by his anxiety to secure justice from Lord Stanley. How far Van Diemen's Land preyed on his mind as he faced key decisions in the Arctic will never be known, but the implication of failure made it unlikely he would return without completing his mission. To have come home without the success everyone so blithely anticipated would have been even more damning than being dismissed from his post in Hobart.

8

Magnetic Empires

THE ORIGINS OF FRANKLIN'S final expedition were more complex than existing accounts assume, and it required a far more sophisticated leader than the brave, blundering Franklin of popular myth. Franklin did not set off on his final tragic mission to 'discover' the North West Passage: the Victorians were not so foolhardy as to risk two ships and 129 men in pursuit of a geographical curiosity of no practical utility. Instead his expedition was designed to address a high-profile scientific agenda, and the decision to send him was driven by the political power of organised science. The mid-century revival of Arctic voyaging can be understood only by shifting the focus from ice and death in the Arctic to policy decisions made in London.

Magnetic science dominated polar exploration after 1836. In the case of the Antarctic the scientists had to admit this, because there was no geographical consideration that could possibly justify a large expedition. In the Arctic the old obsession with the North West Passage could be revived as a suitable cover story, but the men who mattered, the men who secured Franklin's expedition, were scientists, not geographers. Even Beaufort was more concerned with magnetic variation than polar navigation.

Magnetic science settled the size, character, timetable and agenda of Franklin's expedition because observations taken at or near the magnetic pole had become a scientific obsession. The Franklin expedition built observatories on Beechey Island and at Cape Felix, while Sabine's anxiety to recover the data outlived any hope that the men might be alive. Beyond the specific value of being obtained close to the magnetic North Pole the Arctic measurements were intended to be combined with others from around the globe to pave the way for a general theory of terrestrial magnetism. Franklin is invariably omitted from the list of British scientists inspired by the writings of Alexander von Humboldt, the greatest scientist of the age, but this is a serious mistake. Franklin was at the heart of the magnetic crusade and his magnetic credentials secured his final command. Like Ross in Antarctica, Franklin would combine naval command with the direction of scientific observations that furthered Edward Sabine's agenda.

Sabine's triumph

Shortly after Franklin sailed, Sabine's magnetic empire reached its zenith. The BAAS Magnetic Committee met at Cambridge and, as Sabine intended, recommended that the observatories in Britain and the colonies should be kept open for three more years, 'unless in the mean time arrangements can be made for [their] permanent establishment'. As president of the 1845 meeting of the British Association, Herschel declared his support for Sabine's observatories, despite his private concern that data gathering had overwhelmed analysis and theory.[1] They remained in commission for another term.

Sabine also persuaded his fellow scientists to call for additional staff at Woolwich, to reduce the data to order, and for further magnetic survey work 'in regions not hitherto surveyed'.[2] These were put to Prime Minister Peel in a joint Royal Society–British Association request and accepted on 25 June 1845. Franklin had sailed to complete the magnetic chart of the polar regions, but Gauss and Airy believed such missions were unnecessary: any point on earth would produce observations of equal validity for Gauss's theory, and privately Herschel agreed. They were right: Sabine's crusade was built on sand, the scientific and theoretical results were trifling when set against the cost in blood and treasure. Not that he or any of his contemporaries would have admitted their role in the human sacrifice. As for treasure, Ross's expedition to the Antarctic had cost £100,000, but the very fact that this was government money somehow validated the research. Despite his reservations Herschel, indebted to Sabine for research grants, provided the high-level political connections that proved critical in selling the practical value of Sabine's science to the Admiralty and the Board of Ordnance.

Having used the BAAS to extend the life of his magnetic empire,

Sabine settled down to await Franklin's results. By November 1845 the Admiralty was committed to continuing the Hobart Observatory.[3] A survey in Hudson's Bay had been arranged with Beaufort to complement the Franklin voyage: 'I need not urge to you, that the [magnetic] charts on which I am engaged have been and are considered as a public service rendered under the Admiralty.'[4] Elected foreign secretary of the Royal Society in May 1845, Sabine's pluralist approach was paying dividends.[5] The following year the BAAS met at Southampton to lecture invited Norwegian and Swedish scientists on the need to establish 'a magnetic and meteorological observatory in Finnmarken, as a station where the Phenomena of these sciences could be most advantageously studied'.[6] This would complement British research.

Unable to escape the magnetic pull of ice and science Owen Stanley, who had turned down the post of magnetic officer on Franklin's mission, was dispatched to the South Pacific in early 1846. Commanding HMS *Rattlesnake* he was ordered to survey the coast of New Guinea and if necessary rendezvous with Franklin in the Bering Straits, 'as it is contemplated to accomplish the object of a north-west passage over land, if not possible by water.'[7] Stanley remained in the tropics until 1850, when Beaufort ordered him to come home across the Pacific, conducting a series of magnetic observations for Sabine.[8] He died before he could begin this voyage.

By mid-1846 Sabine could anticipate publishing the results of the Ross expedition along with those sent in by Beaufort's surveying ships, including Francis Blackwood's *Fly*, 'and by the expedition under Sir John Franklin. All these observations are made on one general scheme and for a definite purpose, that of making magnetic maps of the whole globe corresponding to a particular epoch.' Such success led Herschel to recommend Sabine for the Royal Society Royal Gold Medal, having completed the first stage in the creation of a practical magnetic science.[9] In turn Sabine relied on Beaufort to secure government funds for publication as the cost would be beyond the means of any learned society.[10] Lord Minto was primed to act in the House of Lords.[11] Moreover, as if he were not satisfied with one global empire of assembled data, Sabine was trying to build another, studying tides and ocean currents.[12]

Rossbank and the imperial mission

The naval magnetic observatory at Rossbank endured after Franklin's recall. The replacement officer who arrived in 1844 was Francis Simpkinson, the son of Jane's sister and another protégé from the 'Celestial *Rainbow*'.[13] Franklin insisted that any staff must be gentlemen, and therefore officers. He did not approve of the Artillery habit of using sergeants.[14] The observatory continued under Admiralty authority until 1852, when it was transferred to the colony. Predictably Lieutenant-Governor Denison closed it eighteen months later, on the last day of 1854.

Sabine used data from Hobart and the Cape to produce a magnetic chart of the Southern Ocean. This was a matter of immediate utility for ships making the long passage to Australasia, and became ever more important when iron steamships like the SS *Great Britain* supplanted wooden sailing ships in the Roaring Forties. This was the type of practical success that had been turned to account when the British Association asked the government to sustain the imperial observatories in 1845. Sabine also exploited Ross's location of the magnetic South Pole, a small triumph for the empirical emphasis in British science. In addition data from Rossbank contributed to the dawning realisation that magnetism had both terrestrial and cosmic origins, a question that had exercised Franklin since the early 1820s.

The completion of Ross's expedition closed the heroic phase of work in the southern hemisphere; henceforth only the steady production of magnetic data at the Hobart observatory would remind the world of the other pole. Although desperate to return to the magnetic north, Sabine did not put all his faith in a naval expedition. Long before Ross could return to the magnetic pole he dispatched a mission to Canada. In 1840 Captain John Lefroy RA set up a magnetic observatory in Toronto which would produce a new series of readings in the high latitudes. Sabine persuaded Herschel to produce a public call for additional magnetic research because it was 'eminently practical' and it would be discreditable to allow other nations to take the lead in this research.[15] Herschel's *Quarterly Review* essay of 1840 pointed to the need for further work in North America, 'the deficiency of trustworthy magnetic observations in all that vast region being lamentable'.[16] This carefully targeted paper was followed up by the president of the Royal Society, the Marquis of Northampton, who begged the Treasury to provide funds. The approach succeeded, securing a grant of £910 for an overland mission into the Canadian north-west in 1843.

The mission, led by Lefroy, was designed to confirm existing data, much of it from the two Franklin expeditions, notably that the point of maximum total magnetic intensity was not coincident with Ross's magnetic pole but well to the south of it.[17] Delighted with Lefroy's results, all Sabine needed were Franklin's latest observations, but here he would be disappointed.[18] Realising the continuing importance of territorial possession in Arctic exploration, he repaid the Hudson's Bay Company for transporting and housing his expedition by recalculating the location of the magnetic North Pole, figures that remained the best guide to the approximate position of the pole for many years.[19]

Although successful, the Lefroy expedition only emphasised the value of naval missions for magnetic science. Not only could they get far closer to the magnetic pole, they also provided a better method of transporting heavy, delicate equipment to key locations. Several of Lefroy's instruments were literally shaken to pieces during overland transport: little wonder when his two dip circles alone weighed twenty-seven and thirty-eight pounds in their travelling cases.

Magnetic observations were the principal object of the Antarctic expedition, reversing the relationship between discovery and observation on the earlier polar missions. Although the voyage had been a resounding success, Ross did not make a complete magnetic survey of the Southern Ocean. Sabine was aware of the problem by 1842, working with Beaufort to fill in the gap. Sabine instructed Lieutenant Clark RA, director of the Cape Town observatory, to complete the project. This was possible because the latest instruments made observations aboard ship nearly as accurate as those taken ashore.[20] In June 1844 Sabine was ready, using the Physics Committee of the Royal Society to make his case at the Admiralty. The voyage was expressly limited to conducting magnetic experiments over approximately one quarter of the Southern Ocean.

Following Admiralty orders the commander-in-chief at the Cape, Admiral Sir Josceline Percy, hired the new 360-ton barque *Pagoda* while Beaufort and Ross selected Lieutenant T. E. L. Moore, an experienced observer from Crozier's *Terror*, to command her.[21] Moore reached Cape Town in January 1845, where *Pagoda* was ready, manned by thirty-four petty officers and men drawn from Percy's flagship. The voyage took in western Australia and Mauritius before paying off at the Cape in July. Linked observations in Singapore and India were arranged.[22] Moore would be elected FRS in June 1854 for his 'skill and sense in making magnetic observations at sea', but by then he had made further contributions to marine science.[23]

Sabine's empire

While Sabine's fixed observatories lacked the drama of a naval expedition, they produced extensive quantities of data for his empire of numbers. Relying on his influence with the Master General of the Ordnance (a senior army officer), Sabine created a bureaucratic power base at Woolwich with unrivalled data-processing capabilities. When the Royal Society rejected the offer of King George III's old Kew observatory, Sabine persuaded the British Association to take it. He turned it into a permanent base for magnetic work in 1846, an 'earthly tabernacle of Humboldtian science'. His empire was complete. Sabine had exploited the goodwill of his scientific colleagues to an almost unimaginable extent. With Kew he had two separate reporting processes, and could use this administrative fact to ensure neither the army nor the scientists would close his project. Magnetism was Sabine's subject, and he did not care what anyone else said, however eminent. This science defined the British Association world view; an elite leadership used the evidence provided by willing observational labourers to secure government funding. This was Sabine's triumph because he and he alone made magnetic science into a career. 'From 1839 Sabine exploited the Royal Society as much as the British Association to superintend and maintain what in reality had become his private magnetic empire.'[24]

The twin poles of this empire were the increasing spread of observation and the development of observing equipment and potential results. By 1838 Humphrey Lloyd had worked out how to use three magnetometers in a small confined space without mutual interference. Consequently the colonial observatories were significantly smaller than the typical European station, while naval and overland expeditions could conduct a variety of readings. Fixed and portable observatories sent out in the 1840s were all equipped with instruments of Lloyd's design.[25]

However, Sabine's scheme did not meet with universal approval. Fellow 'military' scientists had no problem with the passion for data collection and neat charts, but those possessing a more elevated post-Humboldtian vision of the objects of science lamented the glaring lack of theoretical development from the data. Both John Herschel and Astronomer Royal George Airy favoured stopping the data gathering to focus on theory, but Sabine's superior lobbying and administrative powers were committed to imperial expansion. This was a global empire of data collection which Sabine kept 'unconnected with hypothesis of any sort'.[26] Given his mathematical limitations it was perhaps as well that Sabine took this view; he was merely another labourer in Humboldt's *Cosmos*. Right or wrong his methods produced the results he sought. These were closely linked to Beaufort's charts and the ability to predict future compass variation that mariners needed. Sabine's promise to produce this 'prodigiously important arm of navigation' kept Beaufort tied to his chariot, 'because we have no time for patient investigations of that nature'.[27] By the end of the decade the Hydrographer required all recorded positions to include magnetic variation.[28] In pursuit of this eminently practical navigational information Sabine secured a major mission to the Arctic, the renewal of his colonial observational empire for another three years and additional staff for data reduction at Woolwich. In 1849 the government awarded the Royal Society an annual grant to support science: Sabine made sure the Committee of Recommendation, which controlled the distribution of the money, was chaired by Murchison, with himself as secretary. In the first year the Kew observatory received £100, one-tenth of the total available. By 1852 the award had gone up to £150.[29] Despite his central role in the genesis of the Franklin expedition and his obsession with the results, Sabine took a back seat for much of the Franklin search. He had other aims, and saw no reason to endanger his agenda by linking it to a failure.

Aftermath

In the 1840s Humboldt opened his last project. The multi-volume work *Cosmos* was a summation of current thinking about the physical world. Following Kant's argument that it should be possible to detach science from theology Humboldt produced science without God. This, the culmination of Humboldt's working life, occupied his last two decades, and he was anxious to complete it before his natural span expired. The first volume appeared in 1845, but hard as he worked Humboldt could not reach the finish line: the fifth and final volume was posthumously assembled from his notes. As he wrote, he circulated proof sheets across the European scientific community, opening new links between different disciplines and prompting key developments in several fields. (Sabine's knowledge of sun spots came from one such exchange.)[30] Well aware that a wider audience awaited his work outside Germany, Humboldt sanctioned Sabine and his wife to translate the book, a task that must have occupied the pair over the winter of 1845–6. The first volume of the translation was published in August 1846, just as Franklin sailed towards the magnetic pole.

Humboldt had given Sabine permission to 'add such notes as he might think desirable, particularly in the branches of science in which he has himself engaged'.[31] The invitation to boost his own agenda must have been hard to resist, but Sabine added relatively little, enlarging a mere eight footnotes in the first volume. A convinced proponent of further observational research, Humboldt had provided perfectly good promotional copy. The 'magnetic crusade' received a magisterial endorsement: it was to Sabine's work that science was 'principally indebted for the knowledge of the variation of the magnetic intensity over the whole surface of the globe, and for their laws so far as we are able to determine them'.[32] Furthermore, even if scientists could not yet determine the ultimate cause of such phenomena they could measure and discern laws. This Humboldtian measure had

recently made the most brilliant progress in the determination of mean numerical values. From Toronto, in Canada, to the Cape of Good Hope and Van
Diemen's Land, and from Paris to Pekin since 1828, the globe has been covered
by magnetic observatories, [from] which every movement or manifestation, regular or irregular, of the Earth's magnetic force is watched by uninterrupted and
simultaneous observation.

When it came to discussing the pursuit of his peculiar favourite among the systems of knowledge, the great philosopher waxed lyrical:

We accompany, in thought, the bold navigators of the Polar Seas; and, amid the
realm of perpetual ice, view with them that volcano of the Antarctic pole, whose
fires are seen from afar, even at the season when no night favours their bright-
ness. The intellectual objects, both of these adventurous voyages, and those
stations of observation recently established in almost every latitude, are not
strange to us; for we can comprehend some of the wonders of terrestrial magnetism, and general views lend an irresistible attraction to the consideration of
those magnetic storms, which embrace the whole circumference of the earth at
the same instant of time.[33]

While both Humboldt and Sabine praised Ross's work in the Antarctic, the mission was ongoing, and the other pole was in view. Franklin was mentioned several times, notably for his work on aurora. Here, in the most prestigious science text of the decade, Sabine answered his critics. Once Humboldt had spoken, George Airy could not question the need for further observational work. The politics of translation was once more at the forefront of Sabine's agenda. He needed to ensure this text reached the British Association and key supporters of science. While Herschel was happy to read the German original, Sabine's empire required an English edition, which he quickly dispatched to colleagues and patrons.[34]

Although soon replaced by a superior translation, Sabine's edition served its purpose and helped secure Humboldt massive sales and laudatory reviews.[35] Writing in the *Edinburgh Review* in 1848 Herschel noted that Humboldt had done much of his best work by suggesting lines of enquiry and stimulating the efforts of others.[36] Herschel had been a disciple, but he was not alone: Sabine, Lloyd,

Ross, Beaufort and Franklin were only the more obvious followers in the field of magnetic science. Humboldt was the last to see the world of earth and life sciences as a whole, and master the details. Under his imperial sway minions scurried across the earth in pursuit of his ideas. In 1852 the Royal Society awarded Humboldt the Copley Gold Medal for his work on geophysics, although the great man was now too old to collect it in person.[37] If Humboldt's legacy was immense, his prestige soon waned. New, more precise scientists raised in the school of Gauss developed grand theories from evolution to electromagnetism that made better use of his data, and overturned his pioneering attempt to create a systematic explanation. In the process Sabine and his science would be replaced.

BOOK THREE

THE POLITICS OF TRAGEDY

9

'Till our provisions get short'

FEW WERE CONCERNED when Franklin had failed to report after a year in the Arctic. He had urged his friends and family not to expect him until his supplies had run out. Instead the Arctic event of 1846 was the publication of Sir John Barrow's second Arctic book, *Voyages of Discovery within the Arctic Regions from the Year 1818 to the Present Time*, another polemic masquerading as a narrative history. Since he had reviewed every significant Arctic text to appear in the interval the task only took six months. The Admiralty purchased three hundred copies for the libraries of all warships, not least because the book stressed the moral and professional advantages of leading men without resort to corporal punishment.[1] He also reopened an old wound with a venomous account of John Ross's proceedings: Barrow had not mellowed with age. He did not live to follow the unfolding tragedy, ceding his place to his son, another John Barrow.[2]

The Admiralty finally began to think about sending a relief mission in late 1846, prompted by Lady Franklin and those two stormy petrels of the Arctic, Sir John Ross and Dr Richard King. Sir John Ross had condemned the design of the Franklin expedition from the outset. Believing the ships were too large and drew too much water, he had promised to rescue Franklin if he had not returned by February 1847. As good as his word, Ross turned up at the Admiralty with a plan, only to be sent away without a hearing. While the public justification for such brusqueness was that it was too soon for such concern, this opinion was not universal.

Within the Admiralty Sir Francis Beaufort was worried; he persuaded the Board to consult Parry, James Ross, Sabine and Richardson. He asked if they had any idea where Franklin might look for a stores depot, or any other useful information. Typically the expedition had set off without making any preparation for rescue or resupply. The Admiralty had not offered such support, and Franklin had not requested it. Beaufort was also interested to know what form a search mission should take if nothing were heard during the year. Their replies were largely harmonious, especially those of Richardson and Parry, who worked together at the Haslar Royal Naval Hospital from December.[3] Far from sharing Beaufort's concern Parry had 'rather been rejoicing <u>not</u> to have heard anything of the Expedition up to this time, as affording a good hope of its success'. As a naval search would require two more ships as well equipped as Franklin's to follow his orders, he preferred offering whalers and Hudson's Bay traders £1,000 for information.[4] James Clark Ross agreed:

It is perfectly absurd to entertain the smallest degree of alarm on their account. We never could expect them to get through without twice wintering – and if they are far advanced on their way & sufficiently near the continent I have no doubt he will endeavour to communicate with the Hudson Bay people early this spring and we may hear of him by the first dispatch boat.

He believed a relief expedition should meet the ships in the Bering Strait in 1849, when their stores would be near exhausted, and stressed his willingness to take command if required.

Although he deferred to the polar experts, Beaufort could not shake off a sense of foreboding:

though I would not let a whisper of anxiety escape from me yet one must perceive that if he be not forthcoming by <u>next</u> winter, some substantive step must be taken in 1848 – and for that step certain measures must be set on foot in 1847.

He agreed with Parry that this meant preparing two ships, either strengthening bomb vessels or building stout shallow-draught steamers. Anxious and fearful, Beaufort begged James Ross to raise the issue, hoping that would prompt the Board to seek his advice.[5] This was hardly proper conduct for a civil servant.

Having digested the opinions of Ross, Parry and Barrow the Board decided there was no cause for alarm, and little prospect of any news from Franklin before September 1847. It would be enough to offer rewards for information to the annual whaling fleet, and the

Hudson's Bay Company. A naval expedition to the Bering Strait could be postponed until 1848.[6] Yet the matter would not rest. Parry, James Ross, Sabine and Richardson were called to discuss John Ross's letter in February 1847. Although Richardson agreed that any concern was premature, he set out three distinct routes that might be followed and offered to lead an overland expedition in 1848 if nothing had been heard in the interval. James Ross advised sending a naval expedition in May 1848, following Franklin's instructions.[7] The Hudson's Bay Company had standing instructions to transmit any intelligence, and stood ready to assist Richardson's projected overland mission.[8] Orders were given to build the necessary boats.

Edward Sabine joined the discussion in March, reminding Parry that Franklin had expressed no wish for relief and that he had three years' supplies. However, if there had been no news by November 'then decisive steps' should be taken to provide succour at both ends of the Passage. As no rendezvous point had been arranged by Franklin, Sabine advised conducting a steam-powered search around Baffin Bay, and especially in the Wellington Channel. He did not mention the expedition's magnetic objectives, surely the vital point to stress when designing a search-and-rescue mission.[9] Reward notices were issued to the whaling fleets in mid-March, but, as one owner observed, they had no idea where to look. Not that anyone else was better informed. Franklin's course was a complete mystery.

Frederick Beechey, a late addition to the Arctic advisory group, put his finger on an intractable problem. If Franklin was stuck in the area north of Back river his men would be 'quite unequal' to a long overland march. Richardson categorically rejected the idea of looking in an area where there was no food, and the Hudson's Bay posts were far from the coast, because 'I do not think that under any circumstances Sir John Franklin would attempt that route.' Indeed:

Were Sir John Franklin thrown upon the North Coast of the continent with his boats and <u>all</u> his crew, I do not think that he would attempt the ascent of any river except the Mackenzie. It is navigable for boats of large draught, without a portage for 1300 miles from the sea or to within 40 miles of Fort Chipewyan, one of the Company's principal depots, and there are 5 other posts in that distance.[10]

Richardson's mistake was to think Franklin would have any choice in the matter, and to ignore the magnetic motives.

Among the first outside the Arctic circle to express concern was Edward Griffiths, master of the *Barretto Junior*. Writing in June 1847 Griffiths focused on basic logistics: Franklin would have no more than thirteen months of supplies left, and men need a great deal of food in the Arctic. Convinced 'the missing ships will be found between Banks's Land and Wollaston Land' he suggested placing fresh supplies at Point Franklin and Point Belcher.[11] Barrow considered the concern somewhat premature, although if nothing had been heard by the autumn he expected the Admiralty would 'no doubt take measures for every possible inquiry to be made into their fate'. He had already been consulted by Lord Auckland, the First Lord of the Admiralty, and agreed with Parry that the first step would be to enter the region and consult any Esquimaux or Indians. Barrow saw no point guessing where the party was; his only fear was that progress through the ice had been hampered by the vessels' screw propellers. The Arctic experts simply ignored the magnetic mission, despite many of them pointing to the region around the magnetic pole.

Richard King resumed his one-man campaign to lead the search, and as usual managed to alienate all the key decision-makers by his arrogance.[12] He mocked Richardson's plan to travel down the Mackenzie, and he was perfectly correct, but his strident advocacy of the Great Fish river only diverted attention from the area. Franklin died the day after King's letter appeared in the *Times*, not far from where King predicted he would be found, although that information did not reach London until a decade later. While Jane was prepared to entertain such ideas, she drew the line at King.[13] Barrow preferred to put up another straw man, producing a letter of January 1845 in which Fitzjames expressed a strong conviction that the Passage lay north of Parry's Island. He argued that Fitzjames would have pressed this opinion on Franklin.[14] He did not say why Franklin would act on ideas he had categorically rejected in July 1845. Despite that, Barrow's delusion would persist long after he had departed the stage, and deflect much of the search effort in the process.

If nothing else King's prompting revived the search question. Parry, Richardson, Sabine, Beechey, Ross and deputy surveyor John Edye were consulted on practical measures. Edye advised two 350-ton merchant vessels be built for Arctic service. They would take seven months to construct and cost at least £11,000.[15] This advice conveniently allowed the subject to be left pending for the next two months. By November 1847 Jane had secured copies of Franklin's orders and Ross advised Lord Auckland to send the storeship HMS *Plover* into the Bering Strait with supplies and orders to search towards the Mackenzie river for a rendezvous with Richardson, who planned to revisit both the Coppermine and the Mackenzie. The Admiralty persuaded the Hudson's Bay Company to release Dr John Rae, their outstanding traveller and cartographer, to accompany the expedition.[16] Although best known as a heroic footslogger and effective map-maker, Rae had recently been trained in magnetic observation by Captain Lefroy at the Toronto observatory.[17]

Richardson knew that Franklin would not return that year from Lancaster Sound, and was still hoping against hope that the expedition had reached the Bering Strait. He sailed for Hudson's Bay the following spring with a full set of overland magnetic instruments provided by Sabine.[18] Richardson and Rae travelled down the Mackenzie river, coasted east and returned by way of the Coppermine. Being at least 400 miles west of the disaster they found nothing. Richardson evinced little enthusiasm for Sabine's magnetic observations, which he left to Rae, but his life-science research was highly significant.[19]

Still recovering from a serious illness Sabine was suddenly called upon to provide comfort: Jane was now deeply concerned. He outlined the three-pronged rescue effort and repeated his view that Franklin might still be trying to complete his mission. The situation was not desperate, the ships were stored until the following July, by which time relief ships would arrive at both ends of the passage.[20] His own concerns were reflected in the fact that when HMS *Plover* sailed for the Bering Strait on New Year's Day 1848 she was commanded by magnetic veteran Lieutenant Moore. *Plover* carried enough food for her own crew and Franklin's people. Before entering the Arctic, Moore would contact the Russians at Petropavlosk, in part because Fitzjames had mentioned returning by way of St Petersburg.[21] The plan was for *Plover* to push north-east, find a winter anchorage and search for the lost travellers. The winter would provide ample opportunity for magnetic observations. Moore would link up with one of Beaufort's favourite surveyors, Captain Henry Kellett of HMS *Herald*. In March 1848 Kellett was ordered to give up his survey of the coast of California to look for Franklin. While this would be 'vexatious', Beaufort trusted Kellett would not 'grumble': 'any effort on behalf of poor Franklin, and his anxious friends here no one with any heart can grudge. Besides there is no one on that station who has the resources of mind and the physical activity you have.'[22] *Plover* reached the Siberian coast in late 1848 and moved across to Kotzebue Sound in July 1849 to rendezvous with *Herald*. After working north-east to Wainwright Inlet and taking up a secure winter berth Moore dispatched Lieutenant Pullen with a boat party towards the Mackenzie river delta, hoping to rendezvous with Richardson or Franklin.

In three successive Arctic seasons Kellet pushed through the Bering Strait, making a significant addition to knowledge of the area, including the Russian coast of Siberia. He found no trace of the lost expedition. He was also instructed to settle the question of what lay to the north, a continent or an open sea. Beaufort, like Barrow, favoured a continent, but the answer turned out to be a mass of ice. Beaufort claimed the search was 'for the satisfaction of those most interested as well as for the consistency and credit of the country',[23] but he took care to fit in some serious surveying and magnetic work. There was no sense in wasting a chance to chart in Russian waters – no one expected war would be long delayed.[24]

The Ross expedition, 1848–9

Understandably such strategic considerations did not feature in the public debate. In November *Blackwood's Edinburgh Magazine* rounded on those who doubted the purpose of further Arctic effort in magisterial fashion: 'The evident design of Providence in placing difficulties before man is to sharpen his faculties for their mastery.'[25] When the autumn of 1847 came and went without a scrap of news, the Admiralty had no option but to launch the last, and most costly, of their three search missions – following Franklin into Lancaster Sound in the summer of 1848. Beaufort urged James Ross to take command, declaring that 'to no other person would the country be satisfied to delegate that exploit', and hinting that Ross would not be able to live with himself if he didn't go. Despite the promise to his family and the alcohol problems that had precluded his taking the 1845 mission Ross accepted. Many felt that, at forty-seven, he had lost some of his energy and drive. Even so, the Board accepted his offer without hesitation.

Ross and Beaufort agreed that the best hope of finding Franklin lay in following his orders. The key to success would be an extra weapon. Franklin planned to travel by sea: Ross would extend his search with sledges. Beaufort left the details of the mission to be settled privately between Ross and Lord Auckland, First Lord of the Admiralty.[26] Once the decision had been taken the Admiralty moved quickly. John Edye was directed to find two 400–450-ton sailing ships (there were no suitable warships in hand), ready to sail at the end of April.[27] Although his mission was to follow in Franklin's tracks, Ross would not hear of using steamships. This would prove to be a serious error. Suitable ships were purchased, reinforced and fitted with iron-plated bows, internal heating systems and a removable winter roof. HMS *Enterprise* and HMS *Investigator* would be the first and the last naval vessels to search for Sir John. In lieu of steamships Ross demanded two steam launches, though he made little use of them.[28] The ships' stores included significant quantities of pemmican, the obvious preparation for sledging.[29] Ross's lightweight sledges, based on Inuit designs, would be used by all future British expeditions.

In the spring Richard King revived his argument, but the Admiralty ignored him. Yet King's constant, irritating refrain would open a very different aspect of the search. Having deferred to the experts thus far Jane Franklin insisted on being heard. At an interview with Lord Auckland she reminded him that it was her husband they were looking for, an approach that could hardly fail. From that moment she left no avenue unexplored, and valued results over reputations. Although she shared the almost universal dislike of King, she took his ideas seriously, hoping the Hudson's Bay Company would search the area – however unlikely it seemed.[30] Nor did she restrict her interests to overland searches, offering a £1,000 reward for any useful information the whalers might provide.[31] Concerned that the Admiralty notice had missed the sailing of the annual Dundee whaling fleet she asked Ross to distribute her notice at sea. She asked Beaufort, a friend of thirty years and her most important ally, to make sure Lord Auckland knew what had been done, without taking up any more of his time.[32]

Meanwhile Auckland acknowledged the scientific purpose of the Franklin expedition when he linked the search mission with the preparation of an *Admiralty Manual of Scientific Enquiry*. This project had been in gestation since the time he called on John Herschel at the Cape in 1836.[33] Herschel's *Admiralty Manual* provided naval officers with a handy compendium of current thinking on the observational sciences, and guidance on how to record useful information.

Ross's largely self-penned orders were issued on 9 May 1848. He would examine the shores of Lancaster Sound, Barrow Strait and Wellington Channel, if they could be reached that season. To search the openings between Cape Clarence and Cape Walker he would split the expedition, *Investigator* examining the west coast of the Boothia Felix isthmus and Prince Regent Inlet while *Enterprise* was expected to reach Melville Island and survey Banks Land as far as Cape Parry or Cape Bathurst on the American mainland. Another party would attempt to link up with Sir John Richardson's overland expedition on Victoria Land or Wollaston Land.[34] Ross's plans reflected his experience sailing with Parry in 1820, but the Arctic would prove a fickle field for human endeavour. Less fortunate than Parry, luckiest of the polar navigators, his plans proved hopelessly optimistic.

After an inspection by Lord Auckland and Captain Milne, the Naval Lord responsible for stores, the ships sailed on 12 May. Ross reached Franklin's last known location, the Whale Fish Islands off the west coast of Greenland on 22 June, only to discover that the expedition had arrived in an unusually severe year. Unable to cross ice-choked Baffin Bay, Ross surveyed the islands and took magnetic readings before coasting north. Ross finally crossed to the shore of Baffin Island in late August. Three weeks later he was fortunate to secure the ships in Port Leopold, just as the sea began to ice over. *Enterprise* and *Investigator* were 150 miles short of Cape Walker, the point where they had planned to begin the search. Those miles would matter. After using his sledges to stock an advanced base, Ross had the ships housed over for the winter and the inevitable magnetic observatory was built. Back in London Sir John Barrow died on 23 November: it was the end of an era.[35]

The following May, Ross set off with Lieutenant Francis McClintock, twelve men and two sledges for the Wellington Channel. Realising the way was choked with thick ice he altered course south into Peel Sound. Ross led the party, going ahead to select the route, map the area and direct McClintock, who commanded the sledges. It soon became clear that Ross had not packed enough food for men working at the outer limits of human endurance in appalling conditions. After twenty-one days half their rations had been used. Ross stopped at a headland he named Cape Coulman in honour of his wife. Here the men built a large cairn and McClintock conducted magnetic surveys; Ross marched on alone to the next headland, where he secured a commanding view south. He knew the sledge party could not go on, but his single-minded determination to find his friend made him go the extra day. He returned without finding a scrap of evidence. Had Franklin left a marker the greatest mystery of the nineteenth century would have been solved at the first attempt, saving many lives, six ships and a king's ransom. Ross had stopped a hundred miles short of the magnetic pole and less than two hundred miles from the locus of the Franklin disaster. But such distances were meaningless numbers to exhausted, scorbutic sledge crew without the food to go on.

The following day, 6 June, Ross returned and the party headed for the ship. Although he had not found a trace of Franklin, no one would come as close for another decade. In addition Ross had charted a significant addition to the map of the Arctic, with characteristic precision. Before heading back Ross left directions to the nearest relief supplies in a prominent cairn: the lack of such markers persuaded him that Franklin had not come this way. It took fifteen days to reach the ship; every man of the party was in poor shape, apart from McClintock. In their absence other parties had set up markers and checked the depot at Fury Beach. Ross prepared a supply depot at Port Leopold comprising a steam launch, food and stores; although ostensibly created for Franklin, Ross feared he would need it if the ice conditions did not improve. His forebodings proved exaggerated, but only slightly.

Ross's men were in poor health. Four died and many more were hospitalised, including the scurvy-ravaged sledge party. Selected without medical examination, their condition had not been helped by poor food: the canned goods were appalling, while incompetent preparation robbed the lemon juice of any anti-scorbutic properties. The fatal mistake had been made by the Naval Victualling Yard at Haslar, overwhelmed by the demands of Irish famine relief. Health problems only compounded another grim year for ice navigation in Lancaster Sound. The ships finally escaped Port Leopold on 29 August and once in the main channel Ross realised he had no hope of working to westward – his way was blocked by multi-year ice. Melville Island and the Wellington Channel were inaccessible. On 1 September the ships were frozen into the pack ice, which was drifting east at eight to ten miles a day. Only on the 20th, close by Possession Bay, were the ships released, taking another five days to work clear. They had been carried in the ice for 250 miles. Ross had no choice but to return home. It was too late to find a winter harbour; any suitable inlets were already frozen solid and in any event the poor health of his crew made a second winter unthinkable. By mid-October the ships had left the Arctic Circle. Ross disembarked at Scarborough, taking the train to London to brief the Admiralty on 5 November. The ships paid off at Woolwich on the 26th.

Disappointed hopes prompted unjustified criticism. Ross's inability to follow orders became a matter of censure, while his returning after only one winter led Jane to conclude that he was irresolute. The Board minutes reveal a desire to seek explanations and apportion blame, but the bland official letter sent five days later required nothing more from Ross.[36] Embittered by public criticism, Ross resolved not to try again. The Admiralty gave him an annual good-service pension of £150, but that was the end of their generosity. He had not solved their very public problem, and his voyaging days were done.[37]

Ross had come so close to success because he knew that Franklin was heading for the magnetic pole. Yet the central role of magnetic science in the Franklin expedition was allowed to pass without comment and the search soon became fixated on the Passage. Consequently Ross's expedition was followed by a decade of futile searches, each more distant from the disaster than the one before until the mystery was solved by accident. It is striking how quickly the purpose of Franklin's mission was forgotten. From the Banksian beginnings through the Humboldtian heyday Arctic voyages had been driven by magnetic science. We now know that Franklin's men built magnetic observatories at Beechey Island, and at Cape Felix. They may have visited the magnetic pole, and they died in pursuit of scientific data, not the mythic North West Passage. Ross knew that.

Uninterested in such matters, Jane was not inclined to be generous. She arrived in London in November 1849 'very indignant at the return of Ross, and little inclined to listen to the real merits of the case'.[38] While Beaufort managed to improve relations – the three of them dined together in January – she had rejected Ross. Instead she clung ever closer to Beaufort, a decision that spoke eloquently of her desire to hear good news, or at least the most positive interpretation of events, rather than realistic reports from the ice. It marked a major turning point in her campaign, one that coincided with the end of any rational hope that Franklin had survived. Turning to deskbound polar innocent Beaufort for counsel helped her to avoid the grim realities of life and death in the Arctic, realities she would never fully acknowledge.

Ending the search

Long before Ross returned the Admiralty was anxious to close down the search. Having acted on a generous scale in 1848 by sending three interlocking search missions, Lord Auckland's Board was unwilling to countenance further expense. These were hard times: fear of a war with France had put the naval estimates under severe pressure, the Treasury was unsympathetic and old John Barrow, master of the Admiralty agenda, was gone. In early 1849 his son responded to depressing reports from Ross by suggesting that supplies and fresh orders be sent to Baffin Bay. Lord Auckland was decidedly against further expenditure, although he was prepared to consult the Arctic experts or 'Friends of Sir John Franklin' in private. Those friends were Beaufort, Parry, Beechey, Belcher, Back, deputy hydrographer Captain John Washington and Scoresby: Edward Sabine was added only later, although the initial omission was probably unintentional. This process was derailed when Auckland died suddenly over the Christmas holiday. He was replaced by former Chancellor of the Exchequer Sir Francis Baring.

When the Board assembled on 12 January, the senior members were not sympathetic. First Naval Lord Admiral Sir James Dundas observed:

I am decidedly of opinion that no new Expedition or ship should be sent to the Polar Seas & that the late Lord Auckland often told me – he should object to send. Sir Jas Ross's orders were clear & decided – I trust that he will be left to them & his own judgement.[39]

Second Naval Lord Captain Berkeley found it painful to declare against a further expedition, but did so anyway. The most outspoken opponent of any fresh effort was William Cowper MP, the 'financial' Lord of Admiralty.[40] 'I consider that we did enough in sending out the extensive and costly expedition of last year, & we are not called upon to send another'. He reminded colleagues of Ross's opinion that if there was no news by the autumn of 1849 the case would be hopeless: 'I think the advantages likely to accrue from sending another vessel not commensurate with the expense to the country & the risk to which the crew will be exposed.'[41] This was wise, and even statesman-like, but he reckoned without 'Franklin's Friends'. Beaufort and young Barrow assembled a committee. Scoresby, Sabine, Parry, Beechey, Back and Belcher produced eighteen recommendations, including sending a supply ship, which Parry submitted. As a junior civil servant Barrow did not sign the report.

The intervention of the 'Friends' persuaded the Board to send out a supply ship; sentiment overrode sense, sympathy outweighed

Treasury parsimony. The appeal succeeded because Franklin was universally loved and admired. He was the reason men kept on searching, and his wife made sure they never forgot him. Consequently the supply ship would not be left out over the winter. Fourth Naval Lord Milne took a more practical view. While he urged the Board to send supplies, Ross's ships were

to return home in the autumn of 1850, as it must be obvious, that unless the ships have met with Sir J. Franklin's expedition either before this time, or during this summer, there can be little hope of their falling in with our unfortunate countrymen whose store of provisions must have been expended in 1848.[42]

Milne tried to establish that this was the last mission, but his sound judgement would be overwhelmed by Lady Jane's emotional appeal, together with the subtler efforts of Sir Francis Beaufort and John Barrow Jr. The conservative *Morning Herald* helped set the mood, declaring that no one would blame the government for the cost of any rescue attempts, even if the missing expedition returned without their aid.[43] The Admiralty filed the article with a paper from the lost expedition, dated 30 June 1845, recently recovered at sea. HM supply ship *North Star* sailed in May 1849, failed to find Ross, wintered in north-west Greenland and left a large depot at Navy Board Inlet in 1850.[44]

The Admiralty was beginning to weaken and Jane, who had friends inside the building, was quick to exploit the opportunity. Anxious to mount the largest possible effort in what she believed would be the last year in which the party could be saved she suggested that a notice to whalers be sent to the American ports, which dispatched some 600 vessels a year into northern waters. She was also seeking assistance from Sir Roderick Murchison's friend Baron Brunnow, the Russian ambassador. Not only was the exclusion of foreign influence from the region a central if unspoken agenda point of the Arctic mission, but Anglo-Russian relations were bad, and those with the United States were no better. Four days later an Admiralty reward notice offering £20,000 for information leading to the recovery of the ships was printed. With the Admiralty conceding on all fronts Jane turned up the heat. Even radical MPs Richard Cobden and Joseph Hume agreed that more should be done. Her conservative spokesman Sir Thomas Acland raised the question of a reward in the House of Commons. Jane insisted the original reward had been ill considered because it ignored the safety of the men and therefore excluded claims from land-based searchers such as Dr Richardson or the Hudson's Bay travellers.[45] Her point was accepted: a revised notice offered rewards of £10,000 each for the men and the ships, or £20,000 for the entire expedition. In the event Jane's revised reward notice would enable the Admiralty to end the search.[46]

On a visit to Scottish whaling ports Jane discovered that thirty-nine British ships had been in Greenland waters and the Davis Strait in 1848, and as it was too late to influence those already on station in 1849 she wanted another £5,000 reward to persuade others to act. Trying to draw some diplomatic capital from the American president's friendly response to Jane's eloquent appeal Foreign Secretary Palmerston claimed that 'such expeditions are among the most honourable which maritime countries could undertake, and brought upon their originators a degree of glory which could never be achieved by the mere triumph of conquest.'[47]

Scientists

By the time Ross returned in November 1849, British science was already hurrying to distance itself from the inevitable catastrophe. Jane's approach to the Royal Society elicited only a feeble response; Darwin's was typical, when he declared in early 1848: 'I believe old sinner Sir J. Barrow has been at the bottom of all the money wasted over the naval expeditions . . . The country has paid dear for Sir John's hobbyhorse . . . geography is . . . now the chief object'.[48] The scientists who had exploited his geriatric enthusiasm to push their mission into the Arctic would exploit the fact that he would soon be dead to turn him into a scapegoat. For all his faults John Barrow did not deserve that. And yet the scientific impulse remained strong, and its objects unchanged. Sabine supplied Ross's search mission with the correct equipment, trained four officers in magnetic observations and ensured they had duplicate copies of his instructions.[49] Every expedition that went to search for Franklin conducted magnetic observations, their officers suitably equipped and trained by Sabine and his staff to master the arcane, almost religious rituals that had taken over his life. From the start Sabine had intended the Franklin mission to advance his agenda, and his aims did not change when Franklin failed to reappear. Desperate to recover Franklin's magnetic records he ensured that those who searched for Franklin carried on the magnetic work. The object of his endeavour remained a predictive system of magnetic variation as an aid to navigation. In early 1849 he persuaded Beaufort to recover Ross's Antarctic records from his wife, to develop the necessary information for a new South Pacific chart.[50] For all the prominence of magnetic science in the search Sabine remained in the background. He ceded leadership of the search agenda to Murchison, who was a more adept operator and not in public employ. Murchison's campaign relied heavily on the fact that the key political players behind the initial dispatch of the Franklin expedition and the agitators for the search missions were all members of the British Association. As the autumn of 1849 wore on and hope began to fade, Murchison asked Sabine, 'What does James Ross really think of the possibility of saving poor Franklin?'[51] Both men knew Ross would say, 'None whatsoever,' but they pressed on anyway. Together they would sustain the Franklin search for another decade, in the interests of science.

Persuading the public

Jane, one of the few who had not given up hope, would use every trick in the book to keep that hope alive in the hearts of others. She sent the Admiralty an American offer, which was politely declined, but when the pensions of the expedition officers were discussed Admiral Dundas minuted: 'I will not give Franklin & his party up for another year'. Even so, he was preparing for the worst, promoting officers to ensure their dependants received a higher pension.[52] Whaler, scientist and now man of the cloth, the Reverend William Scoresby also continued to hope. Faith and practical experience led him to believe an Esquimaux rumour that the ships were in Prince Regent Inlet, presumably having found alternative sources of food to tide them over. His opinions were a comfort for Jane.[53] She took up new Arctic advisers whenever old ones brought her unpalatable news.

Richardson had returned in November and been widely praised. Sabine soon published Rae's magnetic observations.[54] While Ross's return proved less happy, he too had made significant additions to the knowledge of the region, recording the geography of much of the east coast of Peel Sound. McClintock's geological work was soon incorporated into the map and an eighteen-month series of meteorological and magnetic observations was digested. In the longer term Ross passed his sledging expertise to McClintock, providing the basis for all future search expeditions. Yet it would be an understatement to say that the voyage had been a disappointment. Ross had set out with the aim of finding his friend, the Admiralty had been anxious to be seen to do the right thing and Lady Franklin had invested all her hopes in Ross's expertise. Having arrived in a 'bad' year there was nothing more Ross could have done.

The Times was persuaded that enough was enough: 'With the map of the Arctic regions lying spread before us, we ask ourselves in vain what single object worthy of the venture could by any contingency be gained by any further voyage of discovery in this direction?' The Arctic could never 'be turned to any practical account' and should therefore be given up, 'until some vast change shall occur in the temperature and meteorological arrangements of the globe . . . All the wonders of modern civilisation are palsied in the presence of the eternal ice and snow.' Declaring the Suez and Panama routes were the best way to the Pacific, *The Times* saw no scientific reason for further effort.[55] After reading Ross's dispatches the newspaper repeated the message: 'We trust that any government will for the future discountenance such mad attempts, which are productive only of a great waste of money, and what is of far more importance, of much and useless sacrifice of valuable lives . . . let us hear no more of Arctic expeditions.' The money would have been better spent building a Panama Canal.[56] This assertion was not so disinterested as might at first appear. Although Humboldt had suggested the idea three decades earlier, a canal through Panama had recently become a live subject. British warships were surveying the Pacific coast of Latin America for a suitable terminus and British companies were promoting the idea. No one was looking for an Arctic route.[57]

Despite *The Times*, and in defiance of common sense, Beaufort clung to his delusion that Franklin, his men and one of his ships had survived. He recommended that *Enterprise* and *Investigator* be refitted and sent to the Bering Strait, despite the fact that *Herald* and *Plover* had already searched the area. He hoped that Franklin had pushed through the Passage. Once again Cowper dissented and Milne reminded the Board that Franklin's supplies had run out in July 1848. Yet the Board deferred to the emotional guesswork of an old man unable to separate public office from personal feelings. Although the situation was hopeless, the Admiralty seemed strangely impotent, quite unable to resist the siren call for another rescue mission. Milne, for one, thought Beaufort's proposal 'one of <u>Discovery</u> and not of assistance to those we are so anxious to aid'.[58] The Arctic experts were divided on the best route, some accepting Beaufort's Bering Strait idea, others favouring a return to Baffin Bay. True to form, Parry stressed the need to send small steamers. Cowper, eventually accepting that a new mission was inevitable, favoured George Back's scheme to travel up the Mackenzie and then search east and west along the coast, probably because it would be cheaper than a naval mission.[59] In similar vein *The Times* gave its reluctant blessing to the new mission but warned against any diversion into exploration and declared that this must be the last effort.[60]

Having secured a significant victory over common sense, Beaufort reinforced his triumph by advising the Board to consult the Council of the Royal Society, which contained many of his friends and allies. He also reminded the Board that their actions were subject to public scrutiny: the Franklin search had become 'the great object on which the eyes of all England and indeed of all the world are now intimately fixed'.[61] This was the line that Jane advocated. Two days later, with an air of resignation, the Board accepted his recommendation for yet another search mission through Baffin Bay. Two naval expeditions were planned, from east and west. After a decent interval Sir Robert Inglis MP moved in the House of Commons for copies of correspondence about renewing the search. While he urged the need for steamships, and stressed that Britain was obliged to search for her lost sons, his real object was to elicit a public statement. In reply Sir Francis Baring came close to confessing that Admiralty policy was being driven by an unholy alliance of expert advice and public opinion:

He [Baring] thought it right to state that in an expedition of this nature the pecuniary cost would not be a consideration in the slightest degree. Of course the time might come when they would no longer have a right to risk the lives of men in such a search. That had been to him a subject of consideration; but from the opinion of those who were best able to form an opinion, he trusted there still was such a hope as justified the government in taking every measure which they fairly and properly could take, to render assistance if possible – at any rate, to ascertain the fate of their unfortunate fellow-countrymen. It was not for the purpose of nautical science, or for the extension of geographical knowledge, the importance of which he hoped he did not underrate, but solely for the purpose of saving life, that this expedition was about to be undertaken.[62]

This was not strictly true. Sabine and Beaufort had already ensured that both expeditions would carry the usual magnetic instruments and instructions. While Sabine claimed his observations were 'framed on the smallest scale as there appears an indisposition at present to make scientific observations a prominent feature', and would only be made by one ship on each expedition, this was a temporary setback. Pushing at an open door, he warned Beaufort that if he wanted a variation chart of the Pacific he would need well-equipped magnetic observers in both ships. In truth Sabine wanted a set of readings from Cape Horn to the Bering Strait.[63] Captain Collinson, commanding the Pacific expedition with Robert McClure, was persuaded 'of the important nature of the observations you allude to', and told Sabine that he could 'rest assured they shall have all the attention it is in my power to afford them'.[64] This was hardly surprising; Collinson specialised in hydrographic work.[65] Despite explicit orders that the expedition was 'not for the purposes of geographical or scientific research', both of Collinson's ships carried magnetic equipment along with Sabine's freshly prepared printed instructions.[66] Beaufort and Sabine gave their wholehearted support to a renewed search effort because it served their navigational and scientific agendas. They were quick to exploit the opportunity that emerged when the Admiralty bent before Jane Franklin's brilliant public-relations campaign because they were key members of her campaign team.

At the end of January 1850 Jane was mobilising widespread political support, securing Liberal and Conservative, English and Irish
MPs to her cause. The most prominent would be Benjamin Disraeli,
Conservative leader in the House of Commons. After complaining
about the impact Ross's 'premature return' was having on the
prospect of further searches she urged him to support the call for
further action on a cross-party basis. Clearly her opinion of Disraeli
had changed during the twenty years since their first meeting in
Corfu.[67]

While Jane relied on Beaufort for Admiralty intelligence, she did
not confide in him.[68] Her schemes began to take on an alarming
shape when the Americans became involved. As she anticipated, an
appeal to 'Cousin Jonathan' (the dismissive diminutive of 'John Bull'
used to describe Americans) combined with widespread public interest made it impossible for the Admiralty to follow their sensible,
logical and economical inclinations. As Beaufort explained, 'What
we are to do is now the question, for we must not be behind the feeling manifested throughout our own country or suffer ourselves to be
eclipsed by the humane enthusiasm in America.'[69] Although the
Admiralty agreed to a new search, Charles Darwin believed it was
too late, referring to his fellow barnacle collector as 'the late
Goodsir, being with Sir J. Franklin'.[70] The humble barnacle would
play a critical role in the evolution of his theory.[71]

The better to conduct her public campaign Jane moved to 33
Spring Gardens, next to the Admiralty building. Her efforts inspired
a remarkable series of new search expeditions, expeditions exploited
by many different interest groups. No sooner had Beaufort secured
his Bering Strait mission than he returned to press for a four-ship
steam-powered search of the Lancaster Sound area. Ross's expedition had demonstrated that steam was essential. If they found
nothing at Melville Island and Banks Land the ships could search
Wellington Channel and Jones Sound. The last had been added to
the search after a Stromness resident, John Rae's brother-in-law,
belatedly reported a conversation in which Franklin had mentioned
the route. Beaufort was sceptical, but thought it best to check. The
whole mission would be quick, 'and might be the means of really
satisfying the public' as to where Franklin had gone. Parry was

delighted with the 'bold, comprehensive and decisive plan', and praised the use of steam. Richardson declared it would be 'the last effort.'[72]

The Admiralty accepted the plan for a four-ship expedition to Lancaster Sound.[73] The 400-ton sailing brigs *Assistance* and *Resolute* were accompanied by two cattle boats, the 350-ton, 60-horsepower screw steamers *Intrepid* and *Pioneer*. Following an approach by Aberdeen-based whaler captain William Penny, which Jane had passed on, the Admiralty accepted Beaufort's argument that hiring Penny 'would sensibly satisfy Lady Franklin', clearly already a matter of considerable moment. They commissioned two 150-ton sailing brigs for Penny's expedition: *Lady Franklin* and *Sophia*, the latter to be commanded by Alexander Stewart.[74] Jane's own fund-raising supported Captain Charles Forsyth in the 80-ton schooner *Prince Albert*. The Admiralty put a separate budget head for the Arctic expedition at £21,131 in the 1851 estimates, to make sure the legislators understood the cost of their decisions.[75] Not only was the private expedition funded by American ship-owner Henry Grinnell adopted by the US navy, which provided the brigs *Advance* and *Rescue* to examine the Wellington Channel, but John Ross persuaded his old sponsor Felix Booth to fund a steam yacht to search Barrow Strait. After Booth's sudden death the Hudson's Bay Company picked up the bill. Beaufort had always appreciated the eccentric but well-intentioned and capable Ross, and with Barrow out of the way persuaded the Board to support him.

The main expedition would be led by Captain Horatio Thomas Austin, who came highly recommended by Parry.[76] Parry's judgement proved to be sound; Austin was a skilful and humane leader, but his party found little more than scraps since they were looking in the wrong places. When the insufferable Dr King renewed his call for a land expedition down the Back river in February 1850, he was summarily rejected. 'We have sent out expeditions enough', minuted Cowper. In this the Admiralty erred, allowing their distaste for the messenger to obscure his message.[77]

Once again Sabine secured magnetic observers. Not only was Austin 'very desirous to work for you', but the egregious Captain

Erasmus Ommaney of the *Assistance* volunteered for magnetic work. Clearly Sabine's science remained a valuable currency in the race for command and promotion.[78] Having obtained the instruments and paperwork, Ommaney tried to impress Beaufort with his zeal.[79] Aware who held the Arctic strings, Leopold McClintock begged Sabine to help him secure a place on the expedition.[80]

Evidence

The first concrete evidence of Franklin's expedition was found in 1850. Jane had purchased an 80-ton schooner using public subscriptions and renamed it *Prince Albert*, just in case the Palace remained unaware of her efforts. Leaving Aberdeen in June 1850 skipper Charles Forsyth's orders were clear and should have solved the mystery, with a little help from a Londonderry clairvoyant who pointed to the area around King William Land. Forsyth was directed to sail into Prince Regent Inlet, cross North Somerset on foot and proceed down Peel Sound, completing what Ross had been obliged to abandon. Having made some seventy miles down the inlet Forsyth found his path blocked by ice and gave up. He then headed west to join the other ships, arriving at Beechey Island to find a message that Ommaney had located signs of the lost expedition. Easily distracted, Forsyth searched Cape Riley, returning with meat bones and rope ends.

The official expedition had arrived earlier; Austin's two heavily reinforced brigs made slow progress, even under tow. Without steam the Americans were delayed for five weeks in Baffin Bay. All the search ships that year made it into Lancaster Sound as far as Beechey Island, a two-mile-wide appendage of the far larger Devon Island. Here on 23 August Ommaney landed and found the detritus of the Franklin expedition's 1845–6 winter camp. Despite searching the entire island and tearing down a prominent cairn on the summit of the hill, the only written records of the expedition to be recovered were some rough notes of magnetic observations in Fitzjames's hand. On the 27th the expedition's winter quarters were located, along with the graves of John Hartnell, William Braine and John Torrington. They had died in January and April 1846. Clearly

Franklin had used the sheltered bay, which Austin named Erebus, as a winter anchorage. By this time Penny and John Ross had arrived, as had the American expedition commanded by Edwin De Haven. The discovery of three dated graves prompted a flurry of accountancy correspondence as Admiralty bureaucrats removed the men from the pay list.[81]

The discovery of 600 preserved meat and vegetable tins, neatly stacked and for some unknown reason partly filled with stones, excited some comment, but the real mystery was why Franklin had not left a single record of his voyage, or any clue as to his intended course. To do so was standard practice, and the apparent failure to follow it constituted an astonishing oversight by Arctic travellers as experienced as Franklin and Crozier. On reflection Captain Sherard Osborn of the *Pioneer* concluded that the ice must have opened suddenly, and Franklin would not have had time to carry a record up the hill to his cairn, a hard climb of over an hour. Like much of Osborn's guesswork this seems highly improbable. That nothing could be found did not prove that nothing was left; it only proved that nothing could be found. Subsequently it would transpire that in the summer of 1845 Franklin made a significant voyage up Wellington Channel. He reached 77°N and circumnavigated Cornwallis Island, a remarkable feat unequalled for more than half a century. He had then retreated about a hundred miles east to the safe anchorage at Beechey Island, which may have been selected earlier. This was highly significant. Having closed down the Wellington Channel route, one that he had never thought possible, Franklin took up an ideal winter base, ready for an early start in 1846.

In 1850 Ross and Penny found a good harbour in Assistance Bay on Cornwallis Island. Austin pushed twenty miles further west, only for his four ships to be frozen in the open sea off Griffith Island. After getting trapped in the Wellington Channel and drifting north the Americans were fortunate to be caught up in the eastward flow of pack ice and driven out into Baffin Bay, whence they set course for home. Although their ill-equipped ships and lack of experience had all the makings of a first-class disaster, the Grinnell expedition's surgeon Dr Elisha Kent Kane turned this unpromising material into a best-selling romantic narrative, and himself into an icon of the search.

The naval expedition made preliminary sledge journeys that autumn, to lay down food depots for the spring and re-examine Beechey Island. Instructed by McClintock, Lieutenant George Mecham and other officers quickly mastered the sledges. By mid-October permanent darkness, howling gales and very low temperatures made travel almost impossible. The winter routine was designed to sustain morale, keeping men occupied with work, dinners, plays and visits. Although not distinguished by any great intellectual penetration, Austin's sociable nature and good sense helped keep the crews happy and healthy through the worst weather. Given the infuriatingly opaque results gleaned from the debris at Beechey Island, Austin's unimaginative approach was no worse than the visionary schemes advanced by livelier minds.

In mid-April 1851 sledging began in earnest. Each light Inuit-style sledge was hauled by six or seven seamen, led by an officer who picked out the route and navigated. If the opportunity arose a sail was hoisted to aid progress, but all too often rough terrain made this impossible. Each sledge flew a suitably chivalric flag, made by anxious ladies waiting at home. The sledges weighed about 1,400 pounds fully loaded with tent, sleeping bags, cooking gear, food and fuel. Enthusiastic young officers desperate to make their names pushed themselves to the limits of human endurance; seamen with no such expectations suffered severe hardship and unending cold. For all their heroism Austin's sledge teams found nothing. They were too far north. One sledge team looked into ice-choked Peel Sound but went no further. McClintock reached Parry's western extreme at Winter Harbour, covering an unprecedented 770 miles in eighty days. The sledge expeditions added another 1,200 miles of coastline to the Arctic map. By the time the ice broke up Austin had concluded that Franklin was not stuck west of Lancaster Sound, because there were no signs along the obvious route. He did not consider Peel Sound, since polar authorities Ross, Richardson and Back had discounted the idea. Instead he left Lancaster Sound and used his steamers to search Jones Sound to the north. It soon became obvious that this was another dead end, but at least it had been crossed off the list. The expedition was back at Woolwich by late autumn, only one man short of complement. Austin was well aware that a second winter in the ice would have produced a very different result among men who were worn out by their efforts, several suffering from scurvy and frostbite. Austin's expedition was the happiest official search. It also produced an ample haul of magnetic data for Edward Sabine.[82]

Austin left Captain Penny's *Lady Franklin* and *Sophia* to search Wellington Channel. Supported by John Ross's crew they made significant additions to the geography of the Polar Sea. Penny wanted to stay another winter, asking Austin to leave one of his steamers, but Austin knew better. The Wellington Channel search was complete; another winter would not have produced any positive results. Ever one for a mirage, John Ross came home with a horror story that Franklin's ships had been wrecked in north-west Greenland, and some or all of the crew murdered by Inuit. It was one of many frauds perpetrated on men like Ross, men who were willing to suspend disbelief.

These voyages produced fresh, exciting narratives of heroic endeavour. Unconcerned with science, they recorded a big-boy's adventure, ice navigation, close shaves with monstrous bergs, strange animals and the endless night. Then in the spring sledge parties set out to quarter the desolate wastes of the frozen north, each led by a young officer and flying a banner emblazoned with a motto. They turned the search into a chivalric endeavour, a modern quest for the Holy Grail: they were the Crusaders of the Arctic. This was a powerful, appealing image, but it had nothing to do with Franklin.

The Admiralty had been dragged, unwilling but helpless, into a second round of search missions. Franklin had promised that the mission would continue 'till our provisions get short'.[83] The Board knew very well that such a deadline would have passed many years before, yet they were unable to resist the pressure of public opinion, mobilised by Jane Franklin, playing into the hands of scientists with very different reasons for searching. The scale and persistence of the rescue effort said something about Victorian Britain in the decade of the Great Exhibition: it cared. With so little information to guide the search not one of the missions sent by sea – the obvious method to find lost ships – was successful. Altogether some forty vessels were sent; in 1851 there was an Anglo-American logjam in the desolate waters of Lancaster Sound. The three graves on Beechey Island were only the first of many frustrating glimpses of the expedition. Three dead, a blind cairn, empty food tins, and even magnetic notes, but not one word about where the expedition had been going, or where it had been.

10

Defeated, Deceived and Defrauded

THROUGHOUT THE FRANKLIN search the Admiralty struggled to manage the press. Sending official copy to newspaper editors avoided errors and reduced the danger of ill-informed attacks on official policy. When Charles Forsyth returned to England after a summer cruise in Lady Franklin's *Prince Albert*, the Admiralty sent his report, together with Parry's and Richardson's opinions on the discoveries at Cape Riley, to John Delane, editor of *The Times*. Delane dominated the London newspaper industry, and through him the reports filtered down to the other morning broadsheets.[1] When reports from Commander Pullen's river expedition and John Rae's latest exploit arrived, both were rushed to *The Times*.[2]

As Austin had overwintered, Jane prompted young John Barrow, an Admiralty clerk, to urge the dispatch of a steamship with fresh instructions and stores. A few days later the Admiralty dug in its collective heels. Admiral Dundas favoured sending a steamer, but only if Austin were recalled before the winter. 'I consider after this winter 1850/51 all hope must be given up, of restoring them to this country. I would also send to Captain Collinson & direct that his ships & the *Plover* return to Valparaiso.'[3] New Naval Lord Captain Houston Stewart agreed with old hand Milne: 'I cannot conceal from myself that every <u>fresh</u> ship & man sent out will, in all probability become a <u>fresh</u> source of anxiety & alarm to us, without proportionately increasing the chance of being useful to Franklin.' Cowper concluded 'To send another vessel into the ice would be, in my opinion, a wanton act of folly. We have no object to justify the exposure of life & the expense.'[4] Although the Board had finally taken control of the process, resisting the rather muted pressure of public opinion, it did not recall Austin or Collinson. Consequently Milne's fears would be borne out all too soon.

The news that Collinson's expedition had disappeared did not arrive for some time. In the interval the Admiralty moved to close the search. John Barrow Jr was directed to assemble the Franklin expedition and search documents into a special archive group, to settle any outstanding claims and costs.[5] The very first document, a fair copy of his father's December 1844 memorandum in his own hand, prompted a suitably maudlin reflection. 'Thus from the first commencement I have been deeply involved & much occupied in all that relates to this now painful subject.'[6] In creating the record Barrow mixed his private correspondence into the official papers, further muddying the evidentiary trail of responsibility and authority. At the same time it appears that he let Jane know what was afoot.

Jane needed a campaign manager, a skilled political/scientific operator with access to the seat of power, the confidence of scientists and explorers, and the resources to act without recompense.[7] There was only one man. Sir Roderick Murchison was an old friend and a beneficiary of Franklin's voyaging. Rock samples from the Arctic and Van Diemen's Land were a potent reminder of their friendship. If Murchison wanted any more rocks to extend his Silurian empire he needed to act quickly. Within days he had taken up the challenge, writing to an old school friend, Prime Minister Lord John Russell, to secure an audience for his Arctic deputation.[8] Despite numerous high-status signatures on his petition and a public meeting at the Geographical Society, Murchison's initiative had no effect on Admiralty policy. When fellow search supporter Sir Robert Inglis enquired about a relief expedition for Austin in the House of Commons at the end of March 1851, Baring declared that

the government did not think themselves justified in sending other parties to risk themselves in the Arctic seas; that they ought not to risk further the lives of their gallant seamen. They had done all that a generous country would call upon them to do, and they must do their duty now in stopping any future risk of life.

When Baring received solid support from another Liberal MP, and from Second Naval Lord Admiral Sir Maurice Berkeley, the subject was dropped.[9]

The best hope for reviving the search that summer was the annual BAAS meeting at Ipswich: Richardson trusted that the presence of the Prince Consort would attract a crowd.[10] By this stage the aims and arguments of the scientific projectors were becoming quite blurred, and very few expected a successful outcome to another search. As the scientists lost faith, Jane turned to Admiralty contacts Beaufort and Barrow to sustain her dreams. Torn between duty and hope, Barrow found the strain unbearable.

Many a time I have said that I would willingly be in Franklin's ships, wherever they are, than go through what I do, and very small thanks too for it, except the consciousness of having done my duty by those brave, unfortunate men.[11]

It is unlikely that the Lords of Admiralty missed Barrow's emotional involvement; Jane noted he spent 'a little fortune in Arctic Interests', providing libraries, warm clothes and other luxuries for each Arctic ship.[12] By day the official John Barrow, first-class clerk, funnelled incoming correspondence to the secretary, Captain William Baillie Hamilton. By night a private John Barrow conducted an extensive correspondence with key figures: Hamilton, Beaufort, Parry and Jane in London, and his many friends stuck in the ice. Where his father's secretarial office had controlled the flow of information and the agenda, the younger Barrow had to be more subtle.[13] He collected every scrap of public comment on the subject and used it to prompt the debate within the Admiralty whenever Jane needed to stir Whitehall into action.

Three days after lamenting his trials Barrow returned to the charge, supplying Hamilton with a sheaf of newspaper cuttings and petitions which were 'pouring in'. His words were carefully contrived to convey an exact meaning: 'There seems to be but one feeling (out of doors) respecting it. So great is the pressure, that I am sure the wise course will be to yield to it willingly.'[14] Ignoring Hamilton's hint that he might be rewarded for keeping quiet, Barrow lamented that the Board did not seem to care, or understand his argument. Having dismissed his suggestion to send a steamer in the spring, the Board was left to regret the premature if prudent return of Austin's squadron. Having established his prescience, Barrow urged the need to support Collinson and McClure, who had penetrated 'into unknown regions & must be looked after, as well as Franklin. They must have something to fall back upon, as well as something to advance upon, because they must do one or the other, with or without their ships.'[15] Perhaps he had a better insight into McClure's state of mind than he was prepared to admit. Those who knew the man had no doubt that he would attempt the Passage, despite the clearly stated aims of the expedition.

Austin arrived at Woolwich shortly after Penny. While Queen Victoria and the Prince Consort read the dispatches 'with great interest', Jane was convinced that Penny had no business returning when his expedition had demonstrated that the missing expedition must be somewhere up the Wellington Channel. She was anxious to send another expedition in the spring, confident the area to be searched had been significantly reduced.[16] However, the 'evidence' for such a conclusion was thin: three graves and assorted detritus on Beechey Island, Fitzjames's magnetic notes, newspapers and a parcel wrapping, all now were lovingly bound into Barrow's record.[17] Captain Penny would not be employed again; perhaps his fate was sealed by the appearance of an engraved portrait for which subscriptions were sought. The Admiralty had seen quite enough of vainglorious whaling masters without paying for the privilege. Richardson analysed Penny's weather logs, which discredited the widely held notion that the climate became warmer further north, leading to an open Polar Sea.[18] This should have put paid to the Wellington Channel delusion – but that theory now held the field. After examining the latest material Parry confessed himself no wiser as to the whereabouts of the ships.[19] No one commented on Ommaney's discovery that a magnetic observatory had been erected on Beechey Island.[20]

Altogether more difficult for Baring and his Board was the problem of Lady Franklin. Unlike naval officers she was not amenable to discipline, nor did she have any distraction from her obsessive pursuit of the lost expedition. Having taken up residence in Spring Gardens, literally next door to the Admiralty, she continued to receive inside information from Beaufort and Barrow. Jane would remain a constant presence in the deliberations of the Board for a decade, despite an initial rebuff. In June 1851 Baring declared: 'I do not think the Govt. ought to sanction further expeditions or send another steamer.' His Naval Lords agreed and William Cowper later 'acquainted Lady

Franklin accordingly'.²¹ Unwilling to accept defeat, Jane returned to the charge only to receive the same frosty response:

Their Lordships cannot see that anything more is to be ascertained by a new expedition beyond that which the numerous parties now at work are almost certain to determine; nor that any advantage commensurate with its certain risk is to be gained by the dispatch of another ship to the ice this year.

It grieves me to be the channel of this communication, though I can indeed say that it is from no want of attention to your appeal that I am called upon to make it.²²

The second paragraph reveals that Captain Hamilton, the new Admiralty secretary, had become personally involved. In September the *Morning Herald* attacked the ministry for changing its mind and not sending a steamer.²³ The source of the story was obvious.

The return of Penny and Austin that autumn was profoundly distressing for Jane, her cup rendered doubly bitter by the conviction that Franklin was trapped in the Wellington Channel, halfway to the Bering Strait.²⁴ She blamed the Board for not sending a steamer that summer before turning her distress into a potent lobbying asset.

Having established that the 1851 season had produced 'almost nothing at all', *The Times* landed a powerful blow for common sense. Delane let the ministry know that it could not rely on the support of 'The Thunderer':

In fact we are no wiser than we were before, and all our recent exertions have gone virtually for nothing. It is with no kind of satisfaction that we record these conclusions, but we do not see how it is possible to maintain that any material point has been gained by our tenacious perseverance and untiring zeal.

Not only had the idea of a North West Passage been exploded but, Delane observed, this had been known before Franklin departed. 'It was utterly impossible that any permanent way could be maintained through such regions as these.' It mattered not whether the obstacles were solid land or permanent ice. Unaware of the magnetic issues that dominated the project, he lamented that so much had been staked on solving a geographical question that was not worth the crew of a single sloop. It was time for a better organised and more carefully planned rescue effort, with less restrictive instructions: 'but in any case we hope that these efforts may terminate the national propensity for Arctic expeditions.'[25]

The source of this leader was not hard to guess. The following day Sir Francis Baring provided the prime minister with the Admiralty view. After Penny returned he had 'assembled without delay some of the Arctic Officers – Sir E. Parry, Sir Jas. Ross, Captain Beechey, etc. etc. They could not all attend but those named came. They examined Penny and were unanimously of opinion that the sending out an expedition this year was too late for any good.' Austin had reported he would search Jones Sound, 'and if he found any traces there we should have committed a blunder'. In fact the subject was in 'something of a mess at present for the papers. The Arctic clique and the private trade party are making a set against Austin', but there was no occasion for a court martial, so some officers would consider his conduct, both to clear his name 'and at the same time it may assist us as to our future course'. On this point there 'is much difference – some with Penny believe Franklin went up Wellington Channel, of this opinion is Parry. Some that he attempted to return and was lost in the pack coming home. Austin, Sir Jas. Ross & Sir John Ross are of this opinion.'[26]

Jane had other irons in the ice. After the futile effort of 1850 she wanted to send her schooner *Prince Albert* back, under a different commander. Resigned to the fact that none of Franklin's party had survived, James Ross objected to 'uselessly hazarding the lives of many without the possibility of doing good to any'.[27] However, Jane was not interested in his opinions. He had failed. When the *Prince Albert* returned with little to show for her winter stay other than a full crew list, the *Morning Herald* was effusive.[28]

The press was still being worked up: the *Morning Chronicle* criticised Captain Berkeley for denigrating the work of Sir John Ross in the House of Commons, and expressed the hope that Ross's costs would be refunded. It also praised the American effort, using phrases suspiciously similar to those Lady Jane employed.[29]

Franklin and the Americans

Lest it be thought that an obsessive interest in the Arctic was a uniquely British condition the Franklin story soon engaged international attention. The United States had several reasons for taking a close interest in the Arctic. By 1850 American whalers were active in both Baffin Bay and the Bering Strait, and they dominated the business. Whale oil was the only significant economic asset to be found in the Arctic, and each new round of exploration opened fresh killing grounds to exploit the cetacean population. In the post-war years the British enjoyed a brief golden age of Arctic whaling. The War of 1812 had annihilated American competition while rapid industrialisation provided growing demand for high-grade lubricating oil alongside the usual demand for lighting. Down to 1821 the British fleet included up to 150 ships, but thereafter the decline was slow but steady. The removal of tariff protection in 1820 and falling prices reflected the relatively weak political position of the trade when compared with its industrial customers. The Americans were soon back in business, undercutting British suppliers, and they would dominate global whaling for the next three decades – the age of *Moby Dick*. Despite cheaper, more efficient American competition the British industry survived on a steady diet of tariff protection and rising domestic demand. In the search for whales the ships penetrated ever further into Baffin Bay, and took ever greater risks with the ice. Ship losses rose. In 1830 nineteen ships were crushed from a fleet of ninety-one. In 1835 a second disaster, when a sudden shift in the weather sank six ships and froze another nine, prompted the naval relief expedition led by James Clark Ross and played a critical part in sparking the next round of polar navigation. There were plenty of whales, but catching them was a desperate business among the ice floes. Whale-oil production peaked in the second half of the 1840s before being replaced by rapeseed and mineral oils and coal gas for lighting, demand falling more quickly in Britain than America. The trade was already becoming uneconomic when in 1843 protective tariffs on American whale oils were reduced by three-quarters. This was the final nail in the coffin of an industry already in its death throes and reduced to just a few ships sailing north from Hull or Aberdeen.[30]

The link between Arctic exploration and the whaling trade was obvious. Men such as William Scoresby pioneered the Arctic mission and inspired the naval/scientific expeditions that followed him into Baffin Bay. Naval navigators pioneered new routes, and provided charts. While much of the link was indirect, some American exploring expeditions, notably the Ringgold–Rodgers mission of 1855–9 to the North Pacific, were specifically directed to areas of interest to the whaling trade. In the 1840s whalers began to overwinter in the eastern Arctic, and pushed ever deeper into Hudson's Bay until the trade lost economic viability.

American whalers, already active off Kamchatka, began entering the Bering Strait in 1848, opening a vast new reservoir of prey. Whales were mentioned before trade in the Act that authorised the North Pacific exploring expedition, and were the primary justification for the project.[31] In 1852 the number of American whalers entering the Bering Strait peaked at 252, but the industry suffered a rapid decline as other sources of high-grade lubricating oil came on stream.[32]

In addition the Arctic lay to the north of their own continent, a continent over which many Americans believed it to be their 'manifest destiny' to rule. Finally, this simple, one-dimensional world, completely unlike the increasingly complex industrial society of burgeoning East Coast cities like New York, Boston, Philadelphia and Washington, had a special allure for 'civilised' man. The early nineteenth-century British polar voyages sparked considerable interest in the United States, being both widely reported and widely read in pirate editions of the great Barrow/Murray narratives. These stories gave Americans a sense of kinship with the old country, and were told as moral tales of courage and endeavour. Franklin, 'the man who ate his boots', was well known to American audiences long before 1845. He had passed through New York on his second overland expedition, receiving a warm welcome from the state governor and other public figures.[33]

British polar dramas stirred an interest, and by the late 1830s the United States exploring expedition had been dispatched under Charles Wilkes, crossing Franklin's path in a southern hemisphere that many Americans believed had been set aside by God as the stage on which their country would prove itself the equal of European states. For Edgar Allan Poe this was a question of 'national dignity and honor' and he was not alone in considering Antarctica 'a wide field, open and nearly untouched – "a theatre particularly our own"'.[34]

Franklin's disappearance shifted the focus of American interests to the north. American journals provided extensive coverage of the search and by the time Jane wrote to President Zachary Taylor her husband had become so deeply embedded in contemporary American culture that Taylor felt unable to refuse. Typically Jane had already erected a golden bridge to facilitate official generosity. Her New York contact Henry Grinnell would handle the business of mounting an expedition. In this way Jane kept up the pressure on the British government: it would hardly be possible to stop searching if the Americans were going.

Grinnell made his fortune as a New York ship-owner and merchant. Noted for high standards of probity, morality, and conservative commercial practice, Grinnell retired from his business in 1850 already a wealthy man. He was a founder member and one-time president of the American Geographical and Statistical Society, an American analogue of the RGS, and similarly involved in promoting national exploration with an imperial turn. Grinnell's early connection with whaling gave him a lifelong interest in the Arctic region, and he was quick to respond to Lady Franklin's plea for help in 1850. Personally self-effacing, Grinnell was always ready to act in the philanthropic fashion so esteemed by his contemporaries.[35] He would be the key figure in the American response to Franklin's disappearance.

When Congress debated the cost of the search, speakers stressed the symbolic value of the humanitarian gesture, and saw it as a means of raising American prestige on the international stage. Despite some Anglophobe carping and concerns about cost the measure was widely supported. An Arctic search mission would be a unifying national effort, one that offered a welcome relief from divisive intersectional strife over slavery and the rights of states. It was presumed there were no slaves to be made at the North Pole.[36] Grinnell had funded the two vessels, *Advance* and *Rescue*, sent under naval command in 1850, and refitted the *Advance* for the later expedition led by Kane. It was with good reason that these voyages were known as the first and second Grinnell expeditions. Grinnell visited Britain and was very well received. Later he supported the Arctic research of Charles Francis Hall and Isaac Israel Hayes.

With a mission in prospect the American scientific community was anxious to get involved. Humboldtian navigator, oceanographer and electrical pioneer Captain Matthew Fontaine Maury USN, director of the United States Naval Observatory in Washington, was already at work on economically useful sailing and whaling charts to help his countrymen improve their returns.[37] Maury believed that part of the Gulf Stream might flow due north, creating an open Polar Sea. While his theory had a more scientific rationale than Barrow's old mirage, it was no more accurate. The presence of Scoresby among his sources reveals Maury's cetacean quarry. Maury's whaling charts appeared in 1851–2, helping American whalers make bumper catches in the Bering Strait. They also enabled the Confederate Cruiser CSS *Shenandoah* to wreak havoc among them in 1865. The American expedition would be led by Captain Edwin De Haven USN, fresh from a two-year assignment working at the observatory. His instructions included searching for Maury's open Polar Sea. Who could tell where the next hunting ground would appear? There was no such sea, but it was an attractive idea: a warm ocean would be filled with animals, animals that could be harpooned and rendered down for oil.[38]

Despite achieving nothing beyond a fortunate escape from a terrible autumn in Barrow Strait the amateurish and downright dangerous American expedition was taken as a sign of universal sympathy and fellow feeling by transatlantic cousins. This was far from the case, but it suited Jane's purposes to sustain the illusion. She obtained the American instructions and sent them to the Admiralty, playing down the search for an open Polar Sea. She also ensured the Americans received extensive publicity in British journals, and when Sir Francis Baring requested a copy of De Haven's final report American ambassador Abbott Lawrence had to get one from Jane![39] That said, Lawrence was anxious to see the document in the Parliamentary Papers and the Board was happy to oblige, though it did not disclose Jane's role. Altogether more interesting was the input of Captain Charles Wilkes USN, Antarctic pioneer and ardent nationalist. Wilkes realised that it was useless to send more ships; it was time to send men on sledges and boats across the ice:

The cost is nothing compared to the glory of effecting their rescue, worth ten-fold the efforts hitherto made to find and effect a North West Passage.

I cannot conclude without adverting to the anxiety and interest which exists in this country to receive tidings of the lost expedition. It cannot be greater even in Great Britain. It is the cause of humanity, in which all our hearts and minds should assent to intervention. The honour and glory that would ensure to our country in making a decisive effort would be great – the cost but half a million dollars.[40]

Wilkes had identified an American way in the Arctic, a mission that would link up with the concept of 'manifest destiny'. Anxious to apply an American spur to the flagging British effort, Jane offered the Americans a chance to seize the glory. She wrote to the president both to praise Grinnell's first effort and hoping for more. She also took care to have the letter published in the *Morning Post* and Barrow ensured the Admiralty received a cutting.[41]

Murchison raised a testimonial for Grinnell, who replied with a degree of modesty unusual in such company on either side of the Atlantic: 'I feel that the author of an Expedition that accomplished nothing for humanity and little for science is scarcely entitled to the distinguished favour you have conferred.'[42] Perhaps he realised just how far his work had been manipulated to shame the British government into further efforts.

In the event it would be the self-aggrandising Elisha Kent Kane, rather than Grinnell, who dominated the American response to Franklin. America adopted the cadaverously pale, rheumatic invalid surgeon as their ideal Arctic hero. Serving under De Haven, Kane picked out the geographic pole as the American Arctic mission and generated a national audience. When De Haven expressed no interest in writing up his expedition narrative, Kane produced a lively romance filled with narrow escapes and strange sights which distracted attention from the fact that the expedition had been a disaster. The Americans saw Maury's non-existent sea, got stuck in the ice and had a lucky break, but Kane's tale of character turned the voyage from a scientific record into an all-American outdoor adventure. It struck a spark across the nation. His lecture tour made Grinnell's Geographical Society the headquarters of American Arctic exploration. Recognising the value of a media star, Grinnell secured Kane command of the follow-up expedition despite his lack of navigational skill or command experience. Suitably reinterpreted by Lady Jane the fruitless and risky American effort helped to sustain the British search just when the Admiralty was trying to close it down.

How to stop searching

In late 1851 the Admiralty tried to make sense of the latest results. It did not do very well. Captain Penny's expedition should have ended the search in the Wellington Channel; instead the Board rejected his offer to return with a steamship.[43] Hoping that items recovered from Beechey Island 'may throw light on the tides and currents' provided slim pickings for such a costly endeavour.[44] Indeed, so thin were the results of Austin's whole mission that the Admiralty had been obliged to assemble a committee under Rear Admiral Sir William Bowles to enquire into the affair.[45] Beechey, Parry, Back and Admiral Fanshawe considered 'whether everything was done by them to carry into effect their instructions'. Once the committee was satisfied the Board made the usual promotions and rewards,[46] noting the 'sustained courage' of McClintock and the other sledge travellers.[47]

As the chances of there being any survivors receded, 'catastrophe' theories began to emerge. In early 1852 Barrow had to write to *The Times* to discredit the rumour that the empty tins at Beechey Island could be construed as evidence that the provisioner, Stefan Goldner, had supplied inferior and inedible canned food. Fitzjames had been concerned about the untried contractor, but once at sea had not mentioned the subject again.[48] Soon afterwards an icy mirage took hold of the public. A whaler reported seeing two ships stuck in an iceberg. The professionals were convinced they were not Franklin's command, for very good reason, but the Admiralty still conducted a massive research effort to secure as much information as possible about the ships and the colours in which they had been painted.[49]

Just in case there remained a taste for heroic folly Elisha Kent Kane proposed a suicidal boat expedition along Wellington Channel, reflecting his fascination with the North Pole. Jane ensured he received Admiralty support through Beaufort, while Parry, Ross, Richardson and Sabine provided further advice, the latter, predictably enough, on the instruments and methods of magnetic data gathering.[50] In public the charming, sickly American was grateful, but he had no intention of either returning to the Franklin search or conducting magnetic research.[51] In case anyone thought American actions were disinterested the *Liverpool Albion* and *The Times* reminded readers that the Americans had taken control of the whaling industry in the Bering Strait. Following the collapse of the Australian fishery at Hobart, Britain depended on imported American oil.[52]

Murchison takes the helm

With the Admiralty resolved to abandon the search Jane turned to Murchison, arch manipulator of men and measures. Murchison had turned the Royal Geographical Society into a potent propaganda platform. From his presidential headquarters in Waterloo Place he used public lectures to connect the rich and powerful with scientists and explorers, while generating a constant stream of publications. Among the denizens of the RGS were John Barrow Jr and his coterie of young naval explorers. In the absence of a decent war these men sought promotion in the ice with a desperate fervour. Murchison exploited this enthusiastic support team to advertise his efforts in the national press. He was the ideal man to sustain the Franklin search, and he had more reason than most, being the beneficiary of frequent collections of rock samples gathered by his friend at the outer reaches of the known world. He was quick to ask Jane to have the limestone ballast of the *Prince Albert* inspected for fossils, and checked the dead French volunteer Lieutenant Bellot's effects for similar material. Jane paid his price.[53]

The basic argument of the campaign, shared by Beaufort and Lady Jane, was that Franklin had penetrated further north into the Wellington Channel than the last search mission. It was essential 'to push on fearlessly and decide this trying question'.[54] That this plan assumed an open Polar Sea reveals the extent of their wishful thinking.

Pim

The failure of Austin and Penny left the search party desperate for good news, easy prey for visionaries and cranks. Two expeditions that got nowhere near the Arctic reveal more about the aims and methods of the search than any of those that sailed. While only footnotes in Arctic history, these abortive plans witnessed a change in the scientific leadership of the search and exposed the objectives of those who employed political influence to sustain the effort.

The new hope for Jane, and more especially for some of her supporters, was Lieutenant Bedford Clapperton Pim.[55] Recently returned from HMS *Plover* in the Bering Strait and with a successful land journey from Kotzebue Sound to Norton Sound to his credit, Pim proposed searching along the Siberian coast. He argued that Franklin had gone north-west via the Wellington Channel into the Polar Sea, and became trapped to the north of a 'great land barrier of land which on very good grounds is supposed to exist far to the north of Behring's Strait', a theory that echoed Beaufort's version.[56] Pim had been introduced to Murchison by *Investigator* veteran Robert Brown, then one of Jane's closest advisers. Brown explained that 'he <u>assumes</u> they are trapped at longitude of Bering Strait, but north of barrier of land, with food but no people . . . at extreme West'.[57] Although Beaufort, in Ireland on holiday, was anxious to be involved, the Admiralty declined Pim's offer to lead an expedition.[58] Instead it offered to communicate his plan to the Russian government. Unwilling to accept defeat the usual suspects appeared in their accustomed roles. An article in *The Times* on 10 November stated that Pim's plan was warmly supported by Lady Franklin and the RGS, where Pim was going to speak that evening.[59] Murchison wrote to the First Lord, as the voice of the RGS, and revealed more than he intended:

I beg you to believe that this is no scheme solely got up to obtain more geographical knowledge, but is one which, in reference to Franklin's expedition only, has obtained the warm support of Sir Francis Beaufort and many experienced navigators, as well as good geographers.

Had the geographical agenda, and Beaufort's duplicity, become quite that obvious?

Murchison hoped that Pim would be employed at the public expense, either on this mission or attached to another search party, rather than use up 'his slender means, and the exhausted small fortune of Lady Franklin'. If Baring adopted Pim's plan he was promised the thanks of the RGS, but it is doubtful that Sir Francis, scion of a great banking house, would have placed any value on so debased a currency.[60] The Board wisely declined to depart from their usual practice, forcing Murchison and Jane to look for alternative support.[61]

Anticipating a rejection, Murchison appealed to the prime minister Lord John Russell for £500 of public money to support a two- to three-year survey. 'In common with Admiral Sir Francis Beaufort the Hydrographer of the Navy and many scientific friends I participate in the views of Lt Pim who proposes to reach the north eastern shores of Siberia this winter & thence to commence his expedition.' As president of the Royal Geographical Society he had already written to Russia for the tsar's sanction and discussed the project with the Russian ambassador, his old friend Baron Brunnow.[62] Lord Palmerston helped by employing Pim to carry official dispatches to St Petersburg. Through Russell the RGS asked the Admiralty to put Pim on full pay 'during his survey, which must prove of value to the hydrographical department of the Navy'. Murchison hoped that Russell, a liberal supporter of science and of several Franklin search expeditions, would advance this small sum of money 'to enable us as Englishmen to take our proper share in the first survey of this nature which has been sent to the east of Asia'.[63] Although she thanked Murchison for his efforts, Jane made it clear that she considered Pim's mission subordinate to searching the Wellington Channel and the Bering Strait.[64]

After Barrow gave him an over-optimistic interpretation of the Admiralty position Murchison renewed his approach, claiming the Admiralty had endorsed Pim's mission by giving him leave, a complete misrepresentation of the nature of leave in this period. He hoped Russell would 'accede to what I know to be a very strong & general wish of the public as well as of men of science' so that Murchison could announce official support for Pim's mission at the Raleigh Club on the 17th.[65] This time the bluster worked. The following night Murchison thanked Russell for his kind and timely grant. Pim was overjoyed and the Raleigh Club gave Russell a bumper toast. Murchison produced a few lines for *The Times* on Wednesday 19th, the day Pim left for Russia, having told Russell that Pim would 'do justice to your patronage'.[66]

When corresponding with Baring and Russell, Murchison hardly mentioned Franklin. The scientific/geographic agenda was taking over. Sabine had created the original mission for his science; now fellow scientists crowded in to piggy-back their aims onto the tail-end of a hopeless search. How far any of them were prepared to admit this, even to themselves, is unclear. That Murchison emerged as the dominant voice of British science in the second half of the search is revealing, as is Sabine's approval.

In the event Russell was too wily a politician to be caught so easily. He had been careful to say that he would find the money from official sources, but only if the Admiralty approved.[67] The following day Baring reported that the Board had rejected Pim's 'very wild scheme'; it would be referred to the Arctic Committee but no Arctic officer he had met gave it any credence. Nor was he impressed by Murchison's arguments: 'The Geographical Society no doubt will not be sorry to increase their knowledge of these regions.' As to granting public money he passed the buck to Russell: 'I cannot see that it will be the slightest use to our trade – and like much of our Arctic Expeditions merely fills up the map.' The government had not aided private expeditions in 1850, 'and I think they were right for it is a heavy responsibility to tempt men out without having the slightest control over their proceedings'.[68]

Realising the Board would not pay, Barrow hoped that Pim's attendance at a dinner of the Raleigh Club would attract funds. While he urged Murchison to support Pim, he could offer no better reason than his 'fine, gentlemanly' character.[69] After being rebuffed by Baring, Sir Roderick shifted tack, asking the Earl of Ellesmere to use his influence with his 'friend' to alter Admiralty regulations.[70] It required the more incisive vision of Edward Sabine to impose some purpose on Pim's venture. Sabine did not see any purpose searching for Franklin west of the Siberian islands, but magnetic observations on the coast of Siberia 'would be of very great value indeed . . . it would be worth an expedition of itself'.[71]

While better-informed men realised Pim's mission would be very difficult, Murchison opened doors.[72] His direction of the project was widely praised – the Duke of Northumberland gave him all the credit – but while Lady Jane thought Russell's response must be 'very gratifying' her real concern was to secure public funds for her own effort. She treated Russell's act as an 'additional and pleasant assurance that when renewed measures of search are entered upon in another quarter they will have his individual support'.[73] Her optimism was based on a *Times* report of the 19th that Russell had given £500 to Pim's Siberian project.[74] This was not true, but such concerns did not trouble the search party. Instead they deployed new recruit Charles Weld, Royal Society Secretary, Arctic author and an agent of Jane's, to promote the mission.[75] According to Commander Sherard Osborn, Weld was the ideal 'missionary' for the Arctic cause, lecturing in the major cities to raise funds.[76]

Never one to accept no for an answer, Murchison pressed Russell to have Pim put on full pay and attached to a survey vessel in the Bering Strait. Again the Admiralty refused. Boasting that First Naval Lord Sir James Dundas was 'an old friend of mine', Sir Roderick warned that a refusal on purely technical grounds would be 'widely disapproved'. He was sure that Russell's judgement would be followed by Sir Francis Baring and his Board. Then he let the cat out of the bag. He admitted Pim had 'instructions as to any small addition he might be able to make in the course of his research on Terrestrial Magnetism', and repeated Sabine's claim that 'a few observations . . . on the Coast of Siberia . . . would be worth an expedition itself.' Sabine was desperate for such evidence, believing he was on the verge of a general theory of terrestrial magnetism. Murchison declared that either the magnetic mission 'or the great cause of humanity' was good reason enough to back Pim's mission and threatened to make a public appeal if the government was not forthcoming.[77]

Once again the Board had been wiser than their detractors. After meeting Humboldt in Berlin, Pim reached St Petersburg to find that the leading Russian explorers and geographers dismissed his plan, deliberately or accidentally misunderstanding how much of the coast he planned to search.[78] Long-running tension between the two countries ensured he would hardly be allowed to wander through the tsar's northern domains unsupervised.[79] Jane quickly fired off an emotional appeal to the tsar, but Nicholas was not so easily swayed.[80] While the Russians had seen an opportunity to build better relations with Britain, Murchison could not overcome the innately suspicious bureaucracy of tsarist Russia, or the realities of geography.[81] Humanitarian concern was a currency of limited value in nineteenth-century international relations. On his return Pim refunded Jane's £300. She had only supported the mission as an auxiliary to efforts in the Wellington Channel and the Bering Strait, where she was convinced the search had to be concentrated. Nor was Pim the only projector. His messmate on HMS *Plover* Lieutenant William Hooper put forward a scheme, but the Board was quick to reject it, demonstrating a very clear grasp of the issues.[82] At least Pim was an honest optimist.

Beatson

Predictably, the high-profile search mission attracted a number of scoundrels. Each new proposal required cautious handling. Normally an astute judge of men and motives, Jane was taken in by mercantile Captain Donald Beatson's Christian project to sail the 147-ton screw steamer *Isabel* to the Bering Strait, searching the same area of the Russian Arctic coast as Pim, but by sea. Both Beaufort and Barrow were convinced, and they enmeshed Murchison in the scheme. Unsurprisingly, Beatson's project received a strong endorsement from the *Morning Chronicle* in November 1851, complete with a list of subscribers and their contributions. Jane provided £800, Murchison and Beaufort chipped in with £25 each.[83] By the end of the year Jane was getting cold feet about Pim, for financial or geographical reasons, and shifting her attention to Beatson. She took care to bring Sir Roderick, the right hand of the mission, with her.

Jane, now anxious to widen the search area, was concerned that the Admiralty would confine future rescue missions to the Wellington Channel, as 'so timidly recommended by the late Arctic Committee'. Beaufort agreed that Beatson should go to the Bering Strait, where Franklin had told Kellett he expected to be met.[84] She pressed Murchison to secure a testimonial for Beatson, who needed the money, rather than Grinnell, who did not.[85] Murchison did not need to be asked twice, and was soon twisting rich and noble arms to secure funds.[86] Among his friends the Earl of Ellesmere gave £100, believing such efforts should be 'started with the fiat of the experienced, & sustained with the money of the ignorant'.[87] Nor was he above threatening the government. Claiming his actions were 'impelled by a large and active body of geographers', he warned that if the RGS's wishes were not met a public memorial signed by many eminent men and calling for action would be sent to the queen and Prince Albert.[88] He also arranged for Beatson to speak at the RGS, and secured Russian support through his friend Tsar Nicholas.[89]

At least Beatson was grateful, and he read Murchison well enough to flatter his vanity with the promise to name a prominent feature for him.[90] Beatson also fooled Sophia Cracroft. After her experience in Hobart, Jane might have identified Beatson as a rogue, but she did not meet him. Instead she pressed Murchison to secure Admiralty pemmican and coal, raise funds and engage wealthy backers.[91] Everything depended on Beaufort's inside knowledge of what the Admiralty might provide, and Sir Francis would be called on to judge any serious requests. Suitably armed, Murchison was sent into battle, Jane reminding him to play all her high-value cards. As the mission had been endorsed by the RGS, he had a 'right' to plead, and it would not look good if Beatson were to perish for want of Admiralty pemmican. He might follow up by contrasting the British government's attitude with the American decision to adopt Grinnell's mission. Jane identified Captain Edward Belcher as a major opponent of the Bering Strait route. Just in case Sir Roderick was thinking of holding back she played her own ace:

Tho' very unwilling to come forward again & again as a beggar, I am thinking of writing a note to Sir F. Baring myself on Monday & telling him that if the fears of Mr B's ability or intention to pay be any ground for refusal, I will make myself responsible for the payment – tho' I cannot make it immediate.

She would have written to Parry but the latest Arctic report had 'chilled my confidence in him'. Unwilling to hear bad news, Jane simply cast off another of Franklin's old friends and pressed Sir Roderick for better tidings:

The accomplishment of this object is worthy of the exertion of your generous efforts on behalf of your protégé, and you will feel with me that there is not a moment to be lost now that the present Admiralty's days or hours are numbered.[92]

Murchison deputed Sir Robert Inglis to buttonhole ministers in the House. Russell avoided his initial approach, but Inglis cornered both the prime minister and Sir Francis Baring just as the government was about to fall. Russell passed the buck and Baring fudged the issue, promising to sell supplies but not press for payment. He had done the same for Jane's expedition the previous year. Inglis added his own money to the fund.[93]

Propelled by further judicious flattery Murchison worked hard to advance Beatson's project. He applied to the new Tory Admiralty Board for pemmican and coal, telling the First Lord, His Grace the Duke of Northumberland, that Beaufort and Kellet considered the project novel and likely to succeed. Although immensely rich and personally sympathetic, Northumberland recognised this was official business, so passed it to Admiralty political secretary Augustus Stafford.[94] When it became clear that Beatson had no money, Murchison wrote to the Duke, requesting an advance of £2,000 on Franklin's back pay to cover Jane's costs. After ensuring the funds covered an advance the Duke conceded the point.[95]

In a set-piece debate on the Arctic in the House of Commons on 12 March 1852 Stafford refused to offer any rewards to encourage mercantile officers such as Penny, but promised that strenuous efforts were being made to get another expedition to sea. In Baring's absence two members of his Board defended his decisions and the matter lapsed.[96] A desperate Jane swallowed her pride, asking Murchison to approach new prime minister Lord Derby, the man who, as Lord Stanley, had sacked Franklin back in 1843. Having set her 'hopes on this expedition' she was deeply committed to Beatson, with £3,500 invested.[97]

Sustained pressure from Jane and Sir Roderick finally paid off. On 24 March the Admiralty awarded Jane £2,000 from Franklin's back pay, and provided a steamer to tow Beatson's vessel to the anchorage at Downs, off Dover. Once again this generosity had been prompted by the persuasive pen of Jane Franklin:

I hope I did nobody wrong in writing directly to the Duke instead of the Board. I have been generally in the habit of doing so to former First Lords because I can express myself more freely than in a formal letter to their united Lordships . . . so long as my requests are granted I am thankful & content, but I should be sorry his Grace should think I did a thing very much out of order. That good Lord Auckland began by <u>inviting</u> me to write to him, telling him any suggestions I had . . . and he once spent 2 hours with me talking of Arctic matters & granted everything I wanted. That was a First Lord who spoilt me for any other.

But that was the last good news. On 25 March Beatson's accounts were £2,400 short.[98] The following day the project collapsed: HMS *Monkey* arrived to tow the *Isabel* but Beatson was not ready. He could not load his stores because he had not paid for them.[99] Jane finally realised she had put her faith in a man of straw, risking the credibility of the search. 'What the Admiralty will think of it all, I am afraid to conjecture – after their great kindness too in granting your request & mine.' Yet in her anxiety to get the mission to sea she clutched at every excuse Beatson offered. Her encyclopedic knowledge of Arctic exploration provided neat answers to otherwise intractable problems.[100] But it was all to no avail. Either a crank or a crook, Beatson had run through the subscribers' money and could not sail. Murchison acknowledged the facts, but Jane desperately wanted to believe that Beatson was sincere.[101] The ensuing rift between them lasted until late April, by which time Jane had secured control of the ship. She planned to offer it to the Admiralty, but only if they sent it to join the *Plover* in the Bering Strait. Henry Kellett was confident the Admiralty could not refuse. 'It is better to spend £5,000 to have the expedition we want than to throw the half of that sum into the sea & have no expedition at all.' To restore the credibility of the search she planned to make a public spectacle of Beatson, revealing the steely and unforgiving side of her formidable character.[102]

By publicly damning Beatson she hoped to retain the subscriptions already raised. Just in case Murchison thought he might take the moral high ground, Jane reminded him that he had fallen for the 'ships in the iceberg' mirage and she had not. She also refused to believe the latest theory gaining currency among the experts, that the ships might have been crushed and swallowed up by the Arctic seas.[103] Jane renewed links with Murchison when she needed his back-channel access to the Duke of Northumberland and his Board.[104] In the interval Beatson had been arrested for debt. With £2,200 invested Jane now owned the ship, and begged Northumberland for another advance on Sir John's pay to cover her costs. She wanted to pass the vessel to the Admiralty, as any search would be 'better carried out under naval command'. The Board rejected her loaded gift.[105] Murchison tried again a month later, citing Beaufort's opinion on the uses to which the vessel might be put.[106] Pim, then heading north with Belcher's expedition, sent more money recovered from his abortive mission.[107] Richardson also believed in the western mission, and the possibility that some men still remained, 'supposing material for the chase were saved a remnant may support themselves for years in a favourable locality.'[108]

Long after everyone else had abandoned Beatson, Sabine suddenly remembered his mission, prompted by Richardson and Lefroy's magnetic results from the high Arctic. He asked Beaufort to send Pim with Beatson for magnetic purposes, forgetting that Pim had gone with Belcher. He favoured Beatson's approach, not least because it lent credence to Wrangel's open Polar Sea ideas, translated by Mrs Sabine.[109]

In stark contrast to Beatson's visionary project Captain Rochefort Maguire set off to take command of HMS *Plover*, the advanced depot ship inside the Bering Strait. Even so, Barrow had to beg Murchison to secure the necessary letters for the Russian authorities in Alaska; it would take too long to go through official channels.[110] Sabine loaded Maguire's official mission with six new magnetic instruments for use on land or ice.[111] They would be well used.[112] Every winter Maguire would build a new observatory out of ice blocks. The magnetic observations taken at Point Barrow between 1852 and 1854 were the best produced in the western Arctic.[113] A delighted Sabine observed that these instruments 'have been sent with nearly all the expeditions which, in the past twelve years, have wintered within the Arctic Circle'. Such complete observations required 'a greater amount of private zeal' than could be expected, but, 'In one of these expeditions in particular (the only one that unhappily has not returned in safety) the well-known zeal of its commander SIR JOHN FRANKLIN in the cause of science . . .

gave reason for hopes of the highest promise.' Confident Franklin had conducted the necessary magnetic observations, Sabine was still hoping to recover the data.[114]

By the time the Beatson affair had been resolved Jane had pushed the Admiralty into another search mission. Her single-minded campaign had worn down three Admiralty administrations, keeping Sir John Franklin on the public agenda for six years. She achieved this despite the repeated decisions of experienced officials and politicians to abandon the search as hopeless, dangerous and futile. That her campaign relied on Murchison's determined, self-interested political activity was clear to all those who shared the twin concerns of advancing scientific knowledge and finding the lost expedition. Where Murchison balanced those concerns is unclear – but his lobbying, arm-twisting, speeches and press releases translated Jane's passionate determination into concrete results. He was paid in fossils and polar place names. Sabine, his co-adjutor for two decades, exploited a quixotic quest for magnetic ends.[115]

The Admiralty met pressure for further search expeditions with a variety of unofficial and quasi-official responses. The discussions shifted seamlessly from private to public, some individuals appearing in more than one role. That the Board was not consistent allowed those within and outside the Admiralty to introduce their own agendas, consistently outmanoeuvring the Board. External influence had never been more effective in shaping naval policy – and the name of that influence was Jane.

1 A doom foretold: the gothic horror of Caspar David Friedrich's 'The Sea of Ice', painted over twenty years before Franklin's fated expedition, mocked the aspirations of those who sought the North West Passage.

2 The camera does not lie. Sir John Franklin was a stout old man of sixty when he set out to solve the last Arctic mystery in 1845. The only bit of him to return home would be the badge hanging from his neck.

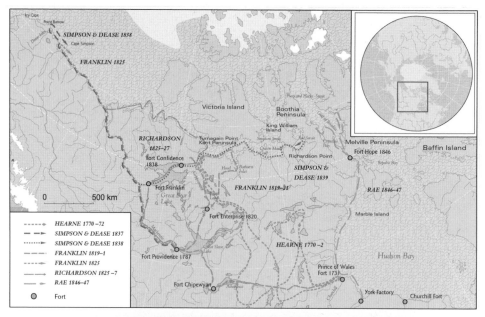

3 In the 1820s Franklin had mapped much of the North West Passage, and realised that it was no more than a geographical curiosity.

4 The reason why. In 1845 Franklin's primary mission was to conduct extensive magnetic observations as close to the magnetic North Pole as possible. One of the many instruments used by the expedition, this dip circle was the last thing his men abandoned before marching to their doom.

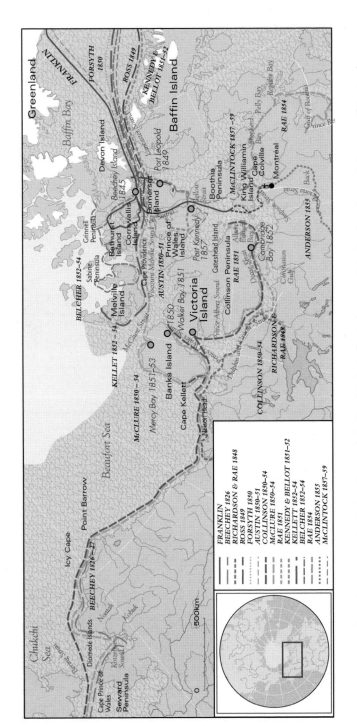

5 Barren victory. After a dozen years of suffering, the search for Franklin had effectively mapped the Arctic and proved that, even if it existed, a North West Passage was utterly useless for commercial navigation.

Map labels

Greenland

Baffin Bay

Devon Island

FRANKLIN

FORSYTH 1850

ROSS 1849

KENNEDY & BELLOT 1851–52

Baffin Island

Beechey Island

Beechey 1845

Somerset Island

Port Leopold 1849

Boothie Peninsula

McCLINTOCK 1857–59

King William Island

Cape Colville

Pelly Bay

Repulse Bay

RAE 1854

Montreal

Gulf of Boothia

Prince Regent

Back River

Bethurst Island

Grinnell Peninsula

Cornwallis Island

Cape Providence

Viscount Melville Sound

Prince of Wales Island

Port Kennedy 1857

Gateshead Island

Albert Edward Bay

ANDERSON 1855

Sabine Peninsula

BELCHER 1852–54

Melville Island

AUSTIN 1850–51

Walker Bay 1851

Victoria Island

Collinson Peninsula

RAE 1851

Dease Strait

Cambridge Bay 1852

Coronation Gulf

Simpson Strait

KELLETT 1852–54

McCLURE 1850–54

Mercy Bay 1851–53

Banks Island

1850

Prince of Wales Strait

Prince Albert Sound

Dolphin and Union Strait

COLLINSON 1850–54

RICHARDSON RAE 1848

Cape Kellett

Nelson Head

Beaufort Sea

Icy Cape

Point Barrow

BEECHEY 1826–27

Chukchi Sea

Diomede Islands

Noatak

Kobuk

Kotzebue Sound

Bering Strait

Cape Prince of Wales

Seward Peninsula

500km

0

Legend

FRANKLIN
BEECHEY 1826
RICHARDSON & RAE 1848
ROSS 1849
FORSYTH 1850
AUSTIN 1850–51
COLLINSON 1850–54
McCLURE 1850–54
RAE 1851
KENNEDY & BELLOT 1851–52
KELLETT 1852–54
BELCHER 1852–54
RAE 1854
ANDERSON 1855
McCLINTOCK 1857–59

6 Edward Belcher's armada ended the official search mission. Belcher abandoned five ships in the ice, and was lucky to get home with most of his men.

7 Looking the wrong way. The mechanics of searching for Sir John were simple: men wracked by scurvy frostbite and hypothermia hauled sledges across the polar wasteland – without a clue where to find Franklin.

8 Anxious friends. Stephen Pearce's composite portrait includes all the key men of the official search mission. Franklin and old John Barrow stare down from the wall while Edward Parry, second left, examines a chart, white haired and distracted James Clark Ross stands at the shoulder of Sir Francis Beaufort, the seated figure at the heart of the story and composition, while to Ross's left are John Barrow junior, and General Sir Edward Sabine – the man who sent the expedition.

9 Forever young. Jane Franklin preferred to be remembered as she had been in 1816, a dozen years before she married Sir John, and fully forty before she took control of the search and remade his reputation.

10 A tragedy in note form. Fitzjames and Crozier left a single enigmatic message at Point Victory, recording Franklin's death, and their decision to march south towards the mainland. It is the only written evidence of the expedition's fate.

11 An American Arctic. Frederic Church's 'The Icebergs' of 1861 hinted at many dreams, an open Polar Sea, and God's divine purpose in the North, indicated by the cross-like wreckage. Rendered irrelevant by the outbreak of the Civil War, the picture would spend the next century in England, art, artist and arctic forgotten.

12 The end of all hope. In 'Man Proposes, God Disposes', Edwin Landseer captured the savage horror of the Franklin story for Victorian Britain. His bears, savage guardians of the icy north, feed on human remains.

13 Redemption. Only a decade later John Millais reversed his old friend Landseer's message. His 'North West Passage' helped to revive the national mission, and send more British sailors to die in the frozen north.

14 And yet men still search for dreams and delusions amid the epic grandeur of the High Arctic. The wilderness of ice and rock, deep inside Smith Sound, would witness further tragedy before the century was out.

15 The truth will out. Discovered on King William Island by a Canadian expedition in the summer of 1945 this pile of skulls marked the expedition's descent from tragedy to horror.

16 The lucky ones. Three of Franklin's men had Christian burials on Beechey Island.

Belcher

WHILE JANE and her acolytes were struggling to make sense of the Beatson fiasco the Admiralty reluctantly came to the conclusion that it must make one last official search. Despite the failure of 1850–1 Jane still believed the Wellington Channel route held the answer. Beaufort agreed, suggesting the expedition must have gone far further north than the last search mission, and that it was essential 'to push on fearlessly and decide this trying question'.[1] Furthermore, as Captain Milne had anticipated, it was no longer just Franklin that was lost. Another expedition had disappeared.

The Bering Strait expedition

The failure of the massive effort in 1850–1 to reveal more than three graves and some camp detritus on Beechey Island was a serious setback. Austin, Penny, De Haven and Ross returned with no better idea of where Franklin had gone, or why, than they had before they left. The Arctic was not ready to give up its secrets. Beaufort's response to the incomplete data was thoroughly in character. He applied logic and experience to the fragmentary evidence. His original Admiralty memorandum of November 1848 had been fundamentally flawed: it presumed the party was still alive, despite the exhaustion of their stores earlier in the year, on the flimsy precedent of John Ross's good fortune in 1829–33. Beaufort maintained that Franklin must have passed Cape Walker before heading southwest, thereby shifting the locus of the search too far west. He assumed suitable ice conditions had allowed the ships to go further west before they became trapped, therefore their overland escape route lay towards the Coppermine or Mackenzie.[2] By 1850 it was obvious that if Franklin could not send a message to the Baffin

Bay/Lancaster Sound area there was little point starting a search for him in that area. Therefore, he argued, current searches should be concluded in favour of a renewed effort inside the Bering Strait.[3]

With the support of Ross, Beechey, Back, Parry and Richardson, Beaufort persuaded the Admiralty to send *Enterprise* and *Investigator*, just returned from Ross's expedition, to the Bering Strait. He also wanted Rae to search the coast, but both expeditions were looking in the western half of the region, not the eastern. To command the new expedition he selected Captain Richard Collinson, another surveying officer, with Commander Robert McClure, recently a lieutenant under Ross, as his second.[4] This was Beaufort's pet project, occupying every waking moment for weeks on end as 1849 turned into 1850. In the event McClure's single-minded ambition wrecked the careful planning, limited the science, and destroyed any chance of completing the tasks Beaufort had delineated with such care.

McClure lost touch with Collinson soon after rounding Cape Horn, and rushed into the ice without waiting for his senior officer, against the orders of Collinson's friend Captain Henry Kellett. Not only did this deprive Collinson of his interpreter, it also ruined Beaufort's basic plan of employing two ships in company for a careful, thorough search.

To his credit McClure made remarkable progress to the east, but it came at a terrible cost in human suffering and naval stores. After two winters his ship was hopelessly trapped in Prince of Wales Strait; only a miracle prevented him from joining Franklin among the lethal mysteries of the Arctic. Then his escape was turned into a successful transit of the North West Passage. That the Board of Admiralty was pleased to accept this 'dubious substitute for what England and the world had had in mind for three centuries'[5] reflected the triumph of very different agendas over the Arctic mission.

Collinson did much better. Delayed by uncertainty over McClure's position, he finally entered the ice the following year. His 300-mile passage east along the north coast of America, through Dolphin and Union Straits, Coronation Gulf and Dease Strait, took him into an area hitherto thought impossible for sailing ships. In the process he came closer than any other naval mission to both solving the Franklin mystery and completing the North West Passage. Passing his second winter in Cambridge Bay the lack of an interpreter prevented Collinson understanding Inuit hunters who knew about Franklin. At one point he was only seventy miles from the abandoned ships; he could have crossed Victoria Strait and visited King William Island, where Franklin's ships were locked in. Instead Collinson spent three torrid winters in the ice and then brought his ship home. By the time he returned the Arctic mania had passed, he received no thanks, and his journal, unlike those of other expeditions, remained unpublished for twenty years.

However, all that lay in the future. Just as the Bering Strait expedition was lost to view the massive armada sent to Lancaster Sound came home. It had failed to find Franklin, and came back convinced he had not gone down the Peel Sound.

Sir Edward Belcher

Before reaching any decision about further searches the Admiralty consulted another expert. Able but pathologically irascible, Captain Sir Edward Belcher was the stormy petrel of the hydrographic service. Although he was not an Arctic expert – his service under Beechey in the 1820s included little time in the ice – Belcher had long been one of Beaufort's favourite surveying officers. He was also a friend of Murchison and Sabine, with whom he shared scientific interests and conservative politics. Sabine considered it 'impossible to speak too highly of Capt Belcher's zeal and indefatigable perseverance, or of his minute & scrupulous attention' in pursuit of magnetic data.[6]

Suitably prompted by the Hydrographer the Arctic Committee recommended a new expedition, using the four ships that Austin had recently brought home. Beaufort had tried to send Belcher to the Bering Strait, but the Admiralty would have none of it. Only by sheer persistence did he secure Belcher the command of HMS *Assistance* and the expedition. Fellow surveyor Henry Kellett, already a stalwart of the Bering Strait search, would command *Resolute*. Leopold McClintock and Sherard Osborn took the steamers *Intrepid* and *Pioneer*; sledge traveller William Pullen commanded the depot ship *North Star*. Many of the junior officers were experienced in and on the ice.

In late 1851 Sir Francis Baring confirmed Belcher would command the expedition, but in a private interview stressed that he should abandon the ships if they became trapped in the ice rather than risk the lives of the men. Like any politician caught between the Scylla of failing to search and the Charybdis of responsibility for a further catastrophe, Baring wanted to limit risk. He need not have worried. Before Belcher sailed the Russell government fell, and Baring was succeeded by the Duke of Northumberland. Northumberland emphasised that the mission should search for Franklin 'and not for the North West Passage'.[7] Belcher's selection had been the last throw of the dice for the Liberal government of Lord John Russell. When Lord Derby's Conservatives took office, Belcher's politics became irrelevant – and the inexperienced new First Lord lacked the insight to foresee problems. Belcher's tempestuous, confrontational leadership was particularly ill suited to the close confinement of a polar winter, and the shared hardships of officers and men in extreme latitudes. He lacked the humanity and consideration that enabled Franklin to lead officers and men without resort to rank and authority. A decade earlier Admiral Sir William Parker had summed up Belcher to perfection: 'A skilful navigator and a clever seaman you may be, but a great officer you can never be, with that narrow mind.'[8] A nit-picking, bullying martinet, Belcher had displayed the same character flaws in every command. Despite that, Beaufort chose him; navigational skill and magnetic science outweighed common humanity.

While Jane was happy to see another official expedition underway, Beaufort had finally given up hope of finding his old friend, or anyone else from the original expedition. But while the public was in the mood for searching he was happy to exploit the opportunity to improve his charts: 'Many of the orders that Captains received would appear to have more to do with surveying than rescue.'[9] While divergent orders may mitigate Belcher's abject and predictable failure as an expedition leader, the blame lay with Beaufort, but he did not act alone.

Beaufort and Sabine chose Belcher for the same reasons they chose Franklin. Beaufort remained deeply committed to Sabine's magnetic project because Sabine never lost an opportunity to link his aims to the Hydrographer's obsessions. All four commanding officers had extensive magnetic experience, while Sabine trainee Lieutenant Bedford Pim was a late addition to the scientific party. Sabine established the research aim of the expedition. Recent observations by John Richardson[10] and Captain Lefroy at Fort Athabasca and Fort Simpson 'shews it to be <u>particularly desirable</u> for the Theory of Terrestrial Magnetism that hourly observations of the magnetic declination should be made by the Arctic Expedition now in preparation during the months in which the ships may be stationary'. To make these 'very simple' observations Sabine prepared a full set of the necessary instruments, and ensured Belcher and Kellett would oversee the work. It only remained for Beaufort to send the magnetic officers to Woolwich to conduct the base observations with their instruments.[11] These were essential 'if those to be made with them in the course of the expedition are to have any scientific value'. The officers did not arrive, forcing a disgruntled Sabine to conduct the base observations without them before letting Beaufort understand that he was not best pleased.[12]

After reading the search record Belcher believed Franklin had gone north up the Wellington Channel, and that he must have left markers, standard practice for Arctic and hydrographic officers. He was equally certain there were survivors. Belcher expected to winter in the ice, reminding Beaufort that he had designed the internal strengthening of the lost ships in 1835. A more immediately useful factor was his confidence that he would find Franklin's report at Beechey Island.[13] Beaufort agreed that 'no one who knows the man can doubt it. It will be found.'[14]

In March 1852, with the expedition preparing to sail, Francis Cresswell, father of Samuel Gurney Cresswell, one of McClure's lieutenants, wrote to the political secretary of the Admiralty. While Cresswell was not alone in his concerns, the Norfolk landowner had useful Conservative connections. Through them he urged that the new expedition should visit Winter Harbour on the south side of Melville Island – because that was where the lost ships had been advised to send for relief.[15] In fact young Cresswell had already left a message at Winter Harbour. With Collinson and McClure now missing in the central Arctic the search mission acquired a new urgency. Supplies would be deposited at Winter Harbour, with advanced markers on Banks Island.[16] After consulting Beaufort and Parry the Duke of Northumberland made rescuing the Bering Strait expedition a major element of Belcher's orders. The Naval Lords were unwilling to send another vessel but Milne, who had particular responsibility for the search, facilitated the new plan by leaving the depot ship at Beechey Island.[17] Once again Parry and Barrow were consulted. Once again optimism, enthusiasm and desperation combined to give the reading public the impression that the Admiralty knew that Franklin was in the Wellington Channel.[18] The sheer size of the expedition posed fresh problems: it would need a store ship after only a year, and Admiralty Secretary Hamilton feared those 'gallant fellows in the ice' might be forgotten.[19] He also recognised that the need to resupply *Plover* in the Bering Strait was a drain on the Pacific squadron.[20] Fresh pemmican was manufactured at Portsmouth in mid-1852 and delivered by HMS *Trincomalee*.[21]

The official Admiralty instructions were drawn up by Beaufort and Belcher. The squadron would enter Barrow Strait and use Beechey Island as a base and final refuge, relying on the depot ship *North Star* as a 'lifeboat'. As the last traces of Franklin had dried up at Cape Bowden, north of Beechey Island, two ships would search the Wellington Channel. The other two would head for Melville Island to deposit food, provisions and directions for Collinson's ships at Winter Harbour and Byam Martin Island. The steam launch left by Ross could be used, but stores should be left at Port Leopold. Belcher was to ensure his squadron kept in frequent contact. Finally, the Board gave him considerable latitude to exercise his judgement.[22]

Encouraged by a steady stream of magnetic data, and the prospect of yet more from Belcher's ships, Sabine exploited every opportunity to maintain the profile of his science. Mutual interest ensured Sabine kept in close contact with Jane.[23] John Rae arrived in London to collect the Gold Medal of Murchison's Royal Geographical Society for an epic 1851 expedition to map missing sections of the Arctic coast. Richardson considered the medal no more than the Orcadian's due. Rae, he declared, had 'completed the N. W. P. At all events he has traced this so far that there is a moral certainty of the existence of the passage.'[24] Recognising the important role that Edward Sabine and his magnetic data could play in generating future Arctic missions, Rae offered to conduct observations on a forthcoming coastal survey for the Hudson's Bay Company.[25] When Kane asked for magnetic advice, Sabine suggested he should receive the same equipment as his British contemporaries and, knowing that Beaufort was anxious to assist the American, seized the opportunity to advise him that the gear was ready should the Admiralty wish to send it.[26] Like most Arctic missions Kane's produced a series of results, published by the Smithsonian Museum in Washington.[27] Another chancer to exploit the magnetic card, Erasmus Ommaney, revived the ridiculous notion of reaching the North Pole by sea. After taking credit for the Austin expedition's magnetic work[28] Ommaney found his desk job in the Coastguard Office rather dull. Sabine was easily persuaded, Beaufort easily enlisted and an approach to the British Association was planned.[29]

Belcher's expedition

Belcher's five ships reached Beechey Island on 11 August 1852. After a brief run ashore he quickly decided the island had witnessed a catastrophe. Three days later Belcher dined his officers and divided his squadron. *North Star* took up her winter station and waited. Belcher made a very short voyage north up the Wellington Channel, reaching 77°53'N, and named Northumberland Sound before being frozen in on the 20th. The expedition sledges were soon in motion, each carrying a proud silken banner twenty-five feet long, made by ladies deeply interested in the search and emblazoned with a stirring motto. There was no trace of Franklin – only ample evidence of earlier searches.

In May 1852 Jane took control of Beatson's ship. She had anticipated inheriting her father's estate and funding another expedition, but her father wisely bequeathed the money to a nephew, leaving Jane with a ship but no funds. When the Admiralty refused to take over the *Isabel*, she turned to Murchison, hoping his scientific standing and personal connection with the Duke of Northumberland would help. They argued that Belcher hoped the *Isabel* would join him, under Captain Edward Inglefield RN, and warned that the

American expedition might have to be fed.[30] Within a month the Admiralty had reversed their decision: *Isabel* was manned, towed to Peterhead and sent to search the shores of Baffin Bay. Captain Inglefield persuaded Jane to endorse a search of Smith Sound, in line with his own geographical interests. *Isabel* entered Smith Sound, achieved a new furthest north at 78°28' and visited Beechey Island, where Inglefield dug up John Hartnell for a rudimentary autopsy. He repaid his debt to Murchison by awarding Sir Roderick a strait,[31] but another scientific supporter earned the honour of furthest north: Cape Sabine on Ellesmere Island. Having pushed further north than any previous navigator and linked up with Belcher, Inglefield was home by the season's end, bringing Belcher's dispatches and proving that fortune favours the bold. Beaufort was not alone in considering Inglefield's achievements remarkable.

With his two ships safely moored for the winter the old Belcher emerged, complaining about his equipment. Sherard Osborn was more concerned to look for an open Polar Sea, naming his sledge for the chief of that faith, old John Barrow. The following spring sledge travellers named a mountain for Beaufort. Further west, *Resolute* and *Intrepid* headed for Winter Harbour, but were iced in a little less than a hundred miles short. They immediately began the search for Franklin, and more realistically for McClure and Collinson. McClintock, Mecham, Pim and others made heroic long-distance journeys in the autumn and the spring. Cold, wet and malnourished men suffered severely for the determination of their leaders. Both McClintock and Mecham made journeys of over a hundred days, covering 1,200 miles. Links were forged with Belcher's party by Lieutenant Richard Hamilton, the most accomplished dog sledge driver, who met Osborn and George Richards, second-in-command of the *Assistance*. Kellett's officers also flew carefully crafted banners on their sledges, as McClintock observed: 'Unconsciously they have created an age of chivalry in favour of our long absent countrymen.' They felt as the Crusaders of old.[32] Saving life proved a more powerful spur to action than the acquisition of geographical information.[33]

However, it was abundantly clear to Kellett and his officers that massive multi-year ice fields made any further progress west or south perfectly impossible. Instead they made contact with *Investigator*, stuck fast on the other side of the ice, through the Arctic post box at Winter Harbour. After debating the options Kellett ordered McClure to abandon his ship and retreat. Lieutenant Cresswell carried McClure's dispatches to Beechey Island, becoming the first man to cross the Arctic from the Pacific to the Atlantic, although a critical part of his journey had been by sledge.

In the summer of 1853 Belcher fell ill and became increasingly difficult. Much of the burden of maintaining harmony fell on George Richards, who had seen it all before on HMS *Sulphur*. Satisfied the Wellington Channel theory was no longer valid, Belcher led his ships south when the ice broke up and wintered for a second year on the west coast of Devon Island. Although only fifty-four miles cross-country from the depot at Beechey Island, the winter base he chose proved to be a trap. Worse still there was no fresh game to be had. By late autumn the ships were in the grip of a scurvy epidemic, with Belcher among those afflicted. One man died.

That winter Kellett retreated east, but did not get back to Beechey Island. His ships, crowded with *Investigator* survivors, were running short of food and clothing.[34] He had intended to search Peel Sound the following year but gave up the plan after hearing that Rae planned to travel that way. Then in May 1854 George Mecham located a cairn Collinson had built on Princess Royal Island, the first news from the missing *Enterprise*. By the time Mecham returned to *Resolute* she had been abandoned, the crew retreating to Beechey Island. Belcher had ordered Kellett to abandon his ships on 30 April, somewhat prematurely as it turned out. Belcher hung on until the end of August, when it became clear that *Assistance* and *Pioneer* could not get out of the winter anchorage. Then Sir Edward precipitately abandoned four perfectly sound ships in the ice, despite the dissenting opinions of his officers, and retreated to *North Star*, Milne's 'lifeboat'. All four crews were crammed into the hold of *North Star* and preparing to sail when the steamer *Phoenix* and the transport *Talbot* arrived under Captain Inglefield. Inglefield reported that a war had broken out with Russia. The men were spread between the three ships, and all were back in Britain by the end of the season. Belcher's decision to abandon five naval vessels in the Arctic provided a suitably dramatic end to the naval search mission.

Politics

In January 1853 another Board of Admiralty assembled to address the ongoing Arctic crisis. Lord Aberdeen's Peelite/Liberal coalition had replaced the Conservatives, bringing a new political master to the Admiralty. At least Sir James Graham was experienced: he had been First Lord when Franklin commanded the *Rainbow*. As the only Naval Lord to have been in office since the search began in 1847, Captain Alexander Milne provided a memorandum. The Board faced a clear choice: it could send out further supplies for Belcher's large force or order it home in August 1853 and abandon the search.[35] In May, with the navigation about to open, fresh orders were drafted for Belcher. If no trace had been found of the Franklin expedition,

it does not appear to us that there is any other direction in which a prospect of their discovery can be expected. Every accessible part of the shores of the Polar Seas, west of Lancaster Sound, will have been visited without finding a trace of the missing ships except their former station at Beechey Island in 1845 and 1846. In such a contingency as this, and if such should likewise be your opinion, after mature consideration with the senior officers under your command, there appears no other course but to abandon all further search.

The letter was dominated by concern for the safety of Belcher's expedition.[36] Franklin was fast fading away. The Admiralty had finally given up: they had wasted enough ships, men and money. The tragedy was that Belcher's mission had been based on a fundamental mistake. The same effort driven down Peel Sound, or across Boothia to King William Land, would have solved the riddle.

Despite the end of the search mission Beaufort and Sabine pressed on with their magnetic enterprise. The Hydrographer wanted to add the latest information on magnetic variation to his charts so that navigators could profit from the work of the last three decades. This work depended on Sabine, the Hydrographer's Department having 'no time for patient investigations of that nature'.[37] Sabine duly extracted his pound of flesh; magnetic observation books would be provided to all ships. 'In short no effort shall be wanting here to rescue this prodigiously important arm of navigation from its present empirical and very unsatisfactory state.' To get his magnetic parallels Beaufort was not above a little flattery: 'thanks to your indefatigable labours the true seeds of magnetic knowledge have been so copiously sown that vigorous plants and abundant fruit must soon spring up and ripen in every country'.[38]

Searching for closure

Although Belcher, McClure and Inglefield headed home at the end of 1854, beaten by ice and storms, Collinson persisted. Not only had he and his ship survived, but he reached much further east than any other ship that had entered the Bering Strait, and explored the area round Cambridge Bay and the east coast of Victoria Land. He spent the winter of 1851–2 close to McClure, but the ships never made contact. His passage through the Dolphin and Union Straits to Dease Strait was a remarkable feat of seamanship, one that inspired Roald Amundsen to take that route. Wintering in Cambridge Bay he nearly met Rae on the west coast of the Victoria Channel in spring 1853, both men being on the wrong side of the strait to find the remains of Franklin's expedition. However, he did find two pieces of door frame, suitably marked with the Admiralty Broad Arrow, on Finlayson Island, and these almost certainly came from Franklin's ships. Collinson left for the west in mid-August, only to find his route blocked at Camden Bay, where he wintered. The next summer he made contact with the long-suffering depot ship *Plover*, now commanded by Captain Rochefort Maguire, received his mail and spent some days at Port Clarence, where both ships prepared to travel home. *Plover*'s six-year Arctic vigil was over, and after conducting the obligatory magnetic observations with *Enterprise*'s equipment the two ships set sail in mid-September. Sabine praised Maguire's magnetic work, the longest and most accurate data set yet gathered from the western Arctic.[39] The last naval vessels had left the Arctic, and none would return for twenty years. When Collinson arrived home in May 1855, he found himself ignored. He wanted the officers who had made the commission difficult to be court-martialled but the Admiralty refused, desperate not to raise the very word 'Arctic' ever again. It had not been a happy voyage. Years of hardship, boredom, monotony and the petty friction of over-familiarity took their toll. The latest account portrays Collinson as a 'suspicious, arbitrary, vindictive martinet' who terrorised his officers while treating his men leniently. Even praise for his remarkable skill in navigating a clumsy sailing ship through ice-choked channels, avoiding the fatal entrapment that befell Franklin, McClure, Belcher and Kellett, is tempered by the accusation of timidity.[40] Among those best placed to judge, Arctic veteran and later Hydrographer of the Navy George Richards considered Collinson's voyage the most remarkable of the search, while his scandalous treatment 'is only to be accounted for by one of those gusts of popular impulse, which at times blind men's understandings, and obliterate their better judgement, until in the end injustice becomes more expedient than honourable recantation'.[41]

Had Beaufort still been in office when Collinson returned something might have been done, but Sir Francis had finally retired and the country was at war. Whatever the cause, the most brilliant achievement of the Franklin search passed without comment, and the most able Arctic navigator had to wait twenty years to be knighted for his services. While Collinson was making the long passage home, his insubordinate, disobedient junior, McClure, had been knighted, promoted and rewarded for reckless folly: the dutiful and correct Collinson was shunned. It was a mark of the Admiralty's anxiety to end this costly and embarrassing episode that it treated an outstanding officer with contempt. A very different fate awaited the next American expedition.

Another American effort

Encouraged by Inglefield's pioneering attempt the second Grinnell expedition followed his route into Smith Sound in 1853, shifting the focus of American efforts to the Polar Sea and the geographical pole. This time Kane was in command, a curious position for a rheumatic invalid doctor, one that can only be attributed to personal magnetism. His instructions from the US navy were scientific, making ample reference to terrestrial magnetism. Neither form of magnetism could stave off a predictable disaster.

De Haven had reported a glimpse of Maury's open Polar Sea at the northern end of the Wellington Channel, 'in confirmation of the theoretical conjectures as to a milder climate in that direction'.[42] Maury then cited this 'evidence' in his pioneering oceanographic study of 1855, *The Physical Geography of the Sea*, devoting a chapter to an open Polar Sea.[43] He also made sure that Elisha Kent Kane attended the Washington observatory to be briefed on this quintessentially romantic vision before he led the second expedition. The open Polar Sea, the scientific component of the package, ensured Kane followed Inglefield's route due north up Smith Sound. The argument was deceptively simple: if there was an open Polar Sea then Franklin might have found it, and still be stuck there, with an ample supply of animals to sustain life. Once again Kane saw exactly what he was meant to see, naming his polar sea for Maury, who wisely renamed it the Kane Basin.[44] That was as serious as the science got on Kane's expedition. De Haven's science had been 'a debacle', despite Kane's assertions to the contrary. His claims were rooted more in establishing his credentials to lead the second expedition than in any vestige of fact, and the science on his mission was no better. Science justified exploration, and kept American scientists onside as indicators of credibility. Kane built and operated a magnetic observatory on his expedition, using British instruments and methods dictated by Sabine.[45] His own contribution was a powerful pen portrait of the observer's existence which reflected his romantic vision of the Arctic, not the steady, chill slog of data gathering. He was the only magnetic observer to ask why they were gathering this mind-numbing data. But he was neither a navigator nor a seaman and did not understand why it was so important. He was happy to base his mission on an open Polar Sea, and then convince himself he had seen it. His scientific results, including the magnetic work, were published by the Smithsonian Institution.[46] They were not notable for their accuracy.

Despite extensive advice, collated by Beaufort,[47] from British friends and officials, and despite the opinion of his own crew, Kane pushed his luck, got stuck, lost his ship and was fortunate to escape with most of his men. After being rescued from certain death by Greenland Inuit hunters Kane led a 'heroic' retreat by sledge and boat, arriving home in late 1855. Kane's expedition was more than a scientific failure, it was a catastrophe. Men died, the ship was lost and the survivors escaped by the skin of their teeth.[48]

Yet such was the popular appetite for heroics that Kane received a tumultuous welcome on his return to New York and his second book became a runaway best seller. He carefully placed what little science had been completed in an appendix, well aware that it would be lost when the popular edition was produced. The role of the Inuit was played down and his own failings overlooked. Making heroes of his fractious, foolish followers pre-empted any serious criticism of his own role. A year later he visited England and took the plaudits of high society and learned societies alike, securing a unique place in Jane's heart. That her ideal Arctic traveller was a man on his death bed, lacking the skill and the science to do the job, is particularly revealing. Her vision was impelled by faith and hope; she was not interested in science or reason. She found comfort in the similarly obtuse ideas of Beaufort and Murchison, not the cold science of Sabine or the advice of veteran Arctic navigators. Kane died the following spring of a long-standing rheumatic heart condition. Death only emphasised the curious fact that he had become an international icon. His voyage made it clear that the United States' polar ambitions were geographical, and perhaps territorial.

Kane and Grinnell had turned the American Arctic mission into a story about explorers, not exploration. In Samuel M. Smucker's *Arctic Explorations and Discoveries during the Nineteenth Century* of 1857 the Americans triumphed in the Arctic. Smucker mentioned Robert McClure's voyage, but treated the entire nineteenth-century impulse as merely setting the scene for Kane's triumph, the final stage of the process. This was the literature of 'manifest destiny', seeking an American route, one which happened to coincide with Maury's mirage and the whaling interest.

Ending the search

The Franklin mystery began as an attempt to shift responsibility. Although the Admiralty had written off the expedition by 1852, presuming all were dead, the Board needed to find the all-important records, establish what had happened and ensure that it was not blamed. Murchison was still trying to browbeat the government into further action, publicly criticising Admiralty delay and inaction. Although the campaign was driven by Lady Jane,[49] Murchison used it to sustain his scientific agenda. Just when it seemed that there would be no end to the cycle of search, fail and search again, fresh news arrived in October 1853 that Lieutenant Gurney Cresswell from Robert McClure's *Investigator* had walked across the North West Passage. Having left a message at Winter Harbour, just as Gurney's father expected, the men of the *Investigator* had been saved from sharing Franklin's fate. This was very convenient for the Admiralty: the North West Passage had been found, and travelled. Parry and Ross were quick to congratulate Barrow on the fulfilment of his father's dream, although Parry had the decency to lament that no trace of Franklin had been found in the process.[50] Admiral Sir James Dundas, First Naval Lord during the early years of the search, spoke for many when he admitted, 'Franklin I now entirely give up.'[51] This was the perfect opportunity to close an embarrassing chapter. It required only a tough politician and a convenient excuse.

Two months later junior Naval Lord Captain Alexander Milne suggested the officers, men and ships of the Franklin expedition should be removed from the Navy List, both to tidy up anomalies – they were still being paid and promoted – and to make it clear time was up. This could be done in the naval estimates then in preparation, and Milne hinted the blow might be softened by promoting everyone, to increase the dependants' pensions.[52] After consulting the Admiralty solicitor, Sir James Graham simply had the names removed from the list with effect from the end of March 1854.

Graham had other concerns. A war with Russia was looming and France would be Britain's main ally! Then the Arctic produced a useful new hero. French Lieutenant Joseph René Bellot, lost in an ice crevasse while marching between two exploring ships, was canonised (not literally, but certainly metaphorically) on 4 November 1853 at a public meeting in Willis's Rooms in Central London. Murchison took the chair and Graham provided the main speech, seconded by Parry. Sabine and Robert Fitzroy moved that any surplus funds be used to provide a pension for Bellot's family. They were followed by John

Barrow, Edward Inglefield, W. A. B. Hamilton, Erasmus Ommaney and Horatio Austin. Sir Robert Inglis MP spoke to a succession of well-meaning motions. Graham was among the subscribers to the fund, as were the prime minister and the foreign secretary Lord Clarendon, both friends of Murchison. They added £25 apiece. Lord John Russell, always strapped for cash, managed £20, but Jane and Lord Ellesmere met the £25 standard. Rubber-boat pioneer Peter Halkett was another £20 man, while local shipbuilder Peter Mare provided £50, the donation of a man thrice bankrupted. John Murray primed the publishing pump with a suitably gentlemanly ten guineas.[53] The subscription funded a stark obelisk on the south bank of the Thames at the Greenwich Naval College, a navigational mark to remind passing mariners of a noble gesture. As mooted, the balance provided the dead man's family with a pension.[54]

To the Intrepid Young
BELLOT
of the French navy,
who in the Endeavour to rescue
FRANKLIN
shared the fate and the glory
of that Illustrious Navigator.
From His British Admirers.
1853–55[55]

Not to be outdone, the French government added a memorial at Rochefort, and another pension.[56]

The prospect of war prompted the *Liverpool Albion* to suggest that Britain's hard-won polar knowledge be exploited to attack 'into the very heart of Siberia' by river.[57] This was a visionary project when the weather in the Crimea proved quite capable of suspending hostilities. Recognising the war would distract the Admiralty from what was in her mind, the paramount duty of rescuing the lost navigators, Jane asked Barrow to have her latest letter 'put aside for a more favourable opportunity'.[58] That opportunity never came.

Then on Friday 20 January 1854 the Admiralty dropped Graham's bombshell. The *London Gazette* carried news that *Erebus, Terror* and their crew were to be paid off and removed from the Navy List. Jane considered the step premature, but Britain was on the verge of war with Russia and the navy had better things to do than look for 126 dead men or pay their relatives as if they were still doing service. Caught off guard, the London press did not get a chance to comment until Monday 23rd. While *The Times* took the official line, the *Morning Herald* denounced the 'indecency and inefficacy' of an administrative exercise to close a 'troublesome and expensive question, heedless of their own and the country's honour'.[59]

This outburst launched Jane's counter-attack, followed up with a public letter to the Admiralty combining a critical résumé of the flaws of every previous search mission and an endorsement of the open Polar Sea concept. Sir Robert Inglis read the draft, which he considered affecting, powerful and beautifully written.[60] Then she co-opted the scientists to her cause, protesting that the Admiralty decision to abandon the search would forego 'discoveries of great scientific interest and importance'. In response the Admiralty observed that since 1845 they had sent fifteen sea-based expeditions at a cost of £610,000, leaving aside private, overland and American efforts.[61] On 17 March the House of Commons was provided with copies of the correspondence, a sure sign that another Franklin debate was imminent. However, time was running out. Jane secured one last set-piece debate in Parliament on 4 April 1854, just a week after war had been declared. Sir Thomas Acland and Sir Robert Inglis demanded copies of Belcher's instructions, which Graham was happy to provide. He had wound up the Arctic campaign because the risk to those searching outweighed any hope of rescuing the lost. *Plover* would remain for another year, specifically to wait for Collinson. Although Disraeli had promised to support Jane's motion, he went home before it came to a vote and the leaderless Conservatives failed to act.[62] This was no time for petty political point scoring, and the House was content.[63]

Predictably Jane was not. Renewing her curious alliance with liberal internationalist and free trader Richard Cobden she urged Murchison to have the usual suspects sign a memorial demanding the current expedition be sustained, not recalled.[64] It was too late for such gestures, and the public would soon have more exciting news to consider. The Admiralty instructed Belcher that once the ice cleared he should withdraw his squadron, making some provision for the missing Collinson. He could, if necessary, abandon the ships he had so carelessly imperilled.[65] News from Collinson turned up just in time, and McClure arrived home to find himself the centre of attention. Murchison's Royal Geographical Society immediately awarded the Founder's Gold Medal for his 'discovery' of the Passage. McClure attended a reception at the Admiralty in early October, during the brief period when it was believed Sevastopol had fallen to an assault shortly after the battle of the Alma.[66] The curious coincidence of an officer being lauded for something he had quite evidently not done and a party being held to celebrate a victory that had not been won should not be overlooked. An overpowering anxiety for good news drove Graham's Admiralty Board in late 1854, reflecting his pathological fear of the print media. Little wonder lies and half truths quickly piled up around the Franklin story.

From the bottomless pit of Arctic despair the Admiralty had finally salvaged some good news. The Board decided that McClure had completed the North West Passage, despite the rather obvious caveat that he had been forced to abandon his ship and complete the navigation on foot across impenetrable ice. McClure should have been court-martialled for hazarding his ship and disobeying a senior officer: instead he was praised and rewarded for resolving a very embarrassing problem. He had taken care to destroy the journals of his junior officers, journals that would have revealed his disobedience of orders and foolhardy lunge for glory. While this allowed the Admiralty to close down half of the Franklin mission, no one noticed that their conclusions were precisely the same as William Scoresby's forty years earlier. The Passage had been found, but was impossible to navigate and could therefore for all practical purposes be ignored. McClure's priority would be contested, but the very fact that he was used to close the search ensured he would receive an undeserved reward. He had not found a navigable sea passage. By rewarding McClure the Admiralty confused the very meaning of the North West Passage, turning the search for a navigable sea route into the futile pursuit of a mere geographic curiosity. In addition the attitude of the Admiralty had a retrospective effect: it allowed men to take credit for achievements that had nothing to do with ocean navigation between the Atlantic and the Pacific.

While McClure could cite superior orders as his authority for abandoning the *Investigator*, Belcher was not so lucky. On 20 October 1854 he faced the court martial required by naval law to account for the loss of his ships. The prime minister's brother Admiral Sir William Gordon presided over an event staged at Sheerness in Kent, the navy's most isolated base. The official line was revealed in *The Times* on Trafalgar Day: Belcher would be indulged because he had brought his men home. If Collinson and his men were safe in England, 'and we were to hear no more of Arctic expeditions, we should be well content to compromise for the loss of the ships'.[67] Indeed the evidence was unequivocal: the men on Belcher's two ships would not have lasted another winter. This was hardly surprising: they had been driven into a part of the Arctic utterly bereft of game, and left to make do with their own stores. Kellett, whose men were in far better shape, having secured considerable supplies of fresh food, was pretty sure his ships could have escaped. He had located Collinson and the *Enterprise* after he had been ordered to abandon his ships. McClintock reckoned the *Resolute* and *Intrepid* would have drifted out of the ice that autumn.

Belcher's defence rested on the Arctic Committee instructions of October 1851, which emphasised that he should take no risks with the lives of brave men. He had searched as far as he could, and the Admiralty's orders of 1853 were to continue, but only if he had information to warrant another season, and could avoid unreasonable risk. The 1854 orders were to withdraw the entire expedition if possible, with considerable discretion to meet the circumstances. He had delayed only through concern for Collinson, but once he heard from *Enterprise* he decided to leave before the winter set in. He expected that either Collinson or one of his officers would appear at the Admiralty in the next two weeks. Predictably the Court heard that Belcher had fallen out with every single officer under his command, even Kellett, a colleague of more than twenty years. While the Court acquitted Belcher, it also censured him for failing to consult Kellett.[68] No one thought to criticise the folly of sending Belcher in the first place.

The acquittal was more a question of saving official face than establishing Belcher's innocence. Not only was Belcher never employed again but the Board emphasised its disapproval by promoting the very officers Belcher wished to court-martial. After the trial Belcher delivered his magnetic data to Sabine.[69] It had not been mentioned at the trial. In 1855 Belcher produced an exculpatory account of the expedition, *The Last of the Arctic Voyages*, which answered the question why, being dedicated to Beaufort.[70] Belcher had killed the official Arctic mission just as the Crimean War of 1854–6 provided an alternative focus for the Hydrographer. Yet even as the war began Beaufort told Murchison it was 'a sacred duty' to keep searching. 'We owe it to the character of our country to leave no stone unturned for that purpose, no spot on earth unexamined that might betray the place and manner of their fate.'[71] He refused to give up, supporting private efforts, British and foreign, on land and sea. For Sir Francis and Lady Jane faith remained stronger than fact, but they would face darker days before the year was out.

12

Martyrs of Science

Mutilated corpses

IN THE AUTUMN of 1854 the news took an unexpected and terrible
turn for the worse. On 22 October word arrived from John Rae, on
a Hudson's Bay expedition in the Repulse Bay area. He had encountered a party of Inuit with Franklin expedition artefacts in their
possession: a gold cap band, silver cutlery and Franklin's
Hanoverian order of Knighthood. They told him the white men had
all died some years before, and the all-important paper record had
been thrown away. (The Inuit were deeply suspicious of such stuff.)
Rae heard that a large group of survivors encountered on King
William Island some years earlier had been in poor condition,
afflicted with scurvy, and 'from the mutilated state of many of the
corpses and the contents of the kettles it is evident that our wretched
countrymen had been driven to the last resource – cannibalism – as
a means of prolonging existence'.[1] Rae's contacts had not met the
sailors, but they had the story on good authority from others who
had.

Rae had never intended the cannibal story to be made public,
expecting the Admiralty to publish a sanitised, official, version.[2]
Instead the unexpurgated text was released. *The Times* published it
on 23 October, reducing Belcher's court martial to a footnote. The
following day 'The Thunderer' majestically declared: 'We have had
quite enough of great Arctic expeditions . . . With the single exception of Captain McClure's they have invariably resulted in
disappointment and disaster.' The only thing left was to recover any
remaining books and papers, and throw full light on the transactions.[3] If only. Rae's sensational news even 'swallowed up interest in
the war'.[4] While the *Army and Navy Register* tried to stem the tide,
it was clear that the Franklin search was over. Only the post-mortem
remained, and that would require hard evidence.

Anxious to forestall any further futile searches in the Wellington Channel, Rae rushed home with a bundle of tragic artefacts. Each piece of cutlery bore the monogram of an officer who had died in the most horrific circumstances that middle-class Victorians could imagine. These quasi-religious 'relics' featured in the pages of the *Illustrated London News* a fortnight later.[5] A relieved Admiralty was quick to thank the Hudson's Bay Company for Rae's report, 'which set to rest the unfortunate fate of Sir John Franklin and his party'. The matter of Sir John was closed: the only remaining anxiety was Collinson.[6] When Beaufort advised the Admiralty that a land expedition to the Back river would establish the details of Rae's report, the task was delegated to the HBC. Rae drew up a plan to complete the Franklin search, and locate Collinson.[7] The Company was happy to oblige, because its charter was up for renewal and its fate lay in the hands of the British government.[8] Furthermore, the opportunity to open a new avenue for commerce at the Admiralty's expense would not occur very often.[9]

Rae's news was not unexpected, but the details were 'even worse than had been anticipated'.[10] Cannibalism struck deep into the self-image of the age; it ripped aside the veneer of civilisation so loudly celebrated at the Great Exhibition of 1851, exposing the brutal reality of human existence.[11] Inuit testimony was unequivocal: these men, emaciated, racked by scurvy and close to death, had breached the ultimate taboo. They had eaten their comrades. Such an accusation carried a terrible burden of horror, blasphemy and alienation. Cannibalism struck at the very heart of the Victorian sensibility, a dark, gothic reminder of man as savage, one that came with a grim baggage of psychosexual fear of the 'other', of non-European peoples, convicts and outsiders. It was most definitely not something that Englishmen did. No one remembered Alexander Pearce, the Tasmanian man-eater; instead questions were asked about the Inuit: these uncivilised heathen savages had told the story, perhaps they were the cannibals? But as anyone with Arctic experience well knew, the Inuit were quite capable of finding food for themselves; they had no reason to kill or eat Franklin's men.

The revelation hit London at a turning point in cultural sensibilities. Tales of sailor cannibalism, the cannibalism of necessity, were not uncommon in the early nineteenth century, notably among New England whalers. They had been a key source for Edgar Allan Poe's *The Narrative of Arthur Gordon Pym* and Herman Melville's *Moby Dick*. But Melville had linked the crime with savage peoples – Englishmen were not expected to eat each other. By the 1850s seafarers were losing their exotic outsider status. Their deeds were increasingly the province of domestic civil courts, their bodies a matter of civic concern. The Franklin story shook the Victorians to the core; it would be a test case for civilisation. In the clamour and furore that followed, the Franklin mission would be largely forgotten. The only things that mattered were English honour, and English civilisation, so when cannibalism joined Franklin in the latest edition of the *Encyclopaedia Britannica* the discussion was wholly concerned with 'savages'.[12] As Brian Simpson's *Cannibalism and the Common Law* made clear, the Victorians would not permit the old ways – the custom of the sea – to persist.[13] Such things were no longer acceptable, especially if the cannibals were English. There were standards to maintain. Not for another century, until a plane crash in the Andes in 1972 reminded modern man about survival cannibalism, were the moral and legal issues revisited. This time Hollywood turned the events into a drama.

Rae's terrible story ended any hope of further searches, just as he identified the area to be searched. After a decade of increasingly futile effort, each mission further from the locus of the disaster than its predecessor, it was clear that the Great Fish river and King William Land held the key to solving the mystery. Black-edged letters revealed that Jane, resigned to widowhood, remained anxious to know what had happened. Still hoping to find survivors, and more realistically documentary evidence, she hoped Rae's news would not prejudice the chances of recovering the records.

While Sir Roderick approved Rae's decision to return home, he considered his report 'must be open to much discussion' and, looking to practicalities, advised Jane to get up a public clamour for an adequate pension while raising the prospect that she would send her own expedition if the government failed to act. Finally, he developed the theme that had Jane's earlier expeditions only followed orders Rae's news would have been pre-empted.[14] Jane picked her preferred options from among Murchison's ideas, dropping the pension appeal, which was too obviously a buy-off clause. Her dreams of a new search were dealt a crushing blow by reports that Collinson was safe. She had hoped that in their collective desperation to find the *Enterprise*, Graham's Board might be persuaded to send a search party for Collinson. News from Collinson arrived on 6 November, ending her last chance of official support. That much was obvious from the decision to consult Parry, Beaufort and Rae.[15] Although she pressed Murchison to use his influence, Jane was already thinking along more realistic lines, planning to employ Franklin's estate to send her own expedition.[16] Over the next two years her objectives slowly changed from search and rescue to sanctify and commemorate.

In a classic example of shooting the messenger Rae was blamed for bringing the news to London. That his account was published by the Admiralty to solve the pressing political problem of how to end the search has been overlooked. As an outsider, a man of trade and the wild frontier, he could be hung out to dry to serve official ends, and paid off later.

Charles Dickens

Having digested Rae's report *The Times* was troubled by his reliance on Inuit testimony, suggesting the 'lying savages' might have murdered the lost party.[17] This approach struck a chord with Charles Dickens. Although better known today as a novelist, Dickens was the pre-eminent contemporary journalist with a prodigious popular output. As a keen student of human nature in adversity he had been fascinated by Arctic voyages, while according to his biographers cannibalism had been an obsession since childhood. Through his journal *Household Words* Dickens had been a stout supporter of the search, and the vision of a pristine Arctic that it implied. He felt compelled to contest Rae's account of cannibalism, although he did not dispute Rae's credibility. Trusting to the character of Franklin and the morality of civilisation he blithely dismissed the Inuit account as 'the chatter of a gross handful of uncivilised people, with a domesticity of blood and blubber'. The basis of Dickens's critique was highly significant. He cited Franklin's first land expedition and a series of contemporary shipwreck narratives to show that 'the coarsest and commonest men of the shipwrecked party have done such things; but I don't remember more than one instance in which an officer had overcome the loathing that the idea had inspired'.[18] Gentlemen simply did not eat other gentlemen; sadly, the lower orders were less discriminating. He may have been closer to the truth than anyone has hitherto suspected.

Drawing on Barrow's 1846 Arctic narrative Dickens produced two articles 'calculated to soothe the minds of their surviving friends' which appeared in *Household Words* on 2 and 9 December.[19] He sent them to Lady Franklin before they appeared in print 'as an assurance of his heartfelt sympathy, and his profound admiration for the character of Sir John Franklin'.[20] While commendable, and not without forensic merit, Dickens's argument that the 'covetous, treacherous, and cruel' Inuit had murdered the survivors was easily demolished by Rae. Rae's article was conclusive, leaving Dickens to append a note that dealt with the Inuit attack on Franklin's boats during his second voyage. More significant were the final words of Dickens's second article, a plea that the explorers be remembered for 'their fortitude, their lofty sense of duty, their courage, and their religion'.[21] With such sentiments animating his pen it was hardly surprising that Dickens was drawn into the Franklin search nexus, linking up with Murchison and attending such core events as the sailing of the last search mission and the exhibition of the greatest Arctic picture. Later he produced Wilkie Collins's play *The Frozen Deep* with stage sets by marine artist Clarkson Stanfield.[22] Catching the public mood to perfection, and exploiting the sensational news, Dickens used his Arctic reading to give the play a serious theme, examining the nature of heroism through the central character's struggle with the temptation to murder. The master of melodrama reduced his audiences, royal, noble and nondescript, to tears, while Murchison took part in one country-house production.[23] Dickens would not be the last to seek some external cause for the disaster. To this day hardly a decade passes without a sensational new explanation that blames someone, or something, for what happened. Such works simply ignore the effective absence of any written records from the expedition.

Like Dickens's output they belong in the category of imaginative fiction.

Despite the sensation caused by Rae's report and the intervention of Britain's leading journalist the Admiralty merely asked the Hudson's Bay Company to check the story. The Admiralty did not want any more information – especially if it was tainted with cannibalism.

Closure

Rae's overland travels had proved the insularity of King William Land, a fact that has led some to contend that he 'found' the North West Passage. The claim is no stronger than McClure's, and does Rae no service. (Neither would he be the last to be credited with its discovery.) He had seen a strait that might, if it was deep enough, allow ships to pass to the east of King William Island. He had not made a sea passage, nor could he chart the strait. If the point needed further proof Rae spent some of his reward money on an unsuccessful attempt to navigate the Passage.[24]

After a period of denial and counter-attack Jane accepted the news was indicative, but incomplete. Hearing that a Hudson's Bay expedition would resolve the question she urged the Admiralty to send a naval officer to take accurate navigational fixes and complete the sacred mission by recovering the remains and effects of brother officers. While still clinging to the faint hope that there might be survivors living with the Inuit, she had begun to stress a new imperative, 'collecting and keeping inviolate the official records of the Expedition, so interesting to the public, and private letters and papers so precious to their surviving friends'. Basing her arguments on the opinions of Kellett, Parry, McClintock and Rae she claimed that these records would establish the achievement of Sir John Franklin. She would use them to build his legend. Because the searchers were acting as executors they should be friends of the lost men, and they needed to find the lost ships. Collinson finally persuaded her that the *Erebus* and *Terror* had sailed down Peel Sound, and become trapped north of King William Land. Little wonder she wanted to see the instructions sent to the HBC.[25]

As ever, she turned to Beaufort for advice and comfort. The aged hydrographer suffered a heart attack that morning, but he replied from his couch in the afternoon. Realising that the only other man at the Admiralty to share his concerns, the second secretary Captain W. A. B. Hamilton, was out of town he sent the letter to John Barrow, hoping he could press the case on 'someone who had soul enough to feel the importance of the object.'[26]

Predictably the Admiralty's response was a crushing rejection. The mission had been entrusted to the Hudson's Bay Company, Lady Franklin could not see the instructions and no naval officer would be sent. 'My Lords are not prepared to recommend any expedition by sea or land which will entail the necessity of passing a winter in the Arctic Regions.'[27] This time Jane had met her match. Sir James Graham was far more able and far tougher than his political predecessors. He was not prepared to have his decisions changed by petticoat influence. Furthermore, Graham may have realised just how deeply his department had been penetrated by Jane's intelligence network. The need to focus on the war with Russia kept Beaufort busy until he retired in early 1855, while Barrow was losing influence and would be passed over for promotion. Although Graham left office in February 1855, his decision against further Arctic searches was upheld by his successor, Sir Charles Wood, a politician only a little less able.

Although depressed by Graham's blunt declaration, Jane was not prepared to give up. Her first act was to contact HBC expedition leader James Anderson. She begged him to find a critical piece of evidence, Franklin's private journal: 'a bound quarto memorandum book . . . It had brass at the corners and a lock and key.' She offered £700 if it could be returned to her unopened.[28] Then she regrouped, recruited more supporters, refreshed those who were wilting and moved to Pall Mall, a more 'accessible part of London', to direct a renewed political campaign. She had already picked Leopold McClintock to lead any privately funded search.[29] Murchison did as he was bid, writing privately to Sir Charles Wood soon after he replaced Graham at the Admiralty, with his usual mix of bluster and moral pressure. He deployed Jane's argument that a single steamship should be sent to check Rae's findings, under McClintock, and

stressed that his approach had the support of the scientific community and a significant body of MPs. Furthermore, if nothing was
done Lady Franklin would spend what remained of her own fortune. 'Lastly, I beg to assure you that this movement has not been
got up by me, but proceeds entirely from the relatives of the unfortunate voyagers with whom I have been urged to co-operate in
promoting this last Arctic adventure for the honour of Britain.'

The closing lines demonstrated just how far Murchison's credit as
a scientific 'expert' had been devalued by overuse and the constant
threat of public action to embarrass the government. Murchison
needed what little capital was left in the bank because there were
many other causes he wanted the government to back.[30] Even so,
Jane was quick to thank him for his effort, while dissociating herself
from Sir Robert Inglis's deputation to Wood. Inglis had been fobbed
off with the promise of a public memorial. She read Wood's gesture
as an attempt to close the subject, and told Inglis that she intended
to carry on. In case no one was listening, Jane dropped hints of failing health and renewed her contact with the Americans.[31]

McClure's claim

Unwilling to accept the Admiralty's decision as final, first Murchison
and then Jane opened communication with new prime minister Lord
Palmerston. Murchison was flattered by Palmerston's response, but
before such contacts could bear fruit McClure added a fresh complication. On 24 April 1855 he submitted a memorial to Parliament
requesting £10,000 for discovering the North West Passage. As the
relevant legislation had been repealed, there was no legal basis for
his claim. Instead McClure's case rested on the fact that the
Admiralty had awarded him a gold watch inscribed: 'Presented to
Captain Robert McClure by the Lords of the Admiralty on his
return to England from the Arctic Sea, after a perilous service in
search of Sir John Franklin in 1850–54, during which he discovered
the North West Passage.' The inscription, probably composed by his
friend John Barrow, was not intended to imply any fiscal obligation.
Nonetheless McClure exploited this marginal opening, claiming his
achievement was a national glory, the Passage being 'an object of

ambition to all maritime countries, the fortunate achievement of which has added another wreath upon the naval records of Great Britain'.[32] Two months later the House of Commons, with Palmerston's wholehearted support, set up a committee to judge the claim.[33] Jane was not impressed. Sophia Cracroft reported to Murchison: 'My Aunt's heart will be fully satisfied if the inscription on the Public Monument [to Franklin] records that the Expedition discovered the N.W. Passage. The Assumption of a Committee of the House of Commons will be as air when set against such an imperishable record.'[34] A permanent public memorial with the appropriate inscription would establish her historical truth.

It took Jane a week to collect her thoughts and write to Palmerston. She denied the validity of McClure's submission, citing two Arctic authorities: 'Sir John Richardson in a letter published in the *Times* of the 23rd has claimed for the *Erebus* and *Terror* under the command of my late husband, the first discovery of a North West Passage, and he treats this as a fact beyond dispute.' Furthermore, Rae's discoveries 'proved' that the Franklin expedition had reached the American coast, completing the passage six months before McClure discovered 'another' passage. Consequently Franklin had priority in discovery. She had no problem with a reward for McClure, rather she was 'advocating the claims of those who cannot speak for themselves, beyond the recognition of a death honourable to the memory of the dead and which detracts nothing from the merits of the living'.[35] Fellow conspirator Murchison received a draft of the letter, which was delivered to 10 Downing Street by 'dear friend' Richard Collinson, her new expert adviser.[36]

Jane spent two decades demonstrating that whatever McClure had discovered Franklin had been first: 'the judgement of those who best understand the question will be in favour of the *Erebus* & *Terror* & . . . this view must eventually prevail'. After discussions with Rae she held out little hope that the Hudson's Bay expedition would reach the mouth of the Great Fish river since the leaders lacked navigational experience. Even so, she offered a reward to recover Franklin's journal.[37] Jane believed the journal would establish Franklin's priority in the Passage and refute the cannibal slur. Richard Cobden advised her to make a direct approach to the

McClure Committee chairman, Conservative MP William Mackinnon, but she left that to Collinson. Jane was at a low ebb, and slightly subdued. A family controversy over Franklin's will had been deeply upsetting, while John Philip Gell's reference to her as 'that Tragedy Queen' was rather too close to the bone.[38]

Despite Collinson's testimony the committee ignored Franklin's prior claim to the passage.[39] After a brief debate on 31 July Parliament awarded McClure and his men £10,000, set aside £800 for a Franklin memorial at Greenwich and ordered that a medal be issued to all those who had taken part in the post-1815 expeditions and the search missions, naval and civilian, British, French and American. They were unable to judge if Franklin had found a passage. As Sir Charles Wood made clear, the purpose of the exercise had been closure: 'Now that his fate and that of his brave companions had become, unfortunately, too certain, there was nothing left for the country to do but to testify to its sense of their services by erecting some suitable monument to their memory.'[40]

The campaign medal for the 'war' on the ice was unusual: suspended by a polar star from a suitably white ribbon, the octagonal medal featured a discovery ship locked in the ice and housed over for winter, a sledge party setting off in the foreground. Altogether more curious was the decision to issue any medal. Such tokens were usually given for successful campaigns and conflicts: the Arctic campaign had been a costly defeat, and the cause had been abandoned.

Adding insult to injury, Chief Factor Anderson's expedition down the Great Fish river proved as ineffective as Jane had feared. Lacking navigational skill and an Inuit interpreter, Anderson merely recovered more silent Franklin artefacts. Despite that, he and his men were awarded the medal. Anderson's 'futile' expedition cost the Admiralty £217, the invoice paid despite the lack of receipts.[41] At least it narrowed the search to King William Island and demonstrated to any neutral observer that it would require a sea-based expedition with extended sledge work to reach the locus of the disaster.[42] Once again Jane urged Murchison to act:

I can hardly believe that after nearly 10 years of godly struggle purportedly to discover the lost Expedition, so that it will become an epoch in the records of the century, for future historians, it will have to be recorded that when the solution of the mystery was within its grasp, the country refused to grasp it. At a small expense & with very little risk, every doubt could be cleared.

The nation had raised a memorial to Bellot, but grudged Franklin and his men a Christian burial when the very location at which they died proved that they had really accomplished all that was needful for the work on which they were sent, and we refuse to snatch from annihilation the records of their struggle. This would never have been the case, I am persuaded, but for this unfortunate war, for tho' the public might be tired of the search, they would not have chosen the moment when the curtain was rising to avert their gaze and say they had had enough.

Although she knew the Americans had their own agenda in the Arctic, which she mistakenly believed was still the North West Passage, Jane was happy to revive their interest, hoping to prompt British action.[43]

Securing posterity

Despite the disappointments of 1854 and 1855 Jane missed no opportunity to advance her cause. An eighth edition of the hugely influential *Encyclopaedia Britannica* was in progress, and the publisher had consulted Barrow about an unsatisfactory entry on Franklin. Jane asked Murchison: 'You may imagine that I cannot be satisfied to leave such an opportunity alone, nor can I bear that the task should fall into incompetent hands.' Finally, Sir Roderick cajoled Richardson.[44] The result was the most commonly consumed version of the Franklin story to appear in the nineteenth century, a beautiful elegy for a noble Christian hero who had laid down his life to complete his mission.[45] No mean student of sentimental writing, Dickens found 'Richardson's manly friendship, and love of Franklin, one of the noblest things I ever knew in my life. It makes one's heart beat high, with a sort of sacred joy.'[46] Lines from Richardson's elegy would achieve timeless power, rendered in brass and stone.

The *Encyclopaedia* proved timely, for by the end of 1855 the Arctic had lost its allure. In December the Admiralty made the position absolutely clear. Two new warships were named *Erebus* and *Terror*, emphasising that Franklin's ships had been lost and that it was time to move on. This decision was one more step in the conscious process of closure.[47] Then Collinson delayed publication of his book, doubting the market would rise to another icy tale. His hope that Anderson would provide closure for Jane by recovering the journals proved well wide of the mark.[48] The Admiralty used Anderson's report to close the subject, and adjudicate Rae's claim to a reward for discovering Franklin's fate.[49]

Kane, the *Resolute* and the Americans

While Jane hoped American activity would shame the government into action, the Foreign Office used the safe return of Kane's North Pole expedition as an opportunity to thank the American government for Grinnell's efforts in the search. Despite new Hydrographer Captain John Washington referring to it as a demonstration of 'international sympathy' the American mission had not been looking for Franklin.[50] In truth the government was pleased to have something positive to say to the Americans after a period of heightened tension.[51] Grinnell accepted the British plaudits, medal and silverware in the spirit that they had been given, as 'a testimonial of the magnanimous spirit of your great and glorious country'.[52] Surely it was over now.

Ice and fate provided the Americans with an opportunity to respond in the same harmonious spirit. Anderson's report reached London on 8 January 1856, accompanied by Kane's gracious reply to the thanks offered by the British ambassador and news that the Americans had salvaged a British ship.[53] In a bitterly ironic footnote HMS *Resolute*, Kellett's ship, had survived her icy ordeal, and been driven out of Lancaster Sound into Baffin Bay by the current. Her hull crazed and leaking, she was salvaged by an American whaler. After the Admiralty had renounced any claim to the ship Grinnell, acting in support of the Arctic mission, had purchased her from her salvors and had persuaded the American government, who saw an opportunity to build diplomatic bridges, to refit the ship and return her to Britain. Buoyed up by the American concession that Franklin had priority among the Passage claims, Jane grabbed at this providential American lifeline, desperately trying to prove that *Resolute* had been returned in the expectation that she would be used in the Arctic.[54]

To profit from this new development, and secure another official search, Jane had to forestall the adjudication of Rae's claim for the parliamentary reward. She argued that Rae had hastened home and helped the Admiralty end the search mission rather than doing his utmost to ascertain the fate of the men. While he deserved a reward, giving him the entire fund would discourage any further effort. She was convinced the decision to hold the discussion in early 1856 was a deliberate attempt to stifle her plans. It was peculiarly ill timed: she had just worked Prince Albert into the frame, using his name to apply some leverage at the Admiralty. While she knew she would be blamed for persevering when others called for the search effort to end, 'Captain Osborn tells me that Captain Milne who is by far the best informed of the Lords of the Admiralty on the Arctic Question, is disposed to think something more should be done. He heard I was at Paris & supposed I had gone to get up a French expedition.' Clearly the methods of Lady Jane were well understood in White-hall. This time she was innocent, although she did express great interest in a new American expedition to the Polar Sea.[55]

By now most Arctic men accepted the search was over. It was time to thank the long-suffering back-room staff, and Sherard Osborn proposed that the Arctic officers recognise their friend John Barrow Jr. Jane was happy to join the memorial: Barrow had been her eyes and ears inside the Admiralty for almost a decade.[56] Furthermore, he shared her views, concluding the official record with a declaration that the search had been 'abandoned' before donating his Arctic collections, the product of many friendships, to the British Museum in November 1855.[57] In late June 1856 the Barrow Testimonial held a dinner and presented him with a suitably grand silver table ornament.[58] McClure emphasised that he had a permanent place in their affections.[59]

Barrow had started the congratulatory merry-go-round by organising a testimonial for McClure, complete with a complimentary address by James Ross.[60] After well-earned leave McClure had cashed in his credit with the Admiralty for a command afloat.[61] He had no doubt that a single ship could resolve the last remaining gaps in knowledge, notably in Peel Sound, travelling from Fury Beach, 'without the least risk or inconvenience' in about eighteen months.[62]

One last time

In June 1856 the Admiralty awarded Rae the £10,000 prize for ascertaining the fate of Franklin.[63] The minute was written by Sir Robert Peel, son of the prime minister who sent the original expedition, against the advice of John Washington, the new Hydrographer.[64] Washington believed Rae's claims remained unproven, and he had not done enough to satisfy a key stipulation of the award, ascertaining the fate of the men.[65] Washington missed the point: Rae's award, like McClure's, reflected a pressing urgency to close the story and clear the Arctic. This should have been obvious when the Admiralty printed Rae's report of cannibalism. By now Arctic death was no longer newsworthy. Many more Englishmen were dying in a far-off land, but they died in battle and their deaths were the news event of the decade. John Franklin's story had been overtaken by the Charge of the Light Brigade, his suffering supplanted by ministering angel Florence Nightingale.

Two pamphlets contested Rae's claim, but they were too little and too late. The Admiralty had closed the subject.[66] In their anxiety to renew the mission the authors of one pamphlet came closer to the truth than they realised, deriding the Admiralty decision to set aside £800 for a monument to the lost navigators, 'martyrs of science' who had discovered the North West Passage.[67] For this, and much else, the original authority was Sir John Richardson, who had coined the memorable phrase 'they forged the last link with their lives' in his brilliant essay for the *Encyclopaedia Britannica*.

Although she protested Rae's reward, Jane waited until the Crimean War was over before returning to the charge. On 14 April 1856, a fortnight after peace had been concluded, she renewed her call for a search. Receiving no reply, she waited until early June and then offered Barrow a portrait of Kane in return for inside information: 'What progress is making in the Arctic papers & when will be the right moment for making an enquiry in the House?'[68] She knew that the Admiralty had done nothing, and time was running out if a mission was to be sent that year. Murchison had approached Prince Albert through the Geographical Society, and Jane thought it might be timely to let the cabinet know the prince's views.[69]

However, Murchison's cross-party coalition was crumbling. While Conservative leader Lord Stanley would not object if the Admiralty went ahead with the limited mission Jane had outlined, he refused to sign a new petition, certain Franklin was dead.[70] Instead Murchison sent Elisha Kent Kane's opinion that there could still be survivors to Palmerston.[71] This material had been provided by Jane, turning Kane's celebrity into a weapon.[72] His populist, romantic version, science-light and full of mystery, was the ideal complement to Jane's 'heroic' Franklin. Between them they obscured the reality of the mission, whether deliberately or in ignorance, and they still dominate the story.

Murchison called for yet another committee of the usual suspects, including Edward Sabine, to determine the best route for 'a final search for the remains of Franklin's vessels'. He urged the prime minister to act quickly so that the search ship could find a good winter base. To catch Palmerston's attention he observed: 'The delay to another year would stimulate the Americans to do it, & deprive our country of the honour.' He knew his man: Americans and honour were enough to pique Palmerston's interest.[73] Murchison was also working *The Times*, although Jane was not entirely happy with his tactics.[74] She knew that Sir Roderick also acted as chief cheerleader for other explorers, notably David Livingstone, and needed to husband his credit with the ministry.[75]

Jane was still receiving inside information from the Hydrographer, John Washington carrying on from where Beaufort had stopped. Suitably prompted, Murchison had assembled another high-profile petition within forty-eight hours, signed by thirty-six luminaries including Sabine, Murchison, William and Joseph Hooker, William Whewell, Charles Wheatstone and even George Airy, and sent it to Palmerston on 5 June. Science backed Jane's desire to solve the mystery, if only because the solution might produce important scientific results.[76]

For Sabine another search would be a wonderful opportunity to follow up Maguire's excellent results from the western Arctic. Reporting in the 1857 volume of *Philosophical Transactions* Sabine praised the latest magnetic research, and revealed his hopes: 'In one of these expeditions in particular (the only one that unhappily has

not returned in safety) the well-known zeal of its commander SIR
JOHN FRANKLIN in the cause of science . . . gave reason for
hopes of the highest promise.' Confident Franklin would have conducted the necessary magnetic observations each winter, he was
desperate to obtain the data. As the record logs were too heavy to be
carried away by men retreating overland, the Royal Society hoped
they would be recovered.[77] This would be possible only if an expedition travelled to the locus of the disaster, exactly what Jane wanted
for her own purposes. Both wanted to recover the written record,
and because Sabine remained hopeful Jane was quick to pass his
advice to Murchison.[78]

Like most obsessive monomaniacs Jane was convinced that everyone else was out to block her plans:

It is the Admiralty policy to conceal this proceeding, just as they have sup-
pressed or cunningly delayed the publication of the Arctic Papers, including my
remonstrance against Rae's £10,000, because they do not want the arguments
for a final search to be known.

Convinced the reward to Rae was illegal, she hoped to embarrass
the Board into acting by offering Kane command of her expedition:

It must prove to them at once that their hope of crushing my efforts by delay &
by presenting the national grant to a wrong purpose cannot avail to put an end
to the question, & they must be well aware of the ill-aspect of a decision which,
in the face of the knowledge of an impending expedition under Dr Kane & his
officers & men, seems to have the direct object of cutting them off from reward
– a sorry return this for that noble compact entered into by the crews of the two
American searching ships of Mr Grinnell, who mutually swore before they
entered the ice that they would touch none of the £20,000 of our Government
however they might earn a title to it. Captain Osborn mentions this in his published Arctic voyages.[79]

This time Sabine provided the ideas and the leadership, which
Murchison employed in a letter to Colonel Phipps, Prince Albert's
private secretary. Sabine offered to contact Lord Ellesmere to ask if
he would advocate an expedition in the House of Lords. To ensure a
favourable reply Sabine would brief the Duke of Argyll, the scientific
cabinet minister, whom he hoped would reply on behalf of the government.[80] He suggested Murchison should contact Delane, hoping

to gain the support of the leading daily: 'Even if you gained nothing but neutrality, it would be worth while.'[81] With a daily sale of 55,000 copies this was the greatest prize in print media.[82] Murchison's ability to work the channels of politics and media was unique in its breadth and fluency.[83] Sabine observed: 'I am the last person in the world to apply to when Court Influence is wanted. You may be able to do something.'[84] The inner history of the Franklin search proves his point: Murchison was the key to opening the doors of power, even if Sabine provided the purpose.

From his active retirement Beaufort advised calling on Lord Ellesmere, president of the Royal Geographical Society, to ask the government how it had responded to the prince's message. He knew nothing had been done, and that the Admiralty remained deeply divided.[85] Any hope that the return of the *Resolute* might occasion renewed Admiralty effort were dashed by Sir Charles Wood's off-hand observations.[86] A few days later Jane sent a fresh letter to their Lordships, part of a new offensive. The area to be searched had been narrowly defined and it would now be possible to settle the question once and for all. As the Admiralty did not bother to answer her letter about Rae, she sent a scientific memorial to Lord Palmerston, and the prime minister replied. It was time to act if they were not to lose another season, although Beaufort, Collinson and Maguire favoured the Bering Strait route. This time the Jane effect did not work: 'My Lords have come to the decision not to send any expedition to the Arctic regions in the present year.' The reason for delay soon became clear: the Board had been trying to find a form of words that would convey unwelcome news, and dampen the premier's romantic impulses.[87]

To keep up the pressure on the Admiralty the remaining elements of the concerted attack went ahead. Lord Ellesmere was ill on the day of his motion, leaving Lord Wrottesley, president of the Royal Society to deliver an appeal that mixed magnetic science and raw emotion.[88] He enquired whether any reply had been made to the memorial calling for an official search in the area pointed out by Rae's discoveries. So far only forty men had been accounted for; others might yet survive with the 'Esquimaux'. At the same time the expedition might find Franklin's journals and records:

It was a great mistake to suppose that the interests of science were in no way concerned in sending out another expedition. In the first place, the scene of the catastrophe had been scarcely at all explored; and, in the next place, it was a great object to recover the magnetic records – for magnetical observations made within the Arctic and Antarctic circles were peculiarly valuable in reference to the theory of magnetism.

As Franklin's officers had been well trained and thoroughly equipped, their observations 'were likely to be very valuable'. A further expedition had been recommended in 'a temperate memorial, signed by influential and well-informed men of almost every grade and profession, and advocated by distinguished Arctic navigators, who supported their opinions by facts and reasonings which carried conviction home to the minds of men accustomed to estimate the bearings of doubtful evidence'. It would gratify the wishes of relatives 'and especially of a widowed lady who had made great sacrifices on behalf of her heroic and lamented husband; and, *above all*, that it would carry out to its legitimate solution an important problem in which the honour of England was largely concerned, and which had excited the curiosity and interest of the whole civilised world'.

To the disappointment of the scientists the government response came not from the Duke of Argyll but from Lord Stanley of Alderley, Owen Stanley's cousin. He had been briefed to reject, noting that Wrottesley's opinions were only to be expected from an interested party. The First Lord of the Admiralty had declared it was too late to sail that year, although he would consider the matter over the recess. Stanley wrapped up by pointedly asking Wrottesley if he would 'incur the responsibility of risking the lives of brave men for such an object'. Wood was prepared to send another expedition while there was any hope of saving lives, but it was a grave matter to send men to find further news of the dead and some scientific records.[89]

Despite Lord Stanley's statement, Murchison's latest effort hit the target. Palmerston accepted many of his arguments, telling Wood: 'I really think that in this and in other papers which I sent you he has established good ground for another expedition in search of the remains of the Franklin Expedition.' The risk was small and the search area much reduced.⁹⁰ Wood hid behind the fact that it really was too late to sail for Lancaster Sound, but he could not avoid the subject. Every time he disposed of an argument for searching, another sprang up, generated or exploited by his indefatigable opponent.

Hard on the heels of his second high-profile book Elisha Kent Kane arrived in London in October. He met the Board of Admiralty, the Hydrographer, Jane and Murchison, and received the Gold Medal of the RGS and the British Arctic Medal. Jane offered him the command of a private expedition, but Kane knew he would not see the ice again. Anxious to exploit the moment, Jane wanted to use Kane, willing or not, to promote her cause. Sabine had no qualms about sending an American. His only concern was the parlous state of Kane's health.⁹¹ However, the American had other ideas, and he was too sick for extended socialising.⁹² All too soon for Jane's purposes Kane set sail for the West Indies. He died at Havana the following spring. His funeral procession from New Orleans became the first great public display of mourning in American history. Jane had idolised the romantic Kane – his portrait hung on her drawing room wall in a velvet frame – but in private she admitted his grim book and early death had played a significant part in closing down the Franklin search.⁹³

The last months of 1856 were a quiet time for Arctic subjects. It was too early to agitate for a summer departure. Then *The Times* weighed in with a pre-emptive strike.⁹⁴ Claiming no officers wished to go, and that any ship sent risked being hurled back, it maintained a determined if ignorant opposition to further searches. Aware that such statements usually reflected government policy, Jane urged Murchison to remind Palmerston that Prince Albert had demonstrated 'very great interest' the previous year, which she was about to rekindle by sending him 'my present proceedings & application'; 'I believe such arguments as these are worth all the others put together.' She also claimed that many people were disgusted with the *Times* article – although she did not name them.⁹⁵

Barrow and Murchison compared notes, and realised that they were outgunned.⁹⁶ Even so, Murchison sent in a response, which Jane and Sophia Cracroft had produced from Collinson's draft. Bolstered by another memorial endorsed by the usual Arctic worthies, Jane's letter appeared in 'The Thunderer' within a week. Months earlier Grinnell had reported that *Resolute* was being refitted for return to England, and overtly linked Washington's decision to the state of Anglo-American relations and of the American Union,[97] whereas he had, in fact, purchased the *Resolute* himself and persuaded the American government to have her refitted. Jane shared the hopes of her Yankee friend, but she read the American gesture of goodwill as a telling argument for action. Surely international amity required the British government to send the *Resolute* back to the Arctic, and just in case it did not she raised the spectral form of Kane, to whose memory the British owed a debt.

With *Resolute* about to leave the United States Jane decided to renew her campaign, although she left the tactics of persuasion to Murchison.[98] The following day Sophia Cracroft equipped Sir Roderick with fresh letters from Collinson and Beaufort, which he duly passed to the prime minister.[99] Jane put her faith in Grinnell's American card: she trusted Murchison's Royal Geographical Society *Resolute* dinner would see the American ambassador declare that *Resolute* should be 'restored to the search as the best compliment that could be paid to the American government and people for fitting her out again and sending her back'.[100] Unfortunately George Mifflin Dallas, a sour cross-grained Anglophobe, wasted the gilt-edged opportunity for diplomatic bridge-building. At least he had the good grace to refer to the 'consecrated ship' when thanking the RGS, although this may have been done to embarrass the British government.[101] If so, his plan worked very well.

In the event the appeal to national honour and the return of the *Resolute*, whatever the deeper objects of the American government, were enough to convince Palmerston:

It seems to me that we cannot well avoid sending out the expedition and that not to do so would be discreditable . . . Having sent ship after ship when we had no idea where to look, now we know where to look can we give up now when we are so close to an answer? We know where to look, there has been little or no loss of life on searches, we have the means at hand, so no expense, and the idea is strongly urged by all Arctic navigators & scientists.

The prime minister assumed that Sir Charles Wood would comply with his wishes.[102] However, Sir Charles was made of sterner stuff.

There was little new in the Arctic papers, apart from the return of *Resolute* and Palmerston's 'concise and forcible summary of the reasons for sending the expedition'. He was singularly unimpressed by the opinions of those who bore neither risk nor responsibility, a line clearly aimed at Murchison, who would be Palmerston's house guest over Christmas.[103] While it had been possible the men might yet be alive he had been prepared to act, but he was convinced Franklin was dead and would not send an expedition to satisfy a curiosity for more information. The risk was unjustified; it might create another Franklin, and yet more rescue missions. Even if they found records they would be of 'no practical utility'. 'My own opinion is against it, Graham I know considered the question as settled & over. [First Naval Lord Admiral Sir Maurice] Berkeley is against it.' Only junior Naval Lord Alexander Milne was in favour. Furthermore, other cabinet ministers opposed the idea. 'In this state of things I think you must bring it before the government as a whole. If they are for it . . . I shall consider myself absolved from a responsibility which I confess I do not like to incur myself.' Palmerston found himself in a difficult position. If he wanted to act he would have to raise the subject in a cabinet where Wood had many political allies.[104]

The reappearance of the *Resolute* countered Wood's argument about cost, and added an international incentive. The restored ship arrived at Spithead on 12 December under the command of Captain Henry J. Hartstene USN, the officer who had rescued Kane's expedition from the Greenland coast. The queen went on board, invited the captain to dine at Osborne House on the Isle of Wight and sent £100 for the crew. Jane stood the crew a Christmas party in Brighton, and sent a suitably grand cake. Hartstene's brief celebrity saw him dine with Palmerston at Broadlands, where he hoped to promote another search.[105] The American served Jane's purposes to perfection. He offered to command a private expedition and when he handed the vessel to the Royal Navy on 30 December he spoke of the mutual interest that both nations took in the Franklin question. Even the usually anti-American media was suitably impressed by so charming an example of diplomatic signalling. Jane reckoned the *Resolute* had been a public relations triumph, and she gave full credit to Murchison's astute tactical work: 'Sir Roderick was my sheet anchor

& never did man exert himself more to make the best of it.'[106]

Yet for all Murchison's skill and determination the search agenda was beginning to fragment. Jane could co-ordinate the opinions of key Arctic officers such as McClintock and Collinson, but the political forum proved far more difficult. When McClintock argued that Palmerston was fearful of risk, she begged to differ: 'The only two things they care about is the money & the <u>trouble</u> – they would fain get rid of the thing altogether.' Even so, she believed it best to make the effort while Palmerston was still prime minister, convinced no one else would do as much. She was finally in a position to act alone, using funds just released by the sale of her land in Australia, but until the future of the *Resolute* was known she could not buy or build her own vessel.[107]

For all Jane's hopes the Admiralty had no intention of sending *Resolute* back north. They politely thanked the Americans and stuck the ship in reserve. Broken up in 1879, a desk was made from her timbers for the American president. John F. Kennedy was the first to use it, and it has remained in the Oval Office ever since. Prime Minister Harold Wilson gave Lyndon Johnson the ship's bell in the late 1960s at a time when Johnson was desperate for a British commitment to Vietnam.

On 6 February 1857 Parliament aired the subject once again, only for radical MP John Roebuck to go off message. He asked if the Admiralty was sending a land expedition, an idea prompted by Lieutenant Pim and Dr King, according to Sophia Cracroft, 'contrary to the express wishes & intimations given to Mr Pim, whom we told that though my Aunt would be very glad of the <u>co-operation</u> of Mr Roebuck, the subject would be in the hands of other parties who had consented to bring it forward'.

Sophia begged Murchison to write to Roebuck. 'He cannot disregard what <u>you</u> say, as he might and probably would a letter from my Aunt, we know that her unsupported testimony is considered suspicious because biased by personal anxiety.' Roebuck's intervention was particularly galling. Working with Crozier's brother Jane had primed prominent Conservative MP Joseph Napier to speak, and was anxious Napier should not think she had anything to do with Roebuck's motion.[108]

Roebuck's intervention ensured the debate did little to clarify the situation. After yet another letter from Murchison detailing Lady Franklin's views Palmerston was largely persuaded.[109] He still required expert opinion on safety, 'for nobody would deny that the expedition ought to be sent out, if it were certain that it would return in safety after one or even two winters in the ice'. Wood's objections were dismissed by Palmerston. They reflected 'the opinions of men who have no practical and local knowledge', notably First Naval Lord Admiral Berkeley, whose family was noted for prejudice and obstinacy:

There is always a prima facie case for doing nothing in any case, but there is a reaction after, and in this instance science and feeling are against you, and may work their way. It would certainly not be honourable to the government if after their refusal the exploration should be undertaken either by the United States or by private enterprise and the undertaking should turn out to be easy and successful.[110]

As Henry Grinnell told John Barrow, 'Your Government must send another expedition to the Arctic Regions or be disgraced in the eyes of the civilised world.'[111] Jane's passionate appeal to honour, patriotism and science had worked.

After discussing the subject with Wood on 18 February Palmerston claimed that the small search area, risk and cost favoured a fresh attempt. He also accepted Jane's argument that the return of the *Resolute* was 'a sort of challenge or invitation to us to endeavour to finish what we have begun'. Palmerston's solution was deceptively simple and politically astute. He would present Parliament with an estimate of the cost and leave the House of Commons with 'the Responsibility of either sanctioning or rejecting the proposal. I think we should hardly be borne out in taking upon ourselves to decide against it, for it is clear that the allegation of extreme danger cannot be maintained.'[112] 'I own it goes against one's grain to run the risk of abandoning any number, however small, of picked English sailors, to end their days wretchedly amid the snow and ice and darkness of an Arctic region associated with Tribes of Esquimaux.' He urged Wood not to overstate the costs, or the risks.[113]

Even so, it seemed that Jane was ready to admit defeat. Thanking a parliamentary supporter for a fine speech, she hinted that her hopes were limited to getting the Admiralty to release a naval officer to command her ship.[114] However, this was no more than a play for the easily raised sympathies of the age. Within a fortnight she had launched the last and most powerful of her many assaults on the administration. She had a powerful support team: Sophia Cracroft ran her office, Murchison drove the political campaign with inside information from John Barrow, while Sherard Osborn, Richard Collinson and Leopold McClintock provided Arctic expertise. Beaufort, now retired, remained a source of ideas, inspiration and inside knowledge.[115] Critically, Murchison had been quick to cultivate new Hydrographer John Washington, largely to draw him into the wider aims of his own imperial geography.[116] The only weakness was that Barrow, for so long the key source inside the Admiralty, retired on 21 March.

Although her hopes for help from the Prince Consort faded, Jane decided to ask Wood for the *Resolute* once Murchison had secured more MPs. In addition Sophia drafted a reward notice for whalers: 'mainly to shew the Admiralty that my Aunt is in earnest, & actively engaged in her work – & to the public that there is yet much to be learned not only about *Erebus* and *Terror*, but the other ships, though the Admiralty profess to consider the subject as sealed for ever'.[117]

By early April Jane was back at the charge, complaining to the First Lord in person about his 'unexpected decision against further searches'. Subtly shifting her ground, she sought partial support to enable her own funds to meet the cost. The *Resolute* was an obvious target, but she had missed the deeper import of the American gesture. The potential for embarrassment made it highly unlikely the ship would be loaned. If the mission succeeded it would leave Britain beholden to the Yankees; if it failed . . . Claiming that the Americans had sent the ship for her was stretching a point, and equally unlikely to elicit the desired response. Had Wood been minded to compromise there were five other Arctic ships lying in reserve – but he had no intention of blinking now. Having been supported by three administrations she wondered why the official attitude had changed after Lord Wrottesley had been promised government support. Her letter was marked 'appeal refused'. Wood was quick to deny that he had promised any help in 1856; he had reached 'the painful conclusion that there was no prospect of saving human life by any further search in the Polar regions'. Consequently he saw no justification for risking more men. Nor would the Admiralty support private ventures, which were likely to be less well funded and equipped, and therefore more dangerous. Well aware that this decision would be considered mean-spirited and economical, he emphasised that danger rather than cost had been decisive: 'Indeed the request made by her does not involve any practical expense.'[118]

Jane reinforced her appeal by arranging for Murchison to contact Wood and Palmerston the day after she sent her letter. Wood was reminded of the same old arguments: although he 'might think public interest has ceased in this matter, there is still a very deep feeling on the part of some of our most powerful & influential publicists and authors (independent of scientific men) who will renew the agitation until the limited (and I think) riskless search which is asked for shall be carried out'. The threat that Dickens and the learned societies would campaign was serious; news that Jane was already looking at a ship to send was the ultimate weapon. But Murchison knew that even the embarrassment of leaving a widow to act alone was unlikely to be an effective argument. Anticipating that Sir Charles would neither send an expedition nor loan the *Resolute*, he added a skilful postscript reminding him that the Admiralty had supported all three of Lady Franklin's private expeditions by permitting naval officers to serve on them, and providing pemmican.[119] This was the minimum that would enable Jane to proceed.

The letter to Palmerston was a carefully crafted appeal to his romantic instinct, warning of potential embarrassment and of international interest from 'our now cordial friends the Yankees'. He enclosed a resolution of the Royal Dublin Society, lately got up by McClintock, appealing for aid to be given (others would follow), while 'some very powerful pens will renew the agitation – men not stimulated by me, but who feel quite as strongly as myself that in some way or other the thing must be done for the honour of the Country.'[120]

Wood rejected the appeal; he found it strange for Murchison to speak of there being 'no danger in going to where one expedition has

<u>been lost</u>'. Sir Roderick was quick to rebut the charge, in the process revealing the real architects of the project:

Allow me to explain that neither Sir F. Beaufort and General Sabine nor myself have advocated the renewal of any attempt to enter by Peel's Sound, or otherwise to follow in the track of former trials . . . In proposing thus to reach the edges of that area which has never been searched, we only recommended that for the honour of our country one final effort should be made, which in our opinion involved little more risk than that which attends almost every maritime survey.[121]

After a decisive rebuff Jane wondered if it would be worth trying to get 'our old enemy the *Times* to say it is reasonable to assist us with the *Resolute*?' McClintock advised calling on the scientists and geographers to combat Delane's opinion. Although an unsigned letter by Osborn appeared in *The Times*, *Resolute* remained out of reach.[122] Delane admitted that he was unable to make a complete volte face on this issue:

My anxiety in the matter has been only to keep good fellows like yourself for such emergencies as the next few years will surely bring us, instead of wasting you upon a search for dead men's bones. We shall want every one of you before ten years are out.[123]

Recognising that his work was done, Jane sent Murchison one of her last prints of the Negelin portrait of Franklin, 'which I reserve for those who do me actual service in the command of Arctic expeditions'.

The Palliser expedition

In fact Sir Roderick had other irons in the Canadian fire. Just as the government decided the Franklin search was over and reduced the North West Passage to the status of a geographical curiosity another round of Canadian scientific exploration opened. The inspiration came from pressing political issues: the future status of the vast area ruled by the Hudson's Bay Company, Canadian desires for devolved government, overland access to the prairies and the need to stabilise the American frontier from Lake Superior to Vancouver. Elected a fellow of the RGS in November 1856, gentleman traveller and militia Captain John Palliser proposed a survey of large parts of British North America, and his proposal was recommended to the government by a committee that included Murchison, Strzelecki, Captains Robert Fitzroy and John Lort Stokes and cartographer John Arrowsmith. Despite the cost the Colonial Office was interested.

The men who set the scientific agenda for Franklin's mission, and the search decade, quickly turned their focus to Palliser's overland project, fixing their parasitic projects onto his transcontinental survey. In effect Sabine and Murchison were admitting their naval dream had died; it could no longer carry their scientific hopes into the frozen north. They would have to find a new vehicle. The Colonial Office opened the door, inviting the Royal Society to advise on the most suitable scientific instruments. Sabine complied, and John Richardson advised him how they should be carried.[124]

Within three months the Royal Society had annexed the project, with Edward Sabine chairing a committee to review the plan. Needless to say a magnetic observer from the Royal Artillery joined the expedition. Murchison, Richardson, William Hooker and Charles Darwin were among those consulted. Palliser was in close contact with Sabine before he set off on his 'scientific expedition' for Canada.[125] Sabine provided the necessary instruments and produced a list of magnetic readings that his young colleague should conduct. Readings taken during the first winter of the expedition were soon on their way to Kew, to be cross-checked and added to Sabine's store. Considering them 'of considerable theoretical importance', Sabine linked them with others taken at the same time across the globe in his 1860 report. The Palliser expedition helped prepare the way for a transcontinental railway, the Canadian Grand Trunk Railway (now the Canadian Pacific), which would replace dreams of a North West Passage with a quicker route between the two great oceans.[126]

That Murchison and Sabine were actively promoting this expedition just when Jane was desperately trying to get government support for her own efforts further north is suggestive. It demonstrated that their agendas coincided perfectly with Jane's project. If another voyage was going to look for Franklin and his priceless records, Sabine would support it. If not, Palliser offered a good alternative. The scientists promoted Arctic exploration for scientific ends. By no coincidence at all Palliser owned a substantial collection of books on the North West Passage.[127]

Palliser's work led directly to the survey of the route for the Canadian Grand Trunk Railway. The railway was a key item in the creation of the Dominion of Canada, along with the surrender of the Hudson's Bay Company's territorial authority and the enshrining of Franklin as a Canadian legend. With the coming of the railway the sea ceased to be the main route into the Canadian midwest, and grain replaced animal pelts as the key export. This development ensured the Hudson's Bay Company lost its territorial role when Canada was confederated in 1867.[128] Canada inherited the British claim to the Arctic, a claim based on the fact that so many Englishmen were buried in the frozen corners of this terrible field.

The passing of Beaufort

Beaufort had retired in early 1855, but continued to advise Jane to the end of his days. Unlike the other 'experts' of the unofficial Arctic Committee, Beaufort had no polar experience. His role was to produce sailing directions based on the combined wisdom of his colleagues. As one might expect from an office-bound manager of charting, they tended to assume too much. Franklin was sought too far west, just because Parry had once managed to make the distance. Because he knew Franklin well, Beaufort was convinced he would follow his orders, so he directed the search towards Melville Island and the west. Consequently he sent missions in from both ends of the possible passage, but focused the search to the north-west of the area where the ships and their crew had perished.

Throughout the Admiralty search Beaufort provided the ideas and the impetus to propel the effort. When the Admiralty wanted to give up after one unsuccessful attempt, he worked against the Board to sustain the hopes of the search party, as a 'Friend of Franklin'. He chose commanding officers with Arctic or surveying experience, linked up the public and private interests, kept the scientific community apprised and involved, and in all but name ran the mission. John Barrow Jr might have handled a large body of correspondence, but he could only do so with the prompting of the man upstairs, the septuagenarian hydrographer, ever more spider-like, at the centre of his web, pulling the strings, without a clue where to look. Had he been gifted with Jane's insight he might have known where to start, but evidence was painfully slow to arrive. Somehow he had clung to the hope that Franklin had made more distance to the west and would be found near the Bering Strait. His work was honoured in the naming of the Beaufort Sea, a sea none of his ships was destined to sail.

Despite Belcher's disgrace, the demands of the Crimean War and the end of the official search Beaufort never gave up. It was a sacred duty, one that transcended wisdom, insight, judgement and perhaps life itself. In retirement he remained a loyal supporter, advising Jane, drafting orders, finding useful sums of money and lending his name to private ventures until his death on 17 December 1857. George Back sneered: 'His judgement was generally clear but he often acted from impulse and was susceptible to flattery: hence the employment of his favourites.'[129] But nobody liked Back, a bumptious little man with ideas far above his limited abilities.

Jane paid Beaufort a suitable compliment at the dedication of the new Church of St Andrew's Waterside in Gravesend, built in his memory with funds largely raised by his daughter Rosalind, Dickens being a significant subscriber. Jane installed a memorial for the crews of the *Erebus* and *Terror* at a point they had passed in May 1845. She chose the church because it was dedicated to 'the faithful friend of her husband, the unwearying advocate of the search for the lost ships and her own wisest counsellor'.[130]

13

Arctic *Fox*

WHEN THE ADMIRALTY conclusively rejected her latest attempt to prompt another official expedition, or even loan her the contentious barque *Resolute*, Jane Franklin was ready with option three. She would buy her own vessel and choose her own captain. That way she could control the aims and objectives of the expedition. The voyage of the steam yacht *Fox* would be at once a triumphant culmination of the search effort, and the key to Lady Franklin's version of events.[1]

Captain Francis Leopold McClintock had already volunteered his services; he came strongly recommended by his earlier exertions and by his tutor, James Ross.[2] Confident that he could escape from any location by sledge and boat, McClintock had been thinking about searching from a base on the Wager river if the *Resolute* did not materialise. With a seaman's eye for the telling detail he had already spotted the key to the mystery:

We have a very interesting proof that there is a channel from Peel Strait down to King William's Land, and therefore a North West Passage there, and which has been discovered by the missing expedition in the fact recorded by Rae, that the flood tide comes from the North.[3]

However, to protect his career McClintock was anxious to secure Admiralty sanction before undertaking an unofficial expedition. Wisely, Jane looked no further, and Sabine concurred.[4] In early April 1857 McClintock inspected a stoutly built second-hand steam yacht, the *Fox*.[5] On 21 April Jane acquired the ship, and registered her in McClintock's name before asking the Admiralty to release him to command the expedition and supply pemmican to fuel the searchers as they marched across the ice. She could not resist reviving the American line, or hinting that *Resolute* would still be welcome as a depot ship and refuge for the *Fox*. Sabine encouraged her because he could see a magnetic outcome. If *Resolute* carried supplies for *Fox* she could also carry a full set of magnetic instruments, and perhaps the odd scientific artillery officer.[6] With his research still in full spate Sabine was anxious to revisit older observation sites like the magnetic pole with new tools and techniques developed by Humphrey Lloyd. After the *Fox* sailed he pestered Ross for the data from his final voyage.[7]

Already primed by Murchison, the Admiralty offered pemmican and gave McClintock leave, but that was all.[8] Well aware of the support he could muster they chose to give way without a fight. Dickens still took the government to task, commissioning an article on 'Official Patriotism' for *Household Words* on 25 April. A month later he spoke at the Royal Geographical Society in support of Jane's expedition.[9] Such high-profile events kept the Franklin mission alive, and ensured the *Fox* voyage achieved everything that Jane wished. It also allowed Dickens another opportunity to argue that he, and not Rae, had been right in 1854 – Franklin and his men died noble Christian heroes, not bestial savages.

Once the decision had been taken a public appeal was launched, handled by Beaufort, which raised £3,000; the Admiralty provided 668 pounds of pemmican, clothes, ice equipment, instruments and books. Jane left Collinson to handle the finances. His letters implicitly offered a name on the map in return for cash. The support of Count Strzelecki, now a councillor of the RGS, earned him an Arctic harbour. A donation of £1,700 from Hobart led McClintock to name a group of barren Arctic rocks off the Boothia peninsula the Tasmanian Islands.[10] With funds in hand McClintock had the 177-ton screw steam yacht strengthened for ice navigation and modified to increase the space for stores. Just before setting off he informed the Admiralty that *Fox*'s crew included fourteen former naval men, eight of whom were Arctic veterans. He asked that their service be counted for pensioned naval service if the expedition proved successful.[11]

McClintock's mission was relatively straightforward. The search area had been closely defined by Rae, and the instructions provided by his formidable sponsor were unequivocal. He was to locate any survivors, recover any records and, lastly, I trust it may be in your power to confirm, directly or indirectly, the claims of my husband's expedition to the earliest discovery of the North West Passage, which, if Dr Rae's report be true (and the Government of our Country has accepted and rewarded it as such), these martyrs in a noble cause achieved at their last extremity, after five long years of labour, and suffering, if not at an earlier period.[12]

There was not a word about cannibalism, and none was needed. McClintock understood that the subject was beyond the pale. Although this last expedition was entirely private, it should come as no surprise to find that it carried magnetic instruments. Sabine's support had been purely self-interested. He hoped McClintock would recover Franklin's magnetic log books, but took care to secure a full set of data from an expedition that planned to pass the magnetic pole. Like every voyage seeking Franklin this would be a magnetic search-and-rescue mission. In May, McClintock wrote to the Council of the Royal Society requesting 'such information and instruction as will enable me, in the continually advancing state of physical knowledge, to make the best use of the opportunity afforded by the voyage, for the prosecution of meteorological, mag- netical and other observations'. He received £50 to buy magnetic instruments, and Sabine's advice on observational techniques to ensure that his time at the magnetic pole 'might not be altogether barren of results'.[13] McClintock's magnetic friend Maguire picked up last-minute advice at the Kew observatory in June, only days before the expedition sailed. He reported 'a long and interesting conversation with General Sabine yesterday. He seems much inter- ested in the Bering Strait route. I am glad to tell you that our magnetic observations at Point Barrow have turned out of great interest.'[14]

McClintock acknowledged the debt that both he and Jane owed to Murchison. 'Be assured I shall not forget the deep interest you take [in] our voyage, nor the great benefits which the cause has derived from your strenuous exertions in its behalf.'[15] In his absence Collinson, Barrow, Maguire, Osborn and others would keep the subject in the public eye.[16] Murchison produced a final article for the *Illustrated London News* and consulted Beaufort before turning his attention to cultivating rising politicians like William Ewart

Gladstone for his global geographic mission.[17] With the costs of the expedition mounting, a final tranche of funds was secured from the Admiralty. Murchison pressed Wood for the widow's pension Jane had refused to claim in 1854 in protest at the decision to pay off the ships. Initially, Wood did not accept that she was entitled to the pension of a rear admiral's widow. As Franklin had been promoted rear admiral by seniority in 1852 and Graham had conceded the point in January 1854, Wood gave way a week later.[18]

McClintock left Aberdeen at the end of June, Jane and Sophia watching from the pier, only to run hard aground on the bar. *Fox* escaped undamaged, made a quick passage to Baffin Bay and then ran into a particularly rough season. Unable to reach Lancaster Sound through the ice floes, *Fox* spent the winter of 1857–8 beset in Baffin Bay, although McClintock remained hopeful.[19] Escaping in the spring of 1858, *Fox* refreshed in western Greenland before entering Lancaster Sound. McClintock stopped to install Jane's memorial to Franklin and his companions on Beechey Island alongside an earlier marker for Bellot before heading south into Peel Strait.[20] Finding his way blocked by thick ice only twenty-five miles in he turned back and entered Prince Regent Inlet. Passing into Bellot Strait he found the route west also blocked by ice, took up a winter harbour and prepared for the spring sledging campaign.

Solution

In late February 1859 McClintock, Lieutenant William Hobson RN and volunteer sailing master Allen Young led sledge parties along well-planned routes. McClintock had designed the search to take in Montreal Island in the estuary of the Great Fish river, the magnetic North Pole, the west coast of King William Island and the shores of Peel Sound. The initial sortie laid out supply depots. After returning to refresh at the ship they set off again in April, following contact with Inuit who had sold them more relics and offered further information.

In early May, Hobson had located the remains of Franklin's magnetic observatory at Cape Felix before following the coast south to a beach two miles past Point Victory. Here the rough limestone ridge was strewn with abandoned equipment, spare clothes, stores, cooking stoves and a six-inch dip circle. The explanation for this curious spectacle came from a cylindrical tin container found in a cairn. It contained the entire written record of the Franklin expedition.

H.M. Ships *Erebus* and *Terror* [. . .] Wintered in the Ice in Lat. 70°5'N Long. 98°23'w.

Having wintered in 1846–7 at Beechey Island in Lat. 74°43'28"N Long. 91°39'15"w after having ascended Wellington Channel to Lat. 77° – and returned by the west side of Cornwallis Island. Sir John Franklin commanding the expedition. *All well.* Party consisting of 2 officers and 6 men left the Ships on Monday 24 May 1847.

Hobson found two copies of this record, both written by Fitzjames. The officers of the landing party were Lieutenant Graham Gore and Mate Charles des Voeux. On the second copy, the one found close to Point Victory, a second note had been hastily added:

1848 HM Ship[s] *Terror* and *Erebus* were deserted on the 22nd April, 5 leagues NNW of this [hav]ing been beset since 12th Septr. 1846. The officers and Crews consisting of 105 souls, under the command [of Cap]tain F. R. M. Crozier landed here – in Lat. 69°37'42" Long. 98°41' [This p]aper was found by Lt. Irving under the cairn supposed to have been built by Sir James Ross in 1831 4 miles to the Northward – where it had been deposited by the late Commander Gore in June 1847. Sir James Ross' pillar has not however been found, and the paper has been transferred to this position which is that in which Sir J. Ross's pillar was erected – Sir John Franklin died on 11 June 1847 and the total loss by deaths in the Expedition has been to this date 9 officers and 15 men.
James Fitzjames, Captain HMS *Erebus*.
F R M Crozier Captain and Senior Officer.
And start tomorrow 26th for Backs Fish River.

The cryptic nature of the report and the lack of any other written evidence has prompted endless speculation. Even careful scholars cannot resist the temptation to complete the story: 'It is probable that they (Gore and des Voeux) reached Cape Herschel on the South Coast of the Island and thus connected a North West Passage.'[21] Such claims have more to do with Lady Jane and Sherard Osborn than history. Many individuals were determined to impose their own version on events, and produce a more complete story. In truth there is no occasion for such speculation. If the Franklin expedition had been sent to complete the North West Passage, as is commonly believed, and the 1847 party had linked the ships with Simpson Strait in the south, Fitzjames and Crozier had ample opportunity to state the fact. Given Fitzjames's concern to record the navigational achievements of the expedition one can only conclude that the Passage had not been completed, or that if it had it was an event of singular unimportance.

McClintock had designed the search routes so that he and Hobson would cross paths approximately halfway down the western coast of King William Island. He let Hobson reach the epicentre of the search first, to ensure that if anything was found Hobson could earn his promotion. McClintock began his search by heading for the Great Fish river. Along the way he met another Inuit party and bartered for relics. Finding nothing on Montreal Island in the estuary of the Great Fish river, where Anderson had searched, he crossed to the south coast of King William Island heading for Cape Herschel. On 25 May he discovered the skeletal remains of a fully clothed white man, lying face down on a low ridge.[22] Despite the wishful thinking of every Passage historian the partly dismantled cairn at Cape Herschel contained no records. Heading north, McClintock found a cairn that Hobson had built, with news that the mission had succeeded, and on 30 May camped beside a boat that Hobson had located in Erebus Bay. The boat had been modified for river navigation, and was lashed to a sledge. It contained some stores, two guns and two sets of human bones, but only a single jawbone, and no skulls. Curiously the boat was pointing back towards the abandoned ships some sixty miles north. McClintock did not speculate on the meaning of the missing skulls, although Rae knew the answer.

After stopping at magnetic north, only to find that Ross's cairn had been demolished, McClintock returned to the *Fox* on 19 June. Hobson had arrived the week before. Allen Young was still tracing the shores of Peel Strait and Franklin Strait. When he returned, *Fox* escaped her anchorage and headed home, arriving at Blackwall Dock on 23 September 1859.

McClintock left the *Fox* at Ventnor on the Isle of Wight on the 21st, rushed up to London and reported to Jane from the United

Services Club. After two years and a series of epic sledge journeys across the frozen landscape he returned with two stained pieces of paper, further relics and a rather better understanding of the chronology of the catastrophe. He provided a full account of his overland travels, but said not a word about the North West Passage, or cannibalism.[23] Collinson quickly analysed the evidence, providing Murchison with the basic facts of the Franklin voyage. McClintock believed the two ships went down Peel Sound and 'attributed their loss to the fact that when the ships left England in the charts then published King William's Land was joined to Boothia Felix. In consequence they struggled to get to the SW instead of to the E where they would have found open water.' He advocated further searches: 'The fact that they got their ships to where they did renders the recovery of the journals of much more importance.' Not only had McClintock 'added 800 miles of important coast line to our maps', but 'he has besides a valuable series of magnetic observations for Gen'l Sabine'.[24] Murchison picked out McClintock's magnetic results for special praise, and admitted that in 1857 'we had every reason to expect that if the ships were discovered, the scientific documents of the voyage, including valuable magnetic observations, would be recovered'.[25] Although he failed to find Franklin's magnetic records, McClintock did all he could to advance Sabine's cause, operating two observatories through the five-month winter. Sabine published his data sets in *Philosophical Transactions*, noting their special interest because they had been made close to the magnetic North Pole, where Ross had observed in 1831. In addition McClintock had observed the dip at the pole on his 1859 sledge journey.[26] However, this magnetic triumph would pass almost unnoticed amid the general euphoria that greeted the resolution of a national obsession.

Now that Franklin's death could be given a date and place even *The Times* celebrated the end of the mystery. Throughout the Franklin search it had taken a critical, rather dismissive attitude, providing few reports, and those predominantly negative or sensational. Rae's cannibal story had been the biggest attraction. McClintock had turned the tables – Jane had won. Compelled to change his editorial line by the weight of national opinion, Delane recreated Franklin as a latter-day King Arthur dying among his friends in an 'imaginary Tintagel'.[27] McClintock's carefully handled report also excused the newly minted 'Arthurian' hero from the stigma of cannibalism, a subject which the paper scrupulously avoided. Even so, the editorial line remained smug: *The Times* had been correct to oppose sending further missions for the past eleven years. To have done so would have 'uselessly sacrificed' the lives of brave men. Having 'offered up the noblest sacrifice even she could find on the altar of science' it would be 'wicked' to expose any more men to the risk. Nature had proved too strong, the Passage was closed to commerce and the nation should 'retire now from the contest with honour, if with grief, and we leave the name of FRANKLIN engraved on the furthest pillars which the energy of mankind has dared to erect as the landmark of its research in the dull and lifeless region that guards the axis of the world'.[28] Yet the desire to wrap up the story and move on was far from universal. Constance Fox Talbot condemned *The Times*'s attitude, believing another expedition should be sent to determine what had caused the disaster.[29] But Victorian Britain was strangely uninterested in the details, perhaps fearful they might provide too clear an insight into human nature. Franklin had been crowned with the laurels of a conqueror, a 'heroic explorer', and national pride had been restored. British naval officers had finished what they started without any help from irritating Americans. The nation did not care about the science, nor did Jane.

It was typical of McClintock's thoroughness that he brought back the letters Belcher had left at Beechey Island for Collinson. The Admiralty showed a rather more balanced view of their worth, consigning them to the Post Office as returned mail.[30] In recognition of the service McClintock had performed in putting an end to the Franklin saga, and more especially in ending Lady Jane's unsettling campaign, the Admiralty granted his men naval sea time for the *Fox* voyage, gave them Arctic Medals and placed several in the Coastguard.[31] The official line was very different: McClintock had been rewarded for adding 800 miles to the Arctic coastline, 'a fit and well merited reward for the enterprise and perseverance displayed'.[32]

The British Association

McClintock's return provided the perfect highlight for the 1859 meeting of the British Association in Aberdeen. It was opened by the Prince Consort on 14 September, dining with the usual galaxy of scientific heroes: General and Mrs Sabine, Murchison, James Clark Ross and others.[33] In his speech Albert held up fellow German Humboldt as the *beau idéal* of an approach to science that codified, connected and completed knowledge, a one-man incarnation of the British Association's mission. Although Humboldt had died on 6 May, just days before Hobson 'solved' the Franklin mystery, he remained the titular deity of the association.[34] The day Albert spoke was, by a curious coincidence, Humboldt's birthday. 'His personal influence with the Courts of Europe enabled him to plead the cause of Science in a manner which made it more difficult for them to refuse than to grant what he requested.'[35] Sabine, Murchison, Herschel and Ross knew exactly what the prince meant, and how hard it had been to replicate the great man's influence in Britain. How far any of them cared to reflect on the uses to which they had put that influence is unknown. The death of Humboldt, coinciding with the resolution of the Franklin mystery, insofar as anyone wished it to be resolved, marked a turning point in science. The Humboldtian impulse had ebbed, replaced by new ideas, new theories and new heroes. God's revealed purpose ceased to be a standard scientific test; there was no place for the cross in a post-Humboldtian landscape. After 1859 Arctic missions lacked the all-embracing enthusiasm and sense of universal purpose that had animated the previous generation. The clash between narrow-focus science and boyish outdoor adventure, first manifest in the career of Elisha Kent Kane, would smash the old consensus.

At the same time there was a change of the guard in Arctic affairs, Beaufort having finally shuffled off this mortal coil; Sherard Osborn begged Murchison to take his place as 'we naval geographers have now no one else to look to but yourself for enlarged and liberal views upon all that relates to geography in the catholic sense of that term'.[36] The shift of focus from charts to maps, from sea passages to land formations, was not accidental. Osborn also brought

Murchison and his young friend Clements Markham together, just as Jane was praising Sir Roderick for his critical role in assembling the *Fox* expedition.[37] Markham would take the subject into another century, and onto another continent.

Triumph

McClintock was an instant celebrity. The high-profile public relations campaign waged to support the mission, especially Dickens's journalism, sustained interest during his absence and made his return a national event. The inevitable round of public appearances and lectures started at the Royal Geographical Society, where he was awarded the Patron's Gold Medal. Murchison offered a preface, although the self-effacing captain had not intended writing a book, let alone requesting an endorsement. He confessed that 'it is LF who is getting it done. I wish you to know this', and begged Murchison to focus his preface on Jane and leave him in the background.[38] Predictably, Sir Roderick took his own line, lauding McClintock's work, celebrating the 'heroic self-sacrifice of Franklin and his associates and stressing the enormous contribution the search mission had made to geographical and magnetic knowledge.[39]

While McClintock did not speculate any further than was required by Jane's instructions, and then largely by omitting awkward subjects, Sir John Richardson continued to take the romantic view that Franklin died 'enjoying the satisfaction of having already accomplished much in the way of discovery'. He argued that with the ships stuck in the ice only sixty miles from open water seen by Dease and Simpson thirty years earlier Franklin must have expected to reach it when the ice cleared in 1847. Richardson explained the heavy losses among officers before the ships were abandoned as evidence of their 'self denial', and believed a boat must have reached Montreal Island. This success left Franklin ready to meet his maker. He trusted Jane would find solace in this fact, and 'the increase of Franklin's already widely extended reputation'.[40] Grinnell provided American corroboration for the new consensus that Franklin had prior claim to discovery of the North West Passage.[41]

Having secured enough evidence to rebut McClure's claim, and

John Rae's horrid stories, Jane was quick to translate her triumph into concrete results. She sent McClintock's Franklin relics to the Palace, courtesy of Edward Sabine. The queen thanked her for the sight of the tragic documents. The following summer the queen and the Prince Consort inspected the *Fox*.[42] For all McClintock's protestations of disinterest John Murray had his book in print by the end of the year, complete with an advertisement for another best-seller, Darwin's startling *Origin of the Species* which appeared on 24 November 1859. Two weeks later Darwin thanked John Murray for a copy of the *Fox* voyage.[43] His work on natural selection had benefited greatly from Richardson's expertise in Arctic zoology.

The Voyage of the Fox was a book with an agenda. Jane had secured a popular audience to prepare the ground for the final stage of her campaign. Then she sent copies to anyone with influence, starting with the Palace.[44] Murchison used the book to highlight the government's folly in failing to sustain the search, leaving the glory and the credit to a small group of 'zealous and abiding friends'.[45] He also pressed Palmerston to have McClintock knighted, an honour duly bestowed in February 1860.[46] Then the Admiralty paid him £1,500 and gave his men double wages.[47] He was also given immediate employment, surveying an Atlantic telegraph cable route via Greenland and Iceland.[48] Unlike so many of his polar peers McClintock rejoined the regular service, becoming an admiral and commanding the West Indies squadron. Having made his career in the Arctic, McClintock never lost sight of the subject, regularly updating his book and advising on polar travel into the twentieth century. He died in 1907, fifty years after the *Fox* set sail.

McClintock's brief, simple narrative was a runaway sales success. Mudie's Circulating Library took 3,000 copies and the book went on to outsell every other title that season, including Dickens's latest novel.[49] It remained in print for half a century, a fact that had a major impact on the development of Franklin scholarship. For all its apparent simplicity this was a carefully constructed text, providing enough evidence to 'solve' the mystery and remove the need for further expeditions, while ignoring the issue of cannibalism. In satisfying the aims of sponsor, service and state McClintock provided the closure that all sought. He revealed that Franklin's ships had been beset in the ice off

King William Island in September 1846, only fifty miles from the magnetic pole and close by the headland James Ross had named Franklin Point in 1832. They never broke free. In 1847 a party had landed at Point Victory to record their activities, and left another record further south. Franklin died shortly after the landing, and the following April Crozier abandoned the ships, leading the surviving officers and men south towards the Great Fish river. McClintock found evidence of their death march, and concluded that the expedition had been destroyed by scurvy, from which his own party had suffered. There was no trace of ships' logs or other large records, which he believed had been jettisoned to save weight, repeating an argument McClure had used to justify suppressing adverse opinion.[50] However, with the snow still deep on the ground the season was hardly ideal for locating burials or other terrestrial features. Having established Franklin's priority over McClure, McClintock was anxious to obtain a public reward for his patron.[51]

McClintock publicly supported Jane's argument that the Franklin expedition, in crossing the Simpson Strait and reaching the mainland, had discovered the North West Passage. His book secured Franklin's primacy, and it closed with a stirring emotional appeal to remember the 'heroic men who perished in the path of duty, but not until they had achieved the grand object of their voyage – *the discovery of the North West Passage*'.[52] Elsewhere he had lauded the contribution of the search missions to geography – hardly surprising when the president of the Royal Geographical Society had made the same argument in the preface. Murchison's hand was evident in the appendices, which included a long report on regional geology. McClintock also argued that the Arctic had been the best school for testing the Royal Navy.

In truth McClintock took a rather different view of the Passage. Had the Bellot Strait been open he would have attempted to reach the Bering Strait. Others would take up the quest, notably his sailing master Allen Young, because the claims of those who walked a passage, saw open water from the shore and even the dead men of the Franklin expedition, were absurd. However, the British had had enough. The cost of the search, the grim results and the taint of cannibalism had done for the Arctic. *The Times* spoke for the government and the nation when it declared an end to the dream on 23 September 1859. Britain had to admit defeat; much had been achieved, and great glory had been gained in the frozen north, but the passage had not been found, and no more brave men should be sent to die there. Nor did the British ever go back. Franklin had killed the Arctic as surely as it had killed him. It didn't help that the official search effort had cost over £600,000, and the total amount spent by 1860 was nearly £2 million.[53]

By early 1861 an exhibition of Franklin relics had been unveiled at the United Services Institution of Whitehall, proving most interesting to a sensation-starved mid-Victorian public.[54] When McClintock was photographed with his finds, the six-inch dip circle took centre stage, but no one commented on the purpose of the instrument.[55] In 1890 the Arctic relics, so lovingly gathered and at such cost, were transferred from the United Services Institution Museum to the Royal Naval College at Greenwich, and thence to the National Maritime Museum.[56]

Commemoration

Although the mystery had been solved, Jane was far from satisfied. She needed to immortalise Sir John (and his companions, for death was now more democratic) and remove the slur of cannibalism. It helped that Sir John had died before the ships were abandoned, and was therefore not involved in the crime as either consumer or consumed. But her work went beyond removing slurs and errors. She was going to rewrite the past. The *Fox* narrative began the process, but she wanted something large, prominent and public in keeping with the Victorian approach. Only a bronze statue would do – a permanent reminder in a public place to ensure the deeds of the dead were not forgotten. The custom of memorialising the illustrious dead was, kings apart, quite new. Franklin would be among the first. Where Nelson's memorials restated the might and majesty of the state through his public persona as the national war god, Franklin's simply recorded his achievements.

It was essential to Jane's purpose that Sir John should receive his memorials. The first was a local affair.[57] Lincolnshire had been anxious to honour him before the *Fox* set sail, Beaufort confidently advising that 'Discoverer of the NW passage' could safely be added to the plinth!⁵⁸ After some dispute about where the Lincolnshire memorial should be placed, and what form it should take – Jane favoured an obelisk on a hill that would serve as a seamark – a large bronze effigy sculpted by Charles Bacon was erected in Spilsby at a cost of £700, the funds having been raised by public subscription. It commemorated Sir John Franklin without mentioning his naval rank and services, his role in the Royal Geographical Society or his scientific and administrative achievements. The only information provided was his birth date and his discovery of the North West Passage. Richardson, high priest of the Franklin cult, gave the inaugural address in late November 1861, in the presence of the local Volunteer Rifle Corps, another harbinger of the new patriotism of sacrifice. The Rifle Movement had been inspired by Franklin's nephew, Poet Laureate Alfred Tennyson.⁵⁹ Jane put a memorial tablet in Spilsby church, alongside those of his brothers Willingham and James. All three had been buried elsewhere.⁶⁰ Lincoln finally commemorated Franklin in the new City and County Museum in 1907.⁶¹

Such local acts of remembrance were never going to satisfy Jane, however, and she used the return of the *Fox* to open her campaign for a national memorial. In mid-January 1860 one of her allies wrote to *The Times* suggesting a memorial in Trafalgar Square to the men who 'perished gloriously, having accomplished the mission on which they were sent, having achieved the grand object of the voyage – the discovery of the north-west passage'. The letter was signed FRS; the sentiments were those of Sir John Richardson FRS.⁶²

From the start Jane had been dissatisfied with the memorial ordered by the Admiralty in July 1855 at the Royal Naval Hospital in Greenwich. Along with the Arctic Medal it had been devised to provide closure, only to be overtaken by events. Not only was it in the wrong place, but it fell far short of the heroic image that Jane required. Richard Westmacott's large marble panel commemorated the lost without listing their achievements.⁶³ His gloomy list of the dead had a doubly funereal quality, offering neither hope nor inspiration. In June 1858 the Admiralty had approved the text, leaving

Westmacott to enter the names and ranks.[64] The memorial to Rear Admiral Franklin was duly carved, only for McClintock to demote him to captain by discovering that his death had occurred before his promotion, so rendering the slab inaccurate. Originally installed in the blind vestibule on the south side of the entrance to the Painted Hall, it was later removed to a space behind the altar of the chapel, conveniently out of public view.[65]

Brazen lies

McClintock's success created an embarrassing situation for Lord Palmerston's new government. Although his previous administration had refused to send an official expedition, he had been in favour, and Sir Charles Wood was no longer at the Admiralty. Jane wanted to complete the process of turning her husband into a hero, and she had a very clear strategy for the endgame. Franklin would be lauded as the man who discovered the Passage, and given a prominent public memorial. In essence, Richardson's *Encyclopedia Britannica* essay would be turned into a public monument. Once again she called on her chief political manipulator Sir Roderick Murchison, and enlisted ex-First Lord of the Admiralty Sir Francis Baring as her parliamentary spokesman. This high-profile elder statesman of the ruling Liberal Party would be by far the most effective political advocate of Jane's cause.

No one doubted that Franklin deserved a monument. William Penny, whaler and searcher found the right words: 'I know of no one better entitled to have his memory perpetuated. He was a Christian hero, faithful to his country and generous to all.'[66] Murchison and Baring favoured securing a parliamentary grant for Jane, but she wanted something quite different. She wanted a public acknowledgement that the

grant was made in recognition (besides other analogous services) of his having with Crozier & his companions laid down his life in accomplishing the mission on which they were sent the discovery of the N W Passage, I do not see how I could decline it, tho' I should prefer to this a grant, which need be very moderate [in] amount, for the erection of a public or national monument to commemorate the fact, & in making which grant there need be no mention of my expenses at all. In no form whatever could I accept anything which did not recognise <u>that discovery</u>, feeling as I do, that it is as much my duty now to endeavour to have justice done to the dead, as it was to try to save them when it was possible they might yet be living. I cannot conceive it possible that there could be any opposition to such a public recognition, unless there are members in the House who are totally unacquainted with recent facts, – it would not stultify any previous act of the House of Commons, it only enables the House of Commons to do an act of consistent justice by rewarding Franklin for the same thing for which they rewarded McClure, each having discovered a distinct North West Passage, though Franklin's was the first in time (by 2 years) & the most navigable, facts which in justification of McClure's Select Committee had not been authentically demonstrated when McClure received his reward.

Both Admiral Walcott MP, a member of the select committee that assessed McClure's claim, and McClure's friend and historian Sherard Osborn accepted Jane's argument that recognising Franklin did no injustice to McClure. She was anxious that the wording of any grant should be drawn up to acknowledge her gratitude to the House of Commons and to Baring, 'to whom I am under a long series of obligations, for his great & generous kindness to me'. She made it clear that while she would refuse any money, even the cost of the *Fox* expedition, 'I can decline no tribute to the memory of my husband or in his honour, if what he has effected be fully acknowledged by it.'[67] Murchison warned the prime minister about the object of Baring's motion, and 'what will be most acceptable to Lady Franklin and her friends'. Explorers and politicians now agreed that Franklin was the first to discover the passage. Among those planning to speak in the debate was Conservative ex-First Lord Sir John Pakington:

Lady Franklin does not seek a pecuniary grant <u>to herself</u>. On the contrary the only way she would feel it possible to accept such, would be that her husband's eminent services and particularly his dying in the discovery of the North West Passage were made the grounds of the award.

She has assured me that in no form whatever could she accept any recompense, if <u>the discovery of the North West Passage</u> was not recognised.

Capt. McClure was justly rewarded for discovering <u>a</u> North West Passage; but the researches of M'Clintock have established the fact that Franklin and his associates had done the same in other latitudes <u>two years earlier</u>.

The House of Commons will therefore do an act consistent [with] justice, if they reward Franklin for the same thing for which they rewarded McClure.

In aiming this statement I beg to assure you that Lady Franklin looks to no large sum (such as was given to McClure) and no pecuniary recompense, but simply to the recognition of her husband's merits by a grant of money sufficient to erect a suitable monument to his memory, & above all that by a vote of the House of Commons, his eminent services should be placed on record.

Confident that Palmerston would agree, Murchison thanked him for securing McClintock's knighthood. Palmerston sent the letter to Murchison's friend Gladstone, now Chancellor of the Exchequer, to ensure the Treasury did not object.[68] He also consulted the new First Lord of the Admiralty, the Duke of Somerset, who confirmed that there were no funds that could be used to reward Lady Franklin. The government would have to go back to Parliament for a fresh vote.[69]

Baring raised a motion to reward McClintock and recompense Jane on 2 March 1860. Well aware that Murchison had adroitly prepared the ground, he made a public show of confidence in the ministry, leaving the solution to Palmerston's judgement. Tory member Mr Whiteside added that Lady Franklin wanted 'recognition of the services and name of her gallant husband, as the true discoverer of the North West Passage, which many men of science said he was, so they might perhaps raise to him a public monument; while in doing so an act of justice might also be rendered to the living'. There was no need to vote, and Palmerston did not speak.[70]

Just in case anyone had forgotten who was responsible for solving the Franklin mystery the Royal Geographical Society presented Jane with its Founder's Gold Medal in May 1860. In accepting the award she restated Sir John's claim to 'the crowning discovery of the N W Passage by himself and his companions which cost them their lives'.[71] The naval estimates passed that August included £2,000 for a monument to Franklin, and Palmerston promised to consult Lady Franklin before settling on the location.[72] He deputed his stepson William Cowper, First Commissioner of Works and the first man to oppose the search mission, to negotiate with Murchison.[73] It took time to settle the details, because Jane had travelled to the United States. Confident the parliamentary decision had dealt with McClure's pretensions she resisted the temptation to press her advantage, merely hoping the statue would be placed in Trafalgar Square. She also advised that Tennyson join the committee with

Murchison and Cowper.[74] That way she could dictate the design of the statue, the bas-relief and the all-important wording.[75]

The statue

Matthew Noble's eight-foot tall statue was suitably heroic. Purporting to represent Franklin telling his men that the Passage had been discovered it was, as Jane had always intended, Richardson's words rendered in bronze. In addition to lists of the two crews the plinth carried two relief panels. The reverse face was accurate enough, illustrating the position of the ships when they were iced in, placed to map the Passage claim. This relief faces into a private garden, and is rarely seen. Instead the public is presented with a wholly imaginary scene of Franklin's suitably Christian funeral.[76] The lies told by this memorial have played a fundamental part in sustaining the mythology of Franklin. While the memorial did not invent the lies, its permanence lent them a credibility they do not deserve.

By accepting Jane's terms Parliament at last managed to end the Franklin search for a very economical £2,000. The *Fox* expedition had cost at least £6,000, and Jane had been offered her costs. She ensured the ministers did her bidding by making them an offer they could not refuse. Noble tendered for £1,700 and the Treasury accepted.[77] The next question was where to put the statue. While Jane favoured Trafalgar Square, the initial thoughts of officialdom focused on St Margaret's Square, now Parliament Square. While Franklin became only the second naval officer to be accorded a statue in central London, service at the battle did not earn him a place in Trafalgar Square. It would have been blasphemous to set him alongside Nelson.

In October 1864 the Office of Works settled on Waterloo Place, the space between Carlton Terrace and the Athenaeum. Use of this site had to be agreed with the occupants of the nearby houses. The only obstacle was Gladstone at number eleven. While he did not object, Gladstone retained the right to do so if anyone else did. At this point it was suggested that the bronze plaques might be damaged by 'mischievous boys and others', so the monument was surrounded by railings. It was completed in late 1866 and Jane was anxious to make the unveiling a last hurrah for the Arctic hero. Murchison was enlisted to make the necessary arrangements:

[A]s the Arctic companions of Franklin wished to have his memory honoured by some little ceremony I was instructed to ask the First Lord of the Admiralty to attend & inaugurate the uncovering of the monument.

Sir J Pakington has fixed on Thursday next at ½ past two O'clock & I intend to announce this to the Geographers at our first meeting tomorrow evening.[78]

Not only did Pakington agree to carry out the ceremony, he also provided a cadetship for nephew Willingham Franklin. Jane had offers of places at the windows of both the Athenaeum and United Services Club (now the Institute of Directors), where she hoped to meet her old friend John Barrow.[79]

On 15 November 1866 Franklin finally received the full establishment treatment. His statue was unveiled by a cabinet minister in the presence of the president of the Royal Geographical Society, numerous Arctic heroes, both officers and men, and crowds of well-wishers. Sabine was there, as were Joseph Hooker, John Murray and Count Strzelecki. Pakington paid a fulsome tribute to Jane. The sentiments were shared by all, with frequent bursts of applause when her name was mentioned. Equally popular was the claim 'that to all future times the name of Franklin would be treasured among the greatest and bravest of those naval heroes of whose glory and memories England was so justly proud'. Murchison took up the laudatory theme, praising Sabine who stood alongside him as the oldest of the Arctic men, and 'a consistent supporter of Lady Franklin', also picking out Collinson, Ommaney and Sherard Osborn before winding up with another commendation of Lady Franklin and complaining that the statue was not in Trafalgar Square. After Pakington, Murchison, and Lady Franklin had been cheered all over again the event closed.[80]

'The last, concluding ceremony' may have been the proudest day of Jane's life.[81] She had overturned the official verdict, crushed her critics and erected a noble monument that made her husband a national hero. She watched in silence, comfortably seated on the balcony of the Athenaeum, Sir John's old club, and acknowledged the applause of the crowd. At the base of the statue was Richardson's motto, 'They Forged the Last Link with their Lives'. Anxious to redeem his friend, Richardson did not live to see the monument unveiled, but his inspired words provided Jane with the central pillar of her triumph. The rest came from the testimony of her own expedition.

The Waterloo Place monument enabled Jane to hard-wire John Franklin into the Victorian consciousness. It was an impressive epitaph, and impressively wrong. From concept to motto the monument was a lie, one that made Jane the widow of a 'great explorer'. In the process it lost sight of the greater man: John Franklin, navigator, scientist and humanitarian, was crushed beneath the granite and bronze of an ill-conceived outsized effigy. By turning Franklin and his men into paragons of the mid-Victorian cult of service, heroes who had willingly sacrificed their lives for the greater good, Jane deliberately obscured the catastrophic failure of the expedition. The appalling fate of the men, men who died in the most horrific circumstances, their hands stained with the blood of their comrades, was simply wiped away. They became Christian gentlemen, idealised compounds of piety, devotion and sacrifice; they were the chivalric heirs of an equally idealised medieval world. It was a Victorian truth, reflecting wider social changes and the creation of the service ethic. Nor was this the end of Franklin's rehabilitation. The statue is little altered by the passage of time. In February 1914 the Board of Works corrected the spelling of des Voeux's name from des Vauex, and changed le Vesconte's middle initial from F to T in 1931, at £2 a time. Then the Board checked the Admiralty record to ensure there were no more errors.[82] Franklin still stands in the shade of a majestic London plane tree, right outside his old club.

In 1860 the Tasmanian legislature voted £1,000 for a Franklin memorial, and Jane ensured Noble produced a second cast so that Sir John's erstwhile subjects might recall his wise, benevolent and liberal administration.[83] Franklin stands in the centre of Hobart, close to the site of the long-vanished Government House, the only governor to be immortalised in this way, and much of his modern celebrity in his other island is a reflection of the power of public art.

Hobgoblin tales

McClintock's voyage closed an epoch in Arctic science; there would be no large government expeditions to the region for sixteen years. In the interval Sabine and his colleagues conducted a highly effective damage limitation exercise. Jane's version of Franklin and his mission ignored science. This was perfect. With remarkable skill Edward Sabine distanced himself and his research from the genesis and catastrophe of the Franklin mission, misleading historians of the Arctic impulse to this day. His adroit tactics enabled him to persist with his research, simply shifting the focus to other regions. The obvious alternative proved to be Africa, where improved tropical medicines, the spread of colonial authority and the career of Murchison's heroic Christian geographer David Livingstone offered a wonderful opportunity for further data gathering. That Livingstone's work was directed by Murchison made the attraction irresistible.[84]

In 1865 Sabine and Murchison backed Sherard Osborn's attempt to launch a mission to the North Pole, through the usual method of a lecture at the RGS. Sabine, Captain George Richards, now the Hydrographer, and Murchison all spoke in the discussion that followed Osborn's impassioned speech. They agreed that it would be 'a discredit to this country, which had taken such a lead in Arctic geographical discoveries, if it left to others the solution of a question so interesting as to what might exist at the North Pole, whether land or whether open sea'. Scientific interest was a key argument, but magnetic research was not mentioned. Osborn was full of optimism, dismissing the risk and praising the officers of the last Arctic campaign. Murchison hoped the RGS 'would be actuated by motives higher than those connected with commerce and trade'. In a letter to *The Times* an unsigned correspondent revived the Franklin disaster, and the decision taken in the mid-1850s to end the search, deprecated the idea of risking lives to resolve geographical curiosities and concluded by reminding readers that the entire region was deeply tainted by the memory of cannibalism.[85] John Delane remained resolutely opposed, telling Murchison that 'it is cruel to poor Osborn and not beneficial to the Society to let the public know you are still thinking of Arctic voyaging'.[86] John Herschel agreed: 'the question is: How are you <u>to get there</u>? And what is <u>the use of getting there at all</u>? [87] Although he had no answer, Murchison kept trying as part of his wider quest to attach scientific work to military activity.[88] While Osborn claimed American explorer Charles Francis Hall's 'fresh hobgoblin tales of the fate of the survivors of Franklin's Expedition' meant it was time to go back, he had other reasons for advancing the idea. Osborn was heavily involved in the creation of the Franklin myth, that of the happy navigator who learned of success at the last, having willingly sacrificed himself to the mission. It was only a romantic step beyond Richardson's version, but it was pure fiction.[89] Osborn, a loose cannon liable to attack the Admiralty just when he needed official support, had to be restrained by cooler Arctic companions like George Richards.[90]

Jane, anxious to get to the truth of Hall's reports that survivors were living among the Inuit, arranged to meet him in America. After the meeting she finally accepted the fact of cannibalism, but she remained anxious to recover the records. Unfortunately Hall had nothing to say 'of any writings, journals or letters, or MS books. This is our heart's anxiety and care.'[91] Publicly McClintock treated Hall's second journey as confirming that Franklin survivors had reached the mainland, but the Inuit had left nothing by way of records.[92] Privately he noted that Hall's account was 'more moderate and less sensational than I expected', but dismissed his notion that a vault had been built near Point Victory for the expedition records as 'one of the wildest guesses I have ever heard of'.[93] It is a pity McClintock's views are not more widely acknowledged. Hall died soon after, and the subject went cold, leaving Jane to indulge her passion for endless travel, including an audience with the pope, and badger new prime minister Gladstone about her husband.[94] This time she secured an eight-foot-high memorial plaque in Westminster Abbey, complete with a pious epitaph penned by his nephew Poet Laureate Alfred, Lord Tennyson:

> Not here! the white North has thy bones; and thou,
> Heroic sailor-soul,
> Art passing on thine happier voyage now,
> Toward no earthly pole.

That Franklin had been seeking 'no earthly pole' was an irony lost on all by the time Tennyson composed his lines, a magnetic truth that had been sacrificed to secure lasting fame. Tennyson's text achieved a degree of celebrity, being translated into Greek and Latin by Gladstone, much to the poet's pleasure.[95] His companions were given less prominent places: the skeletons of Lieutenants John Irving and Henry le Vesconte were reburied in Edinburgh and Greenwich respectively, having been unceremoniously turfed out of the Arctic by American explorers.

Then in a supreme irony Franklin's bust appeared on the Whitehall front of a new Colonial Office building in 1874, as a 'great explorer' rather than a great colonial administrator.[96] Lord Stanley was dead, and no one in the Colonial Office recalled Franklin's government of Van Diemen's Land.

When McClure died in 1873, Jane was disgusted to see him credited with the discovery of the passage, and lost no time telling *The Times* just what she thought. Dr Alexander Armstrong, an old *Investigator* hand, sprang to the defence of his captain, but he could not deal with the core issue of Franklin's priority.[97] Jane had won the last round: she had seen McClure buried and given him his dismissal from the Arctic pantheon. With nothing left to focus her attention Jane did not outlive her last foe by many months: she died on 18 July 1875 aged eighty-three. Another Arctic mission was heading north, but it had not been driven by her agenda. She was carried to her grave by polar pall bearers McClintock, Collinson, Richards, Ommaney and Barrow; Joseph Hooker and the first Bishop of Tasmania were there to recall happier days, along with William Hobson, who had uncovered Franklin's fate, and Matthew Noble who made his effigy.[98] When Allen Young, McClintock's sailing master on the *Fox*, set off to complete the Passage that year, he was determined to search King William Island in summer, to recover the records.[99] *Pandora* did not get that far; the box remained closed.

Sabine eclipsed

Nothing in the Franklin story is so striking as the dexterity with which Edward Sabine managed to generate and direct the mission, sustain his research interest throughout the search and then slip out of the frame when it was time to ask questions and apportion blame. The slippery soldier/scientist simply disappeared from the record. But this was no more than another demonstration of his genius. In 1850 his old rival George Airy wrote to the British Association, arguing that Sabine's Kew observatory should not become involved in continuous terrestrial monitoring – to avoid duplicating the work done at Greenwich. He was ignored. With Sabine controlling both Kew and the British Association no one was going to stand in his way. Airy considered he had been insulted, and the quarrel deepened. In the 1860s Sabine proved that Airy's recordings were unreliable. Nothing could have been more annoying to the Astronomer Royal, but his results disagreed with those of every other magnetic station in Europe. Sabine argued the Greenwich instruments and systems were inferior to those at Kew, and he was right. Airy's instruments were faulty, Sabine's were better. Having persuaded the parsimonious governments of the mid-nineteenth century to fund an astonishing empire of magnetic data gathering, duplicating the existing state-funded observatory at Greenwich, Sabine won his battle.

Although he appeared in Stephen Pearce's Arctic Council picture, Sabine has been quietly omitted from the conventional record of the Franklin voyage. By a cruel irony he was cast into historical oblivion by the collapse of the scientific agenda which had dominated his life. He had sent Franklin north in pursuit of a scientific chimera. Terrestrial magnetism and not Barrow's geographical obsession was the occasion for the 1845 expedition. The political instincts that had worked so well on the magnetic crusade proved useful when a new leader was required for the Royal Society. Sabine was always there, and always willing to do the work. He secured the reward. In 1861 he became the president, his term in office being marked by the personal charm that had smoothed his way to the top for the past forty years, rather than scientific advance.

After 1859 British science witnessed the total eclipse of observational and magnetic interests by biological and botanical work, in both popular imagination and public esteem. The massive shift in scientific ideas that followed the publication of Darwin's *The Origin of the Species by Means of Natural Selection* in 1859 was exactly contemporary with the final resolution of the Franklin mystery. The Humboldtian concept of an orderly world, which could be reconciled with God's will, in which the task of scientists was to observe, record and reduce to order, was simply blown apart by the implications of evolution. Evolution denied the literal truth of the Bible, and this was a step too far for many scientific observers, men who had dedicated their lives to mastering the phenomena before them. None more so than Captain Sir Robert Fitzroy, who had unwittingly provided the opportunity for Darwin's visit to South America, inspired by Humboldt's example, to study nature. It was on Fitzroy's *Beagle* that Darwin first began to comprehend the random, ungodly forces that had shaped the development of animal life. The despairing Fitzroy cut his own throat. Nor was the intellectual crisis restricted to scientists and naval officers. Frederic Edwin Church – master artist of the Humboldtian universe – lost his muse in the massacre of his intellectual world.

Darwinian ideas took control of the scientific world through the agency of powerful figures such as Thomas Huxley and Joseph Hooker, men who shared Darwin's experience as naval travellers and his friendship. The last of the old savants fought a strenuous rearguard action, but even Sabine, the most distinguished of his generation, was quite literally forced out of office by the Darwinian lobby. With biological sciences paramount, the magnetic obsessions and geological impulses that had sent Franklin on his last mission were consigned to the dustbin of exploded scientific interests, to await their historian. In science the fate of the idea before last is to be forgotten. No one suffered more in the massacre of the hard sciences than Sabine. His empire had reached a pinnacle of prestige and power, even as the very concepts that it deified were being smashed.

When Sabine was forced from the presidency of the Royal Society in 1871, it must have given George Airy enormous satisfaction to replace him.[100] Sir Edward died knowing that his science had been exploded. With his passing, his science, and that of Humboldt, was unceremoniously turfed out of the inner sanctum. With a wonderful circularity Sabine would live to taste the fruits of success, and have them dashed from his lips.

The contrast between his ability to secure increased resources and his inability to deal with the ultimate object, the creation of an inclusive theory, reveals the flaw in Sabine's profile.[101] He held profoundly conservative views on the development of science. This caused a heated controversy in 1864 when he refused to cite the theory of evolution when awarding Darwin the Copley Gold Medal. He was also incapable of sophisticated numerical analysis.[102] Sabine had to go because he represented a departed world of amateurism and applied science. Roderick Murchison did not live to see the collapse of this world, but both men dropped off the register of scientific heroes. The new men reconnected themselves with preferred pasts, excluding the two soldiers who had controlled the politics of science for a generation. Sabine's Humboldtian scientific world was shattered beyond recall by Darwin, and amid the wreckage his magnetic science was soon forgotten. The greatest scientific effort of the first half of the nineteenth century, greater by far in scale and scope than any previous scientific collaboration, the mission that had sent Franklin and his men to their deaths, was quietly forgotten. As a result, students of Arctic history have been unable to explain the otherwise astonishing fact that Britain willingly spent an imperial fortune to solve a minor geographical curiosity of no possible economic benefit. If Franklin and his men really did forge any 'last link with their lives', it was the final line on a magnetic chart. But their records were lost, and the science discredited.

American cannibals

By the time Kane returned from his second expedition John Rae's discoveries had broken the hitherto plausible link between searching for Franklin and looking for an open Polar Sea. McClintock's return in 1859 deprived the Americans of any excuse for blundering around in the Canadian Arctic, but that did not stop them. Consequently the American Arctic idea divided. The scientific mission was carried on by Isaac Hayes, who followed Kane's route north, while eccentric Cincinnati newspaper editor Charles Francis Hall tried to find Franklin survivors. Hayes's voyage was ruined as a scientific enterprise by the early death of his scientist, which put a stop to the geomagnetic work, and he arrived home in the middle of the Civil War to find no one cared anyway. Only the claim that he had seen the open Polar Sea kept his name alive with the scientists.[103]

By contrast Hall achieved far greater popular success, living among the Inuit, learning their language and their ways. His expeditions of 1860 and 1864 demonstrated that the Inuit had a powerful tradition of oral history stretching back to Frobisher's voyages in the sixteenth century, and that they had important insights into the Franklin disaster. While Hall conducted pioneering ethnographic studies, he was no scientist. On the second expedition he finally reached King William Island, where Inuit testimony and hard evidence on the ground finally convinced him there were no survivors.[104] He stopped short of the major Franklin sites because it suddenly dawned on him that the Inuit had not been good Christians; they had not offered succour to the Franklin survivors.[105]

Robbed of his romantic illusions about the Arctic, Hall took command of yet another quasi-official American North Pole expedition the year after he returned, only to be poisoned by one of his own officers on the desolate shores of west Greenland. The expedition was a disaster and a disgrace.[106] While some in Britain persisted with Jane's vision of a shared Anglo-American Arctic, hard-headed whaler William Penny was clear that the Americans were following their own agenda and their own interests.[107] At least former cavalry lieutenant Frederick Schwatka's epic sledge journey across King William Island in 1878, supported by the New York newspaper magnate James Gordon Bennett, was well organised. Schwatka used Inuit techniques and Inuit guides to great effect.[108] He also boosted Bennett's circulation figures. Both Hall and Schwatka dug up dead Englishmen and sent them home, as if to undermine the basis of the British claim.

By the 1880s polar science was no longer newsworthy. The subjects that drew popular audiences for exploration were celebrity, tragedy and death. The public did not want their explorers to be scientific, they wanted them to be brave, to suffer and to tell lurid stories. The American love affair with the Arctic was finally killed by the Greely expedition in the early 1880s. US army officer Adolphus Greely led a scientific expedition into Kane Basin in 1881. After two relief attempts had failed the party struggled south to the aptly named Cape Sabine, where they survived by resorting to cannibalism in a very military fashion. The black soldiers were eaten first, then the white, and then the officers by rank. Greely and six other survivors were rescued in 1884.[109] Eventually promoted to major general, he received the Congressional Medal of Honor in 1935, a few months before his death.

BOOK FOUR

THE COST OF THE PAST

14

Big Art, Brazen Lies and the 'Great Explorer'

Big art

THE ARCTIC IMPULSE of the early nineteenth century inspired a significant artistic output. The great majority was literal, even prosaic, created by amateur artists, the majority of whom were naval officers, or worked up from eye-witness sketches and first-hand testimony to achieve an artificial scenic grandeur. Yet the effect was limited, conveying neither insight nor explanation, only spectacle.[1] Only a handful of images achieved true artistic greatness, and all operated in the genre of the sublime – an art consciously designed to inspire fear and dread. In his *Philosophical Enquiry* Edmund Burke had applied the label 'sublime' to anything that, when contemplated, inspired terror – the strongest of human emotions. Kant took the idea a stage further, as 'the extreme tension experienced by the mind in apprehending the immensity or boundlessness of the grandest conceptions'.[2] The Arctic would be the last refuge of the sublime in British art, the only location sufficiently alien and disturbing to terrify the Victorians.[3]

From John Ross to George Nares, nineteenth-century polar expeditions provided sensation-starved Europeans with a succession of powerful, romantic images, combining the unknown with the sublime and the terrible. The most potent Arctic image of the early nineteenth century was Caspar David Friedrich's powerful, eerie premonition 'The Sea of Ice' of 1824, which, while inspired by Parry's first expedition, had far more to say about Franklin's last. The pathetic remains of a crushed sailing ship speak of a catastrophe, and connect the picture with the tragic death of the artist's brother in the ice, many years earlier.[4] These sublime sensibilities animated Franklin on his first overland expedition, leading him to select a picturesque, impractical site for his base camp.[5]

Just as Britain was not alone in the Arctic, British artists were not alone in providing Arctic images. The largest, unsurprisingly, was an American production. Although the connection is unclear, Friedrich's work had more impact in America than in Britain, helping to inspire the 'American Sublime' of Thomas Cole, Frederic Church and Albert Bierstadt.[6] Alongside his artistic training Church (1826–1900) was a devotee of Humboldt, sharing his vision of a comprehensive natural system. After reading the first three volumes of *Cosmos* Church followed Humboldt's South American footsteps, painting several vast scenes in response to Humboldt's call for panoramic images that would awaken interest in nature and inspire other travellers. Science and art were, for him, as close as history and literature.[7] In every case the cross occupied a prominent position, providing a key to Humboldt's natural world. Having painted his vision on a suitably monumental scale, Church sent 'The Heart of the Andes' to Europe to be shown to the master, but it arrived after the old man's death.[8]

Church did not go to Europe with his picture. Inspired by the same curiosity and wonder that had gripped the public on both sides of the Atlantic, he wanted to see the frozen north. A friend observed: 'He desired, if possible, to make his canvas reflect the glint and gloom, the grandeur and beauty, the coldness and desolation of the north, as he had already caused it to glow with the exuberant loveliness of the south.'[9] In late 1858 John Rae lectured in New York on the Franklin search, with some of his 'relics'. A few months later Isaac Hayes was fund-raising for another Arctic voyage. Church, a member of the American Geographical and Statistical Society, knew both Hayes and Henry Grinnell. Lady Franklin's much publicised visit to New York in early 1860 only added to the popularity of the Arctic. In the summer of 1859 Church worked from a hired vessel off the north coast of Newfoundland, producing almost a hundred sketches of icebergs, the raw material for a 'great' picture. By late 1860 he was at work on a vast scale (the picture is 168.3 x 285.7 cm), with the clear intention of repeating the commercial and critical success of such earlier 'great' pictures as 'The Heart of the Andes'. Even as Church was making his sketches McClintock 'solved' the Franklin mystery, leaving American interest in the region focused on the North Pole.

Church was the first great artist to visit the Arctic. His picture, praised for the 'intense solitude of the cool frozen North', first appeared as an empty scene, linked to the American dream of an open Polar Sea. This was an Arctic picture from a very specific moment in time, informed by Matthew Fontaine Maury's notion of an open Polar Sea.[10] Maury invested this concept with a powerful scientific rationale just as John Barrow's similar vision had been laid to rest by British scientific data from the Franklin search.

God's divine purpose revealed through Humboldtian science gave a powerful impulse to the 'manifest destiny' of the United States to rule the entire American continent, from pole to pole. Church's image opened a new proving ground for America, an icon for a self-confident, expanding nation, blessed by God.[11] But such dreams were shattered, not by the discovery of a polar ice cap but by slavery, the dark fracture in the American soul. In late April 1861 'The Icebergs' was presented to the New York public as 'The North', ice and expansion replaced by more immediate concerns. The American Civil War had broken out just twelve days earlier. Church donated the proceeds of the show to a patriotic fund for soldiers' families.

With a war brewing the American public was not gripped by this image.[12] Too vast and singular to attract a buyer without Arctic interests, 'The Icebergs' did not find one in the depressed American art market of the day. Church worked in some human interest, an all-too-obvious fragment of wreckage shaped like a cross hinting at redemption for the dead of the north, before exhibiting the picture in Britain in 1863. The cross only served to emphasise the powerful connection with J. M. W. Turner's 'The Fallacies of Hope'. Little wonder John Ruskin, part of an enthusiastic London audience that supported the one-picture exhibition from June to September, was full of praise. Recognising the potency of the image, *The Times* linked praise for the picture with a warning against further Arctic voyages.[13] The other reason for sending the picture to London was to have a colour lithograph made, which went on sale in 1865. Celebrated visitors to the exhibition included Jane, who approved both image and sentiment, Murchison, Arctic heroes McClintock, Rae, Back, Belcher and Collinson, and at least one famous contemporary artist. The picture eventually found a buyer: British railway magnate Edward William Watkin MP (1819–1901). Watkin had seen icebergs off Newfoundland in 1861 en route to Canada to become director and manager of the Canadian Grand Trunk Railway. This project followed up the Palliser survey, making a vital contribution to the creation of modern Canada. The attraction of the great painting for this eminently practical man was obvious, but he also set out a deeper connection:

The problem of the 'Northwest Passage' has been solved in a new and better way. It is no longer a question of threading dark and dismal seas within the limits of Arctic ice and snow, doubtful to find, and impossible, if found, to navigate. Now the two oceans are reached by land, and a fortnight suffices for the conveyance of our people from London or Liverpool to or from the great Pacific, on the way to the great East.[14]

For Watkin the painting symbolised the heroic but doomed search for a sea passage, and paid tribute to the fallen of that endeavour. Having made his fortune by replacing dreams of an ocean passage with an iron road he was the perfect buyer. A few years later Watkin and Church met in London. After a century hanging in Watkin's Manchester house the picture returned to the limelight, achieving an auction record of $2.5 million for an American painting when it was sold in 1979. Church's picture remains the largest, and by far the most expensive, example of polar art. By the time Church had sold his picture the American Arctic idea that it celebrated had been discarded, like the Franklin search, another victim of the war. The energies of the nation, so important to Church's concept, were focused inward, not to explore but to annihilate. Evidently smitten by the ice, Church painted another Arctic scene from Isaac Hayes's description of the aurora borealis in 1865 and a last small canvas, 'The Iceberg' of 1891, based on the 1859 sketches.[15] Within a decade of painting 'The Icebergs' Church had drifted out of the artistic mainstream. The collapse of Humboldt's scientific universe marked a critical turning point in his career; without the overarching scientific vision and the ability to see the divine in the natural world the energy and grandeur of his oeuvre faded, while the Civil War, the impact of Darwinism and arthritic hands hampered his work. The collapse of 'manifest destiny', God's purpose revealed in nature and

American self-confidence left Church without an audience, he died all but forgotten, his art worthless.[16]

Where Church offered a sublime vision of an unspoiled icy paradise, hinting at new avenues to an open Polar Sea, the great majority of British Arctic painting was uninspired. Most images were worthy literal studies, based on the sketches and watercolours of naval officers and aimed at a sensation-hungry audience. Their primary purpose was to illustrate voyage narratives. While many were chill and grim, none was intended to damn the idea of going north. To celebrate the achievements of the polar officers, Stephen Pearce produced a comprehensive series of Arctic portraits for John Barrow Jr and for Jane. In all, thirty-nine individual pictures were produced, and several were linked in 'The Arctic Council', a stiff, ill-focused group portrait which has inspired many to believe the 'Council' was a formal body.[17] This art was created for the private edification of a man who had done his utmost to advance the search, to commemorate his fellow labourers.[18] Pearce's purpose is rarely considered, but his work has been used to illustrate almost every modern study of the Franklin search.[19] As Barrow and Jane intended, the pictures both made heroes of the men who searched for Franklin and enhanced Franklin's reputation still further. Barrow was happy because they were his friends; Jane knew that the nobler his disciples, the greater Franklin must have been to inspire their efforts.

Having seen Church's picture, Sir Edwin Landseer (1792–1873) took a very different view of the subject, and his grim epitaph is the solitary English masterpiece of the genre. Even as his four colossal bronze lions were adding a suitably Victorian flourish to Nelson's Column, Landseer brilliantly subverted the entire process of lionising Sir John. His Biblical proverb 'Man Proposes, God Disposes' shattered the polite consensus on the meaning of Franklin that Jane had worked so hard to create. While the national war god was supported by four very British lions, Franklin's remains were devoured by hungry bears. British hubris had earned a suitable riposte from the savage guardians of the polar wasteland. The bear on the right of Landseer's picture is crunching a human rib cage.

Already a wealthy man, Landseer had no need to court popularity; he painted through a darkening cloud of loneliness, alcoholism and depression. The picture was commissioned by long-term patron E. J. Coleman, who collected news cuttings on the Franklin story. Taking as models for his central characters the polar bears at London Zoo, Landseer worked quickly, showing the picture at the 1864 Royal Academy Exhibition. The result was highly original and darkly fatalistic. Coming from an artist better known for mawkish, anthropomorphic sentimentality, the complete absence of sentiment is striking.[20] The subject and the eerie, chill light give this picture the power to alarm, but this tragedy has none of the epic grandeur of Frederic Church, or the hope that he offered. Instead it sounded a warning, and a new heroic: 'The idea of death in faraway lands in the service of the nation was to become part of the mythology of latter-day British imperialism.'[21] *The Times* was ecstatic: 'This is a most originally conceived and wonderfully painted picture . . .' panted an overexcited correspondent. 'Sir Edwin goes to the heart of the subject – animal ferocity and desolation. The ice even refuses a grace to those who have braved its terrors, they are to have a living tomb in the maw of the wild beasts.' The critic pointed out a telescope and a notebook, the uniform and the human bones for distant readers.[22] The image and approach reconnected Landseer with his artistic roots in early nineteenth-century romanticism, the apocalyptic sublime of Friedrich.[23]

Lady Franklin was appalled: others, with good reason, doubted Landseer's sanity, but no one could deny the power of his message. Franklin would have recognised Landseer's call for resignation in the face of God. Mad or not, Landseer was telling a higher truth. It was certainly a far cry from 'The Monarch of the Glen'. After his death the Royal Academy judged 'Man Proposes', epitaph of the Arctic impulse, Landseer's 'greatest picture'. Today it hangs in the Great Hall of Royal Holloway College at Egham. Considered 'unlucky', it is covered with a Union Flag, like some dead hero, when students sit exams in the hall.[24]

A decade later John Millais, one of Landseer's young admirers, produced the next major Arctic-related picture. 'The North-West Passage' was exhibited in 1874 with the motto: 'It might be done and England should do it'. Art was thus employed to renew the Arctic mission in the 1870s, and to link it to the heroic totem of

Nelson. An aged sea captain, modelled on the very real Captain Edward Trelawney, friend of Shelley, Byron and the Lake Poets, sits with his maps and charts, a Nelson portrait and an Arctic scene hanging on the wall. His daughter sits at his feet, representing the youth of the nation, listening to the wisdom of their predecessors. The presence of a French tricolour suggests the captain is as heroic as his idol, while the log books tell of his own journeys. The picture includes no sign of the Arctic itself, only the British sense of a task left incomplete, and a heroic example to spur the effort. Millais's greatest popular success expresses the pent-up desires of a nation two decades after the Franklin search, time enough for the horrors revealed by Rae to fade and be replaced by the new model of endeavour and sacrifice. Captain George Nares RN reckoned it had been a vital element in the genesis of his 1875 expedition, a judgement given credence by the critical role of Prime Minister Disraeli in the decision to send a naval expedition north. A popular engraving of 'The North-West Passage' found its way to the four corners of the Victorian imperial world and in 1888 it was purchased by the Tate Gallery.[25] After Nares's return Arctic art tailed off alarmingly. There were no more voyages to inspire, or tales to terrify.[26]

The Franklin disaster was more than a tragedy: it encapsulated the defeat of Western man's ambition to master the globe and impose his order on the natural world.[27] The North West Passage became a metaphor, representing the unknown Arctic 'other', something that gave the international response to the disaster a deeper meaning. While Franklin was only lost from view, the Arctic remained a sublime place of mystery, but when Rae revealed the details of his fate the sublime turned to horror, and the Arctic was damned for ever. Although Jane managed to rescue Franklin's good name from the wreckage, the Arctic had lost its innocence. Landseer's bears were the truth, red in tooth and claw, dispelling illusions, and warning future generations.[28]

More brazen lies

British interest in the Arctic did not benefit from the late-Victorian turn to imperial acquisition. The territory became Canadian in

1867, and therefore of limited concern. When the Americans also gave up, the subject drifted out of time and mind. The collapse of Arctic whaling removed the last reason for looking north. Franklin and his men were reborn as paragons of the Victorian cult of service, heroes who had willingly sacrificed their lives for the greater good.

The impact of the Franklin myth was universal. It inspired the polar efforts of Robert Falcon Scott and Roald Amundsen, both of whom picked up the chivalric 'Crusader' imagery. By the late nineteenth century the popular media had turned such expeditions into sensation-seeking endurance tests, ignoring any scientific or practical objective.[29] Murchison had wrapped his eulogy of McClintock and Franklin in the preface to *The Voyage of the Fox* with stirring sentiments. The Passage had been found 'by the heroic self-sacrifice of Franklin, Crozier, Fitzjames and their associates', while the search mission had 'been the best school for testing, by the severest trials, the skill and endurance of many a brave seaman. In her hour of need – should need arise – England knows that such men will nobly do their duty.'[30] A year later Captain Sherard Osborn chimed in, describing Franklin as an ideal medieval warrior-saint, going 'forth again, in true knightly mood, to ensure, to labour and accomplish much'.[31] Such sentiments were a balm to those who had lost so much, and they also laid the foundations for further endeavour – both Murchison and Osborn would spend the rest of their lives promoting voyages and exploration – but they were a lie. Polish-born seaman-author Joseph Conrad reflected this sentimental line, declaring that Franklin and others had laid down their lives for geography.[32] As cultural historian Mark Girouard has observed, 'One of the advantages (or dangers) of chivalry was that it could lift people to so lofty an emotional level that inconvenient facts could be disregarded.'[33]

Lady Franklin's death in 1875 ended any serious interest in solving the mystery, leaving Franklin a central figure in British culture as the Arctic slowly drifted out of the news. Cannibalism, death and the absence of any economic resources made a fatal combination. Public art was quick to adopt this new Franklin. The Waterloo Place statue was followed by the bust on the Whitehall façade of the new Colonial Office.[34] From this elevation he stares down on the

Cenotaph, Lutyens's stark memorial to a million men who went to do their duty in pursuit of a chivalric ideal and another lie. Under Lady Jane's determined direction Franklin had been shorn of his science and his humanity. He became a late-Victorian hero, a pompous stuffed shirt ripe for reappraisal.

Markham's quest

The process of rewriting the history of the Franklin mission begun by Lady Jane was taken to an inevitable, disastrous conclusion by one of the officers who had gone on the search mission. Clements Robert Markham (1830–1916) left the navy and became secretary of the Royal Geographical Society, in which capacity he was the leading advocate of further Arctic exploration. To this end he rewrote both the Franklin expedition and the search missions as chivalric romances, made heroes of men like McClintock and, with his naval cousin Albert (1841–1918), secured a new mission in 1875. Propelled by an adolescent enthusiasm, Markham would be the Barrow of his generation, the chief advocate and publicist of the process. He created the late-Victorian Franklin, a 'Great Explorer'.[35] Markham would rebuild the polar mission and rewrite much of the history of Arctic exploration.

Having joined the Royal Navy as a cadet in 1844, Markham had been persuaded to join HMS *Assistance* for the 1850–1 expedition by old shipmate Sherard Osborn. In contrast to his practically minded contemporaries, Markham prepared himself for the service by reading everything he could find on the subject, laying the foundation for an unrivalled mastery of the literature, echoing the work of his predecessor Sir John Barrow. Markham experienced an Arctic winter in the Barrow Strait, and the sledging expeditions sent out to search for the missing men. The camaraderie and team spirit of these arduous marches, their naval discipline and sense of purpose, were inspirational, while his literary and organisational talents were employed to the full filling in the long dark months of winter. The vision of exploration as a naval expedition – sledges hauled by loyal and determined men led by heroic, chivalric officers – dominated his approach to polar enterprise for the rest of his life.

Stunned by the scenic grandeur of the Greenland coast, Markham was less impressed by the Inuit, declaring that 'all is grand, majestic, awe-inspiring: all too is pleasant and delightful; all save man'.[36] That early judgement would return to haunt him, not once but twice, as another man fired by the Franklin story adopted the Inuit methods to succeed in the polar regions. Despite his limited experience, Markham was convinced the methods employed in 1850 were the only way to explore the polar wastes. Unwilling to return to regular naval duty after the relative freedom of the Arctic mission, Markham resigned from the service at the end of 1851, in part because of his distaste for corporal punishment, in part because he could not face long years as a subordinate. Instead he wrote about his experiences, and included extensive historical reflections before setting off for Peru.[37] After returning from the Americas, Markham worked at the India Office, and returned to Peru in 1859, spending the next three years acquiring the botanical material necessary to cultivate the cinchona tree on a commercial scale in India. Markham's initiative provided the medicines needed for the control of malaria in that country, a major contribution to the development of the subcontinent, and of British authority. Markham rose to be private secretary to the secretary of state for India: he had the ear of the mighty. Alongside his public career he published extensively in the field of historical geography with the Hakluyt Society and became prominent in the affairs of Barrow's old exploration vehicle, the Royal Geographical Society. In 1863 he was appointed honorary secretary of the RGS, and held the post for twenty-five years. This was an office of labour, but also one of great influence. He could set agendas, promote his own ideas and influence a council containing many influential and prominent men. Working closely with Barrow junior and Murchison he soon became a master of exploration politics. Recognising that the current format of the RGS journal lacked the market appeal to sell his ideas beyond the obvious audience, and with the society unwilling to take his advice, he simply produced his own racier periodical, forcing the society to buy him out and adopt his ideas at second hand.[38]

This talent was used to promote renewed polar exploration. In 1865 Markham's old friend Sherard Osborn read a paper at the RGS calling for a new expedition to explore the region around the North Pole, by way of Smith Sound. With Murchison as president, and Markham as joint honorary secretary, the RGS was quick to urge the cause. However, other opinion formers disagreed, and the government was unimpressed. Only when the Royal Geographical Society and the Royal Society combined was the Conservative government of new imperialist Benjamin Disraeli persuaded. The RGS Committee included six naval heroes and Markham; the Royal Society was headed by Antarctic eminence Sir Joseph Hooker.[39] Echoing old John Barrow's approach, Markham produced a full-scale history of Arctic exploration, *The Threshold of the Unknown Region*, to excite interest.[40] Dedicated to that great survivor George Back, *Threshold* was deliberately long on potential and rather short on real evidence. The object was 'to give the public a correct knowledge of the whole line of frontier separating the known from the unknown region around the North Pole' rather than a simple-minded chase after the polar target.[41] There was nothing remarkable in reaching the pole: improved knowledge of the entire region would be the principal result, and 'ample recompense' for the 'difficulties, perils and hardships of no ordinary character' that would have to be faced.[42] This was a more narrowly focused, navalised version of Murchison's agenda.[43] Few have noticed that Markham clearly and decisively shifted the focus from science to exploration, from useful knowledge to mere curiosity. In the process he continued the trend of diminishing Franklin by association, updating the meaning of the Waterloo Place monument rather than challenging it.

Well aware that Franklin's legacy was a major obstacle to such plans, Markham artfully avoided discussing what had happened and enlisted Jane as his chief witness. In a letter to Murchison written during the 1865 agitation for further exploration Jane deplored the idea that the fate of Franklin should be used to block future official efforts.[44] Magnetic phenomena only rated a brief mention.[45]

Commander Albert Markham, Clements's cousin, went to Baffin Bay on a whaler in 1873, publishing his account the following year as part of the drive for a new naval mission. Clements, long recognised as the historian of the Arctic mission, then produced a slim volume, *The Arctic Navy List*, in 1875, recording the names and achievements of all the officers who had served in the frozen north as the long-anticipated new era of Arctic exploration opened. With his mania for order, Markham divided his heroes into four 'generations'. Cook and Phipps were in the first, Ross, Parry and Franklin the second, the Franklin search group formed the third, while the 1875 party were the fourth. He stressed the importance of the personal transmission of knowledge between generations. Not that his information was necessarily correct. He credited McClintock and not Ross as the 'discoverer of naval sledge travelling'. Curiously, although from personal knowledge, Markham concluded: 'The most valuable qualifications for Arctic service are aptitude for taking part in those winter amusements which give life to the expedition during the months of forced inaction; and for sledge travelling.' Consequently he listed the parts his heroes had played in amateur theatricals alongside the Arctic landmarks which bore their names.[46] Markham assumed his new Arctic heroes would be competent scientific observers, although he hardly mentioned the important work of their predecessors. Instead he stressed camaraderie and the endurance to haul on sledges. It was a chivalric ideal.

The 1875–6 expedition was entirely Treasury-funded, removing control from the learned societies in favour of three Arctic veterans: Osborn, McClintock and Richards. Markham, invaluable as organiser and lobbyist, maintained his influence through these men, because he agreed with their views. They advocated repeating the expeditions of the 1850s – two big ships, large crews, man-hauled sledges and Markham's peculiar contribution: flags and mottoes for each sledging party. They also conducted extensive magnetic research.[47] Commanded by another Arctic veteran, Captain George Nares, with cousin Albert among the officers, the expedition set off in May 1875, Clements Markham travelling with them as far as western Greenland. After wintering on the northern coast of Ellesmere Island, Albert Markham set off for the North Pole, but reached no higher than 83°20'26"N before scurvy and exhaustion forced him to retreat. Men died because Albert forgot the lemon juice, a mistake that overshadowed successful coastal exploration and magnetic fieldwork. The old failing of relying on unscientific 'highlights' to sell the mission had once again betrayed the wider ambitions of the promoters. The anti-scorbutic properties of frozen lemon juice once more proved inadequate, although Albert's absent-minded omission to load any on the sledges did not help. His men died for the same reasons their forerunners had died on the search missions: lack of anti-scorbutics. Unwilling to see his dreams destroyed by an oversight, Clements quickly produced a defence, as if he could wipe away scorbutic death with many, many strokes of his industrious pen.[48] His attachment to the cause was celebrated by the expedition naming Clements Markham Inlet on the northern shores of Ellesmere Island, while personal interest and the inevitable icy agenda prompted him to donate a painting of cousin Albert's furthest-north camp to the RGS. Aware that there were problems, Clements used the preface to the fourth edition of *Threshold* to call for a relief ship to be sent, and elevated this idea into the key to avoiding a repeat of the Franklin catastrophe.[49]

Clements's decision to accompany the expedition to Greenland ended his public career. With customary arrogance and a wilful refusal to consider the necessary routines of the organisation he seriously overstayed his leave, not bothering to tell his superiors where he had gone, or for how long. As the secretary of state minuted: 'Some very decisive measure will be necessary, if anything like discipline or decency is to be maintained in the office . . . and the time has come when he must be told very distinctly that he must obey orders – comply with official rules, or go.'[50] It was typical of Markham that he gave up a promising career to satisfy his obsessions. His next Arctic project was less dangerous, collecting material on Baffin Island for the Hakluyt Society, but no less driven.[51] Thereafter he continued to serve the Royal Geographic and Hakluyt Societies with zeal and effect while earning his living as an industrious writer on history and travel. Unfortunately this development only exacerbated a tendency to be hasty, and somewhat cavalier with evidence.[52]

The international Arctic endeavours of the 1870s produced a new round of literary monuments to record their efforts, and their tragedies, but nothing shifted Franklin from his pedestal. Writing in the *Edinburgh Review*, for so long the liberal alternative to Barrow's *Quarterly*, naval scientist and historian Professor John Laughton recognised the search for knowledge and picked out the Markham cousins for special notice while praising the efforts of all nations. Although these missions were the hardest test of navies outside war, Laughton saw no purpose sending more when the Nares expedition returned with its minor tragedies and trifling triumphs.[53] This expedition finished off the Arctic for the British; they had abandoned the North West Passage after Franklin; after Nares they gave up the North Pole as well. Even so, Albert was promoted, and given a gold watch by the RGS. In 1879 and 1886 he went back to the ice, but only in a private capacity. Albert remained in awe of his cousin,[54] and continued to support his polar causes, for Clements Markham had not finished with the ice. In the following decade he began to lay plans for an Antarctic expedition – once he finished with the Arctic.

Making the 'Great Explorer'

The 1891 Royal Naval Exhibition at the Chelsea Hospital, better known today as the site of the annual Chelsea Flower Show, provided the perfect opportunity to create a definitive version of polar history. Franklin became a central figure in the public display – the Arctic gallery was named for him – while Leopold McClintock helped to collect the necessary relics and add the lustre of his own achievement to the proceedings. Albert Markham compiled a chapter on 'Arctic Heroism' for the exhibition catalogue, leaving no one in any doubt as to the purpose of the show. Earlier that year Clements Markham had lectured the Royal United Services Institution on the need to collect Arctic relics, maps, navigational instruments and other memorabilia at the Royal Naval College in Greenwich to inspire a new generation.[55] His message was echoed by McClintock, who urged the owners of Franklin relics, which had taken on almost religious significance, to loan them to the exhibition. They would be a 'touching memorial' of the fallen and recall the 'extraordinary efforts' made to find the expedition, which he wished to represent with the sledge flags.[56] Having invested Franklin memorabilia with the power of nationalist icons, Markham and McClintock filled the cabinets of the Royal Naval Exhibition with the help of the Admiralty, assembling the large Arctic collection now held by the National Maritime Museum.[57]

The 1891 exhibition was designed to link Britain's mighty naval past with the growing sense of alarm occasioned by the rise of rival fleets in France and Russia. It popularised both past and present in establishing the 'New Navalism' that would sustain naval expenditure down to 1914. With history already established as a major asset in the propaganda offensive, the opportunity was too good to miss.[58] Both Clements and Albert Markham were at the heart of the project, leading the Exhibition Arctic Committee. One wonders who decided that the audience would enter the exhibition through the Franklin Gallery, but the effect was obvious. Between 2 May and 24 October 1891 2.3 million visitors passed a morality tale in ice and artefacts, at the centre of which was the late-Victorian version of Sir John Franklin, loyal, dutiful and not desperately bright. The event was opened by the First Lord of the Admiralty, the man responsible for the latest upsurge in naval expenditure, while the visitors included Queen-Empress Victoria, Edward, Prince of Wales, his son Captain George Saxe-Coburg-Gotha RN and his nephew Kaiser Wilhelm II of Germany. Markham must have been delighted when the prince noted the Arctic relics as 'a source of the highest interest to all' in his speech at the official opening.[59]

The Markhams were supported by McClintock, Allen Young and George Nares. Sophia Cracroft helped with artefacts and advice. Colonel John Barrow lent several Stephen Pearce pictures, including 'The Arctic Council', which became the artistic centrepiece of the exhibition. It would have been inconceivable to have replaced this humdrum offering with Landseer's masterpiece. There was one unexpected presence in Pearce's gallery of 'heroes' – Edward Sabine – but he had been included as a pioneer traveller, not the man who set the magnetic agenda of Franklin's final mission. While the Markhams had no desire to tell that story, the unwitting decision to display the six-inch dip circle found at Point Victory might have pointed up another, very different truth. In the event no one noticed. It was just another brass relic.[60]

The Franklin Gallery opened with a replica of the cairn at Victory Point, the one in which McClintock and Hobson had discovered the 'answer' to the Franklin mystery. This theme continued on a table laden with Franklin artefacts and fourteen sledge flags from various

Arctic expeditions. Albert argued that the benefits of such work were to be seen in the modern navy, and put up Richard Westall's picture of Nelson attacking a polar bear to prove his point. He did not know that the real story of the bear was far less 'heroic'. In the centre of the gallery was a tableau of men hauling sledges. While Albert provided sledges and clothes from the 1875 expedition, the long-term impact of linking British ideas of polar heroism with man-hauled sledges and silk flags would not unfold for another two decades. The display was garnished with samples of Arctic flora and fauna. Outside, an 'iceberg' the size of a gentleman's house, complete with a garnish of bears, was home to a tableau of McClure's *Investigator* trapped in the ice, and an artful electric version of the aurora borealis which might have startled Sir John. Not everyone took the Markhams' Arctic seriously: the correspondent of the satirical magazine *Punch* went off for a suitably cold drink.

The Franklin Gallery revived a heroic name amid scenes of power and pageantry, and gave it a privileged place in the identity of the late nineteenth-century navy. The very episodic nature of naval glory had been a problem for the Victorians. To keep the brand alive they needed to remind the core audience, the British people, of their long line of heroes by refreshing the basic image. Although there had been some heroes in the years since Trafalgar, they were few in number, so the war on the ice was plundered for brave men. Their heroism was positioned as a national contribution, their efforts offered up as role models for future generations. None was more significant than Franklin, the key to a whole dynasty of Arctic death and glory. His noble sacrifice was tied to the hagiography of power. Like David Livingstone and General Charles Gordon, he was a hero who died for Empire.[61]

Of course the exhibition also made heroes of the living, not least Albert Markham. His furthest north was a key brag of Empire, and his clothes were very properly mounted on a dummy. The purpose was to prove that neither Albert nor Franklin had failed. The focus on geography left the real achievements of their expeditions in magnetic and other sciences unspoken, along with the deeply troubling issue of cannibalism. This subject had dropped from sight by the last decade of Victorian Empire. The North West Passage and furthest north were lauded as if they were significant achievements rather than curiosities of the chart. The popular press imbibed the lesson as directed. They celebrated Arctic heroes and praised the noble death march, mercifully unaware of its cannibalistic conclusion, and accorded Franklin the status of a fellow sacrificial offering at the altar of Empire with General Gordon of Khartoum. Suitably impressed, the best-selling popular history of exploration added a new chapter on the Arctic after 1891.[62]

Clements and Albert established that late-Victorian Franklin as a figure of imperial significance, and the foundation stone for further ice exploration. Albert's Franklin hagiography, which also appeared in 1891, a literary version of the Exhibition, had been produced to catch the huge audience that the event would generate. In his anxiety to promote further Arctic work Albert portrayed Franklin as a noble moral crusader. He created a new heroic 'do or die' version, blaming Goldner's meats for the disaster, Belcher's precipitate retreat for killing off the Arctic mission and the government for accepting Rae's evidence as conclusive. He omitted to mention that Lady Jane had instructed McClintock to 'prove' Franklin's priority in finding the Passage: instead he has McClintock initiate the claim. Having stressed the idea that Arctic voyaging was equivalent to military campaigning, Albert urged the renewal of Arctic work. He claimed that the Polar Sea contained abundant animal food to preclude scurvy.[63] His own failure to find such food two decades earlier passed without a word. The book remained in print until 1906, when a new polar hero left Markham's stuffy old Sir John looking rather threadbare.

Albert's text was complemented by a juvenile account of Franklin, a story of bravery, perseverance and, by implication, willing self-sacrifice to inspire future heroes. Heroines were catered for by emphasising Jane's courage and commitment. The Franklins were used to recruit more Edwardian cannon-fodder; no one mentioned the cannibalism. Franklin became a purely biographical subject because no one cared about the Arctic. It wasn't worth anything, white men didn't live there, and so there was no reason to go back.[64] Instead it became a theatre for the sublime and the heroic, not a subject requiring study, analysis or understanding. The Inuit were quietly ignored.

Two years after the exhibition Albert had an opportunity to demonstrate the value of polar work in forming the character of naval officers. On 22 June 1893 off Tripoli on the Lebanese coast, Rear Admiral Markham was confronted with a faulty, potentially lethal signal sent by domineering commander-in-chief Admiral Sir George Tryon. Instead of querying the order, which he knew to be impossible of execution and dangerous to attempt, Markham allowed Tryon to bully him into acquiescence. Three hundred and fifty-eight men died when Albert's flagship smashed into Tryon's HMS *Victoria*, Tryon among them. Albert was exonerated at the resulting court martial.[65] Albert had obeyed his orders, and many men had died as a result, but obedience was the essence, not intelligence. He caused the disaster because he lacked the courage to question a dangerous order. Clearly the Arctic had not shaped him into a superior officer. Although many blamed Albert, his career continued, albeit in a safer shore command. He remained a committed proponent of exploration to the end, loyal, dedicated, but utterly without imagination. That quality was the province of cousin Clements.

At the fiftieth anniversary of his departure, attempts were made to revive Franklin's memory but the highlights – a few imperialist-themed books, a visit to the Franklin Room and the memorial at Greenwich by the Royal Geographical Society, the odd provincial exhibition and an arch painting – proved anti-climactic. The success story was Clements Markham's use of the occasion to launch his Antarctic campaign.[66] He employed Franklin as a useful team player in the construction of a Victorian imperial ethic, backing up Livingstone, Gordon, and other men who had died in more straightforward circumstances. The Arctic was the problem: it had been forgotten. Suitably directed by Clements Markham, the Edwardians shifted their focus from cannibal-tainted Arctic ice to the pristine innocence of the Antarctic, and that has remained the British pole to this day. The emergence of Captain Scott as the latter-day mythic explorer merely cemented the process.[67] The Arctic was left to foreigners: the Norwegians Fridtjoft Nansen and Roald Amundsen were lionised in London for renewing the polar mission and completing the North West Passage respectively.

The poverty of the Markham version was nowhere more obvious

than in the art it inspired. Where Landseer and Millais had offered powerful images which require reflection late-Victorian tastes were simpler. W. Thomas Smith's 'They Forged the Last Link with Their Lives; Sir John Franklin Dying by His Boat during the Search for the North West Passage' of 1895 was blatantly inaccurate and highly romanticised.[68] Inspired by the fiftieth anniversary,[69] Smith used the boat that McClintock had discovered as the central prop in a moral tale of selfless sacrifice, the Richardson view of the mission rendered in oils. The frequency with which this picture is used to package the Franklin story reflects the powerful hold that literal images and simple myths can exercise over the human imagination. This was how the Victorians wanted to remember Franklin, a choice that helps to explain why the disaster would have a tragic refrain in another polar wilderness. The Markhams had reconstructed Franklin as a heroic archetype, swept up in the process that transformed the newly enfranchised working classes into willing cannon-fodder, and provided the upper classes with a self-sacrificing hero to emulate.

The 1890s was a pivotal decade for the British view of the sea. It witnessed the Royal Naval Exhibition and the *Victoria* disaster, the establishment of the Navy League and the Navy Records Society, and ended with the publication of William Laird Clowes's monumental *The Royal Navy: A History* in seven volumes. Clowes was *The Times*' naval correspondent, and it is no surprise that his book amplified the patriotic efforts of the decade and elevated them into a permanent record of why Britain ruled the world. When he began work in the mid-1890s, Clowes solicited help. Always ready to exploit an opportunity, Clements provided a running account of exploration. Significantly, Markham's was the first name cited among the contributors, above American sea-power theorist Alfred Thayer Mahan and American president Theodore Roosevelt. The Markhams were past masters of the narrative of discovery, and far too astute to waste the opportunity to endorse their own message.

Clements's version of the polar expeditions was overtly propagandistic. He made it quite clear that such arduous service developed 'all the qualities that are needed for success in war'. This came before the scientific results, and the improved whale fishery.[70] With an Antarctic expedition in development, Markham penned an effusive treatment of Ross and his work between 1839 and 1843. Although more concerned with danger and exploration than science, he still concluded: 'It was a glorious peace victory.'[71] Franklin's final expedition was always going to be a problem, and Markham's account reveals an underlying tension between evidence and message. He concluded that Franklin was too old, following Barrow in preferring Fitzjames for the command, only to laud his achievement in 1845 as 'the most remarkable voyage that has ever been made in those ice-encumbered straits and channels', reflecting 'sound ability and great judgement'.[72] Thus far the chapter, while laudatory of the Royal Navy and the exploring mission in general, had retained a recognisable basis in fact. It was only when dealing with the Franklin disaster that the agenda overwhelmed the evidence. Markham has Gore and des Voeux reaching Cape Herschel and returning to tell Franklin that they had 'completed' the North West Passage just before his death. This nonsense had been generated by Richardson and Osborn. Markham's chapter transformed it into an accepted part of the Franklin story. He agreed with Albert that the catastrophe had been caused by Goldner's meats, which, being unfit for consumption, led to scurvy.[73] The former accusation remains unproven, the causal connection is incorrect and John Barrow Jr had rejected the claim fifty years before. Cooked food does not retain vitamin C, even if properly preserved.

To wring every last drop of pathos out of the matter Markham continued to invent:

Bravely and resolutely had those gallant sailors stuck to their duty, and died at their posts. Their end, though unspeakably sad and pathetic, was glorious. They died to uphold the honour and prestige of their country. Yet the loss of the Franklin expedition was one of the greatest calamities that ever befell the British Navy.[74]

There was not a shred of evidence for his account of the way the men died, and his assessment of the disaster reads very strangely set against the loss of HMS *Captain* in a gale off Finisterre in 1870 and HMS *Victoria* in 1893, when in both cases several hundred men lost their lives. Perhaps the real calamity for Markham was the impact the Franklin disaster had on the polar mission. The salvation of his cause was provided by the 'unequalled' sledge journeys of 1853–4, which he stressed 'had no dogs', thereby excluding Admiral Sir Richard Vesey-Hamilton, one of the principal supporters of a renewed exploring mission, from his list of heroes. Whatever the cost, 'There is no better nursery to bring out the best and noblest traits in the character of a British seaman.'[75]

The treatment of John Rae's discoveries followed the Lady Jane line. He ignored the issue of cannibalism and condemned the Admiralty for paying him the reward 'in order to close the subject'. Fortunately Lady Jane dispatched the heroic McClintock to search King William Island, and he recovered the story. Fourteen years of searching were over, a mission 'afterwards of great advantage to the service'.[76] It was on these grounds that Sherard Osborn had urged the renewal of the Arctic mission in 1864, and persevered until it was granted in 1874. When Disraeli announced the Nares expedition, he declared that it was intended 'to encourage that spirit of enterprise which had ever distinguished the English people'. Unfortunately, according to Markham, the scientific agenda of the RGS was subverted by Admiralty instructions that encouraged 'a foolish rush to the pole.'[77]

Consequently he was able both to laud the heroics of cousin Albert and excuse the failure by stressing that 'only two men' were lost (he was careful not to say that they died), while the expedition produced 'an exceptionally rich harvest of scientific results'.[78] Having established his case, Markham wrapped up his polemic with a flourish. Exploring was 'legitimate work for the Navy in peace', and he regretted the tendency to abandon this field to other nations.

But it only needs a more thorough study of the history of the Navy, and a more clear appreciation of her needs, in order to restore us to the position we held at the time when Barrow and Beaufort could make their influence felt. For success in war it is not only ships that we need, but also trained officers and men, who have acquired confidence and experience in the course of special service, in addition to the knowledge of the ordinary routine of mastless steamships.[79]

Markham kept up a barrage of work on discovery history to support his belief in a polar mission, gradually shifting his focus south. Here lay a new, pristine wilderness, uncomplicated by people, or the legacy of failure and cannibalism. His work was pivotal to the British Antarctic effort: he would be cheerleader, literary executor and selector of officers.

In 1905 the Earl's Court Naval, Shipping and Fisheries Exhibition included an Arctic section, largely reprising the 1891 event, with the same cast of characters on the committee and Albert Markham's old clothes on display. There was one key difference: the portrait of Franklin on display was 'offered for sale' – a new hero had usurped his space. It was up to Robert Falcon Scott to 'animate the heart and mind' of the nation.[80]

Clements Markham had invented, or at least sustained, the idea that it was 'manly' and 'British' for men to haul sledges across the ice, and had dismissed the use of dogs. He restated this opinion in his 1908 biography of McClintock.[81] In the same year a bright young naval captain wrote an introduction to a reissue of Franklin's first overland expedition narrative.

Another pole

Markham's hard work paid off when he was somewhat surprisingly elected president of the RGS on 13 November 1893, his predecessor having resigned. Markham immediately announced he intended launching an Antarctic mission during his term of office, appointing a council committee to report on the subject. His skills in manipulating information, his energy and his belief were once again harnessed to the cause, and despite many setbacks he overcame the resistance of the doubters, and of those who supported the idea but took a different view of how the job should be done. As if to validate his mission, Markham was knighted for his geographical work in 1896. He packed the Council with his nominees and drove its policy with irresistible energy. He also secured the interest of leading figures in many arenas, all propelled by what one contemporary called his 'impetuous enthusiasm'.[82]

For this national expedition Markham sought the co-operation of the Royal Society, but the society was no longer satisfied that a large-scale party, led by naval officers, was a suitable method. They knew that if the navy led, naval discipline and naval concerns would take priority, to the detriment of the pure science that they were anxious to conduct. The society wanted their nominee to control the scientific work on land, leaving the navy to provide the transport. Markham could not see beyond the past, and wrecked the work of the joint RGS/RS committee that had partitioned the command arrangements. The three retired admirals of the RGS delegation to the joint committee, Albert Markham, Richard Vesey-Hamilton and Anthony Hoskins, promptly resigned. Markham, and most of the RGS, wanted exploration and discovery; the RS wanted science. Markham's clinching argument was that the RGS had raised the majority of the money and built the *Discovery*.

While it is easy to caricature Markham's work as amateurish and destructive,[83] the debate was by no means so simple. That said, the end result was disastrous. The two Scott expeditions were unwieldy, dangerously uncertain of their real purpose and ultimately tragic. Markham won because he was the most determined, and the most effective bureaucrat in the game. His aims were based on the past. He had known many of the men who went south with Ross in 1839–43, and based his planning on Ross's work, including the selection of target area and the insistence on a naval party. He had also selected his officers, including Scott, whom he first met in 1887.

Ultimately Markham lost control of the first expedition to the government because the RGS and RS could not find the money to send a second relief ship to succour the stranded *Discovery*. The Treasury stepped in, severely criticised the running of the project and took over the existing assets, namely the first relief ship then in the Antarctic. With that Markham's power was broken, and after Scott's return he resigned as president. Unfortunately Markham and his ideas lingered. Scott went back, but this time, like Franklin, he did not return.[84] In 1905 Scott's book on the first Antarctic expedition included the observation that Markham was 'the father of the Expedition and its most constant friend'.[85] The depth of Markham's influence on Scott was obvious: his son Peter Markham Scott was born on 14 September 1909.

Unlike Barrow, Markham lived to learn of the disaster that befell 'his' expedition, and helped edit Scott's literary remains. Having shaped the fable of Arctic heroism he was ideally equipped to edit the inevitable consequence: misguided chivalric zeal and manly virtue used to explore one of the most appalling places on earth. Amundsen was successful because he thought clearly, and had learned much in the Arctic. Not only had he made the first real transit of the North West Passage, but he had mastered the use of dogs along the way. In the Antarctic he used dogs to pull his sledges, and then to feed his party. The Markhams had created the late-Victorian Franklin as a mythic hero to excite future emulation, and sell the virtues of polar endeavour.[86] Franklin's sacrifice persuaded the public to back another effort in the ice, only to end with a tragic reprise of earlier horrors. Robert Falcon Scott instantly became what Franklin was turned into long after his death, a hero of selfless sacrifice. Moulded by Jane's version of the story, and pushed on by Markham, Scott had fallen into a ghastly trap. His final expedition narrative was edited by a small group of men, among whom the name of Clements Robert Markham was prominent. Once Scott had replaced Franklin there was no need for the older man. Curiously enough, Amundsen had already removed Franklin from the record books by making the first ship transit of the North West Passage in 1906. In 1912 Scott replaced him as a national totem. As Karl Marx famously observed, 'Hegel says somewhere that all great events and personalities in world history reappear in one fashion or another. He forgot to add the first time as tragedy, the second as farce.'[87] If Scott's first voyage had been something of a farce, his second was all too obviously a tragedy.

The malign effects of Arctic exploration were a direct result of the conscious misrepresentation of their purpose. By 1850 missions dispatched to deal with practical scientific and navigational tasks were written up as little more than expeditions in pursuit of irrational and utterly useless targets like the North West Passage and the geographic poles. The same simplification applied to exploration on other continents. By the early twentieth century such nonsense had become universal. W. Gillies Ross observed of the North Pole: 'That so much effort should be expended, and so much hardship endured, in a quest for this featureless point, set within a frozen ocean, is vivid testimony to the irrational element in exploration.'[88] This development reflected the anxiety to secure a public audience. We should not impose the same concerns on the state-funded expeditions of the early and mid-nineteenth century. While the Franklin expedition may have been described, in shorthand form, as searching for the North West Passage, the official instructions clearly delineate a very different agenda combining scientific and navigational targets. Scott's expeditions have suffered the same fate – misunderstood and misrepresented. Even Susan Solomon, who provides a 'scientific' Scott in *The Coldest March*, is not concerned with magnetic phenomena.[89]

In Marx's terms the failure to own the history of polar exploration, to tell the truth about its aims and objectives, ended in tragedy. Clements Markham succeeded in getting an official expedition sent to the Antarctic in 1901 under Commander Robert Falcon Scott RN (1868–1912). Having sought advice from Fridtjof Nansen and McClintock, Scott conducted a major campaign involving two winters on the ice and extensive sledge travel. He made a 'furthest south' and oversaw extensive scientific work with effective humane leadership. High on the list of scientific projects was geomagnetism. His expedition narrative, like Franklin's eighty years before, was a major success. Scott returned to a hero's welcome at a time when the Edwardians were ready for a new heroic. He was promoted and rewarded, receiving the RGS Patron's Gold Medal like many of his Arctic predecessors. Perhaps the last word on the purpose of polar exploration belongs to Scott. In a letter to Archibald Geikie, Roderick Murchison's protégé and biographer and a member of the Royal Society committee on the 1901–4 expedition, he observed: 'In general I am ready to plead ignorance of the value of our scientific work, but when it comes to magnetic results I make bold to say that our light ought not to be dimmed by anything that other Expeditions can produce.'[90]

The emergence of rival Antarctic expeditions, British and foreign, persuaded Scott to follow Markham's advice and go back. This time he had to raise the funds for the expedition himself. Since the public was only interested in another attempt to reach the South Pole following Ernest Shackleton's heroic failure in 1908, that became the notional purpose of the mission even though Scott did not share this obsession, arguing that the scientific programme was 'the rock foundation of all effort'.[91] Hampered by the inevitable funding shortfall, the expedition reached Antarctica in early 1911. A rival Norwegian expedition under Roald Amundsen, pioneer navigator of the North West Passage was a real concern. The race to the pole, a question of keeping the public happy and satisfying his numerous sponsors, soon dominated Scott's programme.

Scott set out for the South Pole with four companions. Despite the limits of man-hauled sledges and unusually cold and windy conditions they reached their target on 17–18 January 1912, a month after Amundsen's party. The journey back was always going to be hard, but with food short and the weather constantly adverse the men began to fail. Petty Officer Evans collapsed, and Scott put him on the sledge. Although Evans did not last long, the effort of carrying him probably cost the other men their lives. On 16 March Captain 'Titus' Oates, Inniskilling Fusiliers, realising that he could not go on, took himself out of the tent, famously remarking, 'I may be gone some time.' His comrades knew exactly what he was doing, and why. It was the most telling critique of Scott's leadership, one that few have even noticed. Oates knew that carrying Evans had been a fatal mistake, and that Scott would not abandon him either. He acted to save his leader the hardest choice. His sacrifice was in vain. Three days later the survivors were stranded in their tent by a blizzard, unable to make the last eleven miles to their depot. With Scott unable to walk – his gangrenous foot required amputation – it appears that his comrades decided to die with him rather than head for safety. With no more fuel and only two days' food, they could not last long. Scott may have been the last to die, and he kept writing to the end. His final letters and journal entries combined a heartfelt plea that his crew be supported, with the foundations of a new heroic. It was the very thing that Franklin had not been able to transmit, a last testament to heroism. Almost the last line was a message of absolution for Markham; the last emphasised that they were setting a good example by facing disaster like men, like Englishmen: 'We have decided not to kill ourselves but to fight it out to the last for that depot, but in the fighting there is a painless end so don't worry.'[92]

Because the tent, corpses and papers were located just a year later, Scott's sacrifice did far more for polar endeavour than Amundsen's rather clinical triumph.[93] It was heroic, tragic and met the mood of the age. Inevitably and immediately, the link with Franklin was made.[94] The key to the story was death, preferably heroic death, but death – and plenty of it. Nothing sold newspapers like bad news.[95] A memorial was held at St Paul's, the king breaking all precedent by attending in the uniform of an admiral of the fleet. With the royal seal of approval Robert Scott became a national hero, the *beau idéal* of the English gentleman: solid, dependable, brave, and humane.[96] His story still inspires strong opinions, few of which have any basis in fact.

As the secretary of state for war John Seeley declared: 'Our hearts are full to-day of the self-sacrifice of a small band of devoted men who died in the Antarctic . . . We shall never forget those brave sailors who laid down their lives in the cause of their country's honour as truly as the soldier who lays it down on the battlefield . . . we shall not forget the soldier who knew how to die and laid down his life for his friends.'[97] Seeley was only giving official voice to the feelings of a nation, sentiments shared by the navy. Unveiling a memorial plaque at the Naval College in Greenwich a year later, the chaplain of the fleet considered the men had lost their lives for an idea, which might 'set other men on a higher plane of duty, then we had a tragedy in its noblest form. Of such tragedy we needed more. It was the salt of life.'[98] The meaning of those sentiments would be clear before many more months had passed.

To ensure that Scott had not died in vain he was given the same treatment as his northern precursors. A bronze statue sculpted by Lady Scott and paid for by the officers of the Royal Navy was unveiled in Waterloo Place in November 1915, diagonally opposite Franklin's, making them the twin pillars of a brazen lie. That both men were made by their widows is noteworthy.[99] Public subscription funded publication of Scott's scientific results, and founded the Scott Polar Research Institute in Cambridge.[100] Controversy has surrounded Scott since his Edwardian deification. Critics of his leadership and devotees of his cult have, of late, temporarily been set aside by a new Antarctic hero, Ernest Shackleton. That Shackleton, who gave up his expedition to bring home his people, has been chosen as the explorer for the twenty-first century is not surprising. The old heroism imposed upon Franklin and Scott, laying down their lives for country and honour, has outlived its age. After Scott there was no need for other polar heroes. Franklin was abandoned to the Canadians, who had other uses for his expedition.

The First World War

Eighteen months after the deification of Robert Falcon Scott, Britain went to war. An appeal for volunteers met with an overwhelming response. Within days more than a million men had swelled the ranks of the army, and nearly as many would die before the war ended. The sentiments that animated the volunteers were complex and many, but none had such power as duty and honour, of laying down one's life for the mission. The creation of such sentiments had occupied much of the nineteenth century, and they had been disseminated by the cheap press to the newly literate working class. The fallen would be recalled across the land. Public memorials were commissioned in every country town and village church (alongside Franklin's memorial in Spilsby Church are tablets listing those who did not come home in 1918), and in central London public statements in stone and bronze told of an imperishable truth, one that succeeding generations would venerate, just as those who died in the Great War for Civilisation had venerated Franklin and Scott, Gordon and Livingstone.

Such concerns do not appear to have troubled Sir Clements Markham. He died in January 1916 after setting fire to his bedclothes while reading. After supporting the minesweeper service through the First World War, Albert died in October 1918.[101] But even death could not stop Clements, whose history of polar exploration appeared in 1921. *The Lands of Silence* repeated the old mantra that Franklin's party was 'the first to discover the connection of the Atlantic and Pacific Oceans', and that because Franklin lived to hear of this success he 'died happy and full of hope'.[102] As the last and most authoritative statement of a great Victorian lie, such pious nonsense did enormous harm to the history of the Arctic, and warped the mindset of an age. It left Franklin completing a task he had never essayed, while ignoring the real objects of his expedition.

Such self-serving romantic nonsense should be swept aside, for the Franklin story is stranger and more terrible than Markham dared to admit. It retains the power to deprive grown men of their wits, and frighten anyone who believes civilisation is more powerful than animal instinct.

Only in the 1960s did the new heroics of human endurance, and improved cameras, open the eyes of an awestruck public to the majesty that had greeted the first polar voyagers. Today the dominant Arctic image is of an iceberg calving off from a glacier and crashing into the ocean, backed up by frightening statistics about the shrinking polar ice cap. Redundant Soviet-era ice-breakers allow tourists to transit the Passage, or drive up to the pole. John Barrow's dream of an open Polar Sea may become a fact, but in the process Arctic ecology and the Inuit way of life will be annihilated. The North West Passage may bear witness to another human tragedy, on a scale that threatens the very survival of the species.

Terror: What Really Happened?

terror (n.) intense fear, fright or dread.[1]

There is no mystery about the fate of the Franklin expedition. It had been sent to complete an international scientific mission, a critical contribution to the terrestrial magnetic project, under the generic headline of completing the North West Passage. After a benign opening season in which Franklin circumnavigated Cornwallis Island and wintered at Beechey Island he entered Peel Sound, a twenty-mile-wide channel separating Prince of Wales Island from Somerset Island. Hitherto thought to be a dead end, the sound was open, and it led due south. Usually the ice in Peel Strait and Franklin Strait begins to break up in early August as the ice melts; there is no current to help the process:

Clearing of the waterway depends mainly on the warmth of the summer and is not always completed . . . Freeze-up develops among the old floes, if any are present in mid September, but the main ice formation does not occur until the end of the month when general freeze-up of the whole Barrow Strait takes place.[2]

Peel Strait was the nearest major inlet to Cape Walker, the point where Franklin had been directed to start his search for the Passage. It offered a direct route to magnetic north, an irresistible draw for a primarily magnetic mission. James Clark Ross, who understood the importance of magnetic work to Franklin's mission, was able to predict where the ships would get stuck.[3] However, he could not reach the spot, partly because the ice conditions in 1848 were very different from those Franklin encountered in 1846, and partly because he had refused to take steamships.

Stuck

By 1845–6 Arctic navigators understood that ice conditions varied widely between seasons. Although they did not understand the oceanographic and meteorological phenomena at work, they were assembling data to solve the problem. Franklin took a complete library of Arctic exploration, and could call on Crozier, ice masters James Reid, Thomas Blanky and Lieutenant Graham Gore for additional advice. As he pushed south, steam engines enabled him to negotiate a passage partly blocked by multi-year ice fields. For more than a month the two ships made progress, every day taking them closer to Cape John Franklin, and beyond that the Simpson Strait, Point Turnagain and an open coastal route to the Bering Strait. They were approaching James Clark Ross's magnetic pole, a feat no ship would repeat for sixty years. For such small underpowered craft this passage required a lot of luck, and very good ice navigation. Modern research indicates that ice conditions in the Franklin Strait are affected by fairly consistent southerly winds; these prevent the formation of fresh ice and limit the consolidation of multi-year ice. While the south wind held, Franklin's ships made progress, steaming directly into the wind and threading through the pack. On 12 September 1846 they became stuck. In all probability the wind changed direction, leading to a sudden drop in temperature and a rapid consolidation of fresh ice, welding the multi-year pack into a solid, impenetrable mass. This could happen in the space of a single, brief Arctic night. A westerly or west-north-westerly wind would be peculiarly dangerous, helping the light current push heavy ice down the McClintock Channel. The ships were trapped at the entrance to Victoria Strait, just as they emerged from the shelter of Prince of Wales Island:

For most of the year Victoria Strait is filled with very rough ice and evidence has been noted of heavy pressure on all the salient points of King William Island which face the strait. In addition to local ice the strait may receive heavy polar ice and occasional ice islands which have drifted down from McClintock Channel. The northern part of Victoria Channel is never open to any appreciable extent although in most years there is a general loosening of the ice. The southern end of the strait, however, often opens up more or less completely except in severe ice years.[4]

Franklin had reached an area where solid ice formed in early to mid-September. The *Pilot of Arctic Canada* observes that his ships were at the juncture between the most southerly extension of solid ice, up to ten feet thick, and the broken ice of the Peel and Franklin

Straits.[5] Once locked in the ice he could not escape, only drift slowly south. The situation was not ideal. Franklin and Crozier would have preferred a secure winter anchorage like Beechey Island, but they may have expected to escape the following summer. They were less than two hundred miles from the mainland and, being obsessive navigators, would soon notice that they were drifting south at a little under a mile a month.

Everything depended on the summer of 1847. If the ice opened they had a good chance of reaching the Bering Strait, or at least a part of the coast Franklin had charted where they could locate fresh food. In a good year this might have happened, but 1847 was not a good year. The ice did not open. Furthermore, Franklin died at a critical point, a month or so before the potential navigation season. This left Crozier to make the decisions. In normal circumstances a change of leader would have been a minor inconvenience – after all, Crozier was an experienced ice navigator. However, he had no experience of independent command, and began the 1845 expedition in a despondent state of mind. At the very least Franklin's death deprived the mission of an inspirational figurehead.

To make matters worse, Crozier had been left with a very big decision – what to do if the ice did not open. It is inconceivable that he would not have sent sledge parties ashore and across the ice to scout the area. The magnetic observatory Hobson discovered at Cape Felix was a significant feature of the expedition's work, and there are reports of a line of non-magnetic brass poles, the much-derided 'curtain rods', leading away from it towards the magnetic pole. Schwatka discovered two well-built cairns close to Cape Felix. They crowned prominent topographical features, and were visible from a long distance to the north – the route of any ships following their route. While they contained no significant records, Schwatka believed the one nearest the Cape had 'been erected in pursuit of the scientific work of the expedition, or that it had been used in alignment with some other object to watch the drift of the ships'.[6] The second cairn contained a piece of paper with a carefully drawn hand, the index finger of which was pointing south. Any writing had been lost, but the inference was obvious – they went that way. We can assume that Ross would have understood.

However, the area was utterly barren. As McClintock observed, 'Nothing can exceed the gloom and desolation of the western coast of King William Island.' He found the cold foggy atmosphere depressing, his mood darkened by the absence of edible game.[7] This last would be a critical element in Crozier's decision-making – something that can be inferred from the choice he made.

Sick

Inuit testimony left no doubt why Crozier decided to abandon ship: the men were sick. The symptoms the Inuit described so graphically were those of scurvy, a diagnosis confirmed by forensic science. Modern research has established that Arctic scurvy is a more complex phenomenon than the 'normal' version encountered at sea. In addition to ascorbic acid, Arctic travellers were also short of niacin, riboflavin and thiamine.[8] The symptoms of scurvy are well known: weakness, nausea, the reopening of old wounds, receding gums, loss of teeth, blackening of the mouth and skin. Unless sufferers receive fresh food, either animal or plant, it is fatal. Sailors knew about scurvy, the greatest killer of their kind since time immemorial, but lately it had been brought under control by issuing lemon juice. Scurvy appeared on previous Arctic expeditions, usually when too little lemon juice was issued, or it had been frozen, killing the vitamins. Franklin had enough lemon juice for one ounce per man per day for three years. That would have been the bare minimum to keep men healthy in comfortable conditions; it was nothing like enough for men working hard in extreme cold. They needed an adequate supply of fresh food, and they needed the vitamin content of the juice. Unfortunately there was no fresh food and the vitamin C probably fell victim to the temperature in the hold of Franklin's ships as they wintered in the ice. This is the most likely explanation for the scurvy outbreak. When combined with malnutrition or starvation, Arctic scurvy results in rapid loss of body mass, impaired mental and physical function and increased susceptibility to infectious diseases such as dysentery, a common Arctic killer.

Nineteenth-century experience demonstrated over and over again that the key to polar health was a combination of preserved lemon juice and fresh food, mostly wild game but including some vegetation. Some ships even managed to cultivate cress and mustard in useful quantities. The Inuit avoid scurvy by eating raw seal meat, rich in vitamins; they avoid the west coast of King William Island because there is nothing to hunt. Beset in an area without wild game, Franklin and his men would soon be in trouble. Issuing more lemon juice would have helped, but no one understood the causation, or the nature of vitamins, making treatment wholly empirical.

Crozier's immediate concern was to find fresh food. The temptation to contrast his failure with John Rae's heroic overland travels is fatuous. Rae only travelled when he could hunt, and stockpiled frozen game for the winter: he travelled as much by his gun as his snow shoes. Such techniques were only applicable to small groups, and very good shots. Those who followed in Rae's footsteps – Hall, Schwatka and Stefansson – did so in very small parties, often relying on Inuit hunters. Franklin's men could not live off the land, or use Inuit techniques, because they were part of a very large expedition. The size of the expedition reflected the scientific purposes of the mission, and the fact that it was intended to travel by sea. Franklin had been sent to navigate and conduct a major scientific project, not to explore. He could not travel light and fast; he had to watch and wait while needles fluctuated. The objects of the mission were responsible for Franklin ending up beset in the ice off King William Island with more than 120 men to feed. The expedition was unable to hunt enough food to maintain the health of so many men for three years because they had found 'the least favoured spot in the Canadian Arctic' for survival.[9] Across the Victoria Strait, in Cambridge Bay, Rae found plenty of caribou and musk ox, but Franklin did not know where to look.

An earlier voyage by HMS *Terror* suggests what might have happened in 1847–8. In 1836 *Terror* wintered in a similarly barren area. Soon there were sixty men sick, almost the complete complement, and three men died during a single winter.[10] McClure's *Investigator* told the same story. For two years and three months the men avoided any serious outbreak of scurvy because they had access to significant quantities of game, sorrel and scurvy grass. Once the fresh food ran out scurvy quickly set in. A year later men were dying or going insane." The condition of the crew was not helped by inactivity and despair, knowing they could not escape and without hope of rescue. When help arrived, the men's condition improved, despite an unchanged diet, because they had hope. This was the other reason Crozier decided to land: the men were terrified and the only way he could raise their spirits was to promise salvation. He was no fool; he knew it was a lie, albeit a useful lie to keep up morale.

Decision

Crozier and Fitzjames faced a terrible choice: they had to decide which route to take in an attempt to escape their icy prison without letting the men understand that the situation had become almost hopeless. Both men would have known that they had virtually no chance of returning alive – and yet they had to keep up the morale of the men, and keep them occupied to take their minds off the catastrophe that was unfolding before their eyes. Three facts marked the scale of their problem. Food was running short. The men were sick, debilitated and wasting, ravaged by scurvy, if nothing more, and many had died. Finally, they were at least a thousand miles from salvation.

Three days after landing Fitzjames recovered a record deposited the year before and wrote out a bare narrative. He was more interested in where the ships were, where the record had been found, and where Sir James Ross had built a cairn in 1831 than in why the men had abandoned ship, or why so many were already dead. He seemed to be clinging to the navigational certainties of his profession, desperate to avoid anything that smacked of speculation. Crozier signed, and then added the briefest of postscripts. They would start the following day for the Great Fish river. This is the only contemporary written evidence of what happened to the Franklin expedition. It is more interesting for what it does not say than for what it does.

It was a mark of their resignation that neither man added any human, personal touch, nothing for loved ones, the Board of Admiralty who sent them, or any would-be rescuers. Crozier had accepted his fate: he would lead the men south and keep the expedition under military discipline for as long as he could. He knew they had no hope. His job was to keep the men from learning the truth. Crozier's offhand announcement of the route is revealing. He had two choices: seven or eight hundred miles north-east towards Baffin Bay, and the possibility of meeting a whaling ship, or south towards the Great Fish river, and then on to the nearest Hudson's Bay Company post over a thousand miles away. This at least offered the promise of fresh food en route; the Baffin Bay route did not, nor could it be completed in a season, even by men in good condition. Both routes were hopeless, and there is no reason to doubt that Crozier knew as much. His was a rare kind of courage, the ultimate leadership. The decision to depart at the end of April reflected the seasonal nature of Arctic travel. It was the earliest date at which the temperature permitted men to make long journeys, while ice and snow still eased the task of hauling sledges. In summer, rough ground, marshes and mosquitoes made conditions more difficult.

Crozier's men were equipped with three or four strongly built oak sledges, each carrying a boat suitably modified for river travel, tents, food, fuel and other essentials. Even with thirty men hauling the sailors would struggle to overcome the frictional drag of these cumbersome structures, the absolute antithesis of flexible, ultra-lightweight Inuit sledges and boats. Pulling the sledges would be slow work, burning up astonishing amounts of energy, energy the men would be unable to replace for very long. A decade later McClintock calculated that Crozier's sledges held no more than forty days' supply of food and fuel for the team needed to pull them. Unless they discovered alternative supplies along the way the expedition would run out of food. Five to ten miles per day would be the upper limit of progress, so they had enough food for between two and four hundred miles – less than halfway. All the evidence suggests that the majority of the men died within two hundred miles of the original landing.

March

The men who began this doomed enterprise were already in poor health, weakened by scurvy and ill prepared for an arduous route march after three years largely restricted to the narrow confines of their wooden world. They had no specialist clothing, apart from sea boots with brass screws driven through the soles. The major problem they faced was scurvy, a slow, wasting killer that left them exposed to related diseases, notably pneumonia and hypothermia. The sunlight deficiency of a polar winter, the onset of despair and the effects of lead poisoning from the badly soldered food tins did not help, although they were not in themselves lethal.

On 26 April Crozier led his men south, and beyond the reach of history. Once the men abandoned ship their problems increased. Pulling heavy boat/sledges, the combination of severe physical labour, prolonged cold and the heat loss occasioned by sweating in unsuitable clothing meant that fit men would need at least 6,000 calories per day. We do not know if they took any lemon juice with them, but if they did it would have been frozen and next to useless. To facilitate travel the rations would have been reduced, just when the men needed much more food.

Ship's biscuit would have been a tough chew for scorbutic teeth and gums, and although dried and tinned food retained calorific value it required cooking before it could be consumed. This meant carrying fuel, for King William Island has no natural fuel and little driftwood. Dehydration was also a problem. Fresh water could be thawed from sea ice, but that required fuel, which would be in short supply. The catastrophe that overcame Scott's Antarctic party was also largely a result of inadequate rations, too little fuel and critical vitamin deficiencies.[12] Once the men stopped marching the temptation to break up the boats to provide warmth, water and warm rations would have been strong.

Science

In their anxiety to 'solve' the mystery many authors have turned to science, tempted by the delusion of precision. They have discovered that the available evidence resolutely refuses to offer any certainty. For many years scurvy and putrid tinned meat held the field as the obvious 'causes', despite the fact that there was no scientific evidence for either! Then between 1984 and 1986 Dr Owen Beattie's Canadian expedition exhumed the men buried in the permafrost of

Beechey Island. All three had unusually high levels of lead in their bodies, a significant amount of which had been ingested in the previous six months, that is, after the voyage began. Beattie did not say that lead poisoning killed the men, only that it would impair their mental faculties, produce other unpleasant side effects and may have contributed to their deaths. The three men in question actually died of a lethal combination of tuberculosis and pneumonia.[13] However, lead took on a life of its own and is still widely regarded as the 'cause'.

Recently another monocausal disaster theory has emerged. This holds that botulism, either caused by improper canning or acquired from locally killed animals, was the killer.[14] Botulism is lethal, and was present in one of the Beechey Island corpses, but in the absence of tissue samples from King William Island there is no evidence that it caused a single death on the Franklin expedition. More significantly it is simply unnecessary to look for such spectacular external agents as botulism, or lead. Faced with ample evidence that the men died of scurvy and starvation there is no need for speculation. In history the most plausible explanations are the ones that require no flights of imagination, speculation or guesswork, and do not stray beyond the evidence. Historians should check that their evidence would stand up in a court of law.

Bones

Although there are no tissue samples from King William Island, the harsh climate has preserved substantial quantities of human bone. For a century Franklin searchers picked them up. Two sets were sent home, the rest were reinterred. In the process vital evidence was lost, not only the precise location of each bone but the relation between the many bones that make up a skeleton and the possibility of applying more sophisticated pathology techniques. That said, the remains of the expedition litter the way, every discovery revealing another part of the tragedy, mapping out the death march. Human remains have been found on the west and south coasts of King William Island, and on the mainland at Starvation Cove close to the mouth of the Great Fish river. The recovery of evidence from such a distant, bleak and uncompromising land has been a long drawn-out process, and remains incomplete.

In 1949 Inspector Larsen of the Royal Canadian Mounted Police vessel *St Roch* found part of a human skull, later identified as belonging to a European approximately twenty-five years old, near Cape Felix.[15] While this discovery has led to speculation that Franklin may be buried nearby, perhaps on an offshore islet, the underlying truth has been forgotten. Cape Felix would have been the obvious location to bury those who died before the vessels were abandoned, being the nearest point of land to the ships and the location of a quasi-permanent shore base. *If* Franklin was buried on shore this is the most likely location.

The route map of the death march begins just three miles south of Victory Point. In a small bay north of Collinson Inlet, Schwatka found a grave and identified the body as that of Lieutenant John Irving on the basis that it contained Irving's Naval College medal. He sent the remains home to Scotland for burial. More remains were found at Point Le Vesconte, Two Grave Bay and along Erebus Bay, where between six and fourteen bodies lay close to McClintock's horrific boat.[16]

When the march began, Crozier was one of only six surviving officers. Nine others had already died. The officers were critical to maintain the illusion of normality, hope and progress. Without them discipline weakened. With their death went any hope of escape: only the officers possessed the navigational skills to find the way out. Once the men realised their fate the bounds of civilised behaviour were loosed. The majority remained in Terror Bay on the south coast, too sick to carry on or too despairing to try. Terror Bay was an obvious camp site, the first location with adequate game, caribou that cross from the mainland in summer. But the camp soon combined the functions of hospital, mortuary and butcher's shop. Here the living prolonged their existence, but not for long. Inuit witnesses spoke of a large camp, tents, graves, cannibalised bodies and a pile of skulls. They also reported books, manuscripts, a sextant and many watches. Most of the evidence had been dispersed by the sea by the time Schwatka reached the site, leaving a few human bones and a crumpled water tank.

As a small party headed east, men continued to die. The survivors met an Inuit hunting party in Washington Bay, the one uncontested Inuit sighting of the survivors. The Inuit told of sighting a white shape moving in the distance which at first they thought was a bear but which proved to be a party of white men (*kabloona*) dragging a boat on which a sail had been set. Around forty men were present, all were suffering from scurvy and the Inuit were convinced they saw evidence of cannibalism. The meeting was hampered by the lack of a communicating medium, and the Inuit wisely left before they could confirm their grisly suspicions. By reaching Cape John Herschel these men had completed the last link in the North West Passage, if we follow John Richardson's line, but it is doubtful if they cared.[17] They do not appear to have left any message in the cairn. A skull and bones were found here. Further on McClintock found the skeleton of Harry Peglar or Thomas Armitage, a sick, cold, hungry man who simply fell over and died face down in the snow. Two more skulls were found on the beach at Tulloch Point, seven more skeletons in Douglas Bay, where it appears a boat may have been broken up, and at least four on the Todd Islands. In addition Hall removed a skeleton from the islands, one that was tentatively identified as Lieutenant Henry le Vesconte before burial at Greenwich. The skeletal remains of more than half the men seen in Washington Bay have been found further along the coast or on the mainland, a remarkable result, given they were travelling on the coastal margin.

Across the Simpson Strait at the place he named Starvation Cove, not far from the Great Fish river, Schwatka found more human remains. In the twentieth century a skull, three jaws and other large bones were uncovered, together with a coin of King George IV (1820–30). Here the men died; here the Inuit broke up their boat and pillaged their goods, leaving their bones to be buried thirty years later. Schwatka found the remains of a sailor five miles inland from Starvation Cove, perhaps the last man.[18] With that the trail goes cold. The relics found on Montreal Island seem to have been carried there by the Inuit and no bones have been found.[19] This was the end, but it was also the beginning of an enduring horror mystery.

Cannibal

In 1992 a new Franklin site was discovered on a small island, NgLj-2, in Erebus Bay, less than a kilometre from the place where McClintock found two headless men in a ghastly boat. A quantity of human bones, some four hundred items, were found scattered across an area of about three hundred square metres, along with over two hundred Franklin artefacts including wood chips consistent with chopping up boats and sledges for firewood. The bones revealed high levels of lead, consistent with Beattie's findings, levels that would produce sickness, vomiting, and neurological damage. More surprising was the discovery that some 25 per cent showed clear evidence that they had been cut with steel knives, consistent with disarticulation and defleshing for consumption. Furthermore, three major bones had been broken in a manner that would expose the nutritious bone marrow. These findings were consistent with the account of the Inuit hunter In-nook-poo-zhe-jook that the men had sea boots filled with cooked human flesh. The Inuit told Rae that the sailors had cannibalised their comrades, and confirmed his story when interviewed by Hall. Another Inuit, Eveeshuk, reported that a body had been found with the hands sawn off and others with large amounts of flesh removed. For many years this Inuit testimony was the only evidence of cannibalism. McClintock, the first white man to track the death march, simply refused to acknowledge the subject. Then Schwatka picked up similar stories, along with bones that had been sawn through and defleshed.

In 1981 Owen Beattie recovered a femur with knife cuts, and a skull that had been intentionally broken, on the south-eastern coast of King William Island at Kun-ne-ar-be-ar-nu.[20] The site produced a disproportionate quantity of limb bones clustered outside a tent circle, suggesting the men had been carrying the most portable joints on the march. The evidence gathered to date confirms the Inuit accounts, and if more remains are recovered it is likely they will show similar signs of cannibalism. So far no more than seventy sets of remains have been recovered, many having been disaggregated, and few have survived into the modern era when the latest pathology techniques could be applied.[21] In 1997 Keenleyside, Bertulli and

Fricke analysed the NgLj-2 findings, and gave the Inuit back their integrity. Their paper reported convincing proof that cannibalism had occurred on a significant scale at Erebus Bay, at Terror Bay, along the south coast of the island, and perhaps on the mainland as well. Only one question remains: did the Franklin party kill and eat the living, or simply cannibalise the dead? It is unlikely we will ever know.

Yet there was another killer at work on the expedition. All three men on Beechey Island were killed by tuberculosis, a disease that found the hot, damp atmosphere of a ship closed in for winter the ideal breeding ground. Evidence of tuberculosis was also found on bones at NgLj-2.[22] Given the time that elapsed between the deaths at Beechey Island and the final catastrophe, and the known pathology of the aggressive tuberculosis strains found in the remains of expedition members Torrington, Hartnell and Braine, it is possible the disproportionate casualty rate among the officers revealed by Fitzjames's final message was caused by tuberculosis. While such speculation is idle, the fact that Richard Cyriax, author of the standard account of the expedition, was a tuberculosis specialist gives it a certain irony.

The conventional narrative of what happened after Crozier abandoned the ships is simple. The surviving crew marched south and then east, searching for food in a single group pulling several boat/sledges. Schwatka found their camp sites.[23] Along the route men died, some were given 'decent' burials, some were not. The survivors may have camped in Terror Bay and tried to recruit their strength. Most did not leave. The forty men the Inuit encountered in Washington Bay were the last survivors; the rest are accounted for by Inuit testimony of forty dead in Terror Bay and the archaeology of Erebus Bay. This account fits the surviving physical evidence. The Inuit reported breaking up an abandoned boat five miles west of Starvation Cove, and scattering the expedition records.[24] Close by were the remains of five or six men. It is likely all were dead before the winter of 1848. That is the end of the history.

There remains the possibility that further evidence will be found, that the ships might be located, or even the records that have obsessed every Franklin searcher since Lady Jane. But until they do, anything else is speculation. Over the years an understandable anxiety to fill in the blanks has resulted in some interesting creative speculation. The most important of these texts, David Woodman's *Unravelling the Franklin Mystery*, analysed Inuit testimony collected by Rae, McClintock, Hall and Schwatka and developed a more complex chronology in which the ships were reoccupied and some men lived at least another year. After two decades of study Woodman remains convinced the ships will be found and with them the record, a development that would 'render all speculative books', his own included, 'obsolete'.[25] Until then the Franklin story, a unique, unquiet compound of mystery, horror and magic, will continue to haunt the imagination of modern men, a salutary reminder of just how close we are to absolute catastrophe.

Catastrophe and commemoration

If Franklin had brought home the magnetic data that Edward Sabine required, whether he completed the North West Passage or not, he would have been a scientific hero. His achievement would have been annexed to the glory of the state through the medium of imperial science, securing British title to the Arctic, enhancing national prestige and demonstrating once again that the theoretical formulations of German professors were less than half the story. If Sabine had ever finished his magnetic crusade the effect would have been so much more impressive.

Franklin's tragedy had its origins in the remarkable luck of earlier expeditions. It was a fate that had been hanging over British polar travellers since 1818. When Sabine needed fresh magnetic data, only a few Cassandras considered the task dangerous; most assumed it could be done easily and safely. When those assumptions proved wrong, the origins of the expedition were swiftly obscured, leaving Franklin to be recreated as a 'great explorer', something he would not have appreciated, and which was a very long way from the truth. The version that his widow created lasted two generations, helping to send Captain Scott to an icy death and several million Britons to the muddy hell of the Western Front. Little wonder Franklin was added to the pantheon of blundering British officers, debunked like many another Victorian brass totem. The mystery and the horror of the expedition have given him a permanent place in history.

Yet Franklin was neither a bungler nor an explorer. An inspirational leader, the noblest of public men, he made important contributions to polar navigation and magnetic science, wrote a best-selling narrative, governed a colony and commanded a ship of war. He did not 'discover' the North West Passage – instead he discovered that Hell can be found in the hearts of men, in Van Diemen's Land rather than in the high Arctic. He did not live to witness the last days of his expedition, when the veneer of civilisation lifted to reveal primeval savagery, darkness and despair.

By awarding Franklin the dubious distinction of finding a useless geographical curiosity that he was not looking for the Victorians turned a catastrophe into a morality tale, a public endorsement of obedience, duty and resolve. In creating a suitable Franklin they simply ignored reports of cannibalism, and forgot the reason they had done so. By 1900 the public preferred the icy wastes to be primitive and strange, and were completely uninterested in scientific work. In the United States this led to Robert Peary's unscientific dash for the North Pole.[26] In Britain it relegated the science of Robert Falcon Scott's expeditions to appendices, promoting the add-on exploration effort to the starring role. Restoring the central role of magnetic science in the genesis of the Franklin expedition, and analysing the politics of the search missions, reminds us that our ancestors were as intelligent, ambitious, determined and manipulative as ourselves. Above all they were not so stupid as to waste a queen's ransom on a fatuous geography project, one that seemed more complex after it had been 'solved' than it had been before.

Because Franklin's sacrifice could not be represented as 'useful' it proved hard to keep his name alive.[27] Even Jane did not claim the North West Passage was a trade route, and by 1859 Arctic whaling was no longer a British industry. That Scott and the Antarctic provided a perfect replacement sufficed to wipe the Arctic from the national memory. The number of otherwise well-informed Britons who recognise the distinction between the two polar extremities is surprisingly small; many simply assume any ice mass is the Antarctic and wonder where the penguins have gone. Canada, of course, takes a rather different view. Yet the story of Franklin, his men and their tragedy, suitably tweaked by disaster theories, dark tales of cannibalism and a never-ending desire to get a grim laugh out of our ancestors, will endure. Like the Arctic itself, John Franklin's story has the power to deprive grown men of their reason, something that may explain why this book was written, and why it will not be the last.

Karl Marx was right. If we do not own our past we are condemned to repeat our mistakes. Franklin's was the ultimate tragedy – his name and career rendered fatuous by those who loved him most – only for the temper of the times to change. Lady Jane and the Markhams transformed Sir John into a bronze morality tale, making him fair game for twentieth-century revisionists. Having demolished Markham and Robert Falcon Scott, Roland Huntford could not resist an offhand joke at Franklin's expense, describing him as 'one of the great bunglers of polar exploration',[28] unaware that the object of his derision was a cardboard image from the 1891 exhibition, not a real man. This book should be a warning against the cult of celebrity, for behind every bronze hero is a human being, an urgent, flawed life in pursuit of some fragment of immortality. We should listen, not judge, because our ancestors were human, and in seeing their humanity we might recall our own before the lights go out for ever.

Notes

For a list of archive sources, see p. 395.

PROLOGUE: Erebus – the Gates of Hell

1 The *Oxford English Dictionary* (2nd edn, Oxford, 1989) defines Erebus as 'a place of darkness between earth and Hades', from the Greek, meaning the primeval darkness springing from chaos, often used to describe the gates of Hell. The Royal Navy had long used this name for bomb vessels, stoutly built, bluff little craft designed to carry two massive mortars, and fire exploding shell into hostile fortresses and cities.
2 Captain Scott (to Kathleen Scott), 'The Last Word. "To my widow . . . I hope I shall be a good memory"', *The Week*, 20 Jan. 2007, pp. 48–9, reporting the opening of an exhibition of Scott letters at the Scott Polar Institute.

CHAPTER 1: The North West Passage – Designs and Delusions

1 D. Botting, *Humboldt and the Cosmos* (London, 1973), p. 156.
2 H. B. Carter, *Sir Joseph Banks, 1743–1820* (London, 1988) is the standard life.
3 L. Kellner, *Alexander von Humboldt* (Oxford, 1963), pp. 12–14, 207.
4 Kellner, p. 62; the instruments were made by Troughton, Ramsden and Dollond.
5 Botting, pp. 153–6. J. K. Howat, *Frederic Church* (Princeton, 2005) examines the impact of Humboldt's artistic ideas on landscape painting.
6 Botting, p. 176. Carl Friedrich Gauss (1779–1855), German mathematician and astronomer.
7 N. Leask, *Curiosity and the Aesthetics of Travel Writing, 1770–1840* (Oxford, 2002), pp. 6–7 and ch. 6.
8 Kellner, pp. 64–77. Humboldt to Banks, 10 July 1809: W. R. Dawson (ed.), *The Banks Letters* (London, 1958), p. 434.
9 Kellner, pp. 98–100.
10 B. Smith, *European Vision and the South Pacific, 1768–1850* (Oxford, 1960), pp. 151–7.
11 S. Ruskin, *John Herschel's Cape Voyage: Private Science, Public Imagination and the Ambitions of Empire* (Aldershot, 2004), p. 35.
12 For these voyages see G. Williams, *Voyages of Delusion: The Search for the North-West Passage in the Age of Reason* (London, 2002).
13 C. Loomis, 'The Arctic Sublime', in U. C. Knoepflmacher and G. B. Tennyson (eds), *Nature and the Victorian Imagination* (Berkeley, Calif., 1967), pp. 95–112.

14 N. Wolf, *Caspar David Friedrich, 1774–1840: The Painter of Stillness* (Cologne, 2003), pp. 73–7.

15 The British government only settled key locations on the north and west coasts of Australia to forestall the French and Dutch. P. Statham-Drew, *James Stirling: Admiral and Founding Governor of Western Australia* (Crawley, WA, 2003), pp. 102–7.

16 F. Fleming's *Barrow's Boys* (London, 1998) is the best-known account of Barrow's role in this process.

17 T. H. Levere, *Science and the Canadian Arctic: A Century of Exploration, 1818–1918* (Cambridge, 1993), p. 40. Quote from W. Scoresby, *An Account of the Arctic Regions with a History and Description of the Northern Whale Fishery*, 2 vols. (Edinburgh, 1820), II, pp. 537–8.

18 Carter, pp. 505–7.

19 C. I. Jackson (ed.), *The Arctic Whaling Journals of William Scoresby the Younger*, vol. I, *The Voyages of 1811, 1812 and 1813* (London, 2003), pp. xxviii–xxxiii, lv–lxi, 221–31.

20 Levere, p. 41.

21 Carter, p. 508. Banks to Melville, 20 Nov. 1817: N. Chambers (ed.), *The Letters of Sir Joseph Banks: A Selection, 1768–1820* (London, 2000), pp. 334–6.

22 Letters to Charles Blagden and Scoresby: Dawson, pp. 98–104, 739–41.

23 In his famous account of the mutiny on the *Bounty* Barrow stressed the importance of gentlemen officers leading exploring missions. J. Barrow, *The Eventful History of the Mutiny and Piratical Seizure of HMS Bounty, its Causes and Consequences* (London, 1831). The same theme emerges in his 1845 narrative of polar exploration (see n. 27).

24 T. Stamp and C. Stamp, *William Scoresby: Arctic Scientist* (Whitby, 1976), pp. 62–9.

25 J. Burney, 'A Memoir on the Geography of the North East Part of Asia, and on the Question whether Asia and America Are contiguous or Are Separated by the Sea' (11 Dec. 1817), *Philosophical Transactions*, 108 (1818), pp. 9–23.

26 H. Shine and C. S. Shine, *The Quarterly Review under Gifford* (Chapel Hill, 1949), pp. 58–60 for attribution; G. E. Manwaring, *My Friend the Admiral: Rear Admiral James Burney FRS* (London, 1931), pp. 255–61 for the circulation and Burney's view.

27 Transforming a powerful review into a book was an approach Murray had used before, notably with Robert Southey's biography of Nelson. J. Barrow, *A Chronological History of Voyages into the Arctic Regions undertaken chiefly for the purpose of discovering a north-east, north-west or Polar passage between the Atlantic and Pacific from the earliest periods of Scandinavian Navigation to the departure of the recent expeditions under the orders of Captains Ross and Buchan* (London, 1818). He would produce a second volume nearly thirty years later, *Voyages of Discovery within the Arctic Regions from the Year 1818 to the Present Time* (London, 1846), to bring the story up to date.

28 Barrow, *Chronological History*, pp. 348–56.

29 Smith, p. 155.

30 Barrow, *Chronological History*, p. 363.

31 Barrow, *Chronological History*, ch. 5, 'Voyages of Northern Discovery undertaken in the early part of the nineteenth century. Lieutenant Kotzebue – John Ross, David Buchan, William Edward Parry, and John Franklin', pp. 357–79.

32 D. Barrington (ed.), *Col. Beaufoy FRS: The Possibility of Approaching the North Pole Asserted*, 2nd edn (London, 1818 [1775]).

33 A Bill for the more effectually discovering the Longitude at Sea, and encouraging attempts to find a Northern Passage between the Atlantic and Pacific Oceans, and to approach the Northern Pole (9 pp. Bill printed 9 March 1818): www.umanitoba.ca/libraries/inits/archives/arcticbb/viewbb.php?t=1818&p=2.

34 A Bill for the more effectually discovering the Longitude at Sea . . . , pp. 3–4.

35 M. B. Hall, *All Scientists Now: The Royal Society in the Nineteenth Century* (Cambridge, 1984), pp. 14–15.

36 G. A. Good, 'Sabine, Sir Edward (1788–1883)', *Oxford Dictionary of National Biography*, www.oxforddnb.com/articles/24/24436-article.html, accessed 10 Dec. 2004.

37 Carter, pp. 508–11.

38 *Pilot of Arctic Canada*, vol. I, 2nd edn (Ottawa, 1970), p. 48. Claim, possession and title in this region are critical features of all official Canadian literature.

39 M. J. Ross, *Polar Pioneers: John Ross and James Clark Ross* (Montreal, 1994), p. 61.

40 J. Barrow (unsigned) 'Ross's Voyage of Discovery', *Quarterly Review*, 21 (1819), pp. 213–62. Ross's book appeared in March 1819, two months before the *QR* article. Levere, p. 61.

41 Levere, p. 68.

42 Levere, pp. 70–3.

43 Scoresby, I, pp. 1–3. He was using Barrow's *Chronological History*, p. 5n.

44 Scoresby, I, p. 15.

45 Scoresby, I, p. 22; II, pp. 537–9.

46 Scoresby, I, pp. 28–9n. and 33. For Mackenzie and Hearne, see A. Savours, *The Search for the North West Passage* (London, 1999), pp. 24–32, 36–8.

47 Savours, *Search*, p. 40n.

CHAPTER 2: John Franklin – Navigator

1 R. Huntford, *Scott and Amundsen: The Race to the Pole* (London, 1979), pp. 10, 22.

2 H. D. Traill, *The Life of Sir John Franklin* (London, 1896), was the first serious biography. Like those that have followed, it is a study of the bronze statue who found the North West Passage, not the human being.

3 M. Estensen, *The Life of Matthew Flinders* (Sydney, 2002).

4 Flinders to Thomas Franklin, 7 July 1801: Royal Geographical Society (RGS) SJF 1/2.

5 Estensen, pp. 90, 142. J. Fornasio, P. Monteath and J. West-Sooby, *Encountering Terra Australis: The Australian Voyages of Nicolas Baudin and Matthew Flinders* (Kent Town, SA, 2004), pp. 192, 289.

6 Estensen, pp. 211, 216.

7 D. Cordingley, *Billy Ruffian: The Bellerophon and the Downfall of Napoleon* (London, 2003).

8 Franklin to Dr Robert Brown, 18 and 28 Aug. 1814: Scott Polar Research Institute (SPRI) MS 248/296/1 and 3.

9 Brown to Franklin, 25 Aug. 1814: SPRI MS 248/296/2.

10 Franklin to Brown, 9 June 1815: SPRI MS 248/296/5.

11 Franklin to Brown, 9 June 1815: SPRI MS 248/296/5.

12 Franklin to Brown, 5 March 1816: SPRI MS 248/295/4.

13 SPRI MS 248/270.

14 Banks to Scoresby, 18 Feb. 1818: Dawson, p. 740.

15 Franklin to Isabella Cracroft (sister), 6 April 1818: SPRI MS 248/298/7.

16 Kater (1777–1835) was a leading figure in the Royal Society, and a commissioner advising the Admiralty on the *Nautical Almanac*, the navigator's bible. Hall, pp. 12, 18.

17 Franklin to Kater, 9 May 1818: Wellcome MS 7486/84.

18 Franklin to Banks, 7 May 1818: SPRI MS 962/11; MS from McCord Museum, McGill University, Montreal.

19 Trent: SPRI MS 248/274.

20 Barrow minute, 22 Feb. 1819 and Barrow to Goulburn, 26 Feb. 1819: R. C. Davis (ed.), *Sir John Franklin's Journals and Correspondence: The First Arctic Land Expedition, 1819–1822* (Toronto, 1995), pp. xxxiii, 277–8.

21 Davis, *First Expedition*, pp. xxix–xxxiv, xcii, 341–2, 386.

22 Davis, *First Expedition*, pp. xxviii, 277–8.

23 Davis, *First Expedition*. The introduction to this volume is cast as a sustained critique of Franklin because he was an early nineteenth-century naval officer rather than a Hudson Bay traveller or an early twentieth-century explorer. This approach adds little to our understanding of the mission, merely reinforcing existing ahistorical treatment. Franklin, primarily a scientific navigator, was sent to the Arctic coast to make accurate charts and establish reliable bearings. He could not do this with a pocket compass.

24 Davis, *First Expedition*, pp. xci, xix, Earl Bathurst to Franklin, 29 April 1819: pp. 285–8.

25 This disposes of George Simpson's jibe that he could march more than eight miles a day. E. E. Rich (ed.), *The History of the Hudson's Bay Company, 1670–1870*, 3 vols. (London, 1958–9), II, p. 649.

26 J. Cavell, 'The Hidden Crime of Dr Richardson', *Polar Record*, 43 (2007), pp. 155–64, corrects the assertion made in the 1970s that Richardson committed criminal acts, and that these were covered up by Franklin. That such an assertion should be made, and repeated uncritically for decades, reflects a major problem in Franklin scholarship. Franklin and Richardson corrected Hearne's inaccurate position of the mouth of the Coppermine river, and it was one of Hearne's modern editors who made the assertion of murder.

27 Levere, pp. 104–9.

28 Franklin to Richardson, 24 Oct. 1822: Davis, *First Expedition*, pp. 428–31.

29 Botting, pp. 129 and 141 for Humboldt's encounter with cannibalism and his sensationalised account. Barrow reviewed Humboldt's first volume of narrative in the *Quarterly Review* in May 1816, and the first of his appendices in November.

30 Franklin to Isabella Cracroft, 12 April 1823: SPRI MS 248/298/14, quoting the *Literary Gazette* review.

31 Davis, *First Expedition*, p. xli.

32 J. Franklin, *Narrative of a Journey to the Shores of the Polar Sea in the Years 1819–20–21–22*, 2 vols. (London, 1823). The 1970 facsimile reprint is the only modern edition to contain the appendices.

33 Levere, p. 110.

34 A prominent hydrographer.

35 The leading scientific instrument maker.

36 Franklin Election Record: Royal Society GB117.

37 Davis, *First Expedition*, p. xxxiii.

38 Faraday to Franklin, 17 May 1826: F. A. J. L. James (ed.), *The Correspondence of Michael Faraday*, vol. I, *1811–1831* (London, 1991), pp. 406–8. Franklin to Faraday, 7 July n.d.: Wellcome MS 7486/23 refers to one such social occasion.

39 List of members in Faraday to James Ward, 13 March 1824: James, pp. 341–5.

40 Levere, pp. 75, 111.

41 J. R. Bockstoce, *The Opening of the Maritime Fur Trade at Bering Strait* (Philadelphia, 2005).

42 H. Temperley, *The Foreign Policy of Canning, 1822–1827* (London, 1925), pp. 104–5.

43 Shine and Shine, p. xvi.

44 Franklin sketch 'Intended Expedition' to commence February 1824: RGS SJF/2/1. Franklin to Barrow, 26 Nov. 1823: B. M. Gough (ed.), *To the Pacific and Arctic with Beechey: The Journal of Lieutenant George Peard of H.M.S. Blossom, 1825–1828* (Cambridge, 1973).

45 Gough, pp. 12–14. Levere, pp. 112–17.

46 Franklin to Mary Kay (niece), 22 Nov. 1823: FRN/2, National Maritime Museum (NMM).

47 R. C. Davis (ed.), *Sir John Franklin's Journals and Correspondence: The Second Arctic Land Expedition, 1819–1822* (Toronto, 1998), pp. li–lii.

48 F. Woodward, *A Portrait of Jane: A Life of Lady Franklin* (London, 1951), p. 148.

49 Franklin to Beaufort, 6 Feb. 1826: quoted in Levere at p. 125. Franklin to Robert Barrie, late 1825: *Arctic*, 19 (1966), pp. 99–101.

50 Franklin to Edward Kendall, 3 July 1826: FRN/10, NMM. Franklin to Kendall, 12 June 1826: Davis, *Second Expedition*, pp. 372–4, referring to the work conducted at Woolwich Academy by Samuel Christie.

51 Franklin to Murchison, 4 Nov. 1825: SPRI 248/275/1.

52 Davis, *Second Expedition*, p. lii.

53 Gough, p. 39.

54 Franklin to Kendall, 15 Oct. 1827: FRN/15, NMM.

55 Traill, p. 136, from Richardson's narrative.

56 Franklin to Kendall, 3 July 1826, 2 April 1827: FRN/10–11, NMM. Foster to Franklin, 4 Dec. 1827: FRN/12, NMM.

57 Franklin to Kendall, 15 Oct. and 16 Dec. 1827, 29 April 1828, 14 March and 17 April 1830: FRN/15, 16, 18, 23, 24, NMM.

58 Franklin to Kendall and Back, 29 Sept. 1827: FRN/14, NMM.

59 Franklin to Kendall, 15 Oct. 1827: FRN/15, NMM.

60 Davis, *Second Expedition*, pp. lxiv–lxvii.

61 Temperley, pp. 492–3. Levere, p. 112.

62 Franklin to Murchison, 1827 and n.d.: Add. 46,216, ff. 289–91, social correspondence.

63 A. Alexander, *The Governor's Wives* (Hobart, 1999), 'Jane Franklin', p. 153.

64 Alexander, p. 154.

65 Franklin proposal of 17 June 1828: Traill, pp. 140–2.

66 Richardson to his wife, 10 Nov. 1826: SPRI MS 962, McCord Museum Microfilm. Quoted in Levere at p. 124.

67 Gough, p. 49.

68 Ruskin, pp. 48–50.

69 Levere, pp. 136–8.

CHAPTER 3: Another Career

1 Jane to Franklin, Aug. 1830: Traill, p. 155.
2 Franklin to Henrietta Wright, 30 April 1829: Mitchell Library (ML) MSS.
3 Franklin to Arago, n.d.: Wellcome MS 7402/8, 9.
4 Franklin to Mrs Wright (sister), 6 Feb. 1829: ML MSS.
5 Franklin to Henrietta Wright, 30 April 1829: ML MSS.
6 G. L. Harries-Davis, *Whatever Is Under the Earth: The Geological Society of London, 1807–2007* (London, 2007), p. 201. H. Woodward, *History of the Royal Geological Society* (London, 1907).
7 Barrow to Franklin, 5 May 1830: Wellcome MS 7880/4, Franklin to Murchison, n.d. 1830: Wellcome MS 7404/10 and Franklin to Dr William Buckland, 14 June 1830 (ML MSS) are typical.
8 A. Hyman, *Charles Babbage: Pioneer of the Computer* (Princeton, 1982), pp. 49–50, 123–4. Franklin to Jane, 11 May 1829: SPRI MS 248/303/1.
9 Franklin to Henrietta Wright, 30 April 1829: ML MSS.
10 Franklin to Elizabeth Franklin (his sister 'Betsey'), 29 Aug. 1830: RGS SJF 1/11.
11 D. Lyon, *The Sailing Navy List* (London, 1993), p. 133.
12 R. Owen, *The Fate of Franklin* (London, 1978), p. 156.
13 A. Lubbock, *Owen Stanley RN* (Melbourne, 1968), pp. 27–31.
14 J. C. Daly, *Russian Seapower and 'The Eastern Question', 1827–1841* (London, 1991), p. 59.
15 Franklin to Jane, 31 July 1831: SPRI MS 248/303/18. All three men were on the Board: Graham as First Lord, Hardy as First Naval Lord and Elliot as Political Secretary.
16 Franklin to Jane, 7 Oct. 1832: SPRI MS 248/303/26.
17 Sir C. Webster, *The Foreign Policy of Palmerston, 1830–1841* (London, 1951), pp. 259–72. This classic diplomatic history seriously undervalues the economic interests that dominated the day-to-day conduct of British policy.
18 D. C. M. Platt, *Finance, Trade and Politics in British Foreign Policy, 1815–1914* (Oxford, 1968), p. xiv.
19 Franklin to Murchison, 14 Sept. 1831: SPRI MS 248/225/2. Beaufort to Franklin, 8 June 1831: United Kingdom Hydrographic Office (UKHO) Beaufort Letter Book (LB) 3, p. 173. Beaufort to Franklin, 28 Jan. 1835: UKHO LB 6, p. 51. Franklin to Beaufort, 29 March 1832: UKHO Beaufort MS F011.
20 Franklin to Jane, 15 July 1832: Owen, p. 168.
21 Franklin to Mrs Wright, 13 March 1831: ML MSS.
22 Traill, p. 199. R. Blake, *Disraeli* (London, 1966), pp. 63–4, confirms her impression.
23 C. C. Pitcairn-Jones, *Piracy in the Levant, 1827–28* (London, 1934), pp. 168–73, 213.
24 Traill, p. 193.
25 Hardy to Captain Lyons, n.d.: S. Eardley-Wilmot, *Life of Edmund, Lord Lyons* (London, 1898), p. 68.
26 Franklin to Elizabeth Franklin, 12 Aug. 1833: RGS SJF 1/14.
27 Traill chose this as the title for the chapter in his biography of Franklin covering 1834–6. It is in character with Franklin and Jane.
28 Franklin to Elizabeth Franklin, 12 Aug. 1833: RGS SJF 1/14.
29 J. Ross's narrative, 1835, p. xvii, quoted in Levere at p. 94.
30 Franklin to Jane, 15 July 1832: Owen, p. 168.

31 Owen, p. 150.
32 Jane to Franklin, 8 Jan. 1834: Traill, p. 217.
33 Franklin to Jane, 27 Feb. and 3 March 1834: SPRI MS 248/303/61–2.
34 Levere, pp. 85–94.
35 Owen, p. 161.
36 Traill, p. 222.
37 Owen, p. 176.
38 Hall, pp. 199–203.
39 Levere, pp. 138–40.
40 M. Ross, pp. 199–204. Ross would command *Terror*, Edward Belcher the *Erebus*.
41 Levere, p. 140.
42 Back to Franklin, 1827: Traill, p. 228. P. Steele, *The Man Who Mapped the Arctic: The Intrepid Life of George Back, Franklin's Lieutenant* (Vancouver, 2003).
43 Franklin Report on Dr King's Proposal, April 1836: RGS SJF 5/2.
44 Owen, p. 176.

CHAPTER 4: Scientific Empires

1 Now in the National Maritime Museum, London. The museum acquired many Franklin relics from the old Royal Naval Hospital Museum, the United Services Institution and other sources. See J. P. Delgado, *Across the Roof of the World: The Quest for the Northwest Passage* (London, 1999), p. 154 for a photograph.
2 Levere, p. 149.
3 Hall, pp. 199–203.
4 R. A. Stafford, *Scientist of Empire: Sir Roderick Murchison, Scientific Exploration and Victorian Imperialism* (Cambridge, 1989).
5 Barrow minute of August 1830: F. Driver, *Geography Militant* (Cambridge, 2001), p. 40.
6 When he made this statement in 1842 Hamilton was private secretary to the First Lord of the Admiralty. In 1845 he replaced Barrow as permanent secretary. Driver, p. 41.
7 H. Mill, *Records of the Royal Geographical Society* (London, 1930). R. G. David, *The Arctic in the British Imagination: 1815–1914* (Manchester, 2000), ch. 3.
8 Driver, pp. 30–4.
9 David, pp. 65–7.
10 Driver, p. 24.
11 The liberal Humboldt found nothing to admire in the tsarist regime.
12 G. A. Good, 'Sabine, Sir Edward (1788–1883)', *Oxford Dictionary of National Biography*, www.oxforddnb.com/articles/24/24436-article.html, accessed 10 Dec. 2004.
13 Sabine to Ross, 13 June 1840: BJ2/13, f. 11 and R. J. Cyriax, *Sir John Franklin's Last Arctic Expedition: The Franklin Expedition – A Chapter in the History of the Royal Navy* (London, 1939), p. 19.
14 J. Cawood, 'The Magnetic Crusade: Science and Politics in Early Victorian Britain', *ISIS*, 70 (1979), pp. 493–518 at pp. 498–9.
15 C. Babbage, *Reflections on the Decline of Science in England* (London, 1831), pp. 77–97: a savage indictment of pluralism, incompetence and ambition. Hyman, pp. 95–6.
16 J. Samson, 'An Empire of Science: The Voyage of HMS *Herald*, 1845–1851', in

A. Frost and J. Sampson (eds), *Pacific Empires: Essays in Honour of Glyndwr Williams* (Vancouver, 1999), pp. 69–86 at pp. 71–2.

17 Hyman, pp. 95–7.

18 A. Friendly, *Beaufort of the Admiralty: Sir Francis Beaufort, 1774–1857* (New York, 1977), pp. 284–99.

19 Friendly, pp. 290–1.

20 It was perhaps typical that he should record the event in his diary! Friendly, p. 270.

21 Beaufort to James Ross 12.1833: Fleming, p. 319.

22 N. Courtney, *Gale Force 10: The Life and Legacy of Admiral Beaufort* (London, 2003), pp. 270–1, citing L. H. Neatby, *The Search for Franklin* (Edmonton, 1970), p. 92.

23 Franklin and Sabine made significant contributions to scientific understanding of solar phenomena.

24 S. Chapman and J. Bartels, *Geomagnetism*, 2 vols. (Oxford, 1940), II, pp. 898–937 for an overview of geomagnetic history. A. E. Fanning, *Steady as She Goes: A History of the Compass Department of the Admiralty* (London, 1986), pp. xv–xix.

25 W. D. Parkinson, *Introduction to Geomagnetism* (Edinburgh, 1983), pp. 1–2.

26 A. von Humboldt, *Cosmos: A Sketch of a Physical Description of the Universe*, 5 vols. (New York, London, *c.* 1847–52), II, pp. 263, 277. Chapman and Bartels, II, p. 903.

27 Parkinson, pp. 349–51.

28 E. G. Forbes, *Greenwich Observatory: The Royal Observatory at Greenwich and Herstmonceux, 1675–1975*, vol. I (London, 1975), pp. 15–16.

29 W. H. McCrea, *The Royal Greenwich Observatory* (London, 1975), pp. 1 and 5.

30 McCrea, p. 14.

31 McCrea, p. 2.

32 Chapman and Bartels, II, p. 912.

33 Parkinson, p. 352. A. Cook, *Edmond Halley: Charting the Heavens and the Seas* (Oxford, 1998), places Halley's work in the practical sphere of improved navigation. See chs. 3, 7–11.

34 Forbes, pp. 8–9.

35 Chapman and Bartels, II, p. 913 cites J. Churchman, *Magnetic Atlas*, 4th edn (London, 1804). The first edition of 1790 may have been familiar to Flinders, whose patron, Banks, supported Churchman. Dawson, pp. 37, 217–19, 270.

36 McCrea, p. 9.

37 Chapman and Bartels, II, pp. 922–3.

38 Chapman and Bartels, II, p. 914, from Humboldt's *Relation historique*, vol. III at p. 615.

39 Humboldt, *Cosmos*, II, p. 281.

40 See C. I. Jackson.

41 D. Howse, *Greenwich Observatory: The Royal Observatory, 1675–1975*, vol. III (London, 1975), p. 123.

42 Forbes, pp. 164–5.

43 Kellner, pp. 118–19.

44 J. G. O'Hara, 'Gauss and the Reception of His Ideas on Magnetism in Britain (1832–1843)', *Notes and Records of the Royal Society of London*, 38(1) (Aug. 1983), pp. 17–78 at p. 72.

45 Parkinson, pp. 352–3.

46 Parkinson, pp. 47–8.

47 G. W. Dunnington, *Carl Friedrich Gauss: Titan of Science* (1955; new edn Washington, DC, 2004), pp. 156–8.

48 Gauss in Chapman and Bartels, II, p. 928.

49 Gauss in Chapman and Bartels, II, p. 931.

50 O'Hara, pp. 17–19.

51 O'Hara, pp. 43–4.

52 Humboldt letter of 12 Feb. 1838: Chapman and Bartels, II, p. 931, from *Nature*, 141 (1938), p. 299.

53 Dunnington, p. 262.

54 Chapman and Bartels, II, p. 933.

55 O'Hara, p. 42.

56 A. J. Meadows, *Greenwich Observatory*, vol. II (London, 1975), pp. 1–3. W. Airy (ed.), *Autobiography of George Biddell Airy* (Cambridge, 1896), pp. 134–6, 139–40 for compass correction. O'Hara, pp. 33–9.

57 Airy, pp. 124–5.

58 McCrea, p. 7.

59 Beaufort to Herschel, 11 June 1836: Royal Society HS 3 347.

60 Herschel to Beaufort, 29 June 1838 (draft): Royal Society HS 3 355 bis.

61 Airy, p. 170. O'Hara, p. 70.

62 McCrea, pp. 21–4.

63 Royal Society to Admiralty, 1831, ADM 1/4282, cited in A. G. E. Jones, 'Lieutenant T. E. L. Moore RN and the Voyage of the *Pagoda*, 1845', in A. G. E. Jones, *Polar Portraits* (Whitby, 1992), pp. 193–200.

64 J. S. Guest, *The Euphrates Expedition* (London, 1992). James Fitzjames served on this expedition (see ch. 7).

65 Levere, pp. 154–5. Stanley's results were sent to Christie at Woolwich for analysis. Sir George Back, *Narrative of the Arctic Land Expedition* (Edmonton, 1970 [London, 1836]), pp. 625–9.

66 E. Sabine in J. Herschel (ed.), *Admiralty Manual of Scientific Enquiry* (London, 1846), p. 20.

67 O'Hara, pp. 45 and 54. Sabine introduced Lloyd to the aristocracy of European magnetic science. Sabine to Arago, 8 July 1832: Wellcome MS 7404/15.

68 Levere, pp. 149–50.

69 Sabine to Ross, 6 Dec. 1833: BJ2/13, f. 2.

70 Ross to Sabine, n.d. but reply to above: BJ2/13, f. 3.

71 Ross to Sabine, 3 July 1834: BJ3/8, f. 2.

72 Ross to Sabine, 12 Sept. 1835: BJ2/13.

73 Ross to Sabine, 17 Sept. 1835: BJ3/8, f. 5.

74 Harcourt to Humboldt, 28 June 1835: J. Morrell and A. Thackray (eds), *Gentlemen of Science: Early Correspondence of the British Association for the Advancement of Science* (London, 1984), pp. 207–8.

75 Phillips (a colleague on the UK Magnetic Survey) to Ross, 7 Dec. 1835: Royal Society (RS) Sabine MS 260, f. 992.

76 Murchison to Whewell, 21 Nov. 1835: Morrell and Thackray, *Early Correspondence*, p. 222.

77 Whewell to Murchison, 22 Nov. 1835: Morrell and Thackray, *Early Correspondence*, p. 223.

78 Whewell to Harcourt, 27 May 1836: Morrell and Thackray, *Early Correspondence*, p. 227.

79 Royal Society to Admiralty, 29 Feb. 1836: ADM 1/4282.

80 Whewell to Murchison, 22 March 1836: Royal Geological Society, London (LDGSL), Murchison Papers, 838, MW4/14.
81 Ross to Sabine, 10 Oct. 1836: BJ3/8.
82 Humboldt's letter had been addressed to the Duke of Sussex, once a fellow student at Göttingen and now president of the Royal Society.
83 Cawood, p. 500.
84 Hall, p. 156.
85 Morrell and Thackray, *Early Correspondence*, p. 252.
86 Savours, *Search*, p. 177.
87 Sabine to Phillips, 4 July 1838: Morrell and Thackray, *Early Correspondence*, pp. 262–3.
88 Herschel to Humboldt, 31 July 1838: Ruskin, p. 33.
89 Lloyd to Herschel, 4 Aug. 1838: Morrell and Thackray, *Early Correspondence*, pp. 270–1.
90 A. Savours, 'Hobart and the Polar Regions, 1830–1930', in G. Winter (ed.), *Tasmanian Insights: Essays in Honour of Geoffrey Thomas Stilwell* (Hobart, 1992), pp. 175–91 at p. 183.
91 Morrell and Thackray, *Early Correspondence*, pp. 269ff.
92 Northampton to Lord Minto, 6 Jan. 1839: Morrell and Thackray, *Early Correspondence*, pp. 298–9.
93 Daniel to Ross, 5 Aug. 1939: RS Sabine MS 258, f. 383.
94 Sabine to Harcourt, 7 Aug. 1839: Morrell and Thackray, *Early Correspondence*, pp. 317–20.
95 Murchison to Harcourt, 16 Nov. 1839: Morrell and Thackray, *Early Correspondence*, pp. 325–6.
96 Sabine to Gauss, 28 March 1839: O'Hara, p. 56.
97 Herschel to Ross, n.d.: RS Sabine MS 258, f. 647.
98 Hall, p. 206.
99 J. Morrell and A. Thackray, *Gentlemen of Science: Early Years of the British Association for the Advancement of Science* (Oxford, 1981), p. 322.
100 Hall, p. 207.
101 J. C. Ross, *A Voyage of Discovery and Research in the Southern and Antarctic Regions during the Years 1839–43*, 2 vols. (London, 1847), I, pp. xxx–xxxiii.
102 Levere, p. 157.
103 Fanning, pp. 1–45, deals with this subject in detail.
104 Kellner, pp. 169–75.
105 Parkinson, p. 355.
106 Humboldt, *Cosmos*, II, pp. 336–7.

CHAPTER 5: From Van Diemen's Land to Tasmania, 1836–43

1 Franklin to Captain Henry Pelly, governor of the Hudson's Bay Company (HBC), 9 Oct. 1838: Tasmania Archives A10/7/193–4, photocopy from the HBC Archive.
2 Franklin to Captain Cumby, 25 April 1836: ML MSS A, f. 1/24.
3 Franklin to Elizabeth Franklin, 26 March 1836: RGS SJF 1/15. Franklin to Jane, 25 March 1836: SPRI MS 248/303/67.
4 J. West, *The History of Tasmania* [Launceston, 1852], ed. A. Shaw (Sydney, 1971), p. 174.
5 J. Gribbin and M. Gribbin, *Fitzroy: The Remarkable Story of Darwin's Captain*

and the Invention of the Weather Forecast (London, 2003). S. Roberts, *Charles Hotham: A Biography* (Melbourne, 1985). Statham-Drew, *Stirling*. Franklin to Jane, 21 March 1836: SPRI MS 248/303/66.

6 A. G. L. Shaw, *Sir George Arthur, Bart., 1784–1854* (Melbourne, 1980), p. 122.

7 Owen, p. 179. Henry Elliot remained until February 1840. Franklin considered his departure 'a great loss'. Franklin to Sir George Gipps, governor NSW, 19 Feb. 1840: ML MSS A, f. 1/21. Sir Henry Elliot (1817–1907) had a long and successful career in diplomacy; his final posting (1877–84) was in Vienna.

8 Owen, p. 206. C. Lloyd, *Mr Barrow of the Admiralty* (London, 1970), makes no mention of Peter's Tasmanian career, only a minor consular post in France. This problem may have influenced Barrow Sr's opinion of Franklin in 1844–5.

9 F. Woodward, p. 241.

10 Franklin to Gordon Gairdner, 15 Aug. 1836: ML MSS A, f. 1/30.

11 Franklin to Tom (Cracroft, nephew?), 16 June 1836: ML MSS A, f. 1/19.

12 Franklin to Mrs Henrietta Wright (sister), 22 Aug. 1836: ML MSS.

13 Thomas Arnold to Franklin, 20 July 1836: D. Stanley, *Life of Thomas Arnold* (London, 1901), pp. 415–16.

14 Franklin to Captain Cumby, 21 Oct. 1836: ML MSS A, f. 1/25.

15 N. Shakespeare, *In Tasmania* (London, 2004), pp. 76–9. H. L. Malchow, *Gothic Images of Race in Nineteenth Century Britain* (Stanford, 1996), pp. 97–102.

16 Franklin to The Knight of Kerry, 27 July 1836: ML MSS A, f. 1/14.

17 Shaw, pp. 150–1, 217–18, 271.

18 L. Robson, *A History of Tasmania*, vol. I (Melbourne, 1983), pp. 175–314.

19 Owen, p. 153.

20 Franklin to Elizabeth Franklin, 6 Jan. 1837: RGS SJF 1/16. This letter was sent on the day he arrived.

21 M. Hordern, *Mariners are Warned! John Lort Stokes and HMS Beagle in Australia, 1837–1843* (Melbourne, 1989), pp. 98–9.

22 The standard account of Franklin's government, K. Fitzpatrick, *Sir John Franklin in Tasmania, 1837–1843* (Melbourne, 1949), is not concerned with magnetic and polar issues.

23 P. Bolger, *Hobart Town* (Canberra, 1973), p. 32 and elsewhere.

24 See K. Windschuttle, *The Fabrication of Aboriginal History*, vol. I, *Van Diemen's Land, 1803–1847* (Sydney, 2002) for one side of this passionate debate. Ch. 7 discusses Franklin's government.

25 Bolger, pp. 20–2.

26 Bolger, pp. 25–6.

27 Bolger, p. 30.

28 Maconachie was also a friend of George Back, who named an island in the delta of the Great Fish river for him. Back, p. 409.

29 Franklin to Jane, 9 May 1839: G. Mackaness (ed.), *Some Private Correspondence of Sir John and Lady Jane Franklin (Tasmania, 1837–1845)*, 2 vols. (Sydney, 1947), I, p. 75.

30 Franklin to Beaufort, 25 Sept. 1838: Wellcome MS 738/1.

31 Franklin to Jane, 13 April 1841: Mackaness, I, p. 118.

32 West, pp. 146–9, 174–6 and 487.

33 Franklin to Mrs Simpkinson (Jane's sister), 14 April 1839: ML Gell MS 114, Box 2, f. 12. Franklin to Mrs Wright (his sister), 1 June 1839: ML MSS A, f. 1/6.

34 Franklin to Lord Glenelg, 7 Oct. 1837, encl. Franklin minute of that date: Government Print on Convict Discipline, National Library of Australia (NLA).

35 Bolger, pp. 33–4.
36 Robson, pp. 317–35.
37 Jane to Franklin, 28 April 1840: Mackaness, I, p. 93.
38 Fitzpatrick, pp. 80–1. Alexander, p. 143, questions the veracity of this story, but it is too good to omit.
39 The idea was circulated by Montagu and accepted by Lord Stanley. Fitzpatrick, pp. 334–8.
40 Shaw, p. 120.
41 Lady Franklin, Journal of a Tour of the Island 1838: Mackaness, I, pp. 12–33, 42, 43, 49.
42 12,000 serpents were destroyed at a cost of £600: Alexander, pp. 145–6.
43 Franklin to Mrs Simpkinson, 14 April 1839: ML Gell MS 114, Box 2, f. 12.
44 P. Burroughs, *Britain and Australia, 1831–1855: A Study in Imperial Relations and Crown Lands Administration* (Oxford, 1967), pp. 1–11.
45 Burroughs, p. 64.
46 Burroughs, pp. 96–104.
47 Burroughs, p. 214.
48 Burroughs, pp. 332–3.
49 Franklin to Lord Stanley, 24 Feb. 1843: CO 280/153, in Burroughs, p. 335.
50 Land Sales, Revenue, Emigrants and Convicts: Van Diemen's Land: 1835–45

Year	Land sold (acres)	Revenue from sales (£)	Emigrants from UK	Convicts to VDL	Convicts to Australia
1835	48,000	5,319	605	1,860	2,493
1836	25,367	32,875	1,591	3,124	2,565
1837	21,729	34,900	1,731	5,054	1,547
1838	19,936	9,119	571	14,021	2,224
1839	42,451	28,367	328	15,786	1,441
1840	88,788	52,140	299	15,850	1,365
1841	78,946	58,427	806	28,724	3,488
1842	59,543	30,962	2,448	5,470	5,520
1843	49,742	19,804	24	3,135	3,727
1844	4,620	6,817	1	2,161	4,966
1845	1,450	1,609	20	816	3,357

51 Burroughs, p. 382. This is the last sentence of Burroughs's text.

CHAPTER 6: Science, Culture and Civilisation

1 Arnold to J. P. Gell, 15 March 1839: D. Stanley, pp. 503–4.
2 Arnold to James Stephen, 19 March 1839: D. Stanley, pp. 504–5.
3 Franklin to Strzelecki, 28 July 1840: ML MSS A, f. 1/19.
4 Franklin to Cumby, 20 Nov. 1836: ML MSS A, f. 1/25. Ruskin.
5 D. S. Evans, B. H Evans, T. J. Deeming and S. Goldfarb (eds), *Herschel at the Cape: Diaries and Correspondence of Sir John Herschel, 1834–1838* (Austin, 1969), p. 204.
6 Herschel to Caroline Herschel (his scientific German aunt who knew Gauss), 3 Oct. 1836: Evans et al., pp. 220 and 255.
7 Herschel to Captain Lloyd (surveyor of Mauritius), 12 March 1835: RS Sabine MS 258, f. 645.

8 Evans et al., pp. 252 and 256.
9 Jane noted the meetings were held on the first Wednesday of the month, which prevented the Franklins from attending. B. Warner and N. Warner (eds), *The Journal of Lady Franklin at the Cape of Good Hope, November 1836: Keeping up the Character* (Cape Town, 1985), p. 44.
10 Lady Herschel to James Stewart, 16 Nov. 1836: B. Warner (ed.), *Lady Herschel: Letters from the Cape, 1834–1838* (Cape Town, 1991), p. 125.
11 Warner et al., pp. 39–40.
12 Franklin to Herschel, 30 Sept. 1837: Royal Society (RS) Herschel MS HS 7 358.
13 Franklin to Herschel, 7 Nov. 1838: RS Herschel MS HS 7 359 (arrived 16 June 1839).
14 Herschel to Franklin, 16 June 1839: Fitzpatrick, pp. 245–6.
15 E. L. Piesse, 'The Foundation and Early Work of the Society', *Papers and Proceedings of the Royal Tasmanian Society*, 1913, pp. 118–36.
16 Jane to Franklin, 20 June 1839: Mackaness, I, pp. 91–3.
17 Piesse, p. 124.
18 L. Huxley, *Life and Letters of Joseph Dalton Hooker*, 2 vols. (London, 1918), II, pp. 455–6. Davis, *Second Expedition*, p. 2.
19 *Tasmanian Journal of Science*, 1, pp. 124 and 207.
20 D'Urville interview of 28 Feb. 1840, *Tasmanian Journal of Science*, 1, pp. 74–6.
21 Piesse, p. 128.
22 Jane to Mrs Simpkinson, 28 April 1840: Mackaness, I, p. 97.
23 Jane to Mrs Simpkinson, 21 Feb. 1841: Mackaness, I, p. 111.
24 Franklin to John Gould, 21 Feb. 1842: ML Gould MS 2141.
25 Inscription placed in the foundations in English, Greek, Latin, Italian, German and French: ML Gell MS.
26 Currently on display in the Hobart Maritime Museum.
27 Bolger, p. 27.
28 Robson, p. 357.
29 J. Browne, *Darwin's 'Origin of the Species': A Biography* (London, 2006), p. 41.
30 A. Datta, *John Gould in Australia: Letters and Drawings* (Melbourne, 1997), pp. 105–6. Smith, p. 215.
31 Huxley, I, p. 107.
32 Franklin to John Gould, 21 Feb. 1842: ML Gould MS 2141.
33 Smith, pp. 207–9, 218–19. For Lady Franklin's patronage of a major Sydney-based artist see E. Ellis, *Conrad Maertens: Life and Art* (Sydney, 1994), p. 38.
34 L. Paszkowski, *Strzelecki: Reflections of His Life* (Melbourne 2004).
35 Franklin to Strzelecki, 28 July 1840: ML MSS A, f. 1/19.
36 Franklin to Strzelecki, 24 May 1842: ML MSS 114, Box 2, f. 15.
37 Jane to Mrs Simpkinson, 5 Aug. 1842: Mackaness, II, p. 58.
38 Franklin to Murchison, 19 Nov. 1842: SPRI MS 248/225/3. Mackaness, II, p. 57 and Paszkowski, pp. 140–75, 205–7.
39 Piesse, pp. 134–5.
40 Sir W. Denison, 'The Operation of *Teredo navalis* on Colonial Timber', *Papers and Proceedings of the Royal Society of Van Diemen's Land*, 2, pt. 1 (Hobart, 1852), pp. 72–4.
41 Franklin Address to Legislative Council, 10 July 1837: Estimates of Expenditure and the Lieutenant Governor's Report to the Legislative Council, p. 22. Tasmanian Archives Colonial Correspondence.
42 Franklin to Colonial Office, 5 March 1842: Tasmanian Archives Colonial Correspondence.

43 Lady Franklin's Diary, 7 Nov. 1843: Mackaness, II, p. 77.

44 Robson, p. 359.

45 L. Marchant, *France Australe* (Perth, 1982).

46 Jane to Mrs Simpkinson, 3 Feb. 1839: Mackaness, I, p. 56.

47 Charles Bethune, originally Charles Ramsay Drinkwater, then senior officer in New South Wales, saw distinguished service in the First China War of 1839–42 and served as assistant to the Hydrographer from 1846.

48 M. Austin, *The Army in Australia, 1840–1850: Prelude to the Golden Years* (Canberra, 1979), pp. 153–8.

49 A. D. Lambert, 'Australia, the Trent Crisis of 1861 and the Strategy of Imperial Defence', in D. Stevens and J. Reeve (eds), *Southern Trident: Strategy, History and the Rise of Australian Naval Power* (Crow's Nest, NSW, 2001), pp. 99–118 at p. 102.

50 Franklin address to Legislative Council, 30 June 1838: Austin, pp. 161–9.

51 Franklin to Ross, 4 Aug. 1841: SPRI MS 248/316/6. Lady Franklin's Diary, 7 Nov. 1843: Mackaness, II, p. 77.

52 D. Burn, *Narrative of the Overland Journey of Sir John and Lady Franklin and Party from Hobart Town to Macquarie Harbour, 1842*, ed. G. Mackaness (Sydney 1955), p. 63.

53 Robson, pp. 374–5. J. C. Ross, *Voyage*, II, pp. 119–20.

54 Lambert, 'Australia', pp. 100–5.

55 Austin, pp. 94–106, 256–7.

56 Huxley, I, p. 108.

57 Lieutenant Allen Field, an older officer (past fifty), commissioned in 1809 and on half pay since 1823. He joined the navy five years before Franklin. Franklin to John Barrow Jr, 22 June 1837: ML MSS 1214, Box 3, f. 17.

58 Franklin to Henty, 6 Dec. 1842: ML MSS 9342. He had lent Blackwood the plates and charts volume *Atlas de Voyage de Bruny D'Entrecasteaux* (2 vols.; Paris, 1809, folio), which accompanied D'Entrecasteaux's *Voyages à la Recherche de la Pérouse* (2 vols.; Paris, 1808).

59 Franklin to Cumby, 21 Oct. 1836: ML MSS A, f. 1/25. Burnett was thirty-one.

60 Franklin Address to Legislative Council, 10 July 1837: Estimates of Expenditure and the Lieutenant Governor's Report to the Legislative Council, p. 22. Tasmanian Archives Colonial Correspondence.

61 George Frankland to Beaufort, 8 April 1838: UKHO Beaufort MSS F008.

62 Franklin to Jane, 9 May 1839: Mackaness, I, pp. 76 and 124. W. O'Byrne, *Naval Biographical Dictionary* (London, 1849), p. 785. Moriarty died in 1850.

63 O'Byrne, pp. 381–2. Franklin to Ross, 18 Oct. 1840: SPRI MS 248/316/2.

64 Beaufort instructions, 8 June 1837: Hordern, p. 317.

65 Admiralty orders, 8 June 1837: Hordern, pp. 312–13.

66 Hordern, pp. 97–9.

67 Hordern, pp. 242–3; see p. 136 for Owen Stanley's drawing of Low Head lighthouse.

68 Hordern, p. 249.

69 Stokes to Beaufort, 10 Oct. 1842: AD3/100 from J. Gascoigne, *The Enlightenment and the Origins of European Australia* (Cambridge, 2002), p. 94.

70 Franklin to Strzelecki, 24 May 1842: ML MSS 114, Box 2, f. 15.

71 Lady Franklin's Diary, 8 Nov. 1843: Mackaness, II, pp. 77–8. Franklin to Beaufort, 3 Feb. 1845: UKHO Beaufort MSS F019.

72 Franklin to Jane, 20 March 1841: Mackaness, I, pp. 113–14.

73 Franklin to Charles LaTrobe Governor of South Australia, 19 Feb. 1841: ML MSS.
74 Franklin to Mrs Simpkinson, 23 Feb. 1841: Mackaness, I, p. 112.
75 Jane to Mrs Simpkinson, 1 Jan. 1842: Mackaness, II, pp. 41–2.
76 J. Bach, *The Australia Station: A History of the Royal Navy in the South West Pacific, 1821–1913* (Sydney, 1986), pp. 22–6.
77 J. S. Dunmore, *French Explorers of the Pacific*, vol. II (Oxford, 1969), pp. 326–7.
78 Jane to Mrs Simpkinson, 3 Feb. 1839: Mackaness, I, pp. 56–7.
79 J. S.-C. D. d'Urville, *An Account of Two Voyages to the South Seas*, vol. II, *The Astrolabe and Zélée, 1837–1840*, trans. and ed. H. Rosenman (Melbourne, 1987), pp. 449–56, 494, 524–5.
80 D'Urville, p. 494.
81 Franklin to Gipps, 19 Feb. 1840: ML MSS A, f. 1/21.
82 R-Adm. C. Wilkes, *Autobiography, 1798–1877*, ed. W. J. Morgan et al. (Washington, DC, 1978), p. 452.
83 J. C. Ross, *Voyage*, I, pp. 115–16.
84 Owen, p. 206.
85 Franklin to Pelly, 9 Oct. 1838: Tasmania Archives A10/7/193–4. Copy from HBC Archive.
86 Beaufort to Franklin, 16 June 1840: UKHO LB 9, p. 286. Franklin to Sabine, 13 March 1841: BJ3/18, ff. 14–15.
87 Ross's *Voyage of Discovery* was dedicated to Lord Minto, who was First Lord of the Admiralty when Ross was given his orders and was also a member of the British Association. The 'Voyage Instructions of the Royal Society and the Admiralty' appear at pp. v–xlvi.
88 Franklin to Jane, 11 May 1839: Mackaness, I, pp. 79–80.
89 Herschel to Franklin, 16 June 1839: Fitzpatrick, pp. 245–6.
90 Beaufort to Franklin, 17 Nov. 1838: UKHO LB 8, p. 308; 27 March 1841: LB 9, p. 528; 29 Oct. 1842: LB 11, p. 9.
91 Jane to Mrs Simpkinson, 7 Sept. 1841: Mackaness, I, p. 104.
92 Lord John Russell to Franklin, 12 Sept. 1839: cited in A. Savours and A. McConnell, 'The History of the Rossbank Observatory, Tasmania', *Annals of Science*, 39 (1982), pp. 527–64 at p. 531. This was not an ideal location, the sandstone being penetrated by magnetic greenstone outcrops.
93 J. C. Ross, *Voyage*, I, pp. 107–13 and 123–4.
94 Fitzpatrick, p. 247.
95 Sabine to Ross, 10 Jan. 1843: RS Sabine MS 260, f. 1135. The artist was Thomas Bock: Smith, p. 238.
96 Franklin to Buckland, 21 May 1841: ML MSS A, f. 75, cited in Savours and McConnell at p. 537.
97 Franklin to Humphrey Lloyd, n.d. 1842: Wellcome MS 7831/5. Franklin to Barrow (Admiralty), 20 Aug. 1841: cited in Savours and McConnell at p. 538.
98 Franklin to Ross, 9 Sept. and 18 Oct. 1840: SPRI MS 248/316/1–2. Kay in the *Tasmanian Journal*, vol. I (Hobart and London, 1842).
99 Jane to Mrs Simpkinson, 8 Dec. 1840: Mackaness, I, pp. 106–7. Huxley, I, p. 106.
100 J. C. Ross, *Voyage*, I, p. 129. Huxley, II, p. 178.
101 J. C. Ross, *Voyage*, II, pp. 22–3.
102 Franklin to Beaufort, 31 May 1840, 12 April 1841: UKHO Beaufort MSS F012, F015. Franklin to Herschel, 30 Sept. 1837: RS Herschel MS HS 7 358. Franklin to Herschel, 7 Nov. 1838: Royal Society, HS 7 359 (arrived 16 June 1839). Franklin to Colonial Office, 13 April 1843, no. 49, Archive Office of Tasmania.

103 J. C. Ross, *Voyage*, I, p. 116.

104 J. C. Ross, *Voyage*, I, pp. 118–19.

105 Franklin to Jane, 13 April 1841: Mackaness, I, p. 117.

106 Jane to Mrs Simpkinson, 12 Oct. 1841: Mackaness, II, p. 38.

107 Franklin to Jane, 13 April 1841: Mackaness, I, pp. 116–17.

108 Franklin to Ross, 20 April 1841: SPRI MS 248/316/4.

109 Franklin to William Buckland, 21 May 1841: Owen, p. 209.

110 Sophia Cracroft to Mrs Wright, n.d.: Owen, pp. 207–8.

111 Huxley, I, p. 119.

112 *Hobart Town Advertiser*, 4 June 1841, reprinted in the pamphlet *The Nautical Fete, HMS Erebus and HMS Terror* (Hobart, 1841).

113 Jane to Mrs Simpkinson, 18 Sept. 1843: Mackaness, II, p. 68.

114 Whewell to Murchison, 1836: Murchison Papers, LDGSL 838.

115 Franklin to Pelly, 9 Oct. 1838: Tasmania Archives A10/7/193–4, photocopy HBC Archive.

116 Franklin to Lloyd, n.d. 1843: Wellcome MS 7831/5.

117 Jane to Franklin, 21 April 1841: Mackaness, II, p. 17.

118 Franklin to Strzelecki, 25 Dec. 1840: ML MSS.

119 D. Ellison, *Quarter Deck – Cambridge: The Quest of Captain Francis Price Blackwood RN* (Cambridge, 1991), p. 18. Blackwood, a talented surveyor and observational scientist, became a Fellow of the Royal Astronomical Society before his early death in 1854.

120 Jane to Mrs Simpkinson, Sept. 1842: Mackaness, II, pp. 63–4.

121 G. Kerr and H. McDermott, *The Huon Pine Story* (Portland, VIC, 1999).

122 Franklin to Strzelecki, 24 May 1842: ML MSS 114, Box 2, f. 15.

123 Franklin to Strzelecki, 24 May 1842: ML MSS 114, Box 2, f. 15. Burn. J. Calder, *Recollections of Sir John and Lady Jane Franklin in Tasmania* (originally published in the *Tasmanian Tribune*, 1875; repr. Adelaide, 1984).

124 Jane Franklin to Alexander Turnbull (Tasmanian resident), 17 Feb. 1845: Tasmanian Archives Turnbull MS 5737.

125 Franklin to Murchison, 30 Jan. 1845: Murchison MS RGS M/F 17/1. Fitzpatrick, p. 301, citing P. Strzelecki, *Physical Description of New South Wales and Van Diemen's Land* (London, 1845), pp. 38–9.

126 Gascoigne, pp. 86–99, quote at p. 92.

127 Printed form, n.d.: ML MSS.

128 Franklin's distress is evident in his letters to his closest friend, James Clark Ross: Franklin/Ross correspondence, 1842–3, SPRI MS 248/316/8–10.

129 Shaw, pp. 217–18.

130 Jane to Mrs Simpkinson, 12 Oct. 1841: Mackaness, II, p. 35.

131 Shaw, pp. 273–4, 281–2.

132 Alexander, pp. 162, 166. By contrast K. McGoogan, *Lady Franklin's Revenge: A True Story of Ambition, Obsession and the Remaking of History* (London, 2006), accepts and amplifies the charge.

133 Franklin to Ross, 21 July 1843: SPRI MS 248/316/10.

134 Franklin to Captain Philip Parker King, 6 Jan. 1844: ML King MS 7048/1/4.

135 Bolger, p. 41.

136 Robson, pp. 370–86.

137 Franklin to Sidney Herbert, secretary to the Admiralty, 12 Sept. 1843: ML MSS A, f. 1/5.

138 Beaufort to Franklin, 10 June 1840: Mackaness, I, pp. 98–9.

139 Alexander, pp. 1–66.

140 Franklin to P. P. King, 6 Jan. 1844: ML King MS 7048/1/4.

141 F. Woodward, pp. 246–7.

142 Fitzpatrick is conclusive on the Montagu affair.

143 Jane to Mrs Simpkinson, 23 May 1843: Mackaness, II, pp. 66–7.

144 Montagu to Bicheno, 31 Aug. 1844: ML Bicheno MS Ab182, f. 9.

145 For Montagu see *Australian Dictionary of National Biography*, pp. 248–50. His later career at the Cape combined capable public service with financial ruin. He died in 1853.

CHAPTER 7: 'The nucleus of an iceberg'

1 Franklin to Herbert, 12 Sept. 1843: ML MSS A, f. 1/5.

2 Humboldt, *Cosmos*, I, pp. 177, 24. His argument was essentially circular: the key source was Herschel's *Quarterly Review* paper of 1840, an endorsement of Humboldt's original suggestion.

3 Whewell to Murchison, 22 March 1836: Murchison Correspondence RGS M/W4 14. Ross to Sabine, 10 Oct. 1836: BJ3/8.

4 W. Barr (ed.), *From Barrow to Boothia: The Arctic Journals of Peter Warren Dease, 1836–1839* (Montreal 2002), p. ix. Simpson's journals appeared in 1843 – and would have been in Franklin's library in 1845.

5 Sabine to Ross, 13 June 1840: BJ2/13, f. 1. Beaufort sent the book to Franklin in the official mail. For Wrangel/Vrangel see D. Hayes, *Historical Atlas of the Arctic* (Seattle, 2003), pp. 112–15.

6 Franklin to Jane, 28 Dec. 1844: SPRI MS 248/303/81.

7 Franklin to Sabine, 13 March 1841: BJ3/18, ff. 14–15.

8 Lloyd to Sabine, 20 Jan. 1842: BJ3/12, f. 3. Sabine to Lloyd, 21 Feb. 1842, BJ3/83 cites Gauss on the need for hourly simultaneous observations.

9 Sabine to Beaufort, 8 Feb. 1842: BJ3/79, f. 63. Sabine to Beaufort, 8 Feb. 1842: BJ3/79, f. 73.

10 Sabine to Beaufort, 22 Dec. 1842: BJ3/79, f. 86.

11 Sabine to Beaufort, 3 Jan. 1843: BJ3/79, f. 88. This may explain Belcher's appointment in 1852.

12 Lloyd to Sabine, 2 April 1843: BJ3/12, f. 26.

13 Sabine to Ross, 10 Jan. 1843: RS Sabine MS 260, f. 1155.

14 Sabine to Ross, 6 March 1843: RS Sabine MS 260, f. 1156.

15 M. J. Ross, pp. 273–4.

16 General Committee minutes 1843: Dep. BAAS 10, Bodleian Library, ff. 151–2, 185.

17 General Committee minutes 1844: Dep. BAAS 10, Bodleian Library, f. 206.

18 Strzelecki to King, 10 Nov. 1843: ML King MS. For John Lort Stokes see ch. 6.

19 Strzelecki to King, 2 June 1844: ML King MS.

20 Beaufort to Richardson, 26 May 1844: SPRI Richardson Bequest MS 1503/28/3. Franklin to Buckland, 15 June 1844: ML MSS. William Buckland (1784–1856), a geologist and Dean of Westminster, was very close to Sir Robert Peel (British prime minister 1841–6), *Oxford Dictionary of National Biography*, www.offorddnb.com/view/pritnable/3859, accessed, 25 Sept. 2007.

21 Franklin to Adam Turnbull, 20 Sept. 1844: Mackaness, II, p. 87. Franklin to Robert Brown, 23 July 1844: SPRI MS 248/296/10; ff. 10–18 deal with the Montagu affair.

22 Stanley's biographer ignores Montagu's role, ascribing the sacking to the inadequacy of Franklin's 'mild humanity' as a tool of government. A. Hawkins, *The
Forgotten Prime Minister: The 14th Earl of Derby – Ascent, 1799–1851* (Oxford,
2007), pp. 236–7.

23 Franklin to Richardson, 2 Sept. and 5 Oct. 1844: ML MSS 96 and 97.

24 Franklin to Buckland, 5 Sept. 1844: ML MSS.

25 Parry to Buckland, 9 Oct. 1844: ML MSS 116.

26 Franklin to Buckland, 24 Oct. 1844: ML MSS 131.

27 Franklin to Jane, 30 Dec. 1844: SPRI MS 248/303/82.

28 Endorsement on Franklin to Admiralty, 12 July 1845, rec'd 9 Aug. 1845: ADM
7/187, f. 9.

29 J. Barrow: 'Proposal for an Attempt to Complete the Discovery of a North West
Passage', in Cyriax, *Last Expedition*, pp. 19–20.

30 Barrow to Lord Haddington, First Lord of the Admiralty, Dec. 1844: Cyriax, *Last
Expedition*, p. 20.

31 Cyriax, *Last Expedition*, p. 25. Cyriax's account of a search for the North West
Passage frequently hints that the mission had magnetic origins, pp. 17, 25, 35, 38,
43, 51, 54, 56, 58, 62–3, 108, 132 and 198.

32 Barrow to Lord Haddington, First Lord of the Admiralty, 27 Dec. 1844: ADM
7/187, f. 1. Cyriax, *Last Expedition*, pp. 21–2.

33 Magnetic orders for Franklin: BJ3/79, ff. 138–9.

34 Peter Fisher, a veteran of Back's *Terror* voyage, then inspecting captain of the
Coastguard, was available in London. Cyriax, *Last Expedition*, p. 27. C. R.
Markham, *The Arctic Navy List* (Portsmouth, 1875), p. 16.

35 Parry to Haddington, 18 Jan. 1845: ADM 7/187, f. 3.

36 Northampton to Haddington, 18 Jan. 1845, encl. resolution of the Royal Society
Council, 16 Jan. 1845: ADM 7/187, f. 2.

37 Franklin to Haddington, 24 Jan. 1845: ADM 7/187, f. 4.

38 Franklin to Jane 28 and 30 Dec. 1844: SPRI MS 248/303/80–2.

39 Ross to Haddington, 25 Jan. 1845: ADM 7/187, f. 5.

40 Sabine to Haddington, n.d.: ADM 7/187, f. 6. Davis *First Expedition*, p. xxxiv.

41 Cyriax, *Last Expedition*, notes the 'great importance of magnetic observations',
only to drop the subject after two sentences, p. 43.

42 Franklin to Murchison, 12 Feb. 1842: SPRI MS 248/272. Franklin to Murchison,
17 Jan. 1845: Murchison Papers LDGSL 838, MF17.

43 Ross to Beaufort, 19 Dec. 1844: J. C. Ross, *Voyage*, I, p. 275.

44 F. Woodward, p. 257.

45 Franklin to Ross, 24 Dec. 1844: SPRI MS 248/316/16.

46 Franklin to Ross, 9 Jan. 1845: SPRI MS 248/316/17.

47 Franklin to Jane, 31 Dec. 1844 and 1 Jan. 1845: SPRI MS 248/303/83–4.

48 Franklin to Ross, 17 Jan. 1845: SPRI MS 248/316/18. Franklin to Milligen
(Tasmanian resident), 21 Jan. 1845: Wellcome MS 7831/4.

49 Franklin to Jane, 28 Dec. 1844: M. J. Ross, p. 276.

50 Traill, p. 335, quoting Jane's diary of 5 Feb. 1845.

51 Commander Alexander Becher RN (Hydrographic Department) to Franklin, 7 Feb.
1845: UKHO LB 12, p. 316. Franklin to Ross, 8 Feb. 1845: SPRI MS 248/316/21.

52 M. J. Ross, pp. 277–8. Cyriax, *Last Expedition*, p. 35. Franklin to Ross, 10 Feb.
1845: SPRI MS 248/316/22.

53 Franklin to Bowles, 20 Feb. 1845: SPRI, McCord Museum Microfilm 962, f. 6.

54 Traill, p. 335, quoting Jane's diary of 5 Feb. 1845.

55 Franklin to Jane, 1 April 1845: SPRI MS 248/303/85.

56 Franklin to Turnbull, 21 Jan. 1845: Mackaness, II, pp. 87–90.

57 Franklin to Sabine, 23 April 1845 (21 Bedford Square): BJ3/18, f. 21.

58 Parry to Back, 28 Jan. 1845: McCord Museum Microfilm 2731. *The Times*, 29 March 1845 gives the full text of the testimonial.

59 Lloyd to Sabine, 24 March 1845 (Trinity College, Dublin): BJ3/13, f. 8.

60 Lloyd to Sabine, 8 April 1844: BJ3/12. R. W. Fox to Sabine, 3 March 1845: BJ3/19, f. 153, see also fn. 12.

61 Lloyd to Sabine, 13 and 17 May 1845: BJ3/12, ff. 10 and 13. O'Hara, p. 71.

62 C. J. B. Riddell, *Magnetical Instructions for the Use of Portable Instruments Adapted for Magnetical Surveys and Portable Observatories* (London, 1844).

63 Franklin to Sabine, 13 Feb. 1845: BJ3/18, f. 20.

64 E. L. Fanshawe, *Admiral Sir Edward Gennys Fanshawe GCB* (London, 1904), pp. 62–3.

65 Sabine to Beaufort, 8 Feb. 1842 (Woolwich): BJ3/79, f. 63.

66 Beaufort to Sabine, 12 May 1845: UKHO LB 13, f. 16. Sabine to Beaufort, 13 May 1845 BJ3/79, f. 135.

67 J. D. Hooker to Darwin, 2–6 April 1845: F. Burkhardt et al. (eds), *The Correspondence of Charles Darwin* (Cambridge, 1985–) (hereafter *Darwin Correspondence*), III, p. 167.

68 Franklin to Ross 10 and 24 Feb. 1845: SPRI MS 248/316/22–3.

69 Franklin to Jane, 21 March 1845: ML MSS A, f. 1/16. Franklin to Jane, 1 April 1845: SPRI MS 248/303/85.

70 L. R. Croft (ed.), *Diary of a Naval Commander: The Diary of Vice-Admiral James Hamilton Ward, 1843–1846* (Chorley, 1989), p. 33.

71 Franklin to Buckland, 21 April 1845: ML MSS.

72 David, p. 81.

73 Jane Franklin to Gould, 25 April 1845: ML MSS 2141.

74 For Symonds see A. Lambert, *The Last Sailing Battle: Maintaining Naval Mastery, 1815–1850* (London, 1991), pp. 67–87. For the screw propeller see A. D. Lambert (ed.), *Steam, Steel and Shellfire: The Steam Warship, 1815–1905* (London, 1992), p. 35.

75 Parry to Haddington, 18 Jan. 1845: ADM 7/187, f. 3.

76 Franklin to Jane, 2 April 1845: SPRI MS 248/303/86.

77 Franklin to Sabine, 23 April 1845: BJ3/18, f. 21. Franklin to Buckland, 21 April 1845: ML MSS. Jane Franklin to Gould, 25 April 1845: ML MSS 2141.

78 Paszkowski, p. 206.

79 Strzelecki to P. P. King, 5 June 1845: Paszkowski, p. 216.

80 Franklin to Brown, 9 July 1845: SPRI MS 248/296/20.

81 Franklin to Ross, July 1845: M. J. Ross, p. 283.

82 Admiralty to Franklin, 5 May 1845: ADM 7/187, f. 8.

83 Cyriax, *Last Expedition*, p. 51.

84 Lieutenant Bedford Clapperton Pim was another. See ch. 10.

85 Magnetic orders for Franklin: BJ3/79, ff. 138–9. While Levere notes the 'remarkable degree of enthusiasm for magnetic work' (p. 200), he still treats the North West Passage as the primary mission.

86 Crozier to Ross, July 1845: M. J. Ross, p. 285.

87 Franklin to Jane, 7 June 1845: RGS SJF 7/4.

88 Franklin to Buckland, 21 April 1845: ML MSS.

89 Franklin to Dr Adam Turnbull (in Tasmania), 19 May 1845 (the day the expedition sailed: NLA MSS 5737).

90 Jane Franklin to Gould, 25 April 1845: ML MSS 2141.
91 The inn is now called the Sir John Franklin.
92 Franklin to Isabella Cracroft: SPRI MS 248/298/19.
93 Franklin to Turnbull, 19 May 1845: NLA MSS 5737.
94 Murchison, 26 May 1845: Cyriax, *Last Expedition*, p. 56.
95 M. J. Ross, p. 281.
96 R. King, *The Franklin Expedition from First to Last* (London, 1855), pp. 188–91 (italics added).
97 The drawings are held by the National Library of Australia.
98 A. Lubbock, *Owen Stanley of the Rattlesnake* (Melbourne, 1957), p. 158.
99 Franklin to Admiralty, 29 May 1845 (off Aberdeen): ADM 7/187, f. 9.
100 He wrote to Richardson, Parry, Ross, Jane, Sophia Cracroft and Robert Brown. Franklin to Sophia Cracroft, 5 June 1845: LDGSL 838, MS926/9. Franklin to Jane, 3 June 1845: RGS SJF 7/4.
101 Franklin to Isabella Cracroft, 11 July 1845: SPRI MS 248/298/20.
102 Franklin to Jane, 7 July 1845: RGS SJF 7/4. M. J. Ross, pp. 283–5.
103 Franklin to Robert Brown, 9 July 1845: SPRI MS 248/296/19.
104 Fitzjames to Sabine, 11 July 1845 (Whale Fish Islands): BJ3/17, f. 21.
105 Franklin to Sabine, 9 July 1845 (Whale Fish Islands): BJ3/18, f. 32. Sabine to Ross, 25 Aug. 1845: RS Sabine MS 260, f. 1170.
106 Franklin to Admiralty, 12 July 1845, rec'd 9 Aug. 1845: ADM 7/187, f. 9.
107 Franklin to Sabine, 9 July 1845 (Whale Fish Islands): BJ3/18, f. 32. Franklin to Brown, 3 June 1845: SPRI MS 248/296/18.
108 Strzelecki to P. P. King, 1 Dec. 1845: ML King MS. Franklin, *Narrative of some Passages of the History of Van Diemen's Land during the Last Three Years of Sir John Franklin's Administration of its Government*, privately printed, 1845. The facsimile edition (Hobart, 1967) was taken from Murchison's copy.
109 This explains the lacunae in his archive; he took all the material on navigation and magnetic science to the Arctic.
110 Russian hydrographer and Arctic voyager (1770–1846) whom Franklin had met while visiting Russia (see ch. 3 above). See also J. C. Ross, *Memoir of Admiral Krusenstern* (London, 1856).
111 Franklin to Richardson, 7 July 1845: SPRI MS 248/314.
112 Franklin to Robert Brown, 9 July 1845: SPRI MS 248/296/19.
113 Franklin to Ross, 9 July 1845: SPRI MS 248/316/25.
114 Franklin to Parry, 10 July 1845: SPRI MS 438/18/7.
115 Franklin to Isabella Cracroft, 11 July 1845: SPRI MS 248/298/20.
116 Hayes, *Arctic*, p. 80.
117 Map: Wellcome MS 7486/85, reproduced in Hayes, *Arctic*, p. 78.
118 Hayes, *Arctic*, pp. 80–2.
119 John Franklin to Mary Kendall, 12 July 1845: FRN/26, NMM.
120 Franklin to Jane, 1–12 July 1845: RGS SJF 7/4, photocopy.
121 Officially, Franklin had supplies for only three years.
122 Cyriax, *Last Expedition*, pp. 64–5.

CHAPTER 8: Magnetic Empires

1 BAAS presidential address, 1845: cited in Ruskin at p. 34.
2 General Committee minutes, 1845: Dep. BAAS 10, Bodleian Library, ff. 218–31.

3 Sabine to Lt. Hays RN (Hobart Observatory), 22 Nov. 1845: BJ3/83, f. 16.
4 Sabine to Beaufort, 16 March 1846: BJ3/79, f. 158.
5 Murchison to Sabine, 22 May 1845: RS Sabine MS 260, f. 900.
6 Printed report, General Committee minutes, 1846: Dep. BAAS 10, Bodleian Library, f. 256.
7 *The Times*, 6 May 1846, p. 8, 'Naval Intelligence'.
8 J. Goodman, *The Rattlesnake: A Voyage of Discovery to the Coral Sea* (London, 2005), pp. 273–4.
9 Herschel to Sabine, 11 Nov. 1846: RS Sabine MS 258, f. 652.
10 Sabine to Beaufort, 16 July 1846: BJ3/79, f. 172.
11 Minto to Ross, 18 March 1845: RS Sabine MS 260, f. 887.
12 Sabine to Beaufort, 23 Jan. 1846: BJ3/79, ff. 152–3.
13 Savours and McConnell, pp. 562–3. This account is chronologically suspect.
14 Franklin to Lloyd, n.d. (1842?): Wellcome MS 7831/5.
15 'Terrestrial Magnetism', *Quarterly Review*, 66 (1840), pp. 271 and 295; cited in Levere at p. 157.
16 *Quarterly Review*, 66 (1840), p. 304.
17 Levere, p. 158.
18 Levere, p. 161. Lefroy to Sabine, 27 March 1844: G. F. G. Stanley, *John Henry Lefroy: In Search of the Magnetic North* (Toronto, 1955), pp. 96–102.
19 G. F. G. Stanley, pp. xix–xxiii. As governor of Tasmania (1880–2) Lefroy continued his lifelong habit of magnetic observation.
20 Sabine to Beaufort, 8 Feb. 1842: BJ3/79, f. 73.
21 Sabine to J. C. Ross, 24 July 1844: BJ3/81, f. 13.
22 Hall, pp. 214–15 and *Philosophical Transactions*, 135 (1845; pub. 1846), pt. III.
23 A. G. E. Jones, 'Lieutenant T. E. L. Moore', pp. 193. In 1846 Moore made a voyage to Moose Factory on a Hudson's Bay Company ship for magnetic survey work and was retained on full pay to write up his results. In late 1847 he was given command of the *Plover* and sent through the Bering Strait to help look for Franklin. While there he conducted some useful survey work, although when Rae met him in 1851 Moore had an Inuit girl in his cabin and was selling spirits to the natives.
24 Morrell and Thackeray, *Early Correspondence*, pp. 522–31, quote at p. 524. J. Cloake, *Palaces and Parks of Richmond and Kew*, vol. II, *Richmond Lodge and the Kew Palaces* (Chichester, 1996), pp. 49–50, 180–3.
25 O'Hara, pp. 71–2.
26 Sabine published statement of 1855: Levere, p. 161.
27 Beaufort to Sabine, 23 Nov. and 6 Dec. 1853: RS Sabine MS 257, f. 1212.
28 Harbour Department of the Admiralty, House of Commons Return no. 553, 10 July 1849, p. 10.
29 R. M. MacLeod, 'The Royal Society and the Government Grant: Notes on the Administration of Scientific Research, 1849–1914', *Historical Journal*, 14(2) (1971), pp. 323–58 at pp. 327–8, 330.
30 Kellner, pp. 199–213.
31 Humboldt, *Cosmos*, I, p. ix. Humboldt knew and valued the work of English pioneers in magnetic science, including Gilbert's *De Magnete* and Halley's charts.
32 Humboldt, *Cosmos*, I, p. ix (notes) and pp. 174–5.
33 Humboldt, *Cosmos*, I, pp. 178 and 24.
34 R. W. Fox to Sabine, 18 Oct. 1846: RS Sabine MS 258, f. 575. Sabine to Ross, 2 Sept. 1846: RS Sabine MS 260, f. 1171.
35 Longman–Sabine correspondence: RS Sabine MS 257, ff. 800–4.

36 Kellner, p. 210.
37 Kellner, pp. 221–2.

CHAPTER 9: 'Till our provisions get short'

1 J. Barrow, *Autobiographical Memoir* (London, 1848), pp. 486–7 at pp. 480–1. Barrow claimed the only favours he requested on retirement were promotion for Fitzjames and a knighthood for Dr Richardson. Both were granted.
2 J. C. Sainty, *Admiralty Officials, 1660–1870* (London, 1965), pp. 37, 49, 109.
3 A. C. Revell, *Haslar: The Royal Hospital* (Gosport, 1978), p. 35.
4 Ross to Admiralty, 29 Sept. 1846 and Parry to Lord Auckland, 7 Jan. 1847: ADM 7/187, f. 11.
5 Beaufort to J. C. Ross, 20 Jan. 1847: BJ2/3, f. 7.
6 Ross to John Barrow Jr, 31 Jan. 1847 and Board minute, in Lord Auckland's hand, 16 Jan. 1847: ADM 7/187, f. 11.
7 Richardson to Parry, 25 Feb. 1847; Ross to Parry, 2 March 1847: ADM 7/187, f. 12.
8 Pelly to Admiralty, 4 March 1847: ADM 7/187, f. 13.
9 Sabine to Parry, 5 March 1847: ADM 7/187, f. 11.
10 Richardson, 5 May 1847: ADM 7/187, f. 18.
11 Griffiths, 9 July 1847; Griffiths to Hamilton, 12 July 1847: ADM 7/187, f. 11.
12 *The Times*, 14 June 1847, p. 6.
13 F. Woodward, p. 257.
14 Fitzjames to Barrow, Jan. 1845: King, Ross and Weld correspondence in the *Athenaeum* of 12 June 1847: ADM 7/187, f. 18.
15 Auckland to Jane, 13 Nov. 1847: SPRI MS 248/372. Edye memo, 1 July 1847: ADM 7/187, f. 11.
16 K. McGoogan, *Fatal Passage: The Untold Story of John Rae, the Arctic Adventurer Who Discovered the Fate of Franklin* (Toronto, 2001). Admiralty to Hudson's Bay Company, 28 Dec. 1847: ADM 7/187, f. 22.
17 Levere, p. 194.
18 Richardson to Beaufort, 5 Oct. and 6 Dec. 1847 (2): UKHO LB 1857 7/4/3, 4 and 5.
19 Levere, p. 204: Savours, *Search*, p. 188.
20 Sabine to Jane, 13 Nov. 1847: Wellcome MS 7846/89.
21 Ross to Admiralty, 8 Nov. 1847 and endorsement, 9 Nov. 1847. Orders to fit *Plover*, 16 Nov. 1847: ADM 7/187, f. 19.
22 Beaufort to Kellett, 16 March 1848: Friendly, p. 311.
23 Beaufort to Kellett, 16 Nov. 1849: Friendly, p. 313.
24 J. H. Gleason, *The Genesis of Russophobia: A Study of the Interaction of Policy and Opinion* (Cambridge, Mass., 1950).
25 'The Navigation of the Antipodes', *Blackwood's Edinburgh Magazine*, Nov. 1847, p. 516, cited in Loomis, 'Arctic Sublime', p. 104.
26 Beaufort to Ross, 6 Nov. 1847: UKHO LB 15, f. 42a. Also in Friendly, p. 310.
27 Admiralty to Edye, 16 Nov. 1847: ADM 7/187, f. 19.
28 Auckland to Ross, 14 March 1848 and Ross to Auckland, 15 March 1848: RS Sabine MS 257, f. 50 and 261, f. 1097.
29 A high-protein mixture of pounded beef, lard and berries.
30 Savours, *Search*, p. 189.

31 King to Admiralty, 3 March 1848; Ross to Admiralty, 29 Feb. 1848; reward notice, 20 March 1848: ADM 7/187, f. 21. See also *The Times*, 13 March 1850, p. 4, copied from the *London Gazette*.

32 Jane to Beaufort, 27 March 1848: ADM 7/187, f. 21.

33 Auckland to Herschel, 19 Nov. 1847: RS Herschel MS HS 7, f. 9. Herschel's *Admiralty Manual* was a critical tool for the advancement of scientific agendas by naval officers. Predictably, Sabine wrote on terrestrial magnetism.

34 Ross was already too late. In late April Crozier had landed with the surviving men and set off for the mainland.

35 Lloyd, p. 184.

36 Admiralty to Richardson, 21 Nov. 1849. Jane received copies of Richardson's correspondence, and thanked the Board on 4 and 5 Nov. 1849. Admiralty minutes, 12 Dec. 1849; Admiralty to Ross, 17 Dec. 1849: ADM 7/188, sections 17 and 18.

37 This section, unless otherwise noted, is based on: A. G. E. Jones, 'Sir James Clark Ross and the Voyage of the *Enterprise* and *Investigator*, 1848–49', in A. G. E. Jones, *Polar Portraits*, pp. 243–57.

38 Beaufort Diary, 8 Nov. 1849: Friendly, p. 312.

39 Dundas minute, 12 Jan. 1849: ADM 7/188, section 1.

40 The junior civil lord had assumed an unofficial financial role because MPs lacked naval expertise.

41 Cowper minute, 19 Jan. 1849: ADM 7/188, section 2.

42 Milne minute, 20 Jan. 1849: ADM 7/188, section 2. Beaufort to Lady Ross, 17 Jan. 1849: SPRI MS 1226/3/2.

43 *Morning Herald*, 21 Feb. 1849: ADM 7/189, section 13.

44 Savours, *Search*, p. 191.

45 Sir T. D. Acland: Hansard, vol. CIII, p. 1188, 23 March 1849.

46 Jane to Admiralty, 19, 27 and 29 March and 21 April 1849; Admiralty to Jane, 28 March 1849; reward notices of 23 March and 7 May 1849: ADM 7/189, section 16.

47 Lord Palmerston: Hansard, vol. CVI, p. 106, 12 June 1848. Disraeli also spoke in the debate.

48 Hall, p. 204: Darwin to Edward Cresy, before May 1848. *Darwin Correspondence*, IV, p. 134.

49 Sabine to Beaufort, 8 May 1848: BJ3/79, ff. 216–17.

50 Beaufort to Lady Ross, 17 and 20 Jan. 1849: SPRI MS 1226/3/1–2.

51 Murchison to Sabine, 12 Nov. 1849: RS Sabine MS 259, f. 908.

52 Jane to Admiralty, 3 Oct. 1849 and minutes: ADM 7/189, section 2. Dundas minute, 1 Oct. 1849: ADM 7/189, section 1.

53 Scoresby to Barrow, 9 Oct. 1849: ADM 7/189, section 13.

54 Richardson to Sabine, 15 Jan. 1851: BJ3/32, f. 17.

55 *The Times*, 21 Nov. 1849, p. 4.

56 *The Times*, 24 Nov. 1849, p. 4.

57 Belcher report, 28 Feb. 1849: Southampton University, Hartley Library, Palmerston MS GC/BE 574. Samson, pp. 79–81.

58 Milne minute, 3 Dec. 1849: ADM 7/188, section 7.

59 Cowper minute, 3 Dec. 1849: ADM 7/188, section 7.

60 *The Times*, 31 Jan. 1850, p. 4.

61 Beaufort minute, 28 Jan. 1850: ADM 7/188, section 9.

62 Inglis and Baring: Hansard, vol. CVIII, pp. 386–92, 5 Feb. 1850.

63 Sabine to Beaufort, 14 Dec. 1849 (Hastings): BJ3/79, ff. 236–7.

64 Collinson to Sabine, 31 Dec. 1849 (at Woolwich Dockyard while fitting out ships): BJ3/52, f. 47.

65 T. B. Collinson (ed.), *Journal of HMS Enterprise, 1850–1855, by Captain Richard Collinson RN* (London, 1889), pp. 447–58.

66 Admiralty orders, 15 Jan. 1850, signed by Sir Francis Baring: W. Barr, *Arctic Hell Ship: The Voyage of HMS Enterprise, 1850–1855* (Edmonton, 2007), pp. 15–16. Printed magnetic instructions: BJ3/52, f. 60.

67 Jane to Disraeli, 30 Jan. 1850: Bodleian Library, Oxford, Disraeli MS A/IV/N/7. For Corfu opinion, see p. 50 above.

68 Beaufort to Jane, 13 Nov. 1849: SPRI MS 248/343/1.

69 Beaufort to Admiral Sir William Parker, 7 Nov. 1849: Friendly, pp. 312–13.

70 Darwin to J. D. Dana, 24 Feb. 1850: *Darwin Correspondence*, IV, pp. 313–14.

71 Browne, pp. 54–5.

72 Beaufort memorandum, 28 Jan. 1850: SPRI MS 248/344/2.

73 Parry to Beaufort, 2 Feb. 1850: UKHO MISC 12/1/21.

74 Beaufort 12 (Feb.?) 1850: SPRI MS 248/344/1. Beaufort to Jane, 18 Dec. 1849: SPRI MS 248/343/2.

75 Inglis and Baring: Hansard, vol. CIX, p. 738, 12 March 1850. 29 Navy estimates: Hansard, vol. CXIII, p. 472, July 1850.

76 Parry to Captain Hamilton (private), 7 Feb. 1850: ADM 7/190, section 1.

77 Minute on Dr King's proposal of 23 Feb. 1850: ADM 7/188, section 12.

78 Beaufort to Sabine, 2 March 1850: RS Sabine MS 257, f. 117. Ommaney to Ross, 25 Feb. 1850: BJ2/9 7–8. Sabine to Beaufort, 23 April 1850, BJ3/79, f. 245.

79 Ommaney to Beaufort, 8 March and 27 and 30 April 1850: UKHO MISC 7/3/1–3.

80 McClintock to Sabine 17 and 26 Jan. and 9 Feb. 1850: RS Sabine MS 259, ff. 847–51.

81 ADM 7/190, section 2.

82 Sabine to Beaufort, 3 Dec. 1851: BJ3/79, f. 288.

83 Franklin to Robert Brown, 9 July 1845: SPRI MS 248/296/19.

CHAPTER 10: Defeated, Deceived and Defrauded

1 Delane to Hamilton, 15 Oct. 1850: ADM 7/190, section 4. A. I. Dasent, *John Thadeus Delane: Editor of "The Times"*, 2 vols. (London, 1908).

2 Admiralty minute, 28 Oct. 1850: ADM 7/191, section 1. Richardson to Hamilton, 10 Oct. 1850 encl. telegraph message Rae to Richardson requesting Richardson's consent to publish on 11 Oct. 1850. The letter appeared in *The Times* on 13 Oct. 1850.

3 Dundas minute, 11 Feb. 1851: ADM 7/190, section 2.

4 Stewart, Milne and Cowper minutes, 14 March 1851: ADM 7/190, section 2.

5 Decision of February 1851. These files ADM 7/187–200 are the basis of Franklin studies.

6 Barrow note, Feb. 1851: ADM 7/187, f. 1.

7 David, p. 64. Stafford.

8 Russell to Murchison, 26 March 1852: Add. 46,217, f. 485.

9 Inglis, Baring, Buxton and Berkeley: Hansard, vol. CXV, pp. 340–2, 31 March 1851.

10 Richardson to Murchison, 24 June 1851: Add. 46,217, f. 436. T. Martin, *The Life of His Royal Highness the Prince Consort*, 5 vols. (London, 1875–80), II, pp. 379–81.

11 Barrow to Hamilton, 29 Oct. 1851: ADM 7/190, section 2.

12 Jane to Murchison, 12 Feb. 1852: Add. 46,216, f. 184.

13 In the end he was passed over for promotion, retiring in 1857, apparently unsuited to leading the office.

14 Barrow to Hamilton, 1 Nov. 1851: ADM 7/190, section 2.

15 Barrow to Hamilton, 3 Nov. 1851: ADM 7/190, section 2.

16 Colonel Phipps to Hamilton, 15 Sept. 1851; Jane to Admiralty, 12 Sept. 1851: ADM 7/190, section 3.

17 Cyriax, *Last Expedition*, p. 108.

18 Richardson to Parry, 3 Oct. 1851: ADM 7/192, section 1. Both men worked at Haslar Hospital.

19 Parry to Captain Hamilton, 30 Sept. 1851: ADM 7/192, f. 448.

20 W. Barr (ed.), *Emile Frédéric de Bray, A Frenchman in Search of Franklin: Arctic Journal, 1852–1854* (Toronto, 1992).

21 Board minutes, 14 June 1851; Cowper minute, 20 June 1851: ADM 7/192, ff. 290–2.

22 Admiralty to Jane, 2 July 1851: ADM 7/192. Hamilton signed the letter as secretary, and the convention was that he could employ a degree of personal input when corresponding with known individuals.

23 *Morning Herald*, 11 Sept. 1851: ADM 7/192, f. 112.

24 Jane to Captain Hamilton, 24 Sept. 1851: ADM 7/192, section 28.

25 *The Times* leader article, 7 Oct. 1851: ADM 7/192, ff. 104–5.

26 Baring to Russell, 8 Oct. 1851: PRO 30/22/9G, f. 81.

27 Printed appeal for the funds to send the *Prince Albert* on another mission: MPI 315 (5). Ross to John Barrow, 20 Feb. 1851: ADM 7/192, section 23, f. 334.

28 *Morning Herald*, 13 Oct. 1852: ADM 7/192, f. 365.

29 *Morning Chronicle*, 8 April 1851: ADM 7/192, f. 337.

30 G. Jackson, *The British Whaling Trade* (London, 1978), pp. 117, 120–1, 127–30. L. E. Davis, R. E. Gullman and K. Gleiter, *In Pursuit of Leviathan: Technology, Institutions, Productivity and Profits in American Whaling, 1816–1900* (Chicago, 1997), pp. 477–80.

31 D. Hayes, *Historical Atlas of the North Pacific Ocean* (London, 2001), pp. 154–5. J. Schroeder, *Shaping a Maritime Empire: The Commercial and Diplomatic Role of the American Navy, 1829–1861* (Westport, Conn., 1985), pp. 159–60.

32 Davis, Gullman and Gleiter, p. 342.

33 Davis, *Second Expedition*, pp. 15–24.

34 M. F. Robinson, *The Coldest Crucible: Arctic Exploration and American Culture* (Chicago, 2006), p. 25.

35 *Dictionary of American Biography*, vol. VIII (New York, 1932), p. 2.

36 Robinson, pp. 26–8.

37 F. L. Williams, *Matthew Fontaine Maury, Scientist of the Sea* (New Brunswick, 1963), pp. 202, 539–40.

38 J. R. Bockstoce, *Whales, Ice and Men: The History of Whaling in the Western Arctic* (Seattle, 1986), pp. 299 and 369.

39 Sophia Cracroft to Admiralty, 8 June 1850; Lawrence to Baring, 4 Jan. 1852: ADM 7/192, section 3. B. Wilson, *America's Ambassadors to England, 1785–1928* (London, 1928), pp. 260–70.

40 Wilkes to *National Intelligencer*, 26 Jan. 1852. Half a million dollars was about £100,000 in contemporary English money.

41 Jane to President Zachary Taylor, 27 Jan. 1852; *Morning Post*, 22 Jan. 1852: ADM 7/192, section 3.

42 Parry to Murchison, 11 March 1852: Wellcome MS 7401/14. Grinnell to
Murchison, 29 March 1852: Add. 46,216, f. 338.

43 Admiralty to Penny, 18 Sept. 1851 to Jane 19 Sept. 1851 and to Commodore Eden
(Woolwich), 30 Sept. 1851: ADM 7/193, ff. 7, 12 and 13.

44 Admiralty to Austin, 9 Oct. 1851: ADM 7/193, f. 9.

45 Bowles was the brother-in-law of the foreign secretary Lord Palmerston and a
friend of Franklin.

46 Admiralty to Bowles, 5 Dec. 1851: ADM 7/193, ff. 144–6.

47 Board minutes, 2 Oct. 1851: ADM 7/193, f. 233.

48 Barrow to The Times, 5 Jan. 1852: ADM 7/192, section 2.

49 Published in The Times on 14 April 1852: ADM 7/194, ff. 4, 8, 91.

50 Jane to Admiralty, 20 April 1852: ADM 7/194, f. 247. Sabine to Beaufort, 18 Feb.
1853: ADM 7/195, f. 650.

51 Kane to Beaufort, 18 May 1853: ADM 7/195, f. 654.

52 ADM 7/195, ff. 685–713.

53 Murchison to Jane, 4 and 6 Nov. 1852: SPRI MS 248/221/1–2.

54 Jane quoted in The Times, 26 Aug. 1852 and Beaufort memo for the Duke of
Northumberland (First Lord), 24 March 1852: ADM 7/194, ff. 4, 166.

55 W. Barr, 'Franklin in Siberia? – Lieutenant Bedford Pim's Proposal to Search the
Arctic Coast of Siberia 1851–52', Arctic, 45 (1992), pp. 36–46.

56 Murchison to Russell, 12 Nov. 1851: PRO 30/22/9H, f. 99.

57 Robert Brown to Murchison, 21 Oct. 1851: Add. 46,215, f. 250.

58 Beaufort to Sophia Cracroft, 21 Oct. 1851: SPRI MS 248/342/1.

59 The Times, 10 Nov. 1851.

60 Board minutes, 13 Oct. 1851 and Murchison to Baring, 12 Nov. 1851: ADM
7/192, f. 129.

61 Board minute, 14 Nov. 1851: ADM 7/192, f. 127.

62 Brunnow to Murchison, n.d.: Add. 46,215, f. 278.

63 Murchison to Russell, 12 Nov. 1851: PRO 30/22/9H, f. 99. G. P. Gooch (ed.),
Later Correspondence of Lord John Russell, 2 vols. (New York, 1925), I, p. 204,
contains a letter from Murchison to Russell of 1850 about science, the Royal
Society and Sir John Herschel, whom he knew well.

64 Jane to Murchison, Nov. 1851: Add. 46,216, f. 175.

65 Murchison to Russell, 16 Nov. 1851 (Sunday): PRO 30/22/9H, f. 131.

66 Murchison to Russell, 17 Nov. 1851 (Monday night): PRO 30/22/9H, f. 129.
Official thanks from the RGS came later: Woodbine Parish to Lord J. Russell, 25
Nov. 1851: Add. 46,217, f. 353.

67 Lord John Russell to Murchison, 13 Nov. 1851: Add. 46,217, f. 487.

68 Baring to Russell, 14 Nov. 1851 (Admiralty): PRO 30/22/9H, f. 119.

69 Barrow to Murchison, 15 Nov. (1851): Add. 46,215, ff. 103–6.

70 Ellesmere to Murchison, 19 Nov. 1851: Add. 46,216, f. 86 reports his failure.

71 Sabine to Murchison, 15 Nov. 1851: Add. 46,218, f. 9.

72 Both Woodbine Parish, vice-president of the Geographical Society, and Sir
Hamilton Seymour, ambassador at St Petersburg, were discouraging. Parish to
Murchison, 16 Nov. 1851: Add. 46,217, f. 349 and Seymour to Murchison: Add.
46,218, ff. 56–85.

73 Duke of Northumberland to Murchison, 20 Nov. 1851: Add. 46,217, f. 279. Jane
to Murchison, 21 Nov. 1851: Add. 46,216, f. 179.

74 Murchison to The Times, 18 Nov. 1851: The Times, 19 Nov. 1851: ADM 7/192,
f. 125.

75 C. R. Weld to Murchison, 27 Nov. 1851 (Royal Society): Add. 46,218, f. 269. Charles Richard Weld (1813–69) married Franklin's niece Agnes, younger sister of Tennyson's wife, in 1842: *Oxford Dictionary of National Biography*, www.oxforddnb.com/view/printable/28982, accessed 13 Oct. 2005. Weld was author of *A History of the Royal Society* (London, 1848) and *Arctic Expeditions* (London, 1850).

76 Osborn to Barrow, 'Friday' (Dec. 1851?): Add. 35,306, f. 42.

77 Murchison to Russell, 14 Dec. 1851: PRO 30/22/9J, f. 155.

78 Barr, 'Franklin in Siberia?', pp. 40–1.

79 *The Times*, 31 Jan. 1852: ADM 7/192, f. 143. Barr, 'Franklin in Siberia?', p. 44. Markham, *Arctic Navy List*, pp. 42–3. Pim had a fascinating career after he left the Arctic. He went on the *Resolute* under Kellett in 1852–4, commanded gunboats during the Crimean War and became a significant figure in Murchison's geological empire.

80 Barr, 'Franklin in Siberia?', p. 43.

81 Sir Hamilton Seymour (ambassador at St Petersburg) to Murchison, 24 Feb. 1852: Add. 46,218, ff. 56–7.

82 Board minutes, 19 Nov. 1851: ADM 7/192, section 21.

83 *Morning Chronicle*, 28 Nov. 1851: ADM 7/192, section 24, f. 383.

84 Jane to Murchison, 31 Dec. 1851: Add. 46,216, f. 177.

85 Jane to Murchison, 10 Jan. 1852: Add. 46,216, f. 182.

86 Earl of Ellesmere to Murchison, 7 Jan. 1852: Add. 46,216, f. 88 gives £100 for Beatson. Fitzhardinge to Murchison, 17 Jan. 1852: Add. 46,216, f. 163 sends £5.

87 Ellesmere to Murchison 7 (?) 1852: LDGSL 838, ME19/3.

88 Murchison to Russell, 29 Jan. 1852: PRO 30/22/10A, f. 161.

89 Beatson to Murchison, 5 March 1852: Add. 46,215, f. 140. Barr, 'Franklin in Siberia?', p. 44.

90 Beatson to Murchison, 21 and 31 Jan. 1852: Add. 46,215, ff. 136–8.

91 Jane to Murchison, 12 Feb. 1852: Add. 46,216, f. 184.

92 Jane to Murchison, 21 Feb. 1852: Add. 46,216, ff. 188–91.

93 Inglis to Murchison, 17 and 26 Feb. 1852: Add. 46,216, ff. 469, 471. Inglis lived at 7 Bedford Square, close to Franklin.

94 Murchison to Northumberland, 9 March 1852: endorsed, ADM 7/192, f. 391. Augustus Stafford (first secretary to the Admiralty) to Murchison, 9 March 1852: Add. 46,218, f. 111. Northumberland was a friend of Franklin.

95 Murchison to Northumberland, 18 March 1852 with Admiralty marginalia for the Accountant General: Northumberland to Murchison, 22 March 1852: ADM 7/192, f. 391.

96 Hansard, vol. CXIX, pp. 967–701, 2 March 1852. The speakers were Chisholm Anstey, Augustus Stafford, Sir Robert Inglis, Captain Scobell, John Parker and Maurice Berkeley. Inglis and Stafford were Conservatives.

97 Jane to Murchison, 21 March 1852: Add. 46,216, f. 194.

98 Jane to Murchison, 25 March 1852: Add. 46,216, f. 192.

99 Beatson to Jane, 26 March 1852: Add. 46,215, f. 142.

100 Jane to Murchison, 26 March 1852: Add. 46,216, f. 196.

101 Jane to Murchison, 28 March 1852: Add. 46,216, f. 197.

102 Jane to Murchison, 20 April 1852: Add. 46,216, f. 199.

103 Jane to Murchison, 26 April 1852: Add. 46,216, f. 201.

104 Jane to Murchison, 28 April 1852: Add. 46,216, f. 203.

105 Jane to Duke of Northumberland, 29 April 1852; Board minute, 1 May 1852: ADM 7/192, ff. 394–5.

106 Murchison to Northumberland, 27 May 1852: ADM 7/192, f. 400.
107 Pim to Murchison, 28 April 1852: Add. 46,217, f. 391, HMS *Resolute* at Stromness.
108 Richardson to Murchison, 4 May 1852: Add. 46,217, f. 446.
109 Sabine to Murchison, 29 June (1852?): Add. 46,218, f. 26.
110 Barrow to Murchison, 30 Jan. 1852: Add. 46,215, f. 107.
111 Sabine to Beaufort, 30 Jan. 1852: BJ3/79, f. 292.
112 Levere, pp. 215–16.
113 J. Bockstoce, *Journal of Rochefort Maguire, HMS Plover, 1852–1854*, 2 vols. (London, 1988), I, pp. 109–11, 131–4, 286–91.
114 E. Sabine, 'On Hourly Observations of the Magnetic Declination . . . HMS *Plover* 1852, 1853 and 1854, at Point Barrow', *Philosophical Transactions*, 147 (1857), pp. 497–532 at pp. 506–7.
115 Parry to Murchison, 11 March 1852: Wellcome MS 7401/14.

CHAPTER 11: Belcher

1 Lady Franklin quoted in *The Times* of 26 Aug. 1852 and Beaufort memo for the Duke of Northumberland (First Lord), 24 March 1852: ADM 7/194, ff. 4, 166.
2 Beaufort memo, 24 Nov. 1848: Friendly, p. 315.
3 Beaufort to McCormick, 17 Jan. 1850: Friendly, p. 315.
4 Beaufort to Collinson, 10 Dec. 1849: Collinson, p. 11.
5 Friendly, p. 317n.
6 Stafford, pp. 54, 148. Sabine to Beaufort, 3 Jan. 1843: UKHO Minute Book 4, p. 72.
7 Belcher's testimony at his court martial: ADM 1/5645, f. 174.
8 Parker to Belcher, n.d.; also Parker to Belcher, 18 Sept. (?). A. Phillimore, *Life and Letters of Admiral Sir William Parker*, vol. II (London, 1878), pp. 616–19. Sadly Belcher did not take the hint, ending his career under a similar cloud.
9 Courtney, p. 283.
10 Sabine to Lefroy, 7 Oct. 1852: ADM 1/4282, ff. 22–5.
11 Sabine to Beaufort, 8 April 1852: BJ3/79, f. 293.
12 Sabine to Beaufort 15 and 16 April 1852: BJ3/79, ff. 295–6.
13 Belcher memo, 1 Jan. 1852: ADM 1/5615, ff. 467–81.
14 Beaufort memo, 22 Jan. 1852: ADM 1/5615, f. 458.
15 Cresswell to Stafford, 23 March 1852: ADM 1/5615, Pro. C194. D. Harrod (ed.), *War, Ice and Piracy: The Remarkable Career of a Victorian Sailor. The Journals and Letters of Samuel Gurney Cresswell* (London, 2000), pp. 79–80.
16 Parry to Northumberland, 25 March 1852: ADM 1/5615, f. 453.
17 Milne memo, 27 March 1852: ADM 1/5615, f. 461.
18 Beaufort, Milne, Barrow, Parry to Admiralty, April 1852, and *Morning Chronicle*, 11 Oct. 1852: ADM 7/194, ff. 264–91.
19 Hamilton to Barrow, 5 Nov. 1852: ADM 7/194, f. 422.
20 Hamilton to Milne, 5 Nov. 1852: ADM 7/194, f. 423.
21 Barrow to Hamilton, 30 June 1852: ADM 7/191, section 12. A. D. Lambert, *Trincomalee: The Last of Nelson's Frigates* (London, 2002), pp. 85–106.
22 Admiralty instructions to Belcher, 16 April 1852: Add. 35,307.
23 Jane to Murchison, 4 Nov. 1852: Add. 46,216, f. 209.
24 Hayes, *Arctic*, map at p. 90. Richardson to Murchison, 4 and 25 March 1852: Add. 46,217, ff. 438 and 442.

25 Rae to Sabine, 8 June 1852 (Hyde Park): BJ3/32, f. 74. Rae to Murchison, 11 June 1852: Add. 46,217, f. 408.

26 Sabine to Beaufort, 24 Feb. 1853: BJ3/79, ff. 307–8.

27 E. K. Kane, *Magnetical Observations in the Arctic Seas, 1853–1855* (Washington, DC, 1859).

28 Ommaney to Beaufort, 23 June 1852 (Whale Fish Islands): UKHO MISC 7/3/4.

29 Ommaney to Beaufort, 26 July 1852: UKHO MISC 7/3/10.

30 Jane to Murchison, 22 May 1852: Add. 46,216, ff. 205–8.

31 Inglefield to Murchison, 14 Sept. 1852: Add. 46,216, ff. 456–68. Savours, *Search*, pp. 247–9.

32 H. N. Wallace, *The Navy, the Company and Richard King* (Montreal, 1980), p. 129.

33 Wallace, p. 138.

34 The investigators found their situation cramped and awkward: W. Barr, 'A Warrant Officer in the Arctic: The Journal of George Ford, 1850–1854', in A. Frost and J. Samson (eds), *Pacific Empires: Essays in Honour of Glyndwr Williams* (Vancouver, 1999), pp. 101–23 at pp. 111–13.

35 A very positive view of Kellett's mission is recorded in Barr, *Emile Frédéric de Bray*, pp. 9, 66, 84–5, 155. Bedford Pim turned out to be a fine magician and capable geology lecturer. Milne memo, 27 Jan. 1853: ADM 7/194, f. 416.

36 Admiralty orders to Belcher, 11 May 1853: ADM 7/194, f. 432.

37 Beaufort to Sabine, 23 Nov. 1853: RS Sabine MS 257, f. 121.

38 Beaufort to Sabine, 6 Dec. 1853: RS Sabine MS 257, f. 122.

39 Beaufort to Sabine, 21 Sept. 1857: RS Sabine MS 257, f. 125, Levere, pp. 215–16.

40 J. Bockstoce, introduction to Barr, *Arctic Hell Ship*, p. viii.

41 Richards to T. Collinson, 2 Oct. 1889: Collinson, p. xi.

42 G. Williams, p. 539.

43 M. F. Maury, *The Physical Geography of the Sea*, 6th edn (London, 1874; 1st edn New York, 1855), pp. 199–207.

44 G. Williams, p. 540.

45 Levere, p. 221.

46 Levere, pp. 221–3.

47 Richardson to Beaufort, 14 Feb. 1853: UKHO LB 7/20/27. Parry to Beaufort, 16 Feb. 1853: UKHO MISC 12/1/22.

48 Robinson, pp. 31–45.

49 Revd John Barlow (British Institute) to Murchison, 6 Oct. 1853: Add. 46,215, f. 95.

50 *The Times*, 24 Oct. 1853. Parry and Ross to Barrow, 10 Oct. 1853: ADM 7/195, ff. 78–86.

51 Dundas to Barrow, 27 Oct. 1853: ADM 7/195, f. 99.

52 Milne memo, 26 Dec. 1853 and Graham minute, 30 Dec. 1853: J. Beeler (ed.), *The Milne Papers*, vol. I (Aldershot, 2004), pp. 374–5.

53 Parry to Murchison, 5 Nov. 1853: LDGSL 838, MP30 and Bellot Fund Testimonial MB50.

54 ADM 7/195, f. 107. The Bellot memorial cost £494 10s 2d with foundations: Add. 46,216, f. 383.

55 Text on the reverse of the monument.

56 French foreign minister Drouyn de l'Huys to Murchison: Add. 46,216, f. 62.

57 *Liverpool Albion*, 31 Oct. 1853: ADM 7/195, f. 103.

58 Jane to Barrow, 7 Nov. 1853: ADM 7/195, f. 134. This letter, like many more in what is ostensibly an official collection, is quite clearly unofficial and personal to Barrow. Like his father, John Barrow Jr had conflated his public and private spheres.

59 *London Gazette*, 20 Jan. 1854 and *Morning Herald*, 23 Jan. 1854: ADM 7/195, ff. 735, 752.

60 Inglis to Jane, 6 March 1854: SPRI MS 248/429.

61 Jane to Admiralty, 24 Feb. 1854: Levere, pp. 218–19. Arctic Blue Books, University of Manitoba Web Site: www.umanitoba.ca/faculties/arts/anthropology/bluebooks/.

62 Disraeli to Jane, 7 April 1854: B. Disraeli, *Benjamin Disraeli Letters: 1852–1856*, ed. M. G. Wiebe and M. S. Millar (Toronto, 1997), pp. 334–5.

63 Hansard, vol. CXXXII, pp. 437–41, 4 April 1854.

64 Jane to Murchison, 5 April 1854 (4 Spring Gardens): Add. 46,216, f. 215. Cobden to Jane, 11 April 1854 (Midhurst): Add. 46,216, f. 219 (copy). Jane to Murchison, 12 April 1854: Add. 46,216, ff. 217–18.

65 Admiralty to Belcher, 28 April 1854: ADM 7/199.

66 Wallace, p. 139: Maclure to J. C. Ross, 15 Sept. and 3 Oct. 1854: BJ2/10, ff. 20–5.

67 *The Times*, 21 Oct. 1854: ADM 7/199, f. 326.

68 Belcher court martial: ADM 1/5645.

69 Belcher to Sabine, 11 Nov. 1854: RS Sabine MS 257, f. 128.

70 E. Belcher, *The Last of the Arctic Voyages: Being a Narrative of the Expedition in HMS Assistance* (London, 1855); Savours, *Search*, p. 243.

71 Beaufort to Murchison, April 1854: Friendly, p. 321.

CHAPTER 12: Martyrs of Science

1 Rae to Admiralty, 29 July 1854 (Repulse Bay), rec'd 24 Oct. 1854: ADM 7/199, f. 237.

2 W. Barr (ed.), *Searching for Franklin: The Land Arctic Searching Expedition. James Anderson's and James Stewart's Expedition via the Back River* (London, 1999), pp. 13–18.

3 *The Times*, 23 and 24 Oct. 1854: ADM 7/199, ff. 327–8.

4 *Morning Herald*, 25 Oct. 1854: ADM 7/199, f. 330.

5 *Illustrated London News*, 4 Nov. 1854: ADM 7/199, f. 335.

6 Admiralty to Hudson's Bay Company, 24 Oct. 1854: ADM 7/199, f. 280.

7 Rae Report, 26 Oct. 1854: *The Times*, 27 Oct. 1854, p. 8.

8 Rich, *History*, II, pp. 794–7.

9 Barr, *Searching for Franklin*, p. 81.

10 Lord Malmesbury, *Memoirs of an Ex-Minister*, 2 vols. (London, 1884), I, pp. 441–2, diary entry 25 Oct. 1854.

11 J. A. Auerbach, *The Great Exhibition of 1851: A Nation on Display* (New Haven, 1999).

12 Malchow, pp. 105–10.

13 A. W. Brian Simpson, *Cannibalism and the Common Law: A Victorian Yachting Tragedy* (Chicago, 1984).

14 Murchison to Jane, 12 Nov. 1854: SPRI MS 248/221–3.

15 Kellet, Richardson and Back to T B. Collinson (Collinson's brother), 27 and 28 Oct. 1854; Graham to Mrs de Winter (Collinson's sister), 7 Nov. 1854: Collinson MS NMM CL 47.

16 Jane to Murchison, 6 Nov. 1854: Add. 46,216, f. 220. Sophia Cracroft to Murchison, 6–7 Nov. 1854: Add. 46,215, ff. 428–33.

17 *The Times*, 26 Oct. 1854.

18 Dickens to Mrs Watson, 1 Nov. 1854: G. Storey, K. Tillotson and A. Easson (eds), *The Letters of Charles Dickens*, vol. VII, *1853–1855* (Oxford, 1993), pp. 455–6. Slater, pp. 254–68.

19 Dickens to Miss Burdett-Coutts, 20 Nov. 1854: Storey et al., vol. VII, p. 471.

20 Dickens to W. H. Wills, 27 Nov. 1854: Storey et al., vol. VII, p. 473. Dickens to Jane, 30 Nov. 1854: Storey et al., vol. VII, p. 474.

21 'The Lost Arctic Voyagers', 23 Dec. 1854, in H. Stone (ed.), *The Uncollected Writings of Charles Dickens: Household Words, 1850–1859*, vol. II (London, 1969), pp. 513–22. Slater, p. 268.

22 G. L. Carr, *Frederic Edwin Church: The Icebergs* (Dallas, 1980), p. 89.

23 P. van der Merwe, *Clarkson Stanfield, 1793–1867* (Gateshead, 1979), pp. 160–1. Murchison to Sophia Cracroft, n.d.: SPRI MS 248/224.

24 McGoogan, *Fatal Passage*, p. 273.

25 Jane to Admiralty, Dec. 1854: ADM 1/5642, Pro. F374.

26 Beaufort to Jane, 20 Nov. 1854: SPRI MS 248/343/4.

27 Memo on the above dated 4 Dec. 1854: SPRI MS 248/343/4.

28 Sophia Cracroft to Anderson, 15 Dec. 1854: Barr, *Searching for Franklin*, pp. 61–2.

29 Sophia Cracroft to Murchison, 19 Jan. 1855: Add. 46,215, f. 438.

30 Murchison to Sir Charles Wood, 15 March 1855: Add. 49,554, f. 147.

31 Stafford emphasises Murchison's truly global ambitions. Jane to Murchison, 19 March (1855) (60 Pall Mall): Add. 46,216, ff. 223–4.

32 McClure to MPs, 24 April 1855: Add. 35,307, f. 69. McClure's printed memorial to House of Commons, 24 April 1855: Add. 35,308, f. 71.

33 Hansard, vol. CXXXVIII, pp. 2242–6, 19 June 1855.

34 Sophia Cracroft to Murchison, 7 June 1855: Add. 46,215, f. 449.

35 Jane to Palmerston, 26 June 1855, Southampton University, Hartley Library, Palmerston MS GC/FR3, endorsed 'wishing another expedition to the Arctic Region'.

36 Sophia Cracroft to Murchison, 28 June 1855: Add. 46,215, f. 442.

37 Jane to Murchison, n.d. (60 Pall Mall): Add. 46,216, f. 230.

38 Sophia Cracroft to Murchison, 6 July 1855: Add. 46,215, f. 444.

39 Richard Collinson to Sophia Cracroft, 6 July 1855: Add. 46,215, f. 448.

40 Committee of Supply: Hansard, vol. CXXXIX, pp. 1585–8, 31 July 1855.

41 Captain Washington minute, 12 May 1858: ADM 1/5707, Pro. S222. Barr, 'A Warrant Officer in the Arctic'.

42 F. Woodward, p. 290.

43 Jane to Murchison, 15 Nov. 1852 (is 1855) (162 Albany St): Add. 46,216, f. 211.

44 Jane to Murchison, 20 and 30 Nov. 1855 (162 Albany St): Add. 46,216, ff. 225–7.

45 The piece was also reprinted as a pamphlet.

46 Dickens to John Forster, 2 March 1856: G. Storey and K. Tillotson (eds), *The Letters of Charles Dickens*, vol. VIII, *1856–1858* (Oxford, 1995), p. 66. Jane had sent him the article.

47 D. Lyon and R. Winfield, *The Sail and Steam Navy List* (London, 2004), pp. 241–2.

48 Collinson to Barrow, 24 Dec. 1855: Add. 35,308, f. 66. The book did not appear in Collinson's lifetime.

49 For a full collection of Rae's correspondence on the subject see E. E. Rich (ed.), *John Rae's Correspondence with the Hudson's Bay Company on Arctic Exploration, 1844–1855* (London, 1953), p. xc.

50 Foreign Office to Admiralty, 2 Nov. 1855; reply, 7 Jan. 1855 and Washington minute, 5 Nov. 1855: ADM 7/200, f. 2.

51 K. Bourne, *Great Britain and the Balance of Power in North America, 1815–1908* (London, 1967), pp. 179–205 for a more confrontational perspective on Anglo-American relations at this period. A. Dowty, *The Limits of American Isolation: The United States and the Crimean War* (New York, 1971).

52 Admiralty memo, 25 April 1856 and Grinnell to Ambassador Crampton, 18 March 1856: *The Times*, 28 April 1856, p. 9.

53 *The Times*, 9 Jan. 1856, p. 10.

54 Sophia Cracroft to Murchison, 4 March 1856: Add. 46,215, f. 451.

55 Jane to Murchison, 26 Jan. 1856 (60 Pall Mall): Add. 46,216, f. 234.

56 Collinson to Sophia Cracroft, 12 Dec. 1855: Add. 35,308, f. 33. Collinson to Barrow, 17 Dec. 1855: Add. 35,308, f. 35. Jane to Barrow, 3 Dec. 1855: Add. 35,308, f. 392.

57 British Museum to Barrow, 23 Nov. 1855: Add. 35,308, f. 409. Barrow: ADM 7/200, f. 1.

58 Barrow Testimonial, 28 June 1856: Add. 35,308, f. 39; table piece, f. 42.

59 McClure to Barrow, 20 June 1857: Add. 35,308, f. 74.

60 McClure to Barrow, 24 May and 4 June 1856 (HMS *Esk*, Devonport): Add. 35,308, ff. 82, 84.

61 McClure to Ross, 9 Oct. 1855 (13 Welbeck Street): BJ2/10, f. 17. McClure to Ross, 3 May 1860: BJ2/10, ff. 3–11.

62 McClure to Barrow, 8 June 1856: Add. 35,308, f. 88.

63 Rich, *John Rae's Correspondence*, pp. lxxxviii–xcii, 265–97.

64 Washington minute, 2 June 1856; Peel minute, 6 June 1856; Admiralty minute, 20 June 1856: ADM 7/200, f. 272.

65 Washington minute, 2 June 1856: ADM 7/200, f. 272.

66 'The Great Arctic Mystery' and 'Arctic Rewards and Their Claimants of 1856' (31pp., London, 1856), are the last items in the official record: ADM 7/200.

67 'Arctic Rewards and their Claimants', p. 30.

68 Jane to Admiralty, 15 April 1856: ADM 7/200, f. 204. Jane to Barrow, 2 June 1856: Add. 35,305, f. 331.

69 Sophia Cracroft to Murchison, 2 June 1856: Add. 46,215, f. 457.

70 Lord Stanley (15th Earl of Derby, son of the Lord Stanley of 1843) to Murchison, 6 June 1856: Add. 46,218, f. 115.

71 Kane to Grinnell, n.d.: Add. 49,531, f. 154.

72 Jane to Admiralty, 9 May 1856: ADM 7/200, f. 204.

73 Murchison to Palmerston, 8 June 1856: Add. 49,531, f. 152.

74 Jane to Murchison, 20 June 1856 (60 Pall Mall): Add. 46,216, f. 239.

75 Jane to Murchison, 18 Feb. n.d.: Add. 46,216, f. 238. For Murchison's long-term links with *Times* editor John Delane, see LDGSL 838, MD34/1–11.

76 Levere, p. 225.

77 Levere, pp. 215–16. Sabine, pp. 506–7.

78 Jane to Murchison, 22 June 1856 (60 Pall Mall): Add. 46,216, f. 241.

79 Jane to Murchison, 22 June 1856 (60 Pall Mall): Add. 46,216, f. 241.

80 George Douglas, 8th Duke of Argyll, *Autobiography and Memoirs*, vol. I (London, 1906), p. 577. Argyll, a noted amateur scientist, was an early member of the BAAS.

81 Jane to Murchison, 6 p.m., n.d. (1856?): Add. 46,216, f. 249.

82 David, pp. 81-9.

83 His correspondence contains friendly and supportive letters on this and a host of other geographical, geological and scientific issues from leading politicians, foreign ambassadors and John Delane.

84 Sabine to Murchison, 10 Feb. n.d.: LDGSL 838, MS1/2.

85 Beaufort to Murchison, 6 July 1856: Add. 46,215, f. 144. Beaufort to Sophia Cracroft, 15 July 1856: SPRI MS 248/342/2. Francis Egerton (1800-57), 1st Earl of Ellesmere, *Oxford Dictionary of National Biography*, www.oxforddnb.com/view/printable/8585, accessed 17 Nov. 2004.

86 Hansard, vol. CXLXIII, pp. 401-2, 7 July 1856.

87 Jane to Admiralty, 11 July 1856: ADM 1/5679.

88 John, 2nd Baron Wrottesley (1798-1867), astronomer, *Oxford Dictionary of National Biography*, www.oxforddnb.com/view/printable/30089, accessed 17 Nov. 2004.

89 House of Lords 'Further Arctic Expedition': Hansard, vol. CXLCIII, pp. 1,008-13, 18 July 1856; Wrottesley, my italics.

90 Palmerston to Wood, 18 Aug. 1856: Add. 49,531, f. 150.

91 Sabine to Sophia Cracroft, 27 Oct. 1856: SPRI MS 248/469/1.

92 Jane to Murchison, n.d.: Add. 46,216, f. 251.

93 F. Woodward, p. 291.

94 *The Times*, 27 Nov. 1856.

95 Jane to Murchison, 6 p.m., 30 (?) 1856: Add. 46,216, f. 245.

96 Barrow to Murchison, 27 Nov. 1856: Add. 46,215, ff. 111-13. Sophia Cracroft to Murchison, Sunday night, n.d.: Add. 46,215, f. 473.

97 Grinnell to Barrow, 19 Sept. 1856: Add. 35,305, f. 332.

98 Captain John Lort Stokes RN to Murchison, 3 Dec. (1856?): Add. 46,218, f. 146.

99 Sophia Cracroft to Murchison, 4 Dec. 1856: Add. 46,215, f. 461.

100 Jane to Murchison, 6 p.m., 8 Dec. 1856: Add. 46,216, f. 247.

101 Wilson, pp. 294-311. F. Woodward, p. 292.

102 Palmerston to Wood, 13 Dec. 1856: Add. 49,531, f. 158.

103 Stafford, p. 174.

104 Wood to Palmerston, 16 Dec. 1856: Add. 49,531, f. 161.

105 Jane to Murchison, n.d.: Add. 46,216, f. 256. Hartstene to Murchison, 16 and 17 Dec. 1856: Wellcome MS 5220/51-2.

106 Jane to Barrow, 10 Jan. 1857: Add. 35,307, f. 393.

107 McClintock to Sophia Cracroft, 8 Feb. 1857 (Dublin): SPRI MS 248/439, f. 10. Jane to Murchison, Friday, n.d.: Add. 46,216, f. 253.

108 Sophia Cracroft to Murchison, 7 Feb. 1857: Add. 46,215, f. 465. McClintock to Sophia Cracroft, 2 Feb. 1857: SPRI MS 248/439/9. Sir Joseph Napier (1804-82), MP for Trinity College, Dublin, Irish Attorney General in Lord Derby's 1852 administration, *Oxford Dictionary of National Biography*, www.oxforddnb.com/articles/19/19759-article.html, accessed 16 Nov. 2004.

109 Murchison to Sophia Cracroft, n.d., rec'd 16 Feb. 1857: SPRI MS 248/224.

110 Palmerston to Wood, 17 Feb. 1857: Add. 49,531, f. 167.

111 Grinnell to Barrow, 24 Feb. 1857: Add. 35,305, f. 341.

112 Palmerston to Wood, 19 Feb. 1857: Add. 49,531, f. 169.

113 Palmerston to Wood, 22 Feb. 1857: Add. 49,531, f. 172.

114 Jane to Monckton Milnes, 25 Feb. 1857: T. W. Reid, *The Life, Letters, and Friendships of Richard Monckton Milnes, First Lord Houghton*, 2 vols. (London,

1890), II, pp. 15–16. In the 1860s, if not before, Milnes was on close terms with Sabine and Murchison in the RGS/RS nexus.

115 Beaufort to Sophia Cracroft, rec'd 13 and 17 March 1857: SPRI MS 248/342, ff. 3–4.

116 Washington to Murchison, 22 April 1857: Add. 46,218, f. 254; first of three letters about Livingstone, Africa, the Zambesi and deep-sea soundings. Stafford, pp. 41–55, 95, 150, 176–7 and 213.

117 Sophia Cracroft to Murchison, 16 March (1856?): Add. 46,215, f. 471.

118 Jane to Wood, 4 April 1857: ADM 1/5688, f. 83 and Wood's draft reply.

119 Murchison to Wood, 5 April 1857: Add. 49,560, ff. 26–31.

120 McClintock to Jane, 6 April 1857: SPRI MS 248/439/22. Murchison to Palmerston, 5 April 1857: Southampton University, Hartley Library, Palmerston MS GC/MU, f. 5, encl. resolution of the Royal Dublin Society, 3 April 1857.

121 Murchison to Wood, 8 April 1857: Add. 49,560, f. 37. Murchison to Jane, n.d., rec'd 9 April 1857: SPRI MS 248/221/4.

122 'A Friend to the Cause', 16 April 1857: *The Times*, 17 April 1857, p. 10. McClintock to Jane, 18 April 1857: SPRI MS 248/439/23.

123 Delane to Osborn, n.d., rec'd 16 April 1857: SPRI MS 248/367.

124 Colonial Office to PRS, 6 March 1857: Royal Society MM/4/38. Richardson to Sabine, 15 March 1857: Royal Society MM/4/40.

125 Palliser to Sabine, 8 Dec. 1857: RS Sabine MS 260, f. 958.

126 I. M. Spry, *The Papers of the Palliser Expedition, 1857–1860* (Toronto, 1968). For the magnetic work of the expedition see pp. xxii–xxv, xxix–xxxii, xliii–xlvi, l–lii, lvii, lxxx–lxxxv, civ–cv, 550–6 and 618. Spry's earlier book *The Palliser Expedition* (Toronto, 1963), ch. 2, covers the magnetic work.

127 Wallace, p. 166.

128 Rich, *John Rae's Correspondence*, pp. 794–5, 808.

129 Back, n.d.: Back Papers, RGS, quoted in Friendly at p. 323.

130 Friendly, p. 334.

CHAPTER 13: Arctic *Fox*

1 See David Murphy's McClintock biography *The Arctic Fox – Francis Leopold McClintock: Discoverer of the Fate of Franklin* (Cork, 2004).

2 He had been promoted to captain on the return of Belcher's expedition.

3 McClintock to Sophia Cracroft, rec'd 28 Feb. and 10 March 1857: SPRI MS 248/439/11–12.

4 Jane to McClintock, 17 April 1857: J. W. Lentz, 'The *Fox* Expedition in Search of Franklin: A Documentary Trail', *Arctic*, 56 (2003), pp. 175–84 at pp. 178–9.

5 Jane to Murchison, 9 and 10 April 1857: Add. 46,216, ff. 257–9. McClintock to Jane, 18 April 1857: SPRI MS 248/439/23.

6 Sabine to Jane, n.d.: SPRI MS 248/469/2.

7 Sabine to Ross, 13 and 19 Sept. 1858: SPRI MS 1226/27/2–3.

8 Jane to Admiralty, 21 April 1857 and reply, 23 April 1857: ADM 1/5688, Pro. F83 and F89.

9 M. Slater (ed.), *'Gone Astray' and other Papers from Household Words, 1851–59* (London, 1998), pp. 268–9.

10 Fitzpatrick, p. 364. Murphy, pp. 179–80. Savours, 'Hobart and the Polar Regions', p. 178. For the fund-raising effort see W. P. Kay to Robert Wales (two local Tasmanian worthies), 24 June 1852: ML MSS A, f. 1/5.

11 McClintock to Admiralty, 6 Aug. 1857: ADM 1/5684, M153.
12 Jane to McClintock, 29 June 1857 (Aberdeen): F. L. McClintock, *The Voyage of the Fox into the Arctic Seas*, 3rd edn (London, 1869 [1860]; repr. Cologne, 1998).
13 McClintock (1998), p. 28. Levere, p. 228.
14 Maguire to Barrow, 22 June (1857): Add. 35,308, f. 194.
15 McClintock to Murchison, 22 and 28 June 1857: Add. 46,217, ff. 134–6.
16 Collinson to Barrow, 2 July 1857: Add. 35,308, f. 47 re search funds.
17 Beaufort to Murchison, 5 July 1857: Add. 46,215, f. 146. Stafford, pp. 25, 174. Murchison to Gladstone, 22 May 1858 (Geological Survey Office, 22 Jermyn Street): Add. 44,389, f. 218.
18 Murchison to Wood 8, 9 and 16 July 1857: Add. 49,560, ff. 100, 103, 116.
19 McClintock to Washington, 6 May 1858, rec'd 28 Aug. 1858: ADM 1/5696.
20 Originally called Peel Sound when it was believed to be a dead end for ships, it became Peel Strait when it was shown to be an open passage (when ice free).
21 The interpolations inserted into the recovered records in square brackets are areas where the paper has been destroyed, or is illegible. Savours, *Search*, pp. 292–5.
22 Cyriax, *Last Expedition*, p. 170.
23 McClintock to Jane, 21 Sept. 1859: SPRI MS 248/439/32 in W. F. Rawnsley (ed.), *The Life, Diaries and Correspondence of Jane Lady Franklin, 1792–1875* (London, 1923), pp. 144–6.
24 Collinson to Murchison, 22 Sept. 1859: Add. 46,215, f. 402.
25 Levere, p. 229. McClintock (1998), pp. 16–19.
26 *Philosophical Transactions*, 153 (1863), pp. 649–63. Levere, p. 230.
27 David, p. 107 from *The Times*, 15 Nov. 1859.
28 *The Times*, 23 Sept. 1959, p. 6, leader, 'The Last Ray of Light'.
29 Constance Fox Talbot to Henry Fox Talbot, 25 Sept. 1859: WHFT 07961. Fox Talbot Collection, Laycock Abbey, http://foxtalbot.dmu.ac.uk./letters/transcriptDate.php?month=9&year=1859&pageNumber=19&pageTotal=25& referringPage=0, accessed 4 Jan. 2005. The Fox Talbots knew Sir John Richardson.
30 McClintock to Admiralty, 28 Sept. 1859: ADM 1/5714, M194.
31 McClintock to Admiralty, 23 Sept., 28 Oct. and 29 Nov. 1859: ADM 1/5714, M197, M214.
32 Order in Council, 22 Oct. 1859: ADM 1/5726.
33 Taking the chair of the Geographical Section at Aberdeen was James Clark Ross's last public appearance. After his last Arctic voyage he drifted out of public life. The death of his wife exacerbated his drink problem and he died on 3 April 1862, a forgotten lonely man. M. J. Ross, p. 386.
34 Howat, p. 88.
35 Martin, IV, pp. 492–5.
36 Osborn to Barrow, 13 Feb. 1859 (Canton): Add. 35,309, f. 51. Osborn to Murchison, 20 Aug. 1859: Add. 46,217, f. 310.
37 Osborn to Barrow, 20 Aug. 1858 (China): Add. 35,308, f. 503. Jane to Murchison, n.d. 1859 (152 Albany St, Regent's Park): Add. 46,216, f. 263.
38 McClintock to Murchison, 20 Oct. 1859: Add. 46,217, f. 138.
39 McClintock (1998), p. 21. Levere, pp. 229–30.
40 Richardson to Jane, 11 Oct. 1859: Rawnsley, pp. 147–50.
41 Grinnell to Jane, 12 Oct. 1859: Rawnsley, pp. 150–1.
42 Belcher to Sabine, 26 Oct. 1859 in Sabine to Jane, 27 Oct. 1859: SPRI MS 248/469/3.
43 Browne, p. 83. Darwin to Murray, 14 Dec. 1860: *Darwin Correspondence*, vol. VII, pp. 482–3.

44 Jane to Barrow, 27 Dec. 1859: Add. 35,307, f. 395.
45 Murchison's presidential address to the British Association Meeting at Oxford, 1860: SPRI MS 248/223.
46 Evelyn Ashley (Palmerston's private secretary) to Murchison, 20 Feb. 1860: Add. 46,215, f. 66.
47 Washington minute, 26 Nov. 1860: ADM 1/5743, f. 334.
48 McClintock to Admiralty, 6 Sept. 1860: ADM 1/5738.
49 David, p. 80.
50 McClintock (1869), pp. 312–13.
51 McClintock to Weld, 13 Jan. 1860 and Sophia Cracroft, 18 Jan. 1860: SPRI MS 248/439/16 and 37.
52 McClintock (1869), p. 314. The italics are McClintock's.
53 Wallace, pp. 205–6.
54 Caroline Fox Talbot to Henry Fox Talbot, 3 May 1861: WHFT 08357 (see n. 29).
55 Lentz, p. 179.
56 ADM 1/5730, f. 285. K. Littlewood and B. Butler, *Of Ships and Stars: Maritime Heritage and the Founding of the National Maritime Museum, Greenwich* (London, 1998), pp. 12, 19 and 22.
57 Arthur Wright (Franklin's nephew) to Murchison, 25 Oct. 1856: Add. 46,218, f. 337.
58 Beaufort to Jane, 21 July 1856: SPRI MS 1100/5.
59 *The Times*, 28 Nov. 1861, p. 8. I. F. W. Beckett, *Riflemen Form: A Study of the Rifle Volunteer Movement, 1859–1908* (Aldershot, 1982).
60 Jane to Murchison, 7 Nov. 1860 (New York): Add. 46,216, f. 267.
61 Sir F. Hill, *Victorian Lincoln* (Cambridge, 1974), p. 229.
62 'FRS', *The Times*, 19 Jan. 1860, p. 9.
63 Westmacott to Sir Charles Wood (First Lord of the Admiralty), 26 July 1855: ADM 1/5669, W430.
64 Westmacott to Admiralty, 28 June 1858: ADM 1/5707, W276.
65 J. Bold, *Greenwich: The Architectural History of the Royal Hospital for Seamen and the Queen's House* (Princeton, 2000), p. 260: http://www.nmm.ac.uk/memorials/Memorial.cfm?Topic=21&MemorialPage=5&MemorialID=M2370, accessed 17 Sept. 2008.
66 Penny to Barrow, 6 Feb. 1860: Add. 35,306, f. 141.
67 Jane to Murchison, 18 Feb. 1860: Add. 46,216, f. 263.
68 Murchison to Palmerston, 22 Feb. 1860: Add. 44,393, f. 148. The letter is still in the Gladstone MS.
69 Somerset to Palmerston, 24 Feb. 1860: Southampton University, Hartley Library Broadlands MS, GC/SO 27.
70 Hansard, vol. CLVI, pp. 2147–54, 2 March 1860.
71 Jane to Murchison, 24 May 1860 (5 Park Place, St James's): Add. 46,216, f. 265. F. Woodward, p. 304.
72 Hansard, vol. CLX, pp. 1546–7, 18 Aug. 1860.
73 William Cowper to Murchison, 5 Oct. 1860: Add. 46,215, f. 424.
74 Jane to Murchison, 7 Nov. 1860 (New York): Add. 46,216, f. 267.
75 McGoogan, *Lady Franklin's Revenge*, pp. 388–9.
76 B. Read, *Victorian Sculpture* (Princeton, 1982), pp. 149–50.
77 Mathew Noble to Cowper as First Commissioner of Works, 8 July 1861: TNA WORK 20/85.
78 Murchison to Mr Russell (Board of Works), 11 Nov. 1866: TNA WORK 20/85.

79 Jane to Barrow, 13 Nov. 1866: Add. 35,308, f. 398.
80 *The Times*, 16 Nov. 1866, p. 10, col. A, 'Statue to Sir John Franklin'. web3.info-trac.galegroup.com/itw/infomark/807/979/78432037w3/purl=rcl_TTDA, accessed 24 Aug. 2004.
81 McClintock to Jane, 24 Dec. 1866 (Port Royal, Jamaica): SPRI MS 248/439/36. McClintock was serving, so unable to attend.
82 TNA WORK 20/195 for 1931.
83 Cyriax, *Last Expedition*, p. 202.
84 Livingstone to Sabine, 6 Feb. 1860, 17 Jan. 1861 and 13 Dec. 1865: RS Sabine MS 259, ff. 791–5.
85 'A Fellow (of the RGS)', 'Polar Expeditions': *The Times*, 26 Jan. 1865, p. 9.
86 Delane to Murchison, 25 Feb. (1865?): LDGSL 838, MD39/11.
87 Herschel to Murchison, 31 April 1865: Add. 46,216, ff. 402–3.
88 Charles Francis Adams (American ambassador) to Murchison, 14 May 1867: Add. 46,215, f. 5, agreeing to transmit the RGS medal to American polar explorer Dr Isaac Hayes. Lord Stanley (foreign secretary) to Murchison, 6 Aug. 1867: Add. 46,218, f. 123. Stafford Northcote (secretary of state for India) to Murchison, 24 Sept. 1867: Add. 46,215, f. 153.
89 Osborn to Murchison, 14 Oct. 1867: Add. 46,217, f. 314.
90 Richards to Murchison, 30 Jan. 1868: Add. 46,217, f. 432.
91 F. Woodward, pp. 354–7. McGoogan, *Lady Franklin's Revenge*, p. 450.
92 McClintock (1869), p. xxxvi.
93 McClintock to Sophia Cracroft, 13 Oct. 1869: SPRI MS 248/439/17. R. J. Cyriax, 'The Unsolved Problem of the Franklin Expedition Records Supposedly Buried on King William Island', *Mariner's Mirror*, 55 (1969), pp. 23–32.
94 Jane to Murchison, 21 Dec. 1869: Add. 46,216, f. 285. F. Woodward, pp. 347–8. Jane to Gladstone, 15 Dec. 1869, draft enclosing a 3rd edition of *The Voyage of the Fox*: McCord Museum Microfilm 2755.
95 Add. 44,498, f. 246. C. Y. Lang and E. F. Shannon, *The Letters of Alfred Lord Tennyson*, vol. III, *1871–1892* (Oxford, 1990), pp. 113–15.
96 M. Port, *Imperial London: Civil Government Building in London, 1851–1915* (Princeton, 1995), p. 259.
97 Dr A. Armstrong, 30 Oct. 1873: *The Times*, 31 Oct. 1873, p. 6. F. Woodward, p. 361.
98 F. Woodward, p. 364.
99 D. Woodman, *Unravelling the Franklin Mystery: Inuit Testimony* (Montreal, 1991), p. 234.
100 Meadows, pp. 96–120. Hall, pp. 107–8.
101 Morrell and Thackray, *Early Years*, p. 101.
102 Hall, p. 105.
103 Robinson, pp. 56–66.
104 Robinson, pp. 73–5.
105 C. Loomis, *Weird and Tragic Shores: The Story of Charles Francis Hall, Explorer* (New York, 1971), p. 220.
106 Robinson, pp. 79–80.
107 Penny to Barrow, 17 Jan. 1875: Add. 35,305, f. 156.
108 Robinson, p. 86. David, pp. 111–12. W. H. Gilder, *Schwatka's Search* (New York, 1881).
109 Robinson, pp. 83–106.

CHAPTER 14: Big Art, Brazen Lies and the 'Great Explorer'

1 David, pp. 30–45.
2 A. Wilton and T. Barringer, *American Sublime: Landscape Painting in the United States, 1820–1880* (Princeton, 2002), pp. 11–13.
3 David, p. 240.
4 Wolf, pp. 73–6.
5 B. Riffenburgh, *The Myth of the Explorer* (Oxford, 1994), p. 13.
6 Wilton and Barringer, p. 14.
7 Carr, p. 35.
8 Howat, pp. 43–6 and 88.
9 H. Tuckerman, *Book of the Artists: American Art Life* (New York, 1867), quoted in Howat at p. 91.
10 F. L. Williams, pp. 202, 539–40.
11 Carr, pp. 11–28.
12 Carr, p. 83.
13 Carr, p. 90.
14 E. W. Watkin, *Canada and the States, 1851 to 1886* (London, 1887), quoted in Howat at p. 106, and E. J. Harvey, *The Voyage of the Icebergs: Frederic Church's Arctic Masterpiece* (Princeton, 2002), p. 69.
15 Howat, p. 184.
16 Carr, pp. 105–7.
17 R. Ormond, *Victorian Portraits* (London, 1973), pp. 548–9.
18 Ormond, *Victorian Portraits*, pp. 562–3.
19 M. O'Neill, 'Stephen Pearce (1819–1904)', *Oxford Dictionary of National Biography*: www.oxforddnb.com/articles/35/35435-article.html, accessed 12 Dec. 2004. The pictures are now together in the National Portrait Gallery.
20 The quotation originates in Proverbs 16:9. R. Ormond, *Sir Edwin Landseer* (London, 1980), pp. 207–8.
21 Ormond, *Landseer*, p. 207.
22 *The Times*, 30 April 1864.
23 Ormond, *Landseer*, p. 201.
24 C. Lennie, *Landseer: The Victorian Paragon* (London, 1976), pp. 207–9, 243.
25 J. E. Millais, *The Life and Letters of Millais*, 2 vols. (London, 1902), II, pp. 48–52. H. G. C. Matthew, 'Millais', in P. Funnell and M. Warner (eds), *Portraits* (London, 1999), p. 149. K. Flint, *The Victorians and the Visual Imagination* (Cambridge, 1999), pp. 308–12.
26 David, pp. 47, 165–6.
27 Loomis, 'Arctic Sublime', p. 104. David, p. 240.
28 Loomis, 'Arctic Sublime', pp. 110–11.
29 Riffenburgh, p. 14.
30 R. Murchison, 'Preface' to McClintock (1998), p. 21.
31 M. Girouard, *The Return to Camelot: Chivalry and the English Gentleman* (London, 1981), p. 8, from S. Osborn, *The Career, Last Voyage and Fate of Captain Sir John Franklin* (London, 1860), pp. v and 26.
32 Riffenburgh, p. 25.
33 Girouard, p. 230.
34 Port, pp. 258–9.
35 See, for example, Albert Markham's biography of Franklin in the 'Great Explorers' series (London, 1891).

36 A. Savours, 'Clements Markham: Longest Serving Officer, Most Prolific Editor', in P. Hair (ed.), *Compassing the Vast Globe of the Earth: Studies in the History of the Hakluyt Society, 1846–1996* (London, 1996), pp. 165–88 at p. 168.
37 C. R. Markham, *Franklin's Footsteps* (London, 1853).
38 Savours, 'Clements Markham', pp. 183–4.
39 C. R. Markham, *The Threshold of the Unknown Region* (London, 1873), p. 336.
40 *Threshold* ran to four editions by December 1875; the last included Nares's voyage and appeared in French.
41 *Threshold*, 4th edn (Dec. 1875), p. vii.
42 Savours, 'Clements Markham', p. 180, quoting from the 3rd edn of 1875, p. 325.
43 David, p. 70.
44 Markham, *Threshold*, pp. 281–3.
45 Markham, *Threshold*, p. 293.
46 Markham, *Arctic Navy List*, pp. iii–iv.
47 F. J. Evans, *Memorandum on the Magnetical Observations Made during the Voyage of HMS Challenger, 1872–1876* (London, 1878).
48 C. R. Markham, *A Refutation of the Report of the Scurvy Committee* (Portsmouth, 1877). Savours, 'Clements Markham', p. 181.
49 Markham, *Threshold*, preface to 4th edn.
50 Savours, 'Clements Markham', p. 179.
51 C. R. Markham (ed.), *The Voyages of William Baffin, 1612–1622* (London, 1881).
52 *Oxford Dictionary of National Biography*: www.oxforddnb.com/articles34/34880-article.html, accessed 19 Oct. 2004.
53 J. K. Laughton, (unsigned), *Edinburgh Review*, 1875, pp. 447–81 and 1877, pp. 155–69.
54 Albert compiled *The Life of Sir Clements Markham* (London, 1917).
55 H. W. G. Lewis-Jones, '"Heroism Displayed"; Revisiting the Franklin Gallery at the Royal Naval Exhibition, 1891', *Polar Record*, 41 (2005), pp. 185–203 at p. 200. I am indebted to Huw Lewis-Jones for a copy of this important paper.
56 F. L. McClintock to *The Times*, 30 Jan. 1891: *The Times*, 4 Feb. 1891, p. 3.
57 Admiralty to Royal United Services Institution, 9 June 1890: ADM 1/5730, f. 25.
58 A. D. Lambert, *The Foundations of Naval History* (London, 1997).
59 David, pp. 158–9.
60 Lewis-Jones, pp. 192–7.
61 Lewis-Jones, pp. 195–7.
62 Lewis-Jones, p. 198.
63 A. H. Markham, *Life of Sir John Franklin and the North West Passage* (London, 1891): 'do or die', pp. 233–4; Goldner, pp. 245–6; link to war, p. 250; Belcher, p. 256; Rae, p. 258; mission, pp. 314–15.
64 David, pp. 190, 193–5.
65 A. Gordon, *The Rules of the Game: Jutland and British Naval Command* (London, 1996), pp. 208–12.
66 Lewis-Jones, p. 199. David, pp. 162–3.
67 Riffenburgh, p. 7.
68 National Maritime Museum catalogue BHC 1273.
69 David, p. 242.
70 C. R. Markham, 'Voyages and Discoveries, 1815–1856', in W. L. Clowes (ed.), *The Royal Navy: A History from the Earliest Times*, vol. VI (London, 1901), pp. 507–37 at p. 517.
71 Markham, 'Voyages and Discoveries, 1815–1856', p. 526.

72 Markham, 'Voyages and Discoveries, 1815–1856', pp. 528–9.

73 Markham, 'Voyages and Discoveries, 1815–1856', p. 529.

74 Markham, 'Voyages and Discoveries, 1815–1856', p. 530.

75 Markham, 'Voyages and Discoveries, 1815–1856', pp. 536–7.

76 C. R. Markham, 'Voyages and Discoveries, 1857–1900', in W. L. Clowes (ed.), *The Royal Navy: A History from the Earliest Times*, vol. VII (London, 1903), pp. 562–9 at p. 564.

77 Markham, 'Voyages and Discoveries, 1857–1900', p. 566.

78 Markham, 'Voyages and Discoveries, 1857–1900', p. 567.

79 Markham, 'Voyages and Discoveries, 1857–1900', p. 368[?568].

80 Lewis-Jones, p. 200.

81 C. R. Markham, *Life of Admiral Sir Leopold McClintock* (London, 1909).

82 Savours, 'Clements Markham', p. 184.

83 Huntford, p. 128.

84 For Markham's highly revealing personal account of the genesis of the Antarctic mission see his *Antarctic Obsession: The British National Antarctic Expedition, 1901–04*, ed. and intro. C. Holland (Harleston, Norfolk, 1986). There is in Markham's self-satisfied prose more than an echo of John Barrow.

85 Savours, 'Clements Markham', p. 167, from R. F. Scott, *The Voyages of the 'Discovery'* (London, 1905).

86 Lewis-Jones, p. 201.

87 K. Marx, *The 18th Brumaire of Louis Napoleon Bonaparte* (London, 1852), section I.

88 Cited in Robinson at p. 163.

89 S. Solomon, *The Coldest March: Scott's Fatal Antarctic Expedition* (New Haven, 2001).

90 Scott to Geikie, 19 Oct. 1904: RS Sabine MS 261. Quite how this letter came to be in the papers of a man who had died two decades earlier is not clear.

91 R. F. Scott, *Scott's Last Expedition*, 2 vols. (London, 1914), I, p. 167.

92 Scott to Kathleen Scott, 'The Last Word. "To my widow . . . I hope I shall be a good memory"', *The Week*, 20 Jan. 2007, pp. 48–9, reporting the opening of an exhibition of Scott letters at the Scott Polar Institute.

93 David, p. 118.

94 M. Jones, *The Last Great Quest: Captain Scott's Antarctic Sacrifice* (Oxford, 2003), pp. 26, 96.

95 Riffenburgh, p. 199.

96 Girouard, pp. 2–5.

97 Colonel J. E. B. Seeley, 3 Feb. 1913, reported in *The Times*, 14 Feb. 1913, p. 5.

98 Archdeacon H. S. Wood, 29 March 1914: *The Times*, 30 March 1914, p. 5.

99 M. Jones, pp. 155, 221.

100 Unless otherwise stated, this section is based on *Oxford Dictionary of National Biography*: www.oxforddnb.com/articles/35/35994-article.html, accessed 10 Oct. 2004.

101 *Oxford Dictionary of National Biography*: www.oxforddnb.com/articles/34/34879-article.html, accessed 10 Oct. 2004.

102 C. R. Markham, *The Lands of Silence* (Cambridge, 1921), p. 243.

CHAPTER 15: Terror: What Really Happened?

1 *Oxford English Dictionary*, 2nd edn (Oxford, 1989).
2 Canadian Hydrographic Service, *Pilot of Arctic Canada*, 3 vols., 2nd edn (Ottawa, 1970–6), I, p. 149.
3 Cyriax, *Last Expedition*, p. 125.
4 *Pilot of Arctic Canada*, III, p. 213.
5 *Pilot of Arctic Canada*, I, p. 141 map.
6 Gilder, pp. 134–5, 147.
7 Woodman, *Franklin Mystery*, p. 108.
8 R. E. Johnson, 'Doctors Abroad: Medicine and Nineteenth Century Arctic Exploration', in J. Watt, E. J. Freeman and W. F. Bynum (eds), *Starving Sailors: The Influence of Nutrition upon Naval and Maritime History* (London, 1981), p. 106.
9 Woodman, *Franklin Mystery*, pp. 323–4.
10 A. Savours and M. Deacon, 'Nutritional Aspects of the British Arctic (Nares) Expedition of 1875–76 and its Predecessors', in J. Watt et al., pp. 131–62 at pp. 136–9.
11 Savours, 'Clements Markham', pp. 144–6.
12 A. F. Rogers, 'The Influence of Diet in Scott's Last Expedition', in J. Watt et al., pp. 172–3.
13 O. Beattie and J. Geiger, *Frozen in Time: The Fate of the Franklin Expedition* (London, 1987), p. 161.
14 B. Z. Horowitz, 'Polar Poisons: Did Botulism Doom the Franklin Expedition?', *Clinical Toxicology* 41 (2003), pp. 841–7, is suitably cautious. S. Cookman, *Iceblink: The Tragic Fate of Sir John Franklin's Lost Polar Expedition* (New York, 2000) is altogether more sensational.
15 Richard Cyriax admitted that this discovery altered his narrative. Woodman, *Franklin Mystery*, p. 91.
16 McClintock found six, but modern research has discovered more.
17 Woodman, *Franklin Mystery*, remains wedded to the Passage concept, even as he attempts to overturn the death-march chronology, p. 94.
18 Gilder, p. 211.
19 I have taken these locations from Woodman, *Franklin Mystery*. L. A. Learmonth, 'Notes on Franklin Relics', *Arctic*, 1 (1948), pp. 122–3 is also useful.
20 Beattie and Geiger, pp. 58–62.
21 A. Keenleyside, M. Bertulli and H. C. Fricke, 'The Final Days of the Franklin Expedition: New Skeletal Evidence', *Arctic*, 50 (1997), pp. 36–46.
22 R. Bayliss, 'Sir John Franklin's Last Arctic Expedition: A Medical Disaster', *Journal of the Royal Society of Medicine*, 95 (2002), pp. 151–3 at p. 153. Keenleyside et. al., p. 38.
23 Gilder, p. 151.
24 Gilder, p. 106. Woodman, *Franklin Mystery*, pp. 144–7.
25 Woodman, *Franklin Mystery*, p. 324 and D. Woodman, *Strangers Among Us* (Montreal and Kingston, 1996).
26 Robinson, pp. 3–9.
27 David, pp. 242–3.
28 Huntford, p. 22.

Bibliography

ARCHIVE SOURCES

The National Archive, Kew (TNA)

Official Records
    ADM 1/5684 McClintock 1857
    ADM 1/5696 McClintock's report to the Admiralty on the *Fox* voyage
    ADM 1/5714, 5718, 5726 McClintock correspondence, 1859
    ADM 1/5738 McClintock on *Bulldog* deep-ocean sounding between Greenland and
        Labrador, 1860
    ADM 1/5743 334 *Fox* rewards
    ADM 1/5544–5731 Miscellaneous correspondence, 1844–1860
    ADM 7/187–200 The Arctic search papers.
    ADM 7/608–13 Arctic search, Arctic Committee, petitions for the relief of Franklin

Private Papers
    BJ2 James Clark Ross papers: Meteorological Office
    BJ3 Sabine papers
    BJ7 Fitzroy
    PRO 30/22 Lord John Russell MS

British Library, London (Add. MSS)
    Wood, Palmerston, Gladstone, Murchison papers; Barrow bequest

National Maritime Museum, London (NMM)
    Flinders Project, Collinson, Franklin, McClure, McClintock papers

Bodleian Library, Oxford
    British Association for the Advancement of Science (BAAS) collection
    Disraeli MS

Southampton University, Hartley Library
    Palmerston and Cowper MSS (BR)

Geological Society, London (LDGSL)
    Murchison papers

Scott Polar Research Institute, Cambridge (SPRI)
    Franklin, Beaufort, James Clark Ross, Parry, Richardson bequest

McCord Museum, McGill University, Montreal
    Microfilm records

BIBLIOGRAPHY

Royal Geographical Society, London (RGS)
  Franklin collection

Royal Society, London (RS)
  Sabine and Herschel MSS

United Kingdom Hydrographic Office, Taunton (UKHO)
  Beaufort MSS
  Hydrographic Office records

Wellcome Institute, London
  Miscellaneous MSS

National Library of Australia, Canberra (NLA)
  Franklin and Owen Stanley MSS

Mitchell Library, Sydney (ML)
  Franklin MSS; also Bicheno, Buckland, Gell, Gould, King MSS

Tasmanian Archives, Hobart
  Colonial Correspondence
  Turnbull MS

ELECTRONIC RESOURCES

Oxford DNB online

Fox Talbot Collection, Laycock Abbey: http://foxtalbot.dmu.ac.uk/letters/letters.html

University of Manitoba Archives and Special Collections: Arctic Blue Books on Line
http://www.umanitoba.ca/libraries/units/archives/arcticbb/preliminary.shtml is the
guide. A typical example would be: 'A Bill for the more effectually discovering the
Longitude at Sea, and encouraging attempts to find a *Northern* Passage between the
Atlantic and *Pacific* Oceans, and to approach the *Northern* Pole. 9pp. Bill printed
9.3.1818' online as: http://www.umanitoba.ca/libraries/units/archives/arcticbb/
viewbb.php?t=1818&p=2

BRITISH OFFICIAL PUBLICATIONS

Harbour Department of the Admiralty. House of Commons Return no. 553 10.7.1849
Hansard (parliamentary debates)

JOURNALS AND NEWSPAPERS

Edinburgh Review
Illustrated London News
Quarterly Review
Philosophical Transactions
Tasmanian Journal of Science
The Times

BOOKS AND ARTICLES

Airy, W. (ed.), *Autobiography of George Biddell Airy* (Cambridge, 1896)

Alexander, A., *The Governor's Wives* (Hobart, 1999)

Auerbach, J. A., *The Great Exhibition of 1851: A Nation on Display* (New Haven, 1999)

Austin, M., *The Army in Australia, 1840–1850: Prelude to the Golden Years* (Canberra, 1979)

Babbage, C., *Reflections on the Decline of Science in England* (London, 1831)

Bach, J., *The Australia Station: A History of the Royal Navy in the South West Pacific, 1821–1913* (Sydney, 1986)

Back, Sir George, *Narrative of the Arctic Land Expedition* (Edmonton, 1970 [London, 1836])

Barr, W., *Arctic Hell Ship: The Voyage of HMS Enterprise, 1850–1855* (Edmonton, 2007)

— 'Franklin in Siberia? – Lieutenant Bedford Pim's Proposal to Search the Arctic Coast of Siberia, 1851–52', *Arctic*, 45 (1992), pp. 36–46

— 'A Warrant Officer in the Arctic: The Journal of George Ford, 1850–1854', in A. Frost and J. Samson (eds), *Pacific Empires: Essays in Honour of Glyndwr Williams* (Vancouver, 1999), pp. 101–23

Barr, W. (ed.), *Emile Frédéric de Bray, A Frenchman in Search of Franklin: Arctic Journal, 1852–1854* (Toronto, 1992)

— *From Barrow to Boothia: The Arctic Journals of Peter Warren Dease, 1836–1839* (Montreal, 2002)

— *Searching for Franklin: The Land Arctic Searching Expedition. James Anderson's and James Stewart's Expedition via the Back River* (London, 1999)

Barrington, D. (ed.), *Col. Beaufoy FRS: The Possibility of Approaching the North Pole Asserted*, 2nd edn (London, 1818 [1775])

Barrow, J., *Autobiographical Memoir* (London, 1848)

— *A Chronological History of Voyages into the Arctic Regions undertaken chiefly for the purpose of discovering a north-east, north-west or Polar passage between the Atlantic and Pacific from the earliest periods of Scandinavian Navigation to the departure of the recent expeditions under the orders of Captains Ross and Buchan* (London, 1818)

— *The Eventful History of the Mutiny and Piratical Seizure of HMS Bounty, Its Causes and Consequences* (London, 1831)

— 'Ross's Voyage of Discovery', *Quarterly Review*, 21 (1819), pp. 213–62 (unsigned)

— *Voyages of Discovery within the Arctic Regions from the Year 1818 to the Present Time* (London, 1846)

Bayliss, R., 'Sir John Franklin's Last Arctic Expedition: A Medical Disaster', *Journal of the Royal Society of Medicine*, 95 (2002), pp. 151–3

Beattie, O. and J. Geiger, *Frozen in Time: The Fate of the Franklin Expedition* (London, 1987)

Beckett, I. F. W., *Riflemen Form: A Study of the Rifle Volunteer Movement, 1859–1908* (Aldershot, 1982)

Beeler, J. (ed.), *The Milne Papers*, vol. I (Aldershot, 2004)

Belcher, E. *The Last of the Arctic Voyages: Being a Narrative of the Expedition in HMS Assistance* (London, 1855)

Blake, R., *Disraeli* (London, 1966)

Bockstoce, J. R., *Journal of Rochefort Maguire, HMS Plover, 1852–1854*, 2 vols. (London, 1988)

— *The Opening of the Maritime Fur Trade at Bering Strait* (Philadelphia, 2005)
— *Whales, Ice and Men: The History of Whaling in the Western Arctic* (Seattle, 1986)
Bold, J., *Greenwich: The Architectural History of the Royal Hospital for Seamen and the Queen's House* (Princeton, 2000)
Bolger, P., *Hobart Town* (Canberra, 1973)
Botting, D., *Humboldt and the Cosmos* (London, 1973)
Bourne, K., *Great Britain and the Balance of Power in North America, 1815–1908* (London, 1967)
Browne, J., *Darwin's 'Origin of the Species': A Biography* (London, 2006)
Burkhardt, F. et al. (eds), *The Correspondence of Charles Darwin* (Cambridge, 1985–)
Burn, D., *Narrative of the Overland Journey of Sir John and Lady Franklin and Party from Hobart Town to Macquarie Harbour, 1842*, ed. G. Mackaness (Sydney, 1955)
Burney, J., 'A Memoir on the Geography of the North East Part of Asia, and on the Question whether Asia and America Are Contiguous, or Are Separated by the Sea' (11 Dec. 1817), *Philosophical Transactions*, 108 (1818), pp. 9–23
Burroughs, P., *Britain and Australia, 1831–1855: A Study in Imperial Relations and Crown Lands Administration* (Oxford, 1967)
Calder, J., *Recollections of Sir John and Lady Jane Franklin in Tasmania* (originally published in the *Tasmanian Tribune*, 1875; repr. Adelaide, 1984)
Canadian Hydrographic Service, *Pilot of Arctic Canada*, 3 vols., 2nd edn (Ottawa, 1970–6)
Carr, G. L., *Frederic Edwin Church: The Icebergs* (Dallas, 1980)
Carter, H. B., *Sir Joseph Banks, 1743–1820* (London, 1988)
Cavell, J., 'The Hidden Crime of Dr Richardson', *Polar Record*, 43 (2007), pp. 155–64
Cawood, J., 'The Magnetic Crusade: Science and Politics in Early Victorian Britain', *ISIS*, 70 (1979), pp. 493–518
Chambers, N. (ed.), *The Letters of Sir Joseph Banks: A Selection, 1768–1820* (London, 2000)
Chapman, S. and J. Bartels, *Geomagnetism*, 2 vols. (Oxford, 1940)
Cloake, J., *Palaces and Parks of Richmond and Kew*, vol. II, *Richmond Lodge and the Kew Palaces* (Chichester, 1996)
Collinson, T. B. (ed.), *Journal of HMS Enterprise, 1850–1855, by Captain Richard Collinson RN* (London, 1889)
Cook, A., *Edmond Halley: Charting the Heavens and the Seas* (Oxford, 1998)
Cookman, S., *Iceblink: The Tragic Fate of Sir John Franklin's Lost Polar Expedition* (New York, 2000)
Cordingley, D., *Billy Ruffian: The Bellerophon and the Downfall of Napoleon* (London, 2003)
Courtney, N., *Gale Force 10: The Life and Legacy of Admiral Beaufort* (London, 2003)
Croft, L. R. (ed.), *Diary of a Naval Commander: The Diary of Vice-Admiral James Hamilton Ward, 1843–1846* (Chorley, 1989)
Cyriax, R. J., *Sir John Franklin's Last Arctic Expedition: The Franklin Expedition – A Chapter in the History of the Royal Navy* (London, 1939)
— 'The Unsolved Problem of the Franklin Expedition Records Supposedly Buried on King William Island', *Mariner's Mirror*, 55 (1969), pp. 23–32
Daly, J. C., *Russian Seapower and 'The Eastern Question', 1827–1841* (London, 1991)
Dasent, A. I., *John Thadeus Delane: Editor of "The Times"*, 2 vols. (London, 1908)
Datta, A., *John Gould in Australia: Letters and Drawings* (Melbourne, 1997)
David, R. G., *The Arctic in the British Imagination: 1815–1914* (Manchester, 2000)
Davis, L. E., R. E. Gullman and K. Gleiter, *In Pursuit of Leviathan: Technology,*

Institutions, Productivity and Profits in American Whaling, 1816–1900 (Chicago, 1997)

Davis, R. C. (ed.), *Sir John Franklin's Journals and Correspondence: The First Arctic Land Expedition, 1819–1822* (Toronto, 1995)

— *Sir John Franklin's Journals and Correspondence: The Second Arctic Land Expedition, 1825–1827* (Toronto, 1998)

Dawson, W. R. (ed.), *The Banks Letters* (London, 1958)

Delgado, J. P., *Across the Roof of the World: The Quest for the Northwest Passage* (London, 1999)

Denison, Sir W., 'The Operation of *Teredo Navalis* on Colonial Timber', *Papers and Proceedings of the Royal Society of Van Diemen's Land*, 2, pt. 1 (Hobart, 1852), pp. 72–4

D'Entrecasteaux, B., *Atlas de Voyage de Bruny D'Entrecasteaux*, 2 vols. (Paris, 1809, folio)

— *Voyages à la Recherche de la Pérouse*, 2 vols. (Paris, 1808)

Disraeli, B., *Benjamin Disraeli Letters: 1852–1856*, ed. M. G. Wiebe and M. S. Millar (Toronto, 1997)

Douglas, George, 8th Duke of Argyll, *Autobiography and Memoirs*, vol. I (London, 1906)

Dowty, A., *The Limits of American Isolation: The United States and the Crimean War* (New York, 1971)

Driver, F., *Geography Militant* (Cambridge, 2001)

Dunmore, J. S., *French Explorers of the Pacific*, vol. II (Oxford, 1969)

Dunnington, G. W., *Carl Friedrich Gauss: Titan of Science* (1955; new edn Washington, DC, 2004)

d'Urville, J. S.-C. D., *An Account of Two Voyages to the South Seas*, vol. II, *The Astrolabe and Zélée, 1837–1840*, trans. and ed. H. Rosenman (Melbourne, 1987)

Eardley-Wilmot, S., *Life of Edmund, Lord Lyons* (London, 1898)

Ellis, E., *Conrad Maertens: Life and Art* (Sydney, 1994)

Ellison, D., *Quarter Deck – Cambridge: The Quest of Captain Francis Price Blackwood RN* (Cambridge, 1991)

Estensen, M., *The Life of Matthew Flinders* (Sydney, 2002)

Evans, D. S., B. H Evans, T. J. Deeming and S. Goldfarb (eds), *Herschel at the Cape: Diaries and Correspondence of Sir John Herschel, 1834–1838* (Austin, 1969)

Evans, F. J., *Memorandum on the Magnetical Observations Made during the Voyage of HMS Challenger, 1872–1876* (London, 1878)

Fanning, A. E., *Steady as She Goes: A History of the Compass Department of the Admiralty* (London, 1986)

Fanshawe, E. L., *Admiral Sir Edward Gennys Fanshawe GCB* (London, 1904)

Fitzpatrick, K., *Sir John Franklin in Tasmania, 1837–1843* (Melbourne, 1949)

Fleming, F., *Barrow's Boys* (London, 1998)

Flint, K., *The Victorians and the Visual Imagination* (Cambridge, 1999)

Forbes, E. G., *Greenwich Observatory: The Royal Observatory at Greenwich and Herstmonceux, 1675–1975*, vol. I (London, 1975)

Fornasio, J., P. Monteath and J. West-Sooby, *Encountering Terra Australis: The Australian Voyages of Nicolas Baudin and Matthew Flinders* (Kent Town, SA, 2004)

Franklin, J., *Narrative of a Journey to the Shores of the Polar Sea in the Years 1819-20-21-22*, 2 vols. (London, 1823)

— *Narrative of some Passages of the History of Van Diemen's Land during the Last*

Three Years of Sir John Franklin's Administration of its Government (privately printed, 1845; facsimile edn Hobart, 1967)

Friendly, A., *Beaufort of the Admiralty: Sir Francis Beaufort, 1774–1857* (New York, 1977)

Gascoigne, J., *The Enlightenment and the Origins of European Australia* (Cambridge, 2002)

Gilder, W. H., *Schwatka's Search* (New York, 1881)

Girouard, M., *The Return to Camelot: Chivalry and the English Gentleman* (London, 1981)

Gleason, J. H., *The Genesis of Russophobia: A Study of the Interaction of Policy and Opinion* (Cambridge, Mass., 1950)

Gooch, G. P. (ed.), *Later Correspondence of Lord John Russell*, 2 vols. (New York, 1925)

Goodman, J., *The Rattlesnake: A Voyage of Discovery to the Coral Sea* (London, 2005)

Gordon, A., *The Rules of the Game: Jutland and British Naval Command* (London, 1996)

Gough, B. M. (ed.), *To the Pacific and Arctic with Beechey: The Journal of Lieutenant George Peard of H.M.S. Blossom, 1825–1828* (Cambridge, 1973)

Gribbin, J. and M. Gribbin, *Fitzroy: The Remarkable Story of Darwin's Captain and the Invention of the Weather Forecast* (London, 2003)

Guest, J. S., *The Euphrates Expedition* (London, 1992)

Hall, M. B., *All Scientists Now: The Royal Society in the Nineteenth Century* (Cambridge, 1984)

Harries-Davis, G. L., *Whatever Is Under the Earth: The Geological Society of London, 1807–2007* (London, 2007)

Harrod, D. (ed.), *War, Ice and Piracy: The Remarkable Career of a Victorian Sailor. The Journals and Letters of Samuel Gurney Cresswell* (London, 2000)

Harvey, E. J., *The Voyage of the Icebergs: Frederic Church's Arctic Masterpiece* (Princeton, 2002)

Hawkins, A., *The Forgotten Prime Minister: The 14th Earl of Derby – Ascent, 1799–1851* (Oxford, 2007)

Hayes, D., *Historical Atlas of the Arctic* (Seattle, 2003)

— *Historical Atlas of the North Pacific Ocean* (London, 2001)

Herschel, J. (ed.), *Admiralty Manual of Scientific Enquiry* (London, 1846)

Hill, Sir F., *Victorian Lincoln* (Cambridge, 1974)

Hordern, M., *Mariners are Warned! John Lort Stokes and HMS Beagle in Australia, 1837–1843* (Melbourne, 1989)

Horowitz, B. Z., 'Polar Poisons: Did Botulism Doom the Franklin Expedition?', *Clinical Toxicology*, 41 (2003), pp. 841–7

Howat, J. K., *Frederic Church* (Princeton, 2005)

Howse, D., *Greenwich Observatory: The Royal Observatory, 1675–1975*, vol. III (London, 1975)

Humboldt, A. von, *Cosmos: A Sketch of a Physical Description of the Universe*, 5 vols. (New York, London, c. 1847–52)

Huntford, R., *Scott and Amundsen: The Race to the Pole* (London, 1979)

Huxley, L., *Life and Letters of Joseph Dalton Hooker*, 2 vols. (London, 1918)

Hyman, A., *Charles Babbage: Pioneer of the Computer* (Princeton, 1982)

Jackson, C. I. (ed.), *The Arctic Whaling Journals of William Scoresby the Younger*, vol. I, *The Voyages of 1811, 1812 and 1813* (London, 2003)

Jackson, G., *The British Whaling Trade* (London, 1978)

James, F. A. J. L. (ed.), *The Correspondence of Michael Faraday*, vol. I, *1811–1831* (London, 1991)

Jones, A. G. E., *Polar Portraits* (Whitby, 1992)

Jones, M., *The Last Great Quest: Captain Scott's Antarctic Sacrifice* (Oxford, 2003)

Kane, E. K., *Magnetical Observations in the Arctic Seas, 1853–1855* (Washington, DC, 1859)

Keenleyside, A., M. Bertulli and H. C. Fricke, 'The Final Days of the Franklin Expedition: New Skeletal Evidence', *Arctic*, 50 (1997), pp. 36–46

Kellner, L., *Alexander von Humboldt* (Oxford, 1963)

Kerr, G. and H. McDermott, *The Huon Pine Story* (Portland, VIC, 1999)

King, R., *The Franklin Expedition from First to Last* (London, 1855)

Lambert, A. D., 'Australia, the Trent Crisis of 1861 and the Strategy of Imperial Defence', in D. Stevens and J. Reeve, (eds), *Southern Trident: Strategy, History and the Rise of Australian Naval Power* (Crow's Nest, NSW, 2001), pp. 99–118

— *The Foundations of Naval History* (London, 1997)

— *The Last Sailing Battle: Maintaining Naval Mastery, 1815–1850* (London, 1991)

— *Trincomalee: The Last of Nelson's Frigates* (London, 2002)

Lambert, A. D. (ed.), *Steam, Steel and Shellfire: The Steam Warship, 1815–1905* (London, 1992)

Lang, C. Y. and E. F. Shannon, *The Letters of Alfred Lord Tennyson*, vol. III, *1871–1892* (Oxford, 1990)

Learmonth, L. A., 'Notes on Franklin Relics', *Arctic*, 1 (1948), pp. 122–3

Leask, N., *Curiosity and the Aesthetics of Travel Writing, 1770–1840* (Oxford, 2002)

Lennie, C., *Landseer: The Victorian Paragon* (London, 1976)

Lentz, J. W., 'The Fox Expedition in Search of Franklin: A Documentary Trail', *Arctic*, 56 (2003), pp. 175–84

Levere, T. H., *Science and the Canadian Arctic: A Century of Exploration, 1818–1918* (Cambridge, 1993)

Lewis-Jones, H. W. G., '"Heroism Displayed"; Revisiting the Franklin Gallery at the Royal Naval Exhibition, 1891', *Polar Record*, 41 (2005), pp. 185–203

Littlewood, K. and B. Butler, *Of Ships and Stars: Maritime Heritage and the Founding of the National Maritime Museum, Greenwich* (London, 1998)

Lloyd, C., *Mr Barrow of the Admiralty* (London, 1970)

Loomis, C., 'The Arctic Sublime', in U. C. Knoepflmacher and G. B. Tennyson (eds), *Nature and the Victorian Imagination* (Berkeley, Calif., 1967), pp. 95–112

— *Weird and Tragic Shores: The Story of Charles Francis Hall, Explorer* (New York, 1971)

Lubbock, A., *Owen Stanley the Rattlesnake* (Melbourne, 1957)

— *Owen Stanley RN* (Melbourne, 1968)

Lyon, D., *The Sailing Navy List* (London, 1993)

Lyon, D. and R. Winfield, *The Sail and Steam Navy List* (London, 2004)

Mackaness, G. (ed.), *Some Private Correspondence of Sir John and Lady Jane Franklin (Tasmania, 1837–1845)*, 2 vols. (Sydney, 1947)

MacLeod, R. M., 'The Royal Society and the Government Grant: Notes on the Administration of Scientific Research, 1849–1914', *Historical Journal*, 14(2) (1971), pp. 323–58

Malchow, H. L., *Gothic Images of Race in Nineteenth Century Britain* (Stanford, 1996)

Malmesbury, Lord, *Memoirs of an Ex-Minister*, 2 vols. (London, 1884)

Manwaring, G. E., *My Friend the Admiral: Rear Admiral James Burney FRS* (London, 1931)

Marchant, L., *France Australe* (Perth, 1982)

Markham, A. H., *The Life of Sir Clements Markham* (London, 1917)
— *Life of Sir John Franklin and the North West Passage* (London, 1891)
Markham, C. R., *Antarctic Obsession: The British National Antarctic Expedition, 1901–04*, ed. and intro. C. Holland (Harleston, Norfolk, 1986)
— *The Arctic Navy List* (Portsmouth, 1875)
— *Franklin's Footsteps* (London, 1853)
— *The Lands of Silence* (Cambridge, 1921)
— *Life of Admiral Sir Leopold McClintock* (London, 1909)
— *A Refutation of the Report of the Scurvy Committee* (Portsmouth, 1877)
— *The Threshold of the Unknown Region* (London, 1873)
— 'Voyages and Discoveries, 1815–1856', in W. L. Clowes (ed.), *The Royal Navy: A History from the Earliest Times*, vol. VI (London, 1901), pp. 507–37
— 'Voyages and Discoveries, 1857–1900', in W. L. Clowes (ed.), *The Royal Navy: A History from the Earliest Times*, vol. VII (London, 1903), pp. 562–9
Markham, C. R. (ed.), *The Voyages of William Baffin, 1612–1622* (London, 1881)
Martin, T., *The Life of His Royal Highness the Prince Consort*, 5 vols. (London, 1875–80)
Marx, K., *The 18th Brumaire of Louis Napoleon Bonaparte* (London, 1852)
Matthew, H. G. C., 'Millais', in P. Funnell and M. Warner (eds), *Portraits* (London, 1999)
Maury, M. F., *The Physical Geography of the Sea*, 6th edn (London, 1874; 1st edn New York, 1855)
McClintock, F. L., *The Voyage of the Fox into the Arctic Seas*, 3rd edn (London, 1869 [1860]; repr. Cologne, 1998)
McCrea, W. H., *The Royal Greenwich Observatory* (London, 1975)
McGoogan, K., *Fatal Passage: The Untold Story of John Rae, the Arctic Adventurer Who Discovered the Fate of Franklin* (Toronto, 2001)
— *Lady Franklin's Revenge: A True Story of Ambition, Obsession and the Remaking of History* (London, 2006)
Meadows, A. J., *Greenwich Observatory*, vol. II (London, 1975)
Mill, H., *Records of the Royal Geographical Society* (London, 1930)
Millais, J. E., *The Life and Letters of Millais*, 2 vols. (London, 1902)
Morrell, J. and A. Thackray (eds), *Gentlemen of Science: Early Correspondence of the British Association for the Advancement of Science* (London, 1984)
— *Gentlemen of Science: Early Years of the British Association for the Advancement of Science* (Oxford, 1981)
Murphy, D., *The Arctic Fox – Francis Leopold McClintock: Discoverer of the Fate of Franklin* (Cork, 2004)
'The Nautical Fete, HMS *Erebus* and HMS *Terror*' (pamphlet, Hobart, 1841)
O'Byrne, W., *Naval Biographical Dictionary* (London, 1849)
O'Hara, J. G., 'Gauss and the Reception of His Ideas on Magnetism in Britain (1832–1843)', *Notes and Records of the Royal Society of London*, 38(1) (August 1983), pp. 17–78
Ormond, R., *Sir Edwin Landseer* (London, 1980)
— *Victorian Portraits* (London, 1973)
Osborn, S., *The Career, Last Voyage and Fate of Captain Sir John Franklin* (London, 1860)
Owen, R., *The Fate of Franklin* (London, 1978)
Parkinson, W. D., *Introduction to Geomagnetism* (Edinburgh, 1983)
Paszkowski, L., *Strzelecki: Reflections of His Life* (Melbourne 2004)

Phillimore, A., *Life and Letters of Admiral Sir William Parker*, vol. II (London, 1878)

Piesse, E. L., 'The Foundation and Early Work of the Society', *Papers and Proceedings of the Royal Tasmanian Society*, 1913, pp. 118–36

Pitcairn-Jones, C. C., *Piracy in the Levant, 1827–28* (London, 1934)

Platt, D. C. M., *Finance, Trade and Politics in British Foreign Policy, 1815–1914* (Oxford, 1968)

Port, M., *Imperial London: Civil Government Building in London, 1851–1915* (Princeton, 1995)

Rawnsley, W. F. (ed.), *The Life, Diaries and Correspondence of Jane Lady Franklin, 1792–1875* (London, 1923)

Read, B., *Victorian Sculpture* (Princeton, 1982)

Reid, T. W., *The Life, Letters, and Friendships of Richard Monckton Milnes, First Lord Houghton*, 2 vols. (London, 1890)

Revell, A. C., *Haslar: The Royal Hospital* (Gosport, 1978)

Rich, E. E. (ed.), *The History of the Hudson's Bay Company, 1670–1870*, 3 vols. (London, 1958–9)

— *John Rae's Correspondence with the Hudson's Bay Company on Arctic Exploration, 1844–1855* (London, 1953)

Riddell, C. J. B., *Magnetical Instructions for the Use of Portable Instruments Adapted for Magnetical Surveys and Portable Observatories* (London, 1844)

Riffenburgh, B., *The Myth of the Explorer* (Oxford, 1994)

Roberts, S., *Charles Hotham: A Biography* (Melbourne, 1985)

Robinson, M. F., *The Coldest Crucible: Arctic Exploration and American Culture* (Chicago, 2006)

Robson, L., *A History of Tasmania*, vol. I (Melbourne, 1983)

Ross, J. C., *Memoir of Admiral Krusenstern* (London, 1856)

— *A Voyage of Discovery and Research in the Southern and Antarctic Regions during the Years 1839–43*, 2 vols. (London, 1847)

Ross, M. J., *Polar Pioneers: John Ross and James Clark Ross* (Montreal, 1994)

Ruskin, S., *John Herschel's Cape Voyage: Private Science, Public Imagination and the Ambitions of Empire* (Aldershot, 2004)

Sabine, E., 'On Hourly Observations of the Magnetic Declination . . . HMS *Plover* 1852, 1853 and 1854, at Point Barrow', *Philosophical Transactions*, 147 (1857), pp. 497–532

Sainty, J. C., *Admiralty Officials, 1660–1870* (London, 1965)

Samson, J., 'An Empire of Science: The Voyage of HMS *Herald*, 1845–1851', in A. Frost and J. Sampson (eds), *Pacific Empires: Essays in Honour of Glyndwr Williams* (Vancouver, 1999), pp. 69–86

Savours, A., 'Clements Markham: Longest Serving Officer, Most Prolific Editor', in P. Hair (ed.), *Compassing the Vast Globe of the Earth: Studies in the History of the Hakluyt Society, 1846–1996* (London, 1996), pp. 165–88

— 'Hobart and the Polar Regions, 1830–1930', in G. Winter (ed.), *Tasmanian Insights: Essays in Honour of Geoffrey Thomas Stilwell* (Hobart, 1992), pp. 175–91

— *The Search for the North West Passage* (London, 1999)

Savours, A. and M. Deacon, 'Nutritional Aspects of the British Arctic (Nares) Expedition of 1875–76 and its Predecessors', in J. Watt, E. J. Freeman and W. F. Bynum (eds), *Starving Sailors: The Influence of Nutrition upon Naval and Maritime History* (London, 1981), pp. 131–62

Savours, A. and A. McConnell, 'The History of the Rossbank Observatory, Tasmania', *Annals of Science*, 39 (1982), pp. 527–64

Schroeder, J., *Shaping a Maritime Empire: The Commercial and Diplomatic Role of the American Navy, 1829–1861* (Westport, Conn., 1985)

Scoresby, W., *An Account of the Arctic Regions with a History and Description of the Northern Whale Fishery*, 2 vols. (Edinburgh, 1820)

Scott, R. F., *Scott's Last Expedition*, 2 vols. (London, 1914)

— *The Voyages of the 'Discovery'* (London, 1905)

Shakespeare, N., *In Tasmania* (London, 2004)

Shaw, A. G. L., *Sir George Arthur, Bart., 1784–1854* (Melbourne, 1980)

Shine, H. and C. S. Shine, *The Quarterly Review under Gifford* (Chapel Hill, 1949)

Simpson, A. W. Brian, *Cannibalism and the Common Law: A Victorian Yachting Tragedy* (Chicago, 1984)

Slater, M. (ed.), *'Gone Astray' and other Papers from Household Words, 1851–59* (London, 1998)

Smith, B., *European Vision and the South Pacific, 1768–1850* (Oxford, 1960)

Solomon, S., *The Coldest March: Scott's Fatal Antarctic Expedition* (New Haven, 2001)

Spry, I. M., *The Palliser Expedition* (Toronto, 1963)

— *The Papers of the Palliser Expedition, 1857–1860* (Toronto, 1968)

Stafford, R. A., *Scientist of Empire: Sir Roderick Murchison, Scientific Exploration and Victorian Imperialism* (Cambridge, 1989)

Stamp, T. and C. Stamp, *William Scoresby: Arctic Scientist* (Whitby, 1976)

Stanley, D., *Life of Thomas Arnold* (London, 1901)

Stanley, G. F. G., *John Henry Lefroy: In Search of the Magnetic North* (Toronto, 1955)

Statham-Drew, P., *James Stirling: Admiral and Founding Governor of Western Australia* (Crawley, WA, 2003)

Steele, P., *The Man Who Mapped the Arctic: The Intrepid Life of George Back, Franklin's Lieutenant* (Vancouver, 2003)

Stone, H. (ed.), *The Uncollected Writings of Charles Dickens: Household Words, 1850–1859*, vol. II (London, 1969)

Storey, G. and K. Tillotson (eds), *The Letters of Charles Dickens*, vol. VIII, *1856–1858* (Oxford, 1995)

Storey, G., K. Tillotson and A. Easson (eds), *The Letters of Charles Dickens*, vol. VII, *1853–1855* (Oxford, 1993)

Strzelecki, P., *Physical Description of New South Wales and Van Diemen's Land* (London, 1845)

Temperley, H., *The Foreign Policy of Canning, 1822–1827* (London, 1925)

Traill, H. D., *The Life of Sir John Franklin* (London, 1896)

van der Merwe, P., *Clarkson Stanfield, 1793–1867* (Gateshead, 1979)

Wallace, H. N., *The Navy, the Company and Richard King* (Montreal, 1980)

Warner, B. (ed.), *Lady Herschel: Letters from the Cape, 1834–1838* (Cape Town, 1991)

Warner, B. and N. Warner (eds), *The Journal of Lady Franklin at the Cape of Good Hope, November 1836: Keeping up the Character* (Cape Town, 1985)

Watt, J., E. J. Freeman and W. F. Bynum (eds), *Starving Sailors: The Influence of Nutrition upon Naval and Maritime History* (London, 1981)

Webster, Sir C., *The Foreign Policy of Palmerston, 1830–1841* (London, 1951)

Weld, C. R., *Arctic Expeditions* (London, 1850)

— *A History of the Royal Society* (London, 1848)

West, J., *The History of Tasmania* [Launceston, 1852], ed. A. Shaw (Sydney, 1971)

Wilkes, R-Adm. C., *Autobiography, 1798–1877*, ed. W. J. Morgan et al. (Washington, DC, 1978)

Williams, F. L., *Matthew Fontaine Maury, Scientist of the Sea* (New Brunswick, 1963)

Williams, G., *Voyages of Delusion: The Search for the North-West Passage in the Age of Reason* (London, 2002)

Wilson, B., *America's Ambassadors to England, 1785–1928* (London, 1928)

Wilton, A. and T. Barringer, *American Sublime: Landscape Painting in the United States, 1820–1880* (Princeton, 2002)

Windschuttle, K., *The Fabrication of Aboriginal History*, vol. I, *Van Diemen's Land, 1803–1847* (Sydney, 2002)

Wolf, N., *Caspar David Friedrich, 1774–1840: The Painter of Stillness* (Cologne, 2003)

Woodman, D., *Strangers Among Us* (Montreal and Kingston, 1996)

— *Unravelling the Franklin Mystery: Inuit Testimony* (Montreal, 1991)

Woodward, F., *A Portrait of Jane: A Life of Lady Franklin* (London, 1951)

Woodward, H., *History of the Royal Geological Society* (London, 1907)

Index

Aberdeen, Lord, 35, 236, 242

Acland, Sir Thomas, 192, 243

Admiralty: support for exploration, 11–12, 14, 15; and navigational science, 18; relationship with Royal Society, 13; takes control of Royal Observatory, 77; sends out 1818 and 1819–22 expeditions, 18–20, 31; JF reports on second expedition to, 40–1; budget cuts, 42–3; rejects JF's plan for expedition in late 1820s, 42; rota system, 53–4; agrees to observatory at Cape of Good Hope, 77; sends Ross rescue mission, 56; gives funds to Airy for magnetic observatories, 81–2; urged to fund further exploration, 85; assures JF his governorship of Van Diemen's Land will not block future naval employment, 94; sends surveying officer to Van Diemen's Land with JF, 94, 24; official dinner for JF's last expedition, 157; sends Moore's mission to Southern Ocean to make further magnetic observations, 171–2; starts to worry about JF, 179–83; sends out relief missions, 183, 184; unwilling to spend more money on relief missions, 189, 190, 195; 'Friends of Sir John Franklin' persuade them to send supply ship, 190–1; agrees to send further missions, 195, 198, 202; press management of search, 204; refuses to send supply ship to Austin, 204; moves to close search for JF, 205; problems with Jane, 207–8; view of state of search for JF reported to PM, 209; and US search expeditions, 213; Jane uses US search efforts to urge on, 214, 215; and catastrophe theories, 215; supports Kane's Wellington Channel expedition, 215; rejects Pim's expedition, 217, 218, 219, 220; rejects Hooper's scheme, 221; and Beatson's expedition, 223–4; rejects Jane's offer of Beatson's ship, 225; overview of responses to Jane's campaign, 226; approves Collinson's expedition, 227, 228;

and Belcher's expedition, 229, 236; sends Isabel to join Belcher's expedition, 233–4; need to find records of JF expedition, 240–1; starts to close down search for JF, 241–6; releases cannibalism story, 247; asks HBC to verify Rae's report, 248, 252, 253; resists Jane's calls for naval officer to accompany HBC expedition, 253; Jane continues to push for more search expeditions, 260–72; gives partial support to McClintock's Fox expedition, 276, 277, 279; pays Jane widow's pension, 279; pays for Fox expedition after the event, 286, 293; see also Barrow, Sir John; Barrow, John, Jr

Advance, 198, 212

Airy, George Biddell: overview, 80–2; attitude to Sabine, 67; view of importance of magnetic North Pole to geomagnetic science, 142, 168; argues for fewer observations and more analysis, 173, 175; petitions for another search expedition for JF, 261; feud with Sabine, 299; becomes president of Royal Society, 300

Alaska, 35, 41

Albert, Prince: at 1851 BAAS meeting, 205–6; reads Austin's dispatches, 207; appealed to for help in search for JF, 259, 260, 262, 263; opens 1859 BAAS meeting, 284; inspects Fox, 286

American Geographical and Statistical Society, 212

Amundsen, Roald, 237, 314, 324, 330, 332–3

Anatolia, 68

Anderson, James, 253, 256, 258

Anstey, Chisholm, 379n.96

Antarctic: French expedition, 127–8, 132; US expedition, 128, 132–3, 211; James Ross's expedition lobbied for and planned, 59, 71, 80, 86–8; Ross's expedition takes place, 83, 89–90, 129–34; cost of Ross's expedition, 168; Scott's expeditions, 324,

327–8, 328–30, 331–3, 343; Shackleton's expeditions, 90, 331; Amundsen's expedition, 332–3

Antigua, 93

Arago, François, 45, 79, 87, 127

Arctic: popular attraction to, 10; in literature, 10; history of exploration, 10–21, 29–31; reasons for exploration, 11; funding for and promotion of exploration, 13–14; societies promoting exploration, 13; Barrow's histories of exploration, 17–18, 179; exploration drops from favour, 189–90, 194; US interest, 211; first transition from Pacific to Atlantic, 235; campaign medal for all post-1815 explorers, 256; Canada inherits British claim, 274, 314; change in nature of missions after 1859, 284, 296; US exploration, 301–3; paintings of, 307–13, 325; Markham's history of exploration, 317; Markham's list of explorers, 317–18; popular misunderstanding of reasons for expeditions, 330–1; nowadays, 335; ice conditions, 336–7; see also individual explorers by name; North West Passage

'Arctic Council, The' (Pearce), 311, 322

Arctic Navy List, The, 317–18

Argos, 49

Argyll, George Douglas, Duke of, 262, 264, 384n.80

Armitage, Thomas, 346

Armstrong, Dr Alexander, 298

Arnold, Thomas, 95, 111

Arrowsmith, John, 273

art, 307–13, 325

Arthur, Sir George: overview of governorship of Van Diemen's Land, 97–8; treatment of indigenous Tasmanians, 99; penal policies, 101, 102; character and qualities, 110; land ownership polices, 107; founds botanical garden in Van Diemen's Land, 115; breaks with Montagu after misuse of loan, 137–8

Arthur, Lady, 106

Assistance, HMS, 198–9, 229, 235, 315

astronomy, 75, 77, 112

Athenaeum Club, 34–5

Athens, 49

Auckland, Lord: visits Herschel at Cape, 112; consults Barrow about lack of news from JF, 182; James Ross advises on search for JF, 183, 185; Jane appeals to, 185; and Ross's search mission, 185, 186; unwilling to spend more money on search for JF, 189, 190; death, 190; Jane on, 224

aurora borealis, 31, 56, 73, 310

Austin, Captain Horatio Thomas: leads expedition to search for JF, 198, 199–200, 201–2, 204, 205; return home, 207; opinion of JF's whereabouts, 209; inquiry into efficacy of expedition, 215; and Bellot memorial, 242

Australia: Flinders's expedition, 23–5; Parry takes up management of Australian Company New South Wales estates, 44; New South Wales as penal colony, 104, 108; New South Wales granted local government, 105; New South Wales land ownership policy, 107–8; New South Wales wool economy, 108; development of Melbourne and Port Phillip, 104–5, 108; defences, 121; Royal Navy establishes permanent station, 122; improved sea approaches, 126; Moore's voyage to, 172

BAAS see British Association for the Advancement of Science

Babbage, Charles, 34, 45, 67, 69, 70, 88

Back, Captain George: Banks's role in career, 19; goes on JF's 1819–22 expedition, 31–3; goes on JF's 1825–6 expedition, 39; sent on Ross rescue mission, 55, 56–7; 1836 expedition, 57; and Maconachie, 363n.28; attends official Admiralty dinner for JF's last expedition, 157; attitude to JF's last expedition, 160; joins committee to push for more searching for JF, 190; rescue schemes, 195; part of inquiry into Austin expedition, 215; on Beaufort, 275; reputation, 275; visits Church exhibition, 309

Back river (formerly Great Fish river): JF proposes exploring in 1828, 42; Back and King travel down, 56; death march of JF's expedition to, 287, 341–6; Dease and Simpson explore, 164; King advocates as location for JF's last expedition, 182, 198; identified as likely end location for JF expedition, 248, 249; and Fox expedition, 279, 281

Bacon, Charles, 289

Baffin Bay: Scoresby reports open to navigation, 14–15; John Ross confirms existence, 19; John Ross rescued from, 54; James Ross rescues whalers, 57, 85, 210; Sabine advises searching for JF round, 181; James Ross has problems crossing in search for JF, 186–7; and Austin's expedition, 199; and US expedition, 200; whale oil trade, 210; Inglefield searches shores, 234; Fox overwinters in, 279; Albert Markham visits, 317; Clements Markham collects material on, 319

Baffin Island, 19, 187

Bance, James, 112

Banks, Sir Joseph: background, 7, 13; meets Humboldt, 7; lobbying in support of exploration, 13; and Scoresby, 14–15; relations with Barrow, 15; and 1818 and 1819–22 expeditions, 18, 19, 29; and Flinders's Australian expedition, 24; patronage of JF, 27, 29, 30; death, 61–2

Banks Island, 20, 232

Banks Land, 163, 164, 186, 197

Baring, Sir Francis: becomes First Lord of the Admiralty, 190; and hunt for JF, 195–6; refuses to send further search expeditions, 205, 207; reports to PM on state of search for JF, 209; requests copy of report of US expedition, 213; supports Pim's expedition, 217, 218, 219, 220; and Beatson's expedition, 221, 223; and Belcher's expedition, 230; Jane enlists in campaign to mythologise JF, 290; Jane's acknowledgement of help given, 291, 292

barnacles, 155, 197

Barnard, James, 116

Barretto Junior, 160, 161, 165, 182

Barrington, Daines, 18

Barrow, Sir John: background and responsibilities, 11–12, 15; support for exploration, 13–14, 15; as reviewer of expedition narratives, 8–9, 14, 20; relations with Banks, 15; book about Arctic exploration, 17–18; sends out 1818 and 1819–22 expeditions, 18–20, 31, 33; exploits Russian threat to argue for further expeditions, 36; provides editorial support for expedition narratives, 37; sanctions further expeditions for JF and Parry, 37; savages John Ross's expedition narrative, 54; powerlessness to set mission objectives, 57–8; uses RGS to push exploration, 63, 64; hatred of John Ross, 66; engineers Sabine's election as FRS, 66; emphasis on exploration, 69; promotes James Ross's Antarctic expedition, 71; urges Admiralty to fund further exploration, 85; sends son to help JF in Van Diemen's Land, 94; JF introduces Field to, 123; reviews Wrangel's expedition narrative, 129; pushes for another Arctic expedition, 143, 145, 148–50; discusses expedition with JF, 152; retirement, 148, 153, 374n.1; inspects JF's ships, 157; attends official Admiralty dinner for JF's expedition, 157; mistaken belief in an open Polar Sea, 163; publishes second Arctic book, 179; consulted about relief mission for JF, 182; death, 187; scapegoated for exploration expenses and failures, 192

Barrow, Colonel John, Jr (son of the above): takes control of Admiralty library and records, 69; assembles committee to put pressure on Admiralty to search for JF, 190; Jane urges to send supplies to Austin, 204; asked to make archive of JF documents, 205; emotional involvement in search for JF, 206–7, 381n.58; gives Admiralty cutting of Jane's letter praising US expedition, 214; attempts to discredit catastrophe theories, 215; and RGS, 216; and Pim's expedition, 218, 219; and Maguire's expedition, 225; congratulated on Cresswell's walking across Passage, 241; and Bellot memorial, 242; urges Admiralty to send naval officer with HBC expedition to substantiate Rae's report, 253; waning influence, 253, 377n.13; and watch presented to McClure, 254; and JF's *Encyclopaedia Britannica* entry, 257; testimonial for, 259; Jane continues to press for inside information, 260; disheartened with efforts to obtain further search expedition, 265; Grinnell expresses support to for further expedition, 269; retirement, 270; and unveiling of Waterloo Place memorial, 294; at Jane's funeral, 298; Pearce produces portraits for, 311; lends pictures for 1891 Royal Naval Exhibition, 322

Barrow, Peter, 94, 363n.8

Barrow Strait, 186, 232

Bass Strait survey, 125–6

Beagle, HMS, 125, 146, 300

Beatson, Captain Donald, 221–6

Beattie, Dr Owen, 343–4, 347

Beaufort, Admiral Sir Francis: overview, 68–72; supports JF's election as FRS, 34; at Eleanor Franklin's funeral, 38; as friend of JF, 45; JF collects data for, 49; JF consults about his career, 55; founder member of RGS, 64; support for Sabine, 67, 68; strained relations with Airey, 81, 82, close relations with Sabine, 81, 82; tests new instruments, 83; urges Admiralty to fund further exploration, 85; supports and plans James Ross's Antarctic expedition, 70–1, 86–7; selects helpers for JF in Van Diemen's Land, 94; JF explains dismissal

of Maconachie to, 103; dispatches *Beagle* to Australia, 124–5; keeps JF up to date with developments while he's in Van Diemen's Land, 129, 143, 369n.5; JF supplies with tidal and astronomical data from Van Diemen's Land, 132; helps Sabine with geomagnetic data gathering, 144; supports JF in Montagu affair, 147; provides support for idea of another Arctic expedition, 149; discusses expedition with JF, 152; and JF's sailing orders, 158; helps arrange magnetic survey in Hudson's Bay, 169; orders Stanley home from tropics, 169; Sabine asks to find funds to publish geomagnetic data, 169; helps Sabine fill in gaps in magnetic observations in Southern Ocean, 171; selects Moore for Southern Ocean mission, 172; continues to support Sabine's work, 173; consults about relief mission for JF, 179–80; instructs Kellett to help look for JF, 184; urges James Ross to take command of search mission for JF, 185; dines with James Ross and Jane, 189; joins committee to push for more searching, 190; Sabine persuades to recover Ross's Antarctic records, 193; continues to hope for JF's safe return, 195; ensures search missions will carry magnetic instruments, 196; presses for search of Lancaster Sound, 197; supports further search missions, 198; gives inside information to Jane, 206, 207; supports Kane's Wellington Channel expedition, 216; theory about JF's route, 216; supports Pim's expedition, 217, 218; supports Beatson's expedition, 221, 222, 223; gives opinion on uses to which Beatson's ship could be put, 225; opinion of JF's whereabouts, 227–8; supports Collinson's expedition, 228; support for Belcher, 229, 230, 231; finally gives up hope for JF, 230; Northumberland consults about Belcher expedition, 232; and Kane's expedition, 233; admires Inglefield's achievements, 234; mountain named for, 234; continues to work with Sabine, 236–7; collates advice for Kane, 239; considers it sacred duty to carry on search for JF, 246; despite heart attack advises Jane in aftermath of Rae report, 253; retirement, 238, 253; still continues to help Jane's campaign, 263, 266, 270; overview of help given by him to search for JF, 274–5; death, 275; believes JF to have completed Passage, 289
Beaufort Sea, 275

Bedford, HMS, 26–8
Beechey, Captain Frederick: 1825–6 Arctic expedition, 37, 39–40; at Eleanor Franklin's funeral, 38; rescue plan for John Ross, 43; consulted about relief mission for JF, 181, 183; joins committee to push for more searching, 190; examines Penny on his expedition, 209; part of inquiry into Austin's expedition, 215; backs Collinson's expedition, 228
Beechey Island: JF's observatory on, 167; JF winters at, 336; remains of JF's expedition on, 199–200, 203, 207; Penny desires to search further, 215; and Belcher's expedition, 232, 233, 235, 283; Jane's memorial to explorers, 279
Belcher, Captain Sir Edward: background and character, 229; *Sulphur* cruise, 144; helps 'Friends of Sir John Franklin' campaign, 190; opposes Bering Strait as likely location for JF's expedition, 222; expedition to search for JF, 229–36, 243–4, 283, 369n.11; court martialled for loss of ships, 245–6; visits Church exhibition, 309; Albert Markham on, 323
Bellerophon, HMS, 26, 44
Bellot, Lieutenant Joseph René, 216, 241–2, 381n.54
Bellot Strait, 279
Bennett, James Gordon, 302
Berard, Captain, 116, 127
Bering Strait: Russia's control, 11; Burney believes Asia and America to be connected to north of, 16–17; and JF's 1825–6 expedition, 37; Canning secures access for British whalers, 41; as JF's ultimate navigational objective in last expedition, 162–3; Jones's survey work, 373n.23; and relief missions for JF, 183, 184, 195; US whale oil trade, 210, 211, 213; and Beatson's expedition, 221–5; Maguire's mission, 225; Collinson's expedition, 228, 237; favoured by some as location for JF, 263
Berkeley, Admiral Sir Maurice, 190, 205, 209, 267, 269, 379n.96
Bertulli, M., 347–8
Bethune, Captain Charles (Charles Ramsay Drinkwater), 122, 366n.47
Bicheno, James, 140
Bierstadt, Albert, 308
Biot, Jean-Baptiste, 67
Birds of Australia (Gould), 118
Blackwood, Captain Francis, 126, 134–5, 169, 368n.119

Blackwood's Edinburgh Magazine, 184
Blanky, Thomas, 337
Blazer, HMS, 161
Bligh, Captain William, 23–4
Blossom, HMS, 37, 39–40
Bolton, Sir William, 28
Bombay, 113
Booth, Felix, 45, 54, 198
Boothia (Poctes Bay), 57, 129, 164, 186, 282
Borda, Jean-Charles de, 8
botany, 115, 117, 132
botulism, 344
Bounty, HMS, 354n.23
Bowles, Admiral Sir William, 152, 215
Braine, William, 199–200, 348
Bramble, HMS, 134–5
British Association for the Advancement of
   Science (BAAS): foundation, 68, 78; JF
   attends meeting in Dublin, 56; influence,
   62; Murchison made president, 65; publishes Christie's report on Gauss's
   geomagnetic studies, 79; supports Sabine
   over Airey, 82; lobbies government for
   additional geomagnetic research funding,
   83–4, 85; Murchison made general secretary, 86; lobbies for Antarctic expedition,
   87–8, 89; Sabine replaces Murchison as
   general secretary, 66, 67, 88; secures Kew
   observatory and research grants, 145–6,
   172; Magnetic Committee meets in
   Cambridge, 146, 168; urges Scandinavian
   scientists to set up observatory at
   Finnmarken, 169; 1851 annual meeting
   campaigns to continue search for JF,
   205–6; 1859 meeting, 284
Brontë, Emily, 10
Brown, Dr Robert: as Banks's librarian, 27;
   supports JF's election as FRS, 34; and
   RGS, 64; supports JF after dismissal from
   governorship of Van Diemen's Land, 147,
   148, 162; acts as close adviser to Jane, 217
Brunnow, Baron, 191, 218
Buchan, David, 19, 29, 38, 77
Buckland, William, 45, 147, 155, 369n.20
Burke, Edmund, 307
Burnett, Thomas, 94, 124, 125, 366n.59
Burney, Rear Admiral James, 16–17, 18
Byam Martin Island, 232
Bylot Island, 19

Calder, James, 135
Cambridge Bay, 237, 340
Camden Bay, 237
Canada: JF's 1819–22 expedition, 21, 31–4;
   Toronto magnetic observatory, 170;

Lefroy's expedition, 170–1; Palliser's sur-
   vey, 272–4
Canadian Grand Trunk Railway, 310
cannibalism: as taboo, 2; and JF's 1819–22
   expedition, 32–3; among Van Diemen's
   Land's escaped convicts, 96; and JF's last
   expedition, 1, 247–52, 283, 288, 297,
   345–8; sailor cannibalism tales, 248–9;
   and Greely's expedition, 303
Canning, George, 41
Cape Astronomical Observatory, 77, 87,
   112, 171–2
Cape Bathurst, 186
Cape Bowden, 232
Cape Clarence, 186
Cape Coulman, 187
Cape Felix, 164, 167, 279, 338, 345
Cape Herschel, 72, 164, 280, 281
Cape John Franklin, 56
Cape Parry, 186
Cape Riley, 199, 204
Cape Sabine, 234, 303
Cape Town, 112–13
Cape Walker, 163, 186, 227, 336
Capo d'Istria, Count, 50
Captain, HMS, 326
Castlereagh, Lord, 36
Charles II, king of Great Britain and Ireland,
   74–5
Chesney, Colonel, 83
Chimborazo, Mount, 7–8
Christie, Samuel Hunter, 74, 81, 83, 361n.65
Church, Frederic Edwin, 300, 308–11
cinchona, 316
Clarence, Duke of *see* William IV, king of
   Great Britain and Ireland
Clarendon, Lord, 242
Clark, Lieutenant (director of Cape Town
   observatory), 171
Clements Markham Inlet, 319
Clowes, William Laird, 325
Cobden, Richard, 191, 243, 255–6
Cockburn, Admiral Sir George, 41, 46, 155,
   157
cold: effects, 2
Coldest March, The (Solomon), 331
Cole, Thomas, 308
Coleman, E. J., 312
Colenso, Bishop, 116
Coleridge, Samuel Taylor, 10
Collins, William Wilkie, 251
Collinson, Captain Richard: expedition to
   search for JF, 196, 204–5, 206–7, 228–9,
   231–2; Belcher leaves letters for him on
   Beechey Island, 283; search for, 234, 235,

245, 248; return home, 237–8, 250; and
JF's route, 252; acts as adviser for Jane,
255, 270; delays publication of narrative,
258; opinion of JF's whereabouts, 263;
drafts letter for Jane, 265; writes in support
of further search expedition, 266; handles
finances for McClintock's *Fox* expedition,
277; analyses McClintock's evidence, 282;
Murchison commends at unveiling of
Waterloo Place memorial, 294; at Jane's
funeral, 298; visits Church exhibition, 309
Colonial Office bust, 298, 314–15
Columbus, Christopher, 74
compasses *see* geomagnetic science
Congo expedition (1816), 29
Conrad, Joseph, 314
Cook, Captain James: influence, 7; first
Pacific voyage, 12; elected FRS, 13; final
voyage, 16; trains Bligh, 23; later disputa-
tion about findings, 17–18; longitude
calculation, 76
Cooke, Captain John, 26
Copenhagen, battle of (1801), 23
Coppermine river, 31–2, 163, 183, 356n.26
Corfu, 49, 50
Cornwallis Island, 200, 336
Coronation Gulf, 228
Cosmos (Humboldt), 174–6
Cowper, William, 190, 195, 198, 204,
207–8, 292–3
Cracroft, Sophia: on JF's interest in geomag-
netic science, 133; helps JF's defence
against dismissal from governorship of
Van Diemen's Land, 148; sees JF off on
last expedition, 159; rejects Crozier's mar-
riage proposal, 161; taken in by Beatson,
222; writes to Murchison about claim that
JF completed Passage, 255; helps Jane
compose letter to *Times*, 265; help with
the campaign, 266, 268, 270; sees
McClintock off, 279; helps with 1891
Royal Naval Exhibition, 321
Cresswell, Francis, 231
Cresswell, Samuel Gurney, 231, 235, 241
Crimean War (1854–6), 235, 242, 244, 260
Crozier, Captain Francis: goes on Ross's
Antarctic expedition, 130, 134; member of
Tasmanian Society, 116; magnetic observations at Rossbank, 130; made
second-in-command of JF's last expedition,
152; prepares for expedition, 154, 155;
attends official Admiralty dinner for expedition, 157; annoyance at Fitzjames's
geomagnetic responsibilities, 158; last letter home, 161; sends back some of his

supplies, 161–2; magnetic readings, 162;
as ice expert, 337; reaction to being stuck
in ice, 338; takes over as leader after JF's
death, 338; lands surviving men and sets
off for mainland, 287, 341–6, 375n.34;
mentioned in expedition records, 280
Cumby, Captain William Pryce, 26, 44
Cyriax, Richard, 149, 348, 393n.15

Dallas, George Mifflin, 266
Dance, Commodore George, 25–6
Dardanelles, 53
Darwin, Charles: evolution theory, 38, 63,
118, 300–1; contact with JF's last expedi-
tion, 155; scapegoats Barrow for Arctic
failures, 192; gives up hope for JF's expe-
dition, 197; and Palliser's survey of
Canada, 273; *Origin of the Species* pub-
lished, 286; growth in influence, 299–301;
awarded Royal Society's Copley Gold
Medal, 301
Davy, Sir Humphrey, 62, 69
Dayman, Peter, 131
De Haven, Edwin, 200, 213, 214, 239
Dease, Peter, 129, 134, 152, 164
Dease and Simpson Strait, 164
Dease Strait, 228, 237
death: Arctic causes, 2
Decaen, General, 25
declination, 8, 73, 74, 78–9
Delane, John: influence, 204; declares search
for Passage to have been waste of time,
208–9; Murchison works on, 262–3; links
with Murchison, 384n.75, 385n.83; con-
tinues opposition to sending further search
expeditions, 272; mythologises JF, 282–3;
remains opposed to further Arctic expedi-
tions, 296–7
Denison, Sir William, 120, 170
Derby, Lord (14th Earl; formerly Lord
Stanley): dismisses JF from governorship
of Van Diemen's Land, 106, 109; appoints
Eardley-Wilmot to replace him, 138–9; JF
and friends appeal to, 140, 147–8, 162;
Jane appeals to in hunt for JF, 223
Derby, Lord (15th Earl; formerly Lord
Stanley), 261, 264
Devon Island, 199, 235
Dickens, Charles, 250–2, 257, 271, 275,
277, 285
dip circles, 61, 74, 83, 153, 171
Disco, 162
Discovery, 329
Disraeli, Benjamin, 50, 197, 243, 313, 317,
327

Dolphin Strait, 228, 237
Douglas, Sir Howard, 157
Douglas Bay, 346
Drinkwater, Charles Ramsay *see* Bethune, Captain Charles
Dublin Antarctic Committee, 84
Dumont d'Urville, Jules Sébastien César, 116, 123, 128, 132
Dundas, Sir James, 190, 193, 204, 220, 241

Eardley-Wilmot, Sir John, 138–9, 146
Edinburgh Review, 20, 319–20
Edward VII, king of Great Britain and Ireland, 321
Edye, John, 183, 185
Egypt, 53, 126
Ellesmere, Earl of, 219, 222, 242, 262, 263
Ellesmere Island, 234, 318, 319
Elliot, Captain, 48
Elliot, Sir Henry, 94, 363n.7
Encyclopaedia Britannica, 257, 260
energy bars, 2
Enterprise, HMS, 185, 186–7, 228, 235
Enterprise (whaler), 166
Erebus, HMS: fitted out for Arctic service, 57; failed plans to use in new Ross expedition, 84; and Ross's Arctic expedition, 133; importance as expedition ship, 142; refitted for JF's last expedition, 153–4, 155, 156–7; engine, 156; Jane asks Gould to find monkey for, 159; deserted, 280
Erebus Bay, 199–200, 281, 345, 347–8
Ericsson, John, 156
Euphrates, 83, 361n.64
Evans, Petty Officer, 332
Everest, George, 69
evolution, 38, 63, 118, 300–1
expedition narratives: function and typical layout, 36–7

Fanshawe, Admiral, 215
Faraday, Michael, 34, 35, 45
Favourite, HMS, 126
Field, Lieutenant Allen, 366n.57
Field, Joshua, 156
Finlayson Island, 237
First World War (1914–18), 334
Fisher, Commander Peter, 150, 370n.34
Fitzjames, James: goes on Euphrates expedition, 361n.64; Barrow supports to lead Arctic expedition, 153; Barrow obtains promotion for, 374n.1; background and role in JF's last expedition, 154; attends official Admiralty dinner for expedition, 157; geomagnetic responsibilities, 158;

attends divine service led by JF just prior to expedition leaving, 159; letters home, 161; magnetic readings, 162; conviction that Passage lies north of Parry's Island, 182; notes written by him found, 199; expedition record written by him found, 280, 281, 341; concerns about expedition supplies, 215
Fitzroy, Captain Sir Robert, 94, 241, 273, 300
Flinders, Matthew, 22–3, 23–5, 27, 28–9, 360n.35
Flora of Tasmania (Hooker), 132
Fly, HMS, 134–5, 169
food: Arctic requirements, 343
Forster, Georg, 7
Forsyth, Captain Charles, 198, 199, 204
Forth, HMS, 28
Foster, Henry, 40
Fox: Arctic expedition, 276–83, 293, 327, 346; Victoria and Albert inspect, 286
Fox, Robert Were, 83, 153
France: Revolutionary and Napoleonic Wars, 23, 25–7, 28; involvement in Greek politics, 47, 48, 50; builds observatories round the world, 87; Antipodean activities, 121; threat of war with Britain, 122, 127; JF welcomes naval visits, 123; Antarctic expedition, 127–8, 132; rise of fleet seen as threat to Britain, 321
Frankenstein (Shelley), 10
Franklin, Eleanor (JF's daughter) *see* Gell, Eleanor
Franklin, Eleanor (née Porden; JF's first wife), 35, 38, 45
Franklin, Henrietta (JF's sister). 45
Franklin, Isabella (JF's sister), 164
Franklin, James (JF's brother), 22, 45, 56, 289
Franklin, Lady (née Jane Griffin; JF's second wife): background, 41; marries JF, 41, 44–5; on Parry, 44; relationship with JF, 44, 45, 93; interviews Stanley, 47; joins JF in Mediterranean, 50, 51; stays on in Mediterranean after JF's departure, 54; urges JF to try for new polar expedition, 55; visits Ireland with JF, 56; pushes JF to stay in employment, 58; sails for Van Diemen's Land with JF, 95–6; visits Cape Town en route to Van Diemen's Land, 113; unjustified reputation for interfering, 98; fear of snakes, 106; activities in Van Diemen's Land, 106, 111, 115, 117, 121, 128, 130, 132; admiration for Strzelecki, 119; trip to New Zealand, 106, 120, 126;

on Captain Nicolas, 127; helps James Ross buy land in Van Diemen's Land, 134; explores Van Diemen's Land with JF, 135; Montagu's hostility, 137; role in JF's dismissal from governorship of Van Diemen's Land, 106, 138; fights to get JF command of another Arctic expedition, 151; JF entrusts with completion of Van Diemen's Land defence leaflet, 152–3, 162; asks Gould to find monkey for *Erebus*, 159; sees JF off, 159; JF's last letters to, 164, 165; asks for relief mission for JF, 179, 182; concern deepens, 183; backs King's arguments, 185–6; disappointed at short length of James Ross's rescue mission, 188, 189; pushes for more to be done, 191–2; continues to hope, 193–4; public campaign, 196–7, 199; appeals to USA for help, 197, 212; growing influence, 198; supports Penny's and Forsyth's expeditions, 198, 199; prompts Barrow Jr to urge dispatch of supply ship to Austin, 204; supports US expedition, 213; persuades Murchison to campaign, 205; leans on Barrow Jr and Beaufort, 206; anxious to search further in Wellington Channel, 207, 208; strained relations with Admiralty, 207–8; desire to send out *Prince Albert* again, 209; supports Kane's Wellington Channel expedition, 216; asks Murchison to head up campaign, 216; backs Pim's expedition, 217, 218, 220, 221; backs Beatson's expedition, 221, 222–3, 223–4; tries to take over Beatson's expedition, 225; efficacy of her campaign, 226; backs Belcher's expedition, 230; sends *Isabel* to join Belcher, 233–4; admiration for Kane, 240; and Bellot memorial, 242; reaction to removal of expedition members' names from Navy List, 242–3; continues to hope, 246; reaction to Rae's report on expedition's end, 249–50, 252; Dickens sends copies of his articles to, 251; switches her energies to finding the expedition's records, 252–4; reaction to McClure's claim to have completed Passage, 255–6; urges Murchison to ask for another expedition to follow up HBC's, 256–7; and JF's *Encyclopaedia Britannica* entry, 257; continues to push for another expedition, 258–9, 260–72; monomania and paranoia, 262; offers Kane leadership of private expedition, 265; hopes to use *Resolute* in Arctic

dashed, 266, 267–8, 270–2; installs memorial for JF expedition in church built in Beaufort's memory, 275; and McClintock's *Fox* expedition, 276–8; Admiralty pays widow's pension, 279; sees McClintock off, 279; McClintock reports to, 281–2; sends McClintock's relics to Palace, 286; distributes copies of McClintock's *Fox* expedition narrative, 286; memorials and mythologisation for JF, 288–95; awarded RGS Founder's Gold Medal, 292; visits USA, 308; visits Church exhibition, 309; Pearce produces portraits for, 311; reaction to 'Man Proposes, God Disposes', 312; supports Clements Markham's call for further Arctic expedition, 317; meets Hall, 297; death and funeral, 298; Albert Markham on, 323

Franklin, Sir John
GENERAL: books and articles about, 323, 326–7, 334–5; character and qualities, 22, 31, 39, 58, 60; hearing, 26, 98; knowledge of languages, 25; knowledge of marine surveying, 29; knowledge of navigation, 24–5, 61; leadership skills, 39, 40, 47, 158; in paintings, 311–12; physique, 22, 41–2; places named for, 56, 120, 287; popularity, 191; promotion of family, 58–9; relationship with Jane, 44, 45, 93; religious faith, 35, 94, 95; reputation, 58; scientific friendships, 45, 69; sense of public duty, 58; and solar phenomena, 360n.23; statues and memorials to, 100, 288–95, 297–8, 314–15; writing style, 29
LIFE: childhood and family, 22–3; joins Navy, 23; at Copenhagen, 23; sails on Flinders's Australian expedition, 23–6; at Trafalgar, 26; commissioned lieutenant, 26; brother loses family business and savings, 27; Banks adds to list of scientific seamen, 27; in War of 1812, 27–8; 1818 expedition to Spitsbergen, 19, 29–31; earns popular fame, 31; 1819–22 overland expedition in Canadian Arctic, 21, 31–4; elected FRS, 34; founder member of Athenaeum, 34–5; founder member of RGS, 64; marries Eleanor, 35; Eleanor dies, 38; 1825–6 overland expedition in Canadian Arctic, 37–41, 211; knighted, 41; plan for further expedition in late 1820s rejected, 42; visits Russia, 44; marries Jane, 41, 44–5; elected fellow, then councillor, of the Royal Geological Society, 45; Mediterranean service, 46–52; made

Knight Commander of Guelphic Order of Hanover, 52; rescue plan for Ross rejected, 43; helps efforts to get expedition funds from Admiralty, 85; support for Sabine, 67; visits Ireland, 56; made governor of Van Diemen's Land, 58; prepares for government in Van Diemen's Land, 94–6; stops over in Cape Town on way to Van Diemen's Land, 112–13; arrives in Van Diemen's Land, 98–101; penal policies in Van Diemen's Land, 101–5; Jane's role in Van Diemen's Land government, 106; land sales and settlement policies in Van Diemen's Land, 107–9, 364n.50; education and cultural policies, 110–11; founds scientific society and museum in Van Diemen's Land, 113–17; encouragement of science and scientific visitors in Van Diemen's Land, 117–20; encouragement of sea traffic and shipbuilding in Van Diemen's Land, 120–1; and Van Diemen's Land's defences, 121–3; welcomes naval visits to Van Diemen's Land, 123, 126–7; works on charts, navigation and maritime safety in Van Diemen's Land, 123–6; visited by Antarctic travellers in Van Diemen's Land, 127–34; entertains Ross on his way to and from Antarctic, 130–1, 133–4; builds Rossbank, 130–1, 133, 134; explores Van Diemen's Land, 135–6; dismissed from governorship, 106, 109, 137–41; support for idea of another Arctic expedition, 143, 150; prepares to publish his defence against dismissal from governorship, 146–8, 152–3, 159, 162; appointed leader of 1845 expedition, 151–2; prepares, 152–9; good spirits on departure, 159–60; last letters home, 161, 163–4, 165–6; mentioned in *Cosmos*, 175; death, 280, 287, 338; controversy over will, 256; Richardson writes *Encyclopaedia Britannica* entry, 257, 260; mythologisation process, 282–3, 288–95, 297–8, 320–3, 325–6, 334–5, 349–51; myth's impact, 314–15; exhibits about at 1891 Royal Naval Exhibition, 320–3; fiftieth anniversary of departure, 324; Scott takes over as popular hero, 328, 330; likely burial place, 345; achievements assessed, 349–51
1845 EXPEDITION: connection with Ross's Antarctic expedition, 134; fight for funding, 141–52; rationale behind, 141–2, 148–9, 151, 166, 167; JF made leader, 151–2; preparations, 152–9; geomagnetic mission, 61, 153–5, 158, 162, 167–8; other scientific subjects of study, 155; press publicity, 155–6; causes of failure, 156; sailing orders, 158; from Woolwich to Whale Fish Islands, 159–62; route, 162–5, 200; Admiralty starts to worry, 179–83; Richardson/Rae relief mission, 183, 194; Moore's relief mission, 183–4, 373n.23; James Ross's search mission, 184–9, 194, 336; Admiralty sends supply ship, 190–1; rewards offered, 192; Bering Strait search mission, 196; Lancaster Sound search expeditions, 197–204, 212–15; Beechey Island findings, 199–200, 203; press coverage of search, 204; emergence of catastrophe theories, 215; Beaufort's and Jane's theories about route, 216; Pim's expedition fails to get off ground, 217–21; Beatson expedition likewise, 221–6; Collinson's expedition, 196, 204–5, 206–7, 228–9, 237–8; Belcher's expedition, 229–36, 243–4, 245–6, 283, 369n.11; Inglefield autopsies Hartnell, 234; relics, 61, 237; second US expedition, 212, 215–16, 233, 238–40; Admiralty closes down search, 241–6; Rae recovers artefacts from Inuit, 247–8; cannibalism, 1, 247–52, 283, 288, 297, 345–8; Dickens argues with Rae's report, 250–2; HBC expedition sent to verify Rae's report finds nothing but a few more artefacts, 248, 252–3, 256, 258; Rae given parliamentary reward for finding expedition, 260; Jane pushes for further search expeditions in vain, 260–72; memorials, 275, 279; McClintock's *Fox* expedition solves the mystery, 276–83, 293, 327, 346; only written record, 280–1; did it complete Passage?, 280–1, 285, 287–95, 323, 326; McClintock's account in *Fox* expedition narrative, 286–7; cost of search effort, 288; 1861 exhibition of relics, 288; memorials, 288–95, 297–8, 314–15; Hall's belief about survivors, 297; Irving and le Vesconte reburied, 298; Americans dig up bodies, 302; exhibits about at 1891 Royal Naval Exhibition, 321–2; Albert Markham's book about, 323; fiftieth anniversary of departure, 324; Clements Markham's article about, 326–7; author's account, 336–49; causes of death, 343–4, 347–8; may well have completed Passage, 346
Franklin, Thomas (JF's brother), 27
Franklin, Willingham (JF's brother), 22–3, 289
Franklin, Willingham (JF's father), 22

Franklin, Willingham (JF's nephew), 294
Franklin Point, 287
Franklin Strait, 281, 336, 337
Fremantle (Swan River Settlement), 94
Fricke, H. C., 348
Friedrich, Caspar David, 10, 307
Friend, Lieutenant Matthew, 124
Frozen Deep, The (Collins), 251

Gage, Sir William, 155, 157
Gauss, Carl Friedrich: overview, 78–80;
  Humboldt's influence, 8; Sabine's attitude,
  67; influence on Airey, 82; and Britain's
  network of magnetic observatories, 89;
  predicts location of magnetic south, 90;
  Herschel's support, 112–13; disagrees with
  Humboldt over importance of further
  Arctic exploration, 142, 168
Geikie, Archibald, 331
Gell, Eleanor (née Franklin), 35, 45, 111,
  159
Gell, John Philip, 111, 256
Gellibrand, Henry, 74
geodesic science, 18
geology: Lyell's ideas, 38, 49; data collected
  by explorers, 39, 49, 65–6; Murchison
  samples supplied by JF, 49, 136, 151;
  Murchison's developments, 63, 65–6;
  Strzelecki's work in Van Diemen's Land,
  119; McClintock's work in Arctic, 194;
  report in McClintock's *Fox* expedition
  narrative, 287
geomagnetic science: principles and history,
  72–7; instruments, 61, 74, 78, 83, 153,
  171; Humboldt's studies, 7–9; and
  Spitsbergen expedition (1773), 14;
  Scoresby's studies, 14–16; Parry's studies,
  20; JF's initial studies, 25; and JF's
  1819–22 expedition, 31, 33–4; and JF's
  1825–6 expedition, 38; James Ross locates
  magnetic north, 55, 67, 82; Back's studies,
  56; as rationale for expeditions, 57–8,
  82–90; Sabine's studies and data gathering,
  66–8, 82–3, 142–6, 168–9; Gauss's studies
  and data gathering, 78–80; term days,
  129–30, 144, 369n.8; Sabine's network of
  stations, 80, 88–9; arguments among scientists, 80–2; Royal Society Physics and
  Meteorology Committee's procedure manual, 89; Ross's Antarctic expedition
  calculates magnetic south, 89–90, 129–33,
  170; JF's work in Van Diemen's Land,
  130–1, 33, 134–5; Rossbank observatory,
  88, 115–16, 130–1, 133, 134, 170; Lloyd's
  developments, 144; as rationale for JF's

last expedition, 141–2, 148–9, 151, 166,
  167; and JF's last expedition, 61, 153–5,
  158, 162, 167–8, 338; Sabine produces
  chart of Southern Ocean, 170; magnetism
  realised to have both terrestrial and cosmic
  origins, 170; Lefroy's Canadian expedition
  confirms point of maximum total magnetic
  intensity and recalculates position of magnetic north, 171; Moore makes further
  observations in Southern Ocean, 171–2;
  Sabine continues to expand empire,
  172–4; Lloyd improves use of magnetometers, 173; Humboldt endorses progress,
  174–6; readings taken on search missions
  for JF, 183, 184, 186–7, 192–3, 194, 196,
  198–9, 202; Sabine backs Pim's expedition
  in order to get readings from Siberian
  coast, 219, 220; Maguire's readings in
  western Arctic, 225; and Belcher's expedition, 230–1, 246; Beaufort and Sabine
  continue to work together, 236–7; Sabine's
  desperation to recover JF's data, 261–2;
  Sabine promotes Palliser's Canadian survey as vehicle for more data, 273; and
  McClintock's *Fox* expedition, 278, 282;
  McClintock observes dip at pole, 282;
  Sabine switches attention from Arctic to
  Africa, 296; decline in importance,
  298–301; and 1875–6 Nares/Markham
  expedition, 318; and Scott's expeditions,
  331–2; Shackleton reaches magnetic south,
  90
George V, king of Great Britain and Ireland,
  321, 333
Gilbert, William, 74
Gipps, George, 119, 122
Girouard, Mark, 314
Gladstone, William Ewart, 278–9, 292, 293,
  297, 298
Glenelg, Lord, 93, 118
Goldner, Stefan, 215, 323, 326
Goodsir, Dr Harry, 155, 197
Gordon, Admiral Sir William, 245
Gore, Lieutenant Graham, 125, 154, 280,
  326, 337
Gould, John, 106, 118, 156, 159
Graham, Sir James: becomes First Lord of
  Admiralty, 42; and Malcolm, 48; JF
  presses for employment, 53–4; returns to
  Admiralty, 236; removes names of mem-
  bers of JF's last expedition from Navy List,
  241, 243; and Bellot memorial, 241, 242;
  resists Jane's calls for naval officer to
  accompany HBC expedition, 253
Great Fish river *see* Back river

Greece, 47–53
Greely, Adolphus, 302–3
Grey, Earl, 48
Griffin, John, 34, 233
Griffith Island, 200
Griffiths, Edward, 182
Grinnell, Henry: character and background, 212; funds private expedition to search for JF, 198, 212; Murchison raises testimonial for, 214; funds second expedition, 215, 238; FO thanks for help with search for JF, 258; purchases *Resolute*, 266; support for idea of further expedition, 269; supports view JF completed Passage, 285; acquaintance with Church, 308
Gulf Stream, 213
Gunn, Ronald, 106, 115, 117
Gurney, Hudson, 35

Haddington, Lord, 148, 151, 152, 155
Hakluyt, Richard, 15
Hakluyt Society, 319
Halkett, Peter, 242
Hall, Basil, 64
Hall, Charles Francis, 213, 297, 302, 340, 346
Halley, Edmond, 8, 75–6
Hamilton, Lieutenant Richard, 234
Hamilton, Captain William A. Baillie: position at Admiralty, 359n.6; on importance of geography, 63–4; Barrow Jr puts pressure on re search for JF, 206; involvement in Jane's campaign, 208, 377n.22; fears JF will be forgotten, 232; and Bellot memorial, 242; Beaufort's confidence in, 253
Hansteen, Christopher, 67
Hardy, Sir Thomas, 48
Harrison, John, 76
Hartnell, John, 199–200, 234, 348
Hartstene, Captain Henry J., 267
Haslar Royal Naval Hospital, 180
Hayes, Isaac Israel, 213, 301–2, 308, 310, 389n.88
HBC *see* Hudson's Bay Company
Hearne, Samuel, 21, 31, 356n.26
Hecla Strait, 42, 57
Hepburn, Seaman, 32
Herald, HMS, 46, 184
Herschel, John: Athenaeum member, 35; meetings at Beaufort's house, 69; Cape residency, 43, 87, 112–13; influence in promotion of geomagnetic science, 87; and lobbying for James Ross's Antarctic expedition, 70–1, 88; argues for international network of magnetic observatories, 81; on

importance of magnetic observatory in Van Diemen's Land, 88; article stressing importance of geomagnetic science, 89; JF's letters to from Van Diemen's Land, 113–14; and tidology, 132; disagrees with Humboldt over importance of further Arctic exploration, 142; president of BAAS 1845 meeting, 146, 168; lack of belief in geomagnetic aspect of JF's last expedition, 168; recommends Sabine for Royal Society Royal Gold Medal, 169; Sabine persuades to call for additional magnetic research, 170–1; argues for fewer observations and more analysis, 173; on Humboldt, 175; *Admiralty Manual*, 186, 375n.33; opposed to further Arctic expeditions, 297
Hobart: development, 97; appearance, 98–9, 100; society, 101–2; botanical gardens, 115; Ancanthe Museum, 117, 119; Franklin Wharf, 120; regatta, 121; defences, 122; improvements to sea approaches, 125; by-passed by improved sea approaches to Australia, 126; party for Ross after Antarctic expedition, 133–4; collapse of Australian fishery, 216; makes donation to McClintock's *Fox* expedition, 277; statue of JF in, 100, 295
Hobart Town Horticultural Society, 115
Hobson, Lieutenant William, 279–81, 298
Hood, Robert, 31–2, 50
Hooker, Joseph: goes on Ross's Antarctic expedition, 123, 131–2; member of Tasmanian Society, 115, 116; on Gould's *Birds of Australia*, 118; *Flora of Tasmania*, 132; secures Darwin's contact with JF's last expedition, 155; petitions for another search expedition for JF, 261; at unveiling of Waterloo Place memorial, 294; at Jane's funeral, 298; helps spread Darwin's ideas, 300; as head of Royal Society calls for new Arctic expedition, 317
Hooker, Sir William, 115, 261, 273
Hooper, Lieutenant William, 221
Horsborough, James, 34
horizontal intensity, 73
Hoskins, Admiral Anthony, 329
Hotham, Charles, 94
Hotham, Vice-Admiral Sir Henry, 48, 51–2
Household Words journal, 250, 251, 277
Howick, Lord, 103
Hudson's Bay, 169
Hudson's Bay Company (HBC): exploration as aid to trade, 21; supports JF's 1819–22 expedition, 32; Russia as risk to trade, 36; supports JF's 1825–6 expedition, 37; sup-

ports Ross rescue mission, 56; reasons for wishing to continue search for Passage, 72; and Dease and Simpson expedition, 164; supports Lefroy's expedition, 171; stands ready to assist relief missions for JF, 181; releases Rae to look for JF, 183; funds JF search mission, 198; Rae offers to assist in coastal survey for, 233; given task of substantiating details of Rae's report on JF's last expedition, 248, 252–3, 256, 258; loss of authority, 274

Humboldt, Alexander von: expeditions and studies, 7–9, 76–7; Barrow's review of narratives, 356n.29; influence, 12, 63, 67; attitude to Russia, 359n.11; Sabine's translations, 66; credits Columbus with compass correction work, 74; organises first international scientific congress, 77–8; persuades Gauss to look at geomagnetic science, 78; writes to Royal Society proposing international network of magnetic observatories, 79, 81, 86; recommends Gauss's methods to RGS, 79–80; strained relations with Gauss, 80; and Dublin Antarctic Committee, 84; support for British network of magnetic observatories, 88; argues for more state-funded geomagnetic research, 90; continues to push for further Arctic exploration, 141, 369n.2; publishes Cosmos, 174–6; awarded Copley Gold Medal by Royal Society, 176; Pim meets, 220; death, 284; Prince Albert eulogises, 284; influence on Church, 308

Hume, Joseph, 191–2

Huntford, Roland, 351

Huxley, Thomas, 300

Hydrographer's Office, 69; see also Beaufort, Admiral Sir Francis; Washington, Captain John

hydrography, 68–72; see also Beaufort, Admiral Sir Francis; geomagnetic science; Washington, Captain John

hypothermia, 2

'Iceberg, The' (Church), 310

'Icebergs, The' (Church), 309–10

Icy Cape, 37, 39–40

Illustrated London News, 155–6, 278

inclination, 73, 74, 78, 79

India, 113, 316

Inglefield, Captain Edward, 233–4, 235, 242

Inglis, Sir Robert: as Athenaeum member, 35; speaks in Parliament in support of continuing search for JF, 195, 205, 223, 379n.96; on Jane's draft letter to

Admiralty about their decision to end search for JF, 243; speaks in debate about Admiralty decision, 243; deputation to Wood about verifying Rae's report, 254

intensities: horizontal, 73; total, 73, 78

Intrepid, 198, 199, 229, 234, 245

Inuit: Kotzebue meets, 17–18; pilfer from JF's 1825–6 expedition, 39; knowledge of JF's whereabouts, 229; rescue Kane, 239; encounters with JF's last expedition, 247–8, 339, 346, 347, 348; Dickens argues they murdered the expedition members, 250–2; sell more JF relics to Fox expedition, 279, 281; Hall believes survivors from JF's expedition to be living among, 297; Hall's researches into society, 302; Markham on, 316; avoidance of scurvy, 340

Investigator, HMS: on Flinders's Australian expedition, 23–5

Investigator, HMS: on James Ross's search expedition, 185, 186–7; on Collinson's search expedition, 228, 235, 241, 340–1; tableau of at 1891 Royal Naval Exhibition, 322

Ireland, 56, 85

Irving, Lieutenant John, 280, 298, 345

Isabel, 221, 224, 225, 233–4

Isabella, 54

Istanbul, 52, 53, 54

Johnson, Lyndon, 268

Jones Sound, 197, 201–2, 209

Kamchatka, 211

Kane, Dr Elisha Kent: goes on first Grinnell expedition, 200–1, 214–15; leads second expedition, 212, 215–16, 233, 238–40, 258; Jane offers Barrow Jr portrait of, 260; believes there could still be survivors from JF's expedition, 261; Jane uses in attempt to embarrass Admiralty, 262; British honours, 265; refuse Jane's offer of expedition, 265; death, 265

Kane Basin, 239, 303

Kant, Immanuel, 307

Kater, Captain Henry, 18, 30, 35

Kay, Lieutenant Joseph Henry, 47, 116, 130, 131

Keenleyside, A., 347–8

Kellett, Captain Henry: JF speaks to about last expedition, 221; looks for JF in Herald, 184; and Beatson's expedition, 223, 224; and Collinson's expedition, 228; goes on Belcher's expedition, 229, 231,

234–5, 245; Jane consults about Rae's report, 252; ship salvaged by Americans, 258
Kendall, Edward, 40, 165
Kendall, Mary (née Kay), 40, 165
Kennedy, John F., 268
Kew observatory *see* Royal Observatory, Kew
King, Captain (Hobart post officer), 124
King, Captain Philip Parker, 35, 47, 137, 146, 157
King, Dr Richard: character, 161, 179; goes on Ross rescue mission, 56–7; jealousy of JF, 160–1; urges Admiralty to send relief mission, 179; advocates Back river as JF's location, 182, 185–6, 198; suggests land expedition to find JF, 268
King William Island: author travels across, 2–3; JF's expedition stuck off coast of, 287, 338–41; Inuit meet survivors from JF's expedition on, 247; HBC expedition narrows search to, 256; McClintock finds remains of JF's expedition, 281; Hall reaches, 302; Schwatka sledges across, 302; lack of fuel, 343; remains found on, 344, 347
King William Land, 55, 72, 164, 199, 252, 282
Kotzebue, Otto, 17–18, 44
Kotzebue Sound, 184
Krusenstern, Admiral, 44, 163, 372n.110

Lady Franklin (sailing brig), 195, 202
Lady Franklin (whaler), 121
Lambert, General, 28
Lancaster Sound: John Ross believes to be dead end, 19; and JF's sailing orders, 163; missions to find JF in, 186, 197–203, 212–15; McClintock's *Fox* expedition in, 279
Lands of Silence, The (Markham), 334–5
Landseer, Sir Edwin, 311–12
Laplace, Cyrille, 127
Larsen, Inspector, 345
Laughton, Professor John, 319–20
Lawrence, Abbot, 213
lead poisoning, 343–4, 347
Lefroy, Captain John, 170–1, 183, 373n.19
Lempriere, Thomas, 132
Lincoln, 289
Linois, Admiral, 26
Liverpool Albion, 216, 242
Livingstone, David, 261, 296, 386n.116
Lloyd, Humphrey: attends BAAS meeting in Dublin, 56; geomagnetic studies, 79, 85,

87; instruments invented by, 83; visits Humboldt, 88; developments in geomagnetic science, 144; helps prepare for JF's last expedition, 153; improves use of magnetometers, 173
longitude determination, 18, 75–6, 112
Lyell, Charles, 35, 38, 49
Lyon, Captain George, 35, 38

McClintock, Captain Sir Francis Leopold: goes on James Ross's search expedition for JF, 187–8, 194; goes on Austin's expedition, 199, 201, 215; goes on Belcher's expedition, 229, 234; speaks at Belcher's court martial, 245; Jane consults about Rae's report, 252; Jane wants him to lead privately funded search expedition, 253; supports Jane's campaign, 268, 271; as adviser to Jane, 270; *Fox* expedition to search for JF, 276–83, 293, 327, 346; reception back home, 285–6, 292; narrative of *Fox* expedition, 286–7, 314; later career, 286; photographed with finds, 288; success embarrasses government, 290; government pays for expedition, 286, 293; opinion of Hall's beliefs, 297; at Jane's funeral, 298; visits Church exhibition, 309; advises on Nares/Markham expedition, 318; supports 1891 Royal Naval Exhibition, 320, 321; Clements Markham on *Fox* expedition, 327; Clements Markham's biography, 328; advises Scott, 331; on King William Island, 339; calculation of quantity of food carried by JF's men on death march, 342
McClintock Channel, 337
McClure, Sir Robert: goes on Collinson's expedition, 196, 206–7; separates from Collinson and claims to have completed Passage, 228, 340–1; search for, 231–2, 234; Kellett finds, 235; reception back home, 244; knighted, 238; claims prize for having completed Passage, 254–7; at Barrow Jr's testimonial, 259; own testimonial, 259; Jane's view of Passage claims, 291, 298; death, 298
Maguire, Captain Rochefort, 225, 237, 263, 278
Mackenzie, Alexander, 21
Mackenzie river: JF travels down in 1826, 38; delta established as British, 41; and hunt for JF, 181, 182, 195; Richardson and Rae travel down, 183; Pullen travels down, 184
Mackinnon, William, 256

Maconachie, Captain Alexander, 94, 102–3, 104

Macquarie harbour, 135

magnetic science *see* geomagnetic science

Magnetic Union, 79, 80, 112–13

magnetometers, 174; bifilar, 78; unifilar, 83

malaria, 316

Malcolm, Vice-Admiral Sir Pulteney, 48

'Man Proposes, God Disposes' (Landseer), 311–12

Mare, Peter, 242

Markham, Rear Admiral Albert: 1873 trip to Baffin Bay, 317; 1875–6 expedition with Nares, 315, 318–19; Laughton praises, 319–20; later expeditions, 320; and 1891 Royal Naval Exhibition, 320, 321, 322; as hero, 322; book about Franklin, 323; court martialled for smashing into *Victoria*, 324; Clements Markham lauds achievements, 327; clothes displayed at 1905 Naval, Shipping and Fisheries Exhibition, 328; and Scott's expeditions, 329; death, 334

Markham, Clements: background, 315–18; introduced to Murchison, 284–5; history of Arctic exploration, 317, 319; launches Nares/Markham expedition, 318–20; lectures on need to collect Arctic maps and memorabilia, 320; prepares 1891 Royal Naval Exhibition, 320, 321; and Scott's expeditions, 324, 327–8, 328–30, 331; contributes to Clowes's RN history, 325–8; elected president of RGS, 328; knighted, 328; history of polar exploration, 334–5; death, 334

Martin, Captain, 166

Marx, Karl, 330, 331, 351

Maudslay, Son & Field, 156

Mauritius, 172

Maury, Captain Matthew Fontaine, 211, 213, 239, 309

Mecham, Lieutenant George, 201, 234, 235

Melbourne, 105

Melville, Herman, 249

Melville, Lord, 46

Melville Island, 164, 186, 188, 197; *see also* Winter Harbour

Mendelssohn, Moses, 8

Michel (expedition member), 32

Millais, John, 312–13

Milne, Captain Alexander: and Ross's rescue expedition, 186, 191; argues against Beaufort's rescue proposal, 195; fears sending out further search expeditions will mean losing more men, 204, 227; and

Belcher's expedition, 232, 236; starts to close down JF search, 241; supports idea of further search expeditions, 259, 267

Milnes, Monckton, 385n.114

Minto, Lord, 85, 89, 94, 169, 367n.87

Moby Dick (Melville), 249

Monkey, HMS, 160, 161

Montagu, John: dislike of JF's ideas in Van Diemen's Land, 102; JF forced into anti-Maconachie alliance with, 103; orchestrates JF's dismissal from governorship of Van Diemen's Land, 106, 137–8; falls out with Arthur, 137–8; writes to JF's replacement in Van Diemen's Land, 140; JF publishes defence against, 146–8, 152–3, 159, 162; Crozier on ungentlemanly conduct, 162; later career, 369n.145

Montreal Island, 279, 281, 285, 346

Moore, Lieutenant T. E. L., 172, 183–4, 373n.23

Moose Factory, 373n.23

Moriarty, Captain William, 124

Morning Chronicle, 209, 221

Morning Herald, 191, 208, 209, 243

Murchison, Sir Roderick: background and overview, 62–6; JF gathers data for, 49; relationship with JF, 41, 45; supports further exploration to get geomagnetic data, 84–5; as general secretary of BAAS helps Sabine lobby for expedition funds, 86, 89; resigns as BAAS general secretary, 88; JF introduces Strzelecki to, 119; JF sends rocks from Van Diemen's Land to, 136, 151; proposes thanks to Queen for BAAS's acquisition of Kew observatory, 145; support sought in fight for another Arctic expedition, 151; JF dines with at Royal Geological Society, 155; predicts successful return for JF, 160; chairs Royal Society Committee of Recommendation, 173; campaigns for JF search agenda, 193; Jane persuades to campaign for more search missions, 205; raises testimonial for Grinnell, 214; heads up JF campaign, 216; supports Pim's expedition, 217–21; supports Beatson's expedition, 221–4; tries to persuade Admiralty to take over Beatson's ship, 225; reward for fronting Jane's campaign, 226; relationship with Belcher, 229; argues for *Isabel* to join Belcher, 233–4; Inglefield names strait for, 234; continues to urge action on Admiralty, 241; and Bellot memorial, 241; reaction to Rae's report on expedition's end, 249–50; and

Dickens, 251; writes to Admiralty and Palmerston to urge independent naval verification of Rae's report, 253–4; global ambitions, 383n.31; and McClure's claim to have completed Passage, 255; and JF's *Encyclopaedia Britannica* entry, 257; continues to push for another expedition, 260–3, 265, 266–72; relations with Palmerston, 267; relations with Milnes, 385n.114; promotes Palliser's survey, 273; McClintock acknowledges debt, 278; turns to promotion of his geographic mission, 278–9; Collinson analyses McClintock's evidence for, 282; at 1859 BAAS meeting, 284; Osborn begs to take Beaufort's place, 284; meets Clements Markham, 284–5; praises McClintock, 285; uses McClintock's *Fox* expedition to criticise government, 286; preface to and influence on McClintock's *Fox* expedition narrative, 286, 287, 314; Jane enlists in campaign to mythologise JF, 290, 291, 292; makes arrangements for unveiling of Waterloo Place memorial, 294; backs Osborn's call for new Arctic expedition, 296–7; visits Church exhibition, 309; end of career, 301

Murray, John: as Admiralty printer, 12, 37; and *Quarterly Review*, 14, 16; invites Barrow to write book, 17; expedition narratives lucrative for, 37; publishes for RGS, 64; markets *Tasmanian Journal of Science*, 116; JF introduces Strzelecki to, 119; and Bellot memorial, 242; prints McClintock's *Fox* expedition narrative, 286; at unveiling of Waterloo Place memorial, 294

Mycenae, 49

Nafplion, 49
Nansen, Fridjtoft, 324, 331
Napier, Sir Joseph, 268, 385n.108
Napoleonic Wars (1803–15), 25–7, 28
Nares, Captain George, 313, 318, 320, 321, 327
Narrative of Arthur Gordon Pym, The (Poe), 249
National Maritime Museum, 320
Naval, Shipping and Fisheries Exhibition (1905), 328
Navarino, battle of (1827), 47
navigation: compass correction, 14, 20, 25, 38; longitude determination, 18, 75–6, 112; hydrography, 68–72; and astronomy, 75, 112; JF's improvements in Van

Diemen's Land, 123–4; *see also* geomagnetic science
Navy Board, 16
Navy Board Inlet, 191
Nelson, Horatio Lord, 23, 26, 44
New Guinea, 169
New Orleans, battle of (1814–15), 27–8
New South Wales *see* Australia
New York, 211
New Zealand, 106, 120, 121, 126
Nicholas I, Russian tsar, 44, 221, 222
Nicolas, Captain Toup, 127
Noble, Matthew, 293, 295, 298
Norman, Robert, 74
North Somerset, 199
North Star, HMS, 46, 191, 229, 233, 235
North West Bay Company, 32
North West Passage: history of search for, 9–12, 14–21; strategic importance, 9–10; potential economic uselessness, 42, 54; unknown elements decrease, 71–2, 134; geomagnetic science as rationale for further exploration, 84; as rationale for JF's last expedition, 142, 158, 167; known parts at time of JF's last expedition, 164–5; claims that Rae completed, 232–3, 252; McClure erroneously supposed to have completed, 244; Cresswell walks across, 241; McClure claims prize for having completed, 254–7; claims that last JF expedition completed, 280–1; support for view JF completed, 285, 287–95, 323, 326; Jane claims McClure completed different Passage from JF, 291; as metaphor, 313; Amundsen completes, 324, 330; nowadays, 335; JF's expedition may well have completed, 346
'North-West Passage, The' (Millais), 312–13
Northampton, Marquis of, 88, 89, 150, 157
Northumberland, Algernon Percy, Duke of, 34, 220, 223, 230, 232
Northumberland Sound, 233
Norton Sound, 17–18

Oates, Captain 'Titus', 332
Ommaney, Captain Erasmus, 198–9, 207, 233, 242, 294, 298
Origin of the Species (Darwin), 286, 299–300
ornithology, 118
Osborn, Captain Sherard: goes on Austin's expedition, 200; on Weld, 220; goes on Belcher's expedition, 229, 234; and Barrow Jr's testimonial, 259; supports Jane's campaign, 270, 272; begs

Murchison to take Beaufort's place, 284; brings together Murchison and Clements Markham, 284–5; and Jane's claim that JF completed Passage, 291; Murchison commends at unveiling of Waterloo Place memorial, 294; urges new Arctic expedition, 296–7, 316–17; mythologisation of JF, 314; advises on Nares/Markham expedition, 318

Otho, king of Greece, 51, 52

Pagoda, 172
paintings, 307–13, 325
Pakenham, General Sir Edward, 28
Pakington, Sir John, 291–2, 294
Palliser, Captain John, 272–4
Palmerston, Lord: as Athenaeum member, 35; Turkish policy, 48–9; on Taylor's friendly response to Jane's appeal, 192; supports Pim's expedition, 218; relationship with Bowles, 378n.45; asked by Murchison to take up issue of verification of Rae's report, 254; supports committee to judge McClure's claim to have completed Passage, 255; Jane writes to him about McClure's claim, 255; endorses another Arctic expedition, 383n.35; Murchison appeals to for support for another expedition, 261; Jane appeals to, 263; backs idea of further expedition, 264–5, 266–7, 269; relations with Murchison, 267; Jane convinced he will help, 268; leaves matter to Parliament to decide, 269; further appeals to, 271; Murchison presses to knight McClintock, 286, 292; government embarrassed by McClintock's success, 290; and memorials for JF, 292

Panama Canal, 194
Pandora, 298
Parish, Woodbine, 378n.72
Parker, John, 379n.96
Parker, Admiral Sir William, 230
Parry, Sir Edward: background, 19; popularity, 10; Scoresby's influence, 16; 1818 expedition, 19, 30; 1819 expedition, 20–1; exploits Russian threat to argue for further expeditions, 36; 1826 expedition, 37, 54; knighted, 41; appointed to manage Australian Company estates in New South Wales, 44; gains interview for nephew with Jane, 47; and Beaufort, 69; marriages, 93; post-exploration career, 93; consulted by JF on Van Diemen's Land appointment, 94; supports JF in Montagu

affair, 147; provides support for idea of another Arctic expedition, 149, 150; discusses expedition with JF, 152; serious illness curtails his helping JF prepare, 155; helps fit out *Erebus* and *Terror*, 156; attends official Admiralty dinner for JF's expedition, 157; and JF's sailing orders, 158; JF's last letters to, 161, 164; JF confirms position set for Disco, 162; consulted about relief mission for JF, 179–80, 181, 183; works with Richardson at Haslar Royal Naval Hospital, 180; joins committee to push for more searching for JF, 190, 195; approves main Lancaster Sound mission, 197–8; recommends Austin for command, 198; opinions on Cape Riley findings, 204; examines Penny on his expedition, 209; part of inquiry into Austin's expedition, 215; supplies advice for Kane's Wellington Channel expedition, 216; Jane casts off, 222; backs Collinson's expedition, 228; Northumberland consults about Belcher, 232; and Cresswell's walking across Passage, 241; and Bellot memorial, 241; Jane consults about Rae's report, 252

Parry's Fury, 42
Patras, 50–1
Paul I, tsar of Russia, 23
Pearce, Alexander, 96
Pearce, Stephen, 299, 311, 322
Peary, Robert, 350
Peel, Sir Robert, 35, 147, 149, 168, 369n.20
Peel, Sir Robert, Jr (son of the above), 260
Peel Strait (formerly Sound): geography, 387n.20; and JF's expedition, 149, 282, 336; James Ross travels down, 187; Forsyth fails to sail down, 199; Austin expedition gets near, 201; McClintock's *Fox* expedition finds blocked by ice, 279; Young traces shores, 281

Peglar, Harry, 346
Pelly, Henry, 129
Pelorus, HMS, 124
Penny, Captain William: goes on Austin's expedition, 198, 200, 202; return home, 207, 209; on need to build monument for JF, 290; on US Arctic exploration, 302

Percy, Algernon *see* Northumberland, Algernon Percy, Duke of
Percy, Admiral Sir Josceline, 172
Phipps, Colonel, 262
Phipps, Captain Constantine, 14
Phoenix, 235
Pim, Lieutenant Bedford Clapperton: proposed expedition fails to get off ground,

217–21; sends money to fund use of *Isabel* as search ship, 225; goes on Belcher's expedition, 231, 234, 381n.35; suggests land expedition to find JF, 268; later career, 379n.79
Pioneer, 198, 199, 200, 229, 235
plate tectonics, 7–8
Plover, 183–4, 204, 217, 225, 237, 243, 373n.23
Poctes Bay *see* Boothia
Poe, Edgar Allan, 249
Point Barrow, 225
Point Franklin, 56
Point Le Vesconte, 345
Point Sabine, 39
Point Turnagain, 37, 42, 164
Point Victory, 72, 164, 279–80, 287, 297
poles: Parry fails to reach magnetic north, 20; James Ross locates magnetic north, 55, 67, 82; Ross calculates magnetic south, 89–90, 129–33, 170; Lefroy recalculates position of magnetic north, 171; McClintock observes dip at north, 282; Scott's and Amundsen's attempts on south, 331–3; Shackleton reaches magnetic south, 90
Polyphemus, HMS, 23
Pond, John, 77
Port Arthur, 97, 122, 132
Port Clarence, 237
Port Leopold, 187, 188, 232
Possession Bay, 188
Prince Albert, 198, 199, 204, 209, 216
Prince of Wales, 166
Prince of Wales Strait, 228
Prince Regent Inlet, 186, 193, 199, 279
Princess Royal Island, 235
Pullen, Commander William, 184, 204, 229

Quarterly Review: Barrow's reviews, 14, 20; Barrow's articles, 16; Herschel writes essay about need for further magnetic research in North America, 170–1

Radstock, Admiral Lord, 155
Rae, Dr John: background, 183; goes on search mission with Richardson, 183, 194; *Times* publishes news of exploits, 204; considered by some to have completed Passage during 1851 survey, 232–3; in Victoria Channel in 1853, 237; meets Inuit with JF artefacts, 247–50; Dickens argues ineffectually with his report, 250–2; did he complete the Passage?, 252; given parliamentary reward for finding JF's

expedition, 259, 260; lectures in New York on search for JF, 308; visits Church exhibition, 309; Clements Markham on his JF discoveries, 327; reasons for success as overland traveller, 340
Rainbow, HMS, 46–52
Raleigh Club, 218–19
Rattler, HMS, 160, 161
Rattlesnake, HMS, 46, 169
Reid, James, 337
Rennie, George, 35
Rennie, John, 35
Repulse Bay, 42, 247
Rescue, 198, 212
Resolute: on Austin's expedition, 198; on Belcher's expedition, 229, 234; abandoned in Arctic, 235, 245; Americans salvage and return to Britain, 258, 266; Jane's hopes to use in Arctic dashed, 266, 267–8, 270–2; Jane desires as depot ship for *Fox*, 276–7; ultimate fate, 268
Revolutionary Wars (1793–1802), 23
RGS *see* Royal Geographical Society
Rhin, Le, 127
Richards, Captain George: goes on Belcher's expedition, 234, 235; goes on Collinson's expedition, 238; now Hydrographer, speaks in support of further Arctic expeditions, 296; at Jane's funeral, 298; advises on Nares/Markham expedition, 318
Richardson, Sir John: goes on JF's 1819–22 expedition, 31–3; false assertions of criminality, 356n.26; on JF's leadership skills, 34, 40; on utility of Passage, 42; JF recruits to report on collection of fish taken in Van Diemen's Land, 116; supports JF's defence against dismissal from governorship of Van Diemen's Land, 147, 148; recommends JF to lead last expedition, 152; JF's last letter to, 161; Barrow achieves promotion for, 374n.1; consulted about relief mission for JF, 179–80, 181–2, 183; works with Parry at Haslar Royal Naval Hospital, 180; relief mission for JF with Rae, 183, 194; approves main Lancaster Sound mission, 198; opinions on Cape Riley findings, 204; hopes 1851 BAAS meeting will persuade government to continue search for JF, 205–6; analyses Penny's weather logs, 207; supplies advice for Kane's Wellington Channel expedition, 216; continues to hope there are some survivors from JF's last expedition, 225; backs Collinson's expedition, 228; on Rae's 1851 achievements, 232; letter

claiming JF completed Passage, 255; writes JF's *Encyclopaedia Britannica* entry, 257, 260; and Palliser's survey, 273; romantic view of JF's achievements, 285; influence on Darwin, 286; inaugurates Spilsby statue of JF, 289; possible author of letter supporting memorial to JF's last expedition in Trafalgar Square, 289; motto engraved on Waterloo Place memorial, 294–5

Riddell, C. J. B., 153

Rifle Movement, 289

Rikord, Admiral, 51

'Rime of the Ancient Mariner' (Coleridge), 10

Ringgold–Rodgers mission, 211

Robinson, George, 99

Roebuck, John, 268–9

Rosen, Count, 156

Ross, George, 56

Ross, Sir James Clark: Banks's role in career, 19; detects magnetic north while on John Ross's 1818 expedition, 55–6, 67, 82; rescues whalers, 57, 85, 210; tests new instruments, 83; plans to send to Passage fall through, 84–5; co-authors report on geomagnetism in Ireland, 85; optimism about Admiralty giving more exploration funds for Passage, 85–6; disputes Dumont d'Urville's claim to have found magnetic south, 118; member of Tasmanian Society, 116; advocates establishment of permanent Royal Navy Australian station, 122; Wilkes shares information with, 128; refits in Hobart en route to Antarctic, 130–2; Antarctic expedition, 59, 70–1, 80, 83, 86–8, 89–90, 129–34; winters at Hobart on way back from Antarctic, 133–4; JF complains to about Montagu affair, 138; suggested as leader for further Arctic expedition, 142, 143, 145; too drained to take it on, 145, 151; marriage, 145; support for idea of another expedition, 150; supports JF as leader, 151–2; illness of father-in-law prevents his helping JF prepare, 155; against fitting of steam engines in *Erebus* and *Terror*, 156; attends official Admiralty dinner for JF's expedition, 157; and JF's sailing orders, 158; lack of leadership skills, 158; JF's last letters to, 161, 164; John Ross's chart of his Arctic exploration, 164; cost of Antarctic expedition, 168; selects Moore for Southern Ocean mission, 172; consulted about relief mission for JF, 179–80, 181, 183; leads search mission, 184–9, 194, 336; alcohol problems, 185; examines Penny on his expedition, 209; opinion of JF's whereabouts, 209; supplies advice for Kane's Wellington Channel expedition, 216; backs Collinson's expedition, 228; and Cresswell's walking across passage, 241; and McClure's testimonial, 259; recommends McClintock to Jane, 276; his cairn found by JF expedition, 280; last public appearance and later fate, 284, 387n.33; Clements Markham on, 326

Ross, Sir John: Scoresby's influence, 16; Banks's role in career, 19; 1818 Arctic expedition, 19–20, 66, 77; Barrow's feelings for, 66; and Beaufort, 69; 1829–31 expedition, 43, 45–6, 54–5, 56–7; pessimism about JF's last expedition, 160; chart of James Ross's Arctic exploration, 164; denigrated in Barrow's second Arctic book, 179; asks for relief mission for JF, 179, 181; persuades Booth to fund search mission, 198; accompanies Penny on search mission, 200, 202; opinion of JF's whereabouts, 209

Ross, W. Gillies, 330

Royal Astronomical Society, 69, 70

Royal Dublin Society, 271

Royal Geographical Society (RGS): foundation and activities, 45, 63–4, 70; support for exploration, 13; presses for further Arctic missions, 57; Beaufort's role, 70; Humboldt recommends Gauss's methods to, 79–80; public meeting in support of continuing search for JF, 205; Murchison's promotion of, 216; supports Pim's expedition, 217, 218, 219; and Beatson's expedition, 222; awards Gold Medal to Rae, 232; awards Founder's Gold Medal to McClure, 244; awards Gold Medal to Kane, 265; *Resolute* dinner, 266; Dickens speaks at, 277; awards Patron's Gold Medal to McClintock, 285; awards Founder's Gold Medal to Jane, 292; Clements Markham becomes secretary, 315, 316; calls for new Arctic expedition, 316–17; gives gold watch to Albert Markham, 320; Clements Markham elected president, 328; and Scott's first Antarctic expedition, 328–9; awards Patron's Gold Medal to Scott, 331

Royal Geological Society: support for exploration, 13; Lyell's ideas, 38; JF elected fellow, then councillor, 45; Murchison made president, 63; JF dines at, 155

Royal Institution, 34, 45
Royal Naval Exhibition (1891), 320–3
Royal Naval Hospital memorial to JF,
    289–90
Royal Observatory, Greenwich, 70, 75, 77,
    81–2, 85, 299
Royal Observatory, Kew, 145–6, 172, 173,
    299
Royal Society: foundation, 74–5; support for
    exploration, 13, 14–15, 18; and naviga-
    tional science, 18; relationship with
    Admiralty, 13; list of members, 34; JF
    elected fellow, 34; JF's attendance, 45;
    finances expedition to search for Ross, 56;
    loss of interest in exploration, 61–2;
    Murchison made vice-president, 63;
    Sabine's role, 66, 67; Beaufort's role, 68,
    69, 70; issue of admission of amateurs, 70;
    Beaufort lobbies to set up Passage commit-
    tee, 71; relationship with Royal
    Observatory, 75; suggests observatory at
    Cape of Good Hope, 77; Humboldt writes
    to proposing international network of
    magnetic observatories, 79, 81, 86; adopts
    Gauss's methods for collecting geomag-
    netic data, 80; proves inefficient lobby
    group for more magnetic observatories,
    83; lobbies for Antarctic expedition, 87–8,
    89; committees provide manuals for
    Antarctic expedition, 89; asked to report
    on scientific advantage of further Arctic
    exploration, 149; supports idea of another
    Arctic expedition, 150; Sabine elected for-
    eign secretary, 169; Physics Committee
    makes case to Admiralty for further mag-
    netic observations in Southern Ocean,
    171–2; awarded annual grant to support
    science, 173; awards Copley Gold Medal
    to Humboldt, 176; offers scant help to
    Jane in search for JF, 192; advises on
    Palliser's survey of Canada, 273; helps
    McClintock's Fox expedition, 278; Sabine
    becomes president, 299; Airy becomes
    president, 300; awards Copley Gold
    Medal to Darwin, 301; calls for new
    Arctic expedition, 317; and Scott's first
    Antarctic expedition, 329; see also Banks,
    Sir Joseph
Ruskin, John, 309
Russell, Lord John, 103, 205, 218–19, 220,
    223, 242
Russia: poses threat to Britain in Arctic, 11,
    35–7; Kotzebue's Arctic expedition,
    17–18; provokes battle of Copenhagen,
    23; improved relations with Britain, 41; JF

visits, 44; involvement in Greek politics,
    47, 48, 50–1; British desire to use Turkey
    as bulwark against expansion, 48–9; task
    force at Istanbul causes British fears, 53–4;
    Murchison visits, 65; used as threat in
    Barrow's argument for another Arctic
    expedition, 150; and JF's last expedition,
    183–4; threat of war with Britain, 184;
    and Pim's expedition, 217, 218, 220–1;
    and Beatson's expedition, 222; and
    Maguire's expedition, 225; Crimean War,
    235, 242, 244, 260; rise of fleet seen as
    threat to Britain, 321

Sabine, General Sir Edward: overview, 66–8,
    82–5; goes on John Ross's 1818 expedi-
    tion, 77; goes on Parry's 1819 expedition,
    19, 20, 30; supports JF's election as FRS,
    34; relations with JF, 45; attends BAAS
    meeting in Dublin, 56; founder member of
    RGS, 64; and solar phenomena, 360n.23;
    solicits letter from Humboldt to Royal
    Society about geomagnetic data gathering,
    79, 81; achieves network of geomagnetic
    observatories, 80, 88–9; strained relations
    with Airey, 80–1, 82; close relations with
    Beaufort, 81; lobbies for further explo-
    ration as means of gathering geomagnetic
    data, 83, 84, 85; tests new instruments,
    83; effectiveness as scientific promoter, 86;
    urges funds for James Ross's Antarctic
    expedition, 70–1, 86–7, 89; becomes gen-
    eral secretary of BAAS, 66, 67, 88; blocks
    Scoresby's application for grant to study
    magnetic needles, 89; wife translates
    Wrangel's expedition narrative, 129, 143;
    Ross relays Antarctic findings to, 130;
    given painting of Rossbank observatory,
    130; promotion, 133; pushes for another
    Arctic expedition, 142–6, 148–9, 150–1;
    secures Kew observatory and research
    grants for BAAS, 145–6; pushes Ross to be
    leader of next Arctic expedition, 152;
    helps JF prepare for expedition, 153–4,
    156; attends official Admiralty dinner for
    JF's expedition, 157; and JF's sailing
    orders, 158; JF's last letter to, 161; zenith
    of magnetic empire, 168–9; elected foreign
    secretary of Royal Society, 169; recom-
    mended for Royal Society Royal Gold
    Medal, 169; and tidology, 169; produces
    chart of Southern Ocean, 170; sends mis-
    sion to Canada, 170–1; arranges for
    further observations in Southern Ocean,
    171–2; continues to extend empire of

observations, 172–4; knowledge of sun spots, 174; he and wife translate *Cosmos*, 174–5; consulted about relief mission for JF, 179–80, 181, 183; sends magnetic instruments with Richardson/Rae relief mission, 183; comforts Jane, 183; article in *Admiralty Manual*, 375n.33; joins committee to push for more searching for JF, 190; gives magnetic equipment to all JF search missions, 192–3, 196, 198–9; publishes Rae's magnetic observations, 194; supplies advice for Kane's Wellington Channel expedition, 216; backs Pim's expedition, 219, 220; backs Beatson, 225; gives instruments to Maguire's expedition, 225–6; relationship with Belcher, 229; backs Belcher's expedition, 230–1; further promotion of geomagnetic science, 232–3; Inglefield names cape for, 234; continues to work with Beaufort, 236–7; and Bellot memorial, 241; Belcher delivers magnetic data to, 246; asked by Murchison to help establish JF's route, 261, uses idea of another expedition as opportunity to expand research, 261–3; relations with Milnes, 385n.114; promotes Palliser's survey of Canada, 273; encourages McClintock's *Fox* expedition, 277, 278; publishes McClintock's data sets, 282; at 1859 BAAS meeting, 284; at unveiling of Waterloo Place memorial, 294; switches attention from Arctic to Africa, 296; backs Osborn's call for new Arctic expedition, 296; end of career, 298–301; picture of at 1891 Royal Naval Exhibition, 321

St Roch, 345

Schwatka, Frederick, 302, 338, 340, 345, 346

Scobell, Captain, 379n.96

Scoresby, William, Jr: explorations and geomagnetic studies, 14–16; denigrated by Barrow goes back to whaling, 15–16, 18; lack of belief in Passage, 20–1; influences on, 77; Sabine blocks grant application, 89; joins committee to push for more searching for JF, 190; continues to hope, 193; as source for Maury, 213

Scott, Reverend Alexander, 44

Scott, Lady, 333

Scott, Peter, 131

Scott, Peter Markham, 329

Scott, Captain Robert Falcon: on Antarctic death, 2; JF as inspiration, 314; first Antarctic expedition, 329, 331; second Antarctic expedition, 329, 331–3, 343;

mythologisation, 324, 328, 330, 333–4

Scott Polar Research Institute, 333

scurvy: effects, 343; and Dumont d'Urville's expedition, 123, 128; and Laplace's expedition, 127; and JF's last expedition, 326, 339–41; and Ross's search expedition, 188; and Belcher's expedition, 235; and Albert Markham's 1875–6 expedition, 318–19; Albert Markham claims polar animal food can preclude, 323

'Sea of Ice, The' (Friedrich), 10

Seeley, John, 333

Seymour, Sir Hamilton, 378n.72

Shackleton, Ernest, 90, 331, 333–4

Shelley, Mary, 10

Shenandoah, CSS, 213

Siberia, 184, 217–21

Silurian System, The (Murchison), 65

Simpkinson, Francis, 170

Simpson, Brian, 249

Simpson, Sir George, 37, 356n.25

Simpson, Thomas, 129, 134, 142–3, 152, 164, 369n.4

Simpson Strait, 281

Singapore, 172

sledging, 201, 342

Smith, W. Thomas, 325

Smith Sound, 234, 239, 317

Smucker, Samuel M., 240

Smyth, W. H., 64

solar phenomena, 73, 76, 174, 360n.23

Somerset, Duke of, 292

Sophia, 198, 202

Southey, Robert, 354n.27

Spilsby, 289, 334

Spitsbergen: 1773 expedition, 14; 1818 expedition, 19, 29–31; list of years when free from ice, 21; 1826 expedition, 54

Stafford, Augustus, 223, 379n.96

Stanfield, Clarkson, 251

Stanley, Lord see Derby, Lord

Stanley, Captain Owen: serves on *Rainbow* with JF, 47; helps test Fox's improved dip circle, 83; and Torres Strait route, 126; sails in *Beagle*, 134; on Rossbank, 134; one of last to see JF, 161; drawing of Low Head lighthouse, 366n.67; surveys coast of New Guinea, 169; death, 169

Starvation Cove, 344, 346

Stefansson, Viljalmur, 340

Stephen, James, 111, 138

Stewart, Captain Alexander, 198

Stewart, Captain Houston, 204

Stirling, Captain James, 94

Stokes, Captain John Lort, 125, 146, 273

Strzelecki, Count Paul, 119, 146–7, 157, 273, 277, 294
Sulphur, HMS, 144
sun *see* solar phenomena
Sussex, Duke of, 118, 362n.82
Swan River Settlement *see* Fremantle
Symonds, Captain Sir William, 156
Syria, 53

Tahiti, 121, 127
Talbot, 235
Talbot, Constance Fox, 283
Tasmania *see* Van Diemen's Land
Tasmanian Islands, 277
Tasmanian Journal of Science, 116–17
Tasmanian Society, 113–17, 139
Taylor, President Zachary, 212
Terror, HMS: fitted out for Arctic service, 57; 1836 mission under Back, 87, 340; failed plans to use in new Ross expedition, 84; and Ross's Antarctic expedition, 133; importance as expedition ship, 142; refitted for JF's last expedition, 153–4, 155, 156–7; engine, 156; deserted, 280
Terror Bay, 345, 348
Thames, 121
'They Forged the Last Link with Their Lives' (Smith), 325
Threshold of the Unknown Region, The (Markham), 317, 319
tidology, 132, 169
time measurement, 77, 81
Times, The: argues against further Arctic exploration, 194; reluctantly blesses a last mission, 195; influence, 204; declares search for Passage to have been waste of time, 208–9; barrow Jr writes to to discredit catastrophe theories, 215; on US whaling industry, 216; on removal of the names of the members of JF's last expedition from the Navy List, 243; publishes cannibalism story, 247; reaction to Rae's report, 250; Murchison works on to back another search expedition, 261, 262–3; argues against further expedition, 265; Jane's reply, 265–6; Jane considers asking for help, 272; helps to build JF myth, 282–3; declares an end to Arctic dream, 287–8; reviews Church's 'The Icebergs', 309; reviews Landseer's 'Man Proposes, God Disposes', 312; *see also* Delane, John
Todd Islands, 346
Toronto, 170
Torres Strait, 126, 134

Torrington, John, 199–200, 348
total intensity, 73, 78
Trafalgar, battle of (1805), 26
Trafalgar Square, 289, 293
Traill, H. D., 355n.2, 358n.27
Trelawney, Edward, 313
Trent, 29–31
Trincomalee, HMS, 232
Troughton, Edward, 34
Tryon, Admiral Sir George, 324
tuberculosis, 348
Tuckey, James, 29
Tulloch Point, 346
Turkey, 48–9, 52, 53
Turner, J. M. W., 309
Two Grave Bay, 345

Union Strait, 228, 237
Unravelling the Franklin Mystery (Woodman), 349
USA: Antipodean activities, 122; Antarctic expedition, 128, 132–3; Jane appeals to for help finding JF, 197, 212; funds search expedition, 198, 200–1, 212–15; interest in JF affair, 209–15; whale oil trade, 210–11, 213, 216; interest in Arctic, 211; second expedition under Kane, 216, 238–40, 258; returns *Resolute* to British, 266, 267–8; Arctic expeditions, 301–3; artists, 308–11; 'manifest destiny' to rule America from pole to pole, 309

Van Diemen's Land (later Tasmania): Franklin made governor, 58; Rossbank magnetic observatory, 88, 115–16, 130–1, 133, 134, 170; JF's preparations for government, 94–6; cannibalism among escaped convicts, 96; importance to Britain, 96–7; as penal colony, 96–8, 99, 100, 101–6, 121; history, 97–8; JF arrives, 98–101; indigenous Tasmanians, 99–100; renaming as Tasmania, 101; JF's penal policies, 101–6; Jane's activities, 106; JF's land sales and settlement policy, 107–9, 364n.50; JF's education and cultural policies, 110–11; Christ's College, 111; JF founds scientific society, 113–17; JF's encouragement of science and scientific visitors, 117–20; sea traffic and shipbuilding, 120–1; defences, 121–3; JF welcomes naval visits, 123, 126–7; JF's work on charts, navigation and maritime safety, 124–6; starts to decline because of improved sea approaches to Australia, 126; JF visited by Antarctic travellers,

127–34; JF explores, 135–6; JF dismissed from governorship, 137–1; JF's defence pamphlet, 146–8, 152–3, 159, 162; Lefroy as governor, 373n.19; *see also* Hobart

Vesconte, Lieutenant Henry le, 295, 298, 346

Vesey-Hamilton, Admiral Sir Richard, 327, 329

Victoria, queen of Great Britain and Ireland, 207, 267, 286, 321

Victoria, HMS, 324, 326

Victoria Channel, 237, 337

Victoria Land, 186, 237

Victoria Strait, 337

Vindictive, HMS, 127

Voeux, Mate Charles des, 280, 295, 326

volcanoes, 7–8

Wager river, 276

Wainwright Inlet, 184

Wakefield, Edward Gibbon, 107

Walcott, Admiral, 291

War of 1812 (1812–15), 27–8

Washington, Captain John: as secretary of RGS, 118; as deputy hydrographer becomes one of 'Friends of Sir John Franklin', 190; on Kane's expedition, 258; now Hydrographer, believes Rae's claims to have completed Passage unproven, 260; gives Jane inside information and support, 261, 270

Washington Bay, 346, 348

water, drinking, 343

Waterloo Place: statue of JF, 293–5; statue of Scott, 333

Watkin, Edward William, 310

Wauchope, Robert, 112

Weld, Charles, 220, 379n.75

Wellington, Arthur Wellesley, Duke of, 46

Wellington Channel: and JF's route, 163, 200; Sabine advocates searching, 181; James Ross tries to search, 186, 187, 188; Austin to search, 197; Penny's search of, 202; Jane anxious to search further in, 207; some experts believe to be JF's location, 209; Kane's expedition along, 216; as key to JF's location, 216, 221, 227; and Belcher's expedition, 231–6

West, John, 103

Westall, Richard, 322

Westmacott, Richard, 289

Westminster Abbey plaque, 297–8

Whale Fish Islands, 161–2, 186–7

whale oil trade, 210–11, 213, 216, 314

Wheatstone, Charles, 261

Whewell, William, 85, 112, 132, 261

Whiston, William, 76

Whiteside, Mr (MP), 292

Wickham, Captain John, 125

Wilhelm II, Kaiser, 321

Wilkes, Captain Charles, 122, 128, 132–3, 211, 213–14

William IV, king of Great Britain and Ireland (formerly Duke of Clarence): becomes JF's patron, 41, 93; losing control of Admiralty, 42; becomes patron of RGS, 45; JF considers becoming aide de camp, 46; honours JF, 52; questions JF about eastern Mediterranean situation, 53; JF formally presented to as governor of Van Diemen's Land, 95

Wilson, Harold, 268

Winter Harbour, 201, 231–2, 235, 241

Wollaston Land, 163, 164, 186

Wood, Sir Charles: replaces Graham at the Admiralty, 253; Murchison writes to for help in search for JF, 253–4; fobs off Inglis's deputation with promise of public memorial, 254, 256; off-hand comments on return of *Resolute*, 263; Palmerston tries to persuade to send another search expedition, 264–5; continues to refuse, 266–7; Palmerston discusses matter with, 269; refuses Jane use of *Resolute*, 270–1; further appeals to rejected, 271–2; pays Jane widow's pension, 279; no longer at Admiralty, 290

Woodman, David, 349

Woolwich Academy: as Sabine's HQ, 133, 144; observations at, 153, 154; officer training at, 166; Sabine calls for extra staff, 168; data-processing capabilities, 172

Woolwich dockyard, 153

Wrangel, Admiral Ferdinand Petrovich, 66, 129, 143

Wrottesley, Lord, 263–4, 385n.88

Young, Allen, 279, 281, 287, 298, 321

Zanetsky, Captain, 50, 51